DUNMORE'S WAR

DUNMORE'S WAR

THE LAST CONFLICT OF AMERICA'S COLONIAL ERA

∿

GLENN F. WILLIAMS

WESTHOLME
Yardley

Westholme Publishing, LLC
904 Edgewood Road
Yardley, Pennsylvania 19067
Visit our Web site at www.westholmepublishing.com

ISBN: 978-1-59416-317-3
Also available in hardback and as an eBook.

Printed in the United States of America.

Patricia and I dedicate this book to the loving memory of MICHAEL EZRA WILLIAMS, 1978–2016, *our son who departed this life much too soon.*

Contents

Contents

Illustrations

Maps

Halftones

Introduction

DUNMORE'S WAR, named for the last royal governor of Virginia, John Murray, fourth Earl of Dunmore, was the final Indian conflict of America's colonial era. Set mostly in the mountains, valleys, and farmlands of the Virginia backcountry and Ohio River valley from April to November 1774, the conflict started when Indian war parties initiated an aggressive campaign of vengeance with small-scale attacks and raids against homes and settlements on Virginia's frontier. By June 10, after passive defensive measures on the part of local militia failed to stem the violence, Governor Dunmore directed the county lieutenants to respond more vigorously, including limited offensive action. On July 12, the governor took the field to assume personal command. He planned a coordinated response with the combined forces of the most affected counties to take the war to the Shawnee and Mingo towns. About two thousand five hundred militia soldiers, not counting those who remained behind to guard the settlements, marched against approximately one thousand defending Indian warriors, mostly Shawnees, not counting those raiding the backcountry at large. The campaign resulted in only one, but decisive, large engagement in October. By November, the Indian leaders sued for peace and accepted the terms that Lord Dunmore proposed in order to spare their towns from destruction.

This book is, in the main, a campaign history that examines the military operations of Lord Dunmore's War. But it also takes into account diplomatic efforts and political factors. It shows that Virginia called on its colonial militia to achieve strategic objectives consistent with the justified defense of the province and provisions of its royal charter. Furthermore, the narrative demonstrates that the colonial Virginia militia was a more competent military organization than is often portrayed.

Relying almost exclusively on primary sources, the narrative places the 1774 conflict in the context of pre-Revolutionary War Virginia and addresses several themes. First, Governor Dunmore acted in what colonists perceived were the best interests of the colony. As a result, his policies were generally popular and earned him the admiration of those he governed. At times, however, they conflicted with those of the British government and put him at odds with the Secretariat of State for the Colonies, also called the Colonial Office, the ministerial department to which he reported and from which he received his orders and instructions. Second, an Indian war in the Ohio country had become unavoidable in early 1774, and the Shawnees represented the nation with the most hostility toward the British and colonial westward expansion. While Dunmore received at least nominal support from the British Indian Department, he took an active and direct role in diplomacy with the various native peoples living in the Ohio valley and bordering his colony. Third, the Virginia governor led his colony's forces in defense of what they viewed as legally acquired territory and demanded no further land concessions from those they defeated. Fourth, the narrative presents a detailed examination of the organization, training, tactical doctrine, and operations of Virginia's colonial militia, which challenges many popularly held beliefs. Fifth, and finally, Virginia's victory in Dunmore's War held important implications for both sides in the American War of Independence, especially with regard to Indian participation.

Overshadowed by the Revolutionary War, which began six months after it ended, Dunmore's War remains understudied and largely misunderstood. Many historians have either relegated it to the status of a footnote or briefly summarized the episode as a prelude to the Revolutionary War. This is unfortunate because the war is an intrinsically interesting subject with significance in its own right, and its namesake, Lord Dunmore, is a major historical figure.

Many of the currently available histories explain the conflict as little more than an attempt to wrest land from aboriginal inhabitants, and vilify Virginia settlers in general and Lord Dunmore in particular. Others describe it as either a relatively unimportant preliminary to, or an intentional diversion of attention from, events occurring at the same time in Boston and Philadelphia that signaled the approaching revolution. In contrast, this book shows that Virginia called on the colonial militia to defend its border from invasion and secure strategic objectives consistent with the legal acquisition of land and its royal charter. The causes and conduct of the Indian war were not directly connected to origins of the struggle for American independence. However, the results of Dunmore's War held important consequences that manifested themselves early and throughout that approaching conflict.

Various histories of the period that mention Dunmore's War, especially if written since the late twentieth century, almost universally characterize Virginia as the aggressor and its soldiers as land-hungry opportunists at best or lawless and racist banditti at worst. The primary sources cited to support that conclusion reflect the less-than-objective perspective of participants who favored the interests of Pennsylvania in its 1774 boundary dispute and competition for dominance of the Indian trade with Virginia. The different views found in Virginia records and the writings of Virginia participants have been largely ignored, marginalized, or dismissed as "triumphalist" in much of the recent scholarship.

Without ignoring the evidence that has provided the basis of opposing interpretations, this book primarily studies the situation as Virginians recorded it. The documentary evidence from those sources shows that the colony's government did not base its policies only on self-serving aggression. Virginia's acquisition of Indian land between 1768 and 1772 met the established legal requirements, conformed to the restrictions set forth in the Royal Proclamation of 1763, and were ratified by the British Crown. Virginia's expansion into the newly ceded land was allowed by law, as contemporary Virginians and government officials viewed it, and reflected the tenets of Enlightenment philosophy on the settlement of new land.

Many authors cast the Shawnees in the role of innocent victims. While the statement contains a basis in fact, it does not consider the hostile actions committed against Virginians by bands of Shawnee warriors that preceded or precipitated the conflict. Other historians have similarly blamed the war on Virginia aggression and described the Shawnees as trying to protect their homeland in the face of unauthorized white encroachment. When put another way, perhaps without realizing it, the same authors affirm that the Shawnees acted in their own national interests, as any polity would— including the Virginia colony. Similar interpretations fail to mention that the Six Nations, or Iroquois Confederacy, ceded Shawnee hunting ground to the British as part of the Treaty of Fort Stanwix in 1768. The omission maintains the focus on the dispute between the Shawnees and Virginians without an explanation of the Iroquois Confederacy's involvement in creating the contentious situation. The significance of Six Nations suzerainty over other native peoples is essential to a complete understanding of the situation on the frontier in 1774 and the causes of Dunmore's War, and is addressed in detail in this book.

Some historians argue that Virginia sought to fight a war of conquest against Indians, and it mattered little which nation or tribe, in order to take their land. To support that contention, they argue that Dunmore and other Virginians initially viewed the Cherokees as their next target, but then used the raids of the Mingo-leading warrior known as Logan as an excuse to go to war against the Shawnees. *Dunmore's War*, in contrast, shows that Logan's faction of Mingoes had already allied itself with those Shawnees who were predisposed to war. Another interpretation often taken by some historians maintains that after Virginians understood that defeating the Cherokees would not serve their purpose of expansion, they changed their story about Cherokee hostility and provoked the Shawnees into a war instead. The review of primary sources for this book reflects the error in such interpretations. It shows that Shawnee war parties had not only raided backcountry settlements before some infamous Virginia ruffians—not organized as militia—massacred Logan's family, but continued to do so as the Mingo retaliated, while Virginia and Cherokee leaders attempted to resolve their separate dispute peacefully at the same time.

Careful analysis of the comprehensive survey of sources cited in this narrative supports the position that Virginia's soldiers primarily fought a defensive war against unprovoked Shawnee and Mingo attacks on the south bank of the Ohio. Dunmore resorted to conducting an offensive operation only after it appeared to offer the most militarily and cost-effective means to end the war and secure the frontier as soon as possible. It was for this reason that he ordered the militia into the colony's service in July 1774. This book also shows that interpretations that explain that greed—the desire to take booty and Indian land—do not accurately characterize average soldiers' or officers' motivation to serve on Dunmore's expedition. The taking of what one author described as "booty" referred to the possibility of taking Indian horses as an enticement for recruits to join the expedition. Horses represented military resources and therefore legitimate spoils of war, or plunder, to which the victor was entitled according to the conventions of eighteenth-century warfare. Indian raiders certainly sought every opportunity to acquire horses by seizing them from Virginians. While the terms *booty* and *plunder* are often used interchangeably today, a researcher should consider eighteenth-century usage by consulting Samuel Johnson's or other period dictionaries. Choosing the more pejorative *booty*—connoting goods taken by robbery, rather than *plunder*, for spoils taken in war—although possibly unintentional, casts Virginia soldiers in the role of the aggressor.

Perhaps the strongest evidence to support the thesis that Dunmore and the Virginians fought a defensive war is found in its conclusion. When the expedition proved successful in bringing the hostile Indians to negotiate terms, the war-ending Treaty of Camp Charlotte proved far less draconian than one would expect from an aggressor bent on land acquisition through conquest and genocidal extermination. Although Dunmore demanded that the Shawnees and Mingoes return all captives, including those they had never repatriated at the end of Pontiac's War a decade earlier, he required no cession or encroachment of their homeland. The peace terms affirmed the Ohio River as the boundary between the Virginia colony and the land reserved to the Shawnees according to the treaties Crown authorities had negotiated with the Iroquois in 1768 and the Cherokees in 1768 and 1770, but made no demand for a deed to Kentucky from the Shawnees. The surrender of several chiefs or leading warriors to serve as hostages represented the sternest measure Dunmore demanded. A common practice in eighteenth- and early nineteenth-century Indian diplomacy, the surrender of hostages served as security that the Shawnees would honor their promise to release all of their white and black prisoners, as well as guarantee that their headmen would meet Virginia commissioners to sign the final treaty at Pittsburgh the following spring. The defeated party met the condition to demonstrate a sincere desire to negotiate a lasting peace treaty and show the victor that it was not using an armistice in order to disengage from a losing battle so it could renew hostilities later.

Previous treatments of the military institutional aspects of Dunmore's War have been no less unsatisfactory. Like the explanations of the causes and precipitating events, the available literature includes many inaccurate, albeit oft-repeated or broadly interpreted general descriptions of the Virginia forces, with little attention paid to military operations and tactics. In contrast, the pages that follow present a complete and detailed operational account with due consideration of military practice and organization.

The authors who do address the tactical operations attribute any success Virginia militiamen enjoyed to their adopting or copying the tactics of their Indian adversaries, an oversimplification. The reader of this book will see the militia's success resulted more from adapting British tactical doctrine to North America rather than simply adopting Indian fighting methods. Both of Dunmore's principal subordinates, Colonels Andrew Lewis and Adam Stephen, as well as a number of the other officers, had served in Colonel George Washington's 1st Virginia Regiment during the French and Indian War. Stephen, like Washington, had survived Braddock's defeat on the Monongahela in 1755. Such officers learned that victory over Indian enemies came by combining regular and irregular tactics, and they trained their men accordingly. The evidence related in the narrative that follows shows that under the tutelage of veteran officers, colonial militiamen had read instructional texts such as Humphrey Bland's *Treatise on Military Discipline* and applied the lessons about fighting irregulars in Europe to their own experiences fighting Indians. It is important to note, however, that Bland's instructions could not simply be used as written but had to be modified and adapted to the conditions and enemies encountered in North America.

The Virginians adapted conventional European tactics to the American woods and blended them with techniques learned from their native allies and adversaries, as well as the experience of previous conflicts, into their own brand of bush fighting or skirmishing. Virginia's colonial soldiers achieved success in battle against Indian enemies by adhering to a modified British doctrine, which emphasized unit cohesion and fire superiority, although not necessarily by fighting in compact ranks and shunning natural cover, and combined the strategic offense and tactical defense. Similarly, Indian warriors nearly abandoned their traditional tactical doctrine at the Battle of Point Pleasant. Their general practice usually dictated fighting a battle of annihilation rather than one of attrition. The plan of Cornstalk, the Shawnee chief, to advance en masse seeking to surprise, overwhelm, and destroy the opponent in a quick victory was in keeping with this practice. When the attack failed to achieve the desired outcome, Indian forces surprisingly conducted a battle of attrition for several hours before the Shawnees finally disengaged and retired. In addition, the reader will see Virginia's colonial militia as a much more efficient military organization than it has often been portrayed. The army involved in the 1774 campaign likewise effectively followed British—or European—logistical procedures, appropriately adapted to operations in North America, with the protected advance to sustain its forces in the field throughout the campaign.

Much of the currently available literature does not present a completely accurate portrayal of the composition, organization, and training of Virginia's colonial militia. Some authors, for example, explain that the county militias of Virginia were mirror images of those organized in English counties. Although accurate in a general sense, the statement omits the very important distinctions that existed between the Virginia and English militias despite their common heritage. For example, an English parish filled its portion of the county's quota by ballot, or draft, after which the selected men served terms of three years. Following a period of initial training, the militia man joined a unit that mustered periodically and could respond to local alarms or augment the regular British army for homeland defense during emergencies. In contrast, unless exempt by law, all free white male Virginians age eighteen to forty-five had an obligation to serve. They all trained periodically and served whenever the county or colony called them for military service.

Other treatments of Dunmore's War have also tended to impose a formal regimental structure on the administrative organization of Virginia county militias. The reader of the following narrative will note that the administrative groupings of the Virginia militia actually bore less resemblance to such a regular tactical organization. An oft-repeated error is that members enlisted to serve in the militia, and the expedition of 1774 experienced no recruiting problems. The reader of this book will not only gain a more accurate understanding of service in the Virginia colonial militia in general but will also note the difficulty officials encountered when raising forces needed for active duty.

The evidence presented in the following pages shows that the county lieutenants followed the requirements of the colony's militia law and the procedures established for defending their own and assisting neighboring communities, as well as the province at large. It further establishes that the militia of the Virginia colony existed as a pool of available manpower that county, independent borough, or provincial governments could mobilize for military service. The local companies and county regiments constituted administrative—not tactical—units organized according to regional population densities and not mission-oriented considerations. The governor appointed all company officers based on the recommendations of their respective county lieutenants. The governor also signed and issued commissions to the men who the county officials recommended to raise and lead tactical units and authorized them to recruit volunteers and draft individuals to fill their ranks. Ideally, a company embodied for actual service was organized with fifty rank-and-file men, plus officers, sergeants, and musicians, along lines similar to, but not exactly like, those in the British army. While not on a level equal to that found in the regular army, the men of the Virginia militia nevertheless submitted to a level of discipline often not reflected in the popular view of frontier Americans.

Many of the available interpretations depict the Virginia General Assembly as unwilling to support Dunmore with an appropriation of funds and authorization for military action against the hostile Indians. Primary evidence found only in the Pennsylvania records would tend to support such conclusions. The Virginia records contain contradictory testimony. This book demonstrates that although the General Assembly did not agree with Dunmore that the situation warranted the appropriation of funds and authorization to raise an army of provincial regulars, Peyton Randolph, speaker of the House of Burgesses, offered a more appropriate recommendation. Randolph informed the governor that the law titled An Act for Reducing the Several Acts of Assembly, for Making Provision against Invasions and Insurrections, into One Act (often shortened to Invasions and Insurrections Act) already gave him the authority to call militia into service and employ them in this kind of emergency without additional legislation. Perhaps other historians mistook the speaker's explanation that the act for provision against invasions and insurrections constituted a more appropriate application of the governor's war powers for dealing with the emergency as a refusal to act. The reader will also learn that according to the law, the colony's General Assembly normally appropriated the money after the emergency ended and reimbursed military expenses and paid militia soldiers for their service in arrears, not in advance. The record shows that the Virginia government followed the established procedure when it paid its soldiers and the related expenses for the Indian campaign in July 1775, albeit after the Revolutionary War began and Dunmore had fled Williamsburg.

The events related in the following pages occurred during a period in colonial America when resistance to certain British imperial policies had not yet risen to a struggle for independence. Although the Revolutionary War is not the subject of this book, Dunmore's War had an important influence on the events of that later conflict. As long as both sides adhered to the terms of the Treaty of Camp Charlotte and the subsequent councils held at Fort Pitt in 1775 and 1776, the Ohio frontier remained relatively peaceful. Combined with the respite from fighting that ensued in the east between the British evacuation of Boston and the invasion of New York in 1776, the Americans had sufficient time to decide in favor of and declare their independence. When Cornstalk announced the Shawnees' decision to enter the war as British allies and resume hostilities in November 1777, it presented Virginia the motive and opportunity to invade the north bank of the Ohio as a component of the greater struggle. American success in that theater resulted in Britain's recognition of the Northwest Territory, encompassing the present states of Ohio, Indiana, Illinois, and Michigan as within the territorial boundaries of the United States in the 1783 Treaty of Paris.

CANADA

NEW HAMPSHIRE

Ft. Stanwix

NEW YORK

MASSACHUSETTS

CONN

RI

Allegheny R.

PENNSYLVANIA

Ohio R.

Fort Pitt

Philadelphia

NEW JERSEY

Ohio R.

MARYLAND

DE

Kanawha R.

Kentucky R.

New R.

VIRGINIA

Williamsburg

Holston R.

NORTH CAROLINA

SOUTH CAROLINA

GEORGIA

EAST FLORIDA

Atlantic Ocean

Royal Proclamation of 1763
- - - - - - - -

Treaty of Fort Stanwix (1768)
◆◆◆◆◆◆◆◆◆◆◆◆◆◆

Treaty of Hard Labour (1768)
+++++++++++++++

Treaty of Lochaber (1770)
- - - - - - - - - - -

Cherokee Grant (1772)
• • • • • • • • • • • •

N

Indian Territory Ceded by Treaty, 1763–1772.

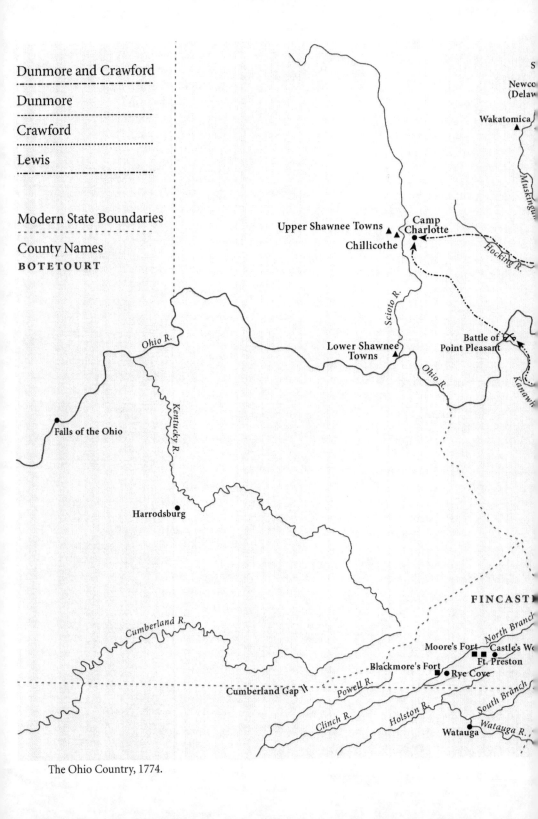

Dunmore and Crawford
-·-·-·-·-·-·-·-·-·-·-·-·
Dunmore
- - - - - - - - - - - -
Crawford
- - - - - - - - - - - -
Lewis
-·-·-·-·-·-·-·-·-·-·-·-·

Modern State Boundaries
· · · · · · · · · · · · · · · · · ·
County Names
BOTETOURT

S

Newco
(Delaw

Wakatomica ▲

Muskingum

Upper Shawnee Towns ▲   Camp
                          Charlotte ●
       Chillicothe
                          Hocking R.

Scioto R.

Lower Shawnee
      Towns ▲   Battle of
                     Point Pleasant ⚔

Ohio R.   Ohio R.

Kanawh

Falls of the Ohio ●

Kentucky R.

Harrodsburg ●

FINCAST

Cumberland R.   North Branch
                          Moore's Fort ■   Castle's W
                                         ■ ● Ft. Preston
                  Blackmore's Fort ■ ● Rye Cove
Cumberland Gap)(Powell R.   South Branch

             Clinch R.   Holston R.
                                    Watauga R.
                          Watauga ●

The Ohio Country, 1774.

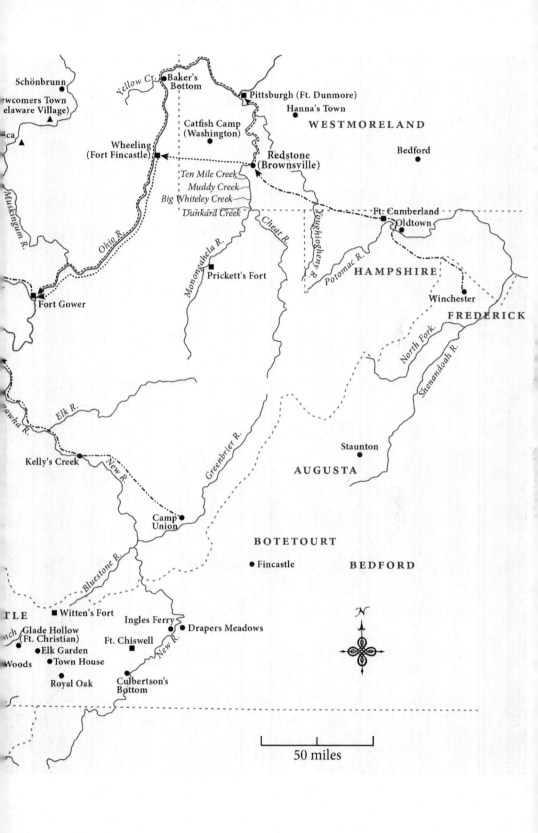

Schönbrunn

ewcomers Town
elaware Village) ▲

ica ▲

Yellow Cr. Baker's
Bottom

Pittsburgh (Ft. Dunmore)

Hanna's Town

WESTMORELAND

Catfish Camp
(Washington)

Bedford

Wheeling
(Fort Fincastle)

Redstone
(Brownsville)

Ten Mile Creek
Muddy Creek
Big Whiteley Creek
Dunkard Creek

Cheat R.

Ft. Cumberland
Oldtown

Ohio R.

Muskingum R.

Monongahela R.

Prickett's Fort

Youghiogheny R.

Potomac R.

HAMPSHIRE

Fort Gower

Winchester

FREDERICK

North Fork

Shenandoah R.

Elk R.

Kelly's Creek

New R.

Staunton

Greenbrier R.

AUGUSTA

Camp
Union

Bluestone R.

BOTETOURT

Fincastle

BEDFORD

TLE

Witten's Fort

Ingles Ferry

Drapers Meadows

nch Glade Hollow
(Ft. Christian)

Elk Garden

Ft. Chiswell

New R.

Woods Town House

Royal Oak

Culbertson's
Bottom

𝒩

50 miles

CHAPTER 1

Our Customs Differing from Yours

Cultural Friction and Conflict on the Frontier

October 1773–March 1774

IT IS 1773 VIRGINIA.[1] Early in the morning on Sunday, October 10, eight men—six whites and two black slaves—lie sleeping in their camp on the west bank of Wallen's Creek in Powell's Valley on the Virginia frontier. Before bedding down the previous night, they had unburdened their pack horses so that bundles of supplies, including sacks of flour and other provisions, were lying about them. Their cattle and tethered horses slept or grazed nearby. The men would soon have to rise, gather the livestock, load the pack animals, and resume the march. They needed to go only a few more miles along this branch of an Indian trail known as the Warriors' Path to rejoin their group's main body.[2] History would soon count members of the caravan among the first victims claimed in a clash of cultures that became the last conflict of America's colonial era. Within months of its conclusion, the first shots of independence at Lexington and Concord would be fired.

As dawn approached, the horses suddenly became restless and agitated. A party of nineteen Indian warriors had observed and shadowed the group ever since it entered the valley. Returning from a congress of several nations' representatives to discuss how to contend with continued white expansion into the hunting ground on the south bank of the Ohio River, the band presumably included fifteen Delaware, two Cherokee, and two Shawnee warriors. No official state of war existed between the British and the several nations whose hunters they might have encountered in these woods. If the members of the caravan had even seen the Indians, they would certainly not have assumed they were hostile, and therefore took no extraordinary security precautions. The braves moved silently forward as they would on a hunt when approaching unsuspecting deer until each came to a position that offered an unobstructed view of their quarry. The warriors raised their muskets, cocked their firelocks, and took aim at the figures huddled near a campfire against the coolness of the early autumn morning.[3]

At daybreak, musket fire and blood-curdling war whoops pierced the stillness as the Indians rushed in and overran the camp. The warriors who killed brothers John and Richard Mendenhall with the opening fusillade immediately pounced on and scalped their lifeless corpses. The braves who fired at James Boone and Henry Russell had intentionally aimed at their hips to disable, not kill. The wounds, though severe, left them alive but writhing in agony on the ground and unable to move. The Indians tortured the unfortunate young men without mercy and made sport of their suffering by repeatedly striking them with knives and tomahawks to prolong the ordeal. Weakened by excruciating pain and loss of blood, the two vainly attempted to fend off the blades with their bare hands. Boone recognized his main assailant as Big Jim, a Shawnee acquaintance of his father's. The young man pleaded with the Indian to spare their lives, but to no avail.[4]

The rest of the warriors split into small groups and continued the carnage. One group captured the horses or plundered the provisions and supplies while the other assailed those who had survived the initial onslaught. Charles, one of the black men, stood paralyzed with fear as two warriors claimed him as their captive. Although wounded, Isaac Crabtree and Samuel Drake fled into the woods and evaded capture. Adam, the other slave, escaped unscathed. From his hiding place concealed in the brush by the river bank, Adam watched the Indians unleash their anger on his companions. The other warriors, impatient to get away, shouted for the braves tormenting Russell and Boone to hurry. After they killed and scalped their victims, the assailants disappeared into the woods with their trophies. One of them left the bloodied war club by the bodies, the traditional sign that boasted the warriors' triumph and warned enemies to pursue at their peril.[5]

The ill-fated party was part of an expedition planned and organized by Captain William Russell and Daniel Boone to "reconnoiter the country, toward the Ohio and . . . settle in the limits of the expected new government" of Vandalia. They had moved in three groups. Boone began the trek on September 25, when his and five other families left their homes on the Yadkin River in North Carolina. After entering Powell's Valley in southwestern Virginia, they halted to rendezvous with a party led by William Bryan, Boone's brother-in-law, which increased their numbers to about fifty men, women, and children. Whereas Boone and his neighbors moved their entire households, including baggage, furniture, domestic animals, and cattle, Bryan's men planned to build houses and prepare their fields over the winter and then return to move their families to the new settlement in the spring. Boone's enlarged column camped and waited for the others to catch up just north of Wallen's Ridge, a few miles from the scene of the fateful incident.[6]

Boone had sent three members of his party, including his seventeen-year-old son, James, with John and Richard Mendenhall to Castle's Woods to obtain tools, farming implements, and additional supplies. Located in the Clinch River valley, the community represented the largest and most distant of Virginia's frontier settlements in the newly established Fincastle County and was home to Captain William Russell. With Russell's assistance, the young Boone and the Mendenhalls acquired the needed supplies, plus additional cattle, horses, and pack saddles. On Friday, October 8, the captain sent them on their way, accompanied by his seventeen-year-old son, Henry Russell, two slaves named Charles and Adam, a hired man known as Samuel Drake, and an experienced woodsman named Isaac Crabtree, to help manage the convoy and cattle. They expected to reach the main body within two days. The next day, after gathering the last of their harvests, Captain Russell followed with thirty men from Clinch River, including his neighbor David Gass.[7]

They had agreed that Russell would assume overall command when he joined the group, while Boone served as the guide into the uninhabited area that the Iroquois called Kain-tuck-ee, or meadowland. A renowned frontiersman as well as a gentleman from a prominent family, Russell represented the natural choice for the leader. He had attended the College of William and Mary, served in the French and Indian War, and become a successful tobacco planter, militia officer, and justice of the peace in Fincastle County. Russell was seeking to claim land due him for his wartime service, and his reputation and leadership skills attracted enough volunteers to give the enterprise a better chance of success. Although Boone exemplified the skills of the consummate woodsman, had visited Kentucky on numerous long hunts, and had scouted their destination the previous winter, his name remained relatively unknown outside of the Virginia and North Carolina backcountry compared to Russell's.[8]

By Sunday morning, Daniel Boone waited in restless anticipation for the arrival of his son's caravan and Russell's contingent from Clinch River. Earlier that morning, following an altercation with another emigrant, one man had quit the venture. While heading home along the Warriors' Path, the deserter happened on the killing field by Wallen's Creek. Fearful of continuing alone, he backtracked to the camp. As soon as the man arrived, Boone learned the news that a number of Indians had attacked "the rear of our company" and his oldest son, James, "fell in the action." While Boone directed the rest of the men to prepare to defend the camp against a similar raid, Boone sent his brother, Squire, with a dozen armed men to investigate.[9]

Traveling in front of the Clinch River men with David Gass, William Russell arrived on the scene first to find Henry's corpse "mangled in an inhuman manner." As the grief-stricken father described, "There was left in him a dart arrow, and a war club was left beside him."[10] As soon as Squire Boone and his men arrived, they searched for any warriors who remained behind in ambush, and then began the grim task of burying the dead. Rebecca Boone, Daniel's wife, had given Squire two linen cloths to use as winding sheets. Russell and Squire Boone wrapped their relatives' remains in one and the Mendenhall brothers in the other, and laid them all to rest. The attack had scattered the cattle and caused such other damage at the main camp that the settlers now found themselves in extreme difficulty. Daniel Boone later recalled, "Though we defended ourselves, and repulsed the enemy," the unhappy affair had so discouraged the whole company that few wished to continue to the Ohio. The men held a council to decide what course of action to pursue, took a vote, and "retreated forty miles, to the settlement of Clinch river." While others returned home, Daniel and Rebecca Boone, who had sold their farm in North Carolina, remained at Castle's Woods for the winter in a cabin on the Gass property.[11]

Several of the men scouted the vicinity but found no signs to indicate whether the missing massacre victims had survived. Crabtree was mentally scarred by the ordeal, but his physical wounds proved minor, and he managed to walk back to Castle's Woods within a few days. The uninjured Adam, possibly disoriented and suffering from shock, took a week and a half to find his way home. The search party presumed the Indians had either killed or taken Drake captive, and no one saw him alive again. After his captors had herded Charles along for some distance, they apparently concluded that an enemy scalp served their purposes as well as a live captive, or possibly argued about who actually owned the prisoner and what to do with him. Scouts later found the man's scalped body by the trail some miles distant from the massacre site.[12]

Once back at home, Captain Russell attempted to account for the dead and missing. He took depositions and compared survivors' recollections with his observations of the detritus at the scene. The captain concluded that the Indian attackers had killed five white men and one black without provocation, and one white and one black man had survived. Russell reported the incident to his superior officer in the militia, Colonel William Preston, the county lieutenant of Fincastle County. The next summer, Virginia's royal governor, John Murray, the fourth Earl of Dunmore, would cite the massacre, along with other incidents, to justify Virginia's hard-line stand when addressing Indian delegations attending a general Indian congress at Fort Pitt.[13]

An account of the "inhuman affair . . . transacted on the frontiers of Fincastle [County]" appeared in the December 23 edition of the *Virginia Gazette* published by Clementina Rind. The article read in part like a military report. Captain Russell's command, which had gone to "reconnoiter," became "separated into three detachments." The Indians attacked the smallest of them, killing five whites and one black. After the unexpected assault, the party retreated after "getting intelligence" of the enemy. The paper asserted that the story came from "good authority," which suggested the Russell-Preston correspondence.[14] A Baltimore newspaper carried a different account of the tragic event on November 27, preceding Rind's by almost a month. Based on a description by "a gentleman of credit lately from New River in Virginia," that version differed in some details such as the circumstances, as well as the numbers of participants and casualties. Several newspapers, including the *Pennsylvania Chronicle and Universal Advertiser* of Philadelphia, reprinted the second-hand version before the presumably more authoritative narrative even went to press in Williamsburg.[15]

Nonetheless, the two accounts renewed the colonists' concern about continued depredations and caused alarm among backcountry inhabitants, those who planned to acquire land in the frontier districts, and Crown officers charged with keeping peace with the Indians. Wondering how hostilities might bear on the land patents promised him and other veterans for military service in the French and Indian War, Dr. Hugh Mercer of Fredericksburg, Virginia, wrote Colonel Preston to inquire if "the Massacre" could be attributed to the "Indian's Jealousy of our settling near them, or to a private Quarrel." He also asked if any party received "certain intelligence" as to what nation of Indians' warriors had killed young "Mr. Russell."[16]

Sharing Mercer's concern, Major General Frederick Haldimand, Lieutenant General Thomas Gage's second in command, who had assumed the duties as acting commander in chief of the king's forces in North America while Gage was on leave in England, asked in a letter to Sir William Johnson, superintendent of Indian affairs for the Northern Department, to be informed of the identity of Indians who attacked Captain Russell's party on its way to the Ohio. The general told Johnson that although "Some say they were Cherokees," he rather suspected them to be members of the "Shawanese than any other."[17] Alexander McKee, posted at Fort Pitt as Johnson's deputy superintendent for the Ohio Indians, heard of the incident from traders returning from downriver and recorded in his journal that another party of Shawnees had returned home from the frontiers of Virginia bringing "a Number of Horses; and . . . had killed Six White Men & Two Negroes."[18] Aware of unrest among the nations of the Ohio country after almost ten years of relative, albeit tenuous, peace, many thought another Indian war might be on the horizon.

Lord Dunmore initially suspected the Cherokees. He wrote to John Stuart, the superintendent of Indian affairs for the Southern Department—and Johnson's counterpart—for his assistance in bringing the guilty parties of that nation to justice. In return, Dunmore told Stuart to assure the Cherokees he would take every step within his power "to prevent any encroachments on their Hunting Ground" by Virginians.[19] Stuart informed Haldimand that the Cherokees' "behaviour and professions" toward the British remained friendly. Although inclined to believe that none from that nation shared in any of the guilt, Stuart nonetheless recommended that Crown officials keep the Cherokees in "good humour," but to be alert for any signs of hostility. He then asked Alexander Cameron, his deputy superintendent for the Cherokees, to investigate further.[20]

Cameron indicated that he had seen or heard nothing that would implicate the Cherokees in the Powell's Valley massacre. Although a war party that had gone out just before the incident returned with the scalps of four white men, Tuckassie Keowee, the son of Oconostota, the "Great Warrior," told Cameron that they had attacked, killed, and taken the scalps from some Frenchmen on the Wabash River after mistaking them for enemy warriors. Tuckassie then told Cameron that seventeen Delawares and three "Seneca [Mingo]" left the Overhill Cherokee town of Chota in early October. He said they went home through Kentucky by way of the Louisa River on the Warriors' Path and may have encountered and killed the whites.[21] In sworn depositions before Fincastle County magistrates, members of Boone's main party identified two Cherokees among a group of Indians they saw in the area days before the massacre.[22] Stuart eventually secured the conviction and execution of only one Cherokee man, leading some Virginians to complain that he had not pursued justice as vigorously as he should have.[23]

The incident caused little concern outside of Virginia and the western counties of Maryland and Pennsylvania. Williamsburg printers Alexander Purdie and John Dixon produced a newspaper that began operation before that of their rival, Clementina Rind, but which shared the name *Virginia Gazette*. Both appeared every Thursday and often ran articles that covered the same events. The day that Rind's printed the story, the Purdie-Dixon

Gazette made no mention of the ambush, even though they issued a two-page supplement to their December 23, 1773, edition. Under the dateline Boston, November 29, an anonymous author, presumably Samuel Adams, announced the arrival of the ship *Dartmouth*, laden with a cargo of 114 chests of detested tea, which he described as the "worst of Plagues," shipped to the colonies by the East India Company in accordance with the Tea Act.[24]

BY LATE 1773, trouble had been brewing on the frontier for some time. Less than a month before the attack in Powell's Valley, Superintendent Johnson sent a report to William Legge, second Earl of Dartmouth, the secretary of state for the colonies, stating that the settlers going from Virginia and seeking new settlements, leaving large tracts of unsettled country behind them, had caused much alarm among the Shawnees. Johnson believed that the Indians had little reason to complain as long as the settlers stayed within the "old claims" of Virginia and not the recently acquired land. The Six Nations of Iroquois and the Cherokees, the two most powerful Indian polities and nominal British allies bordering the thirteen colonies, had recently ceded or relinquished control of the newer claims by the 1768 Treaties of Hard Labor and Fort Stanwix, and the 1770 Treaty of Lochaber. Johnson explained that many settlers could "not be confined by any Boundaries or Limits" without a government presence to enforce Crown policies. While the lawless and disorderly among them committed "Robberies & Murders" and caused concern among the Indians, he conceded that even the law-abiding displayed a general prejudice against all Indians, which in turn caused young Indian warriors or hunters to seek revenge even when slightly insulted.[25]

Of all native peoples inhabiting the Ohio country in 1773, the Shawnee (or Shawanos), western Delaware (or Lenni Lenape), and Mingo (or Minqwe), lived closest to the Virginia settlements. Ironically, they were not indigenous nor had they lived in the region significantly longer than the neighboring colonists. Bands of Shawnees and several little known native tribes had inhabited the Ohio valley until the Iroquois invaded their homelands, destroyed their towns, and dispersed their people during the Beaver Wars of the seventeenth century.[26] The Six Nations then used the conquered depopulated area as a hunting ground for many years before they permitted several bands, which had migrated from their homelands under the pressure of colonial expansion and intertribal disputes, to settle there under its dominion. Superintendent Johnson explained to General Gage that the [then] Five Nations "had conquered all, and actually extirpated Several of the

Tribes there," and placed the Shawnees, Delawares, and others on "bare Toleration in their Stead, as sort of Frontier Dependents," and to act as a buffer for the Iroquois homelands.[27]

In order to better maintain control over their dependents and access to the hunting grounds, the Iroquois sent some emigrants from the Six Nations, mostly Senecas, to settle among the Ohio Indians. Whites knew these Iroquoian people as the Mingo, derived from a name the Delawares applied to all the members of the Iroquois Confederacy. After living removed from under the influence of their chiefs, many Mingo people began to view themselves as autonomous from their parent nations, but they generally remained obedient to the confederacy's central council at Onondaga through the leadership of its local viceroy, the skilled diplomat and leading warrior Guyasuta.[28]

The Six Nations of Iroquois was arguably the most powerful Indian polity in northeastern North America at this time. In the sixteenth century, according to tradition, the Mohawk, Seneca, Onondaga, Cayuga, and Oneida agreed to unite under the Great Law of Peace to become the Haudenosaunee, or People of the Longhouse. To Europeans, they became known as the Five Nations of Iroquois, and the Iroquois Confederacy, or League. Although each remained free to pursue its own interests as long as they were not in conflict with those of other member nations, representative sachems, or civil chiefs, from each moiety assembled around the central council fire at the Onondaga principal town to resolve internal disagreements, discuss issues of mutual concern, and decide on collective action. The Five Nations grew into a powerful political, military, and economic force that first destroyed its nonleague Iroquoian rivals and then struck at various Algonquin stock enemies. During the first quarter of the eighteenth century, the council admitted the Tuscaroras to the confederacy as wards of the Oneida—who represented them at the council fire—and the league thus became the Six Nations.

Victorious in numerous wars of conquest, the Iroquois Confederacy claimed suzerainty over vanquished nations and territory. Through those it considered subordinates and allies, the confederacy extended its diplomatic and economic influence and acted as a conduit for the British to native peoples deep in the interior through an alliance called the Silver Covenant Chain of Friendship.[29] The Iroquois-British alliance proved mutually beneficial and enabled each to use the other's strength and power—whether real or perceived—to leverage its own with friend and foe alike. Under the 1713 Treaty of Utrecht, which ended the War of the Spanish Succession (1702–1713), known as Queen Anne's War in the colonies, other

European nations recognized the Six Nations' people as British subjects and their land within the king's dominion. General Gage cautioned that believing the Six Nations had ever acknowledged themselves as being subjects of the English would be a "very gross Mistake." The general believed that if told so, the news would not please the Iroquois to learn of that status. Gage therefore recommended that the British not treat them as subjects but as allies who accepted the king's promises of protection from encroachment by either his European foes or his white American subjects.[30]

Of all Ohio valley Indian entities, the Shawnees arguably held the most hostility toward British interests. In 1742, Conrad Weiser, the Pennsylvania colony's long-time Indian agent, described them as "the most restless and mischievous" of all the Indian nations. They, and to a lesser extent the western Delawares, felt oppressed by the imperious Six Nations, who looked on them as dependent or tributary peoples. The genesis of this relationship, according to Weiser, came after they suffered a decisive military defeat, after which the Delawares figuratively had "their Breech-Cloth taken from them, and a Petticoat put upon them" by the Iroquois. They humbly called themselves "Women" when they addressed their "Conquerors," which the Six Nations also called them when they spoke "severely to 'em." In less stressful conversations, the Iroquois called the Delawares "Cousins," who in turn addressed them as "Uncles" in recognition of their subordinate status.[31] When Weiser described the subordination of the Shawnees, he explained that it had happened according to a different process. Because the Iroquois had never conquered them, they never officially considered the Shawnees in the confederacy but described them as "Brethren" to the Six Nations. In return for granting permission to settle on land under their dominion, however, the Iroquois claimed "Superiority" over them, and for which the Shawnees "mortally hate them."[32]

Reflecting this animosity, Shawnee representatives repeatedly told Superintendent Johnson and his deputies that the Iroquois Confederacy "had long Seemed to neglect them" and "disregard the Promise ... of letting them have the Lands between the Ohio & the [Great] Lakes."[33] They complained that the Six Nations cared little for the interests of the native peoples they considered under their dominion and appeared more intent on pleasing the British and protecting their own interests when they negotiated matters of war and peace, or the cession and sale of land. The Iroquois ceded land west of the Blue Ridge, including the Shenandoah valley, to Virginia at the 1744 Treaty of Lancaster. Tachanootia, the Onondaga spokesman for the Six Nations, told those attending that treaty, "but as to what lies beyond the Mountains, we conquered the Nations residing there." If the Virginians ever wanted to get a "good Right to it," he continued, it must be only by his peo-ple.[34] Although they disagreed on how far west that cession extended, after white settlers began to occupy it, the Iroquois granted Virginia the remaining land south and east of the Ohio in 1752 at the Treaty of Loggstown. As the Six Nations representative, Tanacharison, the "Half King" leader of the Mingoes and the Ohio country, speaking on behalf of the Six Nations council at Onondaga, signed a "deed" that recognized and acknowledged "the right and title" of the king of Great Britain to all the lands within the colony "as it was then, or hereafter might be peopled."[35]

On both occasions, the Iroquois neither considered Shawnee interests nor recognized Cherokee claims to the same area. To counter the influence of their overlords, the Shawnee expended considerable diplomatic energy attempting to form their own "association" among the Ohio region Indians to help shake their dependency and oppose the military, economic, and political domination of the "6 Nations (& English)."[36] In a somewhat duplicitous effort to convince other native peoples that they served as a channel for Iroquois policy while advancing their own interests, the Shawnees endeavored to draw the "Six Nations emigrants on Ohio," the Mingoes, into their confederacy.[37]

An Algonquin language-stock people, the Shawnee nation functioned as a confederation of five semiautonomous tribal units, called septs, that shared a common language and culture: the Chilabcahtha, or Chillicothe; Assiwikale, or Thawekila; Spitotha, or Mequachake; Bicowetha, or Piqua; and Kispokotha, or Kispoko. Although the system had an uncertain origin, by the latter eighteenth century, each sept had its own council of elders that selected its chiefs and met at its principal town—whose name derived from that of the sept—and participated at a central council as well. Each sept could act independently as long as it did not create conflict with the others, while the central council of elders decided matters of mutual importance, especially those involving diplomatic, military, and economic activities with European or other Indian nations.[38]

When they acted in concert, each sept assumed leadership in a certain facet of governance in which all others recognized its expertise. The two principal divisions, the Chilicothe and Thawekila, held responsibility for managing internal politics and led in matters that affected the tribes when they acted in unison. The Mequachake held responsibility for matters related to health and medicine, and provided healers. The Pequa answered the nation's needs for leadership in spiritual concerns and rituals. Finally, the Kispokos provided the Shawnees with their principal war chiefs and led in military matters.[39]

Indian of the Nation of the Shawanoes.

In his journal, Englishman Nicholas Cresswell gave the following description of Shawnee warriors that he saw in 1774. "They are tall, manly, well-shaped men, of a Copper colour with black hair, quick piercing eyes, and good features. They have rings of silver in their nose and bobs to them, which hang over their upper lip. Their ears are cut from the tips two thirds of the way round and the piece extended with brass wire till it touches their shoulders, in this part, they hang a thin silver plate, wrought in flourishes about three inches in diameter, with plates of silver round their arms and in the hair, which is all cut off except a long lock on the top of the head. . . . They wear white man's dress, except breeches which they refuse to wear, instead of which they have a girdle round them with a piece of cloth drawn through their legs and turned over the girdle, and appears like a short apron before and behind. . . . All the hair is pulled from their eyebrows and eyelashes and their faces painted in different parts with Vermillion. . . . They walk remarkably straight and cut a grotesque appearance in this mixed dress." An engraving of a Shawnee warrior from an original drawing by Georges Henri Victor Collot produced in the late eighteenth century. (*John Carter Brown Library*)

Under the terms of the 1758 Treaty of Easton during the French and Indian War, the Six Nations granted the newly formed confederacy of Shawnee and western Delaware Indians living in the Ohio country a degree of independence, provided that they recognized continued Iroquois dominion over the land, including the exclusive authority to sell it to the British.[40] Although the treaty affirmed Six Nations control over the land they inhabited or used as hunting ground, through the diplomatic skills of the Delaware chief Pisquetomen, the Ohio Indians demanded a boundary to separate Indian from British territory in return for a cessation of hostilities and renunciation of their alliance with the French. When they departed Easton for home, Shawnee and Delaware sachems understood that the British promised not to maintain military posts on Indian land in the Ohio valley after the war.

The Shawnees and other Ohio Indians welcomed the announcement of the Royal Proclamation of 1763 at the end of the Seven Years' War, and viewed it as an affirmation of the promises made at Easton. The proclamation said "that the several nations or tribes of Indians with whom we are connected, and who live under our protection, should not be molested or disturbed in the possession of such parts of our dominion and territories," and it reserved the land between the Appalachian Mountains and the Ohio River as their hunting grounds. As a means of more efficiently managing westward expansion, the proclamation directed the military commanders in chief and the governors of the thirteen colonies, "for the present," to prohibit British subjects from establishing settlements within the boundaries of the colonial charters but beyond a line formed by the heads of any of the rivers that flowed toward the Atlantic Ocean from the west or northwest, or any other land in their territory, that the Indians had not yet ceded to or sold to the Crown, "until our further pleasure is known." Although many British subjects had already settled in the frontier districts on land ceded before 1763, the proclamation put a halt to all purchases of Indian land by private interests. Thereafter, only official representatives of the Crown acting in their official capacity could conduct transactions to acquire Indian land in the context of formal treaties.[41]

These provisions reflected the convention European powers used in their efforts to colonize the New World, which became known as the Doctrine of Discovery. In principle at least, Europeans generally recognized the Indians' right of original occupancy. In the context of colonial America, the doctrine enabled a nation to extend its imperial domain over land previously unknown to, or unclaimed by, other Europeans and thereby preempt the right of any others to do so. When a European nation acquired the unsettled colonial territory of a rival, whether by purchase, diplomacy, or military victory, it only acquired the preemptive exclusion until the Indians ceded or sold them the land.[42]

The British Crown and American colonists saw the acquisition of Indian land as the means of fulfilling their mission to spread civilization, defined as Anglo Christianity and English culture, across the continent. In his *Second Treatise on Government*, English philosopher and apostle of the Enlightenment John Locke wrote that "God and his Reason commanded him [man] to subdue the Earth, i.e., improve it for the benefit of Life, and therein lay out something upon it that was his own, his labour."[43] The colonists moving to the frontier found what they characterized as a vast "desert," meaning a waste country, wilderness, or an uninhabited place, just waiting for them to "improve," or "to advance nearer to perfection" and "raise from good to better."[44] They improved the land by clearing the forest and dividing it into parcels of privately owned property set apart by fences. The settlers altered the land for cultivating crops or grazing cattle and constructed homes, barns, and outbuildings. The new inhabitants established industry and commerce with mills, kilns, mines, and forges. The immigrant populations expanded and established villages and towns with churches, courthouses, jails, taverns, and shops. Finally, they connected their communities with other communities by roads, fords, bridges, landings, and ferries, to advance civilization.

According to Locke, "Land that is left wholly to Nature, that hath no improvement of Pasturage, Tillage, or Planting, is called, as indeed it is, *wast[e]*."[45] American colonists looked to the British Crown, and their colonial governments, to acquire the largely uninhabited wasteland from the Indians, either by force or diplomacy, so they could obtain their own parcels to improve and make their own property. Benjamin Franklin, an American disciple of the Enlightenment, expressed this sentiment in his 1751 essay, "Observation Concerning the Increase of Mankind, Peopling of Countries, &c." He described the filial relationship between the Crown and colonies in part by stating "the Prince that acquires new Territory, if he finds it vacant, or removes the Natives to give his own People Room" fulfilled a paternal obligation. Similarly, a man who invented "new Trades, Arts, or Manufactures" shared the credit with he who acquired land so that both "may be properly called Fathers of their Nation, as they are the Cause of the Generation of Multitudes."[46] The colonists' land hunger should therefore not be characterized as simply motivated by greed but in the context of eighteenth-century attitudes as inspired by Enlightenment ideals.

Regardless of context, enlightened philosophies were alien to the native peoples. In contrast to their white neighbors, Indians believed in a mystical relationship between man and nature in which the Great Spirit, or creator, provided the land and the beasts on it for their use, but not for any one person to alter or possess. Had they been familiar with Locke's work, Indians would have argued that land in which "all the Fruits it naturally produces, and Beasts it feeds, belong to Mankind in common." Since these were produced by the "spontaneous hand of nature," Indians would have maintained that the land needed no improvement.[47] The Six Nations sachem Canassatego recognized this cultural divide when he addressed the Virginia com-

missioner at the 1744 Treaty of Lancaster. "Brother Assaragoa"—an Iroquoian word meaning Long Knife, or Big Knife, in reference to the ceremonial swords Virginia governors wore as a symbol of office and with which
the Indians identified them—"our Customs differing from yours, you will
be so good as to excuse us."[48] Although the Six Nations agreed to cede the
land between the "back of the great mountains" of Virginia and the Ohio
River at that treaty, he expressed the Indians' concern on how the new inhabitants improved the land. When living near them, the settlers' practice
of raising domesticated animals became a source of contention because
"white Peoples Cattle . . . eat up all the Grass, and made Deer scarce."[49]

Similarly, at the Treaty of Easton in 1758, the Seneca sachem Tagashata,
a Six Nations deputy speaking on behalf of all Indians, related that "Our
Cousins [the Minisinks]" complained that they were dispossessed of a great
deal of land due to "the English settling too fast" so that they "cou'd not tell
what Lands [still] belonged to them" and forgot what they sold. He further
maintained that the colonists claimed the wild animals as well as the land
and no longer allowed the Minisinks to "come on . . . to hunt after them."[50]
Indians often felt that even after they ceded land in friendship, white settlers
still dealt harshly with them. With no corresponding concept of private
property and land ownership, Indians believed that the game animals were
still theirs or common to both. They maintained that when they sold land,
they did not propose to deprive themselves of hunting wild deer. They discovered that the settlers not only claimed "all the wild Creatures" on the
land but did not "so much as let us peel a single Tree," or use "a Stick of
Wood" for shelter or firewood. Understandably, many native people took
great offense at such practices.[51] Similar cross-cultural misunderstandings
caused hard feelings, mistrust, and animosity and often led to conflict.

Many colonists did not wait for formal land cessions or purchases from
the Indians. The Royal Proclamation caused dismay among those who already lived or had their eyes fixed on acquiring lands beyond the limits of
settlement. They considered land between the Appalachians and the Ohio
the fruits of victory over the French and their Indian allies, fairly won in a
hard-fought war. Many Americans, including George Washington, understood that what he derisively called the "Ministerial Line" established by the
proclamation had to be "considered by the Government as a temporary expedient."[52] The very wording—"for the present, until our further pleasure
is known"—reinforced this sentiment. Otherwise, many argued, the provision for the governors of the provinces of North America to grant "without
fee or reward" the land bounties promised to officers and soldiers for their
wartime service, and the ten-year exemption from having to pay the same

quitrents as on other purchased lands, would have been hollow.[53] Furthermore, by calling it the ministerial and not royal proclamation, Americans did not fix the blame on the king but on ministers they believed had deceived him.

After the Crown issued the Royal Proclamation, William Johnson and John Stuart, superintendents of Indian affairs for the Northern and Southern Departments, respectively, requested the Lords Commissioners of Trade and Plantations, commonly called the Board of Trade, for permission to conduct negotiations with the Indians to identify and survey the actual boundary. Hoping to avoid another Indian war and satisfy native peoples as well as land speculators, settlers, and colonial officials, the Board of Trade issued its preliminary instructions in 1765. Specifically, the board directed the Indian superintendents to draw the line from Fort Stanwix, at the portage between the Mohawk River and Wood Creek in the north, south, and west to the Ohio River, then along its course to its confluence with the Great Kanawha River, proceeding up the Kanawha to its headwaters, then south to the border of East Florida. In early 1768, the Board of Trade's president, William Petty (who was born William Fitzmaurice before his father changed the family name to Petty in order to inherit the earldom from his wife's family), the Earl of Shelburne, transmitted the king's command to complete the "Boundary line between the several Provinces with the various Indian Tribes . . . without loss of time."[54]

Before any negotiations between Crown officials and Indian nations could begin, the British Indian Department's officers had to mediate peace between the two powerful native polities bordering the colonies. After repeated requests by colonial officials of North Carolina and Virginia on behalf of the Cherokees, Superintendent Johnson invited that nation and the Iroquois Six Nations to send their representative sachems to meet at Johnson Hall, his baronial manor in the Mohawk valley, to discuss ending the war between them. In February 1768, both sides agreed to sign the peace treaty.[55] The Cherokee representatives returned home well pleased and satisfied with the council's results, which opened the way for the next round of negotiations.

In the Northern Department, Indians from several nations began arriving at the abandoned British military post of Fort Stanwix in August. Eventually, three thousand four hundred Indians, including representative sachems, leading warriors, and their families, assembled. They represented the Six Nations and their several dependent and tributary tribes, as well as native peoples from outside of the Iroquois Confederacy such as the Seven Nations of Canada and the Wyandots.

Johnson convened the council. Negotiations began among the various Indians and with William Franklin, the royal governor of New Jersey; commissioners from the colonial governments of Pennsylvania and Virginia; and representatives of the "Suffering Traders" of Pennsylvania. Led by William Trent and Samuel Wharton, the last group sought land cessions for themselves and fellow Indian traders as compensation for the property they lost and other financial hardship incurred during Pontiac's War of 1763 to 1766. Although he attended as Johnson's deputy superintendent for the western Indian nations, George Croghan also had a private interest in the proceedings as one of the aggrieved traders. Dr. Thomas Walker and Andrew Lewis represented Virginia interests, until Lewis departed on October 12 to attend the council with the southern Indians at Hard Labour. The discussions lasted from September 20 until October 24, when the participants began work on formulating the treaty. The sachems of the Six Nations presumed to act as proprietors of all Indian land and affixed their totems to the Boundary Line Treaty and "a deed executed for the lands to the Crown of Great Britain" on November 5, 1768.[56] The final agreement not only established a boundary line on behalf of the Iroquois themselves but for the Shawnee, Delaware, Mingo, and others. Although representative chiefs from those entities attended, the Iroquois signed on their behalf and ceded their interests in land east and south of the Ohio River to the British.[57]

As required by the Royal Proclamation, Johnson, a representative of the Crown acting in his official capacity, purchased the ceded land from the Six Nations, who claimed dominion over it. In return, the favored Iroquois received the entire £10,460 British payment, much to the consternation of the Indian people who actually lived or hunted on the ceded land. The new boundary line ran from just west of Fort Stanwix south to and along the Delaware River, then west to and along the West Branch of the Susquehanna to the Allegheny River at Venango, then followed the latter downstream to Fort Pitt at the Forks of the Ohio River, then down the Ohio, passed the mouth of the Great Kanawha, to the mouth of the Tennessee River, then known as the Cherokee or Hogohege. The treaty therefore extended the boundary prescribed in the Board of Trade instructions much farther west. Part of the cession included the Indiana Grant as compensation to the suffering traders for their losses. To justify extending the cession, the Six Nations' sachems declared "it to be our true Bounds with the Southern [Cherokee] Indians & We Do have an undoubted Right to the Country as far South as that River which makes our Cession to his Majesty much more advantageous than proposed."[58]

Meanwhile, at Hard Labour, South Carolina, Stuart had reached an agreement with the principal Cherokee chiefs that established the southern Indian-colonial boundary on October 17, 1768. To the great relief of British subjects who had already settled there despite the Royal Proclamation, the Cherokees relinquished their claims to all lands between the Appalachian Divide and the Ohio, but only as far as the Great Kanawha River. However, many colonists had settled, and the lands acquired by the Loyal Company of Virginia for speculation were beyond this line. More importantly for Virginia interests, the Treaty of Hard Labour negated much of what the colony had gained in the Treaty of Fort Stanwix. [59]

When Virginia's commissioner, Andrew Lewis, reported on the "ensuing Congress with the Cherokees," the members of Virginia's Colonial Council described the proposed boundary as "highly injurious to this Colony, and to the Crown of Great Britain." They based their objections on grounds that it gave the southern Indians, or Cherokees, "an extensive tract of Land" between the Kanawha and Cherokee Rivers that the Six Nations had owned and ceded at Fort Stanwix. Virginia officials further maintained that Stuart essentially gave the Cherokees land, "a great part of which they never had, or pretended a right to, but actually disclaimed." The council directed Lewis to return to South Carolina, accompanied by Walker, to inform Stuart of the importance of a just boundary before he ordered the line surveyed. Otherwise, Virginia would not cooperate in determining a boundary until it received more explicit and precise instructions from the king. [60]

Superintendent Johnson's Fort Stanwix boundary did not join to form a coherent demarcation with that settled by Stuart in the Treaty of Hard Labour. Johnson maintained that the Six Nations could cede any of the land along that boundary as they held dominion over it by right of conquest, despite claims by those Indians who inhabited or hunted it. Therefore, the Six Nations ceded land on the Susquehanna and Allegheny inhabited by the Delawares and Munsees, as well as the Cherokee and Shawnee hunting ground in Kentucky, and even some arguably Cherokee country in present-day Tennessee, by the treaty signed at Fort Stanwix. [61] Johnson's explanation also affirmed the Virginia position.

Although he expressed displeasure with Johnson for not complying with his instructions and exceeding his authority, Lord Hillsborough, minister of the then newly created Secretariat of State for the Colonies, nevertheless communicated the royal ratification of the treaty and boundary, except for certain private grants, in December 1769. That same month, fifty-three men petitioned Virginia's governor Norborne Berkeley, fourth Baron Botetourt, for permission to "take up and survey" sixty thousand acres on the Cumberland River from the lands situated on the east side of the Ohio "having lately been recognized by the Six Nations of Indians" as conveyed to "his Majesty's Title."[62]

Ratification of the Fort Stanwix boundary required Stuart to renegotiate the southern boundary due to the great loss and inconvenience it caused the many British subjects who inhabited lands that the Cherokees had not ceded but the Iroquois had. Along with commissioners from Virginia and North Carolina, Stuart convened a meeting with sixteen Cherokee chiefs on October 5 at Lochaber, South Carolina, the home of Alexander Cochrane, his deputy for that nation. By the eighteenth, the Cherokee leaders signed the deed relinquishing all claims to the land from the North Carolina and Virginia border west along the Holston River to a point six miles east of the Long Island of the Holston, then north by east on a straight line to the Ohio at the mouth of the Great Kanawha.[63]

Although an improvement, the arrangement still did not please the Virginians much more than the Treaty of Hard Labour had. Authorized by a resolution of the General Assembly to request Stuart to negotiate "a more extensive Boundary," Governor Botetourt urged the southern Indian superintendent to immediately negotiate a treaty with the Cherokees in which Virginia would gain the cession of those lands to which the king had already consented in the Fort Stanwix Treaty. With the necessary appropriations passed, Botetourt commissioned Colonel John Donelson to survey the new boundary as soon as possible after the Indian superintendent and commissioners concluded the new treaty.[64] Botetourt did not live to see it. After he died on October 15, 1770, William Nelson, president of the colonial council, assumed the role of acting governor.

Stuart informed Cochrane that the treaty had not pleased the Shawnees either. They sat as "the head of the Western confederacy" formed for the purpose of maintaining their property in the lands the British obtained from the Six Nations at Fort Stanwix and preventing white people from settling there.[65] Johnson and the Iroquois leaders feared that the Mingoes, residing in the neighborhood of the "disaffected tribes," would feel increasingly alienated. They did not want their emigrants to fall under the influence of the Shawnees, whom they considered no real friends of the Six Nations, to the point where they "followed other councils." Seeking to exert renewed authority on their kin, Johnson called for a congress of deputies from the Six Nations to meet with the Shawnees, Delawares, Wyandots, Miamis, and others to put a halt to their attempts to seduce the Mingoes, or Six Nations on the Ohio, from their allegiance to the Iroquois Confederacy.[66]

WITH THE unexpected death of Governor Botetourt, Lord Hillsborough selected John Murray, the fourth Earl of Dunmore, then serving as royal governor of New York, to succeed him in Virginia. The new governor's father, William Murray, influenced by his wife Catherine's Nairne relatives, and much to the embarrassment of the rest of the Murrays, had joined the losing side in the failed Jacobite Rebellion of 1745. William Murray served the Young Pretender, Charles Edward Stuart, or Bonnie Prince Charlie, as a vice chamberlain, or assistant to the manager of the royal household. Although too young to serve in the rebel army, John left his studies at Eton when his father secured him the honorary position of a "Page of Honour" to the prince. After the forces loyal to King George II decisively crushed the rebels in the April 1746 battle of Culloden Moor, William initially evaded capture, but eventually surrendered to the king's forces. Indicted by a grand jury, he stood trial "by Reason of his having been concerned with the late Rebellion."[67]

Fortunately, William's brother and son's namesake, John Murray, the second Earl of Dunmore, and a "General of Our Foot" in the British army, intervened on William's behalf. The Crown spared William from execution for "High Treason," as well as "all other Treasons, Crimes and Offenses" committed before December 22, 1746, for which he stood convicted. The government commuted the death sentence to confinement. Two years later, in 1748, George II granted William a royal pardon with "license to reside in Beverly, at Yorkshire," which enabled him to succeed the unmarried John as third lord in 1752, when his elder brother died leaving no heirs.[68]

In 1749, the year after the Crown pardoned William, John brought his brother's son into the British army in a manner most appropriate and befitting a young Scottish aristocrat. John, the second Earl of Dunmore, who had served many years as the colonel of the regiment, purchased his nephew and successor to the earldom an ensign's commission in the 3rd (Scottish) Regiment of Foot Guards. Under the unique dual-rank system of the day, the young John Murray's appointment not only included a much sought after membership in the elite unit but a captaincy in the British army as well.[69] When William died in 1756, Captain John Murray became the fourth Earl of Dunmore, with an inheritance that included the additional hereditary titles of Viscount Fincastle and Baron of Blair, Monlin, and Tillimett.[70]

Despite the advantages he enjoyed, Dunmore experienced a series of disappointments as a young officer in pursuit of military distinction and advancement. As soon as Great Britain declared war on France in 1756, he unsuccessfully sought field assignments. Despite the assistance of well-connected friends and relatives, and possibly tainted by his father's treason, his requests for posting to the Anglo-German army commanded by Duke Ferdinand of Brunswick-Lunenburg on the European continent or assignment to that of Brigadier General James Wolfe in North America went for naught. Except for participating in a few raids against the coast of France, he took part in no campaigns of any note. Although Dunmore served in an army engaged in a desperate global conflict, he gained little combat experience and no distinction.[71]

Dunmore's fortunes began to change in 1761, when his fellow Scottish aristocrats elected the brash thirty-year-old to a seven-year term as one of the representative peers of Scotland in the House of Lords. That same year, his friend and army comrade William Fitzmaurice Petty, a military aide-de-camp to King George III, inherited the title second Earl of Shelburne and a seat in the Lords on his father's death. Although nothing prevented serving officers from sitting in Parliament, Dunmore, frustrated in his pursuit of a military career, informed the well-connected Shelburne of his intention to "resign all thoughts of the army" in 1762.[72]

Dunmore eventually received the appointment, and briefly served, as royal governor of New York in 1770. He thoroughly relished his short time as governor and took the opportunity to acquire a sizable holding of land and other wealth in that colony. In an era when realizing personal profit from one's political position did not necessarily constitute a conflict of interest or corruption, Dunmore made the most of his appointment. Although it was considered a promotion, he reluctantly accepted the governorship of Virginia but delayed his arrival in Williamsburg for several months. He assumed his new post in September 1771.

COLONEL JOHN DONELSON set out on his mission to survey and mark Virginia's new western border in fall 1771. Cochrane and "several chiefs of the [Cherokee] Indians concerned," including Attakullakulla, the "Most beloved" or principal chief, whom the British called Little Carpenter, accompanied the surveyors. After they had surveyed the line, Virginia's new governor reported to Secretary of State Hillsborough that the new line did not run exactly according to the instructions and took in a larger tract of the country than the Treaty of Lochaber had defined. During the process of surveying, Donelson secured the several Cherokee chiefs' agreement to adjust the negotiated boundary from that as drawn on the map. The arbitrary line ran through difficult and unremarkable ground, which the Indians described as not good for hunting anyway. The new surveyed boundary fol-

John Murray, fourth Earl of Dunmore. This 1765 portrait by artist Sir Joshua Reynolds depicts Dunmore at age 35, when he was a representative peer of Scotland in the House of Lords of the British Parliament, wearing highland regalia. (*National Portrait Gallery of Scotland*)

lowed easily recognizable terrain features that could never be mistaken and proved less costly to survey. Still short of the limits established by the Fort Stanwix boundary and less area than Governor Botetourt desired for the colony, Virginia's new area extended to the Louisa (or Kentucky) River. From its confluence with the Ohio, the new boundary followed the Louisa to its northernmost fork, ran west along the ridge of mountains to the headwaters of the Cumberland, and then east to the Holston River where it met the cession agreed upon at Lochaber. Although not a formal treaty, the arrangement became known as the Great Grant, or the Cherokee Treaty of 1772.[73]

In February that year, the Virginia General Assembly enacted legislation that created a new county, named Fincastle in honor of one of Dunmore's hereditary titles, by incorporating areas of Botetourt County plus the land acquired by the recent boundary-line adjustments.[74] In April, a group of anxious settlers petitioned the Virginia Assembly for a large grant on the Louisa River. By October, the governor and council ordered a Commission of Peace to establish the county court and appoint justices of the peace, as well as create the militia establishment and commission its field officers.[75]

While the Iroquois and Cherokee relinquished their claims and collected the purchase prices (although evidence exists that the Cherokee may never have received the £500 promised them), none of the diplomatic actions addressed the concerns of the Shawnee for the loss of their hunting ground. For all intents and purposes, especially as colonists, Crown officials, and the Six Nations viewed it, the Ohio River represented the new boundary between the British colonies and Indian country. Not surprisingly, the Shawnees disputed the treaties and looked upon any white encroachment as an invasion. As early as April 1771, Superintendent Stuart informed Lord Hillsborough that the "dissatisfaction of the Western tribes . . . at the extensive cession of land at the Congress at Fort Stanwix" caused them to form confederacies and alliances with other nations. In consequence, they were "indefatigable" in sending messengers and making peace overtures to the Cherokees in order to balance the power of the Iroquois, whom they held responsible for their loss. Stuart further expressed the opinion that the extension of the colonial boundaries into the Indian hunting grounds had "rendered what the Indians reserved to themselves on this side of the mountains of very little use to them." Deer were already becoming scarce because of the influx of white hunters and erection of new settlements.[76]

After reading the reports from the Indian superintendents, General Gage informed Lord Hillsborough that the Ohio tribes had become "discontented" because great numbers of whites had crossed the Alleghenies to settle between the mountains and the Ohio, "so near to the Indians as to occasion frequent quarrels." The general nonetheless had confidence in Johnson's assurance that the Six Nations "resolved to manifest their fidelity to the English" in enforcing the treaty and "bring the Western nations to good order."[77]

The British army relinquished responsibility for frontier security when it ordered a number of posts abandoned and demolished, and their garrisons redeployed to eastern cities. General Gage informed William Barrington, second Viscount Barrington, the secretary at war, "If the Colonists will afterward force the Savages into Quarrells by using them ill, let them feel the Consequences, we shall be out of the Scrape."[78] The evacuation of regulars from Fort Pitt on October 10, 1772, pleased the Indians but caused a vacuum of authority that both Pennsylvania and Virginia sought to fill.

Pennsylvania's Assembly, controlled by the Quaker Party, would never approve the proposal for raising and supporting even a small number of troops that Lieutenant Governor Richard Penn sought to garrison Fort Pitt in the place of the king's forces.[79]

Both virginia and Pennsylvania claimed jurisdiction of the region between the Monongahela and Ohio Rivers, including the strategic Forks. Virginia's government considered the area a part of Augusta County, established in 1738. When Pennsylvania established its Westmoreland County west of the Laurel Ridge in 1772, its boundary overlapped a portion of western Augusta. Virginia's claim ultimately rested on the London Company's corporate charter of 1609, and the royal colony charter that replaced it in 1624, which fixed its area between two hundred miles north and south of Old Point Comfort on the Atlantic, then west to the "Western (Pacific) Sea." Except for specified cessions of land to other colonies at various times, by 1773, Virginia's dominion still stretched in a widening vector to the west and northwest, encompassing present-day Virginia, West Virginia, Kentucky, Ohio, Indiana, Illinois, Michigan, Wisconsin, and part of Minnesota. Pennsylvania based its claim on William Penn's 1661 proprietary charter for a colony between the Delaware River on the east to five degrees of longitude on the west.[80] This description left the western border open to four possible interpretations. The western limit could be defined either by an irregular boundary that mirrored all points on the Delaware, or a fixed straight line corresponding to either the point farthest east, farthest west, or at the median of the two. Any of these solutions for determining Pennsylvania's western boundary encroached on land included in Virginia's charter.

In an attempt to confirm the grants awarded the suffering traders at Fort Stanwix, William Trent and Samuel Wharton traveled to England in 1769 and met with some influential parties to form the Grand Ohio Company. Backed by investors in London and Philadelphia, including merchant and House of Commons member Thomas Walpole and American scientist, author, and printer Benjamin Franklin, who acted as an agent in Parliament for Pennsylvania and other provinces, they approached the Board of Trade with a plan to establish a new inland colony on the recently ceded Indian land. Originally to be called Pittsylvania, they changed the name to Vandalia in honor of Queen Charlotte, George III's wife, as she purportedly descended from the Germanic tribe the Vandals. The proposed venture immediately complicated matters on the frontier.

The Board of Trade cited "the necessity . . . for introducing some regular system of government" to a part of Virginia that the commissioners believed was too far from the civil government at Williamsburg. The distance from that capital, the argument ran, rendered the people living there "incapable of participating of the advantages" of being part of that colony. Therefore, they recommended that the region be separated from Virginia and incorporated into Vandalia by letters patent under the Great Seal of Great Britain. They envisioned the new colony's area as bounded on the west, north, and northwest by the Ohio River, from the border of Pennsylvania to a point opposite the mouth of the Scioto, then down the Louisa to its headwaters and eventually the Holston River, and on the east by the Allegheny Mountains.[81] Although Lord Hillsborough disapproved, the Privy Council overruled him and forwarded the Vandalia plan to the king. The Virginia government opposed the new creation since Vandalia's area would come at the expense of territory granted by the colony's royal charter and recently acquired by the Indian treaties. George Croghan, who expected a settlement based on his suffering trader status, stood to gain either way. Had George III assented to the new colony, Vandalia's boundaries would have encroached on the territory of, and created competing land claims with those issued by, Virginia. The king, however, never signed the charter.

As soon as Dunmore assumed the governorship in 1771, he began receiving petitions for patents on western lands. Presiding over the largest, wealthiest, and most populous British colony on mainland North America, Dunmore seemed eager to establish himself as the king's viceroy and protect the interests of the colony over which he presided. In a personal letter to Hillsborough, he viewed the granting of patents and "settling . . . some of the vacant lands which the new boundary-line now offers . . . as a means of ingratiating myself very much with the people of this colony." Dunmore's ambitions were not unlike those of other colonial officials in using the advantage of government office for personal gain, and he sought to acquire land "advantageous to my family" while in Virginia.[82]

Dunmore found that he and George Washington shared common interests in this regard, and they were on friendly terms. Both aspired to acquire land and gain a return on the investment through speculation. As speculators and other land-hungry colonists joined veterans seeking to redeem their bounties, they desired to have their claims "legally surveyed and patented" as soon as possible.[83] Many settlers had also started flooding into the recently ceded areas since the last war. In a letter to his brother Jonathan, the busy twenty-year-old surveyor George Rogers Clark wrote that "this C[o]untry settles very fast." With the new boundary treaties signed and ratified, Clark added, "the people is a settling as low as ye Siotho [Scioto] River 366 [miles] Below Fort Pitt."[84]

In an effort to establish Virginia authority and bring some order to the situation on the frontier, Governor Dunmore authorized Captain Thomas Bullitt to organize a party to survey the land in northern and eastern Kentucky. Leading about forty men, he started down the Ohio from the Kanawha River. On entering Shawnee country, Bullitt visited the principal Shawnee town of Chillicothe and met with the chief, Keiga-tugh-qua, whom the English called Cornstalk, and other leaders. After informing them that the land on the south bank "had been sold to the white people by the Six Nations and Cherokees as far down the Ohio as the mouth of the Cherokee River," he continued on his way. After reaching the Falls of the Ohio in July, he remained into August to lay out the settlement that later became Louisville, Kentucky. Bullitt's visit understandably alarmed the Shawnee. Meeting at Fort Pitt, Shawnee deputies addressed Guyasuta, the Seneca chief and diplomat representing the Six Nations' interests in the Ohio country and exercising authority over the Mingoes, and Alexander McKee, Sir William Johnson's deputy superintendent, to express their dismay that "our nations had not been considered when the purchases were made."[85]

Meanwhile, Dunmore "thought it might conduce to the good of His Majesty's service" to personally visit the "interior and remote parts" of the colony. The governor planned to go in the summer of 1773, when not much provincial business would be conducted in Williamsburg between the sessions of the General Court.[86] George Washington, actively lobbying for the governor to honor the land grants promised to the veterans of the Virginia Regiment by Governor Robert Dinwiddie and the General Assembly in 1754, and to open the area for settlement, invited Dunmore to visit Mount Vernon on his way. If the governor wished to leave as early as the first of July, Washington offered to accompany his lordship "through any and every part of the Western Country" he thought proper to visit. Washington recommended and arranged for fellow Virginia Regiment veteran William Crawford, a good woodsman who was familiar with the lands in the region, to act as their guide. In addition, Washington offered to contact the now-retired long-time deputy superintendent of the western Indians, George Croghan, to arrange a meeting with some local tribal leaders.[87]

Unfortunately, tragedy struck Mount Vernon on Saturday, June 19, when Martha "Patsy" Parke Custis, Martha Washington's child from a previous marriage, died unexpectedly of an attack of epilepsy. Expressing being "most exceedingly sorry," the governor offered his condolences to the bereaved stepfather and especially the grieving Mrs. Washington for the loss of the "poor young lady." Dunmore understood that Washington could no longer accompany him but communicated his intention to pay his respects to the mourning family in person at Mount Vernon on his way.[88]

Dunmore's mission apparently had two purposes. First, he wished to exert Virginia's jurisdiction over the area to counter the Pennsylvania claims. Second, he opposed the creation of Vandalia and would show the Privy Council and Board of Trade that the frontier districts did not fall beyond the reach of his government's civil and military protection. Formulating his plan, he sought the support of local residents, including some who had accepted Pennsylvania civil offices, like his guide Crawford, who served as the president and chief magistrate for Westmoreland County. While many Virginians lived there, others considered themselves Pennsylvanians. When Dunmore visited his home on the Youghiogheny River, Crawford provided the governor with information about the region and locations of the best land. In return, Dunmore assured Crawford that he would receive the patents for the land Virginia owed him for his wartime service.

On his arrival in Pittsburgh, Dunmore found that the neighborhood had "upwards of ten thousand people settled [but] had neither magistrates to preserve rule and order among themselves, nor militia for their defence in case of sudden attack of the Indians." The withdrawal of the British garrison the previous year left no agency to keep order, and the fort had been partially demolished with the remains in such disrepair that it had little defensive value. Yet, Dunmore noted the presence of an Indian settlement directly opposite to the town on the far side of the river, which presented "the utmost necessity of such establishment." He found many inhabitants who agreed with him, and he claimed that people flocked around him and begged him to appoint magistrates and militia officers in order to remove "these onerous inconveniences under which they labored."[89] To further put their concerns at ease, he assured everyone that his government would honor land patents they received from other valid authorities. Dunmore thus won over a number of Pennsylvanians, including Colonel Croghan, as one of the suffering traders, and Dr. John Connolly, both of whom stood to gain much in the Vandalia project.

ALTHOUGH HIS high forehead, beak-like nose, and steel-eyed gaze gave Connolly a hawklike appearance, Thomas Jefferson described the thirty-two-year-old doctor as "chatty" and "sensible to physic," or the practice of medicine, but who confided that he had always aspired to be a soldier. Connolly proudly stated that he had served as a volunteer—meaning he was

John Connolly met Lord Dunmore during the royal governor's 1773 visit to the frontier. The Pennsylvania doctor became a loyal and leading proponent of Virginia interests, as well as head of that colony's civil government and military establishment in the Pittsburgh area. (*Filson Historical Society*)

unpaid—in two campaigns. These included the British attack on Martinique in the West Indies during the Seven Years' War and on the frontier during Pontiac's War. This participation afforded the aspiring officer an opportunity to observe the "great difference between the *petite guerre* [guerrilla war] of the Indians, and the military system of the Europeans." Not taking the experiences he gained for granted, it was essential and necessary for a good soldier in this service to be a master of both modes of warfare. In addition to experience, Connolly's military service had also earned him a patent for land.[90] Dunmore enhanced Connolly's interest with the promise of an additional two thousand acres at the Falls of the Ohio and invited him to discuss the matter with him more fully in Williamsburg in the autumn. An excited Connolly wrote to George Washington that since "Lord Dunmore hath done us the honor of a visit," he had come to share the Virginian's high regard for the governor as "a Gentleman of benevolence & universal Charity." In September, Washington wrote to congratulate the governor on his safe return to the capital. He also hoped to build on the governor's interest in land acquisition following his "Tour through a Country," which even "if not well Improv'd" had at least been "bless'd with many natural advantages."[91]

Meanwhile, Superintendent Johnson wrote William Legge, second Earl of Dartmouth, secretary of state for the colonies, and president of the Board of Trade, with "intelligence" received from Fort Pitt. His deputy, Alexander McKee, reported that "a certain Captain Bullet with a large number of people from Virginia" had gone down the Ohio beyond the proposed boundary of Vandalia to survey and lay out lands "which are to be forthwith patented." The news disturbed the Indians "a good deal" and left the Shawnee, in particular, "much alarmed at the numbers who go from Virginia in pursuit of new settlements."[92]

Coincidentally, King George III and the Privy Council issued new guidance concerning the disposal of His Majesty's land on April 7, 1773, which Dunmore received in early October. The king and his ministers realized that the authority to grant Crown lands conveyed by each governor's commission and instructions needed to be further regulated and restrained. Additionally, those receiving grants of Crown land should also be subjected to other conditions than previously enumerated. Therefore, George III ordered all governors, lieutenant governors, and other persons "in Command of his Majesty's Colonies in North America" to cease issuing any warrants of survey or to pass any patents for lands, or grant any license for the private purchase of any lands from the Indians without special direction from the king until further notice. The new regulation exempted only veterans of the regular service, not provincials, entitled to the military grants as prescribed in the Royal Proclamation of 1763, although Dunmore vigorously advocated for the latter.[93]

Three weeks had elapsed following McKee's warning about Shawnee restlessness before a party of nineteen braves made their way through the Kentucky hunting grounds on their way home from Chota in Cherokee country. Having just attended a congress where representatives from several nations discussed the continued white encroachment on those very hunting grounds, the warriors' blood was up, and they were spoiling for a fight. When they crossed paths with eight men leading cattle and packhorses, the Indians seized the opportunity to strike. After a quick and violent attack on the morning of October 10, 1773, that left six of the eight dead, fear of a new war spread along the frontier.

CHAPTER 2

Extraordinary Occurrences

Intercolonial Boundaries and Indian Relations

October 1773–March 1774

ONCE BACK in Williamsburg, Dunmore met with the Council of Virginia to review the government business that had transpired during his absence. Composed of twelve prominent residents appointed to life terms by the monarch, the council performed all three functions of government. As a legislative body, it constituted the upper house of the General Assembly. With the governor acting as chief justice, council members served as associate justices on the General Court, the supreme judicial body of the colony. While some members also held appointive offices, they collectively served as a Council of State, or an executive board that advised the governor on matters of colonial administration and policy.[1] After Dunmore weighed his options and developed a preliminary plan to counter Pennsylvania's annexation of western Augusta County, he convened the council in a private session. When they met on Monday, October 11, 1773—by coincidence, the day after the bloodshed in distant Powell's Valley—the governor and councilors took up the matter of the king's recent order on the disposal of Crown land and ordered commissions to fill vacated seats on a county court.[2]

Dunmore then turned to the situation at the Forks of the Ohio and laid "the Petition of Sundry Inhabitants in the Neighborhood of Fort Pitt" before the board. The signatories complained that the Pennsylvania government had encroached on Virginia territory and oppressed several landowners when it established a court with jurisdiction over Virginia citizens residing in a Virginia county, and thus caused them great hardship.

The petitioners requested Lord Dunmore to redress their grievances by taking them under the protection of the Virginia government, to "which they
conceived themselves to properly belong."[3] With the advice and consent of
the council, Dunmore issued a new commission of the peace for Augusta
County and ordered that seven gentlemen who resided in or near Pittsburgh
be added to the slate of justices seated at Staunton. The new justices of the
peace were George Croghan, his cousin Thomas Smallman, Dr. John Connolly, Dorsey Pentecost, John Gibson, John Campbell, and Edward Ward.
The board further recommended that the governor formally complain to
Lord Dartmouth, who was the secretary of state for the colonies, and Governor Penn about the Pennsylvania government's actions in establishing a
court with jurisdiction within what they considered the boundary of Virginia.[4]

Connolly arrived in Williamsburg in early December to keep his appointment to discuss the situation on the Ohio frontier with the governor.
As he took in the sights, he compared it to Philadelphia, with which he was
more familiar. The Pennsylvania capital was the largest city in the British
colonies of North America, a busy seaport and bustling commercial center
with a population of about thirty-five thousand residents. More than seven
thousand structures, including a number of substantial buildings, stood
within the one square mile that defined its municipal limits. In some of its
neighborhoods, densely arranged buildings with adjoining walls were
grouped into square or rectangular blocks along roads of hard-packed
earth, or in some places paved streets, so that Philadelphia looked very
much like a city in England. In contrast, the seat of government and "me-
tropolis" of Virginia had a population of about one thousand people and
about five hundred buildings within limits that measured one mile in length
and one-half mile in width. Connolly would have noticed, as the contemporary British visitor John F. D. Smyth described in his travel log, that, "All
the public buildings are built of brick, all the streets of sand, and the houses
mostly constructed of wood painted white, every one detached from the
other."[5]

On the appointed date, as meeting time approached, Connolly walked
west along Duke of Gloucester Street, the city's primary east-west thorough-
fare, to the Palace Green, which represented the main north-south axis. He
turned right and followed the street that ran on the eastern boundary of
the common to his destination at the Governor's Palace. Captain Augustine
Prevost, a British army officer who visited in September 1774 while on recruiting duty, described the governor's residence as "a commodious building, tho not elegant, with a cupilloe on top." A servant dressed in Dunmore's

The Governor's Palace served as the symbol of royal authority and the official residence of the monarch's viceroy in the colony of Virginia. Completed in 1722 with funds appropriated by the General Assembly, it was destroyed in 1782, two years after the state legislature moved the state capital to Richmond. During the restoration of Colonial Williamsburg in the 1930s, the palace was rebuilt on the same foundation according to the original plans and using contemporary descriptions, and appears today much as it did when Lord Dunmore occupied the building as Virginia's last royal governor. (*Library of Congress*)

brown and blue livery met Connolly at the gate and ushered him into the palace and through the formal entrance hall, where an impressive display of regimental colors, bladed weapons, and functional firearms adorned the walls to impress and remind visitors of Britain's—and Virginia's—military might. The servant then led Connolly up the stairs to the governor's office on the second floor and announced his arrival. [6]

Dunmore greeted him warmly, and the two took their seats. Getting to the business at hand, His Excellency told Connolly that it appeared the new government of Vandalia had "fallen through." Although it had become increasingly unpopular in England, the Privy Council had not yet canceled the project. In consequence, the Grand Ohio Company continued its preparations to implement its plan for developing the inland colony as if nothing had changed, including the establishment of an interim capital at Pittsburgh until the permanent seat of government could be erected at Point Pleasant. Trusting the veracity of the rumors about the project's demise, Dunmore told Connolly he intended to "take charge" of the area that "falls out Pennsylvania." [7]

The governor had set his sights on the strategic Forks of the Ohio, convinced that it lay within the boundary of his colony. Why else, he reasoned, had the British government ordered one of his predecessors, Lieutenant

Governor Robert Dinwiddie, to send Virginia troops to establish a fort there
to block French penetration of His Majesty's dominion in 1754? Virginia
troops had also participated in both Braddock's and Forbes's campaigns to
capture Fort Duquesne and retake the strategic point from the French. After
the British had regained control and began construction of Fort Pitt, Virginia maintained one regiment of its provincial troops to serve in the garrison until the end of the French and Indian War.

Although a scion of the proprietary colony, Connolly had become "convinced that Pittsburgh, Redstone, & all the other Western Settlements, could
not properly be within the Limits of Pennsylvania." After choosing to consider himself a Virginian, he readily accepted his lordship's directions to organize the region as a district of Augusta until a new Virginia county could
be erected to contain Pennsylvania's expansion in that quarter. As he later
wrote in a letter to George Washington, Connolly believed that resolute and
timely action by the Virginia governor and General Assembly "might bring
the Pennsylvanians to some equitable determination of their Western
Boundary."[8] Any discussions about the district's boundaries would remain
academic until the Crown resolved the colonial border issue, but when
asked, Connolly recommended that the district's boundaries encompass
"Pittsburgh, & at least two miles to the East, & up the Monongahela to the
entrance of Buffaloe Creek," and that "perhaps Grave Creek, below Whealon
[Wheeling] ... might be a good west Boundary." An estimated two thousand
people already resided within the limits Connolly proposed.[9]

To perform his duties, the governor issued Connolly two commissions,
one civil and one military. The civil commission appointed him a justice of
the peace for Augusta County and would officially take effect as soon as he
could swear the necessary oaths before Charles Lewis, the chief magistrate
of the county court in Staunton. A justice of the peace, or magistrate, in
colonial Virginia exercised both ministerial and judicial authority at the
county level of government. In the former role, he executed orders, administered policies, collected taxes, and enforced the laws. In the latter, he served
as a judge of record to hear criminal and chancery, or civil, cases.[10] Connolly
also carried the commissions for the six other justices the council added to
the Augusta County court on October 11.

As with his civil commission, Connolly's military commission in the
grade of captain and appointment as commandant of the district came with
orders to establish a militia "expressly for Pittsburgh and its dependencies."[11]
Given its geographical size and estimated free white military-age male population, Dunmore and the council believed the district could support up
to four administrative companies. Connolly's orders in this regard did not

reflect the usual manner by which new jurisdictions established their militias according to the legislation then in effect.

MEANWHILE, three days before New Year's Day, William Crawford wrote to George Washington from his Spring Garden home. Crawford, who acted as Washington's land agent in the Ohio country, had served in the Virginia Regiment under his now-client's command during the French and Indian War. Crawford informed Washington that the yet-unconfirmed news about the end of the Vandalia project had reached Pittsburgh. Both men held military grants for Virginia land that would have been located within the proposed new colony. Having the area "remain in the hands of Lord Dunmore," Crawford told Washington, would prove more beneficial to them than if Pennsylvania maintained control of the Forks of the Ohio region.[12] Two weeks later, Connolly visited Crawford and told him about what had transpired during his recent visit to Williamsburg. In the course of their conversation, Connolly stated that the Vandalia plan had been canceled "without a doubt." Crawford immediately relayed the news to Washington.[13] Although the news of the project's cancellation was premature, individuals who held patents issued in Williamsburg no longer feared how the loss of Virginia's territorial integrity would affect their holdings and engaged surveyors to mark off their claims. Those with eyes fixed westward believed that the Virginia government was again free to manage expansion and settlement, under which they could reap the associated financial benefits. The process also benefitted Dunmore's personal interests in land acquisition and speculation by gaining the support of influential men like Connolly and Croghan.

Lord Dunmore, as contemporary John J. Jacob later described, had acted "With becoming zeal for the honor of the Ancient Dominion."[14] Connolly may have learned of a proposal by Pennsylvania's Westmoreland County trustees to move their county seat from Hanna's Town to Pittsburgh, which added to his sense of urgency.[15] On New Year's Day 1774, following Dunmore's orders, Connolly walked through town to the gate of the abandoned military post. To the assembled inhabitants he announced that the royal governor intended to "maintain the possession of Fort Pitt and its dependencies" as part of Augusta County, where Virginia's militia act and other laws were now in force.[16] By the governor's authority, the captain commandant summoned all eligible white males to assemble at the fort to enroll in the militia on Tuesday, January 25. Connolly then added that the jurisdiction of Westmoreland County did not extend to, and neither its justices of

the peace nor any other civil officers appointed by Pennsylvania's proprietary government had legal standing in, the district. Instead, Connolly informed the residents that although the Court of Augusta County met in
Staunton, about 170 miles away, he planned to hold an additional court
under its jurisdiction in Pittsburgh on the twentieth day of each month.[17]
After he dismissed the crowd, Connolly posted advertisements notifying
the public at large of the forthcoming muster throughout the area.[18] The
captain commandant appointed three subaltern officers to assist him in organizing the district's militia. He presented commissions and administered
the necessary oaths to John Stephenson and William Harrison, William
Crawford's half-brother and son-in-law respectively, and Dorsey Pentecost,
a Westmoreland County justice of the peace living in the Redstone area.[19]

Captain Connolly's actions may have pleased Dunmore, but they
alarmed local officials and the Pennsylvania colonial government. On receiving the first reports from Pittsburgh, Governor John Penn directed the
clerk of the Westmoreland County court, Arthur St. Clair, to stop Connolly's
activities. Although the letter did not reach him in time, St. Clair had already
travelled to Pittsburgh and took action in the absence of orders. St. Clair
had Sheriff John Proctor place Connolly under arrest on January 24 for "requiring the People to meet as a Militia" without legal authority. When Connolly defiantly refused to post bond to ensure his good behavior until
scheduled to appear at the next court day, the sheriff conveyed him to the
jail at Hanna's Town. St. Clair believed that he had put the matter to rest,
but Connolly's subordinate officers conducted the scheduled muster without him. "About eighty persons in arms assembled themselves" the next day.
Identifying the strongholds of Virginia partisans, St. Clair noted they came
"chiefly from Mr. Croghan's neighborhood," three miles up the Allegheny
River from town, and the communities west of and below the Monongahela.
Casting aspersions on the training exercise, he reported the armed men,
"after parading through town and making a kind of *feu de joy*" to celebrate
and salute the return of Virginia sovereignty, proceeded to the fort where
someone produced a cask of rum and knocked the head of it out on the parade. St. Clair, a former British officer, derisively commented, "This was a
very effectual way of recruiting."[20]

Anticipating trouble, St. Clair assembled six Westmoreland magistrates
from in and around Pittsburgh, plus the Crown's deputy Indian superintendent, Alexander McKee, to a meeting where they would be in position
to take action. St. Clair specifically invited McKee because he learned that
the Indian agent also held a commission from Lord Dunmore as justice of
the peace for Virginia's Fincastle County, which raised suspicion he might

Arthur St. Clair, left, was born to a prosperous family in Scotland. He studied medicine at the University of Edinburgh, and apprenticed as a physician, but in 1757 he purchased an ensign's commission in the 60th "Royal American" Regiment of Foot of the British Army. St. Clair served in North America during the French and Indian War, rising to the rank of lieutenant before resigning in 1762. He settled in the Ligonier Valley of Pennsylvania and became a wealthy land owner, businessman, surveyor, and justice of the county court in Bedford and Westmoreland counties. He led the Pennsylvania faction in that colony's 1774 border dispute with Virginia. (*New York Public Library*)

William Crawford, right, a Virginian by birth, learned surveying and worked with George Washington. He served in the Virginia Regiment under Colonel Washington's command during the French and Indian War. After the war he settled on property he purchased along the Youghiogheny River, and supported his family as a farmer, fur trader, and land surveyor. He was also appointed a justice of the peace in Bedford and Westmoreland counties, before he sided with his native Virginia in the intercolonial boundary dispute of 1774. (*Painting by Robert O. Chadeayne/Wyandot County Historical Society*)

side with Connolly if left on his own. The suspicion proved unfounded, and McKee "behaved very well" on the occasion.[21] Recognizing that the task of maintaining Pennsylvania authority would be difficult, St. Clair assured the magistrates of Governor Penn's support and felt confident they would faithfully discharge their duties. As clerk of the court, he instructed them on how to behave. He then distributed a paper he had prepared for all to sign and that he would read to the crowd if events got out of control before announcing "the necessary cautions with regard to the Riot Act."[22] When read to a group of twelve or more people, the Riot Act declared all persons participating in an unlawful assembly to be guilty of a felony offense and subject to the consequences, including the use of deadly force by the authorities.

By addressing his reading of the Riot Act to their "friends and fellow Country men," St. Clair informed Connolly's followers of the validity of the

Pennsylvania government's claim to the country surrounding Pittsburgh. He reminded them that the settlers already living there had "quietly acquiesced in that claim, and all who subsequently arrived had also acknowledged the fact when they applied for their lands. The matter of fixing a formal boundary line between the colonies, St. Clair continued, awaited only the king's assent to Pennsylvania's petition to conduct the necessary survey. He concluded by telling them "it must be evident" that the governor of Virginia had "no more right" to determine the matter than anyone else, "for this plain Reason." [23]

St. Clair then addressed the grievances that Dunmore cited to justify his action and their assembling. He first emphasized that no inhabitant would suffer a lack of protection under the law from Pennsylvania. He warned that a state of anarchy and confusion would likely ensue throughout the region if both Pennsylvania and Virginia maintained "contending jurisdictions in one and the same country." The magistrate further assured the Virginians that they could depend on the Pennsylvania General Assembly to establish a military force at Pittsburgh for their defense when and if warranted. Since the withdrawal of British regulars from Fort Pitt in 1772, the Pennsylvania government primarily trusted the efforts of the Crown's Indian Department, especially the Pittsburgh-based deputy superintendent, McKee, and the Six Nations to keep peace with and between the Indians of the Ohio country, whom the Iroquois considered dependent or living under their dominion. Conversely, they saw having a militia as counterproductive and warned, as McKee told the colonial assembly when Governor Penn sought an appropriation to raise a small garrison there, "an Indian War would certainly follow establishing a Military force at Pittsburgh." The announcement concluded with "his Majesty's Justices and Protectors of the Public Peace of Pennsylvania," informing the newly raised militia company that its muster constituted an unlawful meeting and ordering the men "in his Majesty's Name" to "disperse, and retire . . . peaceably" to their "respective Habitations." [24]

Fearing the worst, St. Clair returned to the fort to read his prepared announcement and order to disperse. The militia officers answered that they had been invited to a lawful assembly, their intentions were peaceable, and they would eventually go home without molesting anyone. St. Clair let the matter rest but reported "their peaceable disposition forsook them" as twilight faded into darkness. He then noted that the militia became increasingly rowdy and the abandoned fort became a "scene of drunkenness and confusion." Without the means to enforce it, St. Clair admitted that the carefully worded warning followed by a reading of the Riot Act would have had little

John Penn, grandson of William Penn, the Pennsylvania colony's founder, was the proprietary governor in 1774. He was appointed governor of the colony by his uncle Thomas Penn —then chief proprietor—and served from 1763 to 1771. He was appointed again in 1773, and served as the last colonial governor of Pennsylvania until the end of the proprietary government during the Revolutionary War. (*New York Public Library*)

or no effect on an armed and intoxicated mob, and he thought it was "most prudent to keep out of their way."[25] Despite being arrested, Connolly had won the first skirmish in the political battle for control of the Forks.

On the last day of January, after meeting with his province's council, Governor Penn wrote to Dunmore explaining that Connolly had been arrested for acting "without Authority, as that District [Pittsburgh and Redstone] was within Pennsylvania, & was raising great Disturbances." He also informed his Virginia counterpart that local magistrates had only confined Connolly for refusing to post bond. In an attempt to curtail any further challenges to Pennsylvania authority in the region, Penn asked Dunmore to revoke Connolly's orders, as well as his and the other commissions, to act in Virginia's favor.[26] The next day, Connolly wrote to Washington from the Westmoreland County "Gaol" at Hanna's Town to explain he had been arrested for being an "Officer appointed by . . . [and] attempting to act under a Commission from Virginia," and denying that the colony of Pennsylvania had any jurisdiction at Pittsburgh. He took Virginia's side, he said, because Pennsylvania had "usurped Jurisdiction, as well as Territory" and took action as an affront to a royal colony. At the same time, he expressed his surprise that Virginia had neglected its claim, allowing it to lie dormant, which invited Pennsylvania's action. He ultimately justified his actions based on the orders he received from Governor Dunmore.[27]

When Penn's letter to Dunmore arrived in Williamsburg, Dunmore convened his colony's council to discuss and draft a response. Penn's request that Dunmore at least temporarily revoke the commissions until His Majesty resolved the intercolonial boundary dispute received a cool reception. The board advised Dunmore to inform Penn there was good reason to believe that Pittsburgh lay considerably within the boundaries of the Virginia colony. The governor therefore wrote to inform Penn that he could not think of allowing Pennsylvania's claim to the region to stand until the matter had been determined by His Majesty in council. Dunmore insisted that Connolly be immediately released and the charges dismissed, and that Penn punish the Westmoreland County clerk and sheriff for their harsh treatment of a Virginia officer.[28]

Dunmore summarily rejected Penn's request that he rescind the orders and commissions issued to the newly appointed civil and military officers in an area he considered part of Virginia.

Maintaining the right of his colony to that country, Dunmore not only cited the royal charter but challenged Penn with his own previous arguments to Lord Dartmouth representing Pennsylvania's dominion over the Wyoming Valley against Connecticut's encroachment. To further strengthen Virginia's position that its jurisdiction preceded the establishment of Westmoreland County in 1772, Dunmore drew Penn's attention to the "transactions of the late war," which gave sufficient proof that the government of Virginia had always considered the Forks of the Ohio within its boundaries. In view of the evidence, he expressed his dismay that Penn would find his actions surprising or unexpected. Finally, Dunmore pledged to do everything necessary within his power for the "good of the government of that part of the country, which cannot but be considered to be within the dominion of Virginia," until the king should declare to the contrary.[29]

The Pennsylvania governor replied with a lengthy letter that stated his government's position and admonished Dunmore not to grant lands or exercise jurisdiction in the disputed area until they received a royal resolution. On the advice of his council, the Virginia governor did "not condescend to answer."[30] The written debate continued on the merits of each colony's case, citing not only charters but legal opinions issued by the king's attorneys general.

With the backing of the Virginia Council, Dunmore addressed his concerns about the situation in the colony's backcountry in a letter to Lord Dartmouth. In it he communicated the "Remonstrance" he had received from backcountry inhabitants against the establishment of Vandalia. Contrary to the conventional wisdom that prevailed at Whitehall, influenced no doubt by some of the project's high-placed and influential investors, the area's inhabitants did not consider themselves as removed from the reach or protection of Virginia's government as had been portrayed. The people living there, said Dunmore, pleaded that they not be separated from the government to which they had always belonged, and with which they felt pleased and satisfied. Dunmore concluded by drawing Dartmouth's attention to the people's fear that becoming part of Vandalia would cause them *"grievous inconvenience"* from the legal complications and property disputes between them and the new colony's proprietors.[31]

Actual partisan activity increased as the war of letters ensued. Dorsey Pentecost resigned his Pennsylvania peace commission and threatened his fellow Westmoreland County magistrate Van Swearingen to follow suit or continue to serve Pennsylvania "at his Peril."[32] St. Clair countered by warning that anyone who attempted to "molest or oppose" Swearingen in the performance of his duties faced immediate arrest. Soon, every magistrate complained of laboring under increased difficulty and the "avowed determination" of the people living in the area not to submit to their jurisdiction. Some members of the proprietary government suggested that running a temporary boundary line between Virginia and Pennsylvania interests might serve to quiet the people for a while, but St. Clair expressed his pessimism to Joseph Shippen, secretary of the Provincial Council, sometimes also called the Colonial Council. Similar to its Virginia counterpart in its executive and advisory roles, the Pennsylvania Council differed in that it did not constitute an upper legislative house of the General Assembly. Meanwhile, Croghan and his "Emissaries" busied themselves by "irritating" the local population against Pennsylvania authority and assuring them they did not reside within the limits of that province. St. Clair charged that the majority of the inhabitants who resided near the proposed line had originally migrated from Virginia and remained unexplainably loyal to and fond of anything that came from that colony. The clerk of the Westmoreland court expressed his concern that if Dunmore did not retreat from the action he had taken, his fellow magistrates would find it nearly impossible to maintain Pennsylvania's civil authority in the region.[33]

Croghan began to openly question the proprietary government's authority. Due to his debts that the earnings from the sale of his considerable land holdings would satisfy, the financially strapped Croghan stood to gain much if Vandalia had become reality. Because he still commanded great respect and influence with the Ohio area Indians, the defection of the retired Crown deputy superintendent and one-time provincial Indian agent represented a significant loss to Pennsylvania interests. On April 5, Croghan told David

Sample, the deputy king's attorney for Westmoreland County, that he long understood that Fort Pitt and its surrounding communities were beyond the limits of Pennsylvania and had therefore never paid the taxes levied by its assembly. In view of the new political situation, Croghan informed Sample he would no longer plead cases in Pennsylvania courts. He argued that he neither had standing in them nor did that colony's courts and laws have any jurisdiction outside its boundaries. He explained that he had submitted to them previously only because he believed "any law better than no law." Since Dunmore extended Virginia authority by raising the militia and appointing civil officers, Croghan said he would no longer "Countenance the Laws of your Province," and any cases brought against him had to be heard in a Virginia court.[34]

Five days later, Croghan wrote to Dunmore to inform him that he would comply with the Virginia colony's terms and have his property submit to the quit rent the same as the rest of His Majesty's subjects. He then applied to the governor and council to direct Thomas Lewis, the surveyor for Augusta County, to survey all his property for the purpose of assessing the tax. Croghan explained that he had often thought of applying to the Virginia government for redress but believed he could not legally do so until Virginia had its laws in force and stopped the encroachments of Pennsylvania in the area.[35]

While Connolly remained in custody, Captain Pentecost took possession of the abandoned Redstone Old Fort and began to enroll eligible inhabitants in the militia.[36] Originally named Fort Burd during the French and Indian War, the post sat on the right bank atop of an ancient Indian mound near the mouth of Dunlap's Creek and effectively controlled an important ford across the Monongahela River. When Lieutenant John Stephenson took command of the unit forming at the nearby settlement, Pentecost organized another company at the community on the opposite bank. By the third week of February, resident Joseph Spear reported to St. Clair that the Virginians up the Monongahela from Pittsburgh had conducted three musters of their militia. One unit met at the Redstone Old Fort, one at Paul Frohman's property on the opposite side of the Monongahela, and one at "Mr. Pentecost's own House."[37] Dunmore's plan continued to unfold.

After several days' confinement at Hanna's Town, Connolly convinced Sheriff Proctor to release him on his parole that he would return to appear in court for trial. Connolly retuned to Pittsburgh, but only stayed a few days. Spear informed St. Clair that he saw Connolly going in the direction of Redstone, instead of returning directly to the courthouse at Hanna's Town, on Wednesday, February 23, but was unaware of the purpose of his excursion.[38]

At Redstone, Pentecost and Stephenson had a detachment of twenty men from the militia ready to escort Connolly along the road toward Staunton until he passed safely beyond the reach of Westmoreland County authorities.[39] After reaching the Virginia county town, Connolly swore the oaths required of a justice of the peace for Augusta County, met with Colonel Charles Lewis, in his capacity as the county lieutenant, and Sheriff Daniel Smith to discuss the next move in the contest to secure the Forks of the Ohio for Virginia. Dunmore had previously alerted Lewis to have his county's militia stand ready to march on Pittsburgh at short notice to support Connolly in a future confrontation with the Pennsylvanians.[40]

Connolly, now fully vested with both civil and military authority by Virginia, began the 170-mile return trip to Pittsburgh on Monday, March 28, accompanied by Francis Brown, an Augusta County undersheriff. A party of pro-Virginia militia from the Chartier Creek settlement joined him at Fort Pitt two days later. Believing they were up to no good and fearing Pittsburgh would soon become a place of "anarchy and Confusion," Westmoreland County justices Aeneas Mackay, Andrew McFarlane, and Deveraux Smith accompanied Sheriff Proctor to the fort to determine Connolly's intentions. Prepared to read the Riot Act if the assembly became disorderly, they discovered Connolly addressing a gathering of little more than twenty men, not all of whom had arms. They watched as he read them the contents of two letters he had recently received from Dunmore. In the first, the governor commended Connolly for his actions to date and for not giving bond in January when Proctor arrested him while engaged in the plan to secure the district for Virginia. He next read a copy of Dunmore's response to Governor Penn's demands. After he dismissed his troops, Connolly met the sheriff and his party in a room of the barracks. He assured them he would be present at the court in Hanna's Town as promised and had no intention of violating "the Established Rules of law" then in effect—until "after the Court."[41]

On Thursday, March 31, Sheriff Proctor attempted to serve a writ on Lieutenant William Christy, one of the subalterns in the Virginia militia company of Pittsburgh. Connolly immediately retaliated by issuing a King's Warrant, or a writ giving the peace officer authority to capture and hold an offender on criminal charges, with which Undersheriff Brown took Proctor into custody and detained him for a good part of the day. Parties of armed men went in pursuit of Proctor's deputy, Ephraim Hunter, and the township's two constables, which rendered it impossible for the Pennsylvania justices to conduct any business. Before long, the two sworn constables renounced their oaths and defected to the Virginia side. With Fort Pitt occupied, and what Mackay called "a Body Guard of Militia about him," Connolly advanced Dunmore's plans to secure the region. After he admitted that a sizable faction of area inhabitants stood ready to join the Virginians, Mackay alleged Connolly "used every artifice" to "seduce the people" with promises of civil and military employment, as well as offering them easy terms for land grants. Mackay lamented that the "giddy headed mobs" had become so infatuated with Connolly's promises that they allowed themselves to be persuaded. He and his fellow magistrates anticipated another muster before their captain commandant stood trial, after which they expected to see a strong body of militia at the courthouse to rescue Connolly and perhaps attempt something else.[42]

Although originally from Virginia, William Crawford remained outwardly loyal to Pennsylvania for the time being and continued to faithfully perform his duties as a justice of the peace and president of the Westmoreland County court. The recent extraordinary events that occurred in the area prompted him to submit a detailed report to Governor Penn, based on the collective observations of all the magistrates concerning Connolly's activities. As the situation continued to deteriorate, Crawford blamed the confusion and resulting disturbances largely on Connolly's militia, which he described as "composed of men without character and without fortune" who were equally averse to any regular administration of justice under either colony. Crawford said Connolly's men obstructed the execution of the legal process by using force to intimidate the Westmoreland County court as a body, as well as harassed individual magistrates. Connolly's partisans, for example, insulted Justice Mackay but paid him cruel special attention when they invaded his home and injured him in the arm with a cutlass blow. To make matters worse, the magistrates collectively feared that Connolly sought to avenge his arrest and confinement in kind by issuing writs for Proctor's and St. Clair's arrests.[43]

Several days before Connolly's scheduled court appearance, rumors circulated that Virginia officers planned to march their several companies to Hanna's Town and "use the Court ill" as they interrupted its proceedings. To prevent any insult to Pennsylvania authority, the court ordered Sheriff Proctor to raise a posse of armed men for its protection. On Wednesday, April 6, the justices learned that Connolly was on his way at the head of around 180 well-armed men, advancing in what Magistrate George Wilson described as a "hostile manner." In comparison, the few ill-armed and unorganized men who responded to the sheriff's call did not present a deterrent. At about midday, the justices heard the sound of drums and fifes approaching from the direction of Pittsburgh. Knowing Connolly to be at hand, they decided it prudent to adjourn early for dinner and vacated the building. Magistrate Thomas Smith said the Virginians marched along the road "with colours flying and their Captains" and subaltern officers "had their swords drawn." As the column of troops arrived and turned off the road, the companies wheeled into line and paraded before the courthouse. On Connolly's command, they surrounded the building and posted sentinels at the doors to prevent anyone from entering without their commander's permission.[44]

Connolly notified the magistrates that he wished to meet with them. The justices agreed and received him in a "private room" where he presented them copies of Lord Dunmore's March 3 rejection of Governor Penn's demands, and his own address to the court. In the latter, Connolly accused "some of the Justices of this Bench" as the cause for his appearance. He stated that he had only obeyed their summons to satisfy his parole and avoid another illegal arrest, and possibly getting taken to confinement in Philadelphia. Once more, he challenged the right of justices of the peace for Pennsylvania to retain jurisdiction in what he maintained was Virginia territory. To prevent confusion and satisfy his stated desire not to instigate a disturbance but prevent one, he offered a temporary solution. Connolly agreed that the Pennsylvania magistrates could continue functioning in all matters submitted to them for a determination by the people who recognized their authority until he received contrary orders from Williamsburg, or the king's decision on the matter became known.[45]

This time, Pennsylvania's Westmoreland magistrates turned obstinate. They drafted a written reply, which one of them read aloud. They maintained that they only exercised their authority within the boundaries of Westmoreland County, which, Virginia's claims notwithstanding, included Pittsburgh and Redstone. Consistent with their desire to do all within their power to preserve the public tranquility, they intended to exercise jurisdiction granted them under the authority of Pennsylvania's government. They agreed, however, to accommodate any differences between the two colonies' respective adherents "by fixing a temporary line between them."[46]

When justices Mackay, Smith, and MacFarlane returned to their Pittsburgh homes late that night, they learned that Connolly intended to issue King's Warrants for their arrest. Undersheriff Brown served the order at McFarlane's home the next morning at about 9:30. "Connolly's Sheriff" and Philip Reilly, whom McFarlane called "an infamous Missworn Constable" for having recently renounced his oath to Pennsylvania, grasped their prisoner by the shoulder and led him before Connolly, holding court at the fort, to receive his sentence. For their intransigent challenge to his compromise solution the day before, the Virginia magistrate insisted his Pennsylvania counterparts either post bond until required to appear for trial or go immediately to jail in Staunton for performing their duty—just as they had done to him in January. The three stood firm, and before leaving for jail in the afternoon, they wrote letters explaining their predicament to Penn.[47]

Thomas Smith sought the provincial government's assistance on behalf of himself and his fellow justices while on their way to jail, exposed to what he described as "the insults of the rabble who are sent as their Guard." Learning of the incident, Penn instructed the remaining officers of Westmoreland County to remain steadfast in their exercise of Pennsylvania jurisdiction but to avoid any confrontation with the Virginians so as to not "widen the unhappy breach" between the two colonies. Recognizing that Virginia had a well-developed militia establishment and Pennsylvania had none, Penn advised that any attempt to contend with force would be in vain and ordered them not to press any criminal charges against the Virginians for exercising that colony's laws. In the meantime, Penn replied to the three jailed magistrates that he had no objection to their posting bond as he continued working to secure their release. In order to minimize further confrontations, Penn instructed the justices residing in the Pittsburgh area that if Connolly arrested them they should immediately post bond rather than suffer incarceration "so great a distance from your homes" in Staunton. If that came to pass, he promised that he would pledge responsibility for their surety. Finally, after meeting with the provincial council, the governor decided to dispatch James Tilghman, Andrew Allen, and Richard Tilghman as commissioners to Williamsburg to speak directly with Lord Dunmore in an effort to restore peace and quiet.[48]

ALTHOUGH MANY Pennsylvanians like Thomas Smith blamed Connolly's behavior, as well as all the civil commotion and anything else "absurd and unwarrantable" at Pittsburgh, on Lord Dunmore, Mackay initially found the Virginia governor to be reasonable when confronted face to face. Shortly after he arrived in Staunton, Augusta County sheriff Daniel Smith granted him leave and assisted him in obtaining the means to make the six-day ride to Williamsburg for an audience with the governor. On or about Monday, April 25, according to Mackay, he and Dunmore "spoke our minds very free to each other." The magistrate complained of his and other Pittsburgh inhabitants' treatment at Connolly's hands and what he perceived as unruly conduct by the militia he had organized and commanded. Dunmore listened and replied by explaining the validity of Virginia's claim to the region under which he had authorized Connolly to prosecute his plans. He offered a somewhat tepid defense of his captain's practice of taking prisoners by saying that in so doing, he "only imitated the Pennsylvania officers'" actions. The governor then excused himself to prepare for a council meeting and asked Mackay to return to the palace the next day to continue their discussion.[49]

Dunmore asked the council for its advice and consent for a letter he drafted in which he formally reprimanded Connolly for his arrest and imprisonment of the three Pennsylvania officers "in Revenge" for St. Clair's having committed him to jail. Dunmore included his guidance for Connolly and his subordinates to mind their future conduct and admonished his captain "that the more illegal the Proceedings of the Pennsylvania Magistrates have been against him, the more cautious ought we to be on our Part, to refrain from imitating such unjustifiable Acts as we have complain'd of on theirs." The council then ordered a proclamation prepared for the governor's signature requiring the inhabitants of "Pittsburgh and its Dependencies . . . to pay Quitrents and other public Dues" to the appropriate officers appointed, or to be appointed, by his government. The proclamation also directed officers of the militia in the district to "embody a sufficient Force for repelling any Invasion of the Indians" or any attempt by the government of Pennsylvania "to disturb the Exercise of Government of this Colony over that Territory."[50] As soon as it had been signed, an express rider carried a copy to Pittsburgh.

Meanwhile, Mackay followed the Virginia governor's instructions to return, and his one-day visit lasted into three. Dunmore finally met him long enough to give him two documents, a letter addressed to Sheriff Smith and another copy of the proclamation to be forwarded to Connolly, and then dismissed him. A disappointed Mackay rode back to Staunton, unaware that the visit resulted in a reprimand of Connolly for having arrested and sent him to jail. To his surprise, the other letter instructed the sheriff to permit the three detained magistrates to "return to their homes and occupations" in Pennsylvania. Waiving the requirement to post a peace bond, the governor relieved the sheriff of his responsibility for their appearances in court.[51]

W HEN DUNMORE's April 25 proclamation arrived by express rider at Pittsburgh, Connolly had it read before public gatherings and posted the broadsides at various places throughout the district, along with his own previously published circular letter warning district residents to be on their guard. The governor's announcement explained the necessary actions taken by the Virginia government "to support the dignity of his Majesty's Government, and protect his subjects in the quiet and peaceful enjoyment of their rights." It also explained their obligations to Virginia with regard to militia service and the payment of taxes. The news spread quickly. Before the end of April, Reverend David Zeisberger recorded in the journal of Schönbrunn, the United Brethren's mission on the Muskingum River, two Moravian Indians returned from Pittsburgh and said the government there had changed, "and the place now belonged to Virginia." It appeared that Connolly had accomplished his mission.[52]

The coming of spring brought not only the annual freshets that swelled the Ohio and its tributaries but worrisome news from the frontier. While the intercolonial border dispute played out in courthouses and capitols, violence between settlers and Indians in the Virginia backcountry increased, and reports of growing native unrest reached Pittsburgh. Alexander McKee reported to William Johnson that traders returning from native towns told of warriors displaying fresh scalps. Others told him that several families along the Great Kanawha River and the Ohio were "cut off"—or killed— over the winter, and that one party of warriors returned from a raid boasting of having killed six whites, "with some Negroes and a Number of Horses taken." The Shawnee appeared to be preparing for war, as many young warriors traded their pelts for more than the usual amounts of powder and lead, but less for commodities.[53] The Indian Department planned for negotiations to check the violence and calm the concerns of the Shawnees, whose resentment of the recent cession of their hunting ground had grown more intense. Croghan had even invited a number of Shawnee elders to Pittsburgh. They spent the winter—from the end of December to the beginning of April—at his home seeking a solution to the violence. McKee urged the chiefs to "use their Utmost Strength and Influence" to control their young men. He warned that they "must not expect That the White People wou'd long lett their Conduct in this manner pass with Impunity," but that it would cause a reaction that would bring destruction upon them and embroil their people in a hopeless fight.[54]

JOHN J. JACOB later wrote that "a kind of doubtful, precarious and suspicious peace" had existed between Indians and whites since the end of Pontiac's War, although occasional violent incidents had occurred.[55] Violence began to increase again following the signing of the boundary-line treaties. In 1771, the year after the Treaty of Lochaber, Colonel Andrew Lewis, the county lieutenant of the newly established Botetourt County, reported to the government at Williamsburg the murder of seven people at a settlement on the Elk River. The prevailing opinion of the local inhabitants was that unspecified Ohio Indians were responsible for the atrocity and that they sought to bring on a general war. In response, Lewis ordered out scouts to guard the frontier against further irruptions and ordered the captains commanding local companies to tell their men "to hold themselves in readiness" to defend their communities if attacked, or march detachments to the relief of their neighbors. Fortunately, calm returned without further incident, and families who fled the settlements at the first alarm returned home.[56]

In the summer of the following year, Adam Stroud returned to his home on the Elk River after being away some length of time and found that hostile warriors had murdered his entire family, plundered his house, and driven off his livestock. The trail of cattle carcasses headed in the direction of a small Delaware village on the banks of the Little Kanawha River a few miles to the north, which local settlers called Bulltown. A Delaware chief whom many whites knew as Captain Bull had sided with Pontiac in the uprising of 1763, but since establishing the settlement, he and the five families of his relatives who resided there enjoyed friendly relations with their white neighbors.[57]

Although the other settlers attempted to dissuade them, five of Stroud's neighbors concluded that Bull and his relatives were guilty of the massacre and demanded summary justice. Without fanfare, the five, including one who had a reputation as an ardent Indian hater, went to the town and murdered every man, woman, and child, then threw the corpses into the river. They later admitted going to Bulltown but alleged they found it apparently abandoned by its inhabitants before they arrived. When questioned separately, some of the men gave conflicting answers, saying they either saw no Indians or they had and engaged in fisticuffs, but they denied having killed anyone. The men were only consistent in claiming they had observed some of the Strouds' clothing and other property in the Indians' possession, which they insisted confirmed their suspicions. When the more-moderate neighbors went to visit, they found an abandoned village with neither any sign of life nor evidence of foul play. No one ever saw or heard from Bulltown's residents again, although the five instigators were always suspected of having done something terrible to the innocent Indian inhabitants.[58]

Such incidents served to remind Indians and settlers alike of the distrust that remained even when communities of the two groups lived in close proximity, and it began to increase in 1773 before the incident in Powell Valley. Earlier that year, fellow traders suspected that hostile Indians had murdered John Martin and Guy Meek on Hockhocking Creek, a western tributary of the Ohio, and stolen their canoe and its cargo valued at an estimated £200.[59] As at Bulltown, peaceful Indians were also among the victims of similar foul play. A settler named John Collins committed "a most malicious and unprovoked Murder of two Cherokee Indians" as the men refreshed themselves with a meal of victuals in his father's house, for which they had begged.[60]

Neither the commander in chief of British forces nor the colonial governments condoned violence against unoffending or friendly Indians, but the fugitive evaded apprehension despite generous rewards authorized by General Haldimand and the Virginia Council. Although it was the most noteworthy incident, the ambush of the Russell-Boone party in October represented but another in a series of encounters that led to war. Such incidents prompted Jacob to conclude "it is certain that our quarrel with the Indians, or their quarrel with us, is nearly coeval."

Jacob attributed much of the violence equally to, "The restless, roving disposition of the Indians, whose only business is hunting and war, together with the frequent encroachments of the white people on their lands and hunting grounds." As the numbers of whites moving into the backcountry increased, so did the potential for conflict. While tribal elders professed peace, young Shawnee, Delaware, and Mingo warriors occasionally crossed the river to cause mischief. Many settlers remembered the bloody raids committed during the French and Indian War and Pontiac's War. They still harbored a deep hatred of all Indians, mourned for murdered loved ones, and prayed that those taken captive who survived but still were not released according to war-ending peace treaties would escape and return home. Some backcountry whites summarily killed native traders or hunters caught or suspected of stealing horses, killing cattle, or hunting in the woods near their farms without considering whether they were friendly or hostile. Jacob described the attitudes of many backcountry Virginians when he wrote "whoever saw an Indian saw an enemy."[61]

Farther south, Georgia faced similar threats on its frontier. On Christmas Day 1773, Creek warriors attacked the farm of a man named White and murdered his entire family of five, including his wife and two children. John Stuart, the Southern Indian superintendent, at first blamed the farmer for provoking the incident when he either killed or wounded an Indian earlier. White maintained that he had fired as he pursued the marauders who had just stolen some of his horses. Stuart said the Creeks had only returned to exact a private revenge, not start a war. However, about three weeks later, on January 14, 1774, a war party struck at the homestead of a family named Shirrol (or Sherrill) in the same neighborhood. This time they killed four of the six whites, including the mother and daughter, and two of the family's three black slaves. Two sons and one black man "defended themselves bravely" and survived. The local commander mustered about one hundred of his militia in response. Although reinforced with twenty-five provincial rangers, the expedition faltered when the Indians ambushed them on January 23. Frontier inhabitants soon heard the rumor that the Choctaws were attempting to reconcile and form an alliance with the Creeks, their traditional enemy, and parties of Cherokees were also joining them on the warpath to attack more settlements. In the ensuing panic, many settlers fled the backcountry for the safety of the fort at Augusta, while Georgia's governor, William Wright, called one-third of the colony's militia to active service. Stuart and his deputy superintendents, including David Taitt for the Upper Creeks and Alexander Cameron for the Cherokees, met with tribal leaders to resolve the growing conflict without further bloodshed.[62]

By late February, traders and other travelers passing through the Virginia settlements told the inhabitants that the Creeks, Cherokees, and Choctaws had joined in a war against the southern provinces. Virginians also heard that since the Indians first struck, they had killed a number of settlers, including "about 40 families lately murdered on the Okonces [Oconee]" River, and fought several battles in which they had beaten the militia. At first, Colonel Lewis paid little regard to what he considered to only be rumor. Arguably one of the most knowledgeable Virginia officials on matters concerning Indian and military affairs on the frontier, the county lieutenant of Botetourt County became convinced of the "Melancoly truth" by several people who claimed to have witnessed the "dreadful effects of Savage Cruelty." When they heard that five hundred Cherokees planned to attack, "but where no person can tell," the settlers on the Holston and other river communities in that quarter began "Forting up," while militia officers sent scouts to watch for and detect an approaching enemy.[63]

When frontier people "forted," it meant they had left their homes and gathered in a nearby military garrison or neighbor's home that had been hardened with a stockade fence or blockhouse. The temporary living arrangement sheltered the women and children, while the men served as sentinels to provide local security, went on patrol to gather intelligence, and manned the walls to repel an assault. If forted for any length of time during the spring or summer, "it was our practice and custom," wrote militiaman John Patton, "to work our fields as well as we could adjacent to the fort." Therefore, they would "turn out in a body and work our respective places by turns." Once the men arrived, they posted two men to watch and stand guard while the rest labored in the field or tended the cattle that had not been corralled in or closer to the fort. They continued working and watching, so "all of us participated in both employments," until the alarm ended and it became safe to return to their individual homes.[64]

A typical frontier fort consisted of a stockade enclosure within four walls of sharpened logs called pickets, with the lower five feet buried in the ground and the curtain wall rising twelve to fifteen feet above the plain. Defenders could fire over the wall or through loopholes cut into it to provide the shooter with a degree of protection from enemy fire. The defense could be improved by adding bastions or blockhouses on one or more corners to create salient angles. A blockhouse was a fortified building of two or more stories. The larger second story created an overhang provided with additional loopholes in the floor so that the garrison could fire at ground-level targets and thereby deny attackers an opportunity to secure a lodgment where defenders firing from the curtain walls could not engage them. Inside, the stockade held barracks to house the garrison, cabins to accommodate families, and magazines for storing ammunition, supplies, and provisions. In lieu of a stockade, some forts consisted of a single or two or more mutually supporting blockhouses. To differentiate military posts built at government expense from fortified private homes, "Fort" followed by the name designated the former, while the owner's name followed by "fort" represented the latter.[65]

The perennial fear of Crown officials had been the union of all the Indian nations along the frontier in a single confederacy and the general war that would likely follow. Lewis added his concern that the Ohio Indians were already "in the Plot" and well acquainted with "the designs of the Southern Indians." He realized nothing could deter the Shawnees, Mingoes, and Delawares from joining the others on the warpath, except their "being so Near Neghbors to Our Settlements below Fort Pitt." He recommended that the Ohio Indians "ought to be strictly watched." If they appeared to be preparing or starting to move their families away, one could expect they were about to become what he described as "Open Enemies."[66]

Colonel William Preston, the county lieutenant of Fincastle County, had Captain William Russell travel to his Smithfield Plantation home on the New River for a meeting. They discussed the situation on the frontier in general, and Russell spoke "in behalf of Our Holston Settlements" in particular. The colonel instructed the captain that if upon his return to Clinch River he deemed it necessary, he should send out scouts to determine the Indians' intentions, as well as to verify the exact location on the ground of the boundary between Cherokee territory and Virginia. For his part, Preston would ask the General Assembly to have the colony pay for their service.

The blockhouse was a type of many fortifications used on the frontier as either military in-stallations or private defenses in which soldiers as well as civilians could find protection and shelter against an attack. As depicted in the image of Fort Anne—built to defend the saw-mill near Skenesborough, New York, in 1777—the blockhouse was built to a height of two or more stories, with the upper levels extending over the lowest one. Loopholes cut in the walls permitted the defenders to engage targets at a distance, while those cut into the floor of the overhanging upper story permitted them to shoot at ground-level targets below the line of fire of those on the wall. (*John Carter Brown Library*)

After completing his report on the situation in Fincastle County, Preston sent Russell to Colonel Andrew Lewis's Richfield home so he could carry the report for Botetourt County to Williamsburg as well. By March 9, Rus-sell was headed on his way to the capital to deliver the two county lieu-tenants' reports and personally inform Lord Dunmore of the critical situation developing in the backcountry.[67]

Lewis had served under Colonel George Washington in the Virginia Reg-iment during the French and Indian War. After completing his report so Russell could carry it to the capital, he also wrote to inform his former com-manding officer of the military situation and how it might affect the status of the veterans' land grants as well as the ongoing land surveys. Depending on the outcome, he cautioned, an Indian war could "put a stop to Our de-signs On the Ohio."[68]

In mid-March, Daniel Smith, a militia captain, deputy surveyor, and sheriff of Augusta County, found himself in Castle's Woods conducting land surveys for Fincastle County. He reported to Colonel Preston, who was Fin-castle County's chief surveyor as well as its chief militia commander, that the people in the Clinch River settlements appeared "more fearful of the Indians than I expected to find them." Recent reports of hostile Cherokees' incursions had caused such an alarm among them that four families had fled to the relative safety of the Holston River settlements in such haste that they left most of their household furniture and livestock behind them. When they realized the cause for alarm was not as dire as they expected, the families ventured back to secure the rest of their property, which presented Smith the opportunity he needed, and he convinced them to stay.[69]

While the inhabitants of Virginia's frontier counties had the most cause for concern, the most alarming nature of the escalating violence on the frontier did not escape the notice of those in the rest of the colony. An open letter to the governor on the subject appeared in the March 24, 1774, edition of Rind's *Virginia Gazette*. Under the pseudonym "Virginius," one colonist wrote the situation had become "so truly critical" that the frontier counties required the immediate and "instant assistance of both the Legislative and Executive powers" for their defense. Virginius accused "Our treacherous and clandestine foes, the Indians," of having "ever greedily embraced all opportunities of manifesting their inimical affections toward us." He concluded with an appeal to the governor, writing, "Ten thousand incidents conspire to render a war at this time necessary, ney inevitable; and the innocent lives of numbers might be saved by the timely proclamation of it."[70] Purdie and Dixon's *Virginia Gazette* edition for the same day carried a notice that also affected the situation on the Ohio. It directed all "Gentlemen, Officers and Soldiers," entitled to land as authorized by the Royal Proclamation of October 7, 1763, and possessing the necessary warrants from Lord Dunmore, to apply to the chief surveyor of Fincastle County, William Preston. Preston had engaged survey parties to work under his supervision "to locate their lands near the Ohio, below the Great Kanawha."[71]

Captain Russell returned from Williamsburg in April to find that many Clinch River settlers had evacuated their plantations. He knew something had to be done to convince the inhabitants who had not abandoned their homes and farms to desist from so "Ruinous an undertaking." He knew that providing timely and accurate information on the location, strength, and intentions of invading Indians thought to be heading their way provided the best antidote for panic. "Agreeable to Instruction" from the county lieutenant, the captain of the local company turned to his men and asked for four volunteers to perform a special mission "in the service of the Country [Virginia]." From among those who stepped forward, he appointed Richard Stanton, Edward Sharpe, Ephraim Drake, and William Harrel "as Runners to scout, and Reconnoiter, to the Westward of this settlement."[72]

Certain that he had the right men, Russell assembled the scouts. He outlined their mission and what he expected them to accomplish. After entering the head of Powell's Valley just beyond the Clinch River settlements of southwestern Virginia, they would follow on or near the Warriors' Path to possibly intercept the likely Indian route of march and look for signs of activity. If the scouts discovered any warriors, Russell instructed them to determine their numbers, direction, and most important, "as nearly as possible, their Intentions." If the runners observed that the Indians intended to make war by attacking the Clinch or Holston River settlements, he ordered them to immediately bring such information back to him or, in his absence, "the next Officer convenient," in order to pass it on to the county lieutenant. Second, if they discovered no signs of approaching warriors, Russell told the runners to continue down Powell's Valley and identify the actual boundary line "between us and the Cherokees" that Donelson had surveyed as part of the Great Grant of 1772. Therefore, after locating a head, they would have to follow the water's course to confirm that it terminated on the Louisa and not the Cumberland. On their return, the scouts would give sworn depositions stating what they discovered for submission to the General Assembly. Knowing the exact boundary would not only prove important for issuing the military land warrants to deserving veterans but would contribute to maintaining good relations with the Cherokees. With the boundary verified, hunters, surveyors, and settlers would have no excuse or recourse to "Plead Ignorance in going over or Infringing on the Indians' Claim."[73]

Finally, Russell cautioned the men that while Virginians remained apprehensive that the Cherokees and certain "northward Indians [the Shawnees] intend War," he ordered them to avoid any provocation, and all contact if possible, with Indian parties. If unavoidable, or they happened to encounter any warriors by accident, the scouts had to refrain from initiating any action that might be perceived as warlike. Since the Indians appeared "ripe for War," he explained, any untoward behavior at that critical time would "not only blast our fairest hopes of Settling the Ohio Country; and be Attended with a train of Concomitant Evils," but would be sure to involve the Virginia government in a "Bloody War." After Russell concluded his instructions, the scouts headed for Powell's Valley.[74]

CHAPTER 3

A War Is Every Moment Expected

Increasing Frontier Violence

April–May 1774

By early april, backcountry inhabitants and work parties spread the word that "the Indians had placed themselves on both sides of the Ohio, and that they intend war." Virginians were not alone in believing that a conflict seemed imminent. The area's Pennsylvanians, however, held the Virginians, not the Indians, responsible for instigating the potential hostilities. Before John Connolly arrested Aeneas Mackay and sent him and two fellow Pennsylvania magistrates to jail, Mackay had expressed his concern in a letter to Governor Penn that the Virginia captain commandant had "parties of armed men patrolling through our streets daily." Their activities had so alarmed the Indians living across the river from Pittsburgh that they expected the whites to initiate "hostility . . . against them and their country."[1] For their part, the Virginians feared they would not only have to fight the Shawnees in the north, possibly in confederation with other Ohio Indians, but the Cherokees in the south as well—either separately or in an alliance. Connolly and his associates continued to cite Virginia's ability to defend the community from invasion and contrasted it to Pennsylvania's lack of a permanent military establishment, whenever news of violence reached Pittsburgh. Just such an incident then occurred downriver.

The Shawnee chiefs who George Croghan and Alexander McKee invited to Pittsburgh at the end of 1773 to discuss the growing frontier unrest became increasingly impatient and concerned. The chiefs' staying as guests at Croghan Hall to ensure their safety had not prevented irate settlers from firing an occasional angry shot in their direction. Acts of hostility caused some of the chiefs to have "disagreeable Dreams" and heightened their feelings of foreboding. On March 8, after hearing "bad News from our Town" about the increasing violence between whites and Indians, the chiefs told their host that they were anxious to leave. When the final meeting of the council convened, also attended by several Six Nations and Delaware chiefs and officials from both colonies, McKee made a final attempt to defuse the causes of conflict. He urged the Shawnee headmen to do their best "to preserve the peace and Tranquility of this Country" when they returned home. The Shawnees replied that "your wise Men" should also be acquainted with the "very great" numbers of white people who were migrating beyond the boundaries established for their settlements. The settlers, as well as the activities of surveyors and land jobbers, were "overspreading the Hunting Country of our Young Men." When the Shawnees' young men found the woods covered with "white people & their Horses" where game had once been plentiful, the chiefs could do little to prevent the "evil Resolutions" that resulted. When young warriors became disappointed in their hunting, maintaining peace would prove impossible.

The expressed desires of the white people to prevent war had so far not impressed the Shawnee headmen. What they had seen and witnessed since their arrival only confirmed their fears. Distant musket shots had harassed them all winter. They had observed the militia "constantly assembling . . . with red Flaggs [sic]"—meaning the red colonial ensigns used as regimental standards—and learned that the "Long Knife [Virginia] people" proposed to build a large fort lower down the river that summer. They challenged that if the Virginians truly desired peace, they would have "laid aside" such warlike preparations. In not doing so, they had convinced the Shawnees that war remained uppermost in most white people's minds.

In concluding the council, McKee told the Shawnee leaders that bad news from their towns concerned whites and Indians alike. He urged them to use their "utmost Abilities in restraining evil dispos'd people & promoting every good thing," and discourage the warlike intentions of their "foolish young men." For his part, McKee promised that he and the colonial officials would do the same among the white settlers. He further assured the chiefs that they would find the "Great-men" of British America, in their "Uprightness & Wisdom," receptive and ready to redress their complaints with the utmost candor. He concluded by telling the headmen they could expect British and colonial leaders to afford them every justice for the transgressions of unfriendly white people so that they would have no need to resort to arms. Finally, McKee promised to communicate their concerns to William Johnson, his superior and the British official Indians trusted most.[2]

Throughout the early weeks of spring, numerous parties of white men looked for land on the south bank of the Ohio for a variety of purposes. Settlers sought acreage on which to build new homes and lives, while others went to ply a variety of trades. Surveyors measured patents and recorded plats for private owners and county land offices. Parties of craftsmen and laborers under contract with the owners built new or repaired existing structures on previously acquired property. Land jobbers acted as speculators and brokers, seeking available property that they could buy and sell for others at a profit. The combined efforts of these and other groups contributed to the common goal of improving what they saw as a vast, uninhabited country, or desert. Amid the activity, news of unfriendly encounters with Indians and reports of warlike acts continued, as the frontier kindling began to smolder.

On Thursday, April 14, three white employees of trader William Butler departed Pittsburgh in a canoe loaded with goods to exchange with the Shawnee for pelts. After traveling about forty-five miles down the Ohio, they stopped for the night near the mouth of Beaver Creek. Along the way they encountered four Cherokees, three men and a woman, to whom they showed some silver items. The next morning, before they could resume their journey, the Cherokees "waylaid" them on the river bank and opened fire. After they plundered the cargo and took the most valuable merchandise, the robbers escaped, leaving a trader named Murphy dead and another named Stephens wounded; conflicting versions reported the third man had either died, went missing, or escaped. A group of land jobbers arrived on the scene and offered their assistance. Benjamin Tomlinson, a settler who lived nearby, dug Murphy's grave while Dr. William Wood dressed Stephens's wounds.[3]

As soon as news of the incident reached Fort Pitt, Connolly embodied a detachment of militia for active service to pursue the Cherokees and instructed the commanding officer to apprehend and bring them back to stand trial for murder, if possible, or otherwise treat them as declared enemies. The militiamen recovered the traders' canoe and a considerable share of the property but could not locate the offending Indians. Connolly followed the next day with another detachment and transported the wounded man back to town. The captain remarked, "This incident occasion'd a great deal of confusion and as I imagin'd it woud be improper to allow an act so insolent to pass over unnotic'd." When the evidence suggested the Cherokees had headed toward the Shawnee towns, Connolly recommended that McKee send that nation's headmen a demand that they apprehend the outlaws.[4] Guyasuta, who had just returned from an Indian congress at Johnson

Hall with messages for restoring "good order to the Southward," warned the other tribes not to join the Shawnees in starting any fights with the Virginians. Guyasuta then sent a message to Mingo Town, the "small Village of Six Nations [Mingo] Indians living below Logs Town," encouraging them to have some warriors join forces with the militia in the attempt to apprehend the renegade Cherokees.[5] Perhaps indicative of the contrasting views held by those who learned of the incident, Virginian John Floyd described it in military terms as a "skirmish," while Deveraux Smith of Pennsylvania wrote since they were Cherokees, he believed the incident was a simple robbery, not an act of war.[6]

McKee followed Connolly's instruction and sent messengers informing Shawnee and Mingo leaders of the Beaver Creek incident and alerted them that he believed that the offending Cherokees were headed in their direction. Imploring them to capture and send "those Murderers" back to Pittsburgh for trial, the deputy Indian superintendent explained how such action served their own best interest. He reminded them not only of their promises to do everything they could to preserve the "Chain of Friendship" with the British and do justice but that they bore some responsibility for rectifying the situation since the bandits had stayed with them as their guests before committing the crimes. The Shawnee, he said, "must be looked upon in some degree accountable" for the Cherokees' behavior. McKee also appealed for the Shawnee leaders to view the attack as an outrage committed against their own people, since the traders furnished them with "Necessaries."[7]

On April 20, after receiving a complaint from the Delaware chief Coquethagechton, or Captain White Eyes, that some Virginians had insulted and abused him, Connolly composed a public notice and had it printed as a broadside announcement posted throughout the district. He also instructed some traders to take copies downriver and post them in the "most public Settlements" along the Ohio. The notices informed all who read them that "certain imprudent people" inhabiting Virginia settlements had "unbecomingly ill-treated" and threatened the lives of some friendly and well-disposed Indians. He cautioned everyone to avoid such conduct in the future and urged them to act friendly toward any "Natives as may appear peaceable" since the "Tranquility of this country" depended on it. The same day, Croghan informed the captain commandant that the Shawnees had become generally "ill disposed and might possibly do mischief." In response, Connolly composed a "Circulatory Letter" to the inhabitants of the district that advised them of the situation and recommended that they "be on their guard against any Hostile attempts" by unfriendly Indians.[8] Many took Connolly's letter as either a warning that hostile Indians would likely strike at any time or that fighting had already begun, and therefore a de facto declaration of war.

Meanwhile, two days after the attack on the traders, the last few of the Shawnee chiefs who had spent the winter at Croghan's departed Pittsburgh. Before long, they passed Little Beaver Creek on their way to the Muskingum or Scioto. Over the course of the next week, McKee learned that "Eighteen Canoes of the Six Nations [Mingoes]" and others who lived near Logstown and Big Beaver Creek had also passed Little Beaver Creek. Many of them had apparently abandoned their villages and followed the Shawnees downriver.[9] Arthur St. Clair observed that "a small party of these [Mingoes]," much to the consternation of the Six Nations council at Onondaga, lived near the Shawnees and were now "in a manner incorporated with them."[10]

A few days later, John Floyd wrote to Colonel Preston about an incident in Fincastle County where he previously reported "3 or 4 Indians down the River were thought to be killed" in a skirmish with thirteen settlers, but that proved to be an unfounded rumor. When he discovered the facts, he wrote that according to one of the men that should have been in the engagement, the Indians had only robbed them.[11] Reports from elsewhere in the Ohio valley brought additional news and rumors. Reverend David Zeisberger at Schönbrunn, the Moravian mission village near the Delaware towns on the Muskingum River, wrote that he had learned from John Bull, also known as Cosh, and John Jungman that a party of Mingoes had stolen fifteen horses from settlers below Logstown, and, "The white people began to be much afraid of an Indian war."[12] They had good reason to, as several violent incidents occurred almost simultaneously at different points along the Ohio.

Despite the danger, William Butler still needed to move the peltry from the Shawnee towns to Pittsburgh. He engaged a Delaware and a Shawnee to help the recently injured Stephens take trade goods to the Indians and bring the pelts to his factory. On Sunday, April 24, about a week after the affair near Beaver Creek, Stephens and his companions paddled their canoe into the channel and headed downriver toward the mouth of the Scioto.[13]

Guyasuta and McKee met in Pittsburgh the next day to discuss the great deal of confusion and discontent many of the Indian tribes had recently expressed concerning Connolly. They cautioned the captain commandant that it could prove very detrimental to the public interest to allow spirituous liquors to be sold or carried into the Indian towns at this critical time. Until then, the traders had either disregarded or not taken seriously the deputy Indian superintendent's earlier requests to limit the amount of alcohol they shipped to the natives. As the reports of violent incidents increased, so did the demand for liquor. McKee and Guyasuta tried to impress on Connolly that "the Addition of Rum" only served to increase the Indians' disorderly conduct.[14] They therefore sought governmental action to limit the availability of alcohol to the Indians. Meanwhile, in Williamsburg on April 25, Dunmore had signed the proclamation that obliged the district's free adult male residents to be prepared to embody as militia in order to repel an expected Indian invasion, and he sent it by express to Connolly at Pittsburgh.[15]

BELOW THE Great Kanawha, at the same time that the incident at Beaver Creek occurred, a group of Shawnee warriors observed from across the Ohio River as Lawrence Darnell and the six members of his survey party landed their canoes on the south bank. The men constituted an advanced detachment of Floyd's survey expedition. Whether unaware, or aware but not alarmed, that Indians had watched them and crossed to their side of the river, they casually unloaded their instruments and supplies and made camp. Suddenly, the warriors surprised and captured the men, robbed them of everything they had, and took them back across the river to a Shawnee town for tribal judgment. For three days, their captors discussed what they should do with the trespassers. Much to their captives' surprise and relief, the Indians told them in English that although Croghan had allegedly directed them to "kill all the Virginians they could find," but only "rob & whip the Pennsylvanians," they could go free. The Indians also ordered them to get off the river immediately.[16]

After several days making their way on foot, the men reached the camp of the main body of Floyd's survey party, located about thirty miles below the Great Kanawha near the mouth of the Little Guyandotte River. Darnell told Floyd what had happened. Floyd, a deputy surveyor and undersheriff for Fincastle County, relayed the news of the attack in a message carried by Alexander Spottswood Dandridge to Colonel Preston on April 26. The deputy surveyor also asked his superior to let him know as soon as possible after the four runners that Russell had dispatched returned with confirmation on the actual location of the border with the Cherokees so none of his men would inadvertently cross it and further provoke the ire of that nation. Although several survey parties had gone out that spring, tensions with the Indians had increased so much by the last week of April that Floyd observed "our Men are almost daily Retreating."[17]

Dandridge and his party left the survey camp "under great apprehension of danger" from the Indians and brought Preston the additional news that three other men from the survey party had earlier left camp with the com-

pleted plats of George Washington's two–thousand-acre claim on the Great
Kanawha, but no one had heard from them since. With tensions on the
frontier escalating, Dandridge also carried Floyd's request for Preston to
send someone to bring the surveyors' horses, then stabled at the Greenbrier
settlements, forward to the surveyors' camp to facilitate their withdrawal.[18]

While Darnell's party underwent their capture and walked back to
Floyd's camp, a group of about eighty or ninety men encamped up the river
near the mouth of the Little Kanawha also had an encounter with hostile
Indians. One of them was twenty-one-year-old George Rogers Clark, who
had established a farm on Grave Creek a short distance from the settlements
on Wheeling Creek. A trained surveyor, Clark had thoroughly explored the
area of the longest straight-line segment of the Ohio known as the Long
Reach the previous year. He had since joined with a group planning to establish a new settlement in Kentucky. Clark and his associates had previously agreed to meet at a rendezvous to assemble the necessary supplies and
equipment, and descend the river in a single body in the spring. While waiting to embark, they learned that Indians had fired on a small hunting party
out looking for game for their group about ten miles farther down the river.
The hunters fortunately managed to fend off the attackers, and all returned
to camp unhurt. "This and other circumstances," Clark later recalled, "led
us to believe the Indians were determined on war" in spring 1774.[19]

In retribution, the settlers decided to attack the Indian town of Horse-
head Bottom, which was on their way to Kentucky on the north bank near
the mouth of the Scioto. They planned to descend the river, land above their
objective, move across country, and then assault the town from behind on
its land side. Having all the equipment and men necessary, they only lacked
a competent leader. Michael Cresap happened to be in the area, about fifteen
miles upriver from their camp. Cresap had some hands, including a group
of eight to ten carpenters and laborers who were busy clearing and improving property claimed by George Washington, and also settling a plantation
on which Cresap intended to settle his own family. In an earlier meeting,
Cresap indicated that after he established his land, he intended to follow
Clark's party to Kentucky. Remembering the conversation during the discussion, one of the settlers in Clark's party proposed that they ask Cresap
to become their leader, to which all unanimously agreed.[20]

Born in Frederick County on Maryland's colonial frontier in 1742, the
son of the famous pioneer Colonel Thomas Cresap, Michael received a formal education at the school of a Rev. Mr. Craddock in Baltimore County.
A veteran soldier, although too young for regular or provincial service in
the French and Indian War, he grew up in the militia and fighting Indians

in the skirmishes that punctuated the tenuous peace that followed 1765. Michael Cresap had initially followed his father's lead as an Indian trader, operating from the family home at Shawanese Old Town on the Potomac River, east of the Wills Creek site of Fort Cumberland. He relocated to Redstone in 1772, where he established a new store and became a land developer as well as a recognized leader of the Virginia faction in the border dispute with Pennsylvania.[21]

The news of recent Indian depredations had alarmed Cresap and his men, and they combined with other work parties in the area for mutual defense and support until their force numbered about thirty. Hunters from both groups encountered each other somewhere in between the two camps, and in the usual exchange of information that ensued, the men from Clark's party informed their counterparts that their companions intended to ask Cresap to serve as their captain. They hurried to tell their leader the news before the messenger from the southern group arrived with the actual request. Once informed, Cresap headed down the river to meet the members of his new command.

After he arrived, the Kentucky-bound settlers held a council to hear Cresap. Clark remembered "to our astonishment our commander-in-chief . . . dissuaded us from the enterprise"! Cresap told them that they had all heard about Indian depredations lately committed on the south bank. With all the candor he could muster, their new captain cautioned them that "the appearances were very suspicious," and although alarming, he felt there was no certainty that a war had yet actually started. He had no doubt that they could carry a successful attack on the Indian village as had been proposed, but whether they attacked at that time or waited, he believed a war would indeed erupt before much longer. The only difference in choosing to attack sooner rather than later would cause them to justly receive the blame for starting it. If they insisted on voting in favor of an immediate attack, Cresap offered to disregard his own reservations and call the men from his camp to combine their forces and lead them into battle. He then proposed an alternative. Cresap asked them to take post with his men near the Wheeling

Overleaf: This "General Map of the Middle Colonies in America," originally completed by surveyor and geographer Lewis Evans and published in Philadelphia, was subsequently copied and printed by mapmaker Carrington Bowles in London, January 1, 1771. The map graphically depicts the progress of western settlement and the changing nature of the frontier between British America and the adjacent Indian nations. The many notations convey information such as "The Virginia boundary with the six Nations in 1722" just west of the Blue Ridge Mountains, and "The farthest settlements in Virginia 1755" on the Holston River in what would become part of Fincastle County in 1772. (*Library of Congress*)

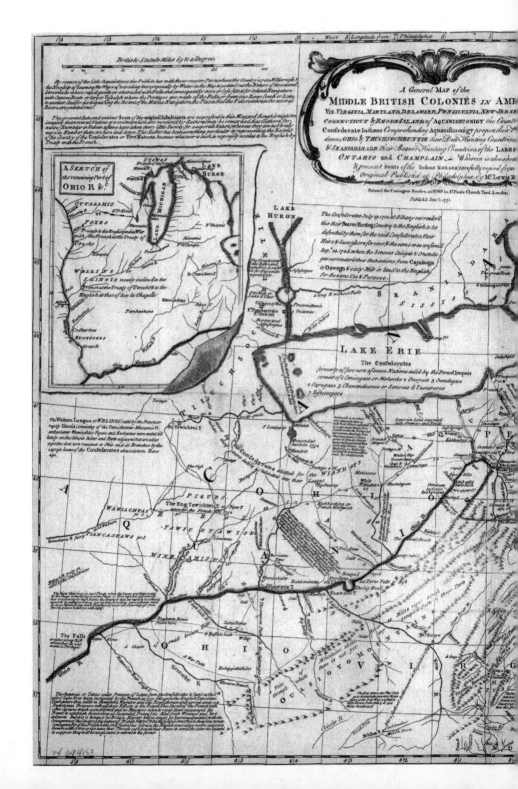

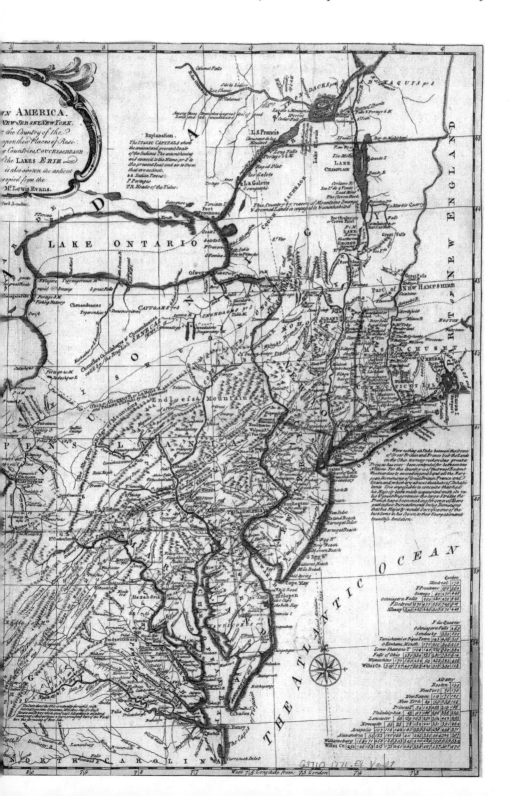

Creek settlement and wait to hear news that confirmed whether a war had actually begun. If there were to be no Indian war that season, he would join them as they proceeded to Kentucky. After a short deliberation, all the men of Clark's band agreed with Cresap.

While on the way to Wheeling Creek, the settlers met a party of Indians led by the Delaware chief Bemino, known to whites as John Killbuck Sr. Now in his sixties, Killbuck had become well acquainted with white people along the frontier. Although he proved a ruthless enemy in past wars, many frontier inhabitants believed the chief had become a reliable friend in the peace that had ensued. While Clark and the group's other leaders went across the river to meet with Killbuck, Cresap remained on the south bank for fear he might be tempted to kill the Indian out of revenge. According to Cresap, the Delaware chief had waylaid his father many times as he traveled the Ohio area as a trader.

When he reached Wheeling, Clark noticed "the country being well settled thereabouts," but strangely "the whole of the inhabitants appeared to be alarmed." Many families from the surrounding countryside had abandoned their isolated homes and sought refuge in the more-densely settled part of the region. To prevent panic and offer protection, Cresap organized his and the local adult male inhabitants into an ad hoc military unit. Clark described it as a "formidable party," since all the hunters and men without families living in the area also joined. Although Cresap offered to send out scouts to provide early warning and security, nothing he said persuaded the refugee inhabitants to return to their homes. It did not take long for Captain Commandant Connolly in Pittsburgh to learn of the presence of Captain Cresap's company at Wheeling. He sent a message that made Cresap aware that a war with the Indians could break out at any time. Connolly therefore requested Cresap to keep his men stationed in the area for a few days, or at least until the question of whether there would be peace or war had been answered. He then confided to Cresap that he was waiting for runners to return from the Indian towns with the latest intelligence. Cresap and his men resolved to stay and comply with Connolly's orders to "be careful that the enemy should not harass the neighborhood."[22]

Meanwhile, back at Fort Pitt, Connolly copied Lord Dunmore's April 25 proclamation and posted it throughout the district, along with his own circular letter for the people of West Augusta to be on their guard. Although it may have had the effect of steeling the officers and men of the militia for the fight, Connolly primarily intended his letter to encourage families not to abandon their homes. While it is unlikely Dunmore's proclamation reached the frontier settlements before the end of the month, Connolly's earlier letter, carried downstream by traders and surveyors, most likely appeared at the Wheeling Creek and other settlements by Monday, April 25. People all along the Ohio had already learned that hostile Indians had effectively closed the river to traffic and threatened parties of surveyors, land jobbers, and laborers on the south bank. Some therefore perceived the Connolly letter as a declaration of war, while others took it as confirmation that war with the Shawnees had already begun. The news affected frontier inhabitants, and the divergent attitudes persisted throughout the conflict. Where some settlers greeted the news with dread and prepared to abandon their homesteads for less vulnerable locations, others resolved to stay in spite of the risks. The letter also inspired some local militia commanders, as well as emergent leaders and their paramilitary bands, to take direct action against any Indian invaders without waiting for orders from a competent authority if they perceived a credible threat to their communities.[23]

Clark later maintained that Cresap received a message in which Connolly begged him to use his influence to have the men of his party protect the country about the settlements by aggressive scouting until the inhabitants fortified themselves by building blockhouses or stockades at their homes. Taking Connolly's letter as official notification that hostilities had commenced, Cresap called his men together for a council of war and read it to them. In the same manner as Indians did, the men planted a war post and declared war against the Shawnees as they struck it with their hatchets, one man at a time. He then summoned all the traders in the area to inform them of the situation as he knew it and cautioned them about the dangers of navigating the river.

Later in the evening, they received unconfirmed reports that marauding warriors had killed two local residents. The news prompted some of Cresap's men to go hunting for Indians with revenge on their minds; and someone brought in two scalps that night. As happened too often, emotions overruled reason. Some men cared little for determining whether the provocative incident had actually occurred, to what tribe the alleged assailants belonged, or the nature of their disposition toward whites. While the Shawnees presented the most likely threat, to some settlers, all Indians were enemies. Many Virginians also believed the Pennsylvania traders were just as bad as, if not worse than, hostile Indians since they profited from supplying muskets, powder, and lead to the warriors who used them against backcountry settlers.[24]

The next morning, Cresap's men learned that a canoe piloted by three men had been sighted as it approached from upriver. Believing they could be Indians intending to cause trouble, Cresap voiced his intention to "way lay and kill" them. Led by Ebenezer Zane, who was a land developer and the founder of Wheeling, a minority of the company's members opposed taking unilateral offensive action for fear of provoking a wider conflict. Considering their argument, the majority sided with Cresap and prepared for action. Two men, named Brothers and Chenoweth, joined the captain. They launched a canoe and paddled upriver to investigate and possibly engage the suspected threat. As it drew closer, Cresap and his companions moved to intercept the boat.[25]

The three in the southward bound canoe were William Butler's employees, including a Shawnee, Delaware, and the previously wounded Stephens, who had left Pittsburgh a few days before on this second attempt to reach the Scioto towns. When he saw Cresap's canoe paddling upstream toward them, Stephens feared it might be hostile Indians like those who had attacked him at Beaver Creek, and so paddled toward the south bank to avoid a confrontation. As the traders headed for the riverbank, someone concealed in the weeds on shore fired a shot that struck and killed the Shawnee. A second shot killed the Delaware. Stephens threw himself into the water. When he noticed three white men paddling the canoe in his direction, he swam toward them. After they helped him aboard, he learned that one of the men was Cresap, who, when asked, denied knowing anything of what happened to the traders in the canoe. Later, after he returned to Pittsburgh, Stephens told McKee that he was "well Convinced" the men who shot and killed his Indian companions were Cresap's "Associates."[26] As Cresap and his men drew alongside the abandoned canoe, Brothers and Chenoweth ruthlessly scalped the lifeless Indians and pushed their bodies into the river. Taking the trader's canoe in tow, the three paddled back toward the landing near camp. When Zane "saw much fresh blood and some bullet holes" in the canoe, he inquired on the fate of the two Indians. Brothers and Chenoweth answered they had fallen overboard.[27]

On Wednesday, April 27, five canoes carrying fourteen Indians went down the river early in the day, unnoticed by Cresap's men. These were most likely some of the Shawnee chiefs returning from the council held at Pittsburgh. A settler named McMahon came to camp and informed Cresap that they had stopped at his home earlier in the morning asking for provisions, which he refused to give them. McMahon warned the Indians that some whites, alarmed by the depredations hostile warriors had recently committed in the area, had killed two Indians in the neighborhood the day before, and he urged them to be cautious. Taking his advice, the Shawnees used the large island off Wheeling to mask their movement from observation and passed down the western channel without being sighted. Soon thereafter, someone brought word that several canoes full of Indians were sighted on the north bank between the mouths of Pipe and Captina Creeks; or from eight to fourteen miles below Wheeling, and opposite Grave Creek. Stephens later claimed hearing Cresap "use Threatening Language against the Indians," saying "he wou'd put every Indian he met with on the River to Death."[28]

The captain gathered fifteen volunteers, loaded into canoes, and pursued the Indians to the mouth of Pipe Creek. Having landed and hidden their canoes on the bank until hardly visible from the river, and suspecting they would be followed after leaving McMahon's, the warriors took position in the bushes on the shore and "prepared themselves to receive the white people." Cresap's men headed toward shore, landed, and advanced against their foe. In the ensuing skirmish, the Indians stubbornly disputed every inch of ground as they retreated. Clark recalled that a few were wounded on both sides, while others said that the volunteers took one Indian scalp but suffered one casualty when "Big Tarrence" Morrison sustained a serious hip wound. The Indians finally broke contact and retired into the woods, leaving their loaded canoes for Cresap's men to capture. Clark observed that the plunder included "a considerable quantity of ammunition and other warlike stores," in addition to trade goods, which Stephens enumerated as sixteen kegs of rum, two saddles, and some bridles.[29]

Once back at Wheeling, Dr. Wood treated and dressed Morrison's wound as the rest of the company discussed their next move, and Cresap sent Connolly a report on what his men had accomplished. When he heard of it, McKee asked Connolly to send an express to Cresap asking what provocation caused him to take his actions and to desist from any further hostilities until he investigated and settled matters, if possible. The Indian Department deputy also dispatched messages to the chiefs, inviting them to attend another council at Pittsburgh as soon as possible in hopes of averting a war.[30]

When questioned by McKee, Stephens claimed that he heard Cresap remark, "if he cou'd raise Men sufficient to cross the River, he wou'd attack a small Village of Indians living on Yellow Creek." Clark's recollection confirmed that the men assembled at Wheeling decided to march the next day, Thursday, April 28, and attack that same Mingo camp. After they had advanced about five miles in the direction of Yellow Creek, Cresap ordered his men to halt for rest and refreshment. He again surprised his followers when he began to question the others "on the impropriety of executing the projected enterprise." A number of those in the group, including Clark, had visited the intended target earlier in the year. They realized, or assumed, the collections of dwellings represented a camp for a hunting party, not a town.

Essentially a temporary village, the camp consisted of shelters and baggage to adequately sustain the hunters, as well as women and children, for an extended period away from their permanent town. War parties, in contrast, traveled light and unencumbered to permit the warriors to move and strike quickly, and without exposing their families to danger. After some reflection, the men agreed with Cresap that the Mingoes they intended to attack, unlike the Shawnees who constantly caused trouble, had indicated no hostile intentions against the settlements. "In short," Clark said, "every person seemed to detest the resolution we had set out with," and they returned to Wheeling that evening.[31]

When he arrived back at camp, Cresap found Angus McDonald waiting for him. Educated in Glasgow, the forty-six-year-old Highlander had left his native Scotland following the defeat of the 1745 Jacobite Rebellion and settled near Winchester. He was a competent soldier, and his military career since arriving in the colonies included service as a captain in the Virginia Regiment during the French and Indian War. In 1769, he was appointed major of the Frederick County militia. Returning from a trip downriver to survey the two thousand acres of his military land grant, McDonald paid Cresap a visit to discuss the military situation on the frontier before continuing homeward. After they finished and McDonald prepared to re-embark, Cresap, Clark, and a number of the others made ready to decamp and head toward Redstone.

Before McDonald shoved off, several men gathered on the bank saw traders John Gibson, Mathew Elliott, and Alexander Blaine descending the Ohio with a cargo of provisions and goods bound for the Shawnee towns on the Scioto. Those on the river bank hailed the traders and requested that they put ashore because they had "disagreeable news to inform them of." On landing, Gibson recalled they encountered approximately 150 men, including Major McDonald and Dr. Wood. The men cautioned the traders about the dangers of heading farther downriver at that time and recounted the series of violent incidents between whites and Indians that occurred in the preceding weeks. Then they added the most recent news, which they had just learned. A work party improving land near the Great Kanawha had encountered and killed all the members of a Shawnee hunting party. Believing an Indian war imminent, the men took the thirty horses loaded with pelts and other plunder from the Indians and fled cross-country toward the relative safety of the Cheat River settlements to escape retribution for the massacre.

Gibson did not believe the story. He had left the Scioto for Pittsburgh earlier that month, after all the Shawnee hunting parties had returned. None

Angus McDonald was a Scottish immigrant with an extensive military background. After serving as a lieutenant in the Jacobite army during the failed Rising of 1745, he fled to America and eventually settled in Virginia. He served as an officer of both provincial regulars, in which he rose to the rank of captain in the Virginia Regiment during the French and Indian War, and in the militia. After the war he received promotion and appointment as major in the Frederick County militia. Called to active duty in colonial service at age 47, he led the expedition against Wakatomika during Dunmore's War.

of them lost any men or reported any violent incidents. To verify, Gibson invited some of the men at Wheeling to accompany him to a place called Canoe Bottom on Hockhocking Creek, where a few members of his company worked pressing skins and building canoes. If these workers were no longer present, they could conclude that the rumor of war was verified and that everything was not right on the frontier. Although Wood and one other man agreed to accompany him, the rest sent someone to consult Cresap. While waiting, some of Gibson's hosts "behaved in a most disorderly manner" and even threatened to kill him and his companions, saying "the damned traders were worse than the Indians and ought to be killed."

When Cresap arrived at the scene early on Friday morning, Gibson informed him what he had proposed and what some of the men said in reply. Cresap spoke with them for about an hour but could not convince any of the men to accept Gibson's proposal. Cresap then personally advised Gibson not to proceed down the river. He confided that he believed the men in the camp "would fall on and kill every Indian they met on the river." Although they had chosen him as their commander and attacked the Indians at Pipe

Creek, Cresap said he would no longer serve as their leader or even continue to stay with them. Instead, he revealed to Gibson his intention to lead his work party, with Clark and some of his associates, "across the country to Red Stone to avoid the consequences."

Despite the warning, Gibson and his companions proceeded by water to the Hockhocking. When they reached Canoe Bottom they found men working on canoes and everything as peaceful as expected, before they continued to the Scioto towns by going over land. When they arrived, Gibson, Elliott, and Blaine heard the Shawnees talking of several recent murders committed against the Indians on the river.[32] At the same time, although Cresap had dissuaded his followers from attacking the camp at the mouth of Yellow Creek, someone else prepared for an engagement there. The smoldering situation on the frontier was about to ignite.

Those Mingoes living at the mouth of Yellow Creek included relatives of a Cayuga leading warrior named Talgayeeta, whom whites knew as Logan or James Logan. His many white acquaintances remarked on the friendship and hospitality he had always shown them. There is also reason to believe that he was white and adopted into his Indian family as a child. Logan had grown up in Shamokin, an Indian town near the Forks of the Susquehanna, where his father, the Oneida chief Shikellamy, represented Six Nations authority to the tributary and dependent tribes, such as the Delaware and Shawnee, living in the area.[33] He was also a diplomat who represented the Iroquois Confederacy's interests with the Pennsylvania government. In that position, Shikellamy developed such high esteem for the Pennsylvania colonial secretary, James Logan, that he chose him as his son's English namesake.[34]

Directly across the Ohio from the Mingo camp stood a white settlement called Baker's Bottom. It took its name from Joshua Baker, who had established a home and farm where he lived with his wife Elizabeth, or Lucy, and his brother-in-law, Nathaniel Tomlinson. Baker also kept a tavern and store, which became the meeting place for neighbors and a source of refreshment, entertainment, sundries, and rum for river travelers, as well as friendly Indians, despite McKee's recommendation. A pregnant Indian woman, Logan's sister (or other close female relative), Koonay, regularly crossed the river to visit Lucy Baker, who kindly gave her milk for her young children. After receiving Connolly's circular letter warning settlers to be on their guard, Baker and other residents decided to evacuate their families from the vulnerable location to Catfish Camp until the situation became less volatile. According to some later accounts, their sense of urgency increased on Friday, April 29, when Koonay warned Lucy that some Mingoes, angered by the recent killings of Shawnees by Cresap's band, planned to cross the river to kill all the white people. When Lucy informed Joshua, he called on his neighbors and friends for assistance.[35]

Upward of twenty or thirty men, mostly from the neighboring Cross Creek area, responded and arrived before morning. They included the Greathouse brothers, Daniel and Jacob, John Sappington, George Cox, Edward King, Michael Myers, and Lucy's brothers Nathaniel, Joseph, and Benjamin Tomlinson. The latter Tomlinson had buried Murphy, the trader murdered by Indians at Beaver Creek earlier in the month. The boisterous Indian-hating Daniel Greathouse took charge and devised a ruthless plan. Most of the men would remain hidden in the "back apartment" of the Bakers' house until they determined the Indians' intentions. If the Mingoes "behaved themselves peaceably," the men agreed, "they should not be molested." If they proved hostile, the whites would "shew themselves and act accordingly."[36]

On Saturday, April 30, the same day Cresap and his followers left Wheeling for Redstone, five Indian men and two women crossed the Ohio to Baker's Bottom. Some accounts attributed their arrival to the Mingoes' daily routine. Others maintained that Daniel Greathouse invited the Indians when he went over earlier in the morning to reconnoiter the warriors' strength. The visitors included Logan's sister Koonay, brother Taylayne, called John Petty by the English, as well as Taylayne's son, Molnah. As soon as the unarmed Indians got out of their canoes, all but Logan's brother went into Baker's tavern for rum. They were all soon intoxicated. Baker, Cox, and Nathanial Tomlinson stayed outside with Taylayne as the rest of their party remained concealed. At one point, Taylayne entered the Bakers' house uninvited and took a military coat and a hat belonging to Nathanial Tomlinson down from where they hung on the wall. After donning the clothes, the Indian, "setting his arms akimbo began to strut about," shouting, "look at me, I am a white man!" When Tomlinson demanded that he return the coat, Taylayne allegedly attempted to strike him while saying, "white man, son of a bitch." When Tomlinson threatened the Indian, Cox advised against taking rash action, saying it would cause a war. Wanting no part of what was about to transpire, Cox left the group and hid in the woods. Although Tomlinson tried to avoid further confrontation, the Mingo's behavior increasingly irritated Sappington. Not able to stand it anymore, he "jumped to his gun" and shot Taylayne as he left the house still wearing the hat and coat.[37]

The rest of the white men emerged from their hiding place. King rushed to the wounded Taylayne as he lay writhing in agony, drew his knife, and said, "Many a deer have I served this way." He ended the man's life and took his scalp.[38] Others rushed and overpowered the drunken Indians in the building and shot every one—male and female alike. Daniel Greathouse proceeded to remove scalps from the warriors he killed and attached the bloody trophies to his belt. As she bled to death, Koonay pleaded with Jacob Greathouse to spare the life of the baby girl strapped to the cradleboard on her back. When the murder spree ended, every Indian except one had been killed. Only the two-month-old baby, the daughter of Logan's sister and the trader John Gibson, survived.[39]

As they surveyed their handiwork, the men noticed two canoes, one with two and the other with five Indians aboard, paddling across the river. Either coming to investigate the fate of their friends after hearing the gunfire or confirming Koonay's warning, Sappington described the braves as "stripped naked, painted, and armed completely for war." The whites took position behind trees and logs along the riverbank and waited for the approaching warriors. As the lead canoe came within a few rods of shore, shots rang out and killed both occupants at close range. Sappington later claimed he killed and scalped one of them himself. The Mingoes in the second canoe turned about and paddled back for the north shore. Shortly thereafter, according to the memories of some participants, two more canoes appeared carrying eleven and seven armed and painted warriors, respectively. They attempted to land below the whites' position, but the settlers engaged them with "a well-directed fire." In the ensuing skirmish, some participants claimed, they killed one warrior who fell dead on shore, and recalled that they killed two and wounded two in the canoes before the Mingoes broke off the engagement and retired, returning fire as they went. Baker later remembered that Greathouse and company killed twelve Indians, including two women, and wounded either six or eight others. In contrast, Indian runners told Moravian missionary Heckewelder that nine had been killed and two wounded.[40] Regardless of the correct butcher's bill, Greathouse and his ruffians brutally murdered innocent people, including at least two, if not three, of Logan's relatives.

News of the massacre spread quickly on both sides of the Ohio, through white settlements and Indian towns alike, with some variations added to the gruesome details. Some of them recounted that the self-appointed leader, Daniel Greathouse, had at first wanted to attack the Indian camp. After crossing the river on a reconnaissance, he found too many warriors to overcome with the numbers of volunteers he had assembled. Instead, he decided on a stratagem. Purporting to be their friend, Greathouse invited the Indians to cross over the river and share some rum. He told Baker to give the Indians all they could drink and that he and the others would assail them after they were intoxicated.[41] In another version, while five of the Indians drank to intoxication, Daniel and Jacob Greathouse challenged the two sober warriors to a contest of shooting at marks, or targets. When they heard the reports of firearms indicating the men had shot the drunken Mingoes at the tavern, the Greathouse brothers took aim at their marksmanship competitors. Because the Indians had already fired, they stood holding empty weapons in their hands, and fell easy victims to the ambush.[42] In the most disturbing and enduring of the variations, as the dying mother pleaded with the men to spare her little girl, Jacob Greathouse aborted Koonay's unborn baby from her womb with his hunting knife, then killed and scalped the infant. In a final act of cruelty, he hung the child's lifeless body on a tree. Whether any of these are accurate, embellished, or exaggerated accounts does not change the heinousness of the acts. What is ironic, however, is that most reports accused Michael Cresap of responsibility and named Daniel Greathouse only as an accomplice.[43] The man who had convinced his followers not to attack the Indian camp only three days before probably arrived at Catfish Camp at the same time the murders that he was blamed for, and forever associated with, were committed.

Greathouse and those who had joined his enterprise knew they had little time to spare. Indians most often went on the warpath to avenge real or perceived injury or insult. They repaid murder with murder, regardless of whether those they killed in reprisal were the actual guilty party. Greathouse's men gathered their families, maybe collected as many head of cattle they might reasonably drive, and loaded what few possessions as would fit on any wagons, carts, or the backs of draft animals they had. Then, in the words of Reverend Zeisberger, the murderers "soon fled and left the [other] poor settlers as victims to the Indians," as they struck the road toward Catfish Camp and Redstone with their two-month-old captive. Others sought refuge in the more-settled areas as well. According to Baker's neighbor, James Chambers, "the settlements near the river broke up," and the inhabitants took the road toward Catfish Camp.[44] Zeisberger reported that "many are fled and left all their effects behind."[45]

Cresap arrived at Catfish Camp at the head of a party of armed men on Saturday, April 30. The men first carried the wounded Morrison on his litter to the home of Dr. William Wheeler for much-needed medical attention. Thus unburdened, they all "lay some time" and rested at the cabin of William Huston. In the conversations that ensued, Cresap's followers learned that the news they had killed three Indians on the Ohio near Wheeling and at Pipe Creek had preceded them. When their host inquired about the stories' veracity, they "acknowledged they had fired first on the Indians" and boasted they had killed some warriors. Cresap's men believed they had complied with legal orders issued by competent authority and therefore felt no need to defend their actions. After they had rested sufficiently, the men continued "on the path from Wheeling to Redstone," leaving Morrison in Wheeler's care.[46]

On Sunday, the day after the bloody incident, the people "who . . . killed some women and other Indians at Baker's Bottom" arrived at Catfish Camp. As the members of Cresap's group had the day prior, some of the party "tarried" at Huston's. Although they had no wounded, they did have a captive "whose life had been spared by the interference of some more humane than the rest," according to their host. One of Huston's neighbors, the widow Martha Jolly, started feeding and dressing the baby, and "Chirping to the little innocent." Her then-sixteen-year-old son, Henry, remembered the baby smiling at his mother and him. The next morning, when Greathouse and his followers prepared to continue "on their march to the interior parts of the country," one of their women took the child from Jolly and explained her intent to send the little girl to her "supposed" father, John Gibson. William Crawford arrived at Catfish Camp on his way from Staunton back to Pittsburgh just before Greathouse's people departed. Being acquainted with Gibson, he took the child into his care and headed toward his Spring Garden home.[47]

Crawford had spent of much of the early spring surveying land in Augusta County for several clients, including his friend George Washington. The volatile situation and escalating violence caused him difficulty in completing his work on two of Washington's claims. The delay prevented Crawford from submitting the surveys to Thomas Lewis, the county surveyor, before the latter departed for Williamsburg to file the latest claims on behalf of their owners. The visit nevertheless proved beneficial, and Crawford "was very friendly treated" during his stay. Colonel Charles Lewis, the county lieutenant, administered Crawford the oaths necessary to be sworn by officers of the Virginia militia and presented him with a captain's commission.[48]

MEANWHILE AT PITTSBURGH, Captain Commandant Connolly faced a serious crisis on Sunday, the first day of May. As the alarm spread, it became impossible to convince many frontier inhabitants not to abandon their homes. Refugees flooded into town and swelled the population. As panic spread across the countryside, he resolved "to make every provision necessary for the defense that this place and opportunity afforded." As authorized by the colony's Militia Law and the Invasions and Insurrections Act, Connolly ordered out the militia companies of Pittsburgh, which totaled about one hundred men. While conducting musters and inspecting the troops, he found many of the townsmen had no weapons. To remedy the situation, he saw it as his duty and within his authority to seize all privately owned firearms and ammunition that could be obtained for military use. With no arms available "but rifle guns intended for Indian trade & of considerable value," he impressed the weapons and then "appraised & distributed to such men" as he thought proper.[49]

As Dunmore had noted on his tour of the district in 1773, Fort Pitt needed extensive work to restore it to a state where it could provide a garrison for the militia as well as a shelter for the inhabitants of the surrounding area in an emergency. When Connolly proclaimed Virginia's sovereignty over Pittsburgh and its dependencies only five months before, the blockhouse, which stood as an outwork, represented the only usable military feature at the post. Since the British army evacuated the garrison and sold the property to a private interest in 1772, the masonry and wooden structures had been largely disassembled, with the bricks and timbers sold as salvage to local inhabitants for building material. With the crisis providing the catalyst, Connolly began the process of making the much-needed repairs and improvements, which the post required to meet the colony's new military contingencies.

Looking beyond the immediate neighborhood of Pittsburgh, Connolly began to raise troops from the district's militia to defend the several dependent communities. He issued orders "to draught one third to this place . . . in order to . . . repair this heap of ruins [Fort Pitt] and to impress provisions, horses, tools &tc."[50] Throughout the first week of May, he reported that militiamen under his command attempted to bring inhabitants into the fort and stopped all men capable of bearing arms who attempted to flee and armed them for service. On Wednesday, May 4, he conceded in his journal that "many of them however deserted." Despite the desertions, Connolly succeeded in amassing a sizeable force and reported that he had every available person employed in "fortifying the fort." The next day he added, "all the inhabitants of the town at work." By Friday, they had made enough progress for him to note that the two western bastions were being strengthened with pickets and "ordered teams to haul in all their . . . timber for that purpose." At the same time, masons repaired the breaches in the angles of the brickwork, while carpenters worked on the gates of the sally ports.[51]

Reverend John Heckwelder, who later wrote a history of the area Indians based on his observations as a contemporary missionary, explained the pro-

tocol followed at an Indian council to prevent war when one nation had insulted or injured another. "If the supposed enemy is peaceably inclined, he
will . . . send a deputation to the aggrieved nation, with a suitable apology."
The deputies would tell the leaders of the injured party that the act they
complained about had been committed without their chief's knowledge by
some of their "foolish young men." After describing that the offending actions were "altogether unauthorized and unwarranted," the offender's nation offered suitable apologies and condolence presents to cover the dead.[52]

On Thursday, Croghan and McKee, with Connolly and others in attendance, met at Croghan Hall with Indian leaders, including Guyasuta, the
deputy for the Six Nations, and the chiefs of several Iroquois and Delaware
bands. Following the established protocol of Indian diplomacy, they opened
with a "Condolence" for the Six Nations, Shawnees, and Delawares "on the
late unhappy death" of some of their friends. In an effort to "wipe the tears"
from their eyes and symbolically bury the bones of the dead by covering
them with gifts, the colonial representatives distributed presents and strings
of wampum to each nation on behalf of their people. The current and retired Indian Department deputy superintendents then requested the assembled chiefs to use their influence with the "distant chiefs" to prevent war
between their peoples. Each Indian leader in his turn spoke in a "most
friendly and reasonable manner" and pledged to honor their treaty obligations and remain loyal to their British allies.[53]

Knowing the importance of diplomacy as well as military preparedness
for security on the frontier, Guyasuta gave a speech that assured the colonial
officials of the Iroquois Confederacy's determination to "take no part with
the Shawanese" and the certainty the Delawares would do likewise. Going
further, Guyasuta said that the Six Nations and Delawares would "never
quarrel with their Brethren the English," but would "live & die" with them
in a fight against the Shawnees. He further recommended that Lord Dunmore build a fort on the Ohio at the mouth of the Great Kanawha to keep
the Shawnees "in awe" and prevent their war parties "from makeing Inroads
amongst the Inhabitants" of Virginia from the Ohio River to "Redstone and
Everywhere." He believed that people living there, although exposed to
depredations, should plant their crops and be guarded by some of the militia until the Shawnee made their intentions known. It was no secret that
the Shawnees had displeased the Iroquois Confederacy and its dependent
nations. Guyasuta assured British officials at Pittsburgh that an attempt to
cause any "Mischief" by the Shawnees would result in their being resented
for it by the Delawares. He added that their conduct over the previous twelve
months made it clear that no other nations would join them in a war against

British interests. If the Shawnees rejected the message calling for them to remain peaceful and did "not listen to Reason," Guyasuta believed "they ought to be chastised," or punished.[54]

The Crown and Virginia officials and Guyasuta agreed to join in sending the Shawnees one message, carried by two respected Delaware chiefs, to articulate the British position. They also decided to share its contents with the assembled tribal representatives as well as any others who could make it to Croghan Hall. Simon Girty, the Indian Department's interpreter, delivered the message and invitation to Koquethagechton, or Captain White Eyes, and Konieschquanoheel, also known as Hopocan, or Captain Pipe, to meet with the English, and escorted them to Pittsburgh on his return trip.[55] Having tirelessly sought to resolve disputes between Indians and whites in the past, White Eyes was regarded by many as the most influential Delaware chief in the Ohio country. Pipe enjoyed a reputation in which his influence among the Delawares and his friendship with the English were equal to those of White Eyes.

Connolly wanted the Delaware chiefs, "to hear what we had to say on the differences which had arisen between us [the Virginians] and them [the Shawnees]."[56] While he busied himself managing the myriad tasks involved with defending the district and making Fort Pitt a respectable defensive installation again, another Indian chief arrived. Connolly presented him with a string of wampum and a speech that expressed a desire to remain at peace. The militia commander also wrote two announcements to be printed on broadsides as well as read and posted throughout the district. One informed the people that the situation appeared to give reason to apprehend "immediate danger from the Indians and particularly the Shawanese." Heeding Guyasuta's advice, the other ordered all traders to refrain from importing liquor into Indian country and reminded them that Virginia law strictly prohibited conducting any trade with an enemy, with the promise that anyone caught conveying liquor to "suspected enemies" would "answer . . . at their peril."

Amid all the bustling activity, the Indian council reconvened on Friday, May 6. Connolly observed as Croghan and McKee conducted the conference, with Guyasuta and some other Six Nations chiefs, and Pipe, White Eyes, and other Delaware leaders attending. The Indian Department men, as the protocol of Indian diplomacy required, distributed presents to the chiefs in condolence for the Delawares that had lately been killed on the river. The Indians, according to Croghan, spoke in a "most friendly and reasonable manner" while discussing the recent violence. All repeated their promises to continue adhering to their professions of peace. As a represen-

tative of the Virginia colonial government, Connolly delivered the speech
and distributed copies that the chiefs could carry for the interpreters to read
to their people on the north bank.

After expressing his sorrow at the disputes and resultant events, which
had bad consequences for both parties, Connolly assured the Indian representatives that Virginia officials "had no act or part" in what happened and
that he had certainly not issued orders to kill any Indians without cause.
He laid the blame entirely on "the folly and indiscretion of our young people," who, like their own young men, were "unwilling to listen to good advice." Connolly promised to investigate and determine exactly what had
happened. He hoped the dispute could remain limited to the "young and
foolish people" of both sides without engaging our "wise men" in a quarrel
in which none of them had a part. He told the Indian leaders that the incidents could not have happened at a worse time, since "the Great Head Man
of Virginia," Lord Dunmore, and "all his wise people"—meaning the General Assembly—were about to meet in their own council to discuss settling
the country bought from the Six Nations. The captain commandant assured
the chiefs that Virginia settlers would "come to be your neighbors . . . [and]
to be kind and friendly towards you." He further expected that "they will
buy goods to cloath your old people and children to brighten the chain of
friendship" between them.

The officer pledged that the Indians would find Virginians as friendly
toward them as their "late neighbors" from Pennsylvania. He concluded by
asking them "not to listen to what some lying people that may tell you to
the contrary"—that although Virginians were always ready to fight an
enemy, they would show their "true & steady friendship" on every occasion
when warranted. After asking Pipe and White Eyes to carry his words home
to their people and the Shawnees, he reassured them he would do all in his
power to bring those guilty of committing the murders at Baker's Bottom
to justice and invited them to a general peace conference at Pittsburgh. The
council adjourned on May 6, and the Indian leaders headed home.

Connolly maintained the stated position that the matters in dispute between the Indian nations and the colony could still be resolved amicably,
notwithstanding the "violent and barbarous treatment" many native people
suffered at the hands of "unthinking and lawless people." When notified
that thirty armed men, not embodied as militia, had gone down the Ohio
in pursuit of Indians, he took quick action to officially disapprove of their
actions and prevent a tragedy. Knowing that White Eyes' family and other
peaceful Indians lived just across the river from Pittsburgh, Connolly sent
the sheriff and a small unit of militia to compel the thirty disorderly white

people to return to Pittsburgh. He also sent an interpreter to locate White Eyes' family and escort them to the Croghan Hall plantation, where they could remain under the colony's protection until the chief returned from his diplomatic mission to the Shawnees. In order to forbid individuals from taking unauthorized action again, Connolly posted advertisements reading that any "attempt to behave so contrary to peace and good order of this country" would be punished by all means available within his power as a magistrate and military commander.

To facilitate the safe assembly of the various Indian chiefs at the next council, Connolly published yet another public notice. He informed the inhabitants of West Augusta that they would join him in welcoming some of the most influential chiefs of the Ohio area nations. "In His Majesty's Name," he commanded all British "subjects of the colony and Dominion" of Virginia to "desist from further acts of Hostility against any Indians whatever, especially those expected to come to the fort for "business in their usual manner." Connolly sent twenty bushels of corn to feed the Indians assembled at Colonel Croghan's.

The same day, Connolly held a conference with some "country people" who had retired to a place about twelve miles south of Pittsburgh, where they requested permission to build a stockade fort for their own protection. The captain cautioned them that their stockade would only afford them "imaginary safety" at best. Dividing the available strength of the country's militia, he explained, might make them feel more secure in their separate communities, but it actually tended to only "lull people into supineness and neglect" and render their defenses ineffective in opposing the enemy. In consequence, they would ultimately be forced to choose between either having to abandon the country or "fall sacrifices to the vindictive rage of the savages." If the refugees still thought that Pittsburgh was too crowded with women and children, he at least wanted their presence to benefit his plan of defense. Connolly agreed to permit them to build a fort upriver on the Monongahela as an intermediate post to keep the line of water communication open with the Redstone settlement. In return, they would have to send one-third of their active young men to assist in repairing and defending Fort Pitt, which, if taken by the enemy, would certainly result in the whole country west of the Allegheny being abandoned. Although they said they agreed at the meeting, Connolly did not expect them to actually comply with his request.

Back in Indian country, the Moravian missionaries at Schönbrunn had finally learned that the Virginians had officially taken control of Pittsburgh and the surrounding country on April 30. That and other news prompted

Reverend Zeisberger to note in his journal that he believed the Virginians feared that the Shawnees had begun preparations for war against them. The runners also informed the missionaries about the recent Indian council at Croghan Hall, during which Guyasuta relayed William Johnson's warning to other Ohio Indians not to join the Shawnees in attacking whites on the south bank. By the end of the first week in May, several Munsee Delawares arrived to inform the missionaries and their congregation that one Shawnee chief had been killed and another wounded on the Ohio—a reference to the skirmish at Pipe Creek. Zeisberger lamented, "It seems Indian war will break out," and feared the Virginians would attack and destroy Shawnee towns.[57] While the clergymen prayed that both sides would resolve their differences without war, worse news followed. An express from nearby Gekelemuckepuck brought the news of the murders of nine Yellow Creek Mingoes and attributed them, as well as the other recent killings, to Cresap.[58]

Gekelemuckepuck sat on the north bank of the Tuscarawas River, a tributary of the Muskingum. Zeisberger described it as a thriving community having more than one hundred log houses in 1770. As the principal town of the region's Unami Delaware, it also served as a political capital for the Lenape people living in the Ohio country. As the home of Netawatwes, a respected Turtle clan Delaware chief whom the English called Newcomer, most whites therefore knew Gekelemuckepuck as Newcomer's Town.[59]

In the aftermath of the massacre, the Mingoes evacuated their camp on Yellow Creek and headed toward Gekelemuckepuck. As members of the injured community arrived, they told their hosts, and anyone else present, of the treachery of the Big Knife and their barbarity to even those who are their friends. Although none of them got close enough to see firsthand, they all alleged that Cresap had not only led the murderers at Baker's Bottom but attributed all of Daniel Greathouse's actual as well as the contrived actions to him.[60] Throughout Indian country, as they had in white communities, facts became intertwined with fiction with each retelling so that the tragedy sounded even more horrifying. By the time William Johnson received it, the report stated that "a certain Mr. Cressop, an inhabitant of Virginia," was responsible, and that he had murdered "forty Indians in Ohio."[61] Even the Pennsylvania partisan Arthur St. Clair stated in a letter to Governor Penn his belief that, "The mischief done by Cressap and Great House had been much exaggerated." Before long, messengers reached the Delaware towns and Moravian communities telling that the Virginians had attacked the Mingo settlement on the Ohio and butchered even the women and the children in their arms, and that Logan's family were among the many slain.[62]

As soon as the aggrieved Mingoes settled in at Newcomer's Town, they began hunting, but not for game. Zeisberger learned they were out "to catch some traders" traveling between towns in order to kill whites—any whites. Many Shawnees, a number of whom already held some animosity toward the Virginians, joined the Mingoes in the endeavor. These hunting parties took no time to determine whether their prey were Virginian or Pennsylvanian. Whoever saw a white man saw an enemy. Seeking allies, the Mingoes sent runners to the towns at Wakatomica on the Muskingum, inviting the Shawnees and Delawares to join them for a council of war at Newcomer's Town.[63]

The Delawares, being more peaceful, kept all traders from using the roads for their protection.[64] Knowing that the Mingoes were likely to take revenge on any white people prompted the Moravian missionaries to "shut themselves up" in their communities. Heckewelder wrote that the friends and relatives of those murdered at Yellow Creek "passed and re-passed through the villages of the quiet Delaware towns, in search of white people." As soon as they became aware of what they were doing, Mingoes also aimed their anger and the most abusive language imaginable at the Delawares who shielded the white devils from their vengeance.[65] The situation caused the white Moravians such great distress that they did not know what action to take. "Our Indians," Heckewelder said, "keep watch about us every night, and will not let us go out of town, even not into our corn fields."[66]

Trying to maintain calm, some of the more moderate Shawnee chiefs sent a message asking "their grandfather, the Delaware nation," to remain peaceful, "easy and quiet." The headmen encouraged all Ohio Indians not to molest or hurt the traders or any other white people in that quarter and the women to continue their spring planting until they determined what would happen. Zeisberger concluded that the Shawnee chiefs desired "to keep the road to Pittsburgh clear, and not hurt the Pennsylvanians," as the source of diplomatic contact and the trade goods on which they depended, as well as firearms and ammunition, but to only contend with the Virginians as potential enemies.[67]

Many on both sides of the Ohio expressed their concern for the safety of traders in Indian country, a number of those finding themselves hunted by people with whom they had usually conducted business. At the end of the first week of May, one trader who made it to Pittsburgh from Newcomer's Town related that a Delaware headman had warned him to flee following the arrival of a wounded Shawnee warrior. The injured man reported that hostilities had commenced, and the English had killed several of his people. Because he expected a Shawnee war party to arrive and threaten his life and those of the Delawares who would try to shelter him, the white man departed in such haste that he left all his property behind him. Many like him, however, still remained.[68]

Meanwhile, the four men Captain Russell had sent out to reconnoiter returned to Castle's Woods on the Friday of the first week of May. They had, according to the captain, "faithfully performed the Service, both as Scouts, and in regard to the boundary Line." After they made their report under oath before a justice of the peace, Russell sent a written copy to Colonel Preston for him to convey to Williamsburg and the General Assembly. The report left no room for any doubt that the Louisa River defined the border between Virginia and the Cherokees. Arriving when it did, the report also helped to determine the legality of any claims still in dispute and afforded the claimants the time and opportunity to adjust their entries at the extraordinary surveyors' expense. Furthermore, having it in possession enabled the General Assembly to appropriate the necessary funds to pay the scouts for their service without making them suffer a lengthy delay.[69]

When William Crawford returned home with his new ward, Koonay and John Gibson's daughter, he sent George Washington copies of the surveys for his Augusta County property and a letter acquainting him with the "truth of matters" on the frontier. Despite having some remaining doubts, Crawford gave Washington the most accurate account possible, from his perspective, on the recent violence. Anticipating retaliation for the massacre of the Yellow Creek Mingoes, he wrote, "Our inhabitants are much alarmed, many hundreds having gone over the mountain, and the whole country evacuated as far as the Monongahela; and many on this side of the river are gone over the mountain." With his new Virginia militia commission, he had mustered one hundred men whom he planned to lead to Fort Pitt, and combined with those posted at Wheeling, "shall wait the motions of the Indians" and act accordingly. Although an Indian council had convened to avert war, he confessed, "What will be the event I do not know," and concluded, "In short, a war is every moment expected."[70]

CHAPTER 4

Trained in Martial Exercise

Escalating Violence and the Militia Law

May 1774

PUSHING HIMSELF to exhaustion, Captain Commandant John Connolly continued his efforts to rehabilitate Fort Pitt, prepare the local militia for action, prevent the flight of fearful inhabitants, and maintain civil order. On Saturday, May 7, 1774, with the authority vested in him by Governor Dunmore's orders appointing him as the district's commanding officer, he started offering militia commissions to reliable people who would recruit volunteers for active service, preferably men without families, and march them to the fort "to enter in the pay of government." That day, he presented an ensign's commission to a man who brought eighteen volunteers to Pittsburgh. Captains William Crawford and John Neville visited the post and recommended that if Connolly issued them "Blank Warrants" to appoint subordinate officers they "would ride about the country and use their utmost endeavors to encourage young men to enter into the service."[1]

Two days later, courtesy of Neville, twenty-four militiamen from Peters Creek arrived to reinforce the garrison, along with "four Negro men . . . with proper working implements" to help repair the defenses. Connolly remarked that Neville's action had rendered "infinite service to me and the country in general," and hoped it would inspire others to exert themselves during that critical time. On Tuesday, Crawford led a welcome reinforcement of about one hundred men into Pittsburgh and expected to meet others there and at Wheeling, where they would wait to see what the enemy would do and take appropriate action. The added strength allowed Connolly to send a forty-man detachment under Captain John Stephenson,

Crawford's half-brother, to protect frontier settlements and prevent any small Indian war parties from attempting to "disturb the tranquility" of the inhabitants, although their chiefs tried to restrain them and remain peaceful.[2]

Amid all the activity and confusion, Connolly heard, and possibly believed, some of the distorted second-hand accounts of Cresap's alleged culpability in the massacre of the Yellow Creek Mingoes. Although many frontier inhabitants had already suffered from the retaliatory raids against their neighbors, it astonished Connolly that they viewed the men who provoked them as meritorious.[3] As if he did not face enough challenges, some obstinate people from the frontiers of Pennsylvania arrived on Wednesday, May 11, behaving in a very disorderly and riotous manner, and threatened to kill the Indians staying at Croghan's nearby plantation. After the captain commandant had the leaders confined, their followers threatened to break them out of jail. In response, Connolly doubled the guard and ordered the officers to fire on any of the armed militia who mutinied and attempted to rescue the prisoners. He also took the precaution of posting two guards and his interpreter at Croghan's home in the event the troublemakers appeared there. By Thursday, the mutineers had apparently come to what Connolly described as a better sense of how they could serve their country, and he dismissed them after they, or someone on their behalf, posted a bond as security for their good behavior.[4]

By week's end, provisions began to arrive at Fort Pitt from the surrounding communities with more regularity, which helped to ease the sense of crisis somewhat, until Connolly received more alarming news. A large body of armed men—not embodied as militia—had gathered at Catfish Camp intent on attacking Shawnee towns in retribution for recent Indian incursions. Unaware that Michael Cresap had called them together, Connolly wrote the men a letter requesting—and ordering—them to return home. He also alerted Captain Stephenson and ordered him to use his company to dissuade any disorderly people from committing any acts of violence against Indians "without the countenance of government."[5]

Connolly needed no more such problems when, on May 19, an Onondaga Indian delivered an insolent message from Daniel Greathouse, Joseph Swearingen, Nathaniel Tomlinson, Joshua Baker, J. Brown, and Gavin Watkins. After identifying themselves as the six people who had killed the Mingoes opposite Yellow Creek, they demanded that Connolly order the Indians to remain on their own side of the river or they would kill more of them. The district commandant dispatched an officer and six men to find and present the ruffians with his reply. He rebuked them for their demands and condemned them for committing barbarous and evil actions for which they deserved the severest punishment the government he represented could impose. After sarcastically observing they had not also murdered their messenger for being an Indian, he concluded with an admonition that if he ever heard that they had either attempted to kill or killed any friendly or unoffending Indians, he would order a party of militia to apprehend them, as well as all those who aided and abetted them, and bring them to justice for "exemplary punishment."[6]

The same day, Connolly alerted commanders of the different corps of militia in the country that recent intelligence warranted a heightened state of readiness. In accordance with the Militia Act, he ordered each captain to immediately call a muster of all the militia in his neighborhood to inspect and examine their arms and accoutrements, and equip those deficient in the best manner possible. Issuing warrants, he authorized militia commanders to impress all necessary provisions, salt, entrenching tools, and other items they needed to perform their duties in accordance with the law for opposing invasions and insurrections. After accomplishing these tasks, he ordered them to detach one-third of their respective companies under the command of their lieutenants and send them with the impressed items to his immediate assistance. Keeping the rest of their men under arms for the defense of their communities until they received further orders, Connolly directed his subordinates to take the necessary measures to stop any people fleeing the district and escort them to Pittsburgh with their belongings. Finally, he cautioned that it may prove necessary to send detachments to assist neighboring communities, or concentrate all their forces at Fort Pitt if hostile Indians wanted that town "to feel the first effects of their resentment."[7]

Such language appeared to contradict Connolly's public insistence that negotiations could settle the disputes without further bloodshed. On May 20, he received a reply from the "disorderly people" at Catfish Camp in which Enoch Innis and Michael Cresap explained that they had assembled in response to recent Indian attacks and challenged Connolly's assurances of peaceful accommodation. If he was so certain that diplomacy would prevent war, the spokesmen invited Connolly, Croghan, and McKee to meet them at Catfish Camp on Monday, May 30, to provide "surety"—essentially agreeing to become hostages—against any Indian depredations for the next six months. Otherwise, the armed band would unilaterally attack the Shawnees. Connolly replied with what he described as a "friendly" letter requesting Cresap to discharge the people he had imprudently assembled without any authority because their presence threatened to render all efforts to prevent conflict meaningless. After waiting two days, Connolly instructed Captain Paul Froman to assemble his militia company, properly armed and equipped, to wait for orders at Redstone. If by noon on Wednesday, May 25, Connolly learned that Cresap and his associates had listened to reason and dispersed, he would order Froman to dismiss the men. Otherwise, Froman's company would march to Catfish Camp and force those gathered "to desist from their destructive scheme."[8]

WHITE EYES arrived at Schönbrunn three days after leaving Pittsburgh on his mission toward the Muskingum to seek an accommodation of concerns with the Shawnees. At McKee's suggestion, two Pennsylvania traders, John Anderson (or Saunderson) and David Duncan, accompanied him as "public messengers" to deliver the appeal for the Shawnees to desist from all hostilities. Concerned for their safety, Zeisberger warned that Indian country had become very dangerous for white people—even those accompanying a respected Delaware chief. Failing to deter the three, the missionary cautioned them to avoid the more heavily traveled road.[9]

On reaching Newcomer's Town, the three men noticed the number of traders who had taken refuge there. The town's headmen also warned them of the perils and advised that only one messenger should continue to Wakatomica with White Eyes while the other waited with them. Following a brief discussion, Anderson accepted the invitation to stay. The others had barely departed the town when an angry musket shot narrowly missed Duncan. White Eyes shouted for the trader to hurry back to the shelter of the village. The chief then "got betwixt" his companion and the assailant, a Shawnee warrior, and disarmed him as he attempted to reload his musket. On his return, the chief personally made the town's Delaware inhabitants responsible for his messengers' safety. The friendly Indians immediately locked all the traders in a "strong house" and had a guard kept on them day and night to protect them from any attempt that might be made on their safety by the Shawnees or Mingoes. Their hosts brought them provisions and anything else they might need to be as comfortable as possible.[10]

Hokoleskwa, the chief whose name translated to Cornstalk—also known to Indians by a name translated as Hard Man—and the other Shawnee headmen politely received White Eyes. They sat around the council fire and listened to the words of apology and condolence for the recently killed Shawnees and the messages delivered on behalf of the colonial commissioners at Pittsburgh. After White Eyes had finished, Cornstalk rose to his feet and responded. He expressed regret that people on both sides had suffered "much ill." The Shawnee held the Virginians responsible for the series of warlike incidents, "All which Mischiefs so close to each other Aggrevated our People very much." As a remedy, Cornstalk demanded that Governors Dunmore and Penn exert their authority more forcefully over the back-country settlers to stop such aggressive actions in the future. He specifically urged that Connolly, as Dunmore's surrogate in the area where most of the violence occurred, "endeavor to stop such foolish [white] People," as Cornstalk had with great pain and trouble prevailed on the Shawnees "to sit still" and refrain from violence until their headmen settled the disputes.[11]

The gathering war clouds had deterred many young Shawnee men from going on the spring hunt. Cornstalk offered to have his nation's warriors escort groups of traders to protect them from the vengeance of friends and relatives of the recently slain who might be waiting along the road to attack them as they traveled home. At the end of the meeting, Cornstalk addressed White Eyes as his "brother" and charged him to deliver his reply to Croghan, McKee, and Connolly, and entrusted him with the string of wampum to testify as the Indians' documentary record, as well as a mnemonic aid for translating the speech.[12]

Pipe joined White Eyes when the grand council convened at Newcomer's Town on Sunday, May 15. Although the envoys urged the leaders representing the Ohio-area Indians to maintain peace, a group of twenty boisterous Mingoes kept "stirring up the Shawnees." Despite the interruptions, Pipe and White Eyes assured those assembled in council that the gang of lawless villains responsible for the recent murders had not acted on Dunmore's orders. While most Delawares seemed amenable, no argument assuaged the anger of the Mingoes and an increasing numbers of Shawnees. When they threatened to kill all white people they met, the town's residents only became even more protective of those they harbored, and determined not to allow the hostiles to take them by surprise.[13]

A few days later, runners brought news from Pittsburgh and a message from Croghan. The retired but still influential deputy Indian superintendent advised all Ohio Indians to "be quiet, and not think of war," and prevent any harm to the traders while Virginia authorities did their utmost to apprehend and bring their peoples' murderers to justice. Croghan added that authorities had already taken one of the villains into custody. After the council had concluded, runners delivered the "agreeable news" to Heckewelder that the Shawnees had decided to remain at peace.[14] No sooner had this raised his hopes than conflicting rumors that the Shawnees had declared war dashed them again.

At places like the Mingo enclave near Gekelemuckepuck and the Upper Shawnee towns of Wakatomika, inhabitants heard the drums beating as groups of young men, eager for martial glory, gathered in front of council houses. They listened to Logan and other captains call on those willing to follow to join them on the warpath to avenge the recent murders of their people at Yellow Creek and on the Ohio. As onlookers watched, the warriors participated in a spectacle, as described in James Smith's captivity narrative, that combined military drill, religious ceremony, and social gathering. Those who had already committed to the enterprise formed into lines and began moving in concert with the beating of the drum, not altogether unlike European soldiers on parade. The braves advanced across the open space to a certain point, and then halted. In unison they gave what one white observer described as a "hideous shout or yell" and stretched their weapons menacingly in the direction of the enemy's homeland, then "wheeled quick about" and danced back in the direction from which they came. After they all returned to the starting point, the leading warrior sang his war song and moved to the painted war post, where he declared his reasons for going to war. After he boasted of his exploits in past battles, he affirmed what he intended to do to any enemies encountered in the next one and struck the post with his tomahawk to demonstrate.

As comrades and spectators applauded in approval and shouted encouragement, the next warrior advanced to the post and repeated the ritual. Whether they sought adulation for performing bravely in battle or just wished to not be left behind by their peers, other young men took up the hatchet as the members of the war party cheered and welcomed them. The ceremony concluded after the last man struck the post. The next morning, warriors bade farewell to friends and loved ones and marched to battle. The news spread quickly through Indian country. Shawnee and Mingo warriors, as well as those of other nations who volunteered to join them—even though their tribal councils decided to remain neutral—repeated the scene in numerous towns north of the Ohio in the months that followed.[15]

Shortly afterward, a group of mission Indians told Heckewelder that while visiting Mochwesung they had witnessed Munsees perform a similar war dance after a party of Mingoes paraded a white man's scalp through the town.[16] Zeisberger's prayers that "the dark cloud" of war would soon pass over and peace be restored went unanswered as he learned that the Shawnees had only agreed to remain peaceful at the council to mollify the Delaware faction. Newcomer arrived at Schönbrunn and broke the news that Shawnee and Mingo leaders had met in a separate council at Wakatomica. Although he had addressed them in a fatherly manner about the "blessings of Peace and Folly of War," the Delaware chief told them the Shawnees and Mingoes had decided to fight. According to Newcomer, Logan had announced that he sought immediate vengeance for the murders of his relatives and took the warpath with nineteen followers to kill the traders who were pressing their peltry at the Canoe Bottom on Hockhocking Creek and make an incursion against Virginia settlements opposite the mouth of Yellow Creek. Newcomer then asked several mission Indians to run ahead to inform Killbuck, who had passed through while escorting a group of fleeing traders toward Pittsburgh.[17]

The missionaries pondered how their flock would meet the crisis. An invasion of the Ohio country would present the greatest threat, according to Zeisberger, as it put their community in danger from both sides. He feared that the conflict might escalate into a general Indian war in which the Pennsylvanians joined the Virginians and possibly targeted the Delawares as well as the Shawnees and Mingoes. Should the community's white brethren feel compelled to flee, Zeisberger believed most of the converted Indians would follow them eastward and reestablish the towns they had abandoned on the Susquehanna. Such a migration involved great risk, and he questioned their ability to gather and carry sufficient quantities of provisions to sustain their entire population while on the move. The missionaries and leaders of the praying Indians joined the headmen of neighboring towns in appealing to Newcomer to assist them in the good work of preserving peace. Although it seemed time would run out, the venerable chief urged all Indians "not to stop the road to Philadelphia, but to let it be free and open" by maintaining friendly relations and trade with the Pennsylvanians.[18]

WHITE EYES returned from his embassy on Tuesday, May 24, and met with Connolly, Croghan, and McKee to inform them of the results of his mission and deliver a letter from Duncan and Anderson. The two men wrote that they and nine other traders, including one George Wilson, had left their shelter at Newcomer's Town and headed toward Pittsburgh with an escort of armed Delawares. Meanwhile, the suspense of waiting at Ligonier proved too much for St. Clair to endure, so he decided to risk the consequences of an encounter with Connolly. His gamble paid off when Pipe and White Eyes returned the very day he arrived.[19]

The same day, Connolly received the news that Cresap had disbanded his men and sent them home. Relieved, he dispatched expresses to inform Froman and the other captains that the danger had passed, and ordered them to dismiss their men with his thanks. A few weeks after he returned home from Catfish Camp, Michael Cresap received a commission in the rank of captain in the Hampshire County militia, signed by Lord Dunmore on June 10. He and Connolly extinguished any personal resentment each

held against the other as a result of the accusations that followed the massacre of the Mingoes from Yellow Creek. The two men now had to work together for the good of their adopted country of Virginia.[20]

The relief Connolly experienced when he learned the situation with Cresap had been diffused was quickly replaced with another source of tension
that evening. As Croghan and McKee prepared for the next day's council,
Connolly received intelligence that some Indians had fired on laborers
working in some fields down on the Old Pennsylvania Road just outside of
Pittsburgh. A man working in one field had suffered a chest wound, while
three laborers last seen in an adjoining field were reported missing and presumed taken captive. Connolly dispatched Captain Abraham Teagarten with
fifteen soldiers to investigate and reconnoiter the area for tracks or other
signs that indicated the presence of marauding Indians.[21]

On Wednesday afternoon, White Eyes delivered messages from the
Delawares at Newcomer's Town as well as Cornstalk's reply on behalf of the
Shawnees to an assembly that included McKee, Connolly, several Delaware
sachems, Guyasuta, the official deputy, plus eight other chiefs from the Iroquois Confederacy, and St. Clair, who represented Pennsylvania at
Croghan's suggestion. Listening intently, no one doubted the Delawares'
sincere desire to remain at peace. However, the "most insolent nature" of
the Shawnees' reply stunned Connolly. Speaking through White Eyes, Cornstalk condemned as lies all that Croghan, McKee, and Connolly told the
Shawnees. In consequence, the Hard Man admitted that twenty warriors
had gone out to get revenge for the recent deaths of their people at the same
time he acknowledged the Virginians' attempt to accommodate their complaints. Cornstalk further infuriated Connolly when he answered the captain's request that the Shawnees "not take amiss the Act of a few desperate
young men" by declaring that Virginians should therefore likewise "not be
displeased at what our Young Men are now doing, or shall do against your
People." Furthermore, the chief ridiculed the Virginians for building forts
on their side of the Ohio, and made it clear that the Shawnees would only
talk peace with Governor Dunmore after they "got satisfaction," or exacted
revenge by killing some white people, "but not before." Shawnee warriors,
he said, were "all upon their Feet" ready for war. St. Clair also characterized
Cornstalk's reply as "insolent" but believed the Shawnees meant no harm
toward Pennsylvania and wrote Penn that they "lay all to the charge of the
big Knife, as they call the Virginians."[22]

St. Clair then stood and addressed the assembled Iroquois Six Nations
and Delaware representatives on behalf of Governor Penn and thanked
them for their good speeches promoting peace. Pennsylvanians, he said, re-

mained determined to maintain the friendship that existed between the Six Nations and Delawares and them. However, since the threatening actions of the Shawnees had alarmed Pennsylvanians, he urged the chiefs to prevent their people from hunting on the south side of the Ohio because some settlers will not be able to distinguish between them and those who may be enemies. St. Clair pledged that his colony's government would endeavor to keep the "Path" of communications and commerce open and "keep bright the chain of Friendship so long held fast by their and our Forefathers."[23]

As the Indian council convened at Fort Pitt, Anderson, Duncan, and company arrived with their nine Delaware escorts. Anderson and Wilson admitted that it took some hard work to get back. The latter added that the Delawares, who still seemed friendly at that time, had enough to do to save their lives from hostile Shawnees and Mingoes. Duncan praised the people of Newcomer's Town for treating them with a great deal of kindness and demonstrated nothing but peace and friendship from all their actions. Wilson remarked that while he had escaped with his life, he had to leave about fifty horseloads of deer skins in the Lower Shawnee Towns. More ominously, the three traders confirmed that before they departed, Logan had set off with about twenty Mingoes and other warriors to strike Virginia settlements near Wheeling. They also worried that hostile Shawnees or Mingoes had gathered for the purpose of finding and killing their fellow traders still in Indian country. Wilson added that no one could tell whether they were dead or alive at that time.[24] About a week later, two messengers from Newcomer's Town reported the Shawnee towns had become quiet again. They said a white man named Connor living at Snake's Town on the Muskingum told them that some moderate Shawnees had taken great pains, together with a group of Delawares, to escort twenty-five or thirty traders, along with their pelts, up the Ohio to Pittsburgh.[25]

While Croghan disagreed, Anderson feared a frontier war would soon erupt. Rumors ran rampant as settlers reported sighting parties of hostile Indians everywhere, although many proved unfounded. Connolly received messages of new depredations almost daily, such as the incident that resulted in one wounded and three men reported missing on May 24, but he could not dismiss any of them without investigation. After three days, Captain Teagarten's patrol returned with the three alleged missing laborers in custody after finding no evidence that they had been attacked by Indians. He determined that they had shot and wounded the other man during a heated dispute over land he was improving and only blamed it on Indians.

The same day, a friendly Indian brought Connolly a letter from "an unfortunate trader in the woods" hiding under the protection of one of the interpreter John Montour's sons. The letter informed the captain that hostile Mingoes had killed and scalped some white people not far from where he took shelter. The stranded man added that some warriors had waited in ambush on the Traders' Path for two days, intent on killing any whites who approached or left Newcomer's Town. The trader believed the warriors had crossed the Ohio to attack the homestead of "some distressed family" to assuage their disappointment at the lack of prey on the north bank.[26]

Reacting to the recent intelligence, Connolly sent Captain Henry Hoagland's company to Wheeling on Thursday, May 26. Hoagland had orders to intercept any Indians he discovered on "our side of the river" and treat any he encountered who were armed, or whose tracks led toward the settlements, as enemies. Erring on the side of caution, Connolly also ordered Ensign Richard Johnston and Sergeant George Cox to follow with reinforcements.[27] The next day, he ordered Captain Joel Reece to immediately march with all the men he could raise and "join any of the companies already out under the pay of the government" to search for, interdict, attack, and pursue any war parties that endangered the frontier communities. Never missing an opportunity to criticize him or the Virginians, St. Clair told Penn that Connolly had sent the troops with orders to fall on every Indian they met, regardless of whether friend or foe. Undeterred, Connolly was constantly improving Fort Pitt's defenses as refugees fled to its protection from the western-most settlements. Under the provisions of the Invasions and Insurrections Act, he ordered "some indifferent cabins" appraised and demolished in order to use the salvaged wood as pickets for the fort.[28]

The news that the "Shawanese were for war" spread quickly from the frontier to Williamsburg and Philadelphia. The traders who returned from Indian country informed militia officers with intelligence that as many as forty enemy warriors—twenty Shawnees and twenty Mingoes—had crossed the Ohio intent on striking somewhere in Virginia. One witness found it "lamentable" that "multitudes of poor people" fled the country to seek refuge in less vulnerable areas while others resolved to stay and defend their homes. Neighbors built and manned stockades and blockhouses in which they could better withstand the expected onslaught.[29] Valentine Crawford commented that erecting such private defenses, such as his own Crawford's fort, provided "a very great means for the people standing their ground." Some who fled from the exposed farms took refuge at these fortified homes instead of heading for the safer areas of the colony and added their numbers to the local militia. Similarly, men who had come to the area to work, such as the hired carpenters and servants George Washington had sent to erect a mill on the bottomland he had acquired near the Little Kanawha River, suspended their projects and volunteered for active militia service and helped the inhabitants build fortifications.[30]

By themselves, the private forts only provided residents a place of refuge unless area militia posted garrisons in them to take an active role in defending their communities. Arthur Trader recalled that in his "15th or 16th year of age," after several captains called their West Augusta District companies to muster, he served in a ranging detachment of fifteen to twenty men from the company commanded by Captain Zackquill Morgan. Posted at the fortified home of fellow company member Sergeant Jacob Prickett, the rangers traversed the country between the Ohio and Monongahela Rivers on patrols that frequently provided the frontier settlers timely warning of approaching danger. Trader said he "remained in this service for four months," during which time his unit engaged in operations "scouting and guarding the settlement against invasion by the Indians."[31]

Although St. Clair maintained that the Shawnees had nothing against the Pennsylvanians, many of that colony's inhabitants from as far away as Bedford took the precaution of forting themselves. Although they had heard of the Delawares' pledge to remain peaceful, many backcountry inhabitants in both colonies expected that nation's warriors to strike before long as well.[32] Calling the reports from the frontier alarming enough, St. Clair informed Governor Penn that the actual incidents of violence had yet to become "equal to the Panic" that had "seized the Country."[33] Events eventually proved St. Clair wrong.

The summary killing of nonoffending Indians in reaction to depredations committed by hostile warriors was not a crime only Virginians committed. At the end of May, St. Clair informed Penn and Connolly that some disorderly Pennsylvania people had brutally murdered a peaceful Delaware Indian named Joseph Wipey and concealed his body under some stones at the bottom of a small stream. According to the Westmoreland County magistrate, Wipey had lived peaceably in the Ligonier area for a long time and had always been on friendly terms with his neighbors. St. Clair suspected John Hinkson, a man he described as "actuated by the most savage cruelty," of the heinous crime. He also alleged that Hinkson had incited James Cooper and others with some kind of religious enthusiasm to join him in the murder. Before the coroner had completed his inquiry, however, Wipey's remains mysteriously disappeared at the hands of some unknown accomplices. Because of a lack of sufficient evidence to make an arrest, Hinkson and Cooper remained at large.[34]

After the chiefs had returned home from Fort Pitt, McKee had time to review the records of the latest council in an effort to determine whether

the two sides faced a further rupture or possible accommodation. He confided to William Johnson that while most Ohio area Indians acted with
moderation, the situation remained critical as the tenuous peace ensued.
McKee believed some "wise interposition of Government" was necessary
for the restoration of a more lasting peace but knew that Generals Gage and
Haldimand had focused their attention on Boston. He recommended finding an effective means of punishing the hostile bands of Shawnees and Mingoes for their "Insolence & Perfidy" without risking a wider and more
destructive conflict for no gain. If a war erupted, he lamented that the backcountry inhabitants would find themselves "involved in misery and distress"
in such an event.[35]

Indian fury fell hard on the Virginia side of the Ohio during the first
week of June. The vengeance-driven Logan led a war party that hit settlements on Ten Mile, Muddy, Whiteley, and Dunkard creeks. All western tributaries of the Monongahela, their selection seemed to validate St. Clair's
belief that the Indians directed their hostility toward Virginia, not Pennsylvania. After arriving in the area, the war party divided into smaller groups
to select their targets. Alerted to the raiders' presence, the authorities warned
local inhabitants to seek shelter at a nearby fort or a neighbor's fortified
home. Some, like William Spicer (sometime written "Spier" or "Spear"),
who had intended to move his wife and seven children to the safety of the
nearby Jenkins's fort on Muddy Creek, had delayed doing so.[36] The hesitation proved fatal.

According to their traditional way of war in such revenge raids, the
braves struck the most vulnerable. Reflecting the attitude of many settlers,
John Jacob described them as not an invading army "but a straggling banditti." Isolated farms presented a favorite target, which they usually assaulted
in the dark of night or at daybreak. They sometimes killed all of the family,
at other times "only a part." The attackers most often killed and scalped
adult and adolescent males outright, as they considered them warriors, as
well as small children. While other family members frequently suffered the
same cruelty, Indians sometimes took women and older children, as well as
some men, prisoner, after which they burned the houses and took all the
horses. Captives not killed in the journey to Indian country still faced an
uncertain reception there.[37] After scouting the area between Dunkard and
Big Whitely Creeks, Logan noticed that the Spicer family still occupied its
farmstead.[38]

On the morning of Saturday, June 4, William Spicer was chopping wood
in the yard near the family cabin. Inside, his wife, Lydia, tended to her two
youngest children while twelve-year-old Elizabeth, or "Betsy," ironed the

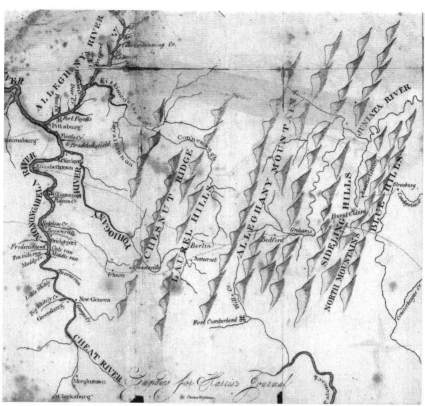

Detail from an 1803 map of western Pennsylvania showing the western tributaries of the Monongahela River where the early settlements which bore the brunt of Indian attacks in June 1774 were located. Below Fredericktown (founded in 1790) are Ten Mile and Muddy Creeks, followed by the Little and Big Whiteley. Dunkard Creek is the unnamed tributary at the confluence of the Cheat and Monongahela rivers above Morgantown. (*Library of Congress*)

family clothes. Outside, sixteen-year-old Job worked in the field while eleven-year-old William Jr. set traps for the squirrels attempting to feed on the young corn in the garden, and their two younger siblings mixed their daily chores with play in the meadow. When Indians emerged from the wood line and approached him, William stuck the axe into a log and headed for the cabin, possibly to retrieve refreshments to offer the visitors as a sign of friendship and peaceful intent. As the warriors followed, one of them—presumably Logan—grabbed the axe and drove it into the farmer's skull from behind. He then burst into the house and treated Lydia and the two little children in the same manner. As the one intruder scalped her parents and siblings, Betsy, still clutching the iron, ran out the rear door.[39]

In her flight, Betsy grabbed little William and attempted to lead him by the hand to safety, but other warriors pursued and caught them, then forced them back to the house. As they drew close to the family cabin, a tall warrior named Snake came outside holding the wounded— but still living— youngest Spicer child upside down by the ankles. Betsy and William watched in horror as Snake bashed the infant's skull against the wall. Out in the field, they saw another brave draw his knife while bending over Job's lifeless body. After breaking its attachment at the hairline with the knife in one hand, he gathered a handful of the boy's locks in the other. The Indian then tore the hair and skin from the crown of Job's head to the nape of his neck, rose to his feet while holding the scalp high with an outstretched arm, and gave the horrific "scalp-yell" to announce his victory. The raiders plundered the Spicers' food supply and possessions as they prepared to leave, while Logan warned the family's two surviving children that he would kill them, too, if they attempted an escape or called out to alert would-be rescuers for help as the war party retreated to the concealment of the woods.[40]

Later in the day, passers-by reported finding Spicer "with a broad-axe sticking in his Breast, his wife lying on her back, entirely naked," the lifeless and scalped corpses of the five children, and carcasses of all of the family's cattle strewn about the property. The neighbors, not able to locate Betsy and little William, surmised the Indians had taken them captive. The same day, Dunkard Creek residents reported three other neighbors missing and presumed they had also been taken captive.[41]

Remaining in the area several more days, the warriors evaded militia patrols and emerged to attack vulnerable settlers when presented the opportunity. Logan and Snake led one group as they crept up on Jenkins's fort and waited for any unsuspecting victims to come out and "fall into their hands." They remained hidden behind a fence as they watched the detachment of militiamen who had buried the Spicer family return, and they waited for a more vulnerable and unsuspecting target. They waited tensely after hearing a female voice from inside the fort ask, "Who will turn out and guard the women as they milk the cows?" A squad of armed men emerged from the gate and scanned their surroundings, alert for any sign of hostile intruders, as the women went about their chores. More than once, Logan feared he and his companions had been discovered, and he contemplated making a run for it when a sentry pointed his weapon in their direction. But they waited until the guards turned their attention elsewhere. Finding no further opportunity to take another scalp or prisoner, the marauders rejoined their war party.[42]

This nineteenth-century painting depicts Elizabeth "Betsy" Spicer—holding her iron at the left—attempting to escape with her younger brother William while members of Logan's war party kill and scalp their parents and siblings, including an infant, and ransack the home. Betsy was repatriated at the end of the war, while William remained with the Indian family that adopted him.

The day after the Spicer massacre, and in the same neighborhood, a man imprudently took leave of his companions to go hunting. A short while later, they heard five shots off in the distance. When their friend's horse returned with an empty saddle, the others went in search. They reported discovering the missing hunter's coat riddled with a number of bullet holes and surrounded by footprints. On Tuesday, a party of Indians waiting outside the walls of Jenkins's fort killed and scalped Henry Wall and a companion named Keener within sight of the people who had taken shelter inside. Connolly received news of these depredations, as well as reports from Wheeling that Indians had killed a man named Proctor at Grave Creek, and thus confirmed fears that at least one more war party, most likely Shawnees, remained at large south of the Ohio.[43]

To counter the raiders "about to annoy our Settlements," Connolly detached one hundred militia soldiers in active service under the command of good officers to find and engage them, if possible. After warriors killed and scalped another settler just outside the fort at Redstone on the Monongahela, a thirty-man patrol met two individuals on the road who swore that they saw thirty Indians about five miles away. The militiamen immediately marched in the direction the informants had indicated but failed to find the enemy. Another thirty-man detachment went in pursuit of those who had murdered the Spicer family and others near Dunkard Creek. The lieutenant in command reported that his men managed to overtake the raiders, who chose to scatter and evade rather than risk an engagement. Although they killed none of the Indians, the militiamen rescued several captives and recovered some horses and other property plundered in the recent attacks. The raids had caused such panic that many people avoided travel on the main roads if they could. Like other well-to-do area families, brothers William and Augustine Crawford had convinced about a dozen families to join them in building forts adjacent to their houses, where neighbors could take shelter instead of abandoning their homes. The Crawford brothers also notified Washington that because of the emergency, William had enlisted the craftsmen and laborers employed at his western property into his company of militia.[44]

On Saturday, June 11, Captain Francis McClure and his second in command, Lieutenant Samuel Kinkade, led their forty-man company in pursuit of Logan's warriors in the neighborhood of Ten Mile Creek above Redstone. Kinkade may have told the captain how his father, St. Clair, and other Pennsylvania officials reacted to the news that he had resigned his recent appointment as a Westmoreland County magistrate to accept a Virginia militia commission. Most of their conversation probably concerned the raids of the previous week in which Logan and his men killed and scalped an estimated sixteen settlers and took several others captive, like young Betsy and William Spicer. After receiving intelligence that someone had seen some Indians, they hastened toward the scene.

As the troops struggled up a steep ascent, the officers pushed ahead "rashly, with insufficient caution," anxious to bring on an engagement and avenge the recent murders. A group of Indians waited in ambush, concealed in the thick foliage at the top of the hill.[45] The warriors fired as the two officers came within range. One bullet struck the captain in the chest and killed him. Another tore into the lieutenant's arm and caused a serious but not mortal wound. As the soldiers advanced to their fallen officers, they saw four warriors running from their concealed positions. Some of the men remained with the wounded Kinkade as the rest went in pursuit. The soldiers believed that they wounded one, but the Indians otherwise escaped without injury. After they buried McClure's remains, the company marched home. Kinkade's report confirmed that the war party remained at large in the Monongahela region.[46]

FEW EXPECTED an Indian war to remain confined to the Pittsburgh region. Colonel Abraham Hite, the county lieutenant, notified Governor Dunmore that hostile Indians had invaded Hampshire County. Warriors had attacked several farms on Cheat River in the first week of June. They killed inhabitants in their homes and cattle in the fields, which prompted the colonel to report "that a scarce day happens that but some cruelty is committed." Opinions between Virginians and Pennsylvanians continued to differ. When he reported to Penn that Indians had caused "some Mischief" on the Cheat River and killed "eight or nine [Virginia] People," St. Clair still questioned whether it signaled revenge for the massacre of the Yellow Creek Mingoes or the beginning of a war. In contrast, Hite wrote to Dunmore "that the many accounts of barbarity" made it "sufficiently obvious to anyone" that the Shawnees had resolved to declare war on Virginia. In consequence, he reported that people in the backcountry had either resorted to forting or moved away from the settlements.[47]

Farther south, warriors, suspected to be Shawnees, attacked a party of Floyd's surveyors on one of the branches of the New River, a tributary of the Great Kanawha, in Fincastle County. The surveyors drove the Indians off, killing eight in a smart skirmish, but suffered the loss of eight men and a boy of their own party.[48] Reverend John Brown wrote to his brother-in-law, Colonel William Preston, that war would probably come. Observing that "a great number under your Care whose dependence for protection (under God) is upon you," the preacher urged Preston to be on his watch and to take every prudent method to prevent a surprise attack.[49] As the county lieutenant, Preston needed no one to remind him where his duty lay. While he also held the posts of county surveyor and sheriff, and had represented his county in the House of Burgesses, he had a wealth of military experience. In addition to a life of service in the militia, he had commanded a ranger company defending the frontier during the French and Indian War.

Preston alerted and directed the captains commanding the Fincastle County militia companies to muster their troops and exert themselves "in keeping the people from abandoning their settlements" and "make them punctually obey orders." Although the Militia Law had expired in July 1773, it remained in force, as everyone expected it would be renewed and continued in the current session of the General Assembly. Captain Daniel Smith agreed that the Invasions and Insurrections Act gave military officers sufficient authority over civilians and to employ the militia during dangerous times, and considered a recent amendment very helpful. The law gave the governor, county lieutenants, and other commanders of militia full power and authority to muster, recruit, levy (draft), and arm men to raise such forces of militia necessary to repel invasions, which included Indian attacks, suppress insurrections, or contend with other danger.[50]

To comply with the intent of the militia laws and the colonel's orders, Smith scheduled a private muster of his company on June 12, or "as soon as the men could get notice as they live much dispers'd." The captain expressed his concern over the scarcity of gunpowder and lead in his part of the county, a situation he described as "a Circumstance as alarming as any that occurs to me now." Although the militia law required each man to keep one pound of powder and four pounds of lead at his home, Smith estimated that if called out to defend the community against an immediate invasion, his company had only an average of five charges of powder per man. Expecting a shipment from Colonel Andrew Lewis of Botetourt County, Smith learned that Major Arthur Campbell, the county battalion's third-ranking field officer, had a large quantity reserved for such emergencies. In consequence, Smith sent Lieutenant James Watson to enquire of its suitability and availability and obtain a quantity for the company.[51]

As CRUCIAL EVENTS transpired at Pittsburgh, Newcomer's Town, and on the frontier, members of the Virginia General Assembly converged on the colonial capital at Williamsburg. Among the items on the agenda, the requirement to revise or continue the two defense-related laws arguably represented some of the most urgent business. Everyone knew that failure to act during the session could complicate matters with regard to the situation on the frontier. Despite their importance, other matters competed for the representatives' attention in the coming legislative session.

In the fifth (1773) edition of his *Dictionary of the English Language*, Samuel Johnson defined "militia" as "that part of the community trained to martial exercise."[52] Earlier editions also included definitions such as "the standing force of a nation" and "The Trainbands," with the latter further explained as "a name formerly given to the militia."[53] Johnson's notes explained that he deduced the meanings from their usage in *The History of the Rebellion and Civil Wars in England*, in which the author, Edward Hyde, first earl of Clarendon, explained "the militia . . . was so settled by law, that a sudden force, or army, could be drawn together, for the defense of the kingdom, if it should be invaded, to suppress any insurrections or rebellion, if it should be attempted."[54] When English settlers established the several colonies, they organized defense forces based on a common English militia tradition. Over time, each of the militias of the colonies adapted to local requirements and established new and unique traditions of their own.

According to his royal commission as governor, Lord Dunmore assumed responsibility for defending His Majesty's colony and dominion of Virginia from invasions, suppressing rebellions, and pursuing enemies to the borders and out of the province. The legislation in effect when Dunmore arrived in 1771, as well as the pertinent clauses in his commission as governor and instructions from the Crown, reflected Johnson's definition of militia and described the force at the governor's command. Delegation of the king's authority empowered the former British army captain "at all times to arm, to levy, muster and command" all persons living within the boundaries of Virginia. As royal governor he could call out, or issue the order to raise, as many regiments and march them anywhere within the province's boundaries as he deemed necessary. In addition to enlisting volunteers, the governor could order the levy, or drafting, of men for active service as soldiers and artificers.[55] The latter group included skilled mechanics and artisans, such as smiths, carpenters, and wheelwrights, along with wagon and packhorse drivers, woodsmen, and cattle drovers. These auxiliaries performed the necessary administrative and logistical functions that supported the line, or fighting forces, during periods of "actual service," or active duty. They could do so either as members of the militia or as civilian employees. In addition, the governor could order the construction of fortifications, and impress, or commandeer, private property such as firearms, sloops, boats, draft animals, wagons, supplies, and provisions for military use. He also held the authority to proclaim martial law and issue letters of marque and reprisal to privateers in the king's name during wartime.[56]

The governor's commission did not grant him absolute military power. Virginia's General Assembly, which mirrored the British Parliament in constitution and power, established the institutional structure of the colony's forces in An Act for the Better Regulating and Disciplining of the Militia, more commonly called the Militia Law.[57] In effect since 1757, the act defined the obligations of those who had to serve, specified their related responsibilities, and qualified the exemptions of those excused from performing service or attending training. It defined the colonial government's role in supporting its military establishment, enforcing the act's provisions, and maintaining order and discipline when its soldiers were not serving on active duty. An Act for Reducing the Several Acts for Making Provision Against Invasions and Insurrections into One Act, more commonly known as the Invasions and Insurrections Act, defined the colonial government's responsibilities for defense and internal security, as well as the operational employment of the militia. The acts included provisions and procedures for raising and supporting militia forces when called into actual service, and enhanced military measures, such as organizing provincial standing forces, or regulars, "in times of danger."[58]

Although based on a common tradition, the latter eighteenth century Virginia militia differed from its English counterpart in many respects. For example, the law that governed the militia in England required all able-bodied males eighteen to forty-five to enroll but required few to actually serve. The anonymous author of the preface to *The Militia-Man*, a handbook published in London circa 1740, wrote, "All men of property should serve in the militia" because they "each have something to lose" and "consequently . . . are fit persons to consider of the means of preserving it."[59] While individuals could volunteer, parishes selected men by ballot to fill their apportioned quotas to the county. After they completed a three-month period of training, militia members served the rest of their three-year terms in units that mustered to train periodically and responded to local alarms or augmented the regular army anywhere in England, but not overseas, during national emergencies. While the English militia recognized the king as its commander in chief, it also performed an important role in the constitutional monarchy as a safeguard against royal excesses. Reflecting the English fear of standing armies in peacetime, the militia existed to protect the rights and property of the citizenry from the army if the king chose to use the regulars as an instrument of domestic oppression. The Virginia militia, like its English counterpart, saw the king as its royal commander but stood ready to protect the rights and property of Virginians if he—or his colonial viceroy—violated the constitution and used the regular army to oppress them.

The Militia Law, like the Mutiny Act that governed the British army, remained in effect for a defined period. The terminating provisions of the Militia Law provided the General Assembly with the opportunity to evaluate laws and incorporate amendments, initiate changes, or repeal them. The process did not always prove easy. For example, when Lieutenant Governor Robert Dinwiddie addressed the General Assembly in November 1753, he reported that he found the militia "deficient in some Points." He then urged the House of Burgesses to revise the Militia Law that had been in effect without substantive changes since 1738.[60] It took the House another four years to pass an effective bill that addressed the problems, but not before the opening campaigns of the French and Indian War proved Dinwiddie's observations correct.

Although the General Assembly had amended it twice and continued it four times to keep it current, the Militia Law enacted in 1757 remained in effect when Dunmore assumed office. Thomas Nelson, president of Virginia's Colonial Council, signed the most recent continuance as acting governor in July 1771, only two months before the earl's arrival.[61] During the February 1772 session, the first over which Dunmore presided, the assembly voted to continue one, but not both, military-related laws. Although the Invasions and Insurrections Act was not due to expire until June the following year, the burgesses viewed it "expedient" to extend it early, for two years, or until 1774. The Militia Law therefore expired in July 1773.[62]

Expiration of the statute, however, did not abolish the colony's militia. On February 6, 1773, Dunmore prorogued, or suspended, the General Assembly's session until March of that year. That was followed by a series of prorogations that postponed resumption of the session until April of the following year, when the governor notified the General Assembly to reconvene in May 1774. When the legislative session was interrupted by this procedure, any law approaching expiration remained in effect until both houses had the opportunity to amend, continue, or repeal it in regular session.[63]

In contrast to the regular British army or other standing forces, an individual did not enlist in the Virginia colonial militia. The law required every free adult white male Virginia inhabitant eighteen to sixty to enroll, which gave the militia a nominal strength of nearly fifty thousand men in the early 1770s. It differed from the English militia of the period in that Virginia's militia principally constituted a pool of manpower available for military service in an emergency rather than an organized reserve of the army. To fulfill his obligation, unless exempt from serving or otherwise excused from participating, each man was required to furnish himself with "a firelock well fixed, a bayonet fitted to the same, a double cartouche-box, and three charges of powder" and attend all musters and training exercises so equipped. Many of the eleven thousand men enrolled in the militia of the counties west of the Blue Ridge, particularly those in the frontier districts, armed themselves with rifles instead of muskets. Colonel Preston, the county lieutenant of Fincastle County in 1774, described the militia of his own and neighboring Botetourt and Augusta Counties as "being mostly armed with rifle guns" and therefore substituted a powder horn and shot pouch for the cartridge box, and a tomahawk in lieu of the bayonet to satisfy the requirements of the Militia Act. The law required every soldier to keep one pound of gunpowder and four pounds of lead, enough for about seventy rounds of ball ammunition for a musket, at his home, and to keep it well maintained and ready to bring whenever directed by his officers in the event of an actual alarm or when ordered into the field for active duty.[64]

The Militia Law did not exempt individuals if they could not afford to purchase the required items. Each county and the corporate boroughs of Williamsburg and Norfolk maintained public magazines with modest supplies of weapons and equipment marked as public property. If a court inquiry verified a member's economic need, the county issued him the necessary arms, accoutrements, and ammunition from its magazine. Once able to do so, the man made payments until he covered the weapon's cost. Otherwise, as soon as the poor soldier who required public assistance could afford to purchase his own arms and ammunition, or had been removed from the muster roles due to age, death, or other reasons, the captain in command of his company retrieved the county's property and returned it to the magazine so it could be issued to another man of limited means.[65]

In 1712, during the War of the Spanish Succession, known in North America as Queen Anne's War, the British government bestowed "a considerable quantity of arms and ammunition for the service of this colony" in order to better equip its militia. Two years later, in 1714, the General Assembly appropriated funds to erect a magazine at Williamsburg where "all arms, gunpowder, and ammunition now in the colony, belonging to the king . . . may be lodged and kept." The weapons stored there, and in the entrance hall of the palace, were then available "to arm part of the militia, not otherwise sufficiently provided." The General Assembly also voted to appropriate funds to employ a staff of two artificers, a "keeper of the magazine" to receive, issue, and account for the weapons and ammunition, and an armorer to maintain and repair them.[66] The arsenal eventually housed other classes of munitions, such as pole and edged weapons, swivel and wall guns, cannon barrels, field carriages and artillery implements, as well as equipment ranging from tents, camp kettles, and entrenching tools to drums. The assembly made it clear that the arsenal did not replace the several local facilities. The munitions and supplies available at "his majesty's magazine and other stores within the colony" improved the province's ability to arm either standing forces or militia ordered on campaign by the government in Williamsburg.[67]

The Militia Act required all free men—white, black, and red—to enroll, but not everyone performed the duties of a soldier. The law traditionally exempted the clergy of the Church of England as well as the "president, masters or professors, and students" of the College of William and Mary, from their military obligations. While still required to enroll, the law also excused holders of public office, members of certain occupations or particular states of employment, and members of other specified classes from attending scheduled training assemblies, but not from owning and maintaining the necessary equipment, or from mustering with their companies in the event of an actual alarm. Quakers and members of other pacifist religious sects were excused from drill, performing military service, and having to possess weapons and accoutrement but had to contribute to the purchase of equipment for poor soldiers and furnish substitutes if they were selected in a draft for active duty. Because other laws prohibited them from owning firearms, the Militia Act required "all such free Mulattoes, Negroes, and Indians as are or shall be inlisted" to participate and assemble without weapons. Not permitted to train as soldiers of the line, these members served as drummers, trumpeters, artificers, pioneers, or "in such other servile labor as they shall be directed to perform."[68]

The General Assembly delegated the means of enforcing order and discipline in its ranks to the militia itself. Officers and enlisted men received no pay for attending but faced fines of up to five pounds or confinement in the county jail and payment of prison fees to the sheriff for missing training assemblies without valid excuse, or failing to pass inspection by not having the required arms and equipment in their possession.[69] Soldiers who committed acts of misconduct, refused to obey the commands of their officers, or behaved "prefactorily or mutinously" during assemblies became subject to stiffer disciplinary action. The Militia Act allowed "the chief commanding officer then present" to summarily impose punishment that included fines of as much as "forty shillings current money" and having an offender "tied neck and heels, for any time not exceeding five minutes," but with no other corporal punishment, such as flogging on the bare back, permitted in peacetime.[70] Courts-martial ordinarily convened the day immediately following a county's general muster, provided the local inferior court had adjourned for the month, or as approved by the General Assembly. Before hearing cases, the empaneled officers swore to "do equal right and justice to all men according to the act of Assembly for the better governing and regulating of the militia."[71]

The General Assembly established rates of pay for militia soldiers when they were called to perform active service or in response to alarms that lasted more than six days. The same per diem rates applied to provincial regulars when the assembly authorized the raising of standing forces. In 1774, soldiers received the following rates of compensation: "the county lieutenant or commander in chief ten shillings per day; a colonel or lieutenant colonel each ten shillings per day; major eight shillings per day; captain six shillings per day; lieutenant three shillings per day; ensign two shillings per day; serjeant and corporal each one shilling and four-pence per day; drummer one shilling and two pence per day; [private] soldier one shilling per day."[72]

In addition, except for criminal charges, the law "privileged and exempted" militia members from arrest while going to, attending, or returning from musters and protected them "from being served with any other process in any civil action or suit" while on duty. At no time could the military items that the law required them to possess be "distressed," or seized, to satisfy creditors in any judgments. When men were ordered to active service in the colony's pay, the law exempted them from having to pay province, county, and parish levies, including any new taxes enacted by the General Assembly during their absence on military duty, as well as "privileged" soldiers' private estates from civil court action for indebtedness.[73]

Although the law mandated compulsory service for all, the militia from time to time suffered a lack of citizen interest or governmental neglect, especially when no apparent or perceived threats to peace and colonial security existed. Understandably, inhabitants on the frontier took more interest in their militia participation than those in more-secure regions, such as the Tidewater, "on account of the frequency of Indian atrocities." Drummer Joseph Tennant, of Captain James Parsons's company of Hampshire County militia in 1774, explained that in the backcountry communities, "Every man learned the use of fire arms from necessity . . . and were taught a certain amount of military discipline."[74]

For whatever reasons, some men preferred paying the fine, or hoped that indifferent county courts would neglect to enforce the law, rather than attend training assemblies. Others refused to turn out when summoned for active service. In contrast, still other Virginians viewed participation in the militia as an avocation. Such officers and members of the rank and file took training and service seriously and developed military skills and prowess that exceeded those of most of their peers. More importantly, their county and colony counted on such men, who usually volunteered at the first alarm and often served repeated tours of duty. In a land devoid of native hereditary aristocracy, most militia officers valued their commissions. Many preferred to be identified and addressed by their titles of rank in public discourse as well as correspondence for the rest of their lives and took them to the grave by having them carved on their headstones.

While many of the colonies were similar in their militia establishments, differences could be found. Where some other colonies elected their leaders, members of Virginia's forces did not. Commanders at various levels appointed subordinate officers and noncommissioned officers. Justices of the inferior courts could suggest candidates for consideration, and members of the council offered their advice and consent on the appointment of field officers, but only the royal governor had the authority to sign and issue commissions.[75] By "reposing special Trust and Confidence . . . in the Loyalty, Courage, and Conduct" of a deserving gentleman, the governor extended the status as an officer, with all the inherent responsibilities as well as privileges involved, in the name of His Majesty.[76]

Each major political subdivision had its "Chief Commander of all his Majesty's Militia, Horse and Foot" who answered to the governor. Given the title of county lieutenant in each of the sixty-one counties, or chief commanding officer in the boroughs of Williamsburg and Norfolk, this officer held "Full power and Authority to command, levy, arm, and muster" all those available for military service residing within the limits of his jurisdiction. In case of a "sudden Disturbance or Invasion" or other emergency, the county lieutenant could "raise, order, and march all or such part of the said Militia" as he deemed necessary to resist and subdue the enemy.[77]

Each chief commanding officer held the rank of colonel, and his commission took precedence before that of any other officer holding equal rank. Otherwise, he observed and followed the orders and directions of the royal governor and "any other . . . superior officer" appointed over him in accordance with the "Rules and Discipline of War." Otherwise, a second colonel often functioned as the deputy county lieutenant and field commander. Some county lieutenants treated their positions more like a civil office and attended only to its administrative requirements while leaving purely military matters to a subordinate field officer.

To organize Virginia forces, the Militia Act required the county lieutenants and chief commanding officers to "list all male persons within this colony (imported servants excepted)" from eighteen to sixty. The county lieutenant then divided the county into nine geographical catchments based on the distribution of the military-age free white male population. Each catchment constituted one company of foot, with possibly one troop of horse organized from the county at large. The county lieutenant placed the soldiers thus organized "under the command of such captains as he shall think fit" to appoint and receive a commission from the governor.[78] After he consulted the subordinate field officers and captains commanding the companies, the county lieutenant appointed the necessary subaltern officers, or the lieutenants and ensigns in companies of infantry, or lieutenants and coronets in troops of cavalry.[79] After an officer received his commission bearing the royal governor's signature, he swore the necessary oaths required to affirm his loyalty and pledged his service "for the security of his majesty's person and government."[80] Each captain appointed the noncom-

missioned officers and musicians in his company as well as a clerk who kept
the muster rolls and maintained the records. Soldiers could not decline appointments to positions of increased authority or responsibility without
consequences. One who refused to serve as a sergeant, corporal, drummer,
or trumpeter "as required by his captain" became subject to a monetary fine
imposed by the county court for every muster that he continued to refuse
the appointment.[81]

Although designated a company and commanded by a captain, the local
unit primarily functioned for administrative and training purposes only.
These administrative companies were often larger than the tactical organization of fifty rank and file established for a company of the line when organized for active service, and they rarely took the field as units except when
called out for an alarm. For example, on being notified of an invasion or
insurrection, the law required every officer to "raise the militia under his
command," dispatch express messengers to inform his immediate superior
commanding officer of his actions, and "immediately proceed to oppose
the enemy" with the number of troops available until he received orders directing him to do otherwise. Similarly, on receiving word of an alarm in an
adjacent county, the law obliged the chief commander of militia to "immediately raise the militia of his county" and detach as many as two-thirds of
his men to engage the invaders or insurgents. The county lieutenant then
organized the remaining third to remain in arms for the "defense and protection of the county," and waited on orders from the governor.[82]

The companies primarily served as sources of trained manpower from
which the colony could organize tactical units for "actual service," or active
duty, in periods of emergency. To make the force "more serviceable," the
Militia Act held officers responsible for their men's readiness and compliance with the law. A captain, for example, ensured that all the soldiers in
his company were properly armed, equipped, and trained. In peacetime,
the statute required him to conduct a "private muster" in the local neighborhood at least once every three months and more often if he or the county
lieutenant deemed it necessary. After the captain inspected his men and
took "particular Care" to see that they all possessed the necessary arms and
ammunition, he trained his company according to the *Manual Exercise as
Ordered by His Majesty* in 1764.[83] The manual reflected the British army's
experience on European battlefields during the Seven Years' War and concentrated on the essential elements of individual and platoon drill, evolutions and maneuvers, and firings.

In addition to observing the several private musters throughout the year,
the militia law required the county lieutenant to train all the companies

under his command once a year at an annual "general muster and exercise," usually in March or April. When wartime necessitated enhanced readiness, the General Assembly often increased the frequency of company musters to once every month, or every other month, and added a second general muster for all counties in September or October as well.[84] It is arguable that British regulars posted in widely dispersed garrisons in peacetime received as much training in regimental-sized formations as Virginia militiamen did by attending their general musters.[85]

Like the company musters, the general musters also began with the ubiquitous inspections to ensure all officers and men had the arms and ammunition the law required. The companies then trained collectively and practiced the elements of the manual that applied to battalion formations. Ideally, two platoons operated in a tactical company-sized unit called a subdivision. Two subdivisions combined to form one grand division. An entire tactical battalion organized on the regular British model consisted of four grand divisions of four platoons each, arrayed in three ranks, and trained to execute the appropriate evolutions and maneuvers with some degree of proficiency. Finally, given the limited time available, a battalion strove to master the most critical elements of all, "firings," either by "ranks entire" or by platoons, subdivisions, and grand divisions in the elaborate sequence and precise order of rolling volleys that enabled it to deliver a near continuous volume of musketry. Victory on the eighteenth-century battlefield often went to the side that could throw the most lead at its opponent in the quickest time.[86] Such exercises would have been the norm in the more settled regions, as reflected in the militia law enacted in 1740, to "establish our Militia on such a Footing, that in case of Invasion or Attack, they may be enabled to contend with regular Troops."[87] Given the threat they would more likely face, the militia of the frontier counties spent more time practicing light infantry-style tactics adapted to the probability of fighting Indians in the woods.

As part of the plan to further enhance readiness and ensure compliance with the Militia Act, Governor Dinwiddie eliminated the office of the single colonial adjutant general on the eve of the French and Indian War. He divided the colony into the Northern, Southern, Middle, and Frontier Military Districts, and assigned an adjutant general to each. Receiving an annual stipend of £100, and usually holding the rank of major, each adjutant general reported to the governor on compliance with the Militia Law in the counties that comprised his district.[88]

In performing their duties, these officers attended all the battalion general musters in their districts. To perform their duties, they were instructed

to "exercise the Officers first" in order "to qualify them to exercise each separate Company" and prepare them for their respective general musters.[89]
During an inspection, they ensured that all company officers had their men
"properly trained up in the use of Arms," and "more perfect and regular in
the Exercise thereof."[90] Finally, performing a role similar to a brigade major
or adjutant in the British army on regimental field days, they inspected "all
detachments before they be sent to parade" and saw that all "their arms be
clean, their ammunition, accouterments, &c. in good order."[91]

With all sixty-one counties and two independent boroughs in the colony
required to conduct their general musters in March and April, the adjutants
general faced challenging spring schedules. The county lieutenants therefore
had to plan their annual training assemblies based on the date they expected
the district officer's presence. The counties involved in Dunmore's War were
among the fourteen that comprised the Frontier Military District, where
Captain Thomas Bullitt served as adjutant general. The veteran officer had
served in the 1st Virginia Regiment throughout the French and Indian War,
remained active in the militia, and had actively sought the assignment before Governor Botetourt appointed him on May 10, 1769.[92]

Due to the remoteness and difficulty reaching some of the locations in
his district, the newly appointed adjutant general used public notices, called
advertisements, in the March 22, 1770, edition of Rind's *Virginia Gazette*
to notify the thirteen county lieutenants of his schedule. (The law that
erected Fincastle County was enacted in 1772.) In 1771, because the General
Assembly had not yet voted to continue the Militia Act due to expire, Bullitt
acted on his "former appointment" to announce his itinerary in the February 5 edition of Purdie and Dixon's *Virginia Gazette*. Unless prevented by
"high water" or other unforeseen circumstances, Bullitt expected to be present at their county courthouses on the dates indicated. Since they all out-
ranked him, and considering the schedule he had to maintain, he requested
that the county lieutenants "oblige him" by assembling their militia "in good
Order, and accoutered as the Law directs" at that time.[93]

Bullitt's responsibilities as a surveyor, which took him on an expedition
to the Falls of the Ohio and the site of present-day Louisville, Kentucky,
prevented him from inspecting the district's general musters in 1773. Fortunately, the counties of the Frontier District benefited from having a number of field officers, senior captains, and noncommissioned officers who
had combat experience in the French and Indian War while serving with
the provincial standing forces. Colonels Adam Stephen and Andrew Lewis,
the county lieutenants of Frederick and Botetourt Counties, respectively,
had served as officers under Colonel Washington's command in the Virginia

Regiment and commanded volunteer battalions in Pontiac's War. Colonels Charles Lewis (Andrew's brother) and William Preston, the respective county lieutenants of Augusta and Fincastle Counties, had served as officers in provincial ranging companies.

With renewal of the Militia Act and the possibility of an Indian war weighing heavily on their minds, the Lewis brothers and William Christian of Fincastle County took their seats in the capitol on Thursday, May 5. In addition to holding elective office as representatives in the lower legislative house, they also held commissions as field officers—colonels—in the militia of the westernmost counties. The men most knowledgeable as well as responsible for the defense of the colony's frontier sat with their fellow members of the House of Burgesses as Governor Dunmore welcomed them for the "necessary business of this Colony" and charged them to "proceed with dispatch which the Publick convenience requires." After making and passing the necessary pro forma resolutions of thanks to the governor for his opening address and congratulating him on the safe arrival of his wife, Charlotte, the Countess Dunmore, and their children, in February, the assembly turned its attention to matters of government.[94]

CHAPTER 5

The Present Exigence

Military Mobilization

May–July 1774

AFTER THE governor's opening address on May 5, Speaker Peyton Randolph brought the House of Burgesses to order to discuss the matters before the lower house for that session. The dispute with Pennsylvania, Indian hostility, and the expiring Militia Act took their places on the calendar. To further complicate their legislative tasks, the burgesses also had to find a way to express Virginia's solidarity with the other colonies in their disapproval of the Boston Port Act before it went into effect on June 1. Before the various bills, resolutions, and even routine matters came to the floor, they made their way through committees.

On Wednesday, May 11, John Blair Jr., the secretary of the council, delivered the governor's address concerning the boundary dispute and military situation on the frontier, which Randolph read to the members of the House. Lord Dunmore explained that he extended Virginia's jurisdiction to the Forks of the Ohio region in order to counter Pennsylvania's "pretended claim to this Country," which, he said, was "founded on a partial survey." He justified his order for officers to assemble a militia in accordance with Virginia's laws after he observed the "defenseless state of a considerable Body of his Majesty's Subjects settled in that part of the Country" and believed it was his duty to defend them. The next day, the governor requested that the speaker read to the burgesses Connolly's recent report about "some Hostility commenced by the Indians."[1] The burgesses agreed with the governor's actions and concurred with his recommendation to establish a temporary boundary until the king approved a "true and proper" permanent border. A committee drafted a formal response in which the members of the House expressed the desire for continued friendship "with our Sister Colony Pennsylvania" and an equitable resolution of the boundary dispute.[2] Governor Penn had previously dispatched three commissioners to Williamsburg to meet with his Virginia counterpart in person, looking to accomplish the same goal.[3]

The General Assembly turned its attention to military matters at the capitol. The king may have delegated the power of the colonial sword to Lord Dunmore by his royal commission as governor and commander in chief of Virginia, but the House of Burgesses held the power of the provincial purse. He had the authority to organize and command provincial standing forces, call the militia into actual service, and order troops to conduct operations, but unless the House of Burgesses consented on behalf of those they represented, and voted to levy the taxes to raise the necessary revenue to pay for military expenses, the governor's war powers had no effect.

Dunmore had informed the burgesses that he did not consider the militia equal to meet the Indian threat on the frontier and urged them to pass legislation to raise and organize a corps of regulars in the colony's pay. He argued that regular soldiers would be subject to military discipline and training as soon as they enlisted, and held the opinion that standing forces, by their very nature, were more effective, economical, and reliable than militia. The governor maintained that simply by having them, the colony would demonstrate its determination to vigorously defend the frontier and have the capacity to conduct timely expeditions of reprisal against the Shawnees, as well as deter other potential enemies in the future.[4]

If the lower house was going to approve Dunmore's request for regulars during this session, its members had to quickly pass the legislation. The lower house members had more confidence in the militia than their governor, and calling militiamen into actual service offered the parsimonious burgesses an attractive alternative to regulars. The county lieutenants could form units, by recruiting volunteers and by draft, to meet the emergency in a relatively short time, and disband them, discharging the men quickly, as soon as hostilities ended. In addition, unlike standing forces, they could appropriate the expenses incurred in arrears by employing the militia. The Militia Act provided a process in which members of the House appointed commissioners who reviewed all the accounts for military expenses, including soldier pay as well as for material and services given voluntarily or impressed, and reported their findings to the committee of the whole. If the House approved payment by majority vote, the speaker instructed the colonial treasurer to disburse the money.[5]

The burgesses determined that using the militia was more appropriate and less expensive than regulars. On Friday, May 13, Speaker Randolph advised Dunmore that the war powers, which were "fully invested" in the governor's office under the existing Invasions and Insurrections Act, sufficiently empowered him to deal with the "hostile and perfidious Attempts of the savage and barbarous Enemies" who had commenced hostilities against his Majesty's subjects.[6] Dunmore replied the next day that while he was aware of the frugal burgesses' desire to "advance the Prosperity" of the colony, he believed the act they had cited did not enable him to "raise a sufficient force for repelling the Attempts of the Indians" in the most economical way. He appreciated their desire for economy but disagreed with their reasoning and maintained their resolution would produce the exact opposite result of what they intended. Although he stated that in the end, a force of regulars would cost the colony— that is, the burgesses' constituents—less money while affording their "dearest interests" more effective protection, he accepted the decision.[7]

As the House turned its attention to other issues, the laws pertaining to colonial defense made their way through the legislative process. On May 19, the representatives voted to continue the Invasions and Insurrections Act, with an amendment, and passed it on to the council for its consent. The bill to renew the Militia Act remained in the House's Committee of Propositions and Grievances. The lower house's Select Committee of Correspondence then informed the committee of the whole that it had read and replied to the legislatures of the other colonies on the status of their collective grievances with the government of Great Britain. Virginians, like most other American colonists, saw the Tea Tax as an unconstitutional attempt to raise revenue without their consent. While they disapproved of the destruction of private property—the East India Company's tea—by Boston's Sons of Liberty the previous December, they deplored the heavy-handed British government's reaction even more.[8]

On Wednesday, May 24, the House met to discuss the Boston Port Act, the first of the Coercive—or "Intolerable"—Acts passed by Parliament, scheduled to go into effect in one week. The burgesses regarded it as the "hostile Invasion of the City of Boston, in our Sister Colony of Massachusetts Bay," and a threat to the liberty of all American colonists. "Being deeply impressed with apprehension" of the act's provisions to close Boston harbor and halt the city's commerce, the lower house resolved to take action in protest. The House ordered that Wednesday, June 1, would be observed as a day of "Fasting, Humiliation, and Prayer." Starting at ten o'clock in the morning, the speaker and mace would lead the assembled representatives in a solemn procession from the House chamber of the capitol down Duke of Gloucester Street to the Bruton Parish Church. Inside, they would devoutly implore God's "divine interposition for averting the heavy Calamity that threatens destruction to our Civil Rights and the evils of civil War." The burgesses intended the action to show their solidarity with the people of Boston and join fellow colonists as loyal subjects of the king to speak with "one heart and one Mind" to firmly oppose "by all just and proper means, every injury to our American Rights." They would offer prayers asking God to inspire the king and "his Parliament" with the "Wisdom, Moderation, and Justice" to remove any threats to the rights of loyal British Americans. After the House of Burgesses directed the order published in the House Journal and newspapers, and on broadsides announcements posted around Williamsburg, the members resumed business to address routine matters for the next two days.[9]

While the representatives worked at the capitol, Pennsylvania's royal attorney general, James Tilghman, secretary of the colony's land office, Andrew Allen, and barrister Richard Tilghman arrived from Philadelphia to address the boundary dispute with Lord Dunmore.[10] He received them at the palace on May 21, and Governor Penn's commissioners began the discussion. They articulated the Pennsylvania position on the proposed location for an interim boundary that could resolve the issue of "clashing jurisdictions" until the king settled the matter permanently. When they submitted their written justification for the proposed line, which put Pittsburgh within Pennsylvania's boundary by five miles, Dunmore rejected it on the grounds that their calculations were in error.[11]

The Virginia governor countered with a "true construction" based on his understanding of the royal grant to William Penn. Using the description of its width to determine the western boundary and "running eastwardly," Dunmore determined that Pittsburgh was located fifty miles outside of the grant's area. The Virginia governor stated, "Your proposals amount in reality to nothing and could not possibly be complied with." When their negotiations ended on May 27, Dunmore told Tilghman, Allen, and Tilghman to inform Penn that his government would not relinquish its jurisdiction of the area without orders from the king. The Pennsylvania commissioners thanked the governor for his polite attention and the "dispatch" he gave their business. They departed Williamsburg the next day.[12] The council "highly approved" of Dunmore's conduct as the "Negotiations came to Nothing."[13]

On May 26, John Blair entered the House chamber during a discussion about the salary of the minister of Shelburne Parish in Loudon County. Ad-

dressing Speaker Randolph, Blair announced that the governor commanded
the House to attend his excellency immediately in the council chamber.
They went upstairs and across to the wing of the capitol where the upper
house convened. When Randolph assured the governor that all had arrived,
Dunmore addressed the speaker and the gentlemen of the House of
Burgesses. He explained, "I have in my hand a Paper published by Order of
your House, conceived in such Terms as reflect highly upon his Majesty and
the Parliament of Great Britain; which makes it necessary for me to dissolve
you." He then announced, "You are dissolved accordingly."[14] Despite dissolution by Dunmore and their collective grievances with recent acts of Parliament, the burgesses remained loyal subjects of the king and still hosted
"A grand ball and entertainment" at the capitol that evening to celebrate
the arrival of the Countess Dunmore.[15]

Dunmore later explained that his "good friends the Virginians" showed
themselves a "little too High spirited" but claimed that he took them by surprise. Satisfied with his action, he told General Gage that he believed his
actions had caused most of the burgesses to "repent sincerely for what they
did."[16] Instead of repenting, eighty-nine burgesses reconvened at the Raleigh
Tavern the next day and agreed to form a nonimportation and nonexportation association, and they called for a Virginia convention and a general
congress of all the colonies.

The dissolution did not abolish the House of Burgesses and representative government in the colony but called on the voting freeholders to re-
constitute it. Dunmore's action was an exercise of the executive prerogative
vested in his office that previous governors had used on occasion. Many
burgesses knew they would return to their seats in the capitol before long.
In the meantime, the governor had to issue writs for new elections, at which
time constituents would vote to reinstate or replace their representatives.
Once accomplished, the governor would call the General Assembly into session and resume the process of enacting laws.

Unfortunately, the dissolution halted progress on some important legislation. The bill for an amended Invasion Act had only made it to the council for consideration. The overdue continuation of the expired Militia Act
had yet to clear the Committee for Propositions and Grievances for its third
and final reading, and a vote by the House. As when the governor had prorogued the General Assembly, all expired laws remained in effect until the
governor called the General Assembly into a new session. Where a prorogued session could continue the legislative process when the session resumed, the new House of Burgesses had to start it anew. The expiration of
the Militia Law did not disband the militia. Until both houses had the op-

portunity to vote whether to continue, amend, or repeal the invasion and militia laws, they remained in effect. Those who might use the expiration of the Militia Act to shirk their military obligations stood vulnerable to prosecution.

Amid the controversy about the closing of Boston harbor; the day of fasting, humiliation, and prayer; and the continuing constitutional crisis between the colonies and mother country, both editions of the *Virginia Gazette* for the week carried news of the simmering hostilities on the Ohio. One article warned readers, "We believe with much certainty that an INDIAN WAR is inevitable, as many outrages have lately happened on the frontier." The causes still seemed unclear to many who did not live in the backcountry. The article accurately concluded that "whether the Indians or whites are most to blame, we cannot determine, the accounts being so extremely complicated."[17]

THE EFFORT to repair Fort Pitt neared completion. Connolly ordered four hundredweight—or 448 pounds—of gunpowder for the militia from the B. and M. Gratz merchant house of Philadelphia to ease the shortage of ammunition. In addition, he ordered a British "union flag of five yards to hoist at the Fort—also to be made of the woolen stuff called bunting." In a letter to Michael Gratz, John Campbell, the company's agent in Pittsburgh, wrote that Connolly's efforts had put Fort Pitt "more in a better posture of defense than I ever saw before."[18]

As leader of the Pennsylvania faction in the border dispute, St. Clair had become an outspoken critic of Governor Dunmore and Captain Connolly. Even Croghan had apparently begun to hint at a renewed allegiance to Pennsylvania. St. Clair and his fellow Westmoreland County magistrates charged that Connolly's Virginia militia had run roughshod over the inhabitants who remained loyal to Pennsylvania. He complained they had "harassed and oppressed the people" and "lay their hands on every thing" they wanted without asking, and "killed people's cattle at their pleasure." Connolly replied that as the Invasions and Insurrections Act required, his officers appraised all the property they impressed for military purposes and presented the citizens thus deprived with "a bill on Lord Dunmore" for payment. St. Clair described the practice as a "downright mockery."[19] It may have surprised the captain commandant, but many Virginians did not hold a high opinion of him either. Although never insubordinate, even William Crawford confided to George Washington that Connolly had "incurred the displeasure of the people."[20]

In a report to Governor Penn, St. Clair expressed his hope that the crisis would reveal "some of the devilish schemes" carried out by Connolly and other Virginia partisans, or possibly Dunmore himself. He even maintained a belief that an Indian War, provoked either on Dunmore's orders or Connolly's own volition, was part of the Virginia plan, which morally strengthened Pennsylvania's position in the boundary dispute. The substantial expenses incurred by repairing Fort Pitt and calling out the militia required an appropriation from the colonial treasury to satisfy, or it would fall to Connolly's personal responsibility. St. Clair knew that the Virginia General Assembly would only levy taxes to cover the expenditure if they appeared sufficiently necessary to justify the debt. St. Clair therefore believed the governor had planned, while Connolly executed, the incidents that had provoked the Shawnees and Mingoes to hostility—if he could only prove it.[21]

It seemed St. Clair and the rest of the Pennsylvania faction did not have to prove anything. At the beginning of June, Major General Frederick Haldimand reported to the secretary of state for the colonies, Lord Dartmouth, that he had received information about the Yellow Creek massacre, "though not from any of the governors or any persons in the Indian department, that one Colonel Cressop from Virginia . . . has of late been on a scout against Indians inhabiting about the Ohio and killed several of them."[22] Later in the month, Sir William Johnson similarly notified Dartmouth that he "received the very disagreeable and unexpected intelligence that a certain Mr. Cressop, an inhabitant of Virginia, had trepanned and murdered forty Indians on Ohio."[23] Johnson further explained to Haldimand that the Indians had considered the attack on their people and scalping of their dead, attributed to Cresap, as a declaration of war.[24]

The roving war parties spread such chaos that it presented the Pennsylvania government an opportunity for recovering the part of Westmoreland County lost to Virginia. Under the threat of attack, but holding to his belief the Shawnees and Mingoes bore no hostility toward Pennsylvania, St. Clair made two recommendations. With no colonial militia to call on, St. Clair, Croghan, McKee, Butler, Mackay, and Smith, along with other pro-Pennsylvania residents of Pittsburgh, entered into a private "Association" to raise, provision, and pay for a ranging company of one hundred men for one month. Optimistic that the company would recruit its volunteers in a short period of time, he asked the governor to request that the Pennsylvania Provincial Assembly assume the expense of keeping the men in service for a longer duration. St. Clair justified the cost by adding that under such protection, Pennsylvania colonists were less likely to desert their homes and farms in panic. Furthermore, he informed the governor that some Pittsburgh inhabitants had proposed to erect a stockade to fortify the town. Should negotiations with Dunmore's government not satisfactorily resolve the boundary dispute, St. Clair suggested that having rangers under arms afforded Pennsylvania the ability of "throwing a few men into that place" to lead the effort, which "would recover the Country the Virginians had usurped."[25]

Carlisle merchant John Montgomery noticed the people of Westmoreland County in "great Confusion and Distress," with many fleeing east and some building forts. He appealed to the governor and assembly to provide enough arms and ammunition to defend the frontier settlements. Montgomery believed that an Indian war that involved Virginia would eventually also include Pennsylvania. Despite the assembly's aversion to military spending, Penn had to convince the house of its obligation and the necessity of raising and paying soldiers. He argued that at the very least, Westmoreland County needed a militia organization. Montgomery further recommended that a unit of full-time soldiers—like St. Clair's rangers—should be enlisted to patrol the settlements, intercept Indian war parties, and build or improve forts at Pittsburgh, Hanna's Town, and Ligonier for the duration of the emergency to encourage Pennsylvanians to make a stand.[26]

If St. Clair and his associates hoped the news of a ranging company forming at Hanna's Town would alarm Connolly and the Virginians, their hopes were realized. Croghan told the Virginians not to worry, because they would only operate between the Kiskiminetas River and Ligonier to help stem the flight of panic-stricken Pennsylvania inhabitants. He envisioned that if circumstances necessitated, the rangers would act in concert with Virginia forces for the general defense of the country against a common foe and not at cross-purposes. Croghan therefore urged St. Clair to exercise prudence and caution and not employ his rangers to "Invade ye Rights of Virginia" and thereby rekindle the war of words between the two governors, which would do nothing to resolve the boundary dispute.[27] St. Clair assured Penn, "In a very particular manner, our Soldiers are directed to avoid every occasion of dispute with the People in the Service of Virginia."[28]

CONCERN FOR the fate of the traders still in Indian country continued to increase despite Cornstalk's pledge to provide escorts and safe passage. The day after the eleven traders from Newcomer's Town arrived in Pittsburgh, Connolly learned that a number of warriors went to the Canoe Place on the Hockhocking River bent on killing some of the whites who frequently gathered there.[29] Word reached Pittsburgh on June 12 that hostile Mingoes had killed and scalped a trader named Campbell at Newcomer's Town, where Duncan and Anderson had found sanctuary the previous month.[30] According to Reverend Heckewelder, other traders found "true friends" among the Delawares, who put themselves in danger for their kindness. The Delawares who escorted many fleeing traders to safety in Pittsburgh not only had to avoid hostile Shawnees and Mingoes but risked the likelihood that jittery militiamen might mistake them for an invading war party and open fire.[31]

A number of friendly Indians guided groups of traders to places of refuge on their side of the Ohio. One Delaware woman, for example, "espied" the Baptist clergyman David Jones and two traders as they traveled together on the Muskingum. After warning of the danger awaiting them if they continued in the direction they were heading, she led them along a route that allowed the men to "escape the vengeance of the strolling parties." Although safer, the terrain proved extremely difficult, and it so fatigued one of the traders that he admitted he preferred death to exhaustion. When the group finally struck a path, he decided to follow wherever it led and bade the others farewell. After he had gone only a few hundred yards, fifteen Mingoes took him captive within sight of White Eyes' Town, about ten miles upstream from Newcomer's Town. He would have reached safety if he had remained with the woman, but as Jones later told Heckewelder, the Mingoes ritually tortured, scalped, and executed him. The warriors dismembered the man's corpse, hung his limbs and flesh on bushes, and celebrated their triumph by yelling the scalp halloo. When White Eyes heard the noise, he led some Delaware warriors to investigate, but they were too late. When they arrived, they could only collect and bury the remains. The next day, angry Mingoes exhumed and rescattered the victim's body parts. Once again, the Delawares recovered and reburied them. The infuriated Mingoes entered the town, condemned the Delawares' conduct, and pledged to "serve every white man they should meet in the same manner."[32] Undeterred by their threats, White Eyes kept most of the Delaware neutral.

A trader's store was located in the Delaware town of the Standing Stone on the Hockhocking River. The men who operated such franchises acquired pelts from Indian hunters in exchange for manufactured wares such as cloth, ammunition, firearms, ornaments, and other goods. During the period the trouble began, the principal trader left on the two-week journey to the company factory at Pittsburgh, where he would exchange pelts for merchandise to bring back to the Indian town. He left John Leith, his seventeen-year-old employee, to mind the store in his absence. John was resting on some skins one morning when an Indian boy entered the store. The boy told John that his father, a local chief, wanted to see him immediately.[33]

On entering the dwelling, the chief motioned for John to sit while a white woman, who Leith assumed to be his wife, translated the Indian's words into English. After they exchanged greetings, the older man asked if John had heard that war had broken out between the whites and Indians. The boy listened with wonder and surprise as the chief told him that Shawnee warriors had recently killed seven white men and captured four others in the area. Recounting the causes of the current hostilities, the elder told the youth that "the Virginians had taken Mingo Town" and massacred Logan's relatives. John answered honestly that he had "heard nothing about it." Believing that he stood accused, John stated, "I had never done any of them harm," and swore he had "no hand in the matter."

The chief then gestured for John to rise to his feet, and with a "fearful expectation" that the chief intended to kill him, he tried to steel himself for the blow of a war club that would surely follow. Instead, the chief put him at ease, pointed to his wife's breasts, and said, "Your mother has risen from the dead to give you suck." He then continued, "Your father has also risen to take care of you, and you need not be afraid, for I will be a father to you." With those words the older man embraced John about the neck to signify that he had formally adopted him. The chief then called on all the town's headmen to meet at the store. After making a brief announcement in their language, "they proceeded to divide the store-goods, spirits, and all that I had care of among themselves."[34]

WITH HOSTILE Indians attacking "the back parts of this Country" to commit "outrages and devastations," Dunmore issued a circular letter to the county lieutenants listing their responsibilities for meeting the crisis. As they could no longer entertain any "hopes of pacification" with the hostile bands of Indians, he took the opportunity to criticize the General Assembly for not having thought it proper to pay more attention to the situation on the frontier, "though they were Sufficiently appraised of it." He alluded to the burgesses' passing the irresponsible resolution to hold the day of fasting and prayer to protest the Boston Port Act before voting on the more pressing necessity of renewing the colony's expired Militia Law. He then outlined the only means left to "extricate ourselves out of so Calamitous a Situation" and explained how the militia would continue to function while faced with an Indian invasion.[35]

The governor informed General Gage that the Indians had "most certainly broke out and murdered a good number of our people," consequently, "all our thoughts must now be turned that way."[36] Under the authority of his royal commission, and responsible for Virginia's defense, Dunmore ordered the county lieutenants to embody—or activate—their militia to stand in readiness to respond to alarms, although he had not yet called them to the colony's service. In the absence of a current militia law, he expected them to exert the powers vested in their offices "that may answer the present exigence." [37]

Dunmore directed the county lieutenants to take the routine precautions found in the Militia Law and every officer's commission. He emphasized the importance of captains holding private musters to ensure the men had the required arms and ammunition and practiced the prescribed drill. Of equal importance, he urged the county lieutenants to "keep up a constant Correspondence" with their counterparts in adjoining counties and assist one another, and if necessary, combine their "respective Corps of Militia into one body." Aware of the shortage of ammunition, Dunmore promised to provide them with powder and ball on his own credit should the General Assembly not appropriate the necessary funds in the next session after reinstating and continuing the Militia Act. He recommended that the county lieutenants have their men erect small forts where the inhabitants could find protection and the county could secure its important documents, and from which, if the militia was compelled to give ground to a large invasion, its retreat could be covered. He left it to their judgment as to where to build the forts and how many to build. The governor believed that the construction of a substantial fort at the confluence of the Great Kanawha and Ohio Rivers would answer several good purposes. While he encouraged them to build such a fort, he left it to the county lieutenants' judgment based on their knowledge of the country if they deemed it expedient. Dunmore added that erecting the new fort and maintaining communications between it and Fort Pitt, now called Fort Dunmore, would offer better protection to area settlers and "awe the Indians." [38]

Finally, Dunmore relied on the "Zeal and discretion" of the county lieutenants "to provide the extraordinary means for any extraordinary occasions that might arise." Ordinarily these officers could not order their men into active service on their own authority except to repel an invasion, or order them—particularly drafted men—to march out of the colony, or more than five miles past the most distant settlements on the frontier. However, Dunmore indicated that if the military circumstances justified doing so, and they could enlist a sufficient number of volunteers, militia officers could conduct operations beyond the limits allowed by law. If they could pursue invading war parties out of Virginia or attack their camps in Indian country, for example, Dunmore encouraged them to take the opportunity to deliver such a stroke. He reasoned that if decisive in stopping Indian depredations, that would certainly justify their actions with the government and "oblige the Assembly to indemnify," or pay them for their service.[39]

After issuing his instructions to the county lieutenants, Dunmore wrote to the commander in chief of His Majesty's force in North America, General Gage, who had just arrived in Boston from home leave in England. The reports from Governor Penn notwithstanding, Dunmore took the opportunity to apprise the general of the situation from the Virginia perspective. His forces had rebuilt Fort Pitt to protect the settlers in the region, "and put it in better condition than it ever was," at least as a defense against small arms. Dunmore said that when those responsible had completed the task, "They have done me the Honor of calling it by my name." With all the nations and tribes to the south and west potentially joined in an alliance against Virginia, Dunmore assured Gage that he had the least doubt his colony's soldiers would soon give a good account of themselves, his earlier comment doubting they were equal to the task notwithstanding. If the few skirmishes that they already had gave any indication of the ultimate outcome, even where the Indians had at least twice the number of men on the field, Dunmore proudly stated, "our people have always kept their ground."[40]

Virginia prepared for war on the frontier even as the people in more-protected counties and those in other colonies discussed the deepening constitutional crisis. While the expiration of the Militia Law did not disband the militia, it complicated the means by which the colony paid for military expenses until the General Assembly reconvened. The next several months would determine whether the militia of Virginia's frontier counties proved equal to the challenge it now faced.

WHEN THE colony needed soldiers, such as for offensive expeditions or the garrisons of frontier forts, the governor would issue a call for troops drawn from the militia to perform actual service in the colony's pay. Addressed to one or more county lieutenants, the call either stated a given number of soldiers, or proportion of his total, such as "one for every twentieth man," to be detached for "immediate service."[41] During the French and Indian War, the House of Burgesses appropriated funds for "Encouragement of militia to go out freely for the defence of the country in all times of danger; with a certain assurance of being paid for their services." Voluntary enlistments were always preferred and sought first. If enough men did not volunteer, the law allowed for drafting men to make up any shortfall. In addition to pay, volunteers and drafted men were promised medical care for illnesses and injuries incurred while on duty, pensions for disabilities that prevented them from earning a living wage after their terms of service expired, and relief for their widows and orphans if they died as a result of service.[42] Ordinarily, the governor sought the assembly's support in appropriating money for soldier pay before issuing the call for men, but he could act without it, albeit in emergencies.

Although written for obtaining recruits to fill the ranks of the standing forces during the French and Indian War, the March 1756 act for frontier defense outlined one method for conducting a draft.[43] The law authorized the chief militia officer to summon the field officers and captains commanding companies of the county or borough to a council of war to implement the draft procedure. The captains brought and delivered lists, derived from court records, of all single free white men living in the precincts that made up their respective company catchments, as well as the company muster rolls showing the names of all those enrolled and participating in the militia. After comparing the documents, the officers added the names of any nonexempt able-bodied men residing in their companies' areas who had not been duly "inlisted and enrolled, according to the militia laws." The county lieutenant then selected a day and time, and called a general muster at the courthouse. Militia and civil officers spread the word by giving public notice, advertising in the *Virginia Gazette*, and posting broadside announcements "at all places of public resort."[44]

The men assembled in their companies outside the courthouse on the appointed day. After roll call, the captains asked volunteers to step forward and took their names. The county lieutenant then reconvened the council of war inside, where the officers prepared a number of blank pieces of paper, one for each available man in the county. The officers then wrote the words, "This obliges me immediately to enter his majesty's service," on the quantity of sheets that reflected the county's quota. After withdrawing one marked paper for each man who volunteered, those who were absent from the muster became the "first pricked down" and "declared to be soldiers duly inlisted in his majesty's service" unless later excused. The remaining sheets were put into a box, "well shaken and the papers therein mixed," and placed in view of all the members of the council of war.

The officers then instructed the assembled men, minus the volunteers, to come forward one at a time to draw one piece of paper from out of the box. As he did so, each man held his paper to "public view." Anyone who displayed a sheet with the writing was "deemed and taken to be an enlisted soldier." The officers could excuse a drafted man if someone present who had not drawn a marked paper chose to take his place. A drafted man could also find an able-bodied man who was not drafted but willing to serve in his stead in return for a payment of money.[45]

Officers received commissions of rank based on the required strength of the units they were to command and were expected to exert their leadership skills and powers of persuasion to recruit a sufficient number of volunteers from a specific administrative company's catchment. Depending on the number of troops required, more than one complement of company officers may have been allowed to recruit from the same catchment. The county lieutenants and their subordinate field officers and commanders took care not to create organizations that proved too top heavy and therefore inordinately costlier by having individuals serve in higher rank positions than was commensurate with the size of the force actually recruited. The law specified that the county lieutenants could "not depute any greater number of inferior officers . . . than one captain, one lieutenant, one ensign, three sergeants or corporals, and one drummer for every fifty soldiers," and in like proportions for greater numbers, in a company of foot.[46]

If the full establishment strength of fifty men for an operational (as distinguished from the administrative) infantry company could not be reached, the number and ranks of the leaders decreased proportionally. A company of foot that consisted of thirty men could not have more than one lieutenant, one ensign, and two sergeants, while a company of fifteen or fewer men required not more than one ensign and one sergeant. Before being taken into pay, the names and numbers on the muster rolls had to be certified by every commanding officer and "attested upon oath" before a justice of the peace of the county where the company had been raised. While they may have been addressed by the titles of higher ranks held in their administrative militia postings, officers received only the pay granted for the ranks approved by the assembly for the command of units on campaign. Commanders who claimed greater numbers of men in order to receive higher rank with corresponding pay, or who appointed more subordinate officers than the actual strength of the unit allowed, faced fines equal to the pay of such "supernumerary officers."[47]

When the colony called the militia to active duty in wartime or other emergency, the district adjutants general or expedition commanders—or county lieutenants if all units came from one jurisdiction—usually established rendezvous camps for organizing and training the force that would take the field. The rendezvous camp represented an important step in the process of preparing militia for active service and campaigning, as well as raising provincial regulars when the General Assembly authorized the es-

tablishment of standing forces. While a soldier received a modicum of training through the quarterly local company and annual general county-wide
musters, what he received at the rendezvous camp improved on that base
and helped transform the ad hoc companies into more-cohesive tactical
units better prepared for the sustained operations in which they would participate.

As the Frontier Department's adjutant general, twenty-one-year-old
Major George Washington conducted the rendezvous camp at Winchester
for the first militia companies embodied for provincial service in 1754. The
training received at other rendezvous camps may have resembled that which
then-Colonel Washington directed the officers of the 1st Virginia Regiment
to institute when he assumed command in 1755. It included drilling the
men in the manual exercise and conventional linear tactics as well as in the
"Indian Method of fighting" and practice "Shooting at Targets."[48] Not ne-
glecting officer training, Washington noted that "there ought to be a time
appropriated to attain this knowledge" and insisted that they read and apply
the lessons found in "Bland's and other treatises which will give the wished
for information."[49]

While the men trained in the school of the soldier according to the 1764
drill manual, officers studied Lieutenant General Humphrey Bland's *Treatise of Military Discipline*, in which he laid down and explained the duty of
the officer and soldier. First published in 1727, its nine editions became
what was arguably the most widely read and authoritative work on British
army tactical operations and unit leadership for much of the eighteenth
century. Based on experience gained on European battlefields but adaptable
to those in North America, the treatise provided a valuable instructional
text for regular and militia officers alike. Its pages contained valuable max-
ims and explanations for officers learning or practicing tactics in chapters
with such descriptive titles as "General rules for Battalions of Foot, when
they engage in the line," and "for the marching of a Battalion, or a Detachment of men, where there is a possibility of meeting the enemy." Lessons
conveyed in the latter were particularly suited to the fluid environment of
petite guerre and fighting partisans in "enclosed or woody country."[50] Although the treatise was developed based on experience gained in or observing operations against the skulking tactics of the irregulars found in
European armies, British and colonial American officers found that many
methods it espoused were adaptable to the terrain and enemy of North
America. Bland's instructions were not simply followed as written; officers
in America combined regular with irregular tactics and blended them with

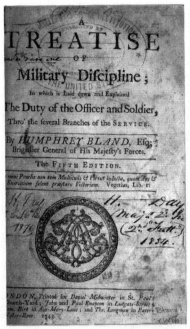
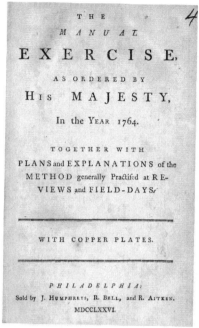

Possibly the two most important military texts available to the officers and men of the Virginia militia in 1774. Humphrey Bland's *Treatise of Military Discipline* was arguably the most influential work on the British army's combat doctrine for most of the eighteenth century. Although its content on training the individual soldiers was superseded by various drill manuals, it remained the standard for instructing officers on how to deal with a variety of scenarios encountered in combat operations. *The Manual Exercise Ordered by his Majesty in the Year 1764* and its several variations, was the standard drill manual used to train individual soldiers and how they functioned in the ranks at the small unit level; and instructed officers at various levels in training their units executing the prescribed formations and "evolutions" used in the linear tactics of the day.

techniques learned from native allies and adversaries and gained from experience in earlier conflicts.

Fighting in the American wilderness required soldiers to use new and diverse methods, skills, and techniques that combined those used in Europe with those found in North America. Using flank guards for marching columns and commanders having their men take advantage of the cover offered by trees, logs, and rocks when attacked by a concealed enemy represents such a combination of both, not the demonstrated superiority of one method over the other. The use of skirmishing tactics in which detachments moving in open order sought to initiate contact with an unseen enemy with a series of small firefights provides yet another example of blended tactics. Skirmishing offered a means of locating and drawing an enemy force into battle where the superior fire of cohesive units determined the outcome of a general engagement.[51]

When they used the term "Indian Method of fighting," Washington and other colonial officers did not mean that they simply copied the tactics and techniques of native warriors but developed and employed a new method of bush fighting that emphasized skirmishing. Operations were usually characterized by acting on the strategic offense and the tactical defense, and applied the same principle on a smaller scale at the tactical level of an engagement. The new method placed an importance on light troops and taking advantage of natural cover and concealment. It also continued to emphasize unit cohesion and fire superiority, although not necessarily by fighting in compact ranks and firing in volleys. During the French and Indian War, for example, light troops on scouting and flanking missions ordinarily employed defensive tactics in battle situations. Although their tactics may have at times appeared similar to those of their Indian opponents, they sought to draw the enemy into a fight so that the main force could bring its firepower to bear with the most effect.[52]

In addition to what they received at musters, the men trained and rehearsed these blended tactics before they conducted an operation. Chaplain Thomas Barton described such an exercise conducted by the provincial regiment in which he served during the French and Indian War that may have resembled the training Washington prescribed for Virginia troops, or that which was conducted at a quarterly general muster or rendezvous camp for militia preparing for campaign:

> [T]he Troops are led to the Field as usual, & exercis'd in this Manner—Viz.—They [the columns] are to, and distant from, each other about 50 Yards: After marching some distance in this Position, they fall into one Rank entire forming a Line of Battle with great Ease & Expedition. The 2 Front-Men of each Column stand fast, & the 2 Next split equally to Right & Left, & so continue alternately till the whole Line is form'd. They are then divided into Platoons, each Platoon consisting of 20 Men, & fire 3 Rounds; the right-Hand Man of each Platoon beginning the Fire, and then the left-Hand Man: & so on Right and Left alternately till the Fire ends in the Center: Before it reaches this Place, the Right & Left are ready again. And by this Means an incessant Fire kept up. When they fir'd six Rounds in this manner they make a [sham] Pursuit with Shrieks & Halloos in the Indian Way, but falling into much Confusion;

they are again drawn up into Line of Battle, & fire 3 Rounds as before; After this each Battalion marches in order to Camp.[53]

The Virginia militia had its unique units and individual specialists. In wartime and periods of increased tensions between settlers and Indians, county lieutenants and local commanders in the backcountry engaged certain individuals as scouts and spies. When the General Assembly provided the authorization and means, they also raised detachments or companies of rangers to better defend the frontier. While all three services sought to accomplish related objectives, and the skills and techniques required of individuals engaged in each may in some cases have appeared the same or similar, rangers, scouts, and spies differed in several ways.

During Queen Anne's War, for example, the government at Williamsburg authorized county lieutenants responsible for frontier defense to raise detachments to "range"—or patrol— the "large vast uninhabited grounds and woods" between settlements.[54] Once posted, these early rangers patrolled the areas between forts and fortified houses—known as stations—on horseback to "observe, perform and keep such orders and in their several rangings and marchings" to detect approaching war parties, or pursue and punish marauders who killed or captured inhabitants at isolated homesteads.[55] Rangers routinely rode in pairs, or "two together," with two such teams covering a chain of four posts from opposite ends. With instructions to meet at an appointed time and place at or near the midpoint, they would exchange information, "report their observations, and when necessary . . . carry information on the appearance of the enemy to the nearest stations" so the militia could respond appropriately to a threat.[56]

When he organized his county's rangers during Queen Anne's and King George's Wars, the chief militia officer appointed a lieutenant to command the detachment. The lieutenant would "choose out and list" eleven ablebodied men who resided conveniently near the frontier station where they were to be posted, and they would report with their own horses, as well as the arms, ammunition, and accoutrement the law required them to keep at home. If the detachment commander could not enlist a sufficient number of volunteers to complete his unit, the county lieutenant drafted the rest from among the enrolled militia. Once formed, ranger units operated only within their home counties. The commander and every ranger received compensation that included pay, based one year of service, plus a stipend for using his own horse and other personal property, that came from the public levy collected in the county. For "greater encouragement" of the ranging service, the General Assembly declared all officers and rangers "free and

exempted" from paying county and parish levies and excused from attendance at scheduled musters.[57]

Through an act of the General Assembly, Virginia called rangers to defend the frontier again in May 1755, during the French and Indian War. The
county lieutenants of Frederick, Hampshire, and Augusta Counties were
each directed to raise one company of fifty men plus officers, organized to
operate on foot, from their respective militias.[58] Paid from the provincial
treasury instead of county levies, the three ranging companies could be deployed to conduct operations anywhere in the colony the governor directed.
During their one-year term of service, rangers answered the immediate orders of the county lieutenant in whose jurisdiction they were assigned and
cooperated with companies of the Virginia Regiment—if posted nearby—
and units of local militia.[59] Although considered part of the province's
standing forces, rangers remained subject to the militia law for discipline
and could not be sent out of the colony or conduct missions more than five
miles beyond the most distant settlements on the frontier unless authorized
by the General Assembly. Conversely, rangers could not be incorporated
with British regulars, placed under command of a British officer, or subjected to the Articles of War.[60] Over the course of the conflict, the service
increased to six companies and included postings to defend the colony's
southwestern frontier. While the governing legislation eventually raised the
authorized strength to one hundred men plus officers, ranger companies
never achieved the full establishment.[61]

Whereas a unit of rangers would seek to intercept and engage an enemy
war party as well as provide early warning, scouts worked in small independent detachments of two or three men to gather intelligence. Those who
supported military operations went ahead of their units to conduct area reconnaissance and surveillance and provided their commanders with information on enemy forces and activities as well as terrain they were likely to
encounter. Other scouts were employed closer to home. They also conducted area reconnaissance but paid special close attention to trails and
other avenues of approach that led to backcountry communities. Once they
obtained information, the scouts returned to a nearby post to report to an
officer of the militia and provide early warning of an attack.

Alexander Scott Withers, an early chronicler of frontier warfare, described those who typically volunteered for duty as rangers and scouts as
men who "made their abode in the dense forest" and spent most of their
time hunting, an occupation he described as "mimicry of war." Such men
were adept at fighting in the wilderness and especially knew how to resist
Indian attacks and retaliate in kind. Withers believed the same skills that

enabled the hunter to approach the "watchful deer in his lair" allowed the ranger or scout to avoid an Indian ambush and frequently defeat those who waited in the ambuscade. The chronicler believed that the long hunters' knowledge and the ease with which they moved about the woods to any location among the settlements to warn the inhabitants of danger made them invaluable to the defense of the backcountry communities.[62]

The spy was neither ranger nor scout—nor even a soldier. More accurately described as a long-range scout in this context, Samuel Johnson's dictionary defined "spy" as "one who watches another's motions" by attempting to "search" or "discover at a distance."[63] Spies did not operate in companies or detachments under the command of commissioned officers but worked individually or in pairs. Certain men, such as William Smith of Augusta County, volunteered to serve as Indian spies. Traveling beyond the limits of settlement and often in the vicinity of Indian towns, they ventured though trackless forests to observe the enemy and his activities in his own country. Despite the hazards, Smith explained that he preferred "this employment" to service in the militia.[64] Although enrolled in the militia, spies were not considered to be in service and were excused from attending musters without suffering fines.

The Virginia militia provided the colony with a force capable of defending its borders as well as taking the fight to an enemy's home territory. It was organized and trained to fight by degrees. At the lowest level, local companies responded to alarms that effected the immediate or neighboring communities. As danger increased, the county lieutenant activated the county's force for its own defense or to assist an adjacent community. The provincial government could call the militia into actual service to repel invasions by external enemies or suppress insurrections and other internal threats. As the likelihood of an Indian war along the Ohio increased in 1774, the militia became more active at each of its levels.

CHAPTER 6

The Warlike Nation of the Cherokee

One Conflict Avoided

June–July 1774

A SCALP HALLOO, the sound of which Reverend John Heckewelder described as a "mixture of triumph and terror, or glory and fear," was heard from the woods beyond the cornfields.[1] Messengers ran ahead to the cluster of villages that made up the town of Wakatomika to announce the approach of a war party returning from the south bank of the Ohio. Men and women, elders and children, all put aside daily chores, ceased play, interrupted routines, and gathered to welcome them home. The returning braves had drawn the first blood on behalf of their people against the enemy Shemanthe or Assaragoa, meaning Big Knife, as the Shawnees and Iroquois, respectively, called the Virginians.

Although not entirely unlike that of a victorious army returning from campaign with captured battle flags and prisoners of war, the Indian celebration was "far more frightful and terrific," Heckewelder wrote. "It is an awful spectacle to see the Indians return home in triumph from a successful expedition with their prisoners and scalps taken in battle." The different perspective reflected the wide cultural divide between European and native peoples. The weary but excited warriors quickened the pace to cover the last few hundred yards as they shouted the "dreadful scalp-yell." The people of the town gathered around them as the braves proudly displayed their trophies, dressed scalps hung from long poles, and recounted the exploits of their victory.[2] Meanwhile, the captives contemplated the fate that awaited them. They had already endured much hardship since their capture and were grief stricken. They reflected on the scalps their captors displayed nearby. Some of them had belonged to family members, friends, and fellow prisoners just a few days before.[3]

Like their counterparts in many Indian societies, Shawnee and Mingo warriors measured victory by the number of "heads" taken in individual combat. Each head represented an enemy conquered, whether killed, wounded, or captured. It mattered little if he had lifted the scalp from the corpse of a slain enemy or a maimed one who still lived. A prisoner, whether eventually executed, sold, or adopted, counted toward a warrior's tally as much as a scalp. According to Heckewelder, both scalps and prisoners provided "visible proofs" of their valor and prowess, and each warrior heralded his arrival in triumph with a separate scalp yell for each head taken.[4]

Embattled Indian nations found the practices particularly effective for terrorizing the inhabitants who settled in the frontier districts of British America, or those individuals who encroached on tribal homelands or exclusive hunting grounds. The taking of scalps and prisoners constituted an important component of national policy and the supporting military strategy when at war against any enemies, regardless of race or culture. Since an Indian nation often went to war to avenge insult of injury committed against it, the taking of heads was also an integral part of the condolence process for families who lost a young warrior in battle, as well as for those who lost any young people to disease or other nonwar-related cause. Grieving families satisfied their need for revenge by accepting an enemy scalp taken on their behalf or by torturing and executing a prisoner. The family could also adopt a captive to take the place of the deceased loved one or redeem the prisoner in exchange for weapons, ammunition, or goods.[5]

Prisoners usually endured tremendous cruelty on the march. Mary Jemison vividly recalled the horrific treatment she received as a prisoner of the Shawnees during the French and Indian War. One of ten captured in the attack on her family's farm, only fifteen-year-old Mary and a neighbor's young son arrived in Indian country alive.[6] Mary's captors deprived their "Extremely fatigued" prisoners of food and water the first day and night, and when the little ones cried for water, the braves made them "drink urine or go thirsty." One Indian followed the party to lash the slower children with a whip in order to maintain the pace needed to evade the militia attempting to rescue the captives. During the first night's rest halt, the warriors "watched [the prisoners] with the greatest vigilance" and permitted them neither shelters nor warming and cooking fires.[7] In contrast, Betsy Spicer and her brother experienced less severe treatment. While Logan threatened to kill them if they attempted to escape or alert rescuers, he also had his men carry the children on their backs when they became too tired to maintain the pace.[8]

After they had traveled a sufficient distance, and any likelihood of an attempted rescue sufficiently diminished, the captors finally permitted hungry prisoners to build fires and offered them food, often plundered from their own pantries. Whereas Logan's Mingoes had already slain all of Betsy and William's relatives in their presence, the Shawnees separated Mary and one other child from the rest, never to see their families and friends again alive. In both cases, the captors separated the surviving children from each other and their previous lives. Mary and Betsy also experienced similar acts of mental cruelty by those who took them prisoner. Both girls recalled that they had to watch as their captors scraped their parents' and siblings' blood, brain matter, and other tissue from their "yet wet and bloody" scalps. The skins were then stretched over hoops fashioned from green wood, then dried and tanned like parchment. After the Indians painted the tanned skin and combed the hair, they hung the dressed scalps on the ends of long poles.[9]

On their arrival, amid the "peculiar shoutings, demonstrations of joy, and the exhibition of some trophies of victory, the mourners come forward to make their claims."[10] The distribution of plundered property satisfied some, while revenge and condolence provided the two major factors in determining the fate of captives. In the absence of a prisoner, returning braves might present the mourning family an enemy scalp to satisfy their vengeance.[11] Some captives, primarily women and children—as well as some men—who survived the journey to Indian country, like the Spicer orphans, found themselves "adopted by the families of their conquerors in the place of lost or deceased relations or friends." The Indians separated Betsy and William and offered them to families from different tribal bands that lived a great distance apart. The two siblings did not see each other again for many years. Repatriated under the terms of the war-ending treaty, Betsy eagerly returned to her Dunkard Creek community. Like more than a few prisoners captured and adopted at a young age, William became domesticated and eventually identified more with his new family. When presented an opportunity to return home, adopted captives like William "never wish themselves away again."[12] Captivity narratives attest to the relative good fortune and happiness of some as well as the cruel suffering and death of many who fell into Indian hands.

An adult male captive's ordeal usually began when his conquerors ordered him to run the gantlet to a painted post from twenty to forty yards away. Reaching the goal required him to pass between two lines of men, women, and children who stood "ready to strike him" with axes, sticks, and other offensive weapons. Warriors stood on the sides to throw sand in his eyes to temporarily blind him as those on the gantlet continued to beat the victim "most intolerably." Beatings became so severe that one survivor, James Smith, when captured by Ohio Indians during the French and Indian War, recalled having wished for his tormentors "to strike the fatal blow" and end his misery, and "apprehended they were too long about it." Willing to accommodate such desires, "some person, longing to avenge the death of some relation or friend slain in battle," always stood ready for the captive to fall and "immediately dispatched" him.[13]

Surviving the gantlet only guaranteed a captive that he would live until female elders or a grieving family determined his fate. If given as a condolence, mourners could elect to receive and adopt him into the family or exact their revenge with merciless treatment in long, protracted tortures, which included burning and other "dreadful executions."[14] The same applied to the community at large. A display of courage while running the gantlet significantly increased, but did not ensure, one's chances of survival. According to the traveling Baptist preacher David Jones, "if any in the town fancy the person for a wife, husband, son, or daughter, then the person purchases the captive, and keeps him as his own." If the elders decided on revenge, the level of pain inflicted significantly increased if the nation had suffered heavy losses in battle or the enemy had committed murders or other atrocities against their innocent women and children.[15]

According to Jones, among the customs of the Shawnee nation, he "reckoned" the cruelty they inflicted on the captives who they did not adopt was "singularly bad." He observed one method of torture in which the captors ran a knife between the victims' "wrist bones," then drew deer sinews through their wounds, and bound them "naked to a post in the long house." He claimed the Indians then enjoyed making "all imaginable diversion" of the helpless and agonizing captives. Some suffered having their noses cut off while their captors made fun of their disfigured appearance. When the sport no longer amused them, the warriors led the prisoners outside, scalped them while still alive, and killed them with tomahawk blows. Finally, they left their victims' bodies where the "fowls of the air" consumed their mangled bodies.[16] James Smith watched his captors prepare "about a dozen men, stripped naked, with their hands tied behind their backs," for burning to death. They tied each victim to a stake and then kept touching him with firebrands and red-hot irons as he screamed "in a most doleful manner" while spectators yelled "like infernal spirits."[17] Mary Jemison recalled that she saw a number of heads, arms, legs, and other fragments of the bodies of some white people who had just been burned at the stake at Shawnee towns in the Ohio country. The Indians fastened the remaining parts and whole bodies to a spit supported at each end by a crotch from a tree branch stuck in the ground, and "were roasted or burnt black as coal" while the "fire was yet burning."[18] Once the celebrations ended, Logan and other leading warriors went about the process of exhorting the young men to join new war parties to go against the Long Knife enemy.

THUS FAR, Mingo and Shawnee raids had fallen hardest on the west district of Augusta County. In early June, Connolly developed a plan of "prudent steps" designed to "put a stop to further cruelties . . . [and] murders committed by the Indians." Outlined in a letter sent to Governor Dunmore on June 7, Connolly proposed to raise and lead a force of three hundred to four hundred men "towards the Enemy's Country." On the way, he planned to halt and build a small fort on the high ground near the settlement at the mouth of Wheeling Creek for the protection of the frontier. Continuing downstream, Connolly planned to build another post at the mouth of Hockhocking Creek, on the opposite side of the Ohio, for use as a magazine, or "repository of Stores," from which small detachments from Wheeling would operate continually on the north bank to alarm the Indians and "if possible keep the Enemy engaged in their own Country." Executing his plan, Connolly believed, would "chastise" and "overawe the Indians" with Virginia's military might.[19]

While waiting for the governor's response and expected approval, the captain commandant began assembling the forces and gathering the supplies needed to execute his planned course of action. Despite their previous differences, continued animosity, and allegiance to opposite sides in the ongoing boundary dispute, Connolly approached the leader of the Westmoreland County magistrates about the possibility of combining their forces to act "in concert." Although Croghan had previously predicted that such cooperation would result if the Indians attacked, St. Clair declined the invitation for the recently organized ranger company, or any other forces the county might raise, to participate in a Virginia expedition. He assured Governor Penn that he remained cautious of taking any step that would potentially "draw this Province into an active share in the War," which Pennsylvania "had no hand in kindling."[20]

Although he sent Captain William Crawford with a company to begin the work of erecting the fort at Wheeling Creek, which they would name Fort Fincastle in honor of another of Dunmore's hereditary titles, Connolly delayed the start of the offensive operation pending the governor's approval. He remained at Fort Dunmore to coordinate the militia response to the attacks, such as Logan's raids, against the district. When Aeneas Mackay learned about the Muddy Creek incident, he incorrectly assumed that Logan's warriors had ambushed McClure's company as it marched to join the forces assembling at Wheeling. The magistrate caustically charged that without suffering any casualties of their own, four Indians had defeated an entire company of Virginians and "knocked" Connolly's scheme "in the head." St. Clair unleashed his own volley of sarcasm, adding that Connolly had "instantly changed the plan" when news of McClure's death persuaded him to remain safely in garrison while others fought the war he had started. Neither St. Clair nor Mackay knew that Connolly had ordered McClure's company toward Redstone and did not receive the governor's approval to execute the plan for offensive action that they derided until more than a week after the ambush.[21]

Because it complemented his instructions to the county lieutenants, specifically the recommendation to build a fort at the mouth of the Great Kanawha and conduct limited offensive operations on the north bank of the Ohio, the governor gave his endorsement on June 20. He directed Connolly to keep a constant correspondence with Colonel Andrew Lewis, the officer he designated to coordinate the efforts of all the frontier counties.[22]

Dunmore also expanded on Connolly's original concept and urged that he either "cooperate with Colonel Lewis, or strike the stroke" himself, provided he could so with minimal risk, and urged "the sooner it is done, the better."

Frederick County had also begun to form units for active service. On Saturday, June 11, Major Angus McDonald sent Captain Daniel Morgan orders to form a unit of fifty to sixty men, in anticipation of the governor's orders to join the force assembling at Wheeling. McDonald also notified the captains commanding three neighboring companies to "call a muster and know what men can be got." If Morgan could not raise the required number from his own, McDonald authorized him to recruit what he needed from these other companies. The major told the captain that he did not want to draft, but only take volunteers, men "such as may be depended on," to "do service to our Country."[23]

Notwithstanding any confidence he had earlier expressed in his abilities, the governor told Connolly that he considered it most necessary for him to remain at Fort Dunmore rather than command in the field. He therefore directed him to select a competent subordinate to lead the proposed expedition into Shawnee country and said he "could not do better" than appoint

Captain William Crawford to command what men he could spare for the mission. Crawford had impressed the governor the year before when, on George Washington's recommendation, he acted as Dunmore's guide during his visit to the frontier district. The governor described the long-time militia member and French and Indian War veteran as a "prudent, active, and resolute" officer, "very fit to go on such an expedition."

In executing the plan, the governor said Connolly should order all officers commanding the detachments going out on missions from Wheeling "to make as many prisoners they can of women and children." The Virginians could use such captives for leverage in bringing hostile nations to a council that could negotiate a peace treaty as well as for arranging an exchange of prisoners. As with Logan's capture of the Spicer orphans, Indian nations had employed and accepted the practice of taking captives when waging war long before European contact. In the division of labor in their societies, women and children usually provided the principal agricultural workforce, and their loss or capture could have an adverse effect on an Indian community's economy. Since war parties often took women and children prisoners, it would seem rational to reply in kind to facilitate a reciprocal exchange and repatriation of captives—provided the officers could maintain order and discipline over their men in order to prevent atrocities like those Greathouse and his followers had committed against the Yellow Creek Mingoes at Baker's Bottom.

Lord Dunmore further instructed Connolly to exert what diplomatic influence he could to "prevail on the Delawares, and the well affected part of the Mingoes" to separate themselves and "move off from the Shawanese." Simultaneously, the Six Nations central council wielded its leadership to isolate the dissident and troublesome Shawnees and keep the Mingoes, Delawares, and other dependents neutral. The governor pledged to all militia commanders on the frontier that after Virginia ultimately prevailed and compelled the Shawnees to "sue for peace," he would not end hostilities until they had effectively punished the enemy Indians for their "insolence." He further pledged to neither grant peace terms nor ratify a war-ending treaty until the Shawnees delivered six chiefs as hostages in order to guarantee their nation's future "good behavior." Every year, on the anniversary of signing the peace treaty, the governor would expect the Shawnees to replace them with different hostage chiefs for the ensuing twelve months. And last, he pledged that the victors would require the vanquished Shawnees "to trade with us only," not the rival Pennsylvanians, "for what they may want."[24]

As RELATIONS between the Virginia colony and the Shawnees and the hostile faction of Mingoes deteriorated, the likelihood of a war with the Cherokees persisted. The tensions that had gripped the Holston and Clinch settlements in the spring had eased but not abated. Virginians, as well as officials of the British Crown, feared the specter of "a Combination of all the Northern Indians together with the Cherokees; the Murders they will be capable to perpetuate, attended with a general Devastation of the Frontiers." Captain William Russell probably spoke for many when he wrote, "I am too much afraid such a Confederacy will be form'd." [25]

Other settlers, primarily from North Carolina, had moved into the Watauga and Nolichucky river valleys on the mistaken premise that the Treaty of Lochaber and subsequent Cherokee cession had opened them for settlement. After negotiating a ten-year lease with the Cherokees in 1772, settlers formed the Watauga Association, which established a five-man court at Sycamore Shoals to perform many local government functions despite the absence of a royal charter. Although outside of the jurisdiction of any colonial government, the inhabitants self-identified as British subjects and informally associated with Virginia. And the Cherokees generally referred to the Watauga inhabitants, as well as all encroaching whites, as "Virginians." Although mistrust ran deep, colonial government and Indian Department officials made efforts to resolve potential grievances before they flared into conflict, such as Captain Russell's measures to curtail the inadvertent crossing of the Cherokee boundary. As a result, relations with that nation remained generally good. [26]

In early June, a number of Cherokees joined settlers in watching horse races and other sporting events during a fair in the Watauga settlement. Without provocation, Isaac Crabtree brutally shot and killed an Indian man whom local residents knew as Cherokee Billy. As the other Indians left to go home, the victim's two companions, a man and a woman, angrily intimated that the whites could expect reprisals from their people for the murder. Inhabitants of the backcountry knew that when warriors took the warpath to avenge such an injury, they did not only target the guilty party but his entire community. Major Arthur Campbell notified Colonel Preston that the news of the threat had greatly alarmed the inhabitants of Clinch and Holston Valleys. While some braced for the expected onslaught and others prepared to flee, Campbell requested reinforcements and ammunition to defend that part of the county. He also sought diplomatic assistance, possibly with an appeal to the respected chief Oconostota, to exert his influence in calming the agitated Cherokees. [27]

Campbell feared that Crabtree and "a few misled followers" would frustrate any efforts to prevent the calamity of a war. The major had learned that the frontier ruffian had recently traveled to Nolichucky, intent on crossing into Cherokee territory to rob or kill some Indians. To his surprise, he found not the two or three "defenseless wretches" that he expected but thirty-seven warriors acquainted with his reputation and intentions who would not fail to "examine" the encroaching troublemaker. Crabtree immediately retreated "with precipitation" to the relative safety of the Fincastle settlements but soon made plans for another attempt. Campbell considered the well-known Indian hater as the principal suspect in Cherokee Billy's murder but doubted the likelihood of bringing him to justice. Although "sober minded" frontier inhabitants detested his act and disapproved of his conduct, they also, however inconsistently, had sympathy for him. They knew that he had survived the ambush in Powell's Valley the previous October, which claimed the lives of six companions, including the son of their neighbor John Drake.[28]

A rumor soon circulated that the Cherokee had initiated their reprisals with an attack that killed a family on Copper Creek, a tributary of the Clinch. As the alarm following the alleged depredations spread, militia companies mustered, and residents became even less inclined to punish a neighbor for killing a single Indian. Campbell turned to the county lieutenant seeking guidance on how to proceed. Colonel William Christian—Preston's deputy and highest ranking subordinate—noted that some settlers were "so desirous" of an Indian war that they "were sorry, exceedingly so," to learn that the rumors concerning the Copper Creek massacre were unfounded. Christian lamented that such sentiment had prompted only "the most worthless" and least dependable men in the county to turn out for military service.[29]

Along with his reply to Campbell, Preston enclosed a personal communication for Oconostota. The county lieutenant explained that Virginia authorities considered Crabtree a fugitive who would receive justice in court and appealed for the chief to dissuade Cherokee braves from taking the warpath. Campbell forwarded the missive to Watauga Association officials at Sycamore Shoals, who had planned a similar mission of peace, for "speedy conveyance" to the middle Cherokee towns. The major added his own letter to his acquaintance, Alexander Cameron of the Indian Department, asking him to use his good offices to resolve the matter. Campbell condemned Crabtree's act with the highest "detestation" but also blamed the southern district deputy superintendent's "Orders . . . to perhaps the profligate part of the nation" when encountering any Virginians on Cherokee lands to summarily act as both their "Judges and executioners . . . for robberies [committed]."[30]

Before composing and forwarding his and Preston's letters to Watauga, Major Campbell ordered Captain John Campbell, his younger brother, to go downriver to the settlement closest to the "Indian Line," the boundary with the Cherokees, for a special task. The captain personally engaged a man familiar with Cherokee country, especially the area on the Holston near its confluence with the French Broad River, to act as a "Spy" to watch the adversary's activities and obtain intelligence.[31]

The captain instructed the volunteer to select a concealed position where he could observe the nearby ford and watch traffic on the path for most of the day. He would break twice each day to range some distance up and down the river looking for evidence that a large party of warriors had passed through the area. If he discovered any indication of an enemy advance toward the Virginia settlements, the spy had orders to return, report his findings, and alert the militia. After informing Preston of the preparations, Major Campbell confided his opinion that the Cherokees would willingly avoid a war unless Crabtree, or someone like him, committed an "affront" that provoked them to it. The major assured the colonel that he would transmit "an account of any true alarm that may happen," as his duty required, and requested the county lieutenant to inform him when and "if the War has actually broke out to the Northward."[32]

While those at Pittsburgh had concerns for traders still in Indian country, the people of Fincastle County worried about the safety of the surveyors with Captain Floyd. Christian remarked to Preston that he believed they remained safe and "would not all be killed if fallen on," or attacked, before returning. He proposed that Preston write to Crabtree's company commander, either Captain James Thompson or William Campbell. The major suggested that the company commander encourage Crabtree to volunteer to go search for the surveyors and warn them to come home lest they encounter hostile Indians. Christian suggested that if Crabtree accepted the assignment and performed his mission well, it might serve to atone for his guilt.[33]

The orders Preston had sent to the captains the previous month remained in effect. With an experience similar to that of Daniel Smith at Indian Creek, Captain Russell reported that at his company's muster on June 25, the men voted to immediately build two forts in the Clinch River area "in as convenient Places as we can get." Russell advised his superior that the shortage of gunpowder continued to hamper his company's ability to defend the settlement, and he trusted that the colonel's efforts to obtain some would meet success. Russell, like Smith, found that invoking the Invasions and Insurrections Act helped him to effectively halt the flight of nervous inhabitants. He was optimistic that in a future emergency he could "call for any Number of Men from Holston" as reinforcements whenever the service required.[34] He added that since his unit covered a large regional catchment with men settled in very remote locations, he requested that Colonel Preston allow his company one additional subaltern. If approved, the colonel could either appoint a new lieutenant or ensign, or provide a blank commission, presigned by Governor Dunmore, so that Russell could select a deserving and qualified man.[35]

Both sensible and sympathetic to the county lieutenant's "Uncommon concern for the Security of Capt. Floyd and the Gentlemen with him," the Fincastle County militia officers turned their attention to finding and notifying the surveyors of the danger they faced. Russell arguably understood their predicament best and expressed his fervent desire to locate and guide the men to safety before "they should fall a Prey, to such Inhuman, Bloodthirsty Devils, as I have so lately suffered." He knew that sending out scouts offered the best chance for securing their survival and safe return, and prayed for God to shield them from harm until they could be found. Russell engaged Daniel Boone and Michael Stoner, "two of the best Hands" in his company, and instructed them "to search the Country, as low as the falls" of the Ohio, and return by way of Mansco's Lick on the Cumberland, and through Cumberland Gap. With no time to spare, he sent them out to warn Floyd's party of the danger and urge them to hasten their return home.[36]

Despite the increased tensions, Preston expressed reservations about his legal authority to order the county's militia into active service before the enemy actually invaded the colony. Christian opined that he could legally "encourage men to rise up and go without expressly ordering them" and bring their own horses and enough provisions to last four or five weeks. Christian believed Preston could easily assemble at least one hundred volunteers willing to take their chance at pay for themselves and stipends for the use of their horses and other private property until the General Assembly resolved the issue of the recently expired Militia Law.

Christian recommended that the county lieutenant seek the volunteers from four companies and embody them under the command of a capable and energetic officer. In accordance with Dunmore's instructions, they would march down the Warriors' Path on the left bank of the Great Kanawha, intercept any invaders coming from the other direction, and build a fort at its mouth. Even if they did not fight them, any Indians who noticed signs of the militia's presence would most likely retreat. With the proposed number of volunteers, they could erect a small fort in about one week. The completed post would then serve to defend the frontier and provide a base from which patrols could continuously operate to "serve the Inhabitants, & perhaps cover the retreat of the Surveyors." Christian knew that when the first volunteers' time expired, the recruitment of replacements might prove difficult. He argued that if a war ensued as anticipated, the General Assembly would no doubt approve the expense, and Preston could order a draft for the necessary men to relieve the garrison.[37]

After considering the recommendation, Preston received intelligence of a "large party of Cherokees," led by a warrior known as the Raven, headed either to or from the Shawnee towns in order to cooperate with them against the Virginians. Realizing the implications, Preston developed his plan. He reasoned that, "The present defenseless Situation of the Frontier Inhabitants of the County of Fincastle make it absolutely necessary [to] Raise & keep on foot a Number of Men, to Protect the Frontiers & annoy the Enemy." He noted that neighboring counties, although no more exposed than Fincastle, had already raised men on the understanding that Lord Dunmore's orders justified the measure. Under his authority as county lieutenant, Preston decided to raise a force of rangers.[38]

Preston selected his deputy, Colonel Christian, to command the ranging force. He could not have chosen better.[39] First commissioned as an ensign in the militia at age fifteen, he had served as an officer in the 2nd Virginia Regiment in provincial service during the French and Indian War and rose to the rank of captain at eighteen. A brave and efficient officer, he participated in the Cherokee Expedition of 1760 and commanded rangers for frontier defense through Pontiac's War. At thirty-one, he now held the rank of colonel. As deputy, Christian served as county lieutenant in Preston's absence and commanded Fincastle County troops in the field. He was married to Anne Henry and studied law with her brother, Patrick Henry. When the General Assembly established Fincastle County, he received an appointment as a deputy clerk of the court and won election as one of the county's two representatives in the House of Burgesses, where he served in the 1773 and 1774 sessions.

Colonel Preston held a council of war at Fort Chiswell, near the county seat at the New River community called the Lead Mines. Preston informed Christian of the mission, and the commanders of the companies what he expected of them. He ordered six captains to muster all the men of their companies, from which they would each raise 20 "good" men, "either as Volunteers or by Draught," and asked for 30 additional volunteers from among the other companies, for a total force of 150 men, not counting the necessary officers. Once all the detachments assembled at the ordinary called the Town House on Holston—an "ordinary" being an inn or tavern licensed to serve food and drink to the public at a fixed price—located on the property of Captain James Thompson on the high ground between the Middle Fork and Sulphur Spring Creek, Christian would organize them into a corps of three companies. Preston had selected Captains Walter Crockett and William Campbell to each command one of the fifty-man companies, assisted by a lieutenant and an ensign. Christian exercised over-all command, as well as that of the remaining fifty-man company. In addi-tion to the normal complement of two officers for that company, Preston allowed him an additional subaltern, Ensign William Buchanan.[40]

The rangers served on foot, but Preston wanted the captains to encour-age as many of the men as possible to bring their own horses to carry the required baggage. Trusting that the General Assembly would authorize pay-ing the troops the necessary stipends, Christian preferred it to impressing pack animals from third parties. In addition to the supplies and provisions the quartermasters could procure, Preston wanted each of the men to bring enough from home so they could "Endeavour to Stay out a month or Six weeks." In accordance with the current Invasions and Insurrections Act, Preston appointed "two honest men on Oath" to appraise the private prop-erty used for public service at the rendezvous, and present the owners with the certificates necessary to file their claims for the government to pay.

According to the original plan, after they assembled and organized at the Town House, Christian would lead the three companies to the Clinch and cross Cumberland Mountain by one of the gaps. After arriving at the "head branches of the Kentucky" River, they would "Range together or in separate parties & at such places" as Christian judged most likely for them to be able to discover, intercept, and repulse the enemy as they approached the Fincastle settlements. With seventy Cherokees reported on the move to "Join our Enemies," many still hoped they would refrain from hostilities and remain neutral. The uncertainty prompted Preston to recommend that Christian exercise the utmost caution and discretion, but left it to his field commander's "Prudence" on how to treat the Indians if encountered and "Judge by the Manner of their approach" before opposing their advance. If the Cherokees came on in a hostile manner, the rangers could anticipate that a number of Shawnees or other enemy Indians accompanied them, which "may render them formidable to your party." Should the rangers en-counter Floyd and the surveyors, Preston wanted Christian to warn them—if they were not already aware—of the danger that attended them and to return to the settlements.[41]

In "Rules for Marching" found in his *Treatise of Military Discipline*, the basic doctrinal manual for officers of the British army, Humphrey Bland wrote, "There is not any thing in which an Officer shews his want of conduct so much, as in suffering himself to be surprised . . . and by not having taken the necessary precautions to prevent it."[42] Familiar with its precepts and armed with his experience, Preston reminded Christian to keep "some active Men" out "to the distance of a mile" on the right and left flanks of his main body, and in his front and rear, while on the march, and to post sentinels when in camp. Such measures prevented surprise attack, "which is too often attended with fatal Consequences" and "above all things ought ever to be Guarded against." Preston further emphasized, "Nor should this part of the duty be Neglected or even Relaxed on any occasion whatever."[43]

Although he probably did not have to tell Christian, Preston added a reminder to "keep up good order & Discipline . . . according to the Militia Law now in force." He stressed the importance of consulting regularly with his subordinate officers, all of whom "will not only be very alert & obedient in their Duty; but they will keep Good order & Discipline in their companies" and remain cooperative and friendly among themselves so that "every Intention of Sending out the Party may be fully answered." By saving the surveyors and performing the duty of rangers, Preston told Christian and his men, they would "render an Essential Service to the Country, as many lives thereby may be sav'd." Preston concluded by telling Christian that he had instructed the captains commanding the companies providing the soldiers to select "none but choice officers & men on this little Expedition" because "the Eyes of the Country" were all on them. He harbored no doubt that every soldier would exert himself to "answer the wishes & expectations of his Country" and serve it as much as was in his power.[44]

After receiving his orders on June 27, Christian notified Preston that he wanted to leave for the rendezvous the following Monday, July 4. Meanwhile, he sought to locate wagons and "a parcel" of seven or eight men willing to volunteer for the expedition whom Captain Daniel Trigg could spare from his company. While the captains mustered their companies, the colonels anxiously waited to learn the latest intelligence before putting the rangers into motion.[45]

As the Shawnees and their Mingo allies prepared for war, runners traveled to neighboring tribes and implored other Ohio country nations, especially the Cherokees, Miamis, Wyandots, the various tribes of Unami and Munsee Delawares, as well as any others who would listen, to join or ally with their

confederation against the Long Knife. They even appealed to the Six Nations, hoping they would join them and bring their dependents and allies
into a pan-Indian military alliance—the worst fear of British America. War
fever raged through the towns and villages of the five septs of the Shawnee
nation and the bands of Mingoes they had taken under their influence and
protection. Moderate voices failed to persuade young men, eager to display
their martial prowess, to stay home. Talk of war was on everyone's lips.

The missionary John Heckewelder described the "Shawanos" as "good
warriors and hunters." From personal observation, he saw them as "courageous, high spirited and manly, and more careful in providing a supply of
ammunition to keep in reserve for an emergency, than any other nation" of
the Ohio valley.[46] Every warrior, he said, possessed the essential and indis-
pensable qualifications of "Courage, art, and circumspection."[47] In contrast,
David Jones did not have such a high opinion of their military prowess or
respect for Shawnee warriors as his Moravian counterpart. The traveling
Baptist preacher described them as having "more timorous spirits, far from
possessing anything heroick." He wrote that they "seek all advantages" and
never engaged in battle "without a manifest prospect of victory." Jones concluded that an opponent need not fear Shawnee warriors "being saucy," unless they had the advantage of "more than a double number [over their
enemy]." While he admitted that they killed many in the last war, Jones hastened to add that most of their victims "were timorous women scared more
than half dead at their sight, or else persons devoid of arms to defend themselves."[48] Regardless of what a contemporary may have thought about their
motivation or skill, the mere rumor of Shawnee warriors moving at large
caused alarm and inspired panic along the frontier.

Indians rarely gave quarter to enemy combatants and often killed noncombatants as well. The practice of taking captives and assimilating them
into their tribal families was intended to diminish an opponent's community as well as offering condolence and replacing their own losses. Unlike
Europeans, they did not look for, but avoided, pitched battles whenever possible and were at their best in individual combat. Unless surrounded with
no chance of escape, Indian warriors would sooner retire from an engagement once they no longer held a tactical advantage rather than accept the
cost of achieving an objective in the European sense. They preferred conducting raids and ambushes in order to inflict casualties as well as terrorize
their enemy.

Regardless of the operation, warriors sought to fight only on their own
terms, according to Heckewelder, by "stealing upon the enemy unawares,
and deceiving and surprising him in various ways."[49] The bloody and dev-

astating raids of the French and Indian War and Pontiac's War, such as those that Cornstalk had led against the Greenbrier Valley settlements in 1763, remained vivid in the memories of many backcountry inhabitants.

A number of chiefs and leading warriors had recruited new war parties in some Shawnee and Mingo towns. The day after the customary war dance, the warriors assembled early in the morning. With their heads and faces painted and packs on their backs, they marched away. As each war party left its village, it proceeded in silence, except for the chief. Leading from the front, he sang the band's traveling song until the last warrior passed the edge of town, at which time they all discharged their firearms, and those who remained behind shouted encouragement and war whoops.[50]

W AR PARTIES crossed the Ohio to strike settlements in Augusta County. To reach their objectives and achieve complete surprise, the braves took great pains to conceal their tracks or any other evidence that gave their presence away. Large war parties divided into smaller ones, and they marched at some distance from each other for a full day at a time. The Shawnees had a well-known ability to deceive enemies by imitating the cries or calls of animals, such as a fawn or turkey during the appropriate season, to decoy or lure them into an ambush or "gain the opportunity to surround them." Similarly, when scattered in the woods, they could easily locate one another by imitating the calls of different birds at appropriate times of the day, repeated from time to time, until they reassembled to camp for the night or to attack.[51]

On some occasions they marched single file, "treading carefully in each other's steps so that their numbers could not be ascertained by the prints of their feet."[52] Captive Mary Jemison explained, "It is the custom of Indians when scouting, or on private expeditions, to step carefully and where no impression of their feet can be left." Whenever possible, they walked on hard, stony, and rocky ground and avoided soft surfaces, to make it more difficult for an enemy to track them. "They seldom take hold of a bush or limb, and never break one," Jemison continued, "and by . . . setting up the weeds and grass which they necessarily lop, they completely elude the sagacity" of any pursuers. Furthermore, the last man followed the file with a "long staff" and picked up all the grass and weeds that were matted down by others walking over them. The amazed Jemison said that he performed the task so well that he made a pursuit impossible, "for each weed was so nicely placed in its natural position that no one would have suspected that we had passed that way."[53]

The warriors became more attentive as they approached closer to the enemy. Jones remarked that Shawnees possessed an astonishing sharpness and quickness of sight. The training and experience that allowed them to notice trodden-down grass or the least impression left on grass or weeds where someone had walked provided another remarkable ability. Watching them in action convinced Jones that a Shawnee warrior could determine the sex and nationality of a person simply by looking at the footprints.[54]

Early in the morning of June 29, the sound of gunfire and war whoops shattered the stillness and reawakened nightmares of 1763, when Shawnee warriors struck the Greenbrier Valley settlements of Augusta County. In an engagement with a unit of local militia, the Indians killed one soldier and wounded the lieutenant in command before compelling them to retreat to Captain John Dickinson's fortified house. Although their action had delayed the attackers long enough for more troops to assemble and noncombatants to find refuge, the Indians soon had Dickinson's fort under siege. The captain sent runners to inform his counterparts commanding the companies in neighboring communities and he requested their immediate assistance.[55]

As the Shawnees and Mingoes spoke of war at Wakatomika and Chillicothe, sent raiding parties across the Ohio, and sought allies, Oconostota called all the principal chiefs of the Overhill Cherokees to Chota, their principal town, or capital, on the Little Tennessee River. One day as they met in council, a serious disturbance disrupted their discussions. James Robertson and William Falling (or Faulin) arrived carrying the conciliatory letters from Watauga Association and Virginia officials on "behalf of the People to endeavor to Compromise the affair of killing the Cherokee at the Races."

When they saw Robertson and Falling, many of the warriors joined the relatives and friends of the murdered Billy in calling for immediate reprisal starting with the two emissaries, despite the messages of peace they carried. Falling said they would have succeeded if not for the "interposition of some of their chiefs" who dissuaded them taking such a "rash step." A number of the traders present in the town saw the commotion, grew timid, and fled for their lives before knowing the outcome. Some "set out for Carolina" or the Holston and Clinch settlements of Fincastle County, where they spread the rumors that caused alarm and resulted in panic and the calling out of additional militia.[56]

The chiefs had discussed and debated the issues surrounding the increased tensions and the potential of war with Virginia. Speaking for all, Oconostota told Robertson and Falling that the discussions covered their

An illustration showing Oconostota, Cherokee chieftain, receiving a French military commission from Louisiana governor Chevalier de Kerlerec in 1761. (*National Archives*)

people's involvement with the murders of young Russell and Boone—and the rest of their party—in Powell's Valley, the recent robberies of Virginia hunters, and Crabtree killing Billy at the races in Watauga. They denied that those guilty of the Boone-Russell murders acted with their approval. Although they admitted their people robbed hunters, they maintained that they did so with "Mr. Cameron's authority." Oconostota told them that The Raven had gone to the Shawnees without the nation's approbation, but no one had heard from him since, and they suspected the Shawnees had killed him. They had rejected Shawnee appeals to join in fighting their common enemy, and as a result, some Shawnees had recently killed one of their people within sight of a Cherokee town.[57] They accepted the messages the two emissaries delivered and promised to give them a reply to carry on their return.

AFTER READING the express from Greenbrier in Augusta County, Colonel Christian had to assume that more war parties roamed at large, including in Fincastle County, and alerted the vulnerable settlements to the danger. He directed Captain Joseph Cloyd to alert the companies at Walker's Creek,

Blue Stone River, and along New River to be on their guard and move their families to shelter until they determined the enemy's strength and intentions. Swollen rivers in the area fortuitously hindered the Indians' ability to make more attacks on the south bank of the New River, but militia leaders knew the short-lived relief would end as soon as the water receded.[58]

Christian directed Cloyd to have the men he had previously ordered to muster for ranger service assemble at the Town House as planned to receive further orders. The colonel directed that all of them should bring a horse loaded with all the ammunition and provisions they could carry, as he could not predict how long they might have to remain in the field before the emergency subsided or others came to their relief. Besides those being called out for actual service, Christian also directed Cloyd to determine the best places where the men of his company who were not marching should immediately erect forts. Christian believed that seeing the activity would encourage the timid local inhabitants to take heart and not flee.[59]

"The hour that I so much dreaded (as to the peace of this Country) is now I am apprehensive near at hand," wrote Major Arthur Campbell to Colonel Preston on Friday, July 1. Fear spread through the countryside as fleeing traders spread the bad tidings throughout the frontier districts. Some of the refugees told Campbell that the Cherokees had murdered the two messengers who carried the conciliatory messages to their chiefs as well as all the traders who remained in their towns when the rampage began. Based on this information, the major reported that the Cherokees had "at length commenced hostilities." Some of the refugee traders also reported seeing at least forty Shawnee warriors arrive in the Cherokee towns, which caused Campbell to expect imminent attacks against the Holston and Clinch settlements. As soon as the bad news spread, the officer expected a number of residents to flee from their homes. As the situation deteriorated further, the captains commanding companies complained that the scarcity of ammunition compromised their ability to defend their communities. As the senior officer in the district, Major Campbell requested reinforcements and expressed his hope that Bedford and Pittsylvania Counties—the adjacent counties east of the Blue Ridge—would recognize the emergency and call out their militias to help. If the three counties joined forces "to face them [the Indians] about the lower settlements on this River," he believed "the War might not be so calamitous." He took the precaution to instruct some of the district's captains to muster half of the men in their companies at the Town House in four days, starting on Tuesday, if not sooner.[60]

Necessity dictated that Preston take every measure in his power to defend the country. In addition to the three ranging companies, he instructed

Christian to call on the commanding officers of seven companies to draft 280 men to defend the Clinch River settlements. That force included fifty men each from the companies of Captains William Herbert and Thomas Madison, thirty each from those of Captains Walter Crockett and Robert Doack, and forty each from the companies commanded by Captains James Thompson, William Campbell, and Major Arthur Campbell. Once they completed the drafts, the men were to assemble at the Town House as quickly as possible. Should they need additional reinforcement, Preston directed the captains commanding the three companies on the Lower Holston River to keep eighty of their men ready to march on the shortest notice.

Meanwhile, Preston directed Christian to use the available forces at his command— drafted militia and rangers—to defend the various frontier communities as best he could. Because the Indians could strike anywhere, Christian sent a thirty-man patrol under a lieutenant and ensign to "range at the heads of Sandy Creek & Clinch" to gather intelligence and provide early warning, and a seventy-five-man detachment, with the necessary complement of officers, from the first draft to reinforce the local militia on the Clinch. Preston wanted his deputy to personally march the rest of his command down the Holston to either the lower road to the Clinch or the road through Moccasin Gap to the Holston. Preston trusted Christian's judgment that from there, based on the latest intelligence, he would either continue to the Clinch or proceed down the Holston. In choosing the latter course, Christian would combine his unit with the drafted militia under his command. If the situation dictated that he use the drafted men as a separate detachment, Preston authorized Christian to place them under the command of such officers as he thought proper to appoint. Furthermore, if the situation dictated a need for additional scouts, Christian had the authority to select "not only good Woodsmen but Men of Property and Veracity" for the service.

As express riders hurried to deliver messages between superior and subordinate officers, Preston knew he could rely on Christian in any situation. To demonstrate the high level of confidence he placed in his field commander, Preston allowed Christian "to take any Measures for the Defense of the Frontiers" not specified in his written instructions. With an eye toward economy, the county lieutenant urged his deputy "not to Incur any Expense to the Country" except those "absolutely Necessary for the Protection of the People." Otherwise, Preston only cautioned Christian not to commit forces far down the Holston unless acting on "well attested" intelligence. He only required Christian to send reports as often as possible, and immediately if "anything Extraordinary" happened.[61]

Panic followed close behind news that an Indian war had started. Many inhabitants deserted the settlements and fled east, but others resolved to meet the danger after seeing to the safety of their families. A number of the people settled on the New River as far up as the mouth of Reed Creek moved to the safety of the fort at Bell's Meadows, where Christian knew some of his officers had also taken their wives and children before returning to their units. Others stayed closer to their farms but sheltered their families at neighbors' fortified homes. Christian placed Captain Daniel Trigg in temporary command of the activated militia so he could remove his own family to safety at Colonel William Fleming's Belmont estate in Botetourt County. Before leaving, he confided to Preston his belief that the panic would soon wane as militia officers exerted their authority. "I can't think the people on the [New] river in the least danger if they would stay home," he continued, "but I am afraid to over persuade them, as they will return of their own accord in some days." Fifty pounds of much-needed gunpowder arrived, but Christian told his superior that in order to keep enough to supply the pending expedition, he would not "undertake to touch it" for distribution to local commanders unless the county lieutenant so ordered, or "the neighborhood is really attacked."[62]

Elsewhere, panic spread. At the end of the first week of July, Captain Daniel Smith informed Preston that the constant rumor of pending Indian attacks had frightened inhabitants from almost the entire settlement at the head of the north fork of the Clinch to the Bluestone. The people at Indian Creek became so frightened from listening to and believing so many "propagators of false reports in the country" that he had difficulty restraining them from panic. Smith had no doubt that hostilities had commenced but lamented that "by passing thro' the mouths of imprudent people," reports that ought to have stirred the inhabitants to the common defense and caused neighbors to rely on each other for strength had the exact opposite effect. The rumormongers exacerbated the actual damage because they incited "timorous people to run away" instead of making a stand.

Captain Smith trusted the many men who said they would return after taking their wives and children to safety. He not only remained optimistic but planned accordingly. Before Lieutenant James Maxwell departed to visit his family in Botetourt County, Smith developed a plan to temporarily reorganize the men into two "separate companies, for the convenience of the inhabitants." Each company, consisting of about half of the enrolled men, would take primary responsibility for defending half of the community and would support or reinforce the other in case of invasion. Such a disposition, they reasoned, provided the entire settlement more protection and would convince more settlers to stay instead of evacuating.

Some of those who had considered or actually evacuated Indian Creek blamed their timidity on a perception that Smith had not sent out the patrols to provide early warning. Without it, they felt the settlement offered a tempting and vulnerable target to Indian raiders. Smith had actually sent two scouts down Sandy Creek to reconnoiter, but they "brought no account of Indians" on their return. Within a short while, Smith sent out two more patrols. One two-man patrol ranged to the head of streams falling to the Louisa, and the other, consisting of Thomas Maxwell (James's brother) and Israel Harmon, scouted down Sandy Creek. Instead of looking for evidence of enemy activity downriver, Maxwell and Harmon went in the opposite direction— to the head of the Sandy. They imprudently told inhabitants that remaining in their homes invited great danger. The two scouts then helped Jacob Harmon move his family and baggage to New River. When he learned that no one had gone down the Sandy, Smith immediately sent two reliable men to do the reconnaissance. As he waited two days for their return, the captain convinced some of the inhabitants who had considered leaving to stay. Smith wanted Thomas Maxwell called to account for his "Highly unworthy" behavior before a court-martial under the still subsisting Militia Law.

In spite of Smith's efforts, his company's strength dwindled. Poor attendance at the most recent muster convinced him that the men who remained suffered low morale, and he would have difficulty providing the drafts Preston ordered. He advised the county lieutenant that keeping a company of fewer than twenty unmotivated men in active service would serve no good purpose if they did nothing but help build forts in the busy time for laying by corn. The captain requested that the colonel instead permit him to keep his men at home but ready to march against any enemy the scouts discovered or join any company that required reinforcement. He knew that allowing them to work their fields between alarms gave purpose to their remaining on their farms and improved their spirits while it kept them available for militia service.[63]

As Preston managed the defense of Fincastle County, an express rider arrived from Williamsburg with Dunmore's reply to his last report. The governor expressed his approval of the measures he and the other county lieutenants had taken and believed they would effectively prevent the "Savages" from inflicting much damage in the frontier districts. Should the Indians attempt to strike, Dunmore expected that the joint forces of the frontier counties would prove sufficient to not only repel but effectively

"Chastise those restless and inveterate Enemys of Virginia." He remained convinced of the need to build a fort for security at the mouth of the Great Kanawha as well as to take offensive action. He told Preston that marching "a Body of Men . . . into the Enemy's Country" would certainly "put a Speedy and effectual end to the War, and Secure you a lasting peace." In response to Preston's request, Dunmore had also enclosed two majors' commissions and authorized Preston to appoint the additional field officers.[64]

Despite rumors of their deaths, Robertson and Falling returned from Chota alive and safe. Major Campbell wrote to Colonel Preston with guarded optimism that after hearing their reports, he "would willingly believe that peace may yet be preserved with the Cherokees." His optimism depended on preventing that "very insolent person" from committing some new provocation, but the major believed that Isaac Crabtree's "timidity . . . will get the better of his ferocity." [65] While making his way to Reed Creek on July 5, Colonel Christian met Falling and promptly informed Preston that his report satisfied him that Virginia had nothing to fear from the Cherokees, and he recommended that the county halt all the last-ordered drafts.[66]

About a week later, Colonel Preston received a letter from Oconostota, addressed to him and Colonel Andrew Lewis, that William Kennedy certified was a "true Copy as Delivered to me from the Interpreters." The chief acknowledged having received the condolence messages the colonels sent Robertson and Falling to read to them, and he replied, "All our Towns are met here [at Chota], and have heard this talk and think it a very good one." The sachem expressed his pleasure and the satisfaction of his people with the Virginians' renunciation of Crabtree's heinous act and pledge to bring the murderer to justice, which made retribution unnecessary. Oconostota said he shared the Virginians' desire for their peoples to "keep the path clean" on both sides of the boundary and to remain at peace. He promised that he would personally urge his nation's young men to refrain from taking the warpath. In return, Oconostota requested that Preston and Lewis exhort Virginians to desist from encroaching on Cherokee country and respect the boundary line surveyed in 1772.[67]

After he forwarded Oconostota's letter to Lewis, Preston composed his reply to "the Chief of the Warlike Nation of the Cherokees, Friends & Brethren." The colonel stated that he shared the desire for both sides to maintain peaceful relations to their mutual benefit. Preston then revealed that he knew that some Cherokees had already gone out to join with the Shawnees and informed Oconostota that Lord Dunmore would soon lead a punitive expedition against Virginia's enemies. The colonel asked Oconostota to admonish his people against letting any French traders in their towns sway them to join with the hostile Shawnees. He warned that those who renounced neutrality would suffer the same consequences that awaited the Shawnees. Given the diminished possibility of war with the Cherokees, the need to maintain all the drafted militia in active service now represented an unnecessary expense. Major Campbell therefore discharged and sent them home to await the next alarm.[68]

CHAPTER 7

The Drums Beat Up Again

Partial Mobilization Becomes General

July 1774

ALTHOUGH THE Cherokee chiefs had promised not to go to war against Virginia, Shawnee and Mingo war parties roamed in search of vulnerable settlements. Messengers carrying the alarms—whether reporting actual depredations, circulating rumors of an attack, or repeating someone's claim to have sighted Indians—helped to spread fear and panic in communities throughout the region. The county lieutenants reported to Governor Dunmore that "skulking parties of Indians (believed to be Shawanese and Delawares) had been discovered lately among the Settlements" in Augusta, Botetourt, and Fincastle Counties, with some of them venturing within twenty-five miles of Botetourt Courthouse.[1] In one attack, Colonel Andrew Lewis of Botetourt County reported that Shawnees had attacked "a Body of men" near his Richfield plantation home, not far from the courthouse town of Fincastle, killing one man and wounding another.[2]

More people continued to shelter in forts throughout Augusta County after the Indian attacks became more "troublesome." On entering active service, Benjamin Cleaver was appointed as a sergeant and detailed with others to guard the "forts of and Frontiers of Tigers [Tygert] Valley," a branch of the Monongahela, for a term of four or five months.[3] Exercising such caution was not misplaced. Indian warriors operating about the neighborhood of Warm Springs shot and slightly wounded one William McFarlon (or McFarland) during the first week of July. The otherwise minor incident nonetheless sent local inhabitants rushing "in ye Greatest Confusion" for the protection of nearby forts. In an attempt to counter the threat and put a stop to their intended hostilities, Colonel Charles Lewis ordered out several companies of Augusta County militia. One of them engaged a group of Indian warriors near the headwaters of the Monongahela. Captain John Wilson was wounded by "a Shot in his Body," which everyone hoped would not prove mortal; the soldiers he commanded killed three warriors in the encounter.[4]

The county lieutenants ordered the captains commanding companies to send out scouts to watch the warrior paths and rangers to rigorously patrol the approaches to settlements in order to detect and provide early warning before enemy raiders struck. Due to their vulnerability to attack along the frontier, the colonels also instructed the captains to send messengers to isolated settlements to warn the inhabitants that a war had begun and to advise them to remove their families to more secure locations.[5]

After dispatching scouts and patrols from his company, Captain John Stuart of Botetourt County sent an express to warn the settlers living in the farthest and most isolated settlements along the Great Kanawha River. Most of them heeded the warning. John Jones, for example, felt "compelled by the incessant incursions of the Indians to take refuge among the inhabitants" of the Greenbrier area. He then volunteered to serve in the company under the command of Captain Matthew Arbuckle to build and garrison a fort on Muddy Creek that would "guard the inhabitants against the incursions of the Indians."[6]

Walter Kelly had a different response. Stuart described Kelly as having a "bold and intrepid disposition" but suspected that he "might be a fugitive from the back parts of South Carolina" who had established his habitation about twelve miles below the great falls of the Kanawha near the mouth of Kelly Creek. When Stuart's messenger arrived at Kelly's cabin, he also found fifty-year-old John Field, the colonel of the militia from neighboring Culpeper County. Accompanied by "several neighbors and one or two Negroes," Field had come to survey the claim on the military grant he received for his service as a captain in the Virginia Regiment during the French and Indian War.[7]

Kelly "received the intelligence with caution" and immediately decided to send his wife and daughter, Sally, along with his livestock, to Greenbrier in the care of his younger brother, William. Stuart described William Kelly as a young man of equally suspicious character. While the others prepared to evacuate, Field expressed different ideas. "Trusting his own Consequence and better knowledge of publick Facts," he persuaded the older Kelly brother to stay. He argued that "[n]othing of the kind" had been heard before and evaluated the new intelligence as "not worth noticing." Although Walter sent his family to safety, he decided to remain on his farm with Field, an unidentified male described only as a "young Scotchman," and a young slave woman.

Later in the day, while Kelly and Field worked at the tanning trough, a party of Indians closed in on the cluster of buildings. As the two men carried some leather toward the cabin, the raiders opened fire and yelled their war whoops. As they ran toward the house to get the muskets kept inside so they could fight back, Field noticed that Kelly had fallen to the ground dead. When he got closer to the house, Field remembered that they had "not charged"—or loaded— either musket, which rendered them useless. Meanwhile, the warriors neared the cabin where "the Negro girl and Scotch boy [were] crying at the door." Realizing the futility of keeping on that course, the unarmed colonel ran out into the adjacent cornfield. He used the concealment provided by the tall stalks to evade any pursuers and avoided capture or death to make his escape. When Field paused to catch his breath, he looked back toward the house and watched helplessly as the warriors killed the boy, scalped both him and Walter Kelly, and carried the girl off as their captive.[8]

When William Kelly and his party arrived safely in Greenbrier, he told Stuart that they had gone some miles from the farm when they heard gunfire. Kelly confided to Stuart that he "expected his brother and Field had been killed." Stuart gathered ten or fifteen volunteers from his company and went to see "what was the consequence" and possibly rescue any survivors. When the patrol met Field coming from the opposite direction, he was naked except for his shirt, his limbs were grievously lacerated from passing through "briars and brush," and he was visibly worn down with fatigue and cold. The exhausted veteran informed the soldiers of the raid, his escape, and the fate of his late companions. Stuart led his men back to Greenbrier to defend the settlement if the Indian raiders chose to penetrate further into Botetourt County.[9]

Writing to Colonel Preston, his Fincastle County counterpart, Colonel Charles Lewis expressed his hope that when the General Assembly convened in August with the newly elected burgesses, they would find some means of ending the war. He did not know that by the time his report on the incident near Warm Springs reached Williamsburg, the governor had already dissolved the assembly, pending new elections. Nor did Lewis know that Dunmore had also departed the capital on Sunday, July 10, to see the situation on the frontier firsthand. He sought to determine the cause of the recent disturbance and, if possible, find a means to settle matters amicably at a conference with the different nations of Indians involved.[10]

DESPITE THE events that transpired elsewhere on the frontier, the Pennsylvania officials in the area surrounding Pittsburgh continued to view the looming Indian war as a crisis instigated by Virginia for its own benefit. In correspondence with Governor Penn, Arthur St. Clair, Aeneas Mackay, Devereux Smith, and Joseph Spear asserted their conclusions that "the Crew about Fort Pitt (now Fort Dunmore) are intent on a war." They charged that John Connolly had express riders constantly on the road between Pittsburgh and Williamsburg with reports that gave the Virginia governor "a flagrant Misrepresentation of Indian Affairs," designed to influence his decisions in that direction.[11] In an attempt to curry favor so the Ohio-area Indians would not view Pennsylvania in the same light as Virginia, St. Clair had Croghan "collect a small present of goods." He then told the retired Indian deputy superintendent to distribute the gifts as a condolence to the Delawares, Shawnees, and Mingoes—the three nations most affected by the recent violence. He instructed Croghan to attribute the gifts to the orders of the generous Pennsylvania governor. St. Clair confided, "Whatever may be Mr. Croghan's real views" on the border controversy, "he is hearty in promoting the general tranquility of the Country [and] ... indefatigable in endeavoring to make up the breaches" to prevent an Indian war.[12]

In order to quiet the intercolonial dispute so they could focus attention on the troubles with the Indians, Lord Dunmore ordered Connolly to discuss settling a temporary boundary with St. Clair and the Westmoreland magistrates. Although the governor still described the Pennsylvania government's demands as "so extravagant he could do nothing with them," he authorized Connolly to propose a line of jurisdiction ten or twelve miles east of Pittsburgh. Knowing the captain's abrasive demeanor often proved counterproductive, the governor further admonished Connolly to give those acting under Pennsylvania authority no just reason to take offense.[13]

Connolly's nature would not allow him to evade controversy. On June 25, twenty-seven individuals signed a petition that protested the "arbitrary proceedings" of Connolly's "Tyrannical Government" and sent it to Philadelphia "On behalf of themselves and the remaining few inhabitants of Pittsburgh who have adhered to the Government of Pennsylvania." The petitioners listed their complaints about the treatment their colony's partisans received and urged Governor Penn to take some action to relieve their distress. In addition, they blamed the "present Calamity & Dread" of frontier war entirely on Connolly's "unprecedented Conduct." Despite the efforts of Pennsylvania authorities to maintain good relations with "our friendly Indians," the petitioners stood convinced of the Virginians' intent to force a war on them.[14]

The subscribers attached a litany of Connolly's lawless acts to their petition. The list recounted examples of Connolly's disdain for Pennsylvania law and authority, such as his surrounding the Westmoreland County courthouse at Hanna's Town with an armed force of two hundred men. They drew the governor's attention to Connolly's attempted interference with the proprietary colony's dominance of commerce with the Ohio tribes and cited Michael Cresap's attack on the Indians employed by the trader William Butler. Finally, they had had enough of Connolly using the Virginia civil and military force at his command to run roughshod over those who remained loyal to Pennsylvania's government. To reinforce these complaints, the petitioners reminded the governor of the several incidents of assault and resulting physical injuries, as well as the destruction of livestock and vandalism or arson of homes and other property directed against them and their families. Many of these incidents also exemplified Connolly's vindictiveness, as they followed the reprimand he received from Dunmore for the unjustified arrest and incarceration of Westmoreland magistrates Mackay, Smith, and McFarlane.[15]

The question of trade as another point of contention between the two colonies went beyond the interference mentioned in the petition. St. Clair expressed his concern to Penn that the Virginians had "determined to put a stop to the Indian Trade with this Province." He learned that Connolly and some associates had received an exclusive privilege to conduct business with the tribes and had imposed a duty of four pence per skin, payable to Virginia, on all traders shipping pelts from Pittsburgh. Furthermore, Connolly had previously sent Captain Henry Hoagland with a company of militiamen across to the north bank of the Ohio to intercept any Pennsylvania traders returning from Indian country. Although they had orders only to stop and examine them, Mackay alleged the soldiers had orders to treat "as Savages & Enemies, every Trader" they found in the woods about Pittsburgh, and kill them.[16]

While patrolling "about four miles Beyond Big Beaver Creek" on July 5, Sergeant Alexander Steele's twenty-man detachment encountered William Wilson with his party of traders and Indian escorts "bringing up a quantity of skins" from the direction of Newcomer's Town. The sergeant halted them and asked Wilson if he employed any Shawnees. The trader replied that he did not and identified his escorts as Delawares. Steele explained that he had orders to conduct the entire party, whites as well as Indians, with their packhorses and skins, to the mouth of the Little Beaver for his commander to examine. Although Wilson later told St. Clair that Hoagland threatened to kill the Indians regardless of nation, the captain released them in the morning after the trader gave his bond for £500 to satisfy Connolly.[17]

The recent petition indicated that the divide between the partisans of the colonies continued to widen, with those in Virginia's interest apparently gaining an advantage. According to Mackay, "the Friends of Pennsylvania" had determined to abandon Pittsburgh and erect a stockade "somewhere lower down the Road" to secure their cattle and other property until they could better determine the direction future events would take. Some Pennsylvanians even proposed erecting a new traders' town at Kittanning that would replace Pittsburgh as the center of their colony's commercial influence in the region.[18] St. Clair and his fellow magistrates also decided to maintain the Westmoreland County ranging company in service for at least another month and, if possible, until after harvest time, in order to assist and protect the people of Pennsylvania. Although they had pledged to raise the money themselves, they applied to the governor, seeking relief from the financial burden.[19]

Alexander McKee, the Indian Department deputy superintendent, called representatives from both colonies to meet on June 29 to hear the latest news from Indian country. Captain White Eyes had just returned from the most recent gathering of Ohio Indian leaders at Newcomer's Town. As the colonial leaders had requested, the Delaware chief dutifully delivered their message to the several assembled nations "to hold fast the Chain of Friendship subsisting between the English and them," despite the disturbances that had happened "between your foolish People and theirs." He reported that the Shawnee headmen had met in a council of their own at Wakatomika and said that they intended to send their "King" to Fort Pitt to hear what the British had to say. According to Aeneas Mackay, White Eyes gave the Pennsylvanians the strongest assurances of their friendship from not only the Delawares, Wyandots, and Cherokees, but the Shawnees as well.[20] At the conclusion of the meeting, the Delaware emissary returned to Newcomer's Town with the speeches the colonial leaders wanted him to deliver in an attempt to end the killing.

Following the council's adjournment, St. Clair initially expressed optimism that "Affairs have so peaceable an Aspect," but after he heard that a large body of Virginian troops was in motion, he feared it would jeopardize the chances for peace. The Westmoreland magistrates soon expressed a new concern from the Pennsylvania perspective when they heard that Dunmore had lately commissioned three new captains, including Cresap, to raise and lead companies of rangers for frontier defense. Even the president of the

Westmoreland County court, Captain William Crawford, accepted a commission and "seems to be the most active" among the Virginia officers. After noting that he had recently marched down the Ohio toward Wheeling in command of a body of troops on his second expedition, the judgmental St. Clair added, "I don't know how Gentlemen account these things to themselves."[21] Privates Evan Morgan and David Gamble could have answered him. Morgan enlisted in Captain Zackquill Morgan's company for the expedition when he "arrived at age, animated with a desire to repel their [the Indians'] inroads— avenge his murdered neighbors—and prevent further invasions." Similarly, Gamble "volunteered at Redstone Old Fort" to serve in Captain Cresap's company on the expedition "to fight against the Indians."[22]

When St. Clair received reports of "four Companies on the march to Pittsburgh," he expressed his usual skepticism. He knew that Connolly had received Dunmore's approval to conduct an offensive operation against the hostile Indians at the end of the previous month, but St. Clair doubted his ability to execute it. Assuming that the expiration of Virginia's Militia Law had restricted that colony's ability to marshal the necessary resources, he told Governor Penn "it is not an easy Matter to conduct so large a Body thro' an uninhabited Country where no Magazines are established."[23]

The Virginians had approximately eight hundred men in motion for the long-awaited operation and relied on their existing militia and invasion and insurrection laws to obtain the necessary provisions and supplies. Connolly appointed an able officer, Captain Dorsey Pentecost, as the conductor of stores and contractor for the army. As such, it fell to him to furnish all the militia soldiers on active service with supplies and provisions. Connolly also appointed officers to serve as commissaries, like Captain William Harrod. The commissary appropriated the livestock, flour, or other foodstuff from private owners, to whom he issued receipts for the appraised value. The commissary then delivered the provisions to the destination designated by the conductor of stores, such as the fort at Wheeling. After delivery, and obtaining the necessary documentation, the commissary settled the accounts for all the associated expenses—including the active-duty pay for the militia soldiers who drove and escorted the cattle, packhorses, and wagons—with the conductor of stores. When the House of Burgesses convened and appointed the required commission to examine and approve the documentation, those holding valid receipts could submit their claims for reimbursement from the colonial treasury.[24]

While the documents may not follow the chain of one single requisition, the following series illustrates an example of the process. On July 4, Captain Harrod presented a receipt to Abraham Van Meter for "Three Steers & one

Cow," with a complete description of each animal, appraised for "Sixteen Pounds Ten Shillings" by Jacob Vanmeeter and Edmund Polke "for the Use of the Government of Virginia." On July 16, Connolly directed Harrod to let Captain Pentecost "have the cattle you bought for Whalin [Wheeling] to be sent down there with all expedition." On July 20, Pentecost instructed Harrod to "Convey them to the mouth of Wheeling as Quick as Possible & Take an acct. of our Expences, what you gave for them," and after delivering them "have them appraised and Take care of all the accts. I may be able to Settle with you." Finally, Captain Crawford, in command at Wheeling, acknowledged receiving "Twenty Fives Beeves for use of the militia at Fort Fincastle" from Harrod on August 2.[25]

John Montgomery, the Carlisle merchant who procured and sold the powder to St. Clair's rangers, expressed his optimism that "the storm will blow over, and yet peace and Tranquility will be Restored to the Back Inhabitants." In a letter, he told the governor that White Eyes' speech in Pittsburgh at the end of June proved the Delawares were all for peace and that Montgomery expected the Shawnees to follow their lead. Incredibly, Montgomery expected no further trouble from them or the Mingoes. Without citing any evidence to support his claim, the merchant declared that Logan, "now satisfied for the loss of his Relations" with the "Thirteen Scalps and one prisoner" he had taken in June, assuredly "will sit Still until he hears what the Long Knife will say."[26]

Montgomery had no sooner expressed this optimism than a war party again terrorized the West Augusta area. Apparently not yet as satisfied for his loss as Montgomery had believed, Logan and seven followers scouted in preparation for their next attack near the mouth of Simpson's Creek on the West Fork of the Monongahela. After observing William Robinson, Thomas Hellen, and Coleman Brown pulling flax in a field on July 12, the Indians crept up on the unsuspecting farmers as if stalking a group of deer. They opened fire and charged out from the woods. One warrior pounced on Brown as he lay dead and bleeding from multiple gunshot wounds and removed his scalp. Others overwhelmed and subdued Hellen, while the rest ran after Robinson as he attempted to escape. After a short chase, Logan and others caught and restrained him and took him back to where their comrades held Hellen.[27]

The search of the home and surroundings for additional settlers to kill, scalp, or take captive proved fruitless. When area inhabitants "forted up" during the recent alarm, Robinson had secured his wife and four children at Prickett's fort, the fortified home of Jacob Prickett, a sergeant and fellow member of Captain Zackquill Morgan's militia company, near the confluence of the Monongahela River and Prickett's Creek. Resigned to taking only one scalp and two captives for their effort, the braves headed back toward Indian country. As they secured the prisoners, the English-speaking Logan became friendly and treated Robinson kindly. He assured his captive that if he went back to his town "with a good heart" and did not attempt an escape, he would spare his life and have him adopted into an Indian family. It was not a simple act of mercy, as Logan had plans for his prisoner that exceeded the immediate satisfaction of his vengeance. Throughout the journey to Wakatomika, Logan maintained a diatribe against Cresap in which he vented his intense hatred for the man who had allegedly murdered his family.[28]

Three days after the incident on the West Fork, John Pollock, David Shelvey, and George Shervor reported that a war party of thirty-five Indians had attacked them and six others as they worked in a corn field on Dunkard Creek. In their deposition to Westmoreland justice of the peace George Wilson, the three testified that although they had escaped, the warriors had killed and "sadly mangled" four of their friends, while two were missing and their fates remained unknown. The men explained that Captain Cresap's company of rangers gave chase, but the Indian raiders had the insurmountable advantage of a full one-day head start.[29]

Between giving his approval in June and reaching Winchester a month later, Governor Dunmore expanded the size and scope of the mission to Wheeling that Connolly had proposed. The governor called on the county lieutenants of Frederick, Dunmore, and Berkeley Counties for additional troops and appointed Major Angus McDonald to command an expedition to raid Wakatomika or other Upper Shawnee towns. With a rank more commensurate with the size of the assembling force, the Frederick County officer superseded Captain Crawford as commander, but the latter continued to play a vital role at Fort Fincastle supporting the campaign.[30]

Crawford had already led two expeditions to the mouth of Wheeling Creek, where his men continued work improving Fort Fincastle. Meanwhile, McDonald departed Winchester with troops raised in Frederick, Berkeley, and Hampshire Counties. Cresap's and other companies joined the battalion as it marched to Pittsburgh by way of Redstone and continued down the Ohio toward Wheeling. As the Virginia governor had ordered, Colonel Andrew Lewis also began raising an additional one thousand five hundred men for active service to defend the settlements and build a fort at the mouth of the Kanawha.

With troops in motion, war appeared more likely than ever. When the Westmoreland County magistrates heard that Connolly had sent the Indians an inflammatory "Speech," it confirmed their suspicions. Acting on

Dunmore's orders, the captain commandant demanded that the Shawnees apprehend Logan, his war party, and any warriors of their nation who had "committed murder last winter" and deliver them, as well as all the prisoners they had taken, to Virginia authorities. If they refused, Connolly threatened that the Virginians would "proceed against them with Vigour & will show them no Mercy."[31]

On July 19, in the wake of the recent attacks, Connolly and St. Clair entered another debate by writing letters that contrasted their respective colonies' approaches to the frontier crisis. In his opening volley, Connolly charged that the Pennsylvanians' naïve reliance on the "pacific dispositions" of the Indians had lulled them "into supineness & neglect" of their own defenses. Such a policy, he said, had tragic consequences, such as the attack of a few days before in which "six unfortunate People were murdered by a Party of thirty-five Indians" at Dunkard Creek. He further warned, "The Country will be sacrificed to their Revenge" if Pennsylvania did not take immediate steps to check the hostile Indians' "insolent impetuosity." He asserted that the people of the frontier wanted nothing more than their government's protection. Connolly concluded that Pennsylvania appeared reluctant, stubborn, and "highly displeasing to all Western Settlers," while Virginia at least took action to protect its inhabitants. As head of Virginia's civil government and military establishment in the Pittsburgh region, Connolly had "determined no longer to be a Dupe to their amicable professions" but had decided to "pursue every measure to offend" the Indians, with or without assistance from the "Neighboring Country"— Pennsylvania.[32]

Three days later, St. Clair countered Connolly by writing that "Such an Effect could never follow from such a Cause." The Pennsylvanian said that "the great armed force" sent down the Ohio on the pretense that it could effectively protect them had actually created the false sense of security into which Virginia's people had fallen. St. Clair agreed that their respective governments had to act to prevent depredations by hostile Indians but argued that Pennsylvania's solution of "ample Reparations . . . for the injuries they had already sustained" would ultimately prove more effective. Only "an honest open intercourse," he said, could immediately establish and maintain peace in the future. St. Clair then stated his hope that Pennsylvania's government would "continue to be founded in Justice, whether that be displeasing to the Western Settlers or not." St. Clair did not see the least probability of a war unless Virginia's maneuvers up, down, and across the Ohio brought about such an event.[33]

Although fellow Pennsylvania magistrate Wilson had sent him the deposition, St. Clair gave the reported recent Indian attack no credibility. On the same day that he countered Connolly's assertions, he informed Penn of the latest occurrences in Westmoreland County. Routinely skeptical of any news about Indian hostility, especially when it originated from or supported the Virginia side, he doubted that "some People were killed upon Dunkard Creek on the 15th instant." He explained that because such news spreads as quickly as the alarm, and this one had not, he questioned its veracity. He believed the deponents started the rumor in order to allow Cresap an excuse for circumventing Connolly's orders "not to annoy the Indians." And although still optimistic that Pennsylvania would escape the "mischiefs of a War," St. Clair noted that so far, the Indians had evidently aimed all their operations at the Virginians. Nevertheless, he took no chances and distributed "Arms all over the Country in as equal proportions as possible" to better enable Pennsylvania inhabitants to defend themselves. The very next day, as if to underscore Connolly's argument, David Griffey reported that he saw five Indians, with "Guns over their Shoulders," on the ridge dividing Brush and Sewickley Creeks, only four miles west of the courthouse. They were armed and obviously not traders, and Griffey described them as ready for battle, "Quite Naked all but their Breechclouts, Marching Towards Hanna's Town."[34]

St. Clair confided a growing uneasiness concerning the Westmoreland rangers. With their second month expiring at a time when the "Country is in such Commotion, and the Harvest not yet in, they cannot be dismiss'd." Consequently, the Westmoreland gentlemen who pledged their financial support stood to assume the expense when the provincial funding terminated. St. Clair sought the governor's assurance of seeking yet another means of relieving them of the burden.[35] On July 20, the Pennsylvania Colonial Assembly appropriated the money and granted the governor authority to "draw Orders on the Provincial Treasurer for any Sum not exceeding Two Thousand Pounds" for "Paying & Victualing" the rangers until August 10. The assembly agreed to extend the appropriation for the same amount until September 20 if it proved necessary, provided that the strength of the force did not exceed two hundred men. By financing the appropriation with the excise tax imposed on the sale of wine, rum, brandy, and other spirits, and the fines collected for failure to pay the excise taxes on liquor, the assembly justified the expenditure as the means for "removing the Panic" caused by the "late Indian Disturbances" on the frontier, as well as to subsidize the costs associated with efforts to maintain the peace and friendship that subsisted between "this Province and the Indians."[36]

In contrast to St. Clair's skepticism about reports of Indian depredations, Valentine Crawford needed no convincing. He wrote to George Washington that marauding warriors had recently "killed and taken [captive] ... thirteen people up about the forks of Cheat River," only about twenty-five miles from his farm on Jacob's Creek. He expressed his deep concern that local inhabitants had seen "savages prowling" about the Monongahela region and expected them to strike somewhere at any time. With "all the men, except some old ones," gone "down to the Indian towns" on the expedition, "all their families are flown to the forts." Two hundred people, mostly women and children from the surrounding area, had taken refuge in Crawford's fort. To further underscore the differences in attitude between Virginians and Pennsylvanians, Crawford took the position that "standing our ground here depends a good deal on the success of our men who have gone against the savages." [37]

AFTER THE late June meeting in Pittsburgh, Captain White Eyes returned to Newcomer's Town carrying the speeches colonial leaders had given him to deliver to the assembled Indians. On his arrival he learned that, "Contrary to their promise before the Chiefs of the Delawares" at the last council, several Shawnee war parties had set out to attack the Virginia settlers. Those same chiefs now instructed White Eyes to tell the Virginians "it would be to no purpose to Treat further with them [the Shawnees] upon Friendly terms." The assembled sachems also informed White Eyes that the Shawnees and their Mingo allies had evacuated their Wakatomika towns and relocated to the area of the lower Shawnee towns near the mouth of the Scioto. The neutral Delawares may have said this to keep the Virginians from attacking so close to their own villages in the area and assured them, saying, "if there is yet one Remaining we would Tell you." They wanted White Eyes to have the Virginians consider crossing the Ohio from the mouth of the Great Kanawha in order to attack their enemies. Otherwise, they feared that Virginia soldiers approaching near the Delaware towns in the area would frighten the women and children and find the "Shawanese are all gone."

Before leaving the last council at Newcomer's Town, the leader of one of the Shawnee war parties boasted that after he struck the Virginians, he would "Blaze a Road" to Newcomer's Town and "do Mischief," just to see if an actual or only a "Pretended" peace existed between the whites and the Delawares. Another Shawnee chief, Keesmauteta, said that since "his Grandfathers, the Delawares, had thrown his people away," they expected that according to ancient custom, such hosts had "Always Turn'd about and Struck them" in the back as they departed. The Delaware envoy had also discovered that another Shawnee war party intended to go to Fort Pitt to kill Croghan,

McKee, and Guyasuta, and intercept and kill White Eyes and his companions so that they could carry "no more news . . . between the White People and the Indians." Before leaving to return to Pittsburgh, White Eyes sent a message to the Wabash—or Miami—Indians "not to Listen to the Shawanese" for they only sought "to draw them into Troubles" and fighting a war they did not want.[38]

As White Eyes headed back to Pittsburgh from Newcomer's Town, Logan gave the "scalp haloo" outside of Wakatomika on July 18. All the warriors in the town came out to greet the returning party and escorted them and their captives to the council house for trial. In accordance with the ritual, the Indians forced Robinson and Hellen to run the gantlet. Although they received merciless beatings every time they fell, both men survived the ordeal. With each captive tied to a stake before them, the Mingoes debated whether to kill and burn them or to present one or both as a condolence to a grieving family. Keeping his promise, Logan convinced the assembled warriors and elders to spare Robinson's life. The conquering warrior untied the captive from the post and fastened a wampum belt around him to signify his adoption, and another family adopted Hellen. Logan took his new ward to a cabin and presented him to his aunt. Logan explained to Robinson that the old woman had lost a son in the massacre at Yellow Creek, and he now took his place in the family to make it whole once more. As Robinson looked around, Logan introduced him to some cousins as his new brothers by adoption.[39]

Three days later, Logan brought Robinson a piece of paper and told him he had to write a letter for him; this was the purpose for which Logan had taken him prisoner and ensured his survival. After he mixed gunpowder and water to make ink, the warrior dictated his words. Addressed to Captain Michael Cresap, he asked, "What did you kill my people on Yellow Creek for?" Although white people had killed other relatives at Conestoga "a great while ago [in 1763]," Logan said he "thought nothing of that." But when Cresap—allegedly—killed his kin on Yellow Creek and took his niece prisoner, the warrior vowed, "I must kill too; and I have been three time[s] to war since." He then added, "the Indians is not Angry only myself." Robinson signed it "Captain John Logan" with the date July 21, 1774. The warrior took the note and set out to war again, telling his scribe that he intended to tie it to a war club and leave it in the house of a family he would murder. Throughout his captivity, Robinson vainly assumed Logan would offer to exchange him for the young girl.[40]

Leaving such a notice by a corpse represented another war ritual common to many Indian nations. Reverend Heckewelder explained that when

Almost two feet long, the fearsome weapon was made of dried and hardened wood that had a metal spike protruding from the round ball at the business end. The Logan war club on exhibit at the Fort Pitt Museum was left by the Mingo leader at the scene of one of his brutal raids on the settlers of the Virginia frontier during Dunmore's War. (*Fort Pitt Museum*)

Indians had decided to take revenge for a murder committed against their people by another nation, they generally tried to make a bold attack to strike terror in their enemies. Sending a war party to penetrate deep, "as far as they can without being discovered," into the enemy's country, they would attack and leave a war club near the body of a person they murdered and "make off as quick as possible." Leaving the war club "purposefully" let the enemy know what nation committed the act so they did not wreak their own vengeance on an innocent tribe. The war club also signified the aggrieved nation's demand that unless the offending nation took action to discover and punish the "author of the original aggression," the club represented the means of further avenging the injury and served as a formal declaration of war. "If the supposed enemy is peaceably inclined," Heckwelder continued, they would send a deputation to the aggrieved nation to offer a suitable apology, which typically blamed "foolish young men" who acted "altogether unauthorized and unwarranted" without the chief's knowledge. Some suitable condolence presents also accompanied the apology in order to "cover," or symbolically bury, the dead.[41]

As sachems of the Ohio nations met at Newcomer's Town, Sir William Johnson convened a "Critical Congress" of Six Nations chiefs and leading

warriors at his Mohawk valley manor, Johnson Hall. The Indian superintendent promised General Gage to do everything in his power of persuasion
to "divert the Storm" gathering on the Ohio. He therefore planned to discuss
the violence committed on the frontier and seek the assistance of the Six
Nations to "bring the troublesome Tribes about the Ohio, Ouabach
[Wabash], &, ca. to make amends." The Iroquois realized that the Shawnees'
own actions had largely led to the disorders and caused trouble among their
confederacy's members, especially alienating many Mingoes. But as they
and Johnson knew, although not an excuse, a "lawless Banditti" of white
settlers who had "surprised, & Murdered near 30 Indians, partly Shawanese,
but principally of the Six Nations [Mingoes]," bore some of the blame as
well.[42]

Johnson first had to convince the Iroquois Confederacy's leaders to help
"preserve the peace & cooperate" with the Indian Department. Together
they could also stop the "irregularities & Murders" and "remedy the abuses"
of which the Indians often complained. Simultaneously, they had to curtail
the "Artifices of the Shawanese and others" who sought to forge alliances
and engage the rest of the Indians of the area, as well as draw the Iroquois
themselves, into the smoldering war on the Ohio. After much negotiation,
Johnson managed to "withdraw the 6 Nations from among them" and concluded a treaty that kept the Iroquois, including the dependents of their
confederacy, from assisting the Shawnees.[43]

On the verge of one of his greatest accomplishments as His Majesty's superintendent of Indian affairs for the Northern Department, Johnson became "seized of a suffocation" after a particular strenuous day of negotiating
and died of a stroke at 8:00 in the evening on July 11. The next day, Colonel
Guy Johnson, William Johnson's nephew as well as son-in-law, sent an express to inform General Gage of his uncle's passing, but even to his last
breath, his final efforts had kept the war on the Ohio from spreading. The
conference observed a recess for the funeral. Two thousand mourners, including a number of Crown and colonial officials, and an impressive array
of Indian leaders attended. The latter, representing many nations and tribes,
paid their last respects to the white man they arguably trusted most. Colonel
Johnson assumed the interim superintendence until the Crown appointed
a permanent successor. Since Indian leaders already recognized him as such,
he took over the conference. Five days after William Johnson's death, July
16, Guy Johnson brought the congress to an "agreeable Termination."[44]

The representative sachems who constituted the central council of the
Six Nations, which usually met at Onondaga, agreed to help "defeat the projects of the Shawanese and their Adherents" by exercising its dominion or

influence over other nations. If necessary, they would "proceed to Extremities" against any that considered an alliance with, or supported, "the measures and designs of the Shawanese" and their allies. Cognizant that the Shawnees would attempt to convince others that the appeal to unite all of them in a general alliance against the British had originated in Onondaga, the council dispatched several deputies to articulate the confederacy's actual position. Carrying wampum that affirmed the message, the deputies warned that any nation or tribe that joined with the Shawnees would face severe consequences. The deputies assured them that all who "acted with Fidelity during the present Troubles" would receive the confederacy's support in reward. Guyasuta, the Six Nations viceroy in the Ohio area, received "private instructions" to "divert other Tribes" and isolate the Shawnees from any potential allies.[45]

In his earlier correspondence asking William Johnson to use his "Interposition with the 6 Nations as Moderators" to prevent a general Indian war, Governor Penn had succeeded giving the old and new Indian superintendents his view of the situation, albeit from his colony's perspective. The Pennsylvania governor's one-sided account of the "distress" on the frontier stated, "Tho in so many Instances aggressors," the Virginians "chuse to consider themselves as the persons injured." The resulting war, he said, would only provide them the pretext to take the opportunity to cross the Ohio and take possession of the "Country even beyond the Limits of purchase" negotiated with the Six Nations at Fort Stanwix in 1768. That made preventing a general war more complicated, since the Indians who were not a party to the treaty could find common cause and join an alliance with the Shawnees. Because he knew it had long been the plan of some Ohio Indians, including some of their Mingo emigrants, to challenge Six Nations suzerainty, Johnson believed it imperative for the Crown to immediately address the Indians' grievances.[46]

Seeking to exercise the leverage that had long benefited the Crown because of their alliance, Johnson urged the Six Nations to immediately express their vehement disapproval of the Shawnees' actions and demand they cease committing all such cruelties against the settlers. Otherwise, he warned, their "Reputation as a powerful Confederacy will greatly suffer in the Eyes of the English." The Six Nations agreed to "check the incursions by their dependents who run about like drunken men and ought to be disarmed by those who are sober." If the Iroquois could not control their people on the Ohio, Colonel Johnson warned, "the English should be obliged to raise their powerful arm against them, which might have dreadful consequences."[47]

Despite the reduced tensions with the Cherokees, rumors of and actual Indian sightings still ran rampant, and Captain William Russell reminded Colonel Preston that Fincastle County inhabitants remained vulnerable to "a Stroke from the Northward [Shawnee] Indians." Captain James Robertson (not the emissary to Chota of the same name) reported that the men of his company had discovered an Indian camp on Paint Creek, and he and Captain Joseph Cloyd had stopped at the Culbertson's Bottom settlement waiting for more men before proceeding. When Colonel Christian learned that local militia had reported seeing "Indian signs" indicating the presence of from fifty to three hundred warriors near their communities, Major Arthur Campbell recommended the rangers not attempt a "long March" beyond the settlements into Indian country until supplied with additional ammunition. Although he had recently received twenty-five pounds of gunpowder, Christian knew that he needed more for the ranger and local militia companies to meet likely contingencies. Christian further recommended that if the county needed additional men, Preston should have the captains of the three "lower Companies" detach them. He knew that between the companies under the command of Captains William Cocke and Evan Shelby, they could easily detach fifty men without putting the security of their own communities at risk. In addition, Christian decided not to order the rangers to advance through Moccasin Gap in the Clinch Mountains as planned. Under the new circumstances, such a move would leave an avenue of approach open by which an Indian war party could advance along Sandy Creek without being detected.[48]

Instead, he assigned a different sector to each company in order to cover the approaches to the settlements, provide mutual support, and reinforce the local militias defending their communities. Remaining active and vigilant, each company could detect a war party moving through its assigned area and either move to "way lay or follow the enemy" and engage them from front or rear. If the Indians managed to strike a settlement before the company could disrupt their scheme, the rangers could pursue them. Christian posted Captain Crockett's company at the head of Sandy Creek with orders to range from there "about the head of the Clinch & Blue Stone" and stand ready to assist the militia guarding the Reed Creek and "head of Holston people" from attack. He further instructed Crockett to keep his men "ready at an hours warning" should it prove necessary for them to go to the aid of the New River communities. Captain William Campbell's company marched to cover the settlements on the lower Clinch and near Long Island on Holston and return through Moccasin Gap and back up the Clinch to rendezvous with Christian at Castle's Woods. Christian positioned the company under his personal command between the other two so that he could "hurry down" to assist the communities on Blue Stone or Walker's Creeks, cover the Clinch settlements, or march wherever else Preston might need him to go.[49]

Despite the troops' presence, a number of Moccasin and Copper Creek families abandoned their farms after hearing someone had sighted Indians—or tracks they perceived as left by Indians—near Sandy Creek. Obeying Preston's order, Captain Robert Doack drafted some men from his company and marched to the heads of Sandy Creek and Clinch River. Upon hearing that Doack had mustered a force of no more than ten, the colonel diverted Crockett's company to relieve the drafted men. On arriving, the ranger captain relayed Christian's instructions that Doack "might as well disband or range a few days" with Crockett until events or orders dictated otherwise. Shortly thereafter, the two captains received an unconfirmed report of sixteen Indians on Walker's Creek. Doack led his men to investigate and take appropriate action, but "not finding any Signs & hearing the News Contradicted," he discharged his drafted men as ordered.[50]

After hearing that residents had fled the Rich Valley and Walker's Creek area "in great Confusion," Christian ordered Doack to send scouts to investigate. The captain noted that although they had left their farms, "The People are all in Garrisons from Fort Chiswell to the Head of Holston." He observed that in the event of an attack, the community only had enough militiamen to adequately man two, but not all three, of the forts they had built. Doack recommended posting a "Sergeants Command" of seven or eight men in actual service—not taken from the rangers—at each fort to increase the "protection & encouragement" of the community. The additional full-time soldiers provided the area's farmers extra security, which also encouraged them to save their crops and not abandon their homes. Furthermore, the next time the Indians attacked, the guards provided a force "Ready to follow the Enemy" immediately, whereas local militiamen would first make sure their families took shelter in the fort before they would be available.[51] "Let the party be ever so small," Doack wrote, offering to command one such detachment regardless of size. Since a fifteen-man detachment required only an ensign and sergeant to command it, Doack indicated his willingness to serve at the pay of a subordinate officer, even if not commensurate to his rank. In seeking any assignment during the crisis, he volunteered to go wherever Preston commanded and wished rather "to be Serviceable than to look for high pay" at that critical time.[52]

When Colonel Christian and his company arrived in Castle's Woods on Sunday, July 10, he found Captain Russell well in control of the situation there. Despite the diminished threat of war with the Cherokees, the competent Russell considered the inhabitants along the Clinch more vulnerable to attack from the Shawnees than their neighbors on the Holston. Two weeks had elapsed since he sent Boone and Stoner in search of Floyd and the other surveyors. Although he had yet heard nothing, he remained confident they would find them safe and expected their return any day. The captain had other scouts "out continually on Duty" at the heads of the Louisa and Big Sandy Rivers, about Cumberland Gap, and down the Clinch, looking for any signs of either the surveyors or approaching enemy raiding parties. Patrols regularly went to "reconnoiter the very Warriours Paths most convenient" to the Clinch River settlement and with which the rangers under Christian's command had not yet become familiar. With no little amount of pride, Russell described those he commanded as "Men that may be depended on" and expressed confidence that any enemy raiders "cannot come upon us, without being discovered, before they make a stroak." Even if they evaded the patrols, Russell knew that his company would meet them with the "probability of Rewarding them well for their trouble."[53]

Although Russell's company originally voted to build two forts for the government, they had altered the plan to add a third. When Colonel Christian arrived, he noticed four forts "erecting on Clinch" to guard the frontier from invasion and shelter the local inhabitants. Russell had named the post at Castle's Woods, which also served as his headquarters, Fort Preston. Twelve miles upriver, on Daniel Smith's property, the men neared completion of Fort Christian.

Fort Byrd stood on the property of William Moore, four miles down the Clinch at the mouth of the creek that also bore the family's name. At Stony Creek, another sixteen miles down, four families had joined to fortify the home of their neighbor, John Blackmore. Although not intended as a military post like the other three, Blackmore's fort provided shelter for travelers and nearby residents. Because of its isolated location and dispersed number of inhabitants, Russell worried for their safety and the adequacy of their defenses.[54]

Despite the measures he had taken, Russell saw room for improvement and requested the county lieutenant's assistance. He described his unit's ammunition supply as "so bad" that he had little usable powder and only "fifty wt. [fifty-six pounds] of Lead." He had dutifully requisitioned more, but a week had passed since Major Campbell assured him that he could expect delivery, with no sign of the powder. The captain also requested that Colonel Preston order some of his men into actual service, or full-time duty, to better defend that part of the county. "Tho' the pay of the Country as soldiers cannot be thought Adequate to such risques," Russell explained that in a small measure it could at least encourage the people to "stand their Ground." Even if the anticipated war never started, the pay would at least offer the men some compensation for their labor in building three fortifications to defend the province's border. They could have easily avoided the drudgery, as Russell reminded the colonel, by deserting the frontier until the danger subsided. The very presence of soldiers encouraged others to refrain from abandoning the Clinch settlements and thereby expose the Holston communities to attack.[55]

Captain Campbell's company arrived in Castle's Woods the next day, Monday, after marching thirty miles up Clinch River from Moccasin Gap. Noting the two ranger companies in his community, Russell no longer concealed his disappointment that Preston and the council of war had not selected him to command one of them. Although "satisfied the gentlemen Officers appointed to the present Detachment, are worthy men . . . as Zealous to serve their Country" as the officers of his own company, he felt slighted at not receiving the assignment. However, Russell conceded that "they might Destroy some of the Enimy in a Week or two." Russell possessed military experience, leadership abilities, and an extensive knowledge of the frontier that few could match. [56] Furthermore, the memory of finding his murdered son's mutilated body just ten months before still haunted him and kindled his desire for revenge. Although the events in Powell's Valley had made this fight personal, Russell, ever the good soldier, placed the country's interests above his own.

In all, Christian now had the one hundred men of the two ranging companies, plus Russell's militia company, within his immediate command, with Crockett's forty men not far away in case of trouble.[57] Before the continued his primary mission, Christian first had to gather provisions for his rangers. He sent parties with packhorses to collect and carry one thousand five hundred pounds of flour and corn back to Fort Preston. Although in need of beef cattle, he hesitated in sending parties to Holston to drive forty head back until he knew Preston's instructions for the next phase of the operation.

Christian concurred with Russell in believing that Boone and Stoner would find the surveyors alive and soon return, although unaware by which route. Christian therefore delayed marching to the heads, or sources of the tributary streams, of the Louisa River to meet them as Preston had originally instructed. Instead, he convened a two-day council of war with the officers present at Castle's Woods to develop a course of action that would satisfy the governor's instruction for the county lieutenant to take offensive action and seek Colonel Preston's approval to execute it. Christian proposed that a force of 150 to 200 men, with five packhorses allowed for each fifty-man company to carry their "Baggage & Blankets & such like" equipage, could march the estimated 120 miles from Castle's Woods to the Ohio opposite the mouth of the Scioto. There, he would leave "the tired & lame Men" incapable of going farther to erect a small blockhouse to support the best men, who would cross the river and cover their retreat in case of defeat. Once on the north bank, the main force of 150 men would move toward the enemy town. With a "good Pilot," or guide, familiar with the trails of the area to "lead us thro' the Woods either by Night or Day," they could advance the last forty-five miles through terrain "where an Enemy would not be expected," to reach the town undetected and conduct a surprise attack.

Christian counted the forces he had available. Russell indicated he could enlist thirty volunteers from the Clinch. The three lower companies on Holston could detach seventy-five. With the 140 rangers and militia already on duty in the area, Christian had the two hundred "choice" men he needed without having to call Captain Crocket's company, which he could leave to protect the frontier. To preserve the element of surprise, the officers agreed to say nothing publicly concerning an attack on the Indian town but only disclosed that they proposed going "to the Ohio & returning up New [Kanawha] River." Although some questioned if they could rely on having a sufficient number of troops willing to cross into Indian country not knowing the plan beforehand, they had confidence that "after going so near the Enemy's Country," enough would certainly do so. In the unlikely event that a sufficient number of volunteers did not step forward to effect the expedition, they agreed that executing the alternate plan of marching up the Kanawha "might be of considerable Service" in providing security for the settlements. If the enemy attacked a settlement on the south bank during his foray, Christian would ask Preston to send him "speedy notification" so that his force could move to intercept the enemy raiders on the banks of the Ohio as they returned.[58]

While he waited for Preston's decision, Christian thought it "better to keep the Men moving slowly than have them remain in camp." He therefore distributed the 115 militiamen in actual service to the various forts to strengthen the garrisons guarding the Fincastle County frontier. As Russell had recommended, he posted thirty men each at Blackmore's fort and at the head of Sandy Creek, and ten at Fort Preston in Castle's Woods. He sent Captain James Thompson with ten men to Fort Byrd on the Moore farm, and another ten men each to James Smith's fortified home and Captain Daniel Smith's, and fifteen to Cove and Walker's Creek.[59]

While Christian and his subordinate commanders waited for Preston's decision, Colonel Andrew Lewis received new instructions from Dunmore. The governor, making his way west from Williamsburg, had now fully digested the county lieutenants' descriptions of the situation on the frontier and recognized that "so great a probability" of an Indian war required immediate action by the colony. He repeated his advice to wait no longer for the Indians to continue their attacks but to "raise all the Men ... willing & Able to go" and immediately march to the mouth of the Kanawha. After building a fort, if Lewis had sufficient forces available, the governor instructed him to advance against the Shawnees and "if possible destroy their Towns & Magazines and distress them in every other way that is possible." He told Lewis that a "large body of Men" had already marched from the Shenandoah valley under Major McDonald's command and could join him there. By keeping communication open with Fort Fincastle at Wheeling and Fort Dunmore at Pittsburgh, the governor believed the militia would prevent any more war parties from crossing the Ohio to attack Virginia inhabitants.[60]

Somewhat taken aback by the governor's apparent lack of understanding about the frontier counties' situation, Lewis immediately wrote to Preston that his lordship had taken for granted their ability to "fit out an Expedition" and ordered one. Although their "backwardness"—meaning reluctance—might have surprised Dunmore, Lewis feared the consequences of mounting an offense while preoccupied with defense elsewhere. He resolved to do something, telling Preston he would rather accept great risk doing something than to allow an unsuccessful outcome by doing nothing. He therefore ordered the county lieutenant of Fincastle to embody a force of at least 250 men to take the field under his personal command.[61]

After he received Lewis's instructions, Preston sent a circular letter to the field officers and captains commanding companies to raise the county's "reasonable" quota of volunteers. Preston believed the men "should turn out cheerfully" to defend their "Lives and Properties," which had "been so long exposed to the Savages," who had enjoyed "too great success in taking [them] away" from the settlers. Moreover, if they neglected to act, they may never have "so Fair an Opportunity of reducing our old Inveterate Enemies to reason." He assured them of Dunmore's commitment to the project's success and confidence that the House of Burgesses would vote the necessary expenditures that would "enable his Lordship to reward every Volunteer in a handsome manner over and above his Pay." With that, Preston added the enticement of a time-honored bonus. "The plunder of the Country," he continued, "will be valuable, & it is said the Shawanese have a great

Stock of Horses." Taking items with intrinsic military value as spoils of war
from the enemy— whether strictly martial and purchased by the government, or sold on the market with the proceeds distributed to the soldiers,
or converted to private use by individual recipients—represented an added
inducement for enlisting. The practice also served as a means of forcing
one's enemy to bear the economic burden of supporting military operations
in his country.

The invasion of Shawnee territory was intended as a reprisal for the series of attacks in the backcountry and not a war of conquest. A successful
campaign offered two immediate benefits. First, it would be the only way
of "Settling a lasting Peace with all the Indian Tribes" whom the Shawnees
had urged to engage in war against Virginia. Second, if the Shawnees suffered the same manner of destruction as they had inflicted, with their towns
plundered and burned, cornfields destroyed, and the people "destressed,"
the punitive expedition could render them incapable of attacking Virginia
again in the future and possibly oblige them to "abandon Their Country."
Preston therefore hoped the men would "Readily & cheerfully engage in the
Expedition." He told the men he and other county lieutenants expected "a
great Number of Officers & Soldiers raised behind the Mountains" to join
the expedition for the same motive of home defense. Preston assured the
Fincastle County men that they would serve in their own units commanded
by their own officers and not be reorganized into units other than those in
which they enlisted. He then informed potential volunteers that fifty-four-
year-old Colonel Andrew Lewis would command the expedition. Despite
his advanced age, the country called on him again for his "Experience,
Steadiness & Conduct on former Occasions." Lewis was respected and ad-
mired throughout the frontier districts, and the knowledge that he was in
command enhanced the effort to attract volunteers.

Preston concluded his letter with an appeal to their pride, as he called
every man to give his utmost exertion because so much depended on the
expedition's success. With "the Eyes of this & the Neighboring Colonies" on
them, he challenged Fincastle County to not leave it to its neighbors to contribute the men, provisions, and any of the other necessities they could
spare. Their governor had called them. Their county stood ready to pay and
support them. Other counties would join and assist them. They fought in
a good cause and had "the greatest Reason to hope & expect" heaven would
bless them with success and defend them and their families against "a parcel
of Murdering Savages." The opportunity for which they had waited and
wished for so long had arrived. "Interest, Duty, Honor, Self-preservation,
and every thing, which a man ought to hold Dear or Valuable in Life," he

Andrew Lewis possessed a wealth of diplomatic and military experience on the frontier. He came to Virginia at a young age when his father fled from Ireland in the 1730s, and settled in Augusta County. He learned surveying and became an officer in the militia. He served as an officer in the colony's standing forces from the beginning and through the French and Indian War, rising to the rank of major in Washington's Virginia Regiment. During Pontiac's War he commanded a battalion in the colony's service, and became the county lieutenant of first Augusta, then the newly established Botetourt County. He also served as a Virginia commissioner at the Treaties of Fort Stanwix, Hard Labour, and Lochaber, and was elected to several terms in the House of Burgesses of the General Assembly. In 1774, Lord Dunmore appointed him as commander in chief of the Southern Division of his army during the Indian war.

said, "ought to Rouze us up at present; and Induce us to Join unanimously as one man to go [on] the Expedition." Preston reminded them of the hardship that awaited them but assured them of the rewards victory would bring.[62]

Virginians in the frontier counties began to hear the strains of the song known as "The Recruiting Officer" with increased frequency in 1774. They heard it played and sung in taverns and ordinaries, at social gatherings, and by soldiers on the march. Although it was an old song that dated from the first decade of the eighteenth century, it remained a popular air, and a most appropriate one for the time and place.

The song originated in 1707 during Queen Anne's War. Following passage of the Acts of Union, which united England and Scotland as the kingdom of Great Britain, Virginians, like other colonists, proudly identified themselves as British subjects. European conflicts increasingly included operations in the New World, and American Britons sacrificed blood and treasure for the empire. *The Recruiting Officer*, George Farquhar's acclaimed musical comedy from the London stage, made its way across the Atlantic and remained in America as a legacy of Queen Anne's War. A professional theatrical company toured the colonies, and as in Britain, the play became an immediate hit and perennial favorite. The first edition of William Parks's *Virginia Gazette* advertised that "The Gentlemen and Ladies of this Country" staged *The Recruiting Officer* in Williamsburg in September 1736.[63]

For the title song, Farquhar adapted the melody of Thomas D'Urfey's familiar ballad "Over the Hills and Far Away," added the accompaniment of a single drum beating the army's "Recruiting Call," and penned new lyrics. Also known as "The Merry Volunteers," the song became popular in its own right, especially among veterans and members of the militia. After Governor Dunmore instructed the frontier county lieutenants to raise troops to fight the Indians, recruiting officers, some accompanied by drummers beating the familiar call, appeared at muster fields, courthouse squares, and wherever military-age men gathered. During summer 1774, Virginians heard "The Recruiting Officer" almost everywhere:

> *Hark! Now the drums beat up again,*
> *For all true Soldiers, Gentlemen,*
> *Then let us 'list, and march, I say*
> *Over the hills and far away.*[64]

WHEN WHITE EYES returned to Pittsburgh on July 23, McKee immediately convened a council for the colonial officials to learn the latest news from the Indian side of the Ohio. The message the Delaware chief delivered to "our Brethren of Pennsylvania . . . and Virginia" laid to rest all doubt as to the Shawnees' intentions. He told them that Sir William Johnson, "with our Uncles the Five Nations, the Wyandots, and all the Several Tribes of Cherokees and Southern Indians," had spoken. They all told the Delaware to "hold Fast the Chain of Friendship" and be strong in refraining from taking the warpath. To that end, he said, the various bands of Western Delawares, including the Munsees, "will sit still at our Towns . . . upon the Muskingum" and maintain the peace and friendship "between You and us."

Since the Pennsylvanians desired to keep the road between them "clear and open" so the traders could pass safely, the Indians asked that the white people not allow their "Foolish young People to Lie on the Road to watch and frighten our People by pointing their Guns at them when they Come to trade with you." Such behavior scared "our People" and "Alarmed all our Towns, as if the White People would kill all the Indians" regardless of whether they were friends or enemies. White Eyes turned to the Virginians and told them that the Delawares "now see you and the Shawanese in Grips with each other, ready to strike." At a loss, they said they could do or say nothing that would reconcile the two sides. He relayed the message that the Delawares only asked that after the Virginians defeated the Shawnees, they neither turn their attention against the other tribes nor start settlements on the north bank of the Ohio. Instead, they urged the Virginians to return to the Kanawha and south side of the Ohio after they had "Concluded this Dispute" with the Shawnees and renew the old friendship with all other nations.

Croghan replied that the Shawnees had exhibited evident proof they did not mean to be friends with either the Delawares or the Virginians. He therefore asked White Eyes to approach the Delawares to ask if they would not think it prudent that some of their warriors accompany the Virginia troops when they go to "Chastise the Shawanese." Such a service would not only shield them from their common enemy, but they could help the Virginia soldiers make a "proper Distinction between our [Indian] Friends and our Enemies." White Eyes replied that he would take that message to the Delaware chiefs at Kuskusky and return with their answer.[65]

Alexander McKee provided Aeneas Mackay a copy the speeches White Eyes had brought back from Newcomer's Town in order to transmit them to Governor Penn. Before forwarding the packet to St. Clair, he met with Devereux Smith, Joseph Spear, and Richard Butler to discuss a plan they wished to recommend to the provincial government in Philadelphia. They felt it absolutely necessary for Pennsylvania to reward the fidelity of the Delawares, especially "such of them as will undertake to Reconnoiter and Guard the frontiers of this Province . . . from the hostile Designs of the Shawanese." Since performing military service on behalf of Pennsylvania would prevent them from following their own occupations of trapping and hunting, the committee thought it "no more than right to supply all their necessary wants while they continue to Deserve it so well at our hands." In the absence of a Pennsylvania armed force, instead of subsidizing a colonial militia, these men of means in Pittsburgh favored a defense policy in which their provincial government hired Delaware warriors as mercenaries to defend them.[66]

St. Clair, in turn, forwarded the speeches along with the latest intelligence concerning the crisis on the frontier to Governor Penn. He said that any prospect of an accommodation between the Shawnees and Virginians was certainly over, and had been for some time. He added his unwavering insistence that it did not appear that the Shawnees had any hostile intentions against Pennsylvania. He then endorsed the recommendation for "engaging the services of the Delawares to protect our Frontier" and believed that it would undoubtedly be a good policy if it did not cost too much. Although

the magistrate anticipated the Indians would be "very craving" of any rewards, he did not think the provincial assembly should overlook the proposal. He recognized a single consistent truth: "These Indian disturbances
will occasion a very heavy Expence to this Province." Therefore, regardless
of whether or not they engaged the services of their warriors, St. Clair urged
that the province secure the Delawares' friendship "on the easiest terms possible." He neither trusted Croghan with a free authorization to spend the
province's money nor wanted to insult the Indians with too parsimonious
a gesture. If the governor thought it was proper to reward the Delawares
with presents, St. Clair recommended that he specify what items he wanted
Croghan to obtain and give them.

Captain White Eyes and John Montour assembled and began preparing
a party of warriors, including Delaware and Six Nations Indians, who
planned to accompany Virginia militia troops if they crossed the Ohio River
to attack the lower Shawnee towns. Connolly once again approached St.
Clair and requested that he order some of the Westmoreland rangers to cooperate and join the expedition as well. The Pennsylvania magistrate again
refused and sent specific orders that they were not to cross the rivers that
defined their area of operation, much less join the Virginians, "who have
taken such Pains to involve the Country in War." Instead, St. Clair still insisted that he wanted the Shawnees to know "this Government [Pennsylva-
nia] is at Peace with them" and would so remain so long as the Indians did
not invade the east side of the Monongahela and cause "mischief." Such action, he warned, would result in an immediate declaration of war and swift
reprisal by the Pennsylvanians. [67]

IN MID-JULY, Governor Dunmore established his temporary headquarters
at Greenway Court, near Winchester, the estate of the county lieutenant of
Frederick County, as well as his fellow peer of the realm, Thomas Fairfax,
Sixth Lord Fairfax and Baron of Cameron. Toward the end of the month,
Dunmore ordered some weapons and ammunition from the provincial
magazine at Williamsburg brought west to supply some of the units he
called out for service. On Wednesday, July 27, a convoy of wagons loaded
with "300 stand of arms, with the proper accoutrements," including muskets, bayonets, and cartouche boxes, as well as eight casks of sifted gunpowder, left the capital for Winchester.[68] Dunmore, the former British army
captain, now commanded a field army preparing for war.

CHAPTER 8

On His Majesty's Service

The Militia Prepares

June–August 1774

SEVEN HUNDRED Virginia militiamen concentrated at Wheeling during the latter part of July. Those under the command of Major Angus McDonald prepared to conduct an operation as the others finished construction of Fort Fincastle under the supervision of Captain William Crawford. Located on high ground that dominated the south bank of the Ohio River at the mouth of Wheeling Creek, the fort guarded the colony's frontier from invasion and offered shelter to area inhabitants in time of danger. The substantial post also served as a base from which patrols ranged the surrounding area to detect approaching enemy war parties and could serve as a forward supply magazine to support offensive operations on the north bank.

As the companies performed routine duties and trained for upcoming missions, McDonald and his subordinate officers completed their plans. Before Lord Dunmore expanded the mission originally proposed by Connolly, he had designated Captain Crawford to lead the foray into Indian country. After the governor assigned McDonald to lead the raid in his stead, Crawford remained in command of a battalion of between two hundred and three hundred men to continue improving the post and its functions as a fortification, logistical base, and communications link between Fort Dunmore (Pitt) and the post planned for construction at the mouth of the Great Kanawha. Their mission went far beyond construction. Crawford's companies also supported local militia units and conducted rigorous local patrols. Most important, Crawford and his men would lend McDonald's expeditionary battalion any assistance it needed, especially to cover its retreat to Fort Fincastle if the mission went badly.

McDonald commanded the larger contingent at the fort. The county lieutenants and Connolly had detached eight companies, or about four hundred men, commanded by Captains Michael Cresap, George Rogers Clark, Hancock Lee, William Linn (or Lynn), Daniel Morgan, Henry Hoagland, James Wood, and John Stephenson (or Stevenson). Just before departing on their mission, McDonald held a council of war at which the officers "unanimously determined" to cross the Ohio and march to and destroy the "Shawanese Town called Wagetomica, situated on the river Muskingum."[1]

Loaded into a flotilla of canoes, the battalion departed Fort Fincastle on Tuesday morning, July 26. After moving the twenty miles down the Ohio to the mouth of Fish Creek—on the Virginia side—the battalion crossed to the opposite bank and landed just below the mouth of Captina Creek. After leaving the canoes, the battalion traveled light, having brought neither packhorses nor wagons and artillery. Each soldier carried enough ammunition and rations to last seven days. The rest of the food remained in the canoes for the trip back to Fort Fincastle. Officers and sergeants quickly reformed and accounted for their men, checked weapons and ammunition one last time, and reported to their captains. Satisfied, the company commanders informed McDonald and stood ready for the major's command.

To advance along the ninety miles by traders' paths—crisscrossed by other minor Indian trails—that defined the route to the Upper Shawnee Towns, the battalion relied on three experienced woodsmen and their familiarity with the area to serve as "pilots," or guides. Jonathan Zane, Thomas Nicholson, and Tady Kelly, all members of the Wheeling settlement's militia company, took their places with the lead element.[2] McDonald gave the march order and the vanguard moved out. The main body followed after waiting the proper interval as prescribed in the chapter on detached service against irregulars in *petite guerre* operations from Bland's *Treatise on Military Discipline*.

As the battalion advanced, the vanguard reconnoitered any "woods, copses, ditches, hollow ways" through or close to which the column had to march, and paid particular attention to "every place where any number of men can lie concealed." Bland's treatise and his own experience told McDonald that the interval between the vanguard and main body must depend on the nature of the country. In such "an enclosed country," that interval at times could "hardly exceed two hundred yards." The main body therefore followed close enough to support the vanguard and come to its relief if ambushed, but not so close that both "should be attacked and cut off by a superior party" at one stroke.[3]

They had gone only a short distance when a violent storm drenched the soldiers and ruined many of the cartridges in their loaded weapons. As soon as the rain stopped and the sky cleared, McDonald ordered a halt so the men could reload with dry powder. Each soldier first attempted to fire his weapon in a hollow log to muffle the sound, thus limiting the chance of inadvertently revealing their presence to any enemy warriors lurking nearby. After extracting misfired charges, every soldier reloaded his weapon with a fresh cartridge.[4]

As the column advanced on Sunday, July 31, the men in the vanguard saw three Indians approaching on horseback at the same time the warriors noticed them. After a brief mutual hesitation, the Indians wheeled their horses about as one soldier raised his weapon and fired. He missed, but before another man could fire, the warriors rode back in the direction from which they had come.[5] With sunset approaching, McDonald ordered the battalion to halt and form a hasty defensive position for the night. With sentinels posted, the men prepared rations for the evening meal and the next morning's breakfast. Except when they stood a tour as sentry, the men slept on their arms until the early morning reveille.[6]

On the assumption that the previous day's encounter had alerted the enemy to the battalion's presence, the officer commanding the vanguard ordered "a Serjeant, and six to twelve men, to advance before him . . . to reconnoiter all suspected places."[7] When the pilots heard what sounded like a man's cough in the distance, it confirmed everyone's suspicion that they were not alone. Suddenly, members of the advance party took cover when they saw three warriors walking on the trail toward them. They remained silent and poised for action until the Indians came within musket range when Private Martin Owens fired but missed. The three braves gave their war whoops and quickly withdrew.[8]

With an engagement imminent, the Shawnees' plan may have resembled a scenario described by Bland where they set "the usual decoy, by which people are drawn into an ambuscade." The leaders posted "small parties" of men "at some distance" from where the main force waited in concealment. The first groups of braves were to open fire as the soldiers approached. After McDonald deployed his battalion and returned fire, the warriors would exchange only a few rounds, then slacken their resistance and begin to withdraw. When the Virginians pressed their imagined advantage, the warriors would "shew as if they were frightened and retire with precipitation" toward the main force's position. The militiamen, flush with apparent victory, would become less cautious as they advanced beyond any support units or potential reinforcements. As the troops broke ranks to pursue what they perceived to be a defeated enemy, the main Shawnee force would open fire from their concealed positions and begin to surround their now-disorganized enemy. The Virginians would realize too late that they had entered a well-planned ambuscade and were now cut off from rescue or retreat.[9]

To counter this tactic, McDonald deployed the battalion into three mutually supporting columns. The center column, which he accompanied, had four companies, while the flanking columns each had two. In the event of trouble, the formation permitted the battalion to quickly deploy into a "Hollow Square" to defend against an attack from any direction, form into line to meet the enemy head on, or conduct a hasty single or double envelopment with the left and right columns maneuvering against the enemy's flanks while the middle column fixed their attention in front.[10]

About a half mile from where the pilots spotted the three Indian scouts, the path entered a swampy area. The soft ground, cut by streams and thickets, slowed the battalion, constricted its intervals, and reduced the room in which it had to maneuver. Adapting the movement to the terrain, the battalion's three columns contracted into a single column of three files until the vegetation began to thin out once more, and pressed cautiously forward. Up ahead, concealed behind trees, logs, and man-made blinds on both sides of the path, about fifty warriors waited quietly and patiently in ambush. When the Virginians came within range, the Indians opened fire. McDonald ordered the companies of the center column to form on line and the right and left columns to "file off" in an attempt to surround the enemy. Maneuvering on the right, Captains James Wood's and Daniel Morgan's companies advanced through the woods, came on line, and attacked the left side of the ambuscade in what Private Evan Morgan described as "some severe fighting." The warriors gave way to the superior numbers but conducted a fighting withdrawal as they fired "from every rising Ground." In order to slow the advance and determine their opponents' strength and intent, the Indians continued the shoot-and-run tactic for about thirty minutes, "when at last they ran" and broke off the engagement.[11]

At one point during the fight, Captain William Linn led his company across a ravine, fording the stream at the bottom, while under enemy fire. Both he and Private Dudley Martin fell wounded as they climbed the far bank and tried to reach the cover of a large tree at the top. Two bullets struck Linn, one in the breast and the other in a shoulder, while Martin took one in his left shoulder, which possibly also hit Linn. As he stood to reload behind a tree, a soldier named Wilson saw the Indian who shot his comrades using the same tree they had tried to reach. Wilson shot and killed the warrior when he emerged from his cover to finish off and scalp Lynn and Martin. Tradition holds that Wilson had not completed his reloading when he saw his target, and in his haste to even the score fired both the bullet and his ramrod at the enemy.[12]

In such circumstances, Bland's manual instructed a commander to keep his men in one body where they can mutually assist one another. It also cautioned that "if they should separate in pursuing those they beat, the enemy may destroy them one after another, with such an inconsiderable number of troops."[13] With the battalion "much scattered in the woods," McDonald halted the advance to permit company commanders to rally and reform their units. While the troops reloaded their weapons, redistributed ammunition, and gathered the wounded, the captains reported that the battalion had suffered two dead and five wounded in the half-hour skirmish. The soldiers had taken no prisoners, and a search of the battlefield found only one dead warrior, presumably a Delaware. Considering the well-known enemy practice of hiding or carrying away their casualties, the Virginians claimed—or believed—they had killed four "and wounded many more" Indians. Major McDonald called his subordinates together to assess and discuss the situation and plan their next move.[14]

Leaving a detachment of twenty-five men to guard and tend to the wounded and bury the dead, the battalion resumed its advance toward the Upper Shawnee Towns, now only five miles away. As they approached, members of the vanguard observed a lone Indian heading up the bank of the nearby creek. Suspecting that the warrior had been in the recent skirmish, one of the soldiers shot and wounded him, but he managed to escape.[15] When they reached the Muskingum River on the opposite side from the town, Virginia scouts observed Indians "posted on the bank, intending to dispute our passage." Both sides commenced a desultory exchange of musketry as men endeavored "to conceal themselves behind trees, logs, &c., watching an Opportunity to fire on each other." The militiamen killed one Indian without suffering any losses of their own in the exchange.[16] When the main body of troops arrived, they deployed along the river facing the Indian town.

Between shots, Joseph Nicholson, one of the battalion's interpreters, called out to the Indians in the Lenape language and told them that he belonged to the Six Nations. A Delaware replied and asked if he was Simon Girty, one of Alexander McKee's Indian Department interpreters. Nicholson answered in the negative and said Girty had remained back at Fort Pitt. The Delaware then asked him to give his name, and when Nicholson identified himself, the two recognized each other as long-time acquaintances. In the conversation, the Delaware said his people wanted peace, and Nicholson invited him over to talk with the promise that no harm would come to him. Trusting the Virginian at his word, the Indian crossed the river to the side held by the soldiers. Recognizing the opportunity thus presented, McDonald issued orders to ensure the man's safe passage and forbade anyone to approach or "molest" the Indian while they talked.[17]

After he entered the battalion's position, the Indian informed McDonald "of the good Disposition of the Delawares to the white people." The envoy told the major that John Gibson and William Wilson, two well-known Indian traders, "had been sent from Pittsburgh," implying on behalf of Pennsylvania interests, to warn them that a party of Virginians had marched against some of their towns to destroy them, but they did not know which ones. McDonald assured the envoy that the Virginians came to only fight the Shawnees and hostile Mingoes. He emphasized that Virginia's governor had given him "particular instructions not to molest any Indians at peace with us, and particularly the Delawares." He added that Governor Dunmore, as well as Virginians in general, remained well aware of the pacific motives of the Delawares, who had on many occasions behaved "friendly to the white people" by rescuing several from the Shawnees and Mingoes and had "taken great pains" to persuade them against attacking the white people.[18]

Hearing that his people were respected by the Virginians brought the envoy great satisfaction. He admitted that when the Pennsylvania traders characterized the Virginians "as cruel, barbarous people, that would spare none of the Indians," his people initially believed them. Because the Delawares wished to remain neutral, what the Pennsylvanians had said left them "in great suspense" in deciding what course to follow, as war in the Ohio valley became more likely. He therefore requested that the Virginians not press the attack against their towns until after he brought the chief named Winganum to meet and talk with McDonald.

A short time after he departed on this diplomatic mission and recrossed the river, the envoy encountered two other Delawares. Believing that their meeting presented another opportunity to avert catastrophe, he convinced his new companions to accompany him back to the Virginians. They fortuitously met a Mingo warrior before crossing the Muskingum, and the three Delawares succeeded in convincing him to join them in their effort. The four-man peace delegation then crossed with a guarantee of safe passage to meet with McDonald, even though the Mingo had fought against their hosts earlier that day.[19]

While McDonald busied himself "commencing a council" with the new Indian delegates, a precarious quiet settled over that portion of the river. Private John Hargiss of Captain Michael Cresap's company watched an Indian "occasionally popping up his head in the fork of a low tree" to observe the Virginians and resolved to shoot the man. After loading his rifle with a double charge of powder and an additional ball, he fixed his point of aim on the space just above the fork and waited for the warrior to raise his head once more. When he saw the brave's painted face appear above his rifle's front sight post, Hargiss squeezed the trigger. The lock released the hammer holding the flint, which struck the frizzen, causing a shower of sparks to ignite the primer in the pan with a flash. Following a discernable split-second delay, the propellant in the chamber exploded. The resulting charge of gas seeking an escape from the bore sent the projectiles spinning toward and then out of the muzzle at the target, while a cloud of dense, acrid smoke engulfed the rifleman. Both bullets struck the warrior in the neck and killed him instantly. Although his companions later dragged the body away from the riverbank and buried it, Hargiss located and scalped the remains the next day.[20]

Back at the council fire, the Mingo and new Delaware arrivals, like their companion before them, said they "were exceedingly pleased" with the friendly reception they received "in that bloody Path" where earlier the same day the "Shawanese and Mingoes had passed to murder" their current hosts. The Indians marveled at the contrast between what they had experienced firsthand and what they had expected from listening to the Pennsylvanians' "terrible accounts of the Virginians intending to cut them off—meaning destroy them—for the sake of their lands." Quite to the contrary, these Delawares found the Chanschican, or Long Knife, "a good people." The "three among so many warriors" could have easily fallen prey to the Virginians to "cut us in pieces" had what the Pennsylvanians told them proved true. Instead, Virginia soldiers welcomed the Delawares as friends, "which will make the hearts" of their "great men and Nation glad when we tell them this good news."

The envoys recounted their nation's effort to remain neutral and explained that the Delaware chiefs had "called our people from among the Shawanese and Mingoes" so that the Virginians would not treat them as enemies as well. In attempting to avert war, Delaware leaders had advised the Shawnees not to attack the whites and warned them of the consequences they could expect if they did. They had told the Shawnees and Mingoes that they would gain nothing from a war but only provoke the whites to retaliate with overwhelming force to destroy them.[21]

With McDonald's battalion poised on the outskirts of Wakatomika, the Pennsylvanians' prediction appeared on the verge of fulfillment. However, the major developed a plan to spare the Shawnee and Mingo towns, including Snake's Town. The soldiers from the Dunkard and Muddy Creek settlements knew that the leading warrior called Captain Snake had accompanied Logan in June when he raided their communities and killed and captured some of their neighbors, including members of the Spicer family. McDonald therefore sent the Mingo warrior, who agreed to act as an ambassador, back to the Indian side of the river with his proposal. The major offered to spare their towns if by the next morning the hostile Mingoes and Shawnees first delivered two of the white women they held captive—possibly including Betsy Spicer—as a sign of good faith. Second, the ambassador and two other warriors had to submit themselves to serve as hostages "until their great Men and ours could talk together." The ambassador then left the camp on his mission to spare the Mingo and Shawnee towns. The three Delawares left in the "most friendly manner," and as neutrals, they sought to warn their Shawnee and Mingo neighbors to evacuate their women, children, and effects before the Virginians attacked.[22]

During a lull in the fighting, the Virginia officers held a council of war to discuss plans for winning the battle. Differences of opinion arose concerning the feasibility and advisability of crossing the river and conducting a frontal assault against an enemy who seemed determined to defend Wakatomika. In addition to the officers, some of the men occasionally "entered warmly" into the discussion and expressed their opinions. Private Patrick Haggerty of Wood's company supposedly exclaimed, "Captain, wherever you'll lead us, even to the hot regions below, I'll follow you!" The officers agreed on a plan in which the main body remained in place "to amuse the Indians" and hold their attention that night while a detachment found a place to cross lower down the river at first light.[23] McDonald therefore ordered Captains Michael Cresap Sr. and Hoagland to lead their companies "some considerable distance" downstream below Wakatomika and cross the river at daybreak. Once in position, they would cover the crossing of the other companies in the morning, and the entire battalion would attack the enemy's flank.[24]

The two companies spent a restless night preparing for the mission. Cresap repeatedly cautioned his men to keep themselves and their weapons ready, concerned that the enemy could launch an attack or ambush them as they crossed the river. In spite of his concerns, he remained confident that his men would perform well. Two hours before dawn on August 2, he silently formed his company, inspected their weapons one last time, and led

A Delaware Indian.
with his Tomohawk Scalping knife &c

While some individual Delaware warriors volunteered to fight the Virginians with the Shawnees and their Mingo allies, most remained neutral and some even served as scouts for Dunmore's forces in the war of 1774.

them forward. As he had anticipated, his and Hoagland's companies encountered some opposition and became engaged in a light skirmish as soon as they crossed the river. They drove the enemy back, established their position on the far bank, and waited for the rest of the battalion to follow. Meanwhile, McDonald remained in position with the six remaining companies and waited for the Mingo envoy to return with the hostages and redeemed captives. When they did not appear, he gave the order to march. After everyone had crossed the river, Major McDonald gave the order for the battalion to advance along the river toward Wakatomika.[25]

About two miles short of the objective, the battalion's scouts encountered the Mingo ambassador walking toward them from Wakatomika. They immediately escorted him to McDonald and the interpreter for interrogation

as the battalion continued its advance. The lead units had not gone another
two hundred yards when the men of Cresap's company, deployed on the
right flank, discovered a party of Indians waiting in ambush under the cover
of the riverbank. When the Virginians outflanked the ambuscade, the Indians abandoned their position and fled. The pursuing soldiers engaged the
retreating warriors in a running skirmish. Cresap killed one straggling brave
with a tomahawk in hand-to-hand combat. Although they counted no other
Indian bodies, blood trails indicated that his men had killed or wounded
several more.[26]

Meanwhile, the ambassador told McDonald he had returned to inform
him that the other Indians would not agree to deliver any hostages. Although the soldiers respected the fact that he had kept his word and returned to inform the major of the results of his negotiation, they suspected
that he had known about the ambuscade and had deliberately not apprised
or warned them of it. To recognize his friendly offices, the troops spared
his life, but they secured and retained him as a prisoner of war.[27] Had the
ambuscade inflicted many casualties among their comrades, the Virginians
might not have proved so forgiving.

The Virginians reached Wakatomika and found "men's scalps hung up
like Colours" but all the towns evacuated. By this eighth day of the expedition, the troops had consumed most, if not all, of the provisions they had
carried from Fort Fincastle. They therefore helped themselves to prepared
food they found at the dwellings and all the provisions they could carry
from the enemy's storehouses to supplement their remaining rations for
the march back to the Ohio. The troops proceeded to burn all the buildings
in the one Mingo and five Shawnee villages and cut down seventy acres of
standing corn in the surrounding fields. In contrast, the soldiers respected
the Delawares' neutrality and peaceful disposition. Except for taking some
corn, "of which the men were much in want," the troops spared the
Delaware villages and left their dwellings and possessions unmolested.[28]

After gathering the plunder it had taken from the enemy, the battalion
returned to the location where the wounded had remained since the August
1 engagement. After allowing the men a short rest, McDonald gave the order
to march cross country toward the Ohio. Subsisting on one ear of corn each
day plus what edible plants they could gather and a "scanty supply of game,"
the men became increasingly famished. Fortunately, no Shawnee or Mingo
war parties interfered with the movement.[29]

After encountering what Private Evan Morgan described as "hardships
and perils that cannot here be detailed," McDonald's exhausted and hungry
battalion completed its dreary return trek to the banks of the Ohio. Near

the mouth of the Captina, they loaded onto their canoes, paddled back to Wheeling, and marched into Fort Fincastle on August 9. The major prepared his report as the men rested and regained their strength before marching home. During those few days, they learned that Governor Dunmore had planned to end the war by invading Shawnee country with two large divisions converging on the principal towns on the Upper Scioto. While some men, like Private William Greenway of Captain Daniel Morgan's company, remained as a frontier guard at Fort Fincastle, McDonald sent most of the others home for a well-earned leave and to prepare for the next campaign. Meanwhile, he went to Winchester to personally brief Dunmore on the results of his operation.[30]

McDonald's expedition had achieved its stated objective. The battalion had penetrated deep into Indian country and destroyed "Wahatomakie, a Shawanese town on the Muskingum . . . with all the plantations round it." The Virginians had successfully executed the mission with little loss of life, friend and foe. When taken to market, the plunder sold for only £35 11s. d3., which was divided among the men. McDonald's force had "taken three scalps, killed several Indians, and made one prisoner," suffered "the loss of only two of his people & six wounded," but offered little in the way of significant results. All factors considered, the operation was little more than a minor tactical success.[31]

The expedition demonstrated to the Shawnees that Virginia could respond in kind with reprisals of its own, but it failed to gain security for Virginia's frontier settlements. The Indian raids continued, and possibly increased in numbers and severity. Considered strategically, the raid on Wakatomika did little to change the course of the war or hasten its conclusion. If it accomplished anything, the expedition convinced Dunmore that only an invasion by overwhelming force directed against the heart of the enemy's country could achieve peace and secure the frontier from continued depredations at an affordable cost. Such an expedition would also force the hostile Indians to accept the terms of the treaties that established the Ohio River as the boundary between Virginia and Indian country.

As MCDONALD's battalion fought its way to Wakatomika at the beginning of August, an Indian war party prowled Botetourt County in the neighborhood of the Greenbrier settlements. Just a few weeks after hostile warriors had murdered Walter Kelly in a raid on his farm, tragedy struck his family again. William Kelly and his niece Sally heard musket shots coming from the direction of Arbuckle's fort as they walked along the road. They did not know that some Indians had fired at a sentry at the post, located just a half mile away at the confluence of Mill and Muddy Creeks, but they immediately realized that it meant trouble. Unfortunately, some warriors had already observed them and moved in for the kill.[32]

The two quickened their pace in an attempt to reach safety. A shot rang out, and Kelly fell to the ground. Wounded but still alive, he told the girl to leave him and run. She tried to escape, but another brave quickly caught and subdued her. The captor then forced his prisoner to watch as one of his companions "Tomhak'd" her uncle and "Cut him Vastly." The warrior then scalped his victim as he bled to death. Captain Arbuckle's men heard the noise and knew that unless they did something immediately, the settlers would never reach the shelter of the fort. The soldiers raced toward the sound of the firing with the knowledge that they represented the victims' only hope. Sadly, by the time they arrived, the warriors had already escaped with two trophies: a dead man's scalp and a young female captive.[33]

EVEN AT THIS late date in the preparations, senior officers still spent large amounts of time appointing officers to raise and command companies for the expedition. As militia leaders recruited volunteers and readied their units for the expedition into Shawnee country, the mission of defending the frontier counties against Indian attacks remained an equally essential concern. By the third week of July, Fincastle County's county lieutenant had to make sure that Majors Arthur Campbell and James Robertson, of the Lower and Upper Holston districts, respectively, took nothing for granted. The complications resulting from having to conduct concurrent offensive and defensive operations against a resourceful and elusive enemy left no room for error. The enormous responsibility rested heavily upon their shoulders. Both field officers had to maintain the credible defense of their respective districts while raising the expeditionary units, which relied largely on volunteers. In many cases this also required adequately compensating for the detachment of what were arguably the best soldiers and most competent officers going on the expedition. That both majors also intended to go on the offensive operation complicated their tasks that much more.

With August 25, the date the county's expeditionary companies expected to assemble at the rendezvous, fast approaching, Major Campbell did his best to prepare the operational contingents and provide for the defense of the Lower Holston district. Finding officers for and filling the necessary numbers of companies, and settling disputes between captains that arose when they recruited volunteers from outside their assigned company catchments, occupied much of his time. Someone had recommended that the county lieutenant consider Evan Shelby Jr., who had relocated to Fincastle County from Maryland in 1773, for a commission. A veteran of the French and Indian War, Shelby had served in both Maryland and Pennsylvania units, where he had risen to the rank of lieutenant. With the need for additional competent officers, Colonel Preston wrote to Shelby, offering and "begging acceptance" of a commission as captain "in our Militia."[34] Shelby accepted.

In the midst of the turmoil of military preparations, Captain Anthony Bledsoe unexpectedly resigned his commission. The French and Indian War veteran ended his active participation in the militia to express his displeasure at not receiving the promotion to major that he expected and believed he deserved. Although the militia would miss his leadership and experience, the county lieutenant took the opportunity to divide and reorganize Bledsoe's former command into two administrative companies. On August 2, Preston appointed Captain William Cocke and Lieutenant Benjamin Logan to form a company with a catchment that encompassed the residents of the "upper part" of Bledsoe's former command. Similarly, the colonel appointed the newly commissioned Captain Evan Shelby and Lieutenant Isaac Shelby, his younger brother, to form an administrative company composed of members from the "lower part" of the old unit's catchment. Preston then instructed Captains Cocke and Shelby to complete the "Division."[35] The Shelbys also had to raise an expeditionary company from the new catchment, plus any volunteers they recruited from Watauga.

Having divided into smaller working groups to complete their measurements of land patents along the Louisa River, Captain Floyd and three other surveyors headed toward safer areas. The group that remained with Floyd returned by way of Cumberland Mountain. They found and followed a "blazed road . . . through the gap of a large mountain" to the head of Powell's River. After the men "lost the Blazes," they moved southeast over the mountains to "Guess's [Guest's] River." Using the tributary to guide their movement, the surveyors finally reached its confluence with the Clinch. Surveyor Thomas Hanson noted in his journal that on Tuesday afternoon, August 9, he and his companions arrived at "Mr. Blackburns near Rye Cove," where they found the local inhabitants forted and prepared for war. When Floyd visited Smithfield four days later to make his report, Preston noted that although other survey parties had not yet returned, there remained "Reason to hope they are safe."[36]

Out on the Louisa [Kentucky] River, as Stoner and Boone searched for the survey parties they warned the inhabitants at Harrod's Cabin—or Harrods Town—about the danger that the commencement of hostilities posed to isolated frontier settlements. James Harrod and his followers, who had established their settlement at the far reaches of Fincastle County earlier that year, immediately decided to abandon their homes and ripening cornfields and move to the relative safety of the Lower Holston settlements until the danger passed. When Harrod learned about Dunmore's proposed expedition and Colonel Preston's call for volunteers, he asked his followers if they would join him on it. After Harrod met with Major Campbell, the field officer responsible for Fincastle County's Lower Holston district, he offered to raise a company of volunteers. Most of the men agreed to enlist on the condition that they would serve together as a single company under their own officers and not simply be assigned to complete another captain's unit. Campbell assured him that the county would honor their proposed arrangement. Harrod received a captain's commission to "Command his own Men . . . and [be] consulted as their Chief officer, on future occasions." Although Harrod's would constitute a separate company, the major explained that it would "be joined [or attached] to Capt. Russell only in making Returns, to the General officer" in order to account for their rations, allowances, and their payroll. The association not only eased Harrod's administrative burden but greatly enhanced his effectiveness as a military officer.[37]

With that resolved, Major Campbell met with Russell and explained the command relationship between the two units. Harrod had favorably impressed the major, who then sent him to meet Colonel Preston. In his letter of introduction, Campbell told the county lieutenant that the new captain "seems very forward to go against the Enemy." Campbell further recommended that Preston "encourage such a Man as Capt. Harrod, with his party, on the present occasion: as far as consistent with the discipline that may be necessary on the Expedition."[38] Meanwhile, left under the charge of his lieutenant, John Cowan, Harrod's men billeted at places that pleased them. To prevent potential friction with the local inhabitants, Campbell instructed Cowan to have the company encamp on the grounds of his own Royal Oak estate until the Holston troops could march with them to the place of rendezvous.[39]

Colonel Preston ordered Major Robertson, the officer responsible for the Upper Holston district, to recruit a company and march immediately down the New River to Culbertson's Bottom. On his arrival, he would also take command of the officers and men who had recently assembled there to perform active service in the colony's pay. Robertson expected to go on the expedition, but he knew the importance of local defense. He threw himself into the assignment with the aim of accomplishing all the necessary tasks before he had to leave for the Fincastle County contingent's rendezvous.

Robertson first addressed the assignment of officers to the district's defense. If he found that the numbers of those present exceeded the proportion that the law allowed, Preston had delegated to him the authority to discharge those who became supernumerary. However, the county lieutenant also gave Robertson the discretion to retain any officers willing to stay as volunteers, as long as they acknowledged the risk that the House of Burgesses had no obligation, and might not approve a claim, to pay them for their active duty. Since the county lieutenant did not assign a commissary officer or purchase agent, it fell to Roberts to acquire provisions and other necessities "on the cheapest and easiest Terms."[40] As specified in his instructions, Major Robertson first supervised the construction of a small stockade fort to protect the local inhabitants and accommodate the posting of a company-size garrison. The county lieutenant instructed him to keep "a just account of the Labour" so that when the colonial government paid them for their military service, Preston could make the case for granting the soldiers extra money for their construction work as well.

The unit posted at the Culbertson's Bottom stockade under Robertson's command did more than erect and garrison the post they named Fort Byrd (not to be confused with the one of the same name built on the Clinch River). When completed, the stockade encompassed a magazine for storing supplies and served as a base for conducting an active defense of the district. Robertson therefore followed Preston's instruction to use his "utmost Endeavours to prevent the Enemy from comeing by that important Pass, & to Protect the Settlers" inhabiting Culbertson's Bottom and Rich Creek. His men conducted continuous operations in which part of them rested from their last missions and prepared for the next ones, while other detachments ranged the area on patrols to detect skulking war parties seeking targets and alert the inhabitants and militia of pending attacks. Robertson's authority and responsibility also encompassed the "Care of any Scouts on that Quarter," which Preston described as "a most important duty & must be carefully looked into."

Robertson knew that the lives of local residents, including the families of militia comrades on active duty elsewhere, depended on him and his men. Although he did not have to, Preston reminded the major that not only his own and his men's lives but the company's reputation as soldiers rested on how well they attended their duty. Therefore, Preston told Robertson "to be constantly on your Guard to prevent a surprise." Given the scarcity of gunpowder, Preston particularly emphasized the imperative for Robertson to ensure the men did not engage in that "detestable practice of wantonly firing Guns without any cause." Those who did not only wasted precious ammu-

nition but unwittingly provided the enemy intelligence that could be used
to advantage. Since it alerted the Indians to their presence, war parties could
then either avoid militia patrols while on their way "to ravage the Country,"
catch them in an ambuscade, or hit them with a surprise attack and thereby
leave the settlements more vulnerable and defenseless.

Wasting or conserving ammunition was one indicator of a military unit's
morale and, by extension, its fighting ability. In addition, Robertson had to
enforce strict discipline among the men and see that the officers punctually
and faithfully executed orders. Preston therefore instructed all of his subordinate field officers, including Major Robertson, to keep "an Account &
Return of any men that proved disobedient, negligent, or mutinous." Just
as their officers read the Articles of War and the potential consequences a
court-martial could impose for violations to British regulars, Virginia officers informed militia soldiers that acts of misconduct "would result in the
forfeiture of pay" and other punishment prescribed by the Invasion Law,
and could result in "not being called upon active duty for the future."[41]

Although "continually on Horse Back among the People," Robertson reported that recruiting volunteers proceeded at a disappointingly slow pace.
With "A Great Deal of Both Good words and Bad ones," by Tuesday, July
19, he had convinced nineteen men to march two days later. With some optimism, he said that four more men had promised to report for duty at Culbertson's Bottom in another week, with an additional three or four to follow
after they harvested and put away their grain.[42]

While making his rounds one week later, on Tuesday, July 26—the same
day McDonald began his expedition against Wakatomika—Robertson visited the New River blockhouse that local residents had named Fort Dunmore. In his inspection, the major found "Six or Seven men" who had
previously left the settlement at Culbertson's Bottom, but he persuaded all
except one to return the next day. He also encountered another seven from
Blue Stone who had abandoned their homes and crops. Although they lived
at some distance from the blockhouse, Robertson promptly engaged them
to be ready for the call to service at any time with the local company. That
call came immediately.

With their tour of duty at Fort Dunmore expiring and their obligations
fulfilled, the men of Lieutenant Henry Thompson's militia detachment intended to leave for their homes in the morning. Unfortunately, the unit expected to relieve them had not arrived. To complicate matters, a returning
detachment reported "fresh Signs of Indians Seen Every Morning" while on
patrol to the nearby Forbes plantation. To garrison the blockhouse until relief arrived, Robertson stationed the men he had just engaged with a few of

Thompson's willing to remain on duty. The ten soldiers proved enough to satisfy the local settlers' security concerns and not feel the necessity to abandon the frontier. Short of both men and ammunition, Robertson expected "a Large Body of Indians" to invade the district at any time. He closed his report to the county lieutenant with uncharacteristic pessimism and pledged to "Stand by the Place" in accordance with his orders, even "if Death Should be my Fate."[43]

After he returned to Culbertson's Bottom on Thursday, Major Robertson reported that Fort Byrd neared completion. He added that he then had twenty-five privates stationed there, with ten more at "old Billy Wood's" fortified home, and repeated his request for reinforcements and more ammunition. This time, his request came with an increased sense of urgency. Under normal circumstances, scouts usually spent three days looking around outside the fort before returning, unless they saw fresh signs of Indian activity. In such cases, they returned and reported immediately. The frequency of sightings had dramatically increased to where scouts reported new intelligence every morning. Telling Preston that he expected the enemy to "give us a Salute when they Assemble their party altogether," Robertson added that they could face the enemy threat with more confidence if reinforced and resupplied with ammunition.[44]

The Fincastle County militia officers met in a council of war at Preston's home on August 2 to develop a plan for "the Defense of the Frontiers, in the absence of the Troops."[45] If the requirement to support offensive and defensive efforts simultaneously had not challenged them enough, the competition among officers trying to recruit volunteers to fill their companies resulted in additional complications. Men who had readily volunteered for active service to defend their communities at the first alarm now sought service in companies going on the expedition. If allowed to go, others had to take their places, and officers would cross-level the strength of the existing companies by transferring men if necessary. Captains commanding companies did not want to release men from their obligations to serve in their units if other captains would benefit without some kind of compensation. Robertson, for example, reported to Preston that many of the men in the Fort Byrd garrison said they would volunteer to serve under his command in the expedition against the Shawnee towns if they could get released from their previous commitments. In contrast, some men wanted nothing more than to fulfill the obligation that the law required of them. Lieutenant Thompson, whose detachment marched from Fort Dunmore—the blockhouse in Fincastle County—for home as soon as the men's active service term expired, now claimed that "his Business was So Urgent at Court" that Robertson could not prevail on him to extend his own tour of duty.[46]

Major Robertson began to suffer with a severe toothache complicated by an upper respiratory infection. Swollen eyes, fever, headache, and difficulty eating and sleeping caused him the "Greatest misery Ever any fellow was in," but he soldiered on and remained on duty. Although in extreme discomfort, he only complained that his responsibilities for coordinating the Upper Holston's district defenses allowed him no chance to raise a company for the expedition. Therefore, the dedicated officer offered to remain at Culbertson's Bottom to command the defenses of that part of the county and, if Preston concurred, requested that the county lieutenant transfer the men he had thus far recruited for the expedition to the company commanded by Captain William Ingles.[47]

Still hampered by shortages of almost every kind of supply, the major pleaded with the county lieutenant to send him some flour, gunpowder, and lead before the units going on the expedition began to assemble at the district rendezvous. On August 6, the soldiers who had served at Culbertson's Bottom since Robertson assumed command asked when they could expect the men who would free them to join the expedition. He could not answer since he had also requested the officer who would replace him to arrive in sufficient time to allow him to recruit men for his own expeditionary company and prepare to go.[48]

Lieutenant John Draper arrived at Culbertson's Bottom with a detachment of thirteen men on the last day of July, which raised the number gathered at Fort Byrd for the expedition to thirty-three. Although Robertson kept scouts out continuously, they had not found any recent signs of Indians near the fort. When Draper reported that his men saw the fresh tracks of an estimated five or six warriors near Wolf Creek, Robertson immediately sent an express with a message warning area inhabitants to be on their guard. Such alerts had become frequent, and with many of the military-age male members of area households performing militia duty, local families had gathered their livestock and a few possessions and took shelter at a nearby military post or a neighbor's fortified home.[49]

IN THE ENSUING WEEK, enemy warriors, including a party led by Logan, prowled about the New River settlements seeking targets. When scouts reported that "three or four Indians Visiting the Waste [ruined] plantations above us on the River" had set John Chapman's vacant home and outbuildings on fire, it prompted Robertson to postpone his leave home. Instead, he remained at his post to coordinate the militia effort to counter the enemy before they could harm any inhabitants or cause more destruction in the neighborhood. Lieutenant Draper marched from Fort Byrd in command of a twenty-man detachment on Sunday morning, August 7. Major Robertson had ordered him to go to Clover Bottom on the Blue Stone to find and destroy the war party. The men seemed eager to take a scalp or two, and before they marched, he offered £5 to any man in the company who brought the first Indian prisoner into the fort.[50] If they found no signs of the enemy there, Robertson instructed Draper to patrol near the Glades before going back into the garrison at Fort Byrd by way of the mouth of the Blue Stone.[51] During the march, Draper's men came across and followed tracks left by a party of four or five warriors. While they had headed in the direction of the New River settlements for some distance, the warriors had apparently scattered and foiled the attempts of the soldiers to track them. They did stop to investigate one of the ruined plantations for Indian signs. At a house the Indians had burned, one of the warriors "Left a War Club . . . well made and mark'd with two Letters I G," which were later determined to be a misreading of "L G," for Logan.[52]

Logan and three warriors, possibly the same ones who evaded Draper's patrol, had scouted the area of the east bank of New River near the mouth of Sinking Creek and observed the farm belonging to Balthazar (also known as Balzer or Palser) and Catherine Lybrook and their children. Because of the emergency, the blockhouse on the property also sheltered the neighbor families of John Chapman, John McGriff, "Widow" Elizabeth Snidow, and someone whose last name was Scott. Despite the fortification, the farm offered the raiders a tempting and lucrative target. They knew that they only had to wait until some of the occupants came out to work in the fields, tend livestock, do other chores, or just enjoy the fresh air and thus become vulnerable.[53]

On Sunday, August 7, the marauders watched as the host family's patriarch, "Old [Balthazar] Lybrook," walked toward the mill located on the creek near the riverbank. Seven boys, ranging in age from a "suckling babe" of a few months to two adolescents of thirteen years, soon appeared from out of the blockhouse. The boys first headed for the spring, about one hundred yards away, but then followed the creek another one hundred yards or so to their swimming hole, where the bank dropped nearly ten feet below the plain to the New River.[54]

The midsummer water level provided a six-foot-wide stretch of sand where the children played. Standing a few yards away in the river, a large rock created a pool where little boys could splash around and wade in shallow water without wandering into water over their heads. On the other side of the rock, the older boys could swim in the deeper water of the river channel while they took turns keeping an eye on the little ones. To reach their swimming hole, the boys descended the steep banks using gullies that erosion had cut and the traffic of thirsty animals had worn into narrow trails over the decades. Shortly after the boys arrived, the two teenaged Lybrook sisters arrived with three younger girls. After loading them into a canoe, the big girls paddled the little ones around the water above the mouth of the creek.[55]

As the children enjoyed an idyllic summer day, three Indian warriors stealthily moved into position to take them by surprise. Startled by a blood-chilling war whoop, the children looked up in horror to see one of the warriors standing at the top of the bank. Although the Indian stood between him and home, eleven-year-old John Lybrook immediately looked for ways to climb the bank and run for safety and warn the others. He managed to evade his assailant and sounded the alarm as he ran to the blockhouse. The two Snidow brothers, thirteen-year-old Theophilus and eleven-year-old Jacob, along with thirteen-year-old Thomas McGriff, attempted to swim to the opposite bank. If they made it, they could run to a neighboring fort to summon help. However, two warriors charged down the bank and splashed into the water in hot pursuit as ten-year-old John Snidow Jr. sat on the rock, frozen by fear. Not knowing what else to do, he held the two youngest Lybrook brothers, one-year-old Daniel and the few-months-old and not yet christened—therefore unnamed—infant in his arms. The two braves paused, struck and killed all three innocents with their war clubs, and, after scalping them, continued the pursuit of Thomas, Jacob, and Theo. They caught and restrained the boys on the far bank, then led their prisoners back to the rock where they forced them to watch the next act of the drama on the river unfold.[56]

When they realized the evil about to befall them, fourteen-year-old Elizabeth and thirteen-year-old Catherine Lybrook turned the canoeful of little girls about, and paddled against the current. In the vain hope that they had reached a safe distance from the danger, the older girls turned the vessel toward the bank. The girls did not know that the third warrior had shadowed their movement, and he sprang from out of the brush as the canoe glided onto shore. With a ferocious war whoop he charged directly into the canoe. Furiously swinging his war club, he murdered Elizabeth, both of the little Snidow sisters, and the Scott's daughter as he made his way aft where Catherine Lybrook sat. From where they watched on the rock, the three captive boys saw the Indian brave "Scalping the Children in the Canoe." Meanwhile, Catherine jumped out of the vessel and ran toward the blockhouse screaming for help. The warrior stood erect amid the welter, held his blood-stained scalp knife at his side in one hand while he raised the other, clutching his newly won trophies high over his head, and gave his triumphant scalp haloo. Enraged that she had escaped his grasp, the warrior chased and nearly caught the fleeing Catherine when the family dog came to her rescue. The protective canine repeatedly charged and bit his mistress's assailant on the legs and ankles. By the time the warrior shook off and struck the dog with his war club, Catherine had reached the safety of the blockhouse. John McGriff—Thomas's father—now had a clear shot and fired his musket at the Indian, whom he believed he wounded. The Indian then retreated to the riverbank.[57]

While his three companions terrorized the children, a fourth raider crept up on the mill. Hard at work, Balthazar Lybrook remained unaware of the events that had transpired outside when a musket shot rang out and wounded him in the arm. Despite the injury, he avoided capture and took refuge in a nearby cave. His attacker eventually gave up searching and re-joined the others; Lybrook remained in hiding until certain that the raid had ended. Even without the senior Lybrook's scalp, the war party had enjoyed a good day of hunting. The warriors had killed seven of their enemies, mangled their bodies, and took three prisoners, a total of ten heads. Two warriors and a "white Indian," referring to Logan, led the three prisoners away "with the greatest Caution . . . Walking on Stoney Hills the worst way Imaginable" to make it more difficult for rescuers to track and follow.[58]

Draper's patrol had returned to Fort Byrd without having found and engaged the four-man enemy war party before it struck. By then, word of Logan's attack on Sinking Creek had spread throughout the county, and on Monday, Major Robertson led another detachment that went "Constantly in Search of them" for the next two days. After the patrol returned empty-handed on Tuesday night, the major reported to Preston his belief that with so few men, the war party had "made not the Least sign we Could follow." Robertson sent the detachment out again on Thursday to "Watch About the Old Plantations" and catch any warriors who came "Skulking About" in an ambush before they did more mischief. The enemy, however, had other plans.[59]

During the two days that followed the raid on Sinking Creek, the warriors maintained a close watch on their three captives and allowed them little to eat. The war party avoided militia patrols as they moved about the area, "away up toward Clover Bottoms on Blue Stone, or Between that and the lower war Road on Blue Stone." Curiously, since that bloody Sunday, the braves neither fell on other defenseless prey nor set a course back toward

Indian country. When they finally halted to allow their captives time to eat and rest on Tuesday evening, their other actions seemed to answer any questions the boys had about the Indians' plans for them. Jacob, Thomas, and Theophilus watched the warriors dividing their powder with each other, and saw less than ten loads in all. Avoiding any combat—even attacking a farmer working alone in his field—conserved ammunition. The boys watched the warriors dress the scalps of the murdered children and realized that their captors could reduce their burden without diminishing the glory of their victory by simply substituting three scalps for three live prisoners. They had also noticed that the warriors had ominously relaxed their guard somewhat. After considering all that they knew, or thought they knew, about their captors' intentions, the boys decided to attempt an escape.[60]

Jacob and Thomas remained awake until about midnight. Certain that all of their captors had drifted sound asleep, the boys made their move. Repeated and increasingly desperate attempts to awaken Theophilus, at the risk of also alerting the Indians, failed. The pair bade their fellow prisoner a sorrowful farewell and walked into the forest. They had not gone far when the youths discovered a hollow log and hid inside. Although only a short distance from camp, their choice represented a careful, quick but not hasty, decision. Jacob and Thomas decided not to flee farther that night because it would have increased the likelihood of their recapture. The short head start they enjoyed would have quickly evaporated had they gotten lost in unfamiliar woods at night, or when they grew more fatigued as fleet-footed, well-rested braves tracked them like prey in the daylight. On the other hand, the boys knew that warriors deep in enemy territory and short on ammunition would not spend much time searching for escaped prisoners before they resumed their search for other targets or returned to Indian country. After the evidence suggested the warriors had moved on, Jacob Snidow and Thomas McGriff, "Intirely naked without Either Blankets or match Coats," eating only what fruit and vegetables they found growing wild, walked along the road until they met some scouts from Fort Byrd.[61]

On Thursday morning, August 11, Robertson and Ensign Thomas Masdin led eight or ten men on patrol and sent other scouts as far as the Glades. None of them reported any signs of Indian activity, leaving the major to surmise that the war party that caused so much damage had advanced along the Sandy River and approached the settlements by the head of the Blue Stone. He therefore ordered scouts to look "High on Blue Stone and Watch the Roads that way."

Robertson reported thirty-six men present for duty at Culbertson's Bottom and fifteen more posted at Wood's fort. The major expected that number to decrease days later when the expedition volunteers departed, but he assured Colonel Preston that Lieutenant Draper and Ensign Henry Patton commanded enough men to garrison the forts and "Likewise have a Smart Party to Range with" for the district's continued defense.[62]

The late reports of war parties encroaching near the settled areas had the soldiers, both new and old hands, "All Distracted Already for Home" and the safety of their families.[63] To address their concerns, Robertson sent a sergeant with eight men to patrol up New River as far as Rich Creek, East River, and Wolf Creek early on Friday morning to see what evidence they could find about recent enemy activity. Meanwhile, some of the scouts met with Jacob Snidow and Thomas McGriff to obtain all the intelligence "a Couple of Poor Little Boys" could provide about the war party that had held them prisoner. Based on that information, the major sent a detachment to scout the place where the boys had escaped their captors. The patrol had not gone more than three miles from Fort Byrd on the north side of the New River when they discovered tracks left by eight or ten Indians who had moved through the area since Tuesday.[64]

When Robertson submitted his next report to Preston, he cautioned the county lieutenant to keep his side of the mountains well guarded. The Upper Holston district had recently contended with numerous "Straggling little party's" of Indians who demonstrated that they could do an abundance of damage. He warned that because of their small size, the marauding parties might be able to get around the scouts and companies without being discovered. In addition to the units that deployed to give the vulnerable settlements early warning or intercept raiders before they could attack, the communities' home units had to stand better prepared to defend themselves. The major suggested that when inhabitants gathered in the protection forts, local commanders should have the authority to enlist as many men as possible in the colony's pay for full-time duty in order to keep them "Ready on any Occasion."[65]

COLONEL ANDREW LEWIS, the county lieutenant of Botetourt County as well as Governor Dunmore's principal subordinate and the commander of the Southern Division of militia defending the frontier, convened a council of war at his Richfield plantation on August 12.[66] The command included the militias of Botetourt, Fincastle, and Augusta Counties, minus the West Augusta district. Those in attendance included his Botetourt deputy and field commander, Colonel William Fleming, and their respective counterparts from Fincastle County, Colonels Preston and Christian. The council clarified the chain of command. The governor had already designated Lewis to command the Southern Division, or left wing, of the army on the expedition to the Ohio and, more recently, instructed Preston to stay behind to command the frontier defenses. Fleming therefore assumed command of the Botetourt troops on the expedition, while Christian did the same for the Fincastle County contingent. The left wing would assemble about seven miles from White Sulphur Springs at a savannah of flat ground called the Great Levels on the Greenbrier River and march on the expedition on August 30. Because it represented the point where units of three counties would join together, they called the general rendezvous Camp Union.

After defining the command relationships, the officers discussed the progress of recruitment of volunteers for the expedition and providing for the effective defense of their two counties when the units going on the operation departed. They realized that the "frequent murders committed by the Indians, & their daily appearance amongst the inhabitants" could cause some reluctance to go on the intended expedition. The colonels also understood that the apprehensive inhabitants of the frontier districts wanted a substantial protection force available in the absence of a sizable detachment of militia to the expedition. This, among other challenges, contributed to the uncertainty that the officers could raise the required numbers of men from their districts. The need to call on assistance from the neighboring Bedford and Pittsylvania Counties, as provided in the law for repelling invasions and suppressing insurrections, had become readily apparent.

The two county lieutenants therefore asked their respective counterparts to each provide two companies, or one hundred men plus the proper officers, so that both counties' frontiers might be protected during the expedition and the defenders' numbers increased. Lewis requested the commanding officer of Bedford to have his detachment march to Botetourt. Preston requested his opposite number for Pittsylvania for a detachment to cover the frontiers of Fincastle County from the head of the Clinch to Culbertson's Bottom. Since Bedford County had already started raising a company of volunteers to go on the expedition, the council of officers decided to request the county lieutenant of Pittsylvania also raise a company for the same service. If these measures failed and the numbers of troops remained insufficient to carry on the expedition, the four colonels believed that Dunmore's instructions and the Invasion Law both provided them the authority to draft men from the militia, and determined "they ought accordingly to be draughted."

With a discussion about resorting to a draft, the field officers had proposed nothing new in the conflict. For example, Privates Jacob Gillespie and

Samuel Gwinn entered Augusta County's service when drafted by their administrative companies in June. Posted to Clover Lick, they helped build and garrison a fort to guard the frontier settlements on the headwaters of the Greenbrier River against Indian raids and had engaged in "some skirmishing." Both men then volunteered to go against the Indians on the expedition when Gillespie joined the company of Captain John Dickenson and Gwinn that of Captain Andrew Lockridge. Before the end of August, they marched to the county and general rendezvous by way of Warm Springs.[67]

As one might expect in a country that relied solely on a militia for its defense, the burden of service fell disproportionately on those willing to volunteer at the first alarm. When Virginia's conflict on the frontier became more protracted, others had to assume some responsibility and fulfill their obligations and contribute to their own protection. The colony needed men to enlist for active service in order to relieve those already on duty who had also volunteered to serve on the expedition. The recent news of war parties striking the frontier showed that the threat remained very real. In a letter to Colonel Preston, Robertson recommended, "You[']l] Please to make the Officers Draft Some of their Company that has not yet been on Duty and Send them out" to Fort Byrd by Monday, August 15. On that day, he intended to allow the men on duty a chance to visit home before marching to the county's rendezvous. The major told Preston he would delay visiting his own family—again—"until I See if we Can Rub up [awaken] these Yalow Dogs A Little," and excite some of the shirkers to volunteer.[68]

Nonetheless, Robertson conceded that like all of his men, his own "helpless family is in Great fear and Indeed not without Reason." Robertson told Preston to expect the settlements closer to his own Smithfield plantation home—only ten to fifteen miles from the site of the Sinking Creek massacre—"to be in A Dangerouser Station" there than the settlements on the Holston. Thinking of the colonel's safety, the major recommended that each of the companies "keep a party Constantly on their Watch, since there is white men amongst them, they [the Indian war parties] Undoubtedly know men of the Best Circumstances," and "they Generally Aim at" their homes in the raids.[69]

PRESTON WASTED no time in seeking additional volunteers from beyond Fincastle County. Hours after returning home from the council of war, he wrote to Captain John Litton Jones to accept his "kind offer" to raise a fifty-man company from North Carolina for the expedition and offered a Virginia commission in the commensurate rank for the number of men he could "engage for that necessary service." The colonel urged him to not delay preparing his men to march to the county's rendezvous at the property of William Thompson "within Ten Miles of New River" by August 24 or 25 so they could reach the general rendezvous at the Levels of Greenbrier before August 30. Once they arrived, he assured the captain, the men would receive the same pay, as well as come under the same regulations and discipline "in the same manner as the militia from Fincastle" and all the "other Counties" and perform the same duties "as the nature of the service will admit." Preston also encouraged Jones to engage ten to fifteen additional men "to stay on the Frontier" and assured him that they would "be well used" under his personal direction.[70]

The next day, Preston wrote to Captain David Long concerning the difficulty experienced in raising his expeditionary company from only his administrative company's catchment. Given no limit to the number who could serve "for the Honour & Interest of the Country [Virginia]," it had become imperative "to send out a large Body of Men on the Occasion." Rather than "breed endless confusion and perhaps retard if not ruin the expedition" by recruiting men from another company, specifically those of Captains Shelby or Campbell, he approved Long's request to accept volunteers from Watauga. Preston also consented to issuing a lieutenant's commission to Robert Lucas if he recruited the twenty-five or thirty Watauga men needed to complete Long's company without further delay.[71]

As soon as news about the attacks on the New River and Sinking Creek reached the Lower Holston district, Major Campbell alerted his subordinates. In particular, he notified Captains Russell and Daniel Smith that "we should be strictly on our guard [lest] some straggling party should visit us." He ordered the two commanders to immediately "endeavor . . . to get the Inhabitants" in their company catchments "collected into 2 or 3 convenient places for forts, and let them keep up strict and regular Duty" until he could send them reinforcements consisting of soldiers on paid full-time duty from elsewhere in the district.[72] The major then ordered the captains in less threatened areas on that side of the district to draft forty men to reinforce Russell's and Smith's companies to keep his promise.

Concerned that the ongoing operations against the war parties in the area would cause at least a one-week delay to the start of the expedition, Campbell told the captains that all young men who volunteered to perform regular duty would receive the colony's pay for performing service at the forts.[73] He then asked Colonel Preston to order thirty more men drafted from Captain Herbert's and "the late Capt. Doack's" companies to join Smith's at his station near the head of the Clinch River. Campbell presented his rationale that by doing so he could form two companies for defense of the Clinch River settlements without interfering with recruitment for the expedition, provided the additional men served in the colony's pay. Recruiting for the expedition elsewhere in the district continued to proceed. Although the recent Indian raids were tragic, Campbell confessed that they had caused sufficient outrage to "Spirit up our people to go on the expedition." Captain Shelby, he wrote, had enjoyed some success in recruiting for his company, including twenty volunteers from Watauga.[74]

On Thursday, August 11, Major Campbell met with inhabitants of the three "upper Company's" on the Holston at the Town House to resolve a problem with the recruitment and fielding of companies. Regrettably, he had found too many officers raising parties, which inhibited building cohesion and the fielding of the required numbers of companies. The problem reached a head when Ensign Alexander Vance of Captain William Campbell's company halted the practice when he discovered men enrolled in Captain Daniel Smith's administrative company going on the expedition under Captain Russell, and Lieutenant Joseph Drake of Captain Floyd's company had actively recruited soldiers living in the catchment of Captain Campbell. When brought to light, the major did all he could to "divert them from such irregular proceedings."

According to Campbell, Drake "persisted and became very noisy" at the meeting. In the detachment Drake had enlisted, Campbell recognized nine men as "late adherents" of Isaac Crabtree's, and therefore potential disciplinary problems. A tenth man, a Private Benjamin Richardson from Campbell's administrative company, refused to go on the expedition under any but Drake's command. To further complicate matters, some of the men recruited from outside the catchment refused to serve alongside Crabtree's friends and insisted that subaltern officers from their parent companies receive appointments to serve over them in Floyd's company as well. Campbell considered assigning Drake to one of the forts instead of going on the expedition, but that would not solve the problems that threatened to disrupt that company. Knowing that he could not resolve all the disruptive issues the units faced before they reported to the rendezvous camp, he decided on another approach.[75]

As if Campbell did not already have enough problems, he learned from Floyd that Russell now seemed inclined to decline going on the expedition and, if offered, would accept command of the forces that stayed behind to defend the frontier along the Clinch River. No one could serve better in such a position. With Floyd now "fond of going" on the military expedition, Campbell knew that Colonel Preston would grant him almost anything he requested, in consideration for having led the successful and extensive survey expedition. To facilitate the substitution, Russell had purportedly offered Floyd the company of men he had raised. Although Preston could appoint Floyd to a company command on the expedition with a minimum of disruption, Campbell recommended that both Russell and Harrod go, while Captain William Herbert remained at home.[76] Preston sought another solution, reluctant to ask Herbert to "drop the Expedition a Second Time" after he willingly agreed to stay back once before already.[77]

In his approach to addressing the several problems facing the companies from his district, Campbell described each controversy in a detailed letter to Preston, leaving their resolution to his superior. Meanwhile, the major used his utmost influence to get as many of the companies as possible on the march to the county's rendezvous camp, where "matters can be more precisely regulated." Isolated from most outside distractions and amid the activities of a highly structured military environment, Preston could more effectively bring his rank and influence to bear in solving the problems. Campbell anticipated that several supernumerary officers would arrive at camp. Although they would lack specific assignments and therefore be ineligible for pay, Campbell told Preston that he expected they would elect to go on the expedition as individual volunteers rather than return home. Captain Robert Doack, who commanded the company at the head of the Clinch, had unexpectedly died in early August. Until Colonel Preston appointed a captain to fill the position permanently, Major Campbell ordered Lieutenant John Stephens to assume command of the company in the interim.

Campbell waited for orders that either assigned him to a position with the expedition or to stay behind to command the Lower Holston district's defenses. Meanwhile, he paid increased attention to logistics, a task as daunting as recruiting. The district's companies going on the expedition, as well as those remaining behind to garrison the forts, lacked sufficient supplies, especially gunpowder and flour. While the former needed to come through the colony's resources, Campbell offered to purchase flour at the going market price at his "own risque"—or personal credit—and receive reimbursement when the General Assembly settled accounts.[78] Preston directed Major William Ingles, the county's commissary officer, to deliver some flour to the district. In forming units for the defense of the district, Preston commissioned Captain David Looney and instructed him to raise a company without encroaching on the catchments assigned to the captains already appointed. In response to Campbell's concern over the number of officers raising units, the county lieutenant confided his apprehension that "there will be Occasion for as many as can be raised." [79]

In describing the situation on the frontier in a letter to George Washington, Preston wrote, "We are greatly harassed in this Country by the Enemy," noting, "In the course of this summer a number of our people have been killed or captivated by the Northern Indians."[80] Feeling "greatly Exposed"—and possibly prompted by Robertson's recommendation—Preston decided "to build a Fort about my House for the Defense of my Family."[81]

In mid-july, as militia commanders recruited companies for the expedition and after the convoy of munitions creaked over the Blue Ridge and rumbled into town, Dunmore composed a letter to the secretary of state, Lord Dartmouth, to inform the British government that he expected a war with the Indians. To justify his actions, he explained that Shawnees, Mingoes, and some of the Delawares had attacked the Virginia frontier and killed, scalped, and "most cruelly murdered, a great many men, women and children." He had ordered out many parties of militia in response, one of which attacked and destroyed one of the enemy towns, Wakatomika on the Muskingum River. The governor reported that although the soldiers killed several Indians, made one prisoner, and destroyed their town and cornfields, the raid failed to force the Indians to recall any of the raiding parties they had on "this side of the mountain."

To underscore the urgency of the situation, Dunmore added that while at dinner the evening before composing his letter, a lone survivor had escaped with news and to spread the alarm that Indian raiders had struck a farm and murdered a family no more than fourteen miles from where he lodged. He then informed the secretary that in about eight to ten days he proposed to march with a body of men "over the Alleghany Mountains, and then down the Ohio to the mouth of the Scioto." If he could take the Shawnees' lower towns by surprise, he believed he could "put an end to this most cruel war in which there is neither honor, pleasure, nor profit."[82]

Events came to a head in the last week of July. From his headquarters at Greenway Court near Winchester, the governor sent Colonel Andrew Lewis a letter in which he enumerated the warlike transgressions that "the general Confederacy of Different Indian Nations" had committed. Dunmore charged that their repeated "Hostilities," directed against Virginians and their settlements, had caused "universal Alarm throughout the frontiers of the Colony." The "Discovery of Indians & the unhappy situation of the Divided People settled over the Mountains" left him no choice other than to not only defend his people but to retaliate. He explained that he would first travel to Fort Dunmore to "put Matters under the best Regulation to Support that Country for a Barrier [and] give the Enemies a Blow that will Breake the Confederacy & render their plans abortive."

For the defensive phase, he planned to have two strong divisions shield the backcountry as they converged from opposite directions. Once the two divisions met, they would join forces to advance west like a dagger thrust deep into Shawnee country. To execute the plan, Dunmore proposed to take as many men as he could muster from between Winchester and Pittsburgh in a short time and move down the Ohio. Meanwhile, he expected Colonel Andrew Lewis, along with his brother, Colonel Charles Lewis, and Colonel William Preston, the county lieutenants, respectively, of Botetourt, Augusta, and Fincastle Counties—the three westernmost—to raise a "respectable Body of Men" that would then join forces with him at either Wheeling or the mouth of the Kanawha, "as is most convenient." The governor cautioned Andrew Lewis in executing his part of the operation that because the Indians had spies watching their movements on the frontier, they had the ability and might attempt to "Bring all the Force of the Shawnees" to bear against his division as he marched to the mouth of the Kanawha—before he could combine forces with Dunmore's division.

The governor supported his adoption of an offensive strategy with two points. First, over time, the expense of the numerous scouting parties and ranger detachments in the different counties would establish a costly but porous barrier that would not effectively prevent the enemy from penetrating it any time or place he chose to do so. Second, an offensive expedition against the enemy's towns, in contrast, would not only cost less but prove "more effectual" in achieving the desired result of halting enemy depredations in a shorter period of time by imposing such terms on them following a decisive victory. Given the alternative, the governor expressed his sincere belief that they "may well depend on the House of Burgesses providing [the funds] for the Expedition" if it represented an alternative to the "greater Expence of Acting on the Defensive at any rate." Since the "Old [Militia] Law" remained in force and thus ensured that the men would get paid and associated expenses reimbursed, their officers could recruit a sufficient number of volunteers.[83] Despite the continuing constitutional crisis, militia officers serving on active duty continued expressing their loyalty and started to address one another in correspondence with the phrase "On His Majesty's Service."[84]

CHAPTER 9

Equal to Any Troops

The Militia Accepts the Challenge

August–September 1774

By MID-AUGUST, the Westmoreland County magistrates learned that when Pennsylvania's Colonial Council, also known as the Provincial Council, met with Governor Penn in Philadelphia earlier in the month, it had taken up a number of matters concerning Pittsburgh and its surrounding area in light of the hostilities between the Shawnees and Virginia, and the continuing intercolonial boundary dispute. It first acted favorably on St. Clair's advice to remove the colony's trading concerns from Pittsburgh due to the "oppressive proceedings of Virginia." The council concurred and recommended that Penn order a town to be immediately laid out "in the Proprietary Manor at Kittanning" to accommodate the traders and other inhabitants of Pittsburgh. Along with the order to lay out the town, the governor cautioned St. Clair that the order to erect a "stockade, or any other work, for the security of the place" that might involve the expenditure of provincial funds had to wait for concurrence of the provincial assembly.[1]

Reports from Pittsburgh suggested that the Shawnees and Delaware remained "entirely pacific" toward Pennsylvania, but the two Indian nations had experienced a rift. As the Shawnees continued to prepare for war against the Long Knife, who "seemed determined to pursue hostile measures against those Indians," the Delaware remained on amicable terms with the Virginians. As a result, the Shawnees living closest to the Delaware removed their communities to their nation's Lower Towns on the Scioto River. In response, the Pennsylvania Council recommended that the governor send messages to both tribes expressing concern over the recent disturbances and reassure them both of Pennsylvania's continued friendship, and another message to Governor Dunmore urging him to seek accommodation with the Shawnees without resorting to war.[2]

In the messages, Penn would declare the province's resolve to preserve the treaties of peace and friendship with both tribes. To the Shawnees, after expressing the great concern of Pennsylvania's proprietary government at "the unfortunate disturbances" that occurred between them and "some of his Majesty's subjects belonging to the Colony of Virginia," he requested that they not strike the Virginians. Penn warned the Shawnees that harming any of His Majesty's subjects would offend the king. He then instructed St. Clair to engage an agent the Indians trusted, suggesting the trader Matthew Elliott, who had done such work for the government in the past, to convey and interpret the written messages and accompanying wampum.[3] Not surprisingly, Penn rejected the suggestion to hire Delaware warriors to defend the province's frontier as "too delicate to intermeddle with," but also deemed it improper to discharge the Westmoreland County rangers when their terms expired on August 10. He decided to "keep them on foot" at least until September, when he would place the matter before the assembly when it next convened.[4]

The governor's correspondence reached Pittsburgh just before a number of Shawnee and Delaware chiefs gathered at Croghan's plantation for a conference on August 21. In order to not offend the Six Nations, St. Clair had a "fair copy" of the original message addressed to the Delaware made for the visiting Iroquois deputies and presented it with some wampum at the meeting.[5] When he then rose to address "the Chiefs and Warriors of the Delaware Indians," St. Clair read Penn's letter aloud. On behalf of the governor, St. Clair apologized for "some of our foolish young men" who had murdered John Weepy and for the Virginians who had killed some of their people below Fort Pitt. He then commended them for their having "a good heart" to not take it as a cause to go to war to exact revenge, but viewed the events in a "proper light." St. Clair continued to tell the assembled Delaware and Iroquois deputies that Governor Penn intended to write the Virginia governor in an effort to restore friendship between the Big Knife and the Shawnees and asked their assistance to persuade the Shawnees to likewise "make up their differences with the Virginians."[6]

After the conference, the Delaware learned that Penn had ordered "a trading place" erected at Kittanning. St. Clair relayed to the governor that the Indians expressed their gratitude and their concern. "They are in want of many things already," he said, "and cannot come to Pittsburgh" owing to the boundary dispute and the looming Indian war.

St. Clair was always critical of the Virginians, and when he wrote the governor at the end of the month, he said he believed it "Impossible to tell what will be the Consequences of the Virginia Operation" into Shawnee country. He continued to deride their military capability and believed "they will not be able to bring on a war." With the campaign season drawing to an end, he hoped Dunmore realized the "Necessity of Peace." In his view, the Virginians' "last Exploit"—the expedition against Wakatomika—did not give them "much stomach for another" military venture. St. Clair perceived "such Confusion amongst the Troops, and Dysention amongst the Officers," that had they attempted another foray, he believed "they most certainly must have been cut off [destroyed]" by the Indians. To heighten his concern even more, St. Clair gleaned some disturbing intelligence from reading a letter from a trader in Detroit to a merchant in Pittsburgh. The trader revealed that the "Indians in that Country" will all join the Shawanees" to fight the Virginians. Braves returning from the Virginia frontier had brought enough scalps to encourage others, and leading warriors, eager to help the Shawnees fight the Big Knife, had a "general Rendezvous appointed on the Oubach [Wabash]."[7]

Instead of engaging a trader like Elliott, St. Clair entrusted the Delaware chief called Captain Pipe to deliver Penn's message to "the Chiefs and Warriors of the Shawanese Indians." On his arrival at their principal town of Chillicothe, Pipe expressed Penn's gratitude for their ensuring the safety of Pennsylvania traders and had "kept fast hold of the chain of friendship" with his colony. He read the Pennsylvania governor's urgent request that they resolve their differences with the Virginians and asked that when "any of the wicked people of Virginia" murdered their people, that the Shawnees not "take revenge upon innocent people" but complain to that colony's governor to punish the guilty.

Pipe relayed Penn's warning that if the Shawnees killed innocent people on account of the actions of some of their countrymen, "the Virginians must do the same thing by you, and then there will be nothing but war between you." As he continued speaking for Penn, he warned the chiefs to "Consider . . . that the people of Virginia are like the leaves of the trees, very numerous," and the Shawnee people "but few." Their warriors might kill "ten thousand of their people for one that they kill of yours," he said, but "they will at last wear you out and destroy you." Any hostile action would only provoke the Virginians to "send a great army in your country and destroy your towns and your corn, and either kill your wives and children or drive them away." Penn, through Pipe, reminded them that Pennsylvanians, Virginians, and Shawnees "were all children of the great King who lives be-

yond the great water." They could therefore expect that the king would take
his anger out on those at fault and punish them accordingly. Urging that
they "forgive what is past and offer to make peace," Penn offered to write
Dunmore and persuade him to "join in mending the chain of friendship"
that had been broken.[8]

THROUGHOUT Fincastle County, units of marching men, convoys of wagons
and packhorses, and herds of cattle began to move. In some units, officers
still had more men to recruit, organize, and train. Quartermaster and commissary officers still shuttled about their districts in the effort to engage
packhorse and cattle drivers, and to gather what the troops needed, whether
they were going on the expedition to take the fight to the enemy or guarding
the backcountry communities from Indian irruption by manning garrisons,
conducting patrols, or scouting the trails. In return, those farmers, herders,
millers, smiths, merchants, and others who, in addition to performing military duty in many cases, gave the army the supplies and services it needed,
received vouchers that acknowledged the colony's debt to them. After the
House of Burgesses convened and appointed the required commissioners
to evaluate the muster rolls and public service claims, the colonial treasurer
would redeem their receipts for payment.

From local company catchments, the men marched to their respective
district rendezvous camp for inspection by the major. Those in the Lower
Holston district reported to Major Arthur Campbell at the Town House on
Holston. The companies of the Upper Holston district marched to Fort
Byrd at Culberston's Bottom and reported to Major James Robertson. The
majors inspected and accepted them into the county's service, issued rations
and camp equipment needed for the march, and sent them on their way.
Some marched in company with packhorse trains laden with supplies and
provisions, or herds of cattle that the quartermasters and commissaries had
acquired and forwarded to the general rendezvous for use on the expedition.

Colonel Andrew Lewis informed Colonel Preston that in addition to
what came for the Botetourt County contingent, packhorse driver John
Criner carried "1 1/2 barrels" of much-needed gunpowder for the Fincastle
troops to the rendezvous. He reminded Colonel Preston, the Fincastle
County lieutenant, to have Colonel Christian give the agent a certificate for
the powder and whatever else he delivered for his men. Because it still remained in short supply, Colonel Lewis asked Preston to ensure the Fincastle
contingent brought "all ye powder that you can possibly spare" to the Great
Levels. With the start of the expedition fast approaching, Lewis turned once

more to the matter of recruiting and asked Preston to inform him of his success as soon as possible lest they have to resort to a draft.[9]

A detachment of eighty men from the companies of Captains William Campbell, Herbert, and Shelby marched "in high Spirits" from Royal Oak for the Lower Holston district's rendezvous at the Town House on August 16, according to Major Arthur Campbell. However, the practices by which Captain Looney and Lieutenant Drake had attempted to recruit men in the catchment areas reserved for Campbell's and Shelby's companies, and Ensign Vance had similarly tried to recruit for Smith's company in the area reserved for Russell's, had hindered the ability of the units assigned to those sectors to achieve their required numbers in a timelier manner. Campbell still sought "to humour all parties" until they arrived at the district rendezvous. There he hoped such contention would become a matter of "indifference" and the men would all decide to "go on the Expedition cheerfully" with the officers to whom they first committed as volunteers. Most of all, he had sought to have all of the Lower Holston volunteers at the district rendezvous for Preston's inspection by August 22.

Captain Russell wrote to Preston to express his disappointment and explain the cause for the delay of his company's departure for the rendezvous. The troops that were expected to replace his men at the forts so the "Volunteers might March to the appointed place of Rendezvous for the expedition" had yet to arrive. Such "relief," he reminded the colonel, had been promised the men when they "Engaged [enlisted]" and agreed to serve in the garrisons in the interim. Likewise, John Brander, the supplier, had not yet delivered the brown linen for making their hunting frocks, as Russell had promised they would receive for joining. His company otherwise stood ready to depart Castle's Woods, and given the distance they had to travel, Russell requested the "same Indulgence" for an increased proportion of packhorses to men as the colonel had granted to Shelby.[10] Russell then made an additional request. One of his men, "a very good Hand," did not have a weapon. He recalled that when he "was in the service before, there was near twenty press'd Guns which the County freely pay'd for." Citing the applicable provisions in the Militia Act for justification and the urgency of the situation, Russell requested his man be issued one without waiting for the court to conduct its inquiry.[11]

The Fincastle County militia officers met in a council of war on August 2 to develop a plan for "the Defense of the Frontiers, in the absence of the Troops [going on the proposed expedition]." The county lieutenant, Colonel Preston, ordered Captain Thompson to "guard the lower settlements on Clinch" with a company of sixty men, but as late as August 25, the "upper settlements" remained "uncovered." The colonel therefore instructed Major Campbell to appoint Captain Daniel Smith, assisted by as many subaltern officers as the major deemed appropriate, to command a similar company to guard that sector. The colonel further instructed the major to form a new sixty-man company, with thirty of them drafted from the administrative companies of Captain Herbert and the late Captain Doack, with the subalterns appointed from the companies that produced the most men. Preston then instructed Campbell to "examine carefully into the number of Scouts on that Quarter," in order to retain the most active and trustworthy, but reduce the overall number.[12]

A number of inhabitants on the Clinch submitted a petition for the county lieutenant to increase the number of troops on duty and employ more of them "in the Service" paid by the colony. Campbell forwarded the petition with his recommendations to Colonel Preston. In the interim, he informed the petitioners that all who performed "regular duty might be continued on the [active duty] Lists until a sufficient Number of Draughts" arrived to complete the companies defending their settlements. If more than the required numbers arrived, he pledged to recommend that in organizing their units, officers keep the "best Woodsmen" from among the locals in pay to serve as rangers before accepting volunteers from Holston or New River. Campbell endorsed the request by warning that a weak defense would cause more settlers to flee the frontier.[13]

Finally on the march, Captain Russell expected to arrive at the district rendezvous on Monday, August 29. With thirty-one rank and file "fit for the business," and more to follow and join him at camp, he planned to have a full company before marching to the general rendezvous. John Brander had still not delivered the brown linen before they left Castle's Woods. With his company "badly fix'd, for the want of Hunting shirts, and Blankets," Russell took a "handful of men" to the supplier's home while the rest continued their march to the Town House. Russell arrived only to discover Brander and his wagon away "on this side of New River," but he was determined to get his men the supplies they lacked before they joined the rest of the army.[14]

Russell had never asked Preston to relieve him, as Major Campbell had suggested, but he knew that the county lieutenant wanted John Floyd to command a company on the expedition. Aware that little time remained for his fellow captain to recruit the required number of men, Russell offered to resign his "Interest . . . of the Volunteers" to Captain Floyd and assist him in recruiting the men still needed (if Preston so desired). In return, Russell requested that he command a company defending the Clinch River inhabitants for as long as the colony needed "to keep Men under pay, in this Quarter." Knowing that Preston had appointed Captain James Thompson to command a company posted at Blackmore's Fort, Russell recommended a shared responsibility. He said that Thompson could command toward the head of the river while he had the lower settlements. Regardless, Russell urged Thompson to use troops "that ought to be Ranging, besides those in the Forts, as Constant Guards" for the settlement. Finally, Russell assured the colonel of his preference to serve on the expedition.[15]

To no one's surprise, Preston wanted the experienced Russell to go on the expedition. Although the county lieutenant accommodated Floyd's request to raise and command his own company, the colonel had no intention of having him replace Russell. By August 26, Floyd had "engaged only 3 men," but Sergeant Ephraim and Lieutenant Joseph Drake claimed they could enlist another eight. The lieutenant, who wished to command his own company, added that forty more men waited to join at the Town House, but he insisted they would only serve under him.[16]

The practices of officers like Drake raised questions and threatened the cohesion of several units. Not only did he lead Floyd to believe he acted on his behalf, Drake had designs on commanding his own unit. Furthermore, he had recruited men who resided in catchments reserved for other captains and thus added needless competition that increased the difficulty of raising expeditionary units. When Major Campbell informed some men that Drake had improperly recruited them, he explained such "former faults or breaches of their Words would now be overlook'd, provided they marched to the Camp" as Colonel Preston had ordered. Most of them agreed and seemed eager to get started on the expedition without further delay. Drake, however, became quite "incensed" at Campbell's actions and accused the field officer of further interference when he learned that Floyd released six men he had recruited to rejoin their original captains' companies upon his arrival at the Town House.[17]

When Captain Floyd conveyed Preston's order for Lieutenant Drake and Ensign Vance to serve as the subalterns, both agreed to march as part of his company. An hour later, after having spoken with some of the men, Vance had a change of mind and refused. Major Campbell publicly gave him a direct order, but the recalcitrant ensign once more refused. When the major ordered someone else to take charge, Drake objected in a "Clamorous manner" and said he would march them himself. Campbell did not wish to cause a further delay in getting the men to the rendezvous. He issued provisions and sent the men with Vance and recommended that Preston consider Drake's behavior grounds for dismissal from the service.[18]

Once he learned the truth about Drake's duplicity in recruiting, Floyd
doubted the ability to raise his company. Counting those Drake had recruited, several of whom either lived within the catchment of Captain
Campbell—from which his officers could not recruit—or had enlisted from
outside of the colony, he had fifteen men on hand. Since Major Campbell
sent them all to the rendezvous, and Captain Campbell's had a full complement, Floyd anticipated no further cause for resentment if the men recruited remained in his. As a possible means of completing Floyd's
company, Major Campbell suggested that Preston appoint Daniel Boone, a
lieutenant in Russell's administrative company, to recruit the balance of
Floyd's unit. According to Russell, Boone had applied to go on the expedition as soon as he returned from his search for the surveyors. A "very popular Officer where he is known," Campbell believed Boone could raise and
march enough men to the Town House in time to complete Floyd's company. [19]

Floyd finally thought everything was in order, and the company ready
to march, when Ensign Vance refused to go. Most of the men then "revolted"
and refused to serve on the expedition with "nobody but Capt. Drake." In
Drake's absence, those men blamed Floyd and accused him of only wanting
them to march under Vance's command to "get some of my own ends answered." Floyd now regretted having "undertaken any such thing as raising
a company," which, if given the choice, he would not do again "for a £100."[20]

By the last day of August, Colonel Christian had a battalion composed
of the better part of six Lower Holston district companies, plus one chaplain, one armorer, and two butchers, prepared to march. After taking roll,
Captains Walter Crockett, William Herbert, William Russell, Evan Shelby,
William Campbell, and James Harrod reported having a total of 15 company officers, 16 sergeants, 2 musicians, and 222 "rank and file"—corporals
and privates— ready to proceed. A packhorse train loaded with baggage,
supplies, and equipment, plus a herd of cattle, completed the unit. Crockett
assigned six of his soldiers to the train, one as the officers' batman, or personal servant, and five as packhorse drivers. In addition, fourteen-year-old
John Canterbury volunteered "to assist in driving Cattle for the supply of
the Army." As the battalion marched, the train and herd increased as Christian accepted additional horses, beeves, and supplies at various points along
the seventy-five-mile route to the Great Levels.[21]

Three men who had not answered the roll call before their units departed
remained unaccounted for, and Christian notified Colonel Preston to "Ad-
vertise them as Deserters." Major Campbell remained at the Town House
to command the district's defenses and forward late-arriving individuals,

units, parts of companies, and supplies to the general rendezvous. Campbell also assumed responsibility for sorting out recruiting controversies, dealing with disciplinary problems, and accommodating the three men left behind as too ill to march with their companies. Once fit for duty, the latter would depart Camp Union with a follow-on unit or convoy escort.[22]

At Fort Byrd, Major Robertson dealt with a number of problems, some of them similar to what Campbell experienced, as he prepared the Upper Holston district companies to march. Although he had "picked up Some" men, he and other commanders experienced "poor Success" in recruitment. To bring their units to strength, they had to "Stir up Some Backward Scoundrels . . . to turn Out or Else force them for neither Honour nor Intreatys will move them [to serve their county]." The time had come to implement impressment, albeit with reluctance.[23] Announcing the likelihood of a draft, he believed, might motivate a few fence-sitting potential recruits to enlist, as a verse of *The Recruiting Officer* suggested:

Hear that brave Boys, and let us go,
Or else we shall be 'prest you know,
Then 'list and enter into Pay,
And o'er the Hills and far away.[24]

Recommending that other commanders follow his example, Robertson called a muster of his administrative company for Saturday, September 3. In accordance with Preston's instructions, he planned to draft only "Hulking young dogs [who had thus far avoided honoring their obligations] that Can well be Spar'd," but no men who had families. Once accomplished, he planned to march to "Overtake the Army" at the Great Levels a week later. Unfortunately, a disappointed Robertson lamented that "not one of the younger fellows Appeared [at the muster] that could go."[25]

In the equally critical task of gathering equipment, supplies, and provisions, Major Robertson's report reflected similar frustrations. On September 4, for example, he waited at Culberston's Bottom for delivery of two beeves and a load of flour, which he would forward wherever the county needed it. One farmer brought two hundred bushels of corn, which he already had ground into flour at a local mill, and would "fondly spare" for the expedition. Such contributions of the civic-minded stood in stark contrast to the likes of "Two Cursed Scoundrels." He referred to a father and son who shirked their own military duty but looked on the emergency as an opportunity to reap a financial harvest while they enjoyed the protection provided by the men who shouldered muskets in the ranks. The opportunists had "Corn, Beef and Old Bacon Plenty to Spare" but refused to accept the receipt to redeem for a public service claim later and would "by no means Let it go with out the Ready Cash." Robertson paid them the money but suspected they "would do all they Can to Hurt the Expedition." [26]

Captain Michael Woods commanded a company but was unable to reach its required strength. Although someone told him he could expect some volunteers from Pittsylvania County, Woods held no illusions he could raise a full company in the time that remained. A few of those whom the captain engaged "some time agone" had since changed their attitudes and refused to march. He asked Preston for advice on how to best proceed with such persons. In a more optimistic vein, Woods reported that his unit had fourteen soldiers "willing to go to the Shawanese towns" and requested to "Join Companies with Major Robertson" and go on the expedition, realizing he would serve in the capacity and pay of a lieutenant. [27]

After going thirty-two miles, Colonel Christian and the lead element of Fincastle troops reached the head of Rich Creek on September 2, with forty-two miles to go. The march had taken longer than expected since the troops spent so much time finding the horses and gathering cattle every morning before they could start. As planned, they had acquired more beeves as they went so that the colonel now counted two hundred head in the herd. Christian recommended that if Robertson had trouble getting enough cattle in his area he could collect the difference at Rich Creek. The colonel estimated it would take Robertson two days to reach Rich Creek, plus two more to drive the cattle to the Great Levels.

Because it would take them too far off his route to get the "between 7 and eight hundred pounds of Flour" stored at Woods's fort, Christian told the captain to move it. He instructed Woods to send four of his active-duty men to obtain or exchange some poor horses and pack saddles at Smithfield for more serviceable ones, and once "better fixed," return to move the flour to the Great Levels. After checking with Colonel Preston, Christian also told Woods to march his men to Culberston's Bottom and join Major Robertson for the expedition. [28]

COLONEL CHARLES LEWIS, the county lieutenant, called the units of Augusta County to assemble in Staunton at the ordinary kept by Sampson Mathews, who was a major in the militia. He established his headquarters at the rendezvous and, except for taking time to execute his last will and testament at the courthouse on Wednesday, August 10, Lewis devoted his time to preparing the battalion for the expedition. Companies soon began to arrive. Captains George Mathews (Sampson's younger brother) and Alexander

McClanahan "Marched with noble Companies all cheerfully willing to go to the Shawnee towns," according to Reverend John Brown of the New Providence Presbyterian congregation. When Captain Samuel McDowell marched into town on August 18, however, his company did not have "the number of men allotted to him."[29]

Like their counterparts in Fincastle County, the company commanders in Augusta worked diligently to bring their units to full strength before they marched to the rendezvous in Staunton. Those militia soldiers already on duty represented a source of men predisposed to military service that they could recruit, although they had to replace them at the forts. While serving at a post defending the Tygert valley settlements, Sergeant Benjamin Cleaver "was called on & volunteered to go." Other captains resorted to a draft if they could not recruit enough privates for their expeditionary companies. A drafted man, such as one named Cox, enrolled in the company of Captain John Dickinson, had to either serve or face legal consequences unless he could furnish a substitute. John Cox, although still "quite a youth, volunteered as a substitute" to go in his father's place.[30] The draft proved less successful in other companies. Reverend Brown heard "25 that were drafted refuse to go" with Captain McDowell "& design to run the hazard of the fine." The clergyman expressed sorrow "that both parents & those that have refused speak & act so unreasonably relative to the present expedition."[31]

Major Mathews, the Augusta County quartermaster, had served as a commissary officer in the French and Indian War and knew his business well. He and his assistants worked tirelessly to gather the packhorses, cattle, provisions, and supplies the Augusta County units needed. Although "several Companies were at the Warm Springs," about six hundred troops had assembled at Mathews's inn. With Colonel Lewis at their head, Augusta "Men & provisions" began marching for the Great Levels on August 30.[32]

DUNMORE HAD designated Winchester, seat of Frederick County, as the place of rendezvous for most units of the expedition's right wing. Located in the lower Shenandoah valley, Winchester had become "one of the largest towns . . . in this Colony" by 1774. The gentleman traveler Nicholas Cresswell, after observing the surveyed half-acre plots aligned on parallel streets, described it as "Regularly laid out in squares the buildings are of limestone," and containing a courthouse and "Two Churches, one English and one Dutch."[33]

As August drew to a close, the pace of militia mobilization quickened. Once the companies from Frederick, Hampshire, Berkeley, and Dunmore

Counties had assembled, including those who previously went on McDonald's raid, they would begin the march to Pittsburgh on the first leg of the expedition. Now Major-Commandant John Connolly, who supervised the raising of companies and gathering of supplies in the West Augusta district, came down from Fort Dunmore to join the rest of Dunmore's staff in planning the operation.

Colonel Adam Stephen wrote from Berkeley Courthouse on August 27 to inform his friend, Richard Henry Lee, that Lord Dunmore had ordered him to the Ohio to "put matters on a footing to establish a lasting peace with the brave natives." Stephen expressed his opinion that the Indians "would behave well, were they not poisoned by the blackguard traders allowed to go among them, [and] to their different towns." Colonel Stephen's military duty precluded his attendance at the congress, where he "would expect to see the spirit of the Amphyctions shine, as that illustrious council did in their purest times, before debauched with the Persian gold."

In his letter, Stephen outlined some of the grievances British Americans wanted redressed and hoped the congress could facilitate that resolution. "The fate of America depends upon your meeting," he told Lee, "and the eyes of the European world hang upon you, waiting the event." Speaking of the unpopular Quebec Act, Stephen warned that "Despotism, and the Roman Catholic religion is established in Canada." Likewise, with regard to the Administration of Justice Act, the colonel questioned if British Americans could "enjoy liberty, if the villain who ravishes our wives, deflowers our daughters, or murders our sons, can evade punishment, by being tried in Britain, where no evidence can pursue him?" At the same time, if "A governor to suppose me of a crime," Stephen said, he could not expect a "fair trial in America." [34]

Stephen said he had written mainly to inform Lee that due to performing military service, he could not attend the General Congress in Philadelphia. His explanation, however, modestly understated the role he would fill. The governor had designated Stephen, the county lieutenant of Berkeley County, to command the right wing of the expedition. When Lieutenant Augustine Prevost of the British 60th Regiment of Foot met Stephen in Pittsburgh a few weeks later, he described the Virginia colonel as "a gentleman . . . who had seen some service during the last war who bears a worthy good character." [35] Stephen had actually served throughout the French and Indian War. Starting as a captain in command of a company in 1754, he rose to the rank of colonel and command of the 1st Virginia Regiment before the conflict ended, and he commanded a provincial rifle battalion that guarded the frontier and accompanied Bouquet's expedition against the Shawnees in

Pontiac's War. In addition to wartime contributions, Stephen was an officer of both the court and militia of Frederick County until a 1772 act of the General Assembly created Berkeley County, at which time Governor Dunmore appointed him its sheriff and county lieutenant.

Although Stephen held the title, Dunmore exercised actual direct command of the wing. Stephen therefore functioned as his second in command and assumed responsibility for executing all of the associated administrative and logistical functions. When the two wings met and combined, Dunmore would become commander in chief while Stephen assumed actual command of the right wing. The unpleasant duty of contending with Lieutenant Colonel Horatio Gates therefore fell to the de facto second in command. Gates, a former major in the British army, had retired on half-pay to Berkeley County and redeemed the land bounty he received for his service during the Seven Years War to acquire the property he named Traveler's Rest. In 1773, Dunmore commissioned Gates "as a lieutenant colonel of militia of Berkeley County, whereof Adam Stephen, Esq., is Lieutenant and Chief Commander."[36] With hope and confidence in the abilities and experience of the former regular officer, the governor appointed Gates to command the Berkeley County contingent on the expedition.

In a shocking and ill-advised August 22 reply to Dunmore, Gates not only declined the appointment but questioned the governor's authority to call him to actual service under the now-expired Militia Act. Two days later, Colonel Stephen informed his subordinate that "his Lordship Testifyd his Surprise that you should Suppose he would act under a Law that had no Existence." Not yet done, Stephen continued on the governor's behalf, "His Lordship therefore Commands me to acquaint you that he expects you will join him directly, & take the Command of the Detachment of Berkley Militia, now marching under Orders by Virtue of that Law."[37] Gates remained unconvinced, but his reply lacked the courage of conviction as he wrote, "I am at present confin'd to my House by a Violent Intestinal Fever." Attempting a graceful withdrawal, Gates replied to Stephen, "as soon as I am able to ride, I shall wait on Lord Dunmore."[38]

The right wing broke camp and began the march along Braddock's Military Road to Pittsburgh in the last week of August. Lord Dunmore then had a force of "upwards of Seven hundred with him," which included the "400 that march'd with Maj. McDonald & three hundred with himself."[39] On August 30, Dunmore halted at Oldtown, Maryland, on the Potomac River about sixty miles from Winchester. After he visited the Cresap family home to pay his respects to Colonel Thomas Cresap, Michael's father, the governor took the opportunity, with Colonel Stephen and Major Connolly "at his elbow," to send a letter informing Colonel Andrew Lewis at Camp Union of a change in plan. Dunmore now instructed Lewis to march the left wing to the mouth of the Little Kanawha to meet the rest of the army.[40]

The Northern Division of the army resumed its march and halted at Redstone, where additional companies joined the expedition and the column split. Dunmore continued on the road toward Pittsburgh at the head of between three hundred and four hundred men and a convoy of twelve wagons. On September 20, the recently promoted Major William Crawford led a detachment of five hundred men with a train of fifty packhorses and a herd of two hundred head of cattle to Fort Fincastle at Wheeling. Connolly rode on ahead to Pittsburgh when the slower moving column stopped at the Great Meadows. He would join Major McDonald, who had previously led a supply convoy to Fort Dunmore, to help direct the efforts of the West Augusta district's officers as they continued recruiting men and as Captain William Herrod, the quartermaster general, and his commissary officers acquired cattle, provisions, and other supplies for the right wing.[41]

COLONEL ANDREW LEWIS had designated the Great Levels, a savannah situated on the Greenbrier River about eight miles from White Sulphur Springs, as the location for the general rendezvous of the left wing, or Southern Division. He named it Camp Union because it represented the place where troops from Augusta, Botetourt, and Fincastle Counties united for the expedition. Due to the close proximity of their home communities to the rendezvous, the Botetourt County companies of Captains John Stuart and Matthew Arbuckle arrived first and established their bivouacs by August 27, but no other units arrived for five more days.

The sound of drums and fifes heralded the arrival of Colonel Charles Lewis and most of the Augusta County contingent, or "line," on September 1, prompting Colonel William Fleming, who arrived shortly behind them, to remark that "Companies have been coming in every day since." Camp Union quickly became a very busy place. Reveille beat every morning before daybreak as the signal to rise in the camps and for sentinels to cease challenging. In the respective lines, captains commanding companies formed their men, called the rolls, and examined arms. Officers met in councils of war to discuss plans. Martial music filled the air as fifers and drummers practiced and beat the required calls at the appropriate times for guard mount and other camp duties. Soldiers drilled, melted lead into molds to make bullets, performed work details and guard duty, and on Sunday attended divine services. Convoys of supply wagons and packhorses, and herds of cattle delivered the sinews of war. Every duty day ended at sunset with the beating of retreat, when the soldiers returned to their tents for the evening and sentries were required to challenge all who approached their posts.[42]

Despite militia troops being posted at the various forts, on the march, and now encamped at the Great Levels, the backcountry remained dangerous. Indian war parties roamed near the settlements and looked for easy targets to attack, which caused the prudent settlers to remain vigilant and cautious. Colonel Fleming had left his Belmont estate for Camp Union on Monday, August 21, but did not arrive until more than a week later. He had "delayed a day or two on purpose," waiting to "fall in with some provision escorts" rather than travel alone. Although he did not find a unit to accompany, his caution proved well founded when he learned that the assembling army had "some Indian Spies attending us" who occasionally fired on "a straggling person" whom they could catch at a disadvantage when "not too near the camp."

Colonel Andrew Lewis, the commander in chief, arrived on September 1. Before he left for camp he ordered three men to guard Fleming's Belmont plantation in his subordinate's absence. Captain Stephen Trigg, who remained behind to command the defenses in the area, would increase, replace, or dismiss the guards if Fleming's wife, Nancy, desired.[43]

First Sergeant William Kennerly, who had volunteered for service in Captain George Mathews's Augusta County company, recalled receiving orders for a detached mission. After they had marched from the county rendezvous at Staunton to Camp Union, Colonel Lewis sent Matthews's and Captain George Moffett's companies to the Tygart River valley, where they built a small post. Named Warwick's fort, for Jacob Warwick, the owner of the property and member of Captain John Dickinson's company, it was to shelter the region's inhabitants. When the two companies returned to Camp Union to participate in the expedition, Kennerly remained to command the sixteen-man detachment left as the garrison.[44]

On September 2, Fleming's first full day at the Great Levels, a messenger brought word that Indians had attacked "Stewart's fort," about four miles away. The detachment of soldiers dispatched to the scene found that Indians had fired on and "slightly wounded" one man, who managed to escape. The next day, a patrol brought "a Countryman from another Quarter," named McGuire, into camp. The "much wounded" McGuire suffered from a "Shot through the Jaw" and had to have "a bullet cut out of his Cheek." Although the braves preferred to target the "country People" who lived "near little Forts about 3 miles" distant, they had otherwise caused little damage. Fleming believed that the frontier would become "altogether safe" after the army marched, since its motions would "fully employ" the warriors in defending their own country and thereby draw their attention away from the settlements.[45]

The troops estimated two enemy war parties of four or five men each operated in the area. The officers therefore took measures to keep the encampment secure while the companies trained and made ready, and quartermaster and commissary officers had their men unload, inventory, and prepare supplies for the campaign. Following the procedure prescribed in General Bland's *Treatise on Military Discipline*, each battalion in camp detailed troops that contributed to a variety of camp guards every day, with the main guard and picket guards considered the most important.

The main guard provided the camp's external security. It usually consisted of a company commanded by a captain, with its men posted as sentinels around the camp's perimeter and at special installations, such as the baggage train, boats, cattle, packhorses, and, if it had one, the artillery park. Each of the camp's tenant battalions also provided a daily picket guard. Under the command of a captain, the picket guard consisted of one lieutenant, one ensign, three sergeants, and fifty rank-and-file soldiers for a twenty-four-hour period.[46]

After standing the daily guard mount, each company-sized body of men maintained themselves "always ready to march at a moment's warning" either to sustain outposts, escort foraging parties, or "in case the enemy should endeavor to surprise . . . [the] camp, to march out and attack them, in order to give the army time to draw up" in line of battle. If an alarm sounded, each captain would form his men and lead them to a designated point of rendezvous with the other battalions' guards. The field officer of the day would then assume command and lead the temporary battalion to meet the enemy while the rest of the army assembled.[47]

The Indians, according to their custom of warfare, approached the camp to cause as much "mischief" as possible while they gathered and seized all the horses they could take. For example, after the captain of the September 4 picket guard from Botetourt County detailed a sergeant and twelve men to march to the ford on the Greenbrier River to escort any baggage trains or packhorse brigades to camp, he assigned the rest of his men to another mission. Dividing them "in such small parties . . . thought most likely to discover & Annoy" any warriors skulking around the camp, the captain sent them beyond the line of picket posts "in quest of the Enemy."[48]

After spending much of the day in fruitless searches, one patrol encountered some men "in the Woods on Horseback." The intruders, "Wearing blankets over their heads to deceive the sentries," dismounted and approached a number of grazing packhorses. After each of the strangers had mounted one and prepared to steal more animals, a sentinel detected the ruse and shouted, "Here they are boys!" The picket guards reacted to the alarm, but the Indians had "time to slip off the Horses without being fired at" and fled into the woods. Although they had "no Opportunity of firing," the picket guards recovered the stolen horses and found "several Buffalo hide halters, a tomahawk," and other items the intruders had dropped nearby. As darkness approached, the captain of the guard recalled his men back to camp.[49]

The next day, in addition to the usual guards, Colonel Charles Lewis, acting as field officer of the day, ordered twenty men "paraded immediately" and provided each with a packhorse. Thus mounted, the guards scoured the woods for two miles all around the camp to "dislodge any Scouting Indians & make it safe for the Pack horse men to gather up their horses." Simultaneously, the captains led that day's picket guards "in quest of the Indians that were discovered" the previous day. Again operating in small units, they had orders to patrol until evening, unless they could overtake and engage the enemy.[50]

Even with the distraction of the daily guard mount, the rendezvous camp provided the captains commanding companies the best opportunity to train their men and develop a degree of unit cohesion not possible by the attendance of a one-day muster every three months. Although it did not make them as attentive as regulars, the military environment also proved conducive to instilling a degree of discipline, a characteristic often lacking in militia organizations. Captains and orderly sergeants read to the men of their companies the punitive articles of the Militia Act, the applicable provisions in the Acts for Repelling Invasions and Insurrections, and "every order by which their conduct is regulated." The leaders let the members know, in no uncertain terms, the consequences for disobeying orders and the punishment that a trial by court-martial could impose on a refractory militiaman. Certain militia members never adjusted well to regimentation, whether on the expedition or in the garrisons. Although cases of insubordination, desertion, and other offenses occurred, the companies generally conducted themselves well. Finally, owing largely to the continuing shortage of gunpowder, the field officers urged captains and subalterns to "exert themselves" in preventing their men from the "infamous practice of shooting away their Ammunition for no good purpose" and demanded that they fire only with their officers' permission.[51]

Although educated as physicians, Captains Thomas Buford, Robert McClennahan, and Colonel William Fleming served as line officers. They, along with the Augusta line's surgeon, Doctor John Watkins, provided the army's left wing with the nucleus of a competent medical staff. As more staff officers arrived in camp, they saw to their respective duties in earnest. Major Thomas Posey, as the quartermaster and commissary general, coordinated the expedition's logistical support. Captains Thomas Ingles and Anthony Bledsoe, quartermaster of Botetourt County and commissary of Fincastle County, respectively, became his principal deputies. Major Sampson Mathews, quartermaster of Augusta, assumed the role of "master driver of cattle," assisted by deputies, or chief drivers of cattle, Captains John Lyle and William McClure. Captains John Hughes and John Taylor became chief packhorse masters. John Warwick was the chief butcher. Largely through the efforts of this staff, supplies and provisions for the expedition arrived steadily. Although shortages continued to plague the force, the subordinate agents in the counties continued to acquire and forward the necessary items to the Great Levels.

Major Posey reported to the commander in chief every evening on the number of packhorses, bullocks, and other cattle. The commissaries had their men find and gather all the cattle lost on the march or wandering around camp into an established "bullock pen" with guards posted. Warwick and the army's butchers had a "Slaughtering pen" made where they could butcher the meat and "kill the Cattle otherwise than by Shooting them."[52]

For transport, by the time the left wing marched, Posey expected to have eight hundred horses "employed" in carrying supplies.[53] Armies of the day usually organized their packhorses into "brigades," each under the control of a packhorse master who held authority over those assigned to the train and staff responsibilities roughly equivalent to a captain of the line. A brigade typically had about forty horses, with one driver controlling a team of two horses, plus additional packhorse men. The latter, often augmented by soldiers detailed from the line companies, assisted the drivers and helped to load, unload, feed, and care for the animals. Furnished with a packsaddle, a horse could carry about two hundred pounds of cargo.[54] John Criner, for example, drove his team into camp and delivered "1 1/2 barrels" of powder for the Fincastle companies, and "1 [whole] & 2 half barrels of gun Powder," plus "16 galls Spirits & Sundry other Articles," which—excluding the liquor and powder—came to about "150 lbs." for the Botetourt County contingent.[55]

Posey informed the battalion commanders that they could expect kettles "to be distributed amongst the whole in equal proportion to the Number [of soldiers] in each line."[56] By the time the army marched, the quartermasters also expected to issue each company entrenching tools, four felling axes, and one broadax. While still on the way to Camp Union, Colonel Christian received word that his men would find "Tents plenty and all goods necessary for the men such as Shirts, Blankets [and] Leggings" when they arrived.[57]

John F. D. Smyth, a British traveler who witnessed the left wing assemble, recorded his impressions about the frontier soldiers' appearance. He described "Their whole dress" as "also very singular, and not very materially different from that of the Indians." Each man wore "a hunting shirt," a functional garment that resembled a "wagonner's frock, ornamented with a great many fringes" that he fastened about the middle with a broad belt. Smyth elaborated on the belt, calling it "much decorated" but utilitarian. Into his belt, a soldier usually secured his tomahawk, "an instrument that serves every purpose of defense and convenience," a tool that functioned as a hammer on one side and a hatchet on the other. The soldiers' kits included accouterments that they would "hang from their necks on one shoulder," such as a shot bag and powder horn. On the latter, many men often carved a "variety of whimsical figures and devices." The preferred headgear was a "flapped hat, of a reddish hue," to protect the wearer "from the intensely hot beams of the sun."

On their legs below the frocks the men often wore "leather britches, made of Indian dressed elk, or deer skins, but more frequently thin trousers" with the addition of the very practical "Indian boots, or leggings." Made from coarse woolen cloth and either wrapped loosely and tied with garters or laced on the outside, the leggings "always come better than half way up the thigh" to offer the wearer "great defense and preservative" against poisonous insect and snake bites, as well as the scratches of thorns, briars, scrubby bushes, and underwood, "with which this whole country is infested and overspread." For footwear, Smyth wrote that frontiersmen sometimes wore pumps of "their own manufacture" but more often wore "Indian moccasins . . . of their own construction also." Made of strong elk or buckskin, which they "dress thence round the fore part of the middle ankle, without a seam," the moccasins fit the wearer "close to the feet, and are perfectly easy and pliant."

As for the hue of their hunting frocks, or rifle shirts, Smyth said that although some men dyed them in a variety of colors, including yellow, red, or brown, "many wear them quite white." Smyth concluded, "Thus habited and accoutered, with his rifle upon his shoulder, or in his hand," the well-appointed "backwoods' man is completely equipped for visiting, courtship, travel, hunting, or war." Smyth added, with a touch of irony, "And according to the number and variety of fringes on his hunting shirt, and the decorations on his powder horn, belt, and rifle," such a man "estimates his finery." Smyth then observed that a Virginian "absolutely conceives himself of equal consequence, more civilized, polite and more elegantly dressed than the most brilliant peer at St. James's in a splendid and expensive birthday suit, of the first fashion and taste, and most costly materials." For the benefit of his European reading audience, he conceded, "Such sentiments as those I have just exposed to notice are neither so ridiculous nor surprising," when one considered the circumstances "with due attention, that prompt the backwoods' American to such a train of thinking, and in which light it is, that he feels his own consequence, for he finds all his resources himself."[58]

Although all of the troops, provisions, and supplies had not yet arrived, the time for the left wing to begin its campaign had come. Such expeditions in the past could usually rely on their accompanying packhorse trains and cattle herds, supplemented by carrying some of the bulk material by canoe, to provide enough supplies and provisions needed to sustain them during the entire operation. This one proved different. Despite the problems some officers had experienced in raising their units, the assembled force had "a much Larger Number than was Expected." Although the officers had already expended a great deal of effort to raise and assemble their half of the expeditionary army, it paled in comparison to the task of getting it where it could do the work for which it existed. While the increased number of troops that had turned out represented an advantage, Lewis realized that the logistical requirements had increased commensurately as well. The estimated distances—140 miles from Camp Union to the mouth of the Kanawha and 70 more to the objective Shawnee Indian towns—further magnified the difficulty of the enterprise. The army had more before it than a walk in the woods.[59]

Colonel Andrew Lewis called the field officers and senior captains together for a council of war and discussed the march to join Lord Dunmore and the right wing on the banks of the Ohio. The size of the force and insufficient number of packhorses necessitated a phased march order of subordinate units and "an Equal addition of Provisions than originally ordered, & Brought out, & carried from this Camp by ye Last Marching Party to ye Mouth of Elk." Instead of simply forwarding some supplies down the Kanawha by canoe, the troops would have to build a magazine "where it must be stored, & taken down by water as we shall have occasion for it."[60] The phased movement of multiple marching units and the more robust and responsive flow of supplies required a well-developed plan executed with a professional level of competence consistent with the best practices of European armies.

Colonel Andrew Lewis proposed "building Canoes, and a Fort at the mouth of Elk," about eighty-five miles away, "and a Fort at the mouth of Kanawha" on the Ohio, sixty more miles distant as the army marched toward enemy territory. The fort on the Elk would include a magazine, or "a small store house, for the provisions." From there, the commissary officers would use canoes to transport the flour and other supplies from the magazine down the Kanawha River to the Ohio. The logistical system would ultimately consist of a rear support base at Camp Union, the intermediate magazine at Elk River, and a forward base at Point Pleasant on the Ohio from which the army planned to enter Indian country. The advanced party, as the first march division, would halt at the mouth of Elk River on the Kanawha to establish a camp. Once the main body arrived, the men would build a fortification, magazine, and canoes. As soon as the packhorse men unloaded their cargo, most of the unburdened pack animals would return to Camp Union for another load and accompany the rear body on its march. Once completed, the quartermaster and commissary officers could send most of the flour forward by canoe, taking maximum advantage of water carriage that not only facilitated movement but made the best use of the limited number of available packhorses. The arrangement also facilitated a continuous flow of provisions, ammunition, and other material forward, as well as the evacuation of the ambulatory wounded back, as the army moved farther from its base of supply.[61]

The wing's commander in chief designated that his brother, Colonel Charles Lewis, would lead the advanced body. Because Captain Matthew Arbuckle of Botetourt County knew the way to Point Pleasant along a branch of the Warriors' Path known as the Kanawha Trail, Colonel Andrew Lewis appointed him as the chief guide and assigned his company to the division. Consisting of the entire Augusta County contingent in camp, nine companies, or "595 officers and men," with Arbuckle's Botetourt company attached, they would march on Tuesday, September 6, accompanied by a commissary officer, a train of loaded packhorses, and a herd of cattle. The main body, or second division, which was commanded by Colonel Fleming and which Colonel Andrew Lewis would accompany, consisted mostly of Botetourt County troops plus packhorses and cattle, and would leave Camp Union six days later. The Fincastle County contingent, under the command of Colonel Christian, which Lewis expected to reach Camp Union any day, would follow with the remaining supplies and provisions, pack animals, and cattle as the rear body, as it brought up the rear as the final division to march.[62]

On Sunday, September 4, while the picket guards engaged Indian marauders skulking around the camp's perimeter and just two days before the
first units marched, a messenger arrived with the letter from Dunmore.
Written from Oldtown, Maryland, five days before, the letter expressed
Dunmore's "warmest wishes" for Andrew Lewis to march his wing to join
the rest of the army at the mouth of the Little Kanawha. Given such short
notice, Lewis replied that "it is not in my Power to alter our route" and explained the circumstances that prevented his complying with the commander in chief's instruction. In a private letter to Colonel Preston, Lewis
said that he wished the governor had explained his reasons for the sudden
change in plan.[63]

On Monday, Colonel Fleming's Botetourt troops took over routine camp
duties and the daily guard mount, which allowed Colonel Charles Lewis's
companies to work without distraction. The men of the first division devoted their energies to preparations for the march. Meanwhile, the packhorse men fixed a quantity of salt, fifty-four thousand pounds of flour, and
all tools not issued to companies for loading on the packhorses. The cattle
drovers gathered their herds to have them ready. Colonel Andrew Lewis issued an order that forbade the sutlers from "distributing Liquors in such
Quantities as will make any of the Troops drunk— otherwise," he threatened, "a total stop will be put to the Retailing of Liquors" in camp.[64] On the
same day in Philadelphia, delegates from twelve colonies convened in the
General Congress—later known as the First Continental Congress—at Carpenters' Hall.

After the fifes and drums of the Augusta line beat the general, used in
lieu of reveille, at daybreak on September 6 as the signal to begin the day
and prepare to break camp and march, the other lines observed the normal
camp routine. The men dressed and ate breakfast, and each captain inspected his men and their weapons. In those companies preparing to depart,
the officers ordered any soldiers deemed not healthy enough to go on the
expedition to remain in camp and rejoin their units by marching with one
of the following divisions or as convoy escorts after they regained their
strength. The quartermasters finally arrived with and distributed camp kettles, axes, and other tools to the companies, and issued enough ammunition
so that each soldier in Lewis's division had "1/4 pound of powder and 1/2
pound of ball" to begin the campaign. The men checked and packed personal gear and unit equipment. When the drums beat assembly, the Augusta
soldiers and those of the attached Botetourt company struck their tents,
loaded their baggage onto packhorses, drew up in their respective companies, and stood ready for the next signal. On hearing the musicians beat a

march, the companies took their places in the formation and marched out of Camp Union, followed by 400 packhorses and 108 head of cattle. Captain John Taylor, although from Fincastle, prepared to march in command of the "Brigade of horses" and would "return as fast as they can" to Camp Union after they unloaded the packsaddles at Elk River.[65]

Not long after Colonel Charles Lewis and the advanced body marched away, Colonel Christian and most of the Fincastle County contingent for the expedition arrived at Camp Union. Colonel Fleming greeted him, and the next day wrote a letter to tell his wife, Nancy, that her "brother & the Companies from Fincastle reach'd this place Yesterday."[66] When the Fincastle County officer reported to the wing's commander in chief, Colonel Andrew Lewis told him that he believed that the number of men present or expected to arrive greatly exceeded his expectations. The next day, Christian wrote to inform Colonel Preston that Lewis had ordered the county lieutenant of Fincastle County to "let but 100 more men follow me." Lewis personally wrote Preston to tell him to only send enough additional men to bring Fincastle County's contingent to about three hundred rank and file, and that he "could employ Any others that are raised to protect your Frontiers." Lewis then added that if Preston sent any more troops to Camp Union, to please "furnish them with Powder," otherwise they would "not have more than 1/4 lb pr Man." Lewis concluded by telling Preston, "It is with pleasure I can inform you that I have had but little Trouble with ye Troops to what I expected and I hope they will continue to do their duty with the same cheerfulness."[67]

Colonel John Field of Culpepper County also marched into Camp Union with one company of thirty-five men soon after the advanced party had departed. When he reported to Colonel Lewis, he informed the commander that he expected another one hundred men to arrive in camp the next day. Field then presented orders that required Lewis to accept the Culpepper County companies for service in the colony's pay as a single corp. Although everyone continued to address him by the title of his permanent rank, Colonel Lewis referred to Field in correspondence as holding the grade of major. According to the Militia Law, given the number of men under his command, "major" reflected the compensation Field could expect to receive after the House of Burgesses voted to settle the colony's military expenses. Without waiting for the rest of the battalion, Field and the single Culpepper company left the following evening to join Colonel Charles Lewis's division on the way to the Elk.[68]

With the army starting to move, many people in the backcountry hoped that the offensive would succeed in bringing enemy depredations against their settlements to an end. Three weeks after the left wing began its cam-

paign, Colonel Preston described the frontier situation in an open letter to
Purdie and Dixon of the *Virginia Gazette*. Reflecting his pride for the soldiers of colonial Virginia, especially his own Fincastle and the neighboring
Augusta and Botetourt Counties, he wrote, "This body of militia being
mostly armed with rifle guns, and a great part of them good woodsmen,
are looked upon to be at least equal to any troops for the number that have
been raised in America." As they marched to face the enemy, he continued,
"It is earnestly hoped that they will, in conjunction with the other party
[the right wing], be able to chastise the Ohio Indians for the many murders
and robberies they have committed on our frontiers for many years past."[69]

CHAPTER 10

To Hold Themselves in Readiness

The Militia Marches

September 1–October 1, 1774

THE SIGHTS and sounds of military activity filled Pittsburgh and the surrounding area in early September. As most of the right wing, or Northern Division, of Dunmore's army marched from its rendezvous camp and Winchester, quartermaster and commissary officers continued to gather supplies and provisions, and company commanders drilled their men and conducted patrols. Like their counterparts in Fincastle, Botetourt, and the rest of Augusta County, they were preparing to support the offensive expedition as well as defend the district and its inhabitants from marauding Indian warriors. Amid the activity, an officer of the regular British army became an observer, as well as a minor participant.

Lieutenant Augustine Prevost, adjutant of the British army's 60th "Royal American" Regiment of Foot, arrived in Pittsburgh on September 3, 1774, at the same time "My Lord Dunmore was expected hourly." The officer had come in his official capacity to recruit men for his unit, then posted in Jamaica, but took time from his duties to visit and conduct personal business with George Croghan, his partner in some land interests as well as the father of his wife, Susannah. Before heading west, Prevost stopped at Williamsburg on July 2 and paid his respects to the governor. He remarked that his lordship not only received him "very politely" but invited him to dine with him and Lady Dunmore at the palace on July 4.[1]

Except for the few days in Virginia's capital, Prevost spent most of the next two months in the company of Pennsylvanians while visiting relatives in Lancaster and stopping at Bedford, Ligonier, and Hanna's Town on the road to Pittsburgh. He exclusively engaged in conversation with individuals whose positions unabashedly favored their colony in its boundary dispute with Virginia and undoubtedly influenced his opinions. By the time Prevost reached Pittsburgh, the views of William Saunderson, who represented Cumberland County in the provincial assembly, William Thompson, a Westmoreland County magistrate, and Alexander McKee of the Indian Department had likely darkened his views of anything Virginian. With their own financial as well as political interests at stake, Indian traders McKee and Thompson, along with Matthew Elliott, Alexander Ross, and Thomas Smallman, added to the Pennsylvania influence reflected in Prevost's actions and diary entries.

Prevost reached Croghan Hall to find his father-in-law "laid up with the gout & rheumatism." The Delaware chief White Eyes waited for Dunmore's arrival with Croghan since, as local members of the Pennsylvania faction claimed, "two or three Virginia militia" had attacked three unarmed Delaware walking along the road from town to Croghan's plantation on September 1. The assailants killed two, but one of the Indians "got off" and swam across the Alleghany to safety. Major Angus McDonald, "happening to be there" in town, immediately issued a reward of £50 to anyone who apprehended the attackers. Prevost did not expect much would come of the gesture and blamed the violence on the "want of discipline among such a set of lawless vagabonds."

When the British officer met Major John Connolly and his wife for dinner at a local tavern two days later, the major impressed the lieutenant as "sincere and friendly" despite "the many accounts . . . heard to his prejudice." The rest of the meeting did nothing to change Prevost's opinion, although when their fellow diners McKee and Ross informed him that someone had threatened White Eyes and his companion, Connolly immediately ordered a party of militiamen to scout the road between the fort and Croghan's to arrest anyone seeking to harm the two Indians. The general situation led Prevost to understand that the crisis had reached the point that "the Indians were all exceedingly alarmed, that a party of Mingoes were out 14 days now in order to strike somewhere; but God only knows."

Dunmore arrived on the evening of September 10, ahead of the rest of his army, after coming down the Monongahela with a small party in three small canoes. The governor landed and immediately went to the "apartments" that Connolly had prepared for his quarters in the fort. "Coming in this manner totally disappointed the poor commandant, who had with vast pain and labor introduced a new mode & system of discipline amongst his veterans," Prevost noted. Connolly had "intended to receive his Lordship with all the pomp &c. imaginable," but instead, "the sentry at the gate," on seeing Dunmore approaching, "laid by his rifle, went up to his Lordship, & with hat off welcomed him heartily." Perhaps the lieutenant added too much gravity in the ceremonial expectations since it "made my Lord laugh heartily."

McKee confided his belief to Prevost that Connolly had "succeeded with his Lordship as to lead him to adopt his measures & way of thinking with respect to the Shawnees, that that nation had a long time since maltreated the Virginians, and that the latter had never scourged them for it, & that now he was come with troops of that Province to chastise them." McKee, as an officer of the Indian Department, informed Dunmore that some representative chiefs, or "deputies from the Delawares, Mingos & Six Nations," had arrived to intercede in behalf of the Shawnees. They had camped across the Allegheny from Pittsburgh, in Indian country, where they felt they could more safely conduct their deliberations without having such a "banditti" about them. Dunmore sent McKee to tell the Indians he desired to meet with them at the fort the next day.

As soon as Major McDonald informed him of the killings earlier in the week, the governor "issued a proclamation by beat of the drum" that offered £100 reward for the apprehension of those guilty of murdering the two Delawares, and for anyone with information to come forward and report it. As to the situation that brought him to Pittsburgh, the governor ordered McDonald to begin the construction of canoes for transporting troops down the Ohio.

Prevost held a low opinion of Dunmore's military competence and described his "schemes & plans of operations" as very much those typical of an amateur, novice, and man "ignorant of the matter he is upon." The lieutenant may not have known that the man he criticized as a military amateur had served as an officer in the elite 3rd Regiment of Foot Guards during the Seven Years War. As a relatively junior officer on a regimental staff, Prevost also may not have known about Dunmore's tenure as royal governor of New York. When it appeared that Great Britain and Spain would go to war in 1770 after the Viceroy of "Buenos Ayres" invaded the British settlement at Port Egmont in the Falkland Islands, Dunmore saw to the repair and improvement of New York's long-neglected and inadequately armed costal defenses. After "putting the province into a condition to resist a sudden attack" by the enemy, he assured his superiors at Whitehall that he had taken all measures necessary for the safety of the colony.[2]

Prevost charged that the governor had no store of provisions, ammunition, or other supplies, but most of all money, and incorrectly believed that the House of Burgesses was very unwilling to appropriate any to him. Fortunately for the governor, according to Prevost, a few individual traders offered to "pay off his soldiers and officers with goods out of their stores, provided they might charge a large, very large, advance such as 300 pr. ct." In fact, Prevost only showed his ignorance of the Virginia government's processes that paid for military activities, as prescribed in the Militia Law and Laws for Repelling Invasions and Suppressing Insurrections.

When Prevost paid his respects to Dunmore at a dinner hosted by McKee, he remarked that "the people of the country seemed happy at his Lordship's arrival as they hoped to see peace & tranquility restored in this part of the country." The governor replied that the "Indian matters . . . would be easily accommodated" but admitted the "troubles fomented by a parcel of bad people were not likely to be so soon adjusted." Obviously with a view diametrically opposed to the opinions Prevost had thus far heard, the governor stated that Pennsylvania partisans, not his colony's militiamen, had murdered the two Delaware "as a stroke of policy in order to throw the odium upon the Virginians."

Meanwhile, Connolly had presided over a court of inquiry on the matter of Richard Butler, a trader who favored the Pennsylvania interests. Two weeks earlier, the major commandant ordered Butler arrested and confined for violating the ordinance against transporting goods, which were seized, from Pittsburgh by way of the new Pennsylvania trading town at Kittanning to the enemy. The court determined that it could find nothing criminal after two days of testimony and remanded the accused back to jail while the magistrates turned to the governor for a determination. Showing what Prevost surprisingly described as "superior sagacity & profound knowledge," Dunmore ordered Connolly to release Butler as soon as the trader posted a security bond and promised to "never prosecute his oppressors."[3]

Led by White Eyes and Custaloga, Indian deputies assembled at the fort on Wednesday, September 14, to begin the long-awaited conference. In the precouncil ritual that governed Indian diplomacy, White Eyes first extended a string of wampum to symbolically "remove the fatigue" of Dunmore's journey, open and clear his ears to what his Indian brothers had to say, and remove every concern from his heart that he held about the Shawnees. Continuing with several affirmations of friendship at this troublesome time, accompanying each again with strings of wampum, the chief expressed that "their hearts, & their wives & children's, were once more rejoiced to see the great man of Virginia & the other brothers of the other provinces" for the efforts at restoring peace on the Ohio. White Eyes concluded by presenting the governor with a belt of wampum to affirm that the gathered Indian deputies "hoped & wanted to assist him in healing up the breach that had been made in the chain of friendship by some rash young people of both parties" and appealed that the Virginians not treat the Shawnees too harshly. With the formalities completed, both sides returned to their respective lodgings to wait to hear Dunmore's reply to their speeches when the council reconvened the next day.[4]

When the council did not reconvene the next day, the Indians seemed very dissatisfied that Dunmore had kept them waiting. They were used to hearing replies to speeches on the following day of a council and were unaware of the governor's practice of keeping even those who called on him in Williamsburg waiting. McKee informed Dunmore about the Indians' displeasure, warning the governor that the chiefs would only wait until noon on Friday for him to do so, "& then would be gone." The Indian Department officer added that many Indians already did not hold a high opinion of him and suspected that he only wanted to keep them near Pittsburgh until his army made ready to go down the river against the Shawnees. They further complained about Dunmore's evasive answers about his intentions and not even providing them "an ounce of provision, powder, and other necessities." Indian leaders expected to receive presents from British and colonial officials when they attended diplomatic councils, and Dunmore's inattention to the practice made them "prodigiously uneasy."[5]

Shortly after the council began on September 16, St. Clair arrived from Kittanning and requested an immediate meeting with the Virginia governor on behalf of the governor of Pennsylvania. He then demanded custody of one of Dunmore's officers, who had committed the murder of a Delaware Indian and for whose apprehension a proclamation had been issued that offered a £50 reward. When they met on the fort's parade, St. Clair delivered a packet from Governor Penn, which Dunmore took but did not open before the meeting ended.

Although he seemed sympathetic to the Pennsylvania faction in the intercolonial dispute, Prevost realized that his father-in-law could not afford to alienate Connolly or the governor while the matter of his land grants remained unresolved. The next day, he began an attempt to repair the apparent rift that had developed between Croghan and the Virginia faction in general and Connolly in particular, and asked the governor what he perceived to be the cause. Dunmore told Prevost that he heard on good authority, other than Connolly, that his father-in-law had slandered him by saying that the governor "had occasioned all this broil between the Indians & the colonies in order to secure a tool for the purpose of ministry." He also told Prevost that Croghan had "strove to set the Shawnees upon the backs of the Virginians by his insidious and dangerous speeches," and that Croghan could be blamed as the "author & sole cause" for the current disturbances. The governor continued that although appointed the chief magistrate of the West Augusta district, Croghan had "denied the jurisdiction of the Province of Virginia" and had "constantly acted a duplicate part throughout the tenor of his conduct."

Following Prevost's intercession with both men, Croghan and Connolly met and repaired their misunderstandings. The next day, September 16, Dunmore also met Croghan and put their differences behind them. The mediation proved mutually beneficial, as Croghan needed Governor Dunmore to validate his land claims in Virginia while Dunmore needed Croghan's assistance in managing diplomatic relations with the Indians, "upon which he frankly owned he believed the whole success of his expedition depended." Having the retired deputy superintendent again in his favor also made Dunmore's negotiations with the Indian deputies much easier and more effective.[6]

After Dunmore received him civilly, Croghan notified the Indians that the governor would respond to their speeches on September 12. When the chiefs arrived the next morning, Dunmore reciprocated the Indian welcome by "condoling with them for the loss they had sustained through the rashness of some vagabonds" to open the discussions. He then answered White Eyes's opening speech by telling the assembled chiefs he appreciated the pains they had taken to "heal the sores made by the Shawanese" and would have preferred to give them a more favorable answer. Instead, he reminded them how little the Shawnees deserved the "treatment or appellation of brethren" from him and charged that they had never complied with the terms of the peace treaty they had made with Colonel Bouquet at the end of Pontiac's War to give up and return their white prisoners, "nor have they ever truly buried the hatchet."[7]

The governor then recounted the numerous violations the Shawnees had committed with the encouragement of the Pennsylvania faction "upon the frontiers of my Government" since 1764. These included, Dunmore charged, "the murder of a man the very next summer" and another "eight of my people upon Cumberland River" the next year. He reminded them of numerous similar incidents, one by one, which included not only attacks but the stealing of horses and goods from Virginia settlers and traders by Shawnee warriors, who "disposed of them (together with a considerable quantity of peltry)" to the traders from Pennsylvania. The governor then reminded his audience that while the Shawnee "banditti" robbed, killed, and injured several Virginians in their country, they allowed Pennsylvania traders to pass unharmed. Dunmore then drew particular attention to the murders of nineteen men, women, and children on the Virginia side of the Ohio from 1771 to 1773, including the family of Adam Stroud on the Elk River and young James Boone and Henry Russell in Powell's Valley. In the latter incident, he added that the guilty warriors "carried off their [victims'] horses and effects" to their towns, where they sold them to Pennsylvania traders. The Shawnees had committed "All these, with many other murders" against Virginians, Dunmore maintained, "before a drop of Shawanees blood was spilt" by Virginians.

The governor concluded that since the beginning of 1774, Shawnee warriors had "continually perpetrated robberies upon my defenseless Frontier inhabitants," which at length irritated them so much that they began to retaliate. While Dunmore assured the Delaware and Iroquois of his colony's friendship and justice to the other nations represented, he posed them a question about how they thought the Virginians should treat the Shawnees. Having stated the dispute "between them and us," Dunmore left it to the deputies to judge what they merited.[8]

Captain Pipe and his delegation, whom the Indian deputies sent to mediate with the Shawnees, returned on September 18. He informed Croghan that the Shawnees "were willing to come to terms" with Dunmore in order to avoid war. They desired to know what the Virginians expected and would willingly make restitution as soon as they were permitted to go hunting. The next morning, the governor's party, which included Colonel Stephen, Major Connolly, two musicians playing French horns, and a "Scotch Piper," arrived at Croghan Hall in two boats that displayed the British flag. The deputies of the several nations waited on the opposite bank to meet with them but requested to consult with Croghan before they answered the governor. Croghan recommended to Dunmore that Connolly and McKee also accompany him to the meeting.

When the council reconvened at the fort on September 23, Pipe announced that the Shawnees stated their desire to restore friendship. Pipe related that in the council held in their towns on the Scioto, Cornstalk claimed he had told the warriors to stay home and "be quiet" and not "molest" the Virginia backcountry inhabitants. Except for a few "rash young men" who went out on their own, he maintained that his nation's people and their Mingo friends had complied. Plukkemehnotee, a Mingo chief whom whites called Pluggy, blamed the recent disturbances on Wyandot, Miami, and Ottawa warriors who had disregarded their own nations' chiefs to fight the Virginians. He said that because the Shawnees and Mingoes desired peace, when the war parties entered their towns to offer their aid, the

Shawnees told their erstwhile allies to return to their homes. Big Apple Tree, a Mohawk deputy who accompanied Pipe, told Dunmore that the Shawnees would "pursue proper measures to restore peace" and meet with the Big Knife and Dunmore wherever he built his council fire, which the Six Nations, Wyandots, and Delaware would attend to restore a proper peace.[9]

Dunmore had heard enough. He thanked Pipe and the delegation for their intercession in attempting to broker a peace. He reminded all those present that the Shawnees had always shown hostility toward the Virginians. On the other hand, Dunmore said that the Big Knife remained ready to do even their greatest enemies justice. He asked Big Apple Tree to invite Cornstalk and the Shawnee chiefs to meet him either at Wheeling, the mouth of the Little Kanawha, or any other place farther down the Ohio they chose. The governor assured them that if they came, he would listen to them and treat them fairly. He then presented wampum as he told the several deputies that if his brethren of the Six Nations, Wyandots, and Delaware led the Shawnees to the council fire, he could trust that the meeting would occur. As a further sign of their desire to see the dispute resolved without war, Pipe and a fellow Delaware chief named Wanganam offered to accompany Dunmore on the expedition to help facilitate any negotiations.[10]

When Croghan returned home that evening, he told Prevost that the Delaware, Wyandot, and Six Nations deputies "seemed extremely pleased" with the outcome of the council. Dunmore waited on the canoes to arrive on the Monongahela. While the Indian council occupied much of the governor's time, Colonel Stephen saw to it that the right wing completed its preparations for the expedition. Three hundred to four hundred militiamen, mostly from the West Augusta district, joined those who had marched from Winchester to raise the division's strength to about seven hundred men. After Majors McDonald and Connolly had the newly constructed or impressed vessels loaded with supplies and provisions, the soldiers climbed aboard and waited for Dunmore. He came to the landing and immediately set off with them to go downriver to join Colonel Andrew Lewis at the mouth of the Kanawha.[11]

COLONEL ANDREW LEWIS's left wing, or Southern Division, had begun its march from Camp Union toward the mouth of the Kanawha. The advance party, the first to leave the Great Levels, marched with scouts out in front, followed by a fatigue party of ax-wielding woodsmen, or pioneers, and their detail of guards. The pioneers cleared the path of obstructions and widened it enough for the packhorses and cattle to pass, and cut blazes on the trees to mark the way the divisions were to follow. A general order, whose execution had been drilled and practiced before leaving Camp Union, provided for the orderly defense of a camp without the need for posting it in the daily plan. In the case of an alarm, "each Company is to form on the Ground [where] they are encamp'd and face outwards, & stand fast until they receive orders." Each morning after the beating of the general, captains inspected their companies as bullock drivers gathered their herds and counted the beeves, the packhorse men loaded their animals with cargo, and all prepared to march.[12]

By the fifth day of marching, the column had gone about thirty miles from Camp Union on its way to the Elk River. Not far away, having taken a different trail and traveling faster, Colonel Field's detachment of Culpepper County men halted near Little Meadow River for the night of September 10, unaware of the location of Colonel Charles Lewis's division. Early the next morning, Privates John Clay and Francis Cowheard (or Coward) of Captain James Kirtley's company went out to gather the packhorses that had wandered away from camp in the night. At the same time, two Ottawa warriors approached Field's camp looking for grazing horses they could easily bridle and lead out from under the very noses of the picket guards. From their hiding place they saw Clay but did not notice Cowheard, who walked about one hundred yards away. One of the Indians shot and killed Clay. Cowheard looked in the direction of the musket's report in time to see an Indian, scalping knife in hand, running toward the body of his dead companion. Reacting quickly, Cowheard evened the score with a shot that killed the warrior before he could take the scalp. The other Indian ran off and escaped but left behind a number of rope bridles in his hiding place. After the soldiers gathered and loaded the horses, they stood ready to resume the march. The Indians' appearance compelled Field to change course, and by the end of the day, the Culpepper men fell in with Colonel Charles Lewis's division.[13]

The advance party reached the Elk River on September 21, fifteen days after leaving, and eighty-five miles from, Camp Union. The men established the camp upstream from its confluence with the Kanawha River and not far from the ruins of Walter Kelly's farm. Colonel Charles Lewis posted guards and sent out patrols to look for signs of recent Indian activity. In accordance with his brother's plan of campaign, he determined the division's priority of work. The men established cattle and horse pens and began working on the fortification, supply magazine, and canoes while they waited for the main body.[14]

THE AUGUSTA COUNTY spies posted on Gauley Mountain, about fifty miles from Camp Union, watched as one war party returned toward Indian country from the direction of the settlements on September 6. Three days later, they saw three more warriors heading east toward the settlements. Except for Major Angus MacDonald's raid on Wakatomika, the Virginians had fought a completely defensive and largely local war. Although Dunmore had decided to take the fight to Shawnee country, the expedition had yet to cross the Ohio River. Virginia's militia forces remained on defense, with Indian war parties active on the south bank, particularly in Fincastle County. The hard-pressed militia struggled to protect the lives and property of the backcountry inhabitants as shortages of all classes of supply, especially ammunition, hampered effective responses to enemy attacks.[15] Fortunately, a convoy had just reached the lower district headquarters carrying, among other stores, one and one-half pounds of much-needed gunpowder. In an effort to stretch the supply as far as possible, Campbell judiciously divided it and kept some in reserve for issue in an appropriate contingency.[16]

Like Augusta, Fincastle County recruited men as "Indian spies" to monitor the likely avenues of approach to the settled regions. Just as the militia companies found it difficult to muster adequate forces that could defend all the places that needed protection, the county had only a limited number of men for that service to observe or detect evidence of approaching war parties at the mountain passes, water gaps, and trails. With no other option, some of the spies had two or more observation posts at such a distance apart that it took several days for them to check them. Consequently, one pair of spies discovered footprints that revealed an enemy party had crossed the Sandy River heading toward Maiden Springs. The spies immediately headed for the settlement to alert the five soldiers of Captain Smith's company who manned the small fort and sound the alarm to muster the local militia. With a two- or three-day head start over the spies, the Indians struck without warning.[17]

Early in the morning on September 8, as his wife and three small children remained in bed, John Henry stood in the door of his home in the Clinch River area. Two Indians concealed in the nearby woods shot him. Although severely wounded, Henry ran into the woods hoping his assailants would pursue him instead of entering the house and harming his family. By chance, he met his neighbor "Old John Hamilton," who concealed Henry in a thicket before running the four miles to Fort Christian to alert the militia. Stopping to check at the house on his way, Hamilton found no one present, and presumed the Indians had taken Henry's family captive. Henry died of his wounds within a day without learning of their fate. Meanwhile, another neighbor, named Bradshaw, had also fled from his farm after notic-ing some "Indian signs" in his cornfield. He met Hamilton, and the two men walked together toward Captain Smith's station. After going about three miles, they came to a place where twelve to fifteen warriors, by their estimate, had evidently "Breakfasted" earlier in the day and left some of their provisions behind when they departed. Hamilton and Bradshaw spread the alarm when they reached Rich Valley, at which several distressed inhabitants fled to Royal Oak or other defended communities. Indian raiders also struck on the North Fork of the Holston. About one mile from "the upper End of Campbell's Choice" near the Clay Lick, warriors captured Samuel Lemmey, but the families of John and Archibald Buchanan narrowly escaped.[18]

In response, Major Campbell ordered Captain Smith to send out patrols in the Clinch area, and for the three nearest companies on the Holston—Crockett's, Herbert's, and the "late Doack's"—to muster all available men on September 10. He expected the raiders to follow their last blow by con-tinuing to advance deeper into the settled areas and striking all the homes, farms, and other improvements in their path. The major also anticipated that the warriors would stop and loot all the abandoned property in their path, which he viewed as a vulnerability that he intended to exploit. He therefore instructed the local commanders to have their men turn out with their arms and bring as much ammunition as possible and enough rations for an operation of several days' duration. When the Holston men assem-bled, Campbell issued enough powder from the contingency stock he had set aside so that the soldiers, including those who brought none, had at least "3 loads apiece."[19] The major divided the Holston men into three units and sent them by different routes to intercept the raiders.[20]

Three days later, about one-half mile from Maiden Spring, three Indian warriors saw a lone white man approaching. Unaware that their intended target was a member of one of Captain Smith's patrols moving in extended order, they decided to kill and scalp him. The warriors opened fire from be-hind the cover of large trees but missed. The soldier returned fire, hitting one of his assailants, then ran to rejoin his comrades. The wounded Indian fell to the ground a few steps from the tree. Although the brave bled pro-fusely, which caused a "plug" to "burst out of the wound," he somehow made his way about eighty yards to the refuge of a large pit or cave, where he later died. The other two warriors fled while the soldiers, although spread out for about three hundred yards, moved toward the sound of the gunfire and gave them "a good chase." A few days later, a patrol went back to the area to find the dead man's corpse. "Anxious to get his scalp," the troops took ropes to lower one man down with "lights" to search the cave for the wounded Indian.[21]

Elsewhere, on the evening of September 13, some of Captain Smith's scouts discovered the tracks of an enemy war party that had captured some prisoners and some horses from the settlements. Once informed, Smith led a twenty-one-man detachment in pursuit. They moved quickly in an attempt to overtake the warriors and rescue the captives. The Indians became aware they were being followed, and before the militiamen drew near, the raiders mounted the stolen horses and escaped with their prisoners.[22]

On September 17, Campbell reported to Preston on the action he had taken to counter the enemy attacks in that part of the county during the preceding week. He praised the conduct of the district's militia in general. Most of them had willingly performed any service asked of them when called out, but a few men caused him concern. He therefore requested Colonel Preston's guidance, as well as the authority to maintain good order and discipline among the soldiers guilty of misconduct. For example, he wanted to know how to best deal with "a few obstinate Wretches, that selfishly refuses Duty," lest they set a bad example that others may follow at the next alarm. Campbell also wanted to know how to proceed against those men who turned out but were derelict in their duty or committed acts of misconduct while in service.[23]

The latter category came to Campbell's attention after the members of one detachment behaved "indifferently" while on a mission. After they arrived at the scene where Indian raiders had wounded John Henry, the men conducted only a cursory search for the invaders before they retired to Captain Smith's station to get provisions from the magazine. They drew three days' rations, including bacon, on the pretense that they needed the food in order to sustain them on an extended patrol operation in which they would search for footprints and other signs of enemy activity in the surrounding country in order to prevent another raid. Instead of performing any service, much less this operation, they immediately started for home. As they made their way, they received the report that someone had discovered fresh signs of Indian activity nearby, but the homeward-bound troops refused to investigate. Although Campbell considered the men's "ill-Conduct" in forsaking their mission egregious enough, he viewed the deceptive acquisition of scarce provisions as having significantly added to the infraction. The misappropriation of the bacon had particularly vexed Campbell. He explained that the magazine kept that item in reserve primarily to sustain the parties ordered out in the arduous pursuit of Indian raiders and for the spies who stayed at their posts for extended periods without the ability to acquire rations from local sources. Furthermore, with any meat—not only bacon—in short supply on the Clinch, the county had difficulty maintaining a sufficient ration for those who deserved it.[24] When rations constitute part of a soldier's pay, the offense equates to men receiving pay without having performed any service to earn it.

The insufficient supply of ammunition continued to threaten the effective defense of the settlements. The wasteful and reckless practice of shooting off ammunition without cause or to no useful purpose in which some incautious inhabitants indulged had exacerbated the problem. Campbell explained that although the garrisons had little gunpowder on hand, if the county could spare one or two pounds more, he would divide it in the same sparing manner as he had before the alarm of September 10. The major assured the colonel that the soldiers of his command could then effectively respond to the next threat.[25] If the shortage of gunpowder did not present enough of a problem, the major added that if not soon replenished, his district's magazine would soon run low on flour as well. Despite these challenges, the major confidently assured the county lieutenant that the soldiers of the district's militia would give a good account of themselves in action if the enemy dared to trouble the area's inhabitants again.[26]

As for the state of the garrisons, Major Campbell had recently inspected the defenses of settlements in his district. Ensign Hendly Moore and Sergeant John Duncan had fifteen men at Fort Christian, or Glade Hollow, twelve miles east of Fort Preston at Castle's Woods. Eighteen men served under Sergeant John Kingkead (or Kinkaid) at Elk Garden. Sergeant Robert Brown commanded five men at Maiden Spring. These numbers indicated that these forts all had their full complements. In contrast, Captain Smith had chosen to fully garrison the station at Maxwell Mill last since no women and children took shelter there, and had expected the recent levies from New River and Reed Creek to arrive before long. Major Campbell therefore sent a patrol composed of some of the most reliable men to see how Captain Smith and the three men posted with him and Ensign John Campbell fared at "Smith's Upper Station" at Maxwell's Mill. The place was sometimes also called Big Crab Orchard or Witten's (Whitton's) fort, at the home of John Whitton.[27]

To help hurry the reinforcements, Campbell asked Preston to have Lieutenant Jeremiah Pierce, who commanded Captain Crockett's administrative unit while the captain was away on the expedition, to send him fifteen men. He explained, "That Company that is covered by so thick a settlement as Reed Creek" could detach them without significantly degrading the local defense. He requested that the county lieutenant order the "upper settlements" on the New and Elk Rivers, which had sent "few if any Men" on the expedition, likewise muster detachments to aid those communities that were left less well defended when their men answered the governor's call. Doack's company was also tasked to detach fifteen men. Twelve of them arrived before another week passed, with two more men expected a few days later, but the fifteenth, Campbell learned, "was an obstinate Gent that despises Authority," and would therefore not turn out as ordered.

Major Campbell explained to Colonel Preston that he frequently traveled about the district to distant localities in the county to acquire provisions for the soldiers on duty at the various stations and "stir up others" to honor their service obligations. Campbell recommended that the county lieutenant consider increasing the number of men on active duty in the district for at least a few weeks to help the "weakly guarded" lower settlements. Of these, Campbell also asked for additional men on full-time duty to also be posted at Royal Oak. When Captain John Wilson arrived with his company of levies from Pittsylvania County, Campbell urged Preston to immediately detach a "Subaltern's Command"—fifteen to twenty-five men—to Maxwell Mill to reinforce Captain Smith's weak garrison there. After he conceded that the additional men expected from several other Fincastle companies could probably not be raised, Campbell recommended that Preston deploy the rest of Wilson's company of Pittsylvania County men on Reed Creek and in Rich Valley in order to protect and encourage the inhabitants to stay in their homes and save their crops.[28]

By Friday, September 23, reports from local militia officers indicated the situation in the Clinch and lower Holston settlements had deteriorated when patrols and scouts discovered signs of a large enemy war party. Logan—the Mingo leader—and his raiders arrived in the vicinity of Fort Byrd. It was built on the property of William Moore and included his fortified home, hence it was often also referred to as Moore's fort. The fort was located in Lower Castle's Woods, and Lieutenant Daniel Boone commanded its twelve-man detachment. As they scouted for weaknesses in the settlement's defenses, the marauders killed or seized and drove off several head of cattle and horses. Others surprised two black men working in the fields and took them prisoner before they could reach safety. The warriors then used the captives as bait by forcing them to run the gantlet within sight of the fort in an attempt to draw its defenders into an ambush. Not strong enough to sally out to attempt a rescue with any prospect of success, the garrison stood helplessly by and watched the prisoners endure the ordeal.[29]

John Roberts and his neighbors thought they had nothing to fear living near Kings Mill on Reedy Creek, a tributary of the Holston North Fork, and close to the Cherokee line. No war parties from that nation had ever ventured or conducted raids there, leading the settlers to believe the very remoteness of the location afforded them enough security that they need not worry. The families chose to not seek shelter in any of the nearby forts when they received the alarm. Focused on a possible incursion by Cherokee warriors, they had not counted on Logan's war party coming across Moccasin Gap after attacking William Moore's—Fort Byrd—on the Clinch and approaching from a direction they did not expect. The folly of such a false sense of security became all too apparent when Logan's warriors attacked. Although Roberts's neighbors managed to escape, his family fell victim to a gruesome assault. The raiders took ten-year-old James captive, killed and scalped his parents and sisters, and left his younger brother "Scalped and Tomahawked" but alive. As they escaped with their trophies, the attackers most likely left the child behind because he appeared dead or dying and therefore had no further value.

The lad, however, had enough life in him to go for help. He started to run when he mistook an approaching patrol for another Indian raiding party, but he stopped and rejoiced for his deliverance when he heard his uncle's voice calling his name. He ran to them and told the soldiers what had happened. Despite his young age and recent ordeal, the boy spoke sensibly in response to their questions and led his uncle to the mutilated bodies of his murdered parents and sisters. The militiamen found a war club, with a message attached, near the corpses. The parchment bore a message dated July 24, 1774, from "Captain John Logan" to Captain Michael Cresap. In it, Logan asked, "What did you kill my people on Yellow Creek for [?]" It was the letter the Mingo warrior had dictated to William Robinson, the man he had taken prisoner near Prickett's fort in June.[30]

In extending his revenge to the Roberts family, Logan and his war party had killed and scalped the mother, father, and daughters, took one boy captive, and left another for dead. It may be recalled that Carlisle merchant and Pennsylvania partisan John Montgomery had expressed his belief to Governor Penn that the Mingo leader had sated the vengeance for the murder of his relatives in June. Now in September, Montgomery's prediction that Logan would "sit Still" had not proven true. The commander of the patrol sent Logan's war club and message parchment up the chain of command to Major Campbell, who forwarded it to Colonel Preston on October 12.[31]

In his report, Campbell described that the Roberts boy had received but one blow to the back of his head with a tomahawk. Although the weapon had cut through the child's skull, the major "believed his Brains is safe." With compassion and sympathy, the district commander sent for "an Old

Man that has some Skill" to attend the young patient and asked Preston to send a Dr. Lloyd, or at least some medicines, to treat the injury. Unfortunately, the boy did not survive long. Campbell reported that after "frequently lamenting 'he was not able to fight enough for to save his mammy,'" the poor child passed away on October 6.[32]

Although the local militia commander, Captain William Cocke, pledged to do his duty and everything in his power "to promote the Honour and Safety of this Frontier," he advised the inhabitants who had not yet forted that they should not repeat the Roberts's error by placing their trust in the remote locations of their settlements to preserve them from harm. He urged them to erect a fort at a suitable place as near as possible to the line that separated the Virginia colony from Cherokee country so as to not yield "one foot of Ground" to the hostile Indians. He warned that by abandoning and fleeing their homes, they not only surrendered their property and means of support but revealed their weakness and inability to resist to the invaders. The captain ordered his sergeant to deploy all available men in the company for the community's protection. In the meantime, he pledged to travel to South Carolina to recruit some volunteers to help them, and he hoped Virginia's government would vote them recompense for their service.[33]

At the first sound of "hallooing, and the report of many guns at several houses" at Kings Mill, an express rode off to Major Campbell's headquarters with the news of yet another attack. The series of frequent alarms and sightings of war parties had convinced many of Fincastle County's backcountry inhabitants that the Cherokees had indeed taken the warpath and committed the latest atrocities. Two traders, Archibald Taylor and a local man named Shoat, had recently returned from Cherokee country. Like other traders who frequently ventured into that nation's towns, Taylor and Shoat were greatly concerned when they saw that the Cherokees "appeared in a very bad temper." They testified to Major Campbell that during their stay they watched two war parties leave their towns but confessed that they did not know whether the warriors intended to join forces with the Shawnee and their allies gathering on the Scioto or to attack Fincastle County settlements on their own.[34]

Back in the settlements, since so many of the militia's best soldiers had gone on the expedition, the men who remained back for home defense responded to many alarms. To make matters worse, since the expedition required such a large quantity of what was available, the forces that remained had only a limited supply of gunpowder and lead. The settlers on the Holston understandably experienced much anxiety because they knew they had little to sustain them in a protracted fight. Major Campbell reflected their sentiment when he confided to Colonel Preston "it would ruin us" if they had to engage the Cherokees in a war at that time. As the people of Kings Mill gathered to build a fort in which to make a stand, Campbell ordered Captain Cocke to take what men he could raise from his company and go to their support and said he would further reinforce them as soon as Captain Wilson's Pittsylvania County men arrived, as well as with whatever forces Colonel Preston could send their way.[35]

After he examined Taylor and Shoat more closely, Campbell determined that Shawnee and Mingo—not Cherokee—war parties were to blame for the recent attacks. The traders told the major that Oconostota had endeavored to remain peaceful with the English, and most of his people wanted no part in the war. Furthermore, the chief pledged that while he had nothing to do with the decision of any of his nation's warriors to fight against the Virginians, a strong faction among them favored the Shawnees. Campbell offered to forward a letter from Preston to Oconostota that he suggested might help the chief "resume his authority" over some of the more impertinent warriors. Campbell also wrote to ask his friend Alexander Cameron, the Southern Indian Department's deputy superintendent for that nation, to intercede. Even if the Cherokees decided to join the Shawnees on the warpath, negotiations might delay hostilities long enough to allow the Virginians time to better prepare their defenses.[36]

The defenders of the Clinch and Holston districts of Fincastle County began to experience frequent alarms and noticed increased signs of Indian activity even in "the very Heart of the Settlement." Except for one man narrowly escaping capture on the South Fork, they had not actually seen warriors in force since the attacks on Reedy Creek earlier in the month. The reports led Major Campbell to believe most of the warriors seen moving about the settlements were only "Spies." Despite the recent enemy activity, the major took some satisfaction from the fact that he had convinced the people not to flee from the settlements, and that the Cherokees had not perpetrated the attacks. He assured Preston that if the county lieutenant could send them more ammunition, they could defend the county even if they did have to fight the Cherokees and the Shawnees as well.[37]

Lieutenant Boone sent Campbell a war club that differed markedly in appearance from the one left at Blackmore's and suggested "it is the Cherokees that is now annoying us." Campbell preferred to believe that some of the Indians who had fled from Wakatomika in the wake of McDonald's raid in August, including Logan, had "taken refuge" just beyond the settlements. He ventured that these refugees would willingly sew confusion and like nothing more than to see a misunderstanding arise between the Virginians

and the old Cherokee chiefs who had thus far kept the peace. Campbell continued to believe the Cherokees had not committed the "mischief." He not
only had the war club and message that Logan left at the Roberts's home
but viewed the circumstances in which someone found Cherokee clubs and
other signs as "suspicious."[38]

Amid the turmoil, a gentleman from "Carolina" contacted Campbell
with an interesting offer to bring fifty Catawba warriors who desired to be
employed against the Shawnees. These warriors would be accompanied by
"fifty prime white men" who wished to come and assist "their Neighbours,"
the Virginians. Before giving the Carolina gentleman an answer, Campbell
consulted Preston. He recommended that the best way they could use such
volunteers was to have them march through Cumberland Gap to the Ohio,
where they could act as scouts against the Shawnees during the coming winter. Campbell heard nothing more of the offer from the Carolina gentlemen.
He then confided a thought to Preston. If war with the Cherokees appeared
likely, he proposed stationing one company at or near the Long Island of
the Holston. Control of that feature would offer the Virginians a decided
advantage in the event of such a contingency.[39]

Defending the frontier had become more complicated since the recent
series of attacks. The companies on the Holston felt they faced as much
danger as those on the Clinch, which made them reluctant to go to their
neighbors' aid at the expense of their own families' protection. Meanwhile,
the defenses at Blackmore's and the head of the Clinch were stretched thin,
and ammunition was in such short supply that neither Captain Looney's
nor Captain Smith's companies could effectively pursue an enemy force of
a dozen or more warriors. With his men unhappy with their lodgings, Captain Wilson told Major Campbell that they would rather have had Colonel
Preston station them in the woods. As a remedy, Campbell suggested the
colonel might better employ them on the Clinch toward the head of the
Blue Stone. There they could effectively defend the frontier as well as the
Reed Creek settlement as they presently did. The major reported that the
middle stations on the Clinch remained strong, but when employed in small
ranging operations, the militiamen who were also local inhabitants feared
leaving the protection of the forts to tend the crops in their fields. And while
Boone conducted an active defense of the Castle's Woods area, the spies
who operated out of the post at Blackmore's had lately become remiss in
reporting signs of the enemy. Despite these concerns, Major Campbell remained confident of the district's ability to guard the inhabitants until the
expedition returned.[40]

During the period between sunset and darkness on Thursday, September 29, Indian raiders fired at three men near Fort Christian on the Clinch, where Ensign Hendly Moore commanded. In the exchange, the warriors killed and scalped Sergeant John Duncan within three hundred yards of the post. As soon they heard the gunfire, the men of the garrison mustered a small detachment that marched out to engage the invaders. The Indians immediately "ran off," and the soldiers pursued them until it became too dark to continue. The ensign sent an express explaining the situation to Campbell early the next morning. Lieutenant Boone prepared to lead a patrol from Fort Byrd in search of any enemy in the area of his station when he received an express from Blackmore's fort. After reading it, the lieutenant relayed the report that detailed the increased enemy activity in the area around Stony Creek and the lower Clinch River during the preceding week. Captain Looney, able to muster only eleven men from his company at that time, reluctantly reported to Campbell that he could neither range in search of the warriors who had raided Fort Christian nor investigate the latest enemy activity.[41]

IN LATE SEPTEMBER, the period of relative calm that had lasted along the Monongahela and its tributaries since July came to an end. War parties returned, and the inhabitants in that part of Augusta County once again experienced the ravages of Indian war. One group of warriors murdered a man and his wife and took several neighbors prisoner in the Tenmile Creek area on the morning of September 28. Another raiding party moved in the vicinity of Prickett's Fort. When they heard cow bells, the Indians took position along the side of a trail and waited in ambush. When Josiah Prickett and Mrs. Susan Ox drove some cows in toward the post for milking, the braves killed and scalped him and took her captive.[42]

As Lord Dunmore conducted his diplomatic efforts at Pittsburgh, Major William Crawford ordered his men to break camp near Redstone. On September 20, his five-hundred man division of the right wing marched overland to Wheeling with a train of fifty packhorses and a herd of two hundred head of cattle. When his men reached Fort Fincastle, the major allowed them only a short respite before they prepared for the next phase of the expedition. His brother Augustine Crawford, a commissary officer, supervised the Fort Fincastle magazine. He and his men would remain to forward provisions and supplies as the division advanced.[43]

Lord Dunmore arrived at Fort Fincastle on September 30, after traveling the ninety miles downstream from Pittsburgh. With the union of Craw-

ford's division and the main body, the men who had been detached to garrison Fort Fincastle since August rejoined their companies. As it encamped
about Wheeling, the strength of the right ring of Dunmore's army stood at
about one thousand two hundred men. The governor then learned about
the recent raids on the Monongahela communities. The news could not
have come at a worse time. Commissary officer Augustine Crawford noted
that it "alarmed his Lordship, much as the Indians had been peaceable [in
the area] for some time, and some of the defiant nations had met him at
Fort Dunmore" for optimistic negotiations about avoiding war. The governor still expected Cornstalk and the Shawnee leaders to meet him near the
mouth of the Hockhocking, but prospects for peace had dimmed in spite
of the optimism expressed when the council concluded at Pittsburgh. Crawford probably expressed the feelings of many when he wrote, "We were in
hopes of a peace being concluded between his Lordship and the Indians,"
but in the wake of the recent raids on the Monongahela, he doubted it
would happen. If the governor could affect a resolution of differences with
the Indians, the commissary officer believed that the Virginians could relieve "the poor distressed Bostonians," referring to a widely circulated but
unfounded rumor that General Gage had attacked the city with artillery.[44]

Early on the morning of October 2, while the drums and fifes of most
of the corps encamped around Wheeling sounded reveille, the musicians
of Major Crawford's division beat the general. On hearing the signal, the
men packed their individual loads and unit baggage, packhorse men loaded
cargo onto their charges, and the cattle drivers gathered the herd. When
they heard assembly, the captains formed their companies and took their
places. When his subordinate notified him that they all were ready, Crawford saluted the governor and gave the order. The musicians sounded the
march, and the column moved forward along the south bank of the Ohio.
Following a plan similar to that of the left wing, Crawford's division, like
that of Colonel Charles Lewis, would establish a forward support base at
the mouth of Hockhocking Creek, where it would await the main body before continuing its advance against the enemy.[45] According to the change of
plan that the governor communicated to Colonel Andrew Lewis from Oldtown, Maryland, on August 30, Crawford expected to meet the left wing
marching up from the Great Kanawha when he arrived, or shortly thereafter.

Crawford's division arrived near the mouth of the Little Kanawha—on
about October 4—after a march of eighty miles and prepared to cross the
Ohio, which the terms of the 1768 Treaty of Fort Stanwix defined as the
boundary between the Virginia colony and the land reserved to the Indians.

When all was ready, Crawford gave the order. Boatmen ferried the soldiers across the river on rafts and canoes, as the horses and cattle swam alongside. Once they landed on the north bank, scouts went forward along the intended route, officers reformed their companies and posted security, and the cattle and packhorse drivers arranged their animals for the next leg of the march. When the captains indicated their units were ready, the division continued its advance, now moving along the north bank to the mouth of Hockhocking Creek "where the whole of the troops [the left and right wings] are to rendezvous." When they arrived, Crawford's men did not encounter any troops from the left wing, nor did his scouts report seeing any signs of them.

As the spearhead of an invading army, the Virginians found themselves in enemy country and acted accordingly. They dutifully took the necessary precautions according to the doctrine contained in Bland's *Treatise on Military Discipline* and what experience had taught them. The division mounted the necessary guard force, with the concomitant picket posts and local patrols. Those soldiers not assigned to guard duty began clearing land and felling trees in order "to build a stockade fort, or large block-house" located—as Crawford noted from having surveyed the tract—just across the Ohio from some "bottom land" owned by George Washington. When completed, the post constituted the first fortified forward supply base on the north bank of the Ohio. Back at Wheeling, Sergeant Ebenezer Zane assumed command of the detachment that remained to garrison Fort Fincastle and guard the magazine operated by Augustine Crawford. That post became important as the last link on the south bank in the logistical chain that conducted supplies and provisions to the right wing, and the entire army after the planned junction with Colonel Andrew Lewis's command, in its protected advance into hostile territory.

With seven hundred men embarked aboard a flotilla of canoes, pirogues, and keelboats, Dunmore gave Colonel Stephen the command to advance, on about October 2. The main body of the right wing moved down the Ohio from Wheeling to the mouth of the Hockhocking. After the boatmen banked the watercraft and the troops disembarked, Dunmore had the entire wing present to wait for Colonel Lewis's wing to join him, and for Cornstalk's delegation to arrive and resume negotiations. As Colonel Stephen assumed command of the encampment on about October 5, the newly arrived soldiers assumed their share of camp duties, including security, and assisted Crawford's men in building the storehouse and fortifications. Dunmore named the post Fort Gower in honor of the lord president of the Privy Council, Granville Leveson-Gower, second Earl of Gower—Lady Charlotte

Dunmore's brother-in-law and the governor's political sponsor.[46] He then
sent Sam Kenton, Simon Girty, and Peter Parchment by canoe to Point
Pleasant carrying orders for Lewis to march to the place of rendezvous without delay.[47] When they found that the left wing had not yet reached the
mouth of the Kanawha, the three scouts deposited the written orders in a
hollow tree, along with an "advertisement," or sign, posted nearby telling
Lewis's men of its presence, before they returned to Fort Gower.

As THE EVENTS on the Ohio transpired, Colonel Andrew Lewis planned to
march to the Elk River with the main body of the left wing, most of the
Botetourt County contingent, and two companies from the Fincastle, approximately six hundred men, on Monday, September 12. In addition to
the companies of Russell and Shelby, Colonel Lewis ordered Christian to
detach some of his men—not drawn from the aforementioned companies—to Fleming's command for driving horses and cattle and to "work at
[building] Canoes" at the Elk River. Private Joseph Duncan of Captain
Crockett's Fincastle County company, for example, was appointed as a
driver of cattle and "to guard the Beeves" during the march to the Ohio.
Since the detail reduced the number of Fincastle County soldiers at Camp
Union to just a few more than one hundred, Christian asked Preston to
"send about 100 rank & file men if they can be got with Convenience" and
without detriment to those garrisons in the forts or units patrolling the
frontier. While some officers believed the frontiers would be in less danger
after the army marched, owing to the Indian war parties' leaving to guard
their own homes, most had confidence that Preston would not leave the
people unguarded.[48]

Although disappointed that he would lead the last element to march and
have responsibility to convoy the last major supply train, Colonel Christian
nonetheless worked tirelessly to prepare the next division, as well as his own,
for the march. He wrote to Colonel Preston and requested that he "hurry
on Majr. Robertson & the men" to Camp Union. Although most of the
county's contingent would bring up the rear, he wanted to leave no one behind and urged that they go on together and try to overtake the rest of the
army at the mouth of the Elk, or at the mouth of the Kanawha by the latest.
Christian wanted neither to cross the Ohio much behind the main body
nor "miss lending our Assistance" to the army in an engagement. Since
Christian assumed any additional Fincastle men would have a good number
of packhorses but only a little flour, he requested they come quick. Although
no beeves remained at camp after the advanced body departed, Christian

expected more to arrive soon through the efforts of Major Posey and his department. Major Mathews, for example, had to bring an additional one hundred sixty thousand weight of beef on the hoof. Of the fifty-four head of cattle expected to go with Colonel Fleming's division, only twenty-six were on hand in camp, with the rest on the way.[49]

More troops had mustered to join the expedition than were expected. Consequently, the quartermasters and commissary officers realized they had not acquired sufficient stocks of supplies or enough provisions to support the force at hand. To remedy the situation, Colonel Andrew Lewis notified Colonel Preston and those who commanded the rear detachments in Augusta and Botetourt Counties of a plan for effectively employing the surplus manpower and reduce the rate of consuming rations that had been gathered for the expeditionary force. Expecting a total of as many as 1,490 men, on September 10, Lewis ordered the captains of the units scheduled to march on September 12 to inspect and report on the physical condition and health of their men by the end of the day. After they identified them, the colonel proposed posting those "not fully fit to undergo the fatigue of the Expedition" to garrison the small forts. This measure ensured that the colony gainfully employed the men taken into pay, improved the defenses of the communities served by those forts, and issued the soldiers stationed there rations from the stores acquired for the subsistence of the garrisons.[50]

Later in the evening, according to Colonel Fleming, one of the spies came in from Gauley Mountain with some new intelligence. On Tuesday the sixth he had observed a war party of five Indians returning toward Indian country from the direction of the settlements with three horses. In the morning three days later, he saw three more warriors heading toward the settled areas. The officers expressed their concern that "Somebody would be killed," since the inhabitants of the neighborhood tended to travel about carelessly. Colonel Christian suggested that the Indians the spies had observed had mainly come only to watch the motions of the army. Regardless of what motives brought the warriors through there, Fleming and his fellow officers agreed that the enemy closely watched the movements and activities of their army.[51]

On Sunday, the Fincastle contingent took over the remaining camp duties and the main guard in order to allow the Botetourt companies, and the others attached to them, to complete their preparations for marching. The order went to the troops from Botetourt, Captain Thomas Buford's company of riflemen from Bedford, and Captains Shelby's and Russell's companies from Fincastle County, to "hold themselves in Readiness to move on the Shortest Notice." Orders also directed each captain to inspect and ex-

amine and report the status of the ammunition distributed in their companies. The staff officers set to their tasks as well. Majors Posey and Ingles
had to "have all the packhorses loaded as early as possible." Ingles therefore
reported on the number of packhorses in camp, excluding those of the Fincastle line, and had "the brigade under his care" loaded with all the ammunition. The main body's commissary officer, Captain Charles Simms,
inventoried and reported on the quantity of salt and other provisions, as
his assistant conductors fixed all the tools not already issued to the companies to pack saddles for loading. Despite the flurry of activity in camp, officers and men made time for the "Divine Service to begin at 12 o'clock"
noon.[52]

The general, the signal for the troops to prepare to march, beat for the
main body at daybreak—in lieu of reveille—on September 12. After the
musicians beat the march, Fleming, accompanied by Andrew Lewis, led his
division out of Camp Union. The first day's march took the troops, packhorses, and cattle seven miles to Camp Pleasant, its next stop on the way to
the Elk River. After the marching men had halted for the day, a man entered
camp with a message for Colonel Andrew Lewis from his brother Charles.
It informed him that the company from Culpepper County that left Camp
Union with Colonel Field in command had caught up with the advance
party on Sunday night after an encounter with the enemy that left one soldier and one Indian dead.[53]

When the division broke camp on Buffalo Creek on the fourth day of
the march, Colonel Andrew Lewis thought it necessary to warn the men
that they had entered onto "ground much frequented by the Enemy." He
also found it necessary to have the captains repeat to their companies the
order that forbade the unauthorized firing of weapons. Not only was it a
matter of preventing the waste of ammunition, but since the enemy could
be present, it also could be a matter of life or death by potentially inviting
an attack. Fleming told the captains to announce to their companies that
any soldier who fired his gun without first obtaining permission would be
considered disobedient and treated accordingly by his comrades. If the
shooter fired against an enemy, however, the admonition did not apply,
since the sound of gunfire served as an alarm for the division that someone
had sighted or engaged the enemy.[54]

With Colonels Andrew Lewis and Fleming gone, Christian assumed
command of Camp Union until his division marched to the Elk River. The
rear body included the last of the Fincastle County contingent and some
Culpepper men, plus the Augusta men ordered to remain behind to wait
for the county's packhorses that went with the lead division to return for

new loads. Major Posey went to Staunton to "hurry out all the flour possible" before the end of the week, while several soldiers were employed to assist the drovers in gathering the beeves scattered around camp. The quartermaster had forwarded about "72,000wt" of flour with the first two march units, leaving about 8,000 in camp, with 130 horse loads expected to arrive in camp by the next evening, 96 more loads at Warm Springs waiting for transport to the Great Levels, and "between 20 and 30,000 wt beyond the Springs."

Christian planned to march by the following Monday, September 19, with all the supplies he could obtain in one or two days so his division could reach the mouth of the Kanawha and cross the Ohio with the rest of the army. He still waited for Major Robertson and the rest of the Fincastle contingent to arrive on Sunday or Monday, in enough time to march, and hoped that he would endeavor to get some more beeves on the way, and perhaps provide thirty more. Although Colonel Lewis had mentioned Robertson as the best officer to leave in command of a detachment to "take on what Provisions" he could not get ready by the time he marched, Christian wanted the major with him on the expedition.[55]

As the division prepared for the campaign, Christian complained that by the time the Fincastle companies had arrived at the rendezvous, the camp equipment in most need, kettles and tents, had mostly been distributed to the other contingents. This left only sixteen or seventeen battered tin kettles and only a few tents for all of his county's companies. The quartermaster assured him on Monday, September 12, that he had ordered enough linen to make the necessary tents to be brought with packhorses expected to arrive the next day. By the end of the week, Captain Floyd expressed his confidence that his men would "make out pretty well" in receiving enough kettles and the allowed sixty yards of tent cloth for each company. Christian meanwhile wrote to Preston for Robertson "to send over that whole Country and try to buy beg or borrow kettles" before he marched for the rendezvous—if he had not yet left. The lack of a simple item threatened the health of the troops. He explained that to do without kettles "is very hard, almost impossible," because men would become ill if forced to subsist on roasted meat without broth. [56]

Back in Fincastle County, as he prepared to leave Woods's fort for Camp Union, Major Robertson reported to Colonel Preston that he had collected some "Beeves and Cattles" at Rich Creek. He and Captain Michael Woods had combined their two understrength units into one company of fifty-five men. The number included some men of the Woods's fort garrison willing to enlist again once discharged from their current terms, which Robertson gladly obliged. When six of Woods's drafted men refused to go, they appealed to Preston to try to get off and not face a court-martial. Robertson and Woods requested that the county lieutenant "not Countenance any of them." Since two of the men had previously served as scouts, Woods threatened to withhold their pay certificates and told them their stopped pay would satisfy their fines for not marching. Despite the controversy, an elated Robertson expressed his gratitude to all of the good friends who assisted him in raising enough men to complete his company to full strength, a task he "thought merely Impossible to do" only a short time earlier.[57]

With Robertson at last heading toward the Great Levels with additional men and cattle, Colonel Christian decided to remain at Camp Union until Monday or Tuesday, September 25 or 26, when he led a large convoy of provisions and about 220 men. On Friday, the colonel issued orders for the division to prepare to march on short notice and for captains to recall all their men from out in the neighborhood back to camp by Saturday evening and have their companies ready for marching. The army had no horses to spare, and Acting Ensign (Sergeant) James Newell of Captain James Herbert's company noted that Christian allowed each captain to have three packhorses and no more for himself and company to carry all personal baggage and camp equipment. The orders directed the packhorse masters to have the road completed if possible and their animals supplied with hobbles and breastplates for their saddles and ready to start off by Sunday evening. The drivers of cattle received similar instructions. Finally, the colonel forbade gambling in camp until further notice.[58]

The general beat at daybreak on Tuesday, September 26, for the men scheduled to march, and they completed their final preparations. After a late start, Colonel Christian led the rear party on the first three miles of its route in the direction of the Elk River before it halted for the evening. According to Captain Floyd, Christian expected that Dunmore would make peace with the Indians before any serious fighting occurred, or certainly before a significant proportion of the Fincastle County contingent reached the Ohio.[59]

Captain Anthony Bledsoe, quartermaster of the Fincastle County expeditionary contingent, assumed command of Camp Union and the small stay-behind detachment. His command included the soldiers of his own company plus a few stragglers and the sick from several units. Christian had instructed him to wait until the six brigades of packhorses that accompanied the advance party returned from the Elk River, which he expected at any day, and to follow. In the meantime, Bledsoe saw that the men prepared supplies for loading as soon as the pack animals returned and had sufficient rest. However, of "two hundred fifty Loads" that did not arrive at Camp Union as expected, 150 had yet to leave Staunton, with the last 100 still waiting at Warm Springs. To further complicate matters, Major Sampson Mathews sent word to inform Bledsoe that he had the supplies waiting in Staunton, but with no means of transporting them to Camp Union, he was obliged to wait for the pack train to return, which certainly caused further delay.

The packhorses returned to the Great Levels late on Friday, September 30. With the animals' condition "so much Worsted," however, they could not go to Staunton and Warm Springs for their next loads without three days of rest first. To add to his burden, Bledsoe complained that he needed a hospital and a doctor to care for all the sick from the whole regiment remaining at Camp Union. Finally, his departure for the Elk much delayed by having to collect the supplies at Warm Springs and Staunton, Bledsoe confessed to Preston, "I Judge every person finds the Expedition more tedious than it was generally expected." [60]

On WEDNESDAY, September 21, after a march of 108 miles in 16 days, the troops of Colonel Charles Lewis's division arrived at the Elk River, where the elder Colonel Lewis intended to build a fortified magazine. The troops established the encampment about one mile upstream from the mouth, where the Elk flows into the Kanawha River. To get there, the route had taken them to the banks of New River just below the falls and passed near the ruins of Walter Kelly's farm, the scene of Colonel Field's harrowing ordeal in July.[61]

Colonel Fleming's division, accompanied by Colonel Andrew Lewis, arrived two days later after marching the same distance in twelve days. Following roll call, the combined returns, or strength reports, showed that the body of troops encamped on the Elk River had 977 officers and men present, with 945 fit for duty. With the two divisions joined, Colonel Andrew Lewis planned to march for the mouth of the Kanawha on October 1. To execute the plan, the men of the left wing had much to do, not the least of which was to secure the encampment from surprise attack from marauding Indians. The next day's order required fifty rank and file with the proper complement of officers and noncommissioned officers for the main guard, as well as the picket guards from each line. To accomplish some of the important tasks required to progress to the next phase of the campaign, commanders reported the number of artificers in the respective corps that were willing to work making canoes and doing other necessary tasks, and quartermasters put all the tools in working order.

With the beating of reveille on Saturday morning, the army fell into a familiar routine of military activity in camp. The main and picket guards established local security for the encampment, and Colonel Andrew Lewis ordered out three different scouts, or small patrols, to determine the extent of enemy activity in the area. One ranged up Elk River, another scouted the right bank of the Kanawha River, and the other reconnoitered the left bank to the mouth of the Coal (or Cole) River. Since Dunmore's original campaign plan intended for both wings to rendezvous at the mouth of the Kanawha, Colonel Andrew Lewis instructed a scouting party to descend the river by canoe to Point Pleasant. On arriving, they were to wait for Lord Dunmore and the arrival of the "Troops from the Northward." Because they first had to mend a split in the hull of their canoe, they did not get under way until Sunday.

Soldiers not posted to guard duty or sent on missions performed fatigue duties. Details helped the packhorse men unload cargo and had the flour and gunpowder lodged in the magazine built for that purpose. Major Ingles had three brigades of recently unburdened packhorses sent back to Camp Union for more flour, and had those kept for the main body, as well as the cattle, turned out to graze. Other fatigue parties chopped wood or erected breastworks to fortify the magazine for when the army marched. The artificers, such as carpenters, masons, and shipwrights, went to work building the storehouse and canoes. One board of officers impaneled as a court-martial convened to determine if a case of misconduct warranted a trial. Another board of officers met to set a bill of prices, or rated each variety of liquor peddled in camp to ensure the sutlers did not gouge the soldiers.

The scouts who headed toward the Coal River followed a trail on the left bank of the Kanawha for several hours until they left the path to encamp for the night. Early in the morning, they discovered the hoof prints left by "3 horses, one of them shod, & two moccasin tracks" on the path about four miles from the Elk River encampment. The lead scout sent Private James Mooney, of Arbuckle's company, back to report to Colonel Fleming as the rest of the patrol proceeded on toward the Coal. Before returning to camp, the scouts discovered a recently abandoned campsite. The signs indicated an estimated fifteen warriors headed upstream in the direction of the New River. Fleming believed the first sighting to be a four- or five-man party returning home from a raid with three captured horses, which did not present a threat. Believing the second report indicated the presence of a dangerous war party, Fleming sent Captain Arbuckle out with a fifty-man company in an effort to intercept them.

The army used the halt at the Elk River to advantage. The men and packhorses got a much-needed rest and chance to recuperate from minor injuries sustained on the difficult march through rugged terrain. Officers and noncommissioned officers took remedial action for some minor acts of misconduct, as some stragglers and deserters who rethought their decisions rejoined their units. Despite the prohibition and consequences concerning the unauthorized discharging of their firearms already posted on September 15, Colonel Fleming ordered the captains to read their companies an even sterner warning. Immediately after reveille at daybreak on the morning of September 27, each company commander assembled and stood at the head of his men and read the final warning. They announced that anyone who continued to disregard the order may rest assured that an officer with a party of men would be ordered out to apprehend and confine them. The captains then inspected arms and ammunition, identified those who were deficient in the amount of gunpowder issued at Camp Union, and added their names to the list of heavy fatigue duties. Due to recent rains, the colonel also ordered the officers to inspect their men's arms for wet cartridges, and if necessary, send them to the armorer in order to unbreech and clear their weapons. With several days in place, the armorer had the time to make mechanical repairs, giving priority to fixing defective gunlocks.[62]

Private James Fowler of Russell's company returned from the scout sent to the mouth of the Kanawha on Thursday, September 29. As he and two companions paddled down the river one night, they saw some suspected Indian fires on the right bank about fifteen miles upstream from its confluence with the Ohio. When they approached for a closer look, the scouts made some noise, at which time whoever tended the fires extinguished them. They banked the canoe and disembarked. Later, two of the men proceed on foot to reconnoiter Point Pleasant. They sent Fowler back to the Elk River in the canoe to report on what they had seen so far and to tell the colonel they would meet him on the march. On his return trip, Fowler paddled close to the left bank and "spied five Indians with three horses" going toward the Indian towns—likely the same party Mooney had reported.[63]

With the army ready to march, the officers left nothing to chance. To prevent any confusion arising in camp by "the Sutlers retailing of Liquors in such Quantities & so frequently as to make many of the troops drunk," Colonel Andrew Lewis deemed it necessary to limit the sale of alcohol to that allowed by the orders of the respective captains in their own camps.

The colonel further forbade the sutlers from bringing any more liquor supplies into camp until further notice, which restricted sales to that which
they already had on hand. [64]

With the date to march approaching, the pace of preparations quickened. Colonel Fleming noted that "Men have been employed in making canoes since we came here." By Thursday evening, the shipwrights had
eighteen large ones ready to receive their cargo with all possible speed. They
needed crews, and the next day the call went out to muster a sufficient number of troops most accustomed to working canoes. The packhorse masters
had their men gather and drive their animals to camp, reported the number
fit for service, and held them ready for the call to load. Similarly, the cattle
drivers gathered their charges to graze and posted grass guards to prevent
their wandering off again, and to have them ready in the morning as early
as possible. Captains inspected their men, arms, and ammunition as they
went through the familiar process of preparing their companies to march,
and the commissary and his assistants issued each soldier provisions for
two days.

The general did not beat at daybreak as planned on September 30. A
hard rain delayed the expedition, and the amended order of the day directed
the posted guard to continue as usual. The men, horses, and beeves waited
for a break in the weather to cross the one-hundred-yard expanse of river.
Another ford lay about one and a half miles above the camp, but the state
of the river offered little advantage to crossing there. Although the rain continued, the order came for the infantry to cross, march down the opposite
bank of the Elk toward its mouth, and encamp for the night. After they arrived, the commissary issued each soldier provisions for two more days.
Back at the magazine, the boatman fixed their loads to the "best Advantage,"
ready to embark in the morning. [65]

As September drew to a close and October began, despite its bad experience with recruiting men and acquiring supplies, Dunmore's Virginia
army was in motion. The right wing, or Northern Division, commanded
by Colonel Adam Stephen, had established one magazine at Wheeling and
descended the Ohio to the mouth of Hockhocking Creek, where it built another. The left wing, or Southern Division, commanded by Colonel Andrew
Lewis, had begun its march to the Ohio as well. After establishing a magazine at Elk River, two of Lewis's three divisions began their march along the
Kanawha to Point Pleasant. While Indian scouts kept Lewis's army under
observation, Cornstalk's army of Shawnees and their allies prepared to meet
the invaders.

CHAPTER 11

A Hard Fought Battle

Point Pleasant

October–November 1774

IN KEEPING open the offer he made at the end of the council held at Pittsburgh, Lord Dunmore waited for Cornstalk and a delegation of Shawnee chiefs to meet for one last attempt to forestall war. As the calendar turned from September to October, winter would soon bring the campaign season to an end. Time was of the essence for a resolution, either diplomatic or military. The governor had yet to hear from Colonel Andrew Lewis and therefore did not know when the two wings of his army would join to execute the invasion of Shawnee country as planned, if the final attempt for a negotiated settlement failed. Recent Indian raids on the settlements seemed to indicate the conflict would continue until the Virginians took decisive action. With time running out, Dunmore faced a situation that offered little cause for optimism.

ON OR about October 7, Cornstalk called a council of war with the Shawnee military chiefs, leading warriors, and the "captains" of the allied warrior bands. He had received accurate and timely intelligence from a variety of sources, which he could use in developing a plan of action. The scouts who had watched Colonel Andrew Lewis's command ever since it assembled at Camp Union and hovered on the flanks of each marching division now had the camp at Point Pleasant under observation. War parties returning from raids against the settlements along the Monongahela and elsewhere in Augusta County, as well as Pennsylvania traders from Kittanning, brought information on the right wing's movements and the camp established at the mouth of the Hockhocking.

All that he heard made Cornstalk aware of the situation he now faced. He knew that Dunmore's army would enjoy a three-to-one numerical advantage over his when the two divisions joined forces. As good as their warriors were in individual combat, the armies of the various Indian nations suffered from a general strategic and logistical weakness in the ability and capacity to conduct lengthy campaigns or endure long battles of attrition. The *petite guerre*, or guerrilla war, offered the American Indian nations the best chance of martial success. They had come to realize that they could prevail in conflicts of short duration if they achieved quick yet stunning victories. Indian forces therefore aggressively took the offensive and fought brutal battles of annihilation when presented with a reasonable chance of winning. Seizing or holding ground did not figure in tactical planning or constitute a measure of success. Indian warriors fought primarily to inflict heavy casualties and thereby destroy or demoralize their opponents.[1]

An astute commander, Cornstalk knew it would take the Virginians several days before they could unite their separated forces. He proposed a bold plan, risky yet tactically sound, to attack with his concentrated strength while the Virginians were still divided. Doing so allowed his forces to fight each of the enemy's wings separately on nearly equal terms to defeat them in detail. It combined the advantages inherent in offensive action as well as what military planners call interior lines, with the element of surprise to multiply the combat power of his army beyond the number of its warriors. If the Shawnees and their allies destroyed one wing of the Virginia army at the mouth of the Kanawha, they could then move to attack the other as it advanced along the Hockhocking before it threatened the principal Shawnee and Mingo towns on the Upper Scioto. Given the native disdain for their enemy's fighting abilities and methods of warfare, Cornstalk believed the warriors could strike devastating blows before the Virginians advanced too far into his people's territory. Furthermore, he believed that inflicting heavy casualties would demoralize the militiamen and convince Lord Dunmore to halt the campaign before it cost more blood and treasure than the colony was willing to pay. Offering the best—if not only—hope, the plan would allow the Indians to forestall strategic defeat even without achieving a decisive tactical victory.

That night, the sound of drumming was heard about the several Shawnee and Mingo towns and villages as the captains of war parties gathered the men who had pledged to follow them. With each warrior holding a tomahawk, spear, or war club, they chanted their war songs and moved forward across a clearing at the town's center by the council house performing their war dance. After taking his place in line, each warrior advanced and struck toward the war post. When the last man finished, the warriors applied their war paint. They reassembled the next morning. Stripped for battle, wearing only breechcloths, leggings, and moccasins, and carrying a few provisions in packs on their backs, the several groups marched away as their families watched them depart.[2]

Although Cornstalk's army consisted mostly of his own people and Mingoes, braves from the Delaware, Ottawa, Miami, Wyandot, and "several Other Nations" increased the size of the force. Whether they were motivated by a desire to gain reputation and status or simply to fight a hated enemy, the opportunity to take some Big Knife scalps led them to ignore their chiefs' orders or defy the pronouncements of their Six Nations overlords to aid the Shawnees. While Cornstalk had some warriors remain behind to guard their families and towns, and raiding parties operated against the settlements, estimates vary of the total number of fighting men who formed "the whole United Force of the Enemy Ohio Indians" and took the warpath. Although one officer who arrived at Point Pleasant after the battle opined that Cornstalk led "not more than five hundred at most," others put their strength as high as about one thousand. Most Virginia participants, particularly those who took part in the engagement, estimated the strength of Cornstalk's mobile force at between seven hundred and eight hundred fighters. Given the contemporary tribal populations with the traditional proportion of warriors as reported by the British Indian Department and colonial Indian agents, the most common estimate, seven hundred to eight hundred, appears to be the most accurate.[3]

White Eyes arrived at Chillicothe amid the preparations to deliver Dunmore's invitation for Cornstalk and other leaders to meet him on the banks of the Ohio for a final attempt at negotiation. John Montour, the widely respected cultural mediator, or go-between, and a trader named William McCulloch (or McCullough) accompanied the Delaware chief. If anyone had a reasonable chance of bringing Cornstalk and the others to a council with the Big Knife, the Delaware White Eyes and the French-Iroquoian-Algonquian métis Montour did. Traders like McCulloch, who often rankled the ire of backcountry settlers for supplying weapons to the Indians, even in time of war, could have also helped White Eyes in his endeavor. Although the trader may have been a Pennsylvania partisan in the border dispute with Virginia, his friendly business relationship with the Shawnee could have maintained rapport in a contentious dialogue. Cornstalk, however, expressed no desire to negotiate further. He essentially informed White Eyes that "700 Warriors" had gone southward to "Speak with the Army there"— meaning Lewis's left wing—instead of to Fort Gower to talk with Dunmore. The Indian commander continued by saying that the warriors heading toward Lewis's force would "begin with them in the morning and their business would be Over by Breakfast time." After that, the Shawnees and their allies would return north and "speak with his Lordship." [4]

WHITE EYES, Montour, and McCulloch arrived at the mouth of the Hockhocking the day after Dunmore established his headquarters at Fort Gower. The governor recorded that he received "disagreeable information" conveyed by "our friends the Delaware." The mediators relayed the Shawnees' defiant reply that they would "listen to no terms" at that time. Instead of resuming negotiations, they had "resolved to prosecute their designs against the people of Virginia."[5] Having received no recent correspondence from Colonel Andrew Lewis to gauge how long it would take his division to reach the rendezvous, the governor once more amended the campaign plan to the new requirements. "Unwilling to increase the expense of the Country by further delay," he decided to press forward into Indian country from both Point Pleasant and Fort Gower, with the two wings converging on the Shawnee towns to join forces "about twenty miles on this side of Chillicossee at a large ridge." The governor drafted the new orders and sent Kenton, Girty, and Parchment back to Point Pleasant, this time accompanied by McCulloch, to deliver them to Colonel Lewis.[6]

White Eyes had offered to raise a force of Delaware warriors to accompany the army against the Shawnees. Keenly aware that backcountry Virginians generally harbored a "natural dislike" of all Indians, even those of the friendly nations, the governor declined the generous offer. As a practical matter, he wanted to avoid any threats to good order and discipline that could result from even a minor misunderstanding between people of different cultures. Dunmore graciously thanked the chief and accepted the services of only a few Delaware scouts. From the intelligence he had received concerning the numbers of warriors the Shawnees and their Indian allies had gathered to fight against him, Dunmore believed that his army had sufficient strength "to defeat them and destroy their Towns" if the Shawnees still refused his last "offers of Peace" when they saw the Virginians approach.[7]

WHEN THE left wing marched from the Elk River on October 1, Colonel Andrew Lewis ordered the troops to form two columns, or "grand divisions," with the Augusta County line constituting the left division and the Botetourt County line constituting most of the right column. Each line posted one company in both the advanced and rear-guard detachments— on the left and right respectively—with four men from each also detached as flankers. The Botetourt County company of Captain John Lewis, Andrew's oldest son, detached a sergeant and twelve soldiers to move with the guides ahead of the advance guard, while a company from the Augusta line detached a similar party to trail behind the rear guard. The main body, about four hundred men, formed with front and rear divisions, or four subdivisions, and with an ensign's command of sixteen men acting as flankers to each side. The cattle herd and packhorse train with their guards "fell in betwixt the Front & Rear sub-divisions" of the main body. The march order reflected the doctrine found in Bland's *Treatise*, albeit modified for use in the North American wilderness, much as Colonel Henry Bouquet had also done with the "marching square" formation he employed on his expedition against the Shawnees during Pontiac's War. The convoy of eighteen supply canoes, plus those of the sutlers who accompanied the army, kept abreast of the marching columns during the day and banked near the latter's camp each night.

With the soldiers deployed in such a formation, Colonel Fleming explained to future readers of his journal how the column had an established and well-practiced battle drill to respond to a threat from any direction. In a head-on meeting engagement, or if the enemy attacked the column in front, the advanced guard would "Free themselves & Stand the Charge" while the right and left columns moved to outflank the enemy and then "Close in &c." to finish them. Regardless of "whatever Quarter, Column or Van or Rear Guard" the enemy attacked, the colonel continued, those directly under attack would "Stand the Charge" while the unengaged "Distant Columns" attacked the enemy's own flanks. The left wing, therefore, moved while deployed in this formation, except where the terrain proved too restrictive and dictated otherwise. After it left the mouth of the Elk, the wing marched to a point on the Kanawha opposite the mouth of Coal Creek and halted. Repeated with little change every day of the march, the order for encamping prescribed the priority tasks that the force had to accomplish before dark. The responsible line held guard mount and posted main and picket guards for security. Cattle drovers and packhorse drivers turned their animals out to graze. Boatmen banked and secured their canoes. The

butchers slaughtered the necessary number of beeves and issued the various
messes their daily fresh meat ration. Officers inspected their companies and
arms. The men cooked their rations for the evening meal and next morning's breakfast. As the sun began to set, the secured camp settled in for the
night.[8]

On October 2, the army marched through "rich Bottoms & muddy
Swamp Creeks," encountering the latter obstacles about every mile or half
mile so that the packhorses, according to Fleming, became "much Jaded."
About two miles from the previous night's encampment, some of the troops
marched through the ruins of an "Indian fort" positioned along a branch
of the warriors' path that also functioned as a trader's trail. Probably the
remnant of an earlier conflict, the oval-shaped feature measured about one
hundred feet in length with a "cellar full of water 8 feet broad," and "banks"
that stood three feet high above the surface of the water. Meanwhile, out on
the Kanawha, one of the sutler's canoes "overset," with the loss of "two guns
. . . & some baggage." Another watercraft, fashioned from two canoes fastened together, also "overset." Although two or three of them got "much
wett," the twenty-seven bags of flour floated long enough for boatmen to
recover the entire cargo. So that the dampened flour would not spoil in
transit, the commissary issued every soldier a two-day ration at the next
halt. While morale generally remained high, Fleming noted that the army
had experienced a few breaches in discipline since it marched from Camp
Union. Since leaving the camp at the Elk, in addition to the theft of some
provisions, infractions included the desertion of a sergeant and three men
who left the army without being granted leave.

The column continued to move through rich bottomland until it
reached the steep and "very Muddy" banks of Pocatalico Creek. The men
trudged through the stream at a ford where the water measured some forty
feet wide and three to three-and-a-half-feet deep before the column continued another mile past the river's mouth and halted to camp for the night.
As the accompanying supply convoy paddled down the Kanawha parallel
to the marching column, another sutler's canoe capsized, and one more of
the supply laden "double canoes Split" and sank. The boatmen's efforts
again saved most of its cargo of flour.

Major Ingles urged the cattle drovers to keep the herd together as much
as possible as the division continued to negotiate several defiles with high
steep banks and along hillsides with steep slopes that came so close to the
water of the Kanawha at times that it forced the two columns to compress
and march together on a single path. On October 5, the lead scouts found
the camp that the advanced "spies" had used before they sent Private Fowler

back to the Elk in the canoe and continued overland to accomplish their mission on foot. A squad of men who stayed behind at the previous night's camp to gather straggling cattle caught up with the main body at the end of the day's march. They reported having observed an Indian warrior, "suppos'd a spy," investigate the now-abandoned bivouac site with great interest.[9]

Finally, on Thursday, October 6, after Colonel Andrew Lewis's Southern Division, or left wing, of the army had marched through "many defiles, cross'd many Runs with Steep high & difficult banks" for about eight miles, the column entered a bottom that stretched along the Kanawha for another three and three-quarters miles to its confluence with the Ohio. Colonel Fleming described the point of land as rising high and affording "a most agreeable prospect" for establishing an encampment. He looked across the two rivers at the confluence to the opposite banks. He estimated the width of the Ohio as seven hundred yards, while the "deep still water of the Kanawha" extended four hundred yards across at the mouth. The colonel determined that the middle ground of the point stood ten feet above the water, and he observed that the elevation gave it "an extensive View up both rivers & down the Ohio." After posting local security for what became the Camp on Point Pleasant, the officer of the guard assigned the now-routine force of an ensign's guard of eighteen men on the canoes and ammunition. The commissary, Major Ingles, reported to Colonel Andrew Lewis on the exact number and condition of the beef cattle and ordered the canoe men to do their best to cover the flour supply in order to protect it from moisture, while the quartermaster, Major Posey, ordered his assistants to take special care to secure and preserve the ammunition.

The advanced scouts—Fowler's companions—reported to Colonel Lewis that they had seen no war parties or signs of the enemy present since they first reached and subsequently ranged about Point Pleasant. The men had observed several Indian hunting parties tracking buffalo but were careful to avoid detection as the hunters pursued their quarry. Of the most consequence, the scouts reported finding no indication that the Northern Division had reached Point Pleasant before them, but they discovered the "Advertisement" Kenton, Girty, and Parchment had posted. The messengers' notice advised members of the Southern Division they would find a letter from Dunmore "lodged in a hollow tree." That document contained the governor's order, which had been overtaken by more recent events, for Lewis to march his men upriver to join forces with the other division at the mouth of the Hockhocking.[10]

COLONEL CHRISTIAN and the Southern Division's rear party left Camp Union on September 26 and reached the mouth of the Elk River in eight days. The men unloaded the supplies from the packhorses and placed them in the magazine. Christian put Captain Slaughter in command of the post, which included the magazine and its staff of assistant quartermasters, and a garrison comprised of "all the Lowlanders," or the men in the companies from Dunmore and Culpepper Counties. He instructed Slaughter to load twenty-four thousand pounds of flour aboard the canoes when they returned from downstream in order to transport it forward to the main body. Christian sent Privates James Knox and James Smith of Robertson's company, along with two other men, to learn the latest news on the situation at Point Pleasant. The men also carried an express to inform Colonel Andrew Lewis that the rear body would march for Point Pleasant with 350 head of cattle on October 6. Christian added a summary of his orders to Slaughter, which included his explanation that when the canoes returned, the Elk River garrison would keep a provision of fifty beeves and some flour.[11] Captain Bledsoe prepared to lead the last division of the rear body from Camp Union on October 16, and hoped to reach Point Pleasant with two hundred loaded packhorses and eighty additional head of cattle in twelve days.[12]

BEFORE THE REVEILLE sounded at Point Pleasant on Friday, October 7, the order went out to all the subordinate commanders to take a complete roll of their units and follow the camp routine established at Camp Union and the Elk River until the division marched again. In its V-shaped camp layout, or castrametation, the Southern Division headquarters occupied the vertex at the point, with the Botetourt County line—including the attached companies—erecting its shelters for one-half mile along the Ohio, while the Augusta line's tents stretched a similar distance along the Kanawha. Fleming described the area between the two lines of tents as "full of large trees & very brushy." The routine of daily camp duties kept the men busy on numerous tasks. In addition to local patrols, picket duty, and daily guard mount, fatigue details occupied much of the soldiers' time. Preservation of the health and welfare of the troops dictated that building a "Necessary House," or latrine, ranked among the first tasks accomplished, lest the camp become "fouled & sickly." Similarly, general orders reminded company officers to encourage their troops to preserve their own "health & Satisfaction," as well as avoid disciplinary action, and to use the latrines rather than "ease themselves" at various locations around the camp.

Getting the canoes unloaded as soon as possible also ranked high among the priority of tasks. Over the next few days, Lieutenants James and Hugh Allen of Captain George Mathews's Augusta County company mustered as many artificers as they deemed necessary to construct a magazine, or "Shelter for the Stores." Every day, Major Ingles had the horse and cattle drivers gather the animals that had wandered away from camp during the night, while Colonel Fleming sent an ensign in command of eighteen privates, six scouts, and some cattle drovers to return to the encampment of Wednesday night to search for and retrieve any beeves lost along the way, and drive them back to Point Pleasant.[13] The next day, October 8, Ingles instructed the "Bullock drivers" to erect a pen large enough to accommodate the herd. The drivers let the animals range about the point and graze all day long but had to gather and confine them in the pen every night before the beating of retreat.[14] After he learned that Colonel Christian's two-hundred-man rear party had arrived at the Elk "with Bullocks and Gun Powder," Sergeant Obadiah Trent, the division's master boatman detailed from Captain Henry Pauling's Botetourt County company, led the flotilla of canoes back upriver to the magazine in order to transport the flour and other stores back to Point Pleasant.[15]

After he read Dunmore's message that directed him to march to join forces at the Hockhocking, Colonel Andrew Lewis conferred with his two principal subordinates, his brother, Charles Lewis, and William Fleming. The three colonels shared the opinion that the governor's order was impractical to execute and offered little advantage to accomplishing the mission of the expedition. As the division commander turned his attention to drafting a reply to Dunmore, Colonel Fleming expressed the same concerns in a letter to Colonel Stephen, hoping that his long-time friend and comrade would share them with the governor as well. The strength returns showed that the division had "800 effective Rank & File"—not including officers, sergeants, musicians, and staff—at Point Pleasant, plus an additional "200 & odd men" following—under Christian's command—within a distance of sixty miles. Colonel Andrew Lewis informed the governor that they had already endured a "very fatiguing march" when the main body reached the mouth of the Kanawha late on October 6, so that the left wing could not possibly leave Point Pleasant before Christian's column—and the rest of the flour, packhorses, and cattle—joined him, and all the men and animals recovered their strength.

Lewis and Fleming also addressed the tactical implications of the new plan Dunmore had proposed. Having reached Point Pleasant, the left wing stood as close—or perhaps closer—to the Shawnee towns as the right wing

did at the mouth of the Hockhocking. Affecting a juncture at that time offered no operational advantage, but only further delayed the advance. Confident of victory, Colonel Lewis explained that his officers and men saw the
enemy as "within their grasp." Furthermore, the officers considered the
mouth of the Kanawha as the "pass into the frontiers" of the Virginia colony,
particularly the backcountry settlements of Augusta, Botetourt, and Fincastle Counties. Marching north at that time, they argued, neglected or
abandoned an important barrier and left the communities of their friends
and families exposed and more vulnerable to invasion.[16]

Colonel Fleming explained to Stephen that the reasons that supported
Dunmore's proposed plan had to be "Overbalanced" by showing their arguments held more weight in order to convince the governor to counter-
mand his order to march to Fort Gower. Fleming then stated that if they
complied with the governor's order as given, the resulting march away from
the perceived critical point would only serve to "blunt the keen edge" of the
Big Knife army pointed toward the enemy at the very time they needed to
keep it honed sharp to deal with the Shawnees. Furthermore, he feared that
it would only "raise a Spirit of Discontent not easily Quelled amongst the
best regulated Troops," much less militiamen unused to the "Yoak" of strict
military discipline who had primarily volunteered to defend their homes.
When the division's field officers completed the response for their commander's signature, Privates William Sharp and William Mann, two drafted
men serving in Captain Andrew Lockridge's company of Augusta County
militia, carried it to Fort Gower for delivery to the governor.[17]

Lord Dunmore's four messengers—Kenton, Girty, Parchment, and now
McCulloch— arrived at Point Pleasant from Fort Gower with personal letters for Andrew Lewis and Fleming from Colonel Stephen, but more importantly, they had the governor's latest orders. He directed the left wing
commander to disregard the previous instruction and march to meet the
right wing at the place "appointed near the Indian Settlements" instead.
Dunmore and Lewis apparently reached the same conclusion, but their respective messages crossed in transiting the seventy-mile stretch of the Ohio
River between the mouths of the Hockhocking and Kanawha. Sharp and
Mann had left Point Pleasant carrying Lewis's recommendation on Saturday, while Kenton, Girty, Parchment, and McCulloch arrived with the governor's new order on Sunday.[18]

With "Guards Properly Posted at a Distance from the camp as usual,"
and as the masters and artificers neared completion of the storehouse, the
soldiers went about their duties on Sunday. Men of the several units attended divine services at noon to hear "a Good Sermon" preached by the

Reverend Mr. Terrey. Some of the men discussed the "disagreeable news from Boston" that Stephen had conveyed in his letter to Lewis. Although the account that British regulars had fired on Massachusetts Bay militia proved to be only a rumor, it caused considerable angst among the soldiers who had been following the constitutional debate with interest. At the evening officers' call, Colonel Lewis reminded the adjutants to send their units' scouts for the next day to his headquarters early in the morning to receive their instructions for Monday's patrols.[19]

McCulloch, the Indian trader who had accompanied the messengers, sought out his former acquaintance, Captain John Stuart, who was serving as officer of the guard. McCulloch found Stuart at his tent, and they talked while the trader waited on his companions to start the return trip. In the conversation, McCulloch mentioned he had recently returned from the Shawnee towns. Intrigued, Stuart asked the trader if he thought the Shawnees were "presumptuous enough to offer to fight" considering that the Virginians outnumbered them. McCulloch answered, "Ah! They will give you grinders, and that before long." McCulloch kept repeating his answer to Stuart until his companions summoned him back to their canoe.[20] In contrast, Major Ingles later reflected that the soldiers felt that they occupied the "Safe Position of a fine Encampment." Given their presumed numerical superiority, the Virginians felt their army was "a terror" to all the Ohio area tribes. Perhaps "Lulled in safety" by overconfidence, after the drums beat retreat, Ingles "went to Repose . . . little Expecting to be attacked."[21]

Despite the Virginians' precautions and sense of security, Cornstalk's forces were indeed close at hand. After arriving on the Ohio approximately six to eight miles upstream that day, the warriors built about eighty rafts and crossed the river. Once across, they advanced to the site of an abandoned Indian village and trading post known to many whites as the Old Shawnee Town, located at the mouth of Old Town Creek and about two miles from the Virginians' camp. There Cornstalk's army halted for the night and made its final preparation.[22] Scouts had kept the enemy camp under observation, so that when Cornstalk and the other leaders met, they had the latest intelligence on their enemy's defenses as they developed the plan of attack.[23]

In accordance with their method of fighting, warriors only sought a battle when they enjoyed a clear advantage and sure prospect of victory with the loss of few men. Therefore, they always looked to surprise and strike an enemy hard during a moment or condition of weakness. Once they lost a crucial advantage and could not easily overcome their opponent, they would—more often than not—disengage to minimize their losses rather

than fight to a decision in the face of mounting casualties. If the tide of battle turned against them, warriors generally saw little reason to continue
fighting. They did not consider breaking contact and quitting the field
under such conditions as a sign of cowardice but a practical means of preserving their strength until they had the opportunity to defeat their enemy
without losing many men. If surrounded, however, they would fight to the
death rather than surrender, regardless of the odds.[24]

After a short night's rest, the Indian warriors were up for the fight. Their
leaders told them they would advance in a large body toward the Virginia
camp, staying on high ground as much as possible, initially marching in
single file and expanding as the terrain visibility dictated.

Just short of the Virginians' camp, they would silently eliminate the pickets and form into a line. If still undetected, they would attack at first light,
advance quickly in a rush to catch the enemy troops by surprise, either still
asleep in their tents or awake but unprepared to form an effective line of
defense against the assault. If all went well, the fury of the warriors' assault
would create such terror and confusion that the Big Knife soldiers would
have to choose between two equally undesirable options, but both of which
the Indians planned to exploit. Warriors would pursue and hound those
remnants of the broken army that scattered and fled in the direction from
which they had marched from the Elk River. Virginians who survived the
onslaught and retreated to the Kanawha would either have to fight to the
death on the bank or enter the water in a vain attempt to swim across the
deep and wide river to safety. The fleeing soldiers would then find, to their
dismay, the far banks lined with Indian warriors waiting to take them under
fire and complete their destruction. Once he had ended the threat from the
south, Cornstalk planned to return toward the Scioto in order to intercept
Dunmore's Northern Division, or right wing, as it advanced along the
Hockhocking toward Chillicothe and the Upper Shawnee Towns.[25]

Stripped nearly naked and all encumbering clothing and equipment dis-
carded, the warriors began "boldly marching to attack." On encountering
their enemy, the Indians at Point Pleasant most likely employed the tactics
James Smith described in his captivity narrative. After his capture and adoption, the band of Canawauaghs (or Kahnawakes) accepted him as a warrior
and trained him in their well-developed and oft-practiced tactics and techniques during the French and Indian War. He therefore experienced combat
from an Indian perspective. He wrote that warriors advanced "under good
command" and were "punctual" in obeying the shouted orders of their leaders. War parties executed a variety of maneuvers in which they changed
from files into lines and stood, advanced, or retreated as quickly as necessary

to fit the tactical situation. In the absence of spoken orders, each man guided his movement and motions by observing those of the companion to his right hand, and the man to his left guided on his. In doing so, according to the situation, they could "march abreast in concert" or in "scattered order." When they sighted an enemy force, the leaders gave general orders with a "shout or yell." In most engagements, they would advance in a semicircular formation to surround an enemy or assail an exposed flank to pin him against a natural obstacle such as a river. When the battle was joined, bands often employed tactics in which part advanced or retreated as the other part kept firing. If their enemy surprised them, the warriors would "take trees" for cover and face outward to prevent being surrounded. Individually, each warrior fought "as though he was to gain the battle himself" and sought every opportunity to gain every advantage over his opponent.[26]

At their camp on the opposite end of the point, some Virginians had just started to rise. Because Colonel Andrew Lewis had directed the commissary to have the butchers slaughter the poor quality beeves first, some company commanders decided to supplement their men's meat ration with game. Early on Monday morning before the reveille beat, two men from each of the two Fincastle County units attached to the Botetourt line turned out to go hunting. Sergeants Valentine Sevier and James Robertson of Shelby's company, and Privates Joseph Hughey and James Mooney from Russell's took two separate paths in the direction of Old Town Creek. They had gone nearly two miles from camp when Sevier and Robertson "discovered a party of Indians" assembled near the abandoned town and immediately ran back to camp. The other two did not fare as well. A party of Indians saw them first and opened fire. Hughey fell dead, and Mooney, pursued most of the way, ran back to camp to give his comrades the alarm.[27] Tradition holds that Tavenor Ross, a Virginian who had been captured and adopted by the Shawnees as a child during the French and Indian War, fired the shot that killed Hughey.[28]

Although concerned that the chance for surprise may have been compromised, Cornstalk gave the order and warriors began "boldly marching to attack." The war parties initially moved in files along the trails that led through the woods. Despite heavy-growth timber, fallen tree trunks, and dense thickets that covered areas of the bottomland along the Ohio River's south bank, the braves made their way forward as the predawn darkness gave way to increasing levels of light. With better visibility, the intervals between warriors expanded until the several files gave way to a large column that could take advantage of the terrain for ease of movement as well as have room to maneuver once it made contact with the enemy.[29]

The reveille had already sounded by the time Mooney reached camp. Giving the password as he raced by a picket, Mooney ran directly to Captain Stuart's tent to inform the officer of the guard. The winded Mooney reported that he "saw above five Acres of land covered with Indians as one could stand one beside another." Men who had heard the shots gathered outside of Stuart's tent, curious to learn the cause, and listened intently. A few minutes later, as men continued to gather, Sevier and Robertson arrived to confirm the intelligence that the enemy was close at hand. Colonel Lewis immediately ordered the drummers to beat the to arms for men to retrieve their weapons, and then the alarm to warn everyone in camp of "sudden danger, so that all may be in readiness for immediate duty." Everyone knew the procedure as drummers throughout the camp took up the beat and the field officers met with Lewis.[30]

After he considered the descriptions provided by the hunters and the lack of intelligence provided by recent patrols, Colonel Lewis assessed the situation. Although the enemy was present in a "considerable body ... who made a formidable appearance," he felt that what his division faced was a scouting party, albeit a large one. For a situation in which a commander's unit encountered a "skulking party" of enemy irregulars, Bland's *Treatise of Military Discipline* recommended that a commander order a "proper detachment" to go out to attack them. However, the treatise advised the commander to exercise extreme caution in execution and resist pursuing a retreating enemy too far for fear of an ambuscade or discovering the size of the enemy force "greater than what they apprehended" and "too advantageously posted to be easily dislodged."[31] Lewis adopted a course of action in keeping with that doctrine. He determined that an immediate reconnaissance in force to destroy, capture, or drive the enemy away presented the most appropriate response. He ordered the two subordinate colonels, Fleming and his brother, Charles Lewis, to each detach 150 men led by the most experienced captains—giving little regard to company integrity—from their respective lines "to go in Quest of them."[32]

Colonel Charles Lewis formed his detachment from the Augusta line with Captains John Dickinson, Benjamin Harrison, Samuel Wilson, and John Skidmore. Colonel Fleming assembled his with Captains Shelby and Russell of Fincastle, Captain Thomas Buford of Bedford, and Captain Philip Love of the Botetourt line. While the arrangement enabled the two lines to parade the most available soldiers quickly, the resulting loss of cohesion—and therefore combat efficiency—inherent in the ad hoc nature of the units soon negated any advantage. As Captain John Floyd later commented, "no one officer ... had his own men." Once formed into columns of two files, the two detachments marched "briskly" from opposite ends of the camp and beyond the line of pickets just after sunrise. Fleming's Botetourt line detachment advanced about one hundred yards in from the Ohio River's bank. Acting as the guide, Mooney took his place with the scouts to pilot the detachment to where he and Hughey had had their fateful encounter with the Indians. Colonel Charles Lewis's detachment of the Augusta line advanced "near the foot of the hills" along Crooked Creek on a somewhat parallel course 150 to 200 yards east of and trailing Fleming by about 100 yards.[33]

Shawnee scouts detected and informed Cornstalk of the approaching Virginians. The chief realized the shots his warriors had fired at the hunters earlier had alerted the enemy to his army's presence on Point Pleasant. Having lost the element of surprise, he altered his plan of attack. The Shawnee chief gave orders to initiate the battle by ambushing the two columns, keeping them separated and unable to provide each other mutual support. After they defeated the immediate threat, the warriors would continue the attack by advancing on the Virginia Southern Division's main body to destroy it.

At about 6:30 A.M., as the Augusta detachment's column began to cross an open area about one-half mile from the camp's line of pickets, the men heard three shots fired in quick succession, which killed the leading scout. The woods ahead of them then erupted with a blast of musketry from Indian warriors positioned "behind Bushes & Trees." Reloading quickly after the "first fire," the Indians all fired another, and then a third shot as the Virginians struggled to deploy into line. The first man of each file stood fast as the next two split respectively to the left and right sides in succession, extending to form a single-rank line while taking advantage of any cover the vegetation provided. Given the nature of the terrain, the shock of enemy fire, and the tendency of inexperienced troops to stay close to comrades rather than in extended interval, it is unlikely that Lewis's men occupied a line more than two hundred or three hundred yards long. The Augusta detachment fought back "with much bravery & Courage," but the volume of enemy fire forced it back with several casualties.[34]

After pulling back, Lewis stood in the open, disregarding the cover a nearby tree provided. As he directed his captains while they re-formed the line on some high ground along Crooked Creek and attempted to tie in with Fleming's line, a musket ball struck the colonel. He immediately realized the severity of the injury. Satisfied he had done all he could, he handed his rifle to his attendant, who then assisted him as he calmly walked back toward camp telling his men, "I am Wounded, but go on & be Brave."[35]

Meanwhile, the Botetourt detachment had advanced about three-quarters of a mile beyond the pickets when Colonel Fleming heard gunfire on his right. "In almost a second of a minute," his unit received fire from in front and also became heavily engaged. One of the first shots struck and killed Mooney, and the men deployed into line in the same manner as their Augusta comrades, except they did not initially also take cover. With their left flank on the bank of the Ohio, officers endeavored to get the men to extend the line so as to join their right flank to the left flank of Lewis's Augusta line. Since Fleming's detachment had moved farther up the point, they had to extend obliquely to the rear to join with that of Colonel Lewis. The men fought back with "with spirit & resolution," but Fleming realized after several exchanges of fire that his men's initial disposition "would never promise success." Under the conditions, they were "forced to quit their ranks & fly to trees."[36]

It is difficult to determine the frontage both detachments would have actually occupied. In addition to the factors already noted, both detachments suffered the consequences of the decision to draw men from every company to form them. Although he was not present, Captain Floyd later wrote that officers had difficulty in getting men to advance when the engagement first started because some troops refused to recognize the authority of any but the officers of their own companies. He added that the Virginians never had more than three hundred or four hundred men in action at once since a number of men avoided combat by sheltering behind "trees & logs the whole way" between camp and the fighting and "could not be prevailed upon to advance to where the fire was." If these statements are true, the detachment frontages could have been considerably less than two hundred yards.

The Shawnees, Mingoes, and their allies enjoyed a numerical superiority and tactical advantage over both Virginia detachments in the opening stage of the battle. They fought with great bravery as they "Disputed the Ground with the Greatest Obstinacy" and pressed attacks that forced both lines of Virginians to retreat from one hundred to two hundred yards from the points where they made initial contact. At that critical moment, enemy bullets hit Colonel Fleming in three places and caused dangerous wounds. Two balls went through his left arm and broke both bones below the elbow, and one went through his left breast three inches below the nipple, which caused part of his lung to protrude. The colonel continued to encourage his men and remained on the field until he felt "effectually disabled" by the injuries. Assisted by one of his attendants, he returned to camp to seek medical care. Fleming later reflected that the Indians fought with such ferocity and skill

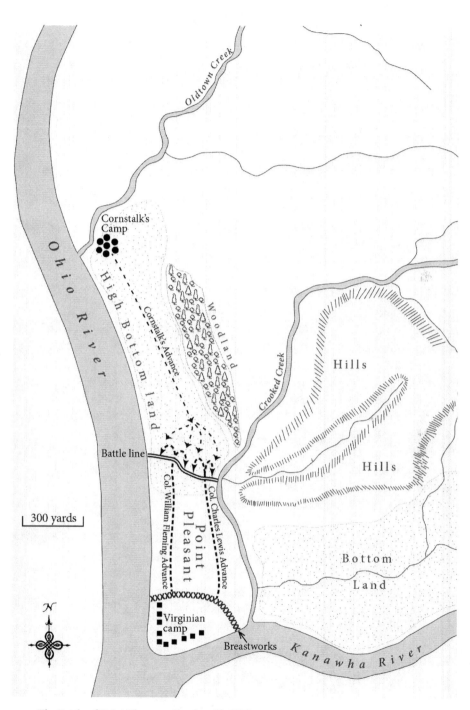

The Battle of Point Pleasant, October 10, 1774.

that the battle "was attended with the death of some of our bravest officers & men, also the deaths of a great number of the enemy." [37]

The Indians' movements aimed to exploit the gap that separated the two Virginia detachments before they could join to form a continuous line. Feeling victory near at hand, some of the more impetuous warriors made rushes, "attended with dismal Yells & Screams," against the Virginians, "often Running up to the Very Muzzles of our Guns where they as often fell Victims to their rage." Fighting in pairs from natural cover, one member firing as the other loaded, the Virginians in both lines maintained a consistent level of fire. In this adaptation of conventional tactics to the woods, they took the tactical defense in which cohesive firepower eventually proved decisive. The surviving captains took charge. On the left, Captain Shelby assumed command from the wounded Colonel Fleming, and, ably assisted by Russell and Love, succeeded in halting the Botetourt line's retreat. On the right, of all the captains, only Harrison remained uninjured to take command, but the situation remained desperate. [38]

Back at camp, the men listened to the sound of the battle that unfolded in the distance. They noted that the first few individual shots had erupted into an exchange of musketry on the right and then extended to the left as it increased in intensity. Casualties soon began to return to camp. Of the wounded field officers, Fleming arrived at the surgeon's station where Dr. Watkins dressed his wounds. Although they were serious, the doctor believed they would heal. Colonel Charles Lewis reached the station just as the surgeon finished with Fleming. Watkins confirmed Lewis's suspicion that his wound was mortal, and there was little a doctor could do except try to make his patient comfortable. Some men helped the dying colonel to his tent, where he expired a few hours later.

By 7:00 AM, the firing along the battlefront had become "very warm," and the Virginia casualties mounted, particularly among the officers. With the initial detachments in trouble, giving ground, and in danger of getting outflanked, everyone concluded that they faced more than scouting parties. It had proved fortunate that the ill-fated hunting parties discovered the enemy and spoiled the element of surprise. What Colonel Andrew Lewis had intended as a reconnaissance-in-force mission against some scouts had become what is known in military parlance as a spoiling attack, a minor offensive action that disrupts the opponent's major attack. In addition to the two injured colonels, walking wounded, and those who assisted other casualties, message runners informed Colonel Lewis of the gravity of the situation. Neither he nor anyone else had expected a general engagement at Point Pleasant, but he knew they now faced one with the two forward detachments driven back by the Indians' initial onslaught. Since the Augusta detachment on the right had retreated farther, Colonel Lewis decided to send it an immediate and significant reinforcement first.[39]

The Augusta detachment had started the reconnaissance in force that morning trailing behind that of the Botetourt. The Indians had forced the Augusta detachment's line to retreat a total of about four hundred yards since the first shots were fired, which put the critical fighting only a short distance from the camp; some participants said within sight of it. The Indians continued to press their attacks against the two detachments that had not yet joined to present a single continuous line of resistance. The gap between the two still represented a vulnerability the Indians might exploit if the Virginians could not close it.

With both of his subordinate colonels down, Colonel Andrew Lewis called on John Field. Although he had entered active service for this campaign in the grade (and pay) of major and commanding a three-company corps of volunteers, he held the permanent rank of colonel and the position of county lieutenant for Culpeper County. Lewis recognized Field in his permanent rank with the commensurate authority and ordered him to lead a reinforcement of two hundred men to stiffen and take command of the Augusta detachment's line on the right of the battlefield. Once Field was in position, Lewis emphasized the need for him to extend the line to the left in an effort to join with the Botetourt detachment. Field went forward leading a composite battalion that included his own and Captain Kirtley's Culpeper County companies, and the Augusta County companies of John Stuart, George Mathews, and Samuel McDowell, complemented by the remnants of the Augusta units whose captains deployed with Colonel Charles Lewis earlier in the day.

Colonel Andrew Lewis anticipated that on the right Cornstalk might also send a force down the bed of Crooked Creek to its mouth on the Kanawha. If the Indians succeeded, they would not only get around the flank of the Augusta detachment's line and be in position to assail the Virginians' camp, but they could cut off the Virginians' retreat and seal the fate of the entire Southern Division. It became critical that Lewis get enough force along the creek on the right to stop such an enemy move. The colonel committed the last three Augusta County companies, about 120 men in all, to prevent the enemy from using the creek bed as an avenue of approach to the camp and to gain control of the key terrain of the adjoining high ground on the east bank. The companies commanded by Captains William Nalle and Joseph Haynes were ready and marched without delay, while Captain George Moffat's company followed in short order. The two leading companies made contact with and engaged a party of the enemy in and astride the creek bed and forced the warriors to withdraw, while Moffat's company ascended and took control of the elevation, which prevented the enemy from using it to get around the militia's flank.[40]

While the engagement for the streambed ensued, Field and his reinforcement reached the battle line just in time to stem the Indian advance. The colonel directed the newly arrived companies into position to strengthen and extend the line to the left as the Virginians continued to fight on the tactical defensive. Summoning all the warriors they could, the Indian leaders made repeated brave and desperate attacks to break the Virginia line. All of their efforts proved futile, and according to Colonel Fleming, the "advantage of the place & the steadiness of the men defied their most furious Essays."

Meanwhile, although holding their positions on the left, the Botetourt men also needed help. Colonel Andrew Lewis sent a runner with a message directing Captain Evan Shelby to assume command of the detachment. He then ordered a reinforcement to the line of about two hundred men. It consisted of the Botetourt County companies of Captains Matthew Arbuckle, Robert McClanahan, Henry Pauling, John Murray, and John Lewis, the last being Andrew and Charles's nephew and cousin of his namesake in the Augusta line, plus the units commanded by the lieutenants who had remained in camp when their captains marched with Fleming.

Despite the desperate situation, Fleming noted that Colonel Andrew Lewis "behaved with the greatest Conduct & prudence and by timely & Opportunely supporting the lines" as he directed the battle. His coolness under pressure and tactical competence ultimately saved the Southern Division of the army from destruction and achieved the victory. That does not excuse his errors. The ability of the Indian army to approach so close to the camp at Point Pleasant without being detected nearly resulted in catastrophe. The plan for patrols and picket guards proved inadequate. The decision to muster some men out of each company and place them under command of the most experienced captains instead of committing entire companies to the two initial detachments had nearly led to defeat. It is therefore of great credit to the courageous officers still in the fight, and the brave men who followed them and acted like soldiers, that the Virginians were ultimately victorious.

Despite the earlier error, Lewis focused on the task before him. Throughout the rest of the battle, Fleming described his commander as "fully employed in Camp" as he sent companies to reinforce parts of the line where they were most needed and directed preparations for the defense of the camp in the event the Indians succeeded in pushing the army to the water's

This image depicts Virginia forces fighting in ranks as well as taking cover behind trees and logs, as they struggle to stem the tide of the Indian attack at Point Pleasant. It captures the desperation and intensity, as well as the scope of the fighting of October 10, 1774. (*West Virginia Archives and History*)

edge. Until he committed their companies to the battle, the colonel instructed the captains who remained in camp to have their men working to clear the area between the two lines of tents and erect a breastwork using the trees and brush they removed. The sick, walking wounded, cattle and packhorse drivers, and all other men detailed "on command" from their companies took position behind the breastwork to defend the camp. Finally, Colonel Lewis held two companies in the rear. Captain Alexander McClanahan's Augusta company, which provided that day's camp guard and therefore constituted the final deployable reserve, and the Botetourt County company commanded by his eldest son, Captain John Lewis, which formed "a line round the Camp for its defense" behind which other companies could rally to make a final stand at the breastwork.[41]

Having "found their strength much increased" when Field arrived at the head of the reinforcements, the Augusta men on the right repulsed another attack and forced the Indians to retreat a short distance. Although the action remained "Extremely Hot," the Indian forces no longer held a numerical advantage along the line of battle, and the Virginians wrested the initiative from them and advanced. The militiamen began to regain some of the ground they had yielded earlier in the day. At about 9:00 A.M., the Augusta line had advanced far enough forward for its leftmost unit to finally make contact with the Botetourt's rightmost. As Colonel Christian later wrote,

"Our People at last formed a line" of battle that ran continuously for about six hundred yards from the bank of the Ohio River on the west to Crooked Creek and the high ground on the east. The Ohio prevented the Indians from getting around the Virginians' left flank, while the high, steep—almost vertical in places—ridge on the right offered no ground on which they could traverse around the Virginia right flank. Given the number of men committed to the fight and the length of the line, the Virginia companies could easily have formed the line two ranks deep. Even with an extended interval and men taking cover behind rocks and trees, the files of two riflemen each would have been one yard or less apart. Such a density optimized both the rate and volume of the Virginians' aimed defensive fire against an enemy that either stood fast or advanced. From 9:00 A.M. to 1:00 P.M., the engagement became the kind of battle the Virginia troops had wanted to fight.[42]

The battle thus became static, but with no sign of slackening fire. In fact, the firing became even more intense as the opposing forces blasted away at each other at ranges of no more than twenty yards in some places. Along the line, some men fought individual combats, either with firearms, "tomahawking one another," or hand to hand. Colonel Field became engaged in such a close-quarters fight. While he stood behind a tree waiting to acquire a target, an Indian warrior hiding behind a tree to his left front began to talk, which distracted him. With his attention thus diverted, two warriors positioned among some logs on higher ground to his right shot and killed him. With Field dead, Captain Shelby assumed command of the entire line of battle.[43]

Amid the sounds of gunfire and screams of the wounded and dying, soldiers heard their officers and sergeants shouting orders and words of encouragement. Those soldiers who understood Indian languages translated for their comrades as they heard chiefs and leading warriors similarly exhorting their own men to "drive the white dogs in," "lie close and shoot," "shoot straight," and "be strong." Those acquainted with Cornstalk heard his distinctive voice telling warriors to "fight and be strong!" All along the line, soldiers and warriors exchanged insults and epithets as well as bullets. Some recalled that their comrades who spoke Shawnee translated, and English-speaking warriors "Damn'd our men for white Sons of Bitches." Other warriors taunted, referring to the field musicians playing their fifes in battle, asking why they did not "Whistle now" and saying that instead of playing they should "learn to shoot!" Other Indians yelled to inform their opponents of expected reinforcements in the night, and with the additional warriors they would again outnumber the Virginians when they finished the battle on Tuesday.

The engagement the Indians had initiated as a battle of annihilation, with a numerical superiority over Colonel Fleming's and Charles Lewis's detachments, had become a battle of attrition in which the Virginia soldiers now outnumbered Cornstalk's warriors. The tide had turned slowly, beginning when Colonel Andrew Lewis committed most of his companies to the engagement. When suffering heavy casualties, Indian warriors generally broke contact in order to renew the fight under more advantageous conditions. At Point Pleasant, however, the Shawnees and their allies faced an unusual circumstance in that withdrawing at this time in order to fight again would cause them to face the combined Virginia army at a location even closer to the towns and cornfields they sought to defend. Withdrawal from this battle gained them no advantage and put them at greater disadvantage.[44]

Cornstalk decided to remain engaged at Point Pleasant in order to inflict more casualties on the enemy. The Indians would do so by allowing the Virginians to advance against a vigorous defense and pay dearly in blood for every foot gained. They would also feign retreat to lure into ambush or surprise small groups of advancing Virginians whom they had deceived into thinking the Indians were on the run. When the opportunity presented itself, they would renew the attack and break the Virginians' line and destroy it.

Colonel Andrew Lewis gave Shelby the order to advance, and the troops pressed forward in a "fierce onset." Weight of numbers eventually began to tell, and the Indians fell back "by degrees" for about one mile. To counter Indian ploys that sought to draw them into small-scale ambuscades, the Virginia officers endeavored to keep the men of their units in "one body," according to Bland's treatise, so they provided mutual support to each other as they advanced. The leaders took care to prevent part of a unit from getting separated from the main body, lest a small number of enemy destroy a larger unit piecemeal. To counter the Indian tactic of feigning retreat to lure the Virginians into an ambush, the Virginia officers adhered to Bland's advice to prevent men from leaving their places in the line to go after the foe individually, or even allowing a few to pursue faster than the rest of the line advanced. Instead, they had men deliver covering fire for others who maneuvered forward, which subjected the enemy to "many brisk fires" that killed or wounded several of their chiefs and leading warriors.[45]

Although continuous, the volume of fire had decreased to the point that the officers considered it "not so heavy." Despite the Virginians' successful advance on the left side of the field, the terrain on the right, with its "Close underwood, many steep banks & Logs," greatly favored the Indians in the defense as they disputed the ground "inch by inch" for about one mile. Between 1:00 and 2:00 P.M., in the course of their long retreat, the Indians "met with an advantageous piece of ground," a long ridge about one and one-quarter mile east of the Ohio between a marsh and Crooked Creek, on which they could make a "resolute stand." As a result, the Virginia line no longer ran straight across the point, but having advanced farther along the Ohio on the left, it skirted southeast then east along the base of the ridge to Crooked Creek. The Virginia officers made a reconnaissance of the Indian line and studied the terrain. They met in a council of war and determined it "imprudent" to attempt a frontal assault to "dislodge" the Indians.[46]

Between 3:00 and 4:00 P.M., the Virginians remarked on the decreased volume of the enemy fire and that the warriors began to appear "quite dispirited." Officers speculated that the chiefs and leading warriors had vainly attempted to rally the braves and renew the fight. Throughout the battle, especially after the Indians began retreating, troops observed parties of warriors stopping to cut saplings to fashion into litters in order to remove the "dead, dying & wounded" from the battlefield. Although they recognized it as a common practice from previous battles, the militia officers were unaware of the details and extent of the evacuation until after the engagement. They had evidently carried wounded men back to the banked rafts and ferried them across. The Virginians found corpses hidden, buried, or "slightly covered" with earth, dead leaves, or foliage, and others that had been "drag'd down and thrown into the Ohio." The fallen warriors who could not be carried off by their friends were intentionally scalped, presumably to deny the Virginians the trophies.

As part of the Indian force carried out the grim task and prepared to cross the Ohio, the other maintained a level of fire to prevent interference by the Virginians, and according to Major Ingles, "Continued Shooting now & then until night put an End to the Tragical Scene and left many a brave fellow Weltering in his Gore."[47] Colonel Fleming's orderly book noted that besides hearing a shot "now & then" to discourage a pursuit, firing ceased at about one-half hour before sunset. The Indians then left the Virginians "in full possession of the field of Battle."[48] Under the cover of darkness, the warriors skillfully withdrew to where the rafts were located five or six miles upstream, crossed the Ohio with their wounded, and retreated toward Chillicothe.[49]

"Victory having now declared in our favor," Colonel Lewis ordered the men to return to camp "in slow pace." Along the way, they carefully searched for and recovered wounded to bring them into camp, "as well as," Fleming added, "the Scalps of the Enemy." It being too late in the day to publish the usual written plan and order, Colonel Andrew Lewis verbally ordered that the guard mount a force double the usual size for the night and designated "Victory" as the "Parole," or password.[50]

Colonel Christian and his rear body were still twelve to fifteen miles from the mouth of the Kanawha when the battle started. He had planned to reach the camp at the mouth of the Kanawha sometime on Tuesday until he received an urgent message from Colonel Andrew Lewis. Informed that the camp was under attack, Lewis ordered Christian to come as quickly as possible. Christian left a small guard detail to remain with the cattle and packhorses and to follow as best they could while he led most of the men forward to Point Pleasant. Privates Joseph Duncan and John W. Howe recalled, "We left the Cattle and marched on to join the battle" but arrived too late, after the battle had "terminated." Captain Floyd recalled that Christian's men marched into camp at about midnight, when they "were kindly received" and told that their arrival had been "much prayed for that day." When the follow-on detachment with the cattle and pack train finally reached Point Pleasant on Wednesday, Private James Brown said they "helped to bury the dead, and attended the wounded & then stayed a considerable time on duty."[51]

When he saw the condition of the dead and wounded, Colonel Christian predicted that many more men would die. Not only did many have two or three gunshot wounds, the colonel added that the casualties were in a "deplorable situation," with "bad doctors, few medicines, nothing to eat or dress with proper." Even more horrifying, Christian remarked that the cries of the wounded prevented the uninjured but exhausted men from resting at all that night.[52]

Fleming described the engagement as "a hard fought Battle" that lasted from sunrise to sunset. While Colonel Andrew Lewis's wing of the army retained the field, it had suffered 75 killed or mortally wounded and 140 wounded of varying severity, with many shot in two places, and some in three. Having started the engagement with nine hundred effective officers and men, the army sustained a casualty rate of about 20 percent, with an extraordinarily high proportion among the officers. These included the two colonels, four captains, and four lieutenants dead. The wounded officers counted one colonel, three captains, and three lieutenants.[53] The Virginians had the "satisfaction" of carrying all their wounded and dead off the battlefield "with Very little Loss of Scalps," while taking about twenty scalps from the enemy.[54]

An exact number of Indian casualties cannot be determined because of their practice of carrying their wounded and dead off the battlefield and disposing of the remains of the latter. Most Virginia participants believed the enemy had suffered an equal number of dead and wounded, but one can reasonably argue that they had fewer casualties. The only indication as to what the battle had cost the Shawnees and their allies rested in what the Virginians found on the battlefield. Major Ingles reported that the Virginia troops took twenty scalps. Two days after the engagement, on Wednesday, October 12, Colonel Fleming enumerated seventeen scalps that the men had collected and "dressed hung upon a pole near the river." The plunder taken on the field included "23 Guns, 80 Blankets, 27 Tomahawks," and assorted "Match coats, Skins, Shot pouches, powder horns, War clubs, &c." Fleming recorded that the plunder "sold by Vendue accounted to near £100."[55]

The battle may have ended but not the war. The men at Point Pleasant expected another engagement, if not there, then when they joined forces with Lord Dunmore. The day after the engagement, heavy patrols searched for Indians within several miles, and Colonel Christian's men located the rafts where the warriors had ferried across the river. Back in camp, with a double guard still mounted, the officers began the process of preparing the Southern Division to continue its mission. All company commanders inspected their men, arms, and ammunition. They then issued a sufficient amount that "completed" each soldier's load to "1/4 lb. Powder & 1/2 lb. Lead as early as possible." The officers then held their units "in readiness" so they could take the field as well as "well repulse" another enemy attack while they gathered the beeves and completed construction of the post at Point Pleasant.[56] Colonel Lewis composed a message to the governor that gave him details of the engagement. He also requested that in view of the recent battle, Dunmore consider marching the Northern Division to Point Pleasant before he advanced against the Shawnee towns. If Dunmore did not concur, Lewis requested that he send a surgeon to assist Dr. Watkins and medicine to help treat the Southern Division's wounded.

Colonel Lewis took the time to commend his men. He asked his subordinate officers to pass on his "Hearty thanks . . . to the brave officers & men who distinguished themselves" in the previous day's battle, and commended their gallant behavior in "a Victory . . . under God obtain'd." The army took time to mourn its losses. Recognizing the high number of casualties, Lewis urged his men not to be dismayed by the deaths of so many brave officers and soldiers. Although they could not help regretting the casualties, the colonel urged that they use the memory of the fallen to inspire them "with a double degree of Courage and Earnest desire to give our perfidious Enemies one thorough Scourge." The army buried the men who died in the battle in different places and interred the "officers & Gentlemen in the Magazine."[57]

In the aftermath of the fighting, Virginia officers and soldiers offered a grudging respect for their opponents. Colonel Christian, for example, recorded that the officers to whom he spoke after the battle described that "the Enemy behaved with inconceivable Bravery" and "exceeded every man's expectations." Fleming said, "Never did Indians stick closer to it, nor behave bolder." He also added that the warriors "came fully convinced they would beat us."[58]

CHAPTER 12

The Treaty of Camp Charlotte and Beyond

November 1774–July 1775

ON THE DAY AFTER the Battle of Point Pleasant, Tuesday, October 11, Lord Dunmore gave the order for his Northern Division to advance as planned. According to one tradition, he decided to do so the day after he heard the sounds of a small-arms infantry firefight in the distance—some thirty-five line-of-sight or seventy watercourse miles away. He had already, before the battle, sent Colonel Andrew Lewis orders to advance directly from Point Pleasant to the nearest Shawnee towns on the upper Scioto as soon as the rest of the left wing troops and supplies caught up to his main body. The intelligence received from White Eyes and Montour that the Shawnees would first go south to engage Lewis before turning their attention to his wing presented Dunmore with the opportunity to steal the march on his opponent and turn Cornstalk's plan against its designer. Before marching from Fort Gower, Dunmore again dispatched messengers who repeated his orders for Lewis "to march soon to the [Shawnee] Towns & Join him on the way" near a region called the Pickaway Plains. With Cornstalk's battle-weary force retreating and encumbered with wounded men, the Virginia army's right wing encountered little opposition as it advanced.[1]

On October 12, Privates Sharp and Mann arrived at Fort Gower with a message for Dunmore from Lewis. Members of the one-hundred-man garrison posted to guard the supply magazines at the fort informed the messengers that the governor had marched with most of the right wing the day before they arrived. The messengers caught up to Dunmore the next day and delivered Lewis's initial report of the engagement at the mouth of the Kanawha. When Dunmore had it announced, the news of the victorious Battle of Point Pleasant "occasioned great joy among the troops." The outcome of the engagement proved "very different from what the Indians had promised themselves."[2]

After a few more days of marching, the right wing of the Virginia army arrived at Pickaway Plains, not far from some important Indian towns. These included Grenadier Squaw's Town on Scippo Creek, about one-half mile above its confluence with Congo Creek, and Cornstalk's Town, another half mile to the north. The most important, or principal, town of the Shawnees was Chillicothe, which had "good Houses & plenty of Ammunition & Provisions." White Eyes and John Montour had provided Dunmore with intelligence that the Shawnees and their allies had assembled five hundred to seven hundred warriors, plus their families, to make a stand. The town was on the west side of the Scioto, where the high bank and only one ford below the site made it a difficult place to attack. The Shawnees had "cleared the Woods to a great distance from the Place" to create fields of fire to improve on its inherent defensive qualities.[3]

As soon as Dunmore's men arrived, they went to work and erected Camp Charlotte. Named in honor of the British queen, it manifested the British-colonial American doctrine for fighting Indians by combining the strategic offense with the tactical defense. Dunmore's right wing had marched deep into Shawnee country, to the very outskirts of the nation's principal towns. The fortified camp provided a secure base from which the Virginians could conduct forays against centers of Shawnee population, commerce, and food production. The Shawnees had to choose between abandoning their towns and retreating, or attacking. If they chose the latter, they would face 1,150 Virginia militiamen fighting on the tactical defense, entrenched behind sturdy earthen breastworks.[4] To make matters more urgent, the Shawnees could expect Colonel Lewis and the left wing of the Virginia army to begin its advance to join forces with Dunmore.

Dispirited, the Indian chiefs and leading warriors held a council. Cornstalk convinced them that seeking terms of peace presented the best option for their nation. The Indian leaders resolved to make no further attempts to challenge the Big Knife, or what Dunmore characterized in his report to Lord Dartmouth as "a Power they saw so far Superior to theirs." Instead of continuing to fight, the Shawnee chiefs decided to "throw themselves upon our Mercy." Knowing that Dunmore had marched with the Northern Division, the Indian headmen went to find and meet him the day he arrived near their towns. They sent Pennsylvania trader Matthew Elliott with a flag of truce to arrange the meeting.[5]

Another Pennsylvania trader, John Gibson, the widower of Logan's sister, Koonay, accompanied Dunmore's expedition as an interpreter. Elliott informed Dunmore that the Shawnee chiefs had sent him to ask the governor to halt his army and send someone to their town who understood their language. Dunmore's officers recommended Gibson. When he arrived, Gibson found Cornstalk and Logan. After Logan shed an "abundance of tears," he delivered his famous lament.[6] "Logan's Lament" was later published in the *Virginia Gazette* to wide acclaim. Thomas Jefferson included it in *Notes on the State of Virginia*:

> I appeal to any white man to say, if he entered Logan's cabin hungry, and he gave him not meat; if ever he came cold and naked, and he clothed him not. During the course of that long and bloody war, Logan remained idle in his cabin, an advocate for peace. Such was my love for the whites, that my countrymen pointed as they passed, and said, 'Logan is the friend of white men.' I had even thought to have lived with you, but for the injuries of one man. Col. Cresap, the last spring, in cold blood, and unprovoked, murdered all the relations of Logan, not sparing even my women and children. There runs not a drop of my blood in the veins of any living creature. This called on me for revenge. I have sought it: I have killed many: I have fully glutted my vengeance. For my country, I rejoice at the beams of peace. But do not harbour a thought that mine is the joy of fear. Logan never felt fear. He will not turn on his heel to save his life. Who is there to mourn for Logan?— Not one.[7]

Logan then agreed to bring in the prisoners he still held. These included the young Roberts boy from the Holston, the two black men captured at Blackmore's, Betsy Spicer, Sally Kelly, and William Robinson. The last was the man to whom he dictated the letter to Cresap that was left on the war club at the Robertses' home. Gibson returned to Camp Charlotte with the Shawnee leaders' answer to Dunmore's invitation to discuss peace terms and "renew and Brighten the Chain of Friendship" between their peoples. Although the Shawnees professed a desire to end the fighting, they also expressed fear for their safety if they went to his location. Dunmore promised they would be in the "utmost safety," and repeated his invitation with a challenge to their sincerity. If they did not come to Camp Charlotte immediately, he would have to assume their professions of peace did not come from their hearts, and he would have to "proceed accordingly."[8]

ON OCTOBER 12, only two days after the bloody Battle at Point Pleasant, the left wing began preparing in earnest for continuing the expedition. Colonel Christian sent fifty men to get the cattle left behind when the Fincastle troops made the forced march to Point Pleasant on the day of the battle. Because many of the beeves and horses had wandered away and "dispersed in different quarters" in the confusion that day, Major Ingles sent the cattle and packhorse drivers out to gather and drive their charges back to camp. Lieutenant James Allen, his brother Hugh having been killed in action, resumed supervising the construction of the storehouse as Colonel Lewis urged the master and artificers to have it "finished as quick as possible." The commanders of the several companies had their men clear away all the "underwood" near their unit's tents. The captains then divided the proposed line according to their companies' strength, and after the quartermaster sergeant issued them the necessary tools, the men began work on the defensive breastwork.[9]

Very early on the morning of October 13, Privates Sharp and Mann returned from Fort Gower with Dunmore's orders to march toward the Shawnee towns and meet him on the way.[10] The next day, Colonel Lewis issued the necessary commissions and appointments to replace those officers killed in the battle, and Captain Slaughter arrived with the soldiers and cattle that Christian had left at the Elk River. Over the next few days, the fatigue details finished building the storehouse and bastion and "running up" a breastwork that measured "two logs high." A detail consisting of three men drawn from each company went out to search for all of the army's horses still on the loose and drive them back to camp, while the cattle drovers gathered and penned their animals.[11]

By Saturday, five days after the battle, the army had regained much of its strength and had the camp in a reasonably good state of defense. Lewis issued the order for company commanders to inspect their men to identify all the sick, lame, and others "Judged unfit for Duty" who would remain at Camp Point Pleasant when the rest of the Southern Division marched.[12] The captains issued each of the men going on the expedition one-half pound of powder and one-half pound of lead to cast into bullets. The commissary directed the butchers to prepare a five-day ration of beef to issue the next day so they could prepare for its "carriage" as the companies completed the breastwork. Lewis called for the scouts to assemble for his instructions for the next phase of the campaign. By Sunday, Major Ingles had selected the sixty strongest packhorses to carry the flour and one horse for each company to carry its tents.[13]

Colonel Fleming, still recovering from his wounds, assumed command of the camp and the 278 men who stayed behind. His command included a garrison of three company-size detachments, "properly officered," with one composed of men from Augusta, one from the Botetourt and Fincastle, and the third from the contingents of the other counties represented, with a total strength of 7 officers, 15 sergeants, 2 musicians, and 156 rank and file, plus a number of cattle and packhorse drivers and boatmen. He also had responsibility for ninety-four sick and wounded and eighteen men who functioned as "waiters on the wounded." While the rest of the army continued the expedition, those remaining served to secure the camp from an enemy attack, send out ranging patrols, and perform the regular camp duties, which included guard mount and work details to complete the fort. When finished, in addition to the storehouse, breastwork, and bastions, Fort Blair would have four curtain walls and barracks constructed of hewn timber. The post would also serve as a magazine to guard, store, and relay supplies and provisions to the expedition as it marched deeper into enemy territory. Private Joseph Hundly, originally of Captain William Leftwich's Bedford County company who served in Captain Slaughter's garrison company, recalled that the men built the stockade to house the sick and wounded, and "there was men left sufficient to protect the garrison at that place." On Monday, October 17, the left wing crossed the Ohio with 1,150 men, 118 beeves, and a ten-day supply of flour. The next morning, it started its march for the Shawnee towns.[14]

In spite of the number of casualties suffered in the recent engagement, the troops of the left wing were confident and eager to face the next challenge. As the main body prepared to cross the Ohio and enter Shawnee territory the next day, Ensign James Newell of Captain William Herbert's company of Fincastle County, one of the units that remained behind to garrison the Camp at Point Pleasant, felt inspired to express his thoughts in verse. On October 17, after he recorded the next day's orders and his company's strength report, or return, Newell entered the poem he composed in his Orderly Book and Journal. It is remarkable not only as a statement of duty and resolve but also for expressions of respect and loyalty to Lord Dunmore and King George III:

Bold Virginians all, each cheer up your heart.
We will see the Shawnees before we part,
We will never desert, nor will we retreat,
Until that our Victory be quite complete. Ye offspring of Britain!

Come stain not your name,
Nor forfeit your right to your father's fame,
If the Shawnees will fight, we never will fly,
We'll fight & we'll conquer, or else we will die.

Great Dunmore our General valiant & Bold,
Excels the great Heroes—the Heroes of old;
When he doth command we will always obey,
When he bids us fight we will not run away.

Good Lewis our Colonel, courageous & Brave,
We wish to command us—our wish let us have.
In Camp he is pleasant, in War he is bold
Appears like great Caesar—great Caesar of old.

Our Colonels & Captains commands we'll obey,
If the Shawnees should run, we will bid them to stay.
Our Arms, they are Rifles, our men Volunteers,
We'll fight & we'll conquer; you need have no fears.

Come Gentlemen all, come strive to excel,
Strive not to shoot often, but strive to shoot well.
Each man like a Hero, can make the woods ring,
And extend the Dominion of George our Great King.

Then to it, let's go with might & with main,
Tho' some that set forward return not again.
Let us quite lay aside all cowardly fear,
In hopes of returning before the new year.

The land it is good, it is just to our mind,
Each will have his part if his Lordship be kind.
The Ohio once ours, we'll live at our ease,
With a Bottle & glass to drink when we please.

Here's a health to King George & Charlotte his mate,
Wishing our Victory may soon be complete,
And a fine female friend along by our Side,
In riches & in splendor till Death to abide.

Health to great Dunmore our general also,
Wishing he may conquer wherever he go.
Health to his Lady—may they long happy be
And a health, my good friends, to you & to me.[15]

W HEN THE Shawnee leaders arrived at Camp Charlotte, Dunmore immediately welcomed them to a conference in which they settled the differences
that existed between the two sides. Dunmore proposed terms that surprised
the Indians as more lenient than they could have hoped. In specifying the
"Terms of our reconciliation," the first article required the Shawnees to "Deliver up all prisoners without reserve." This included not only those captured in the course of this conflict but those captives still held since the end
of the French and Indian and Pontiac's Wars. The Indians also had to "Restore all horses and other valuable effects" they carried off in the course of
their raids on the backcountry settlements. In keeping with the Treaties of
Stanwix, Hard Labor, and Lochaber, the Shawnees recognized the cessions
the Six Nations of Iroquois and the Cherokees made to British colonial officials. Accordingly, they promised to neither hunt on the Virginia side of
the Ohio River "nor molest any boats passing on it." In establishing peace
with the Virginia colony, the Shawnees also had to "Promise to agree" to the
regulations that governed their trade with that colony and its people "as
hereafter dictated by the King's Instructions."[16]

To provide guarantee that they would abide by the articles of the treaty,
Dunmore required the Shawnees to "Deliver . . . certain hostage" chiefs or
their sons for security. The Virginians would keep them in custody at
Williamsburg until convinced of the Shawnees' "sincere intention" to comply with the articles of the treaty. Pleased that Dunmore imposed no punishment, the Indian leaders agreed to the terms "with alacrity and solemn
assurances of their quiet and peaceable deportment for the future." Dunmore reciprocated by promising their nation "protection and good treatment" by his government and the people of Virginia.[17] The Treaty of Camp
Charlotte represented only an interim agreement or an armistice. The parties would meet again, in spring 1775, after the General Assembly reconvened and ratified the terms, at which time they would conclude the formal
treaty at Fort Dunmore.

Cornstalk then stood to address the Big Knife—Dunmore. In accepting
the peace terms without admitting guilt for initiating the war, Cornstalk attempted to mitigate his nation's decision to fight. He expressed regret for
the "Depredations committed on your People by the Shawnees" but alleged

that it was "the Mingoes that occasioned it," who then "stood and looked on" as spectators. Cornstalk pledged that from that day forward, his people would stand together with the Virginians against other Indians, and "never go to war with you again," to which he added "let your heart be strong." He then recommended that Dunmore set one or two of the hostages at liberty among the Mingoes so they could influence "correct affairs" among that polity, and "be of great service towards the Peace."[18]

It looked as though the parties had agreed to peace and the war ended when Shawnee scouts reported to their headmen of another force of Virginians approaching that had come as close as fifteen miles from their towns. The headmen took their concern to Lord Dunmore, and he immediately dispatched an express to order Colonel Lewis to halt his division and advance no further. He informed Lewis that he had "very near concluded a peace." Finding no suitable place to encamp, and because someone had fired on them earlier that day, Lewis ordered his men to continue marching.

The next morning, another express arrived from Dunmore to inform Lewis that a peace treaty "was in a manner concluded" and that the "Shawanese had agreed to his terms." He repeated the order for Lewis to halt, approach no closer, and encamp. The governor also invited Lewis and any of his officers as he deemed proper to come over to Camp Charlotte. Not thinking it "prudent" for a party of a few officers to travel in enemy territory despite the pending treaty, Lewis led his entire division with the intention of joining with that of Dunmore. His guide, however, led them on the wrong path, taking one that led between the Shawnee towns and Dunmore's location instead of the one that led to Camp Charlotte. The Indians, fearing that Lewis would attack their towns, "left his Lordship, and run off."

All the Indians left Camp Charlotte except White Fish, who had accompanied John Gibson. Dunmore headed straight to Lewis's division and arrived at his camp at dusk. He asked Lewis why he had not stopped when he so ordered and if he intended to march on the Indian towns. The colonel explained what had happened and the mistake that had transpired, and he assured Dunmore that he had no intention of attacking the Indian towns after he had received the governor's orders. The next morning, Dunmore addressed the assembled captains and field officers of the Southern Division to explain that the Indians had agreed to terms. Believing the continued presence of Lewis's troops could hinder the conclusion of the peace treaty, Dunmore sent them home, except for fifty Fincastle men who went to the other wing's camp. Following beating of the general the next morning, Lewis's men broke camp and marched in the direction of the Ohio River.

The Southern Division reached Point Pleasant on October 28, and all crossed over to the Virginia side the following day.[19]

The Shawnees had complied with the terms of the agreement, but the Mingoes had not. They objected to some conditions, and Major William Crawford believed that they intended to deceive the Virginians. John Montour confirmed Crawford's suspicion when he informed Dunmore that the Mingoes intended to "slip off" while the Virginians settled matters with the Shawnees. Montour added that they planned to escape to the Great Lakes, where the Virginians would not follow, taking their captives and stolen horses with them.[20] In response, the governor ordered Crawford to lead 240 men to go after them. Private John W. Howe of Robertson's Fincastle company volunteered to join them. He explained that when the Mingoes "defied or failed to come in," the governor ordered Crawford's unit "to go against their town."[21]

In order to deceive the Mingoes about the true nature of their mission, Crawford's men set out at night on October 20 under the pretense of going to the magazine at Hockhocking for provisions. The soldiers changed course and marched swiftly to the Mingo settlement at Salt-Lick Town, forty miles up the Scioto from Camp Charlotte. According to Montour's information, all the Mingoes had planned to rendezvous there the next day before beginning their journey. Crawford and his men reached Salt-Lick Town that night. At daybreak, he sent half of his force around Salt-Lick and the other half to another small village one-half mile away.

As a Virginia scout crept toward the village, he encountered an Indian lying behind a log that blocked his path just outside of town. On being discovered, the Virginian had no choice but to kill the Indian. Crawford's men then attacked and caused much damage, but because the noise alerted the Indians in the process, most of the band escaped. The Virginians killed six and wounded several more of the enemy. The troops also took fourteen prisoners and captured ten guns and all of the Mingoes' baggage and horses, and they rescued two white captives. The plunder later sold for £400. Lord Dunmore kept eleven of the prisoners and returned the rest to their people as a sign of good faith in an effort to persuade them to accept all the terms he had offered.[22]

When Dunmore had arrived at the mouth of the Hockhocking River before beginning the march toward the Scioto towns, John Leith recalled that in Standing Stone, the town where he remained a captive, "Some of the Indians proposed to kill me." Fortunately, the boy's adoptive Indian father "interfered, and prevented their cruel intentions." As the Indians evacuated their towns, Leith said, they "took me with them, with my hands bound behind my back ... on a long and wearisome journey to their camp." Not knowing what to expect, or if his guardian's influence would continue to be sufficient to protect him, Leith "formed a firm and settled resolution to make my escape, if any opportunity should offer." Although he made several attempts, he was "so carefully watched, that all possibility of escape was utterly abortive."

"After the cessation of hostilities," Leith later recalled, "my [Indian] father gave me and his two sons our freedom with a rifle, two pounds of powder, four pounds of lead, a blanket, shirt, match-coat, pair of leggings &c. to each, as our freedom suits." The chief then told the boys "to shift for ourselves." Although free, Leith remained in Indian country, making his life once more as a trader and hunter.[23]

With peace concluded, Lord Dunmore ordered the discharge of the militia from colonial service. The companies of the Northern Division made their way back down the Hockhocking to Fort Gower, then up the Ohio, while most of the Southern Division returned by the way they had come, along the Kanawha Trail to the Elk River and on to Camp Union. Some crossed the Kanawha at its mouth and headed directly for points in Fincastle County. The colony maintained garrisons at the mouth of the Kanawha, at what was later named Fort Blair, and at Fort Dunmore in Pittsburgh. Fort Fincastle, at Wheeling, remained unoccupied but ready for use by the local militia in a future alarm.

Before Dunmore's expeditionary army dissolved in November, some of the Northern Division's officers met at the fortified magazine at the mouth of the Hockhocking, where they drafted and signed a document they titled the "Fort Gower Resolves." The document reflected their loyalty to the British Crown while also stating their commitment to liberty and rights as freeborn Englishmen. The officers affirmed, "That we will bear the most faithful allegiance to his Majesty King George the Third ... [and] at the expense of life, and everything dear and valuable, exert ourselves in support of the honor of his Crown and the dignity of the British Empire." They closed by complimenting the governor: "We entertain the greatest respect for his Excellency, the Right Honorable Lord Dunmore, who commanded the expedition against the Shawanese ... from no other motive than the true interest of this country." While the officers acknowledged that political tensions between the government in London and the colonies had grown worse during their absence, they maintained that their fervent desire for a redress of colonial grievances had not kept them from faithfully performing their duties. But the officers made known to all their sympathies by stating, "We will exert every power within us for the defense of American liberty,

and for support of her just rights and privileges; not in any precipitate, riotous, or tumultuous manner, but when regularly called forth by the unan-
imous voice of our countrymen."[24]

The veterans of the victorious Virginia army were not the only group
moving east after the cessation of hostilities. Nicholas Cresswell, an English
traveler, recorded in his diary that he witnessed "four Indian Chiefs of the
Shawnee Nation" at Winchester in December while he was on his way to
survey land in the Ohio country. He further explained that the Shawnee,
"who have been at War with the Virginians this summer, but have made
peace with them," had sent "these people to Williamsburg as hostages," as
the Treaty of Camp Charlotte required.[25]

Dunmore received a hero's welcome when he triumphantly entered the
capital of Williamsburg. Proclamations of thanks and gratitude abounded
in print on the pages of the *Virginia Gazette* as well as in oratory. They came
from those "most dutiful and loyal subjects," the mayor, recorder, aldermen,
and common council of both of Virginia's major municipalities, the city of
Williamsburg and the borough of Norfolk, and the president and professors
of the College of William and Mary. Everyone, it seemed, congratulated and
thanked him for performing "a dangerous and fatiguing service" and
achieving the "defeat of the designs of a cruel and insidious enemy." The
king's Virginia subjects likewise congratulated their governor on the newest
addition to his family, a daughter, whom he and Lady Dunmore appropriately named Virginia.[26] The celebrations continued in the best traditions of
British America with the illumination of the Capitol and a ball.

The governor also received letters of congratulations from private
sources, like one from Thomas Cresap, father of Captain Michael Cresap.
The colonel wrote that his sources "from the other side of the Mountains"
informed him that the "Delawares and Mingoes, or Six Nations who were
up the Ohio," were all "well pleased" with the outcome of his lordship's campaign against the "Shawnees and Mingoes who had been amongst them."
He told the governor that his sources also said that traders were again taking
gunpowder and lead, and along with others in the "interest of Pennsylvania," were attempting to incite the Ohio Indians to resume the war against
Virginia. These "villains" had spread rumors that Virginia forces had gathered at Point Pleasant, Wheeling, and Pittsburgh to invade Indian country
in the spring, and, on a personal note, continued to represent him and his
son Michael in "very Dark Colours to the Board of Trade."[27]

Celebration, however, only delayed the impact, or masked the reality, of
the bad news. In short order, Dunmore would learn of the true severity of
the worsening constitutional crisis that had developed in his absence. It was

only a matter of time before Americans would learn if Parliament intended to impose more coercive legislation on the other colonies, including Virginia, similar to the laws it had passed to force Massachusetts Bay back to its proper sense of duty. Up to that time, except when he dissolved the General Assembly in June 1774, Dunmore had not taken the visible elements of Virginia's resistance seriously. He provided little or no information about the situation in his province to the secretary of state for the colonies, Lord Dartmouth. While the rumor of bloodshed in Massachusetts in September proved to be fiction, the constitutional crisis inched a little closer to the possibility of an actual rebellion when the First Continental Congress and the Virginia Convention passed resolutions calling for overt colonial resistance to parliamentary rule. The congress that met in Philadelphia resolved to form the Continental Association, a nonimportation and nonexportation agreement that mirrored the Virginia Association in his own colony, in an effort to persuade the British government to repeal the recent laws that colonists found intolerable. The reality of the volatile political situation became painfully obvious in April 1775, when the "Quiet Time" came to an abrupt end with an exchange of musketry. Lord Dunmore found that his popularity had waned as Virginia colonists learned that British regulars had fired on colonial militiamen in Massachusetts, and the constitutional crisis erupted into war. Dunmore had only a few months to reside in the Governor's Palace at Williamsburg.

The colony's General Assembly convened in June 1775, with the recently elected, or reelected, representatives taking their seats in the House of Burgesses. The matter of continuing or replacing the expired Militia Act, ratification of the Treaty of Camp Charlotte and appointing commissioners to negotiate the formal treaty with the Shawnees at Pittsburgh, and paying for the recently concluded Indian war led the list of issues that he would lay before the assembly for action.

The assembly attempted to take up the public's business where the last session had left off the previous year when Dunmore dissolved the House of Burgesses. It being the first session convened following the end of hostilities with the Shawnees, the lower house followed the established procedures and appointed the required number of commissioners to examine the muster rolls to determine the pay soldiers earned for their service. They also examined commissary and quartermaster records to satisfy the claims for reimbursement of the citizens who contributed the goods, materials, services, and animals the army required, whether voluntary or impressed. Unfortunately for those entitled to the money, the General Assembly adjourned shortly after June 8, the day Lord Dunmore fled Williamsburg to seek refuge and send his family back to Great Britain. He reestablished his capital on board HMS *Fowey* anchored in the York River, which made it impossible to conduct the province's business with the legislature still in Williamsburg, despite the latter's guarantee of the governor's personal safety.

THE THIRD Virginia Convention assumed the duties of the colonial legislature when it convened in Richmond on July 17, 1775. The Revolutionary War having begun, in order to defend the colony the convention established a new armed force consisting of regulars, minutemen, and militia, all of whom were answerable to the convention through its executive body, the Committee of Safety. The convention also voted to disband the companies the old government had retained in active service for the garrisons of Forts Blair and Dunmore (Pitt) to defend the frontier, as well as the volunteer militia companies the Second Convention had resolved to raise in March in order to provide for the colony's defense after the old militia law expired without being continued by the General Assembly.[28]

The convention then took up the matter of paying for the recent Indian war, both in its responsibility to pay the soldiers and to satisfy the public service claims. After the commissioners completed their examinations and reported their findings to the committee of the whole, the convention voted to pay the veterans for their service to the colony. The new legislature also made provisions to award pensions for the relief of the wounded whose combat injuries prevented them from supporting themselves by their prewar occupations, as well as to the surviving widows and orphans of the men who died while in service. When the legislature finally settled all accounts, Dunmore's War had cost Virginia approximately £350,000 in colonial currency.[29] In order to raise the necessary revenue to meet these and other expenses, the convention voted to impose new taxes.[30]

It established the following per diem rate for each day of actual service Virginia soldiers performed: commanding officers, 1 pound, 5 shillings; county lieutenants, 1 pound; colonels, 15 shillings; lieutenant colonels, 13 shillings; majors, 12 shillings; captains, 10 shillings; lieutenants, 7 shillings, 6 pence; ensigns, 7 shillings; quartermasters and adjutants, 6 shillings; sergeants, 2 shillings, 6 pence; corporals, 2 shillings; drummers and fifers, 2 shillings; privates, 1 shilling, 6 pence; and scouts, 5 shillings. The convention voted to pay the men called into service by their counties and those who served under Lord Dunmore, including volunteers recruited in Maryland, North Carolina, and Pennsylvania, according to the same scale. The veterans of Dunmore's War therefore received the same compensation as the soldiers who served as Virginia regulars, minutemen, and militiamen in actual service to fight the British or guard the frontier from Indian attack in the early stages of the Revolutionary War.[31]

WHEN THE Revolutionary War came to Virginia, the legacy of Dunmore's War had a significant effect. The victory of the Virginia militia, particularly at the Battle of Point Pleasant, effectively pacified the Ohio frontier with regard to the Shawnees and the faction of Mingoes allied with them. The officers of the British Indian Department did not convince them and other Ohio-area Indian nations to become full participants in the War for American Independence on the side of the British Crown until 1777.

The frontier along the Ohio River had remained peaceful during the two ensuing years, which coincided in part with an absence of British troops in the thirteen colonies and allowed the Patriot side a degree of security to adopt independence. Dunmore's mild terms in the Treaty of Camp Charlotte arguably influenced the Shawnees' and Mingoes' decision to side with the British as a means of halting continued American expansion in the region. The unintended consequence of Ohio Indians' military alliance with and cooperating with Crown forces made the area between the Ohio and Mississippi Rivers enemy-held territory. That situation prompted Governor Thomas Jefferson to order Brigadier General George Rogers Clark to lead Virginia forces in an invasion to reestablish the state's claim in defiance of the Quebec Act of 1774.

It is somewhat ironic that Andrew Lewis, as a brigadier general in the Continental Army, commanded the forces that drove his former governor's British and Loyalist forces out of Virginia in July 1776. Dunmore's time in the colony thus came to an end.

Conclusion

LORD DUNMORE commanded Virginia forces and led them to victory in a war to defend the colony against attacks by a Shawnee-led Indian confederacy. To the casual observer, achieving a defensive objective by pursuing an offensive strategy may seem paradoxical, but it explains Virginia's actions in Dunmore's War. The colony's last royal governor planned and conducted an invasion of an opponent's homeland that achieved a victory not measured by the numbers of enemy combatants killed and noncombatants slain, areas of land ceded, reparations obtained, or the monetary value of a ruined economy, but by the formal recognition of an established border, a promise to cease cross-border incursions, return of captured property, and repatriation of prisoners. The Virginia colony fought a limited war for limited defensive objectives, at the end of which it offered the Indians generous peace terms. While such a view runs counter to those found in some recent scholarship, which contend that the war was nothing more than an unjustified land-grab, it should not come as a surprise. The character of the outcome reflected that of the limited wars fought in Europe during the same period.

Dunmore's War not only reflected eighteenth-century concepts of limited conflict but a more timeless reason the Virginians went to war in 1774. Among lists of governmental responsibilities, security of borders and protection of citizens and their property from foreign invaders have always ranked high. With confidence in the validity of the treaties that defined the Ohio River as the boundary between the area open to settlement and Indian country, the colonists considered the presence of every hunting party on the south bank as a treaty violation. Given the clash of cultures and fre-

quency of such incidents, encounters turned violent until both sides resorted to armed conflict to settle their differences. Virginians justified their
reaction as a response to an unjust aggressor.

From April to August 1774, Shawnee and Mingo military operations
forced thousands of settlers to abandon their backcountry homes and farms
and flee to the safety of less vulnerable areas. Those who remained risked
all as they lived and worked in constant fear of attack. Defensive measures,
such as conducting patrols and building forts in which settlers took refuge,
afforded a degree of protection but did not stop depredations. As the situation grew more desperate, Governor Dunmore offered to lead an offensive
against the Indians. He argued that doing so would achieve a more favorable
military outcome, cost less blood and treasure, and take less time than staying on defense. Forcing the enemy to fight in his own country rather than
in the colony provided the Virginians the motivation for invading Shawnee
country, not the acquisition of territory.

Despite the prowess that Indian warriors exhibited in combat, Virginia
militiamen went to war confident in their own abilities. Although the two
forces shared some apparent similarities in technique, such as men taking
cover to return fire, the militiamen did not simply copy fighting methods
of their Indian opponents. Warriors usually attacked only when they held
such an advantage that guaranteed their success in a battle of annihilation.
When they did not possess such an advantage at the outset, they created it
as the fight developed in order to finish it on their terms. For example, Indian braves typically retreated before a numerically superior army and
traded ground for enemy lives until the opposing force was either lured to
its destruction or so weakened that it retreated.

The Virginia forces developed tactics of their own, known as skirmishing
or bush-fighting, to counter their opponents' advantages. The soldiers of
the backcountry combined techniques learned from native warriors with
the British army's *petite guerre* doctrine as adapted to the terrain and enemy
found in North America and integrated the use of the rifle. A uniquely European contribution to this style of warfare, the rifle provided an individual
soldier with a weapon of greater range and accuracy than the standard musket. Originally developed for hunting, rifle technology's military application
caused a further revision in the tactics Virginia soldiers had honed in previous conflicts.

When on defense, the militiamen relied on aimed fire more than massed
volleys but employed both with effect. When on offense, the Virginians ideally sought to force opposing warriors to either yield ground and disperse
or left them no alternative but to attack at a disadvantage against the disci-

plined firepower of cohesive units. When executed properly, the militia tactic is described by some historians as essentially acting not on the strategic offense but the tactical defense, albeit in a very basic sense. The differences and similarities in the styles of fighting employed by both combatants were demonstrated at the Battle of Point Pleasant. That decisive tactical victory made possible the strategic victory reflected in the terms of the Treaty of Camp Charlotte.

The doctrine of acting on the strategic offense but tactical defense is also evident in the final phase of Dunmore's War at Pickaway Plains. The Virginia army marched deep into enemy country, threatening the Shawnees' principal towns with destruction, thereby demonstrating the strategic offense. The soldiers then built Camp Charlotte and prepared to fight from behind sturdy entrenchments on the tactical defense if the Shawnees chose to oppose them. Given two equally unacceptable options, either abandoning their towns or attacking the fortified camp, the Shawnees agreed to terms dictated by Dunmore.

The actual peace terms did not match those perceived in many current secondary accounts of Dunmore's War. What the Treaty of Camp Charlotte did not require of the Indians is of equal significance. Dunmore neither imposed harsh terms on nor demanded punitive concessions from the defeated enemy. Instead, he required the Shawnees to accept the cessions negotiated by the Six Nations and Crown representatives in 1768. Although sounding harsh to present-day audiences, Dunmore's requirement for the Shawnees and Mingoes to surrender hostages while waiting for a formal treaty was a conventional practice in Indian diplomacy. The holding of hostages guaranteed the Shawnee and Mingo representatives would attend the council to negotiate the formal peace treaty at a later date.

The popular perception that Dunmore's expedition had great success in enlisting volunteers with the promise of generous land bounties is also incorrect. In the accounts of those who volunteered, the desire to acquire Indian land was conspicuously absent. In contrast, soldiers volunteered primarily to serve and defend their country of Virginia. Many also cited the desire to prevent or avenge the murder and abduction of loved ones and neighbors, as well as the destruction of their homes and loss of property, at the hands of Shawnee and Mingo raiders. Given such motivations, it is remarkable that Dunmore's army achieved success without the troops resorting to the indiscriminate killing of noncombatants or large-scale destruction of Shawnee and Mingo towns and cornfields.

A related fallacy about Dunmore's War that has appeared in some recent scholarship holds that recruitment for the expedition was not difficult given the allure of acquiring land and plunder. The records indicate that some officers experienced difficulty in raising their units. In such cases, captains combined understrength companies to form one with sufficient numbers to enter service. In some communities, militia officials resorted to filling their vacant ranks by a draft. Others sent recruiting agents to communities in other colonies, primarily North Carolina and Maryland, to seek individual volunteers. Counties not included in the call-up also responded to the governor's call. Dunmore, Bedford, Culpeper, and Pittsylvania all raised companies for the expedition as well as to defend neighboring Fincastle and Botetourt Counties. Clearly, recruiting troops to serve in Dunmore's War was more difficult than is often asserted.

Although the militia of the western Virginia counties performed reasonably well in general during Dunmore's War and at the Battle of Point Pleasant in particular, it displayed weaknesses that cannot be ignored. Service in the militia on the frontier was markedly different from that in more secure areas of the colony. By necessity, the soldiers of the backcountry took their obligations to attend training assemblies and otherwise participate more seriously than their counterparts in the Tidewater, for example, because of the proximity of an actual threat. Living in communities vulnerable to attack, by necessity they received more practical experience in being called out for alarms or ordered into active service for short, and sometimes frequent, periods of active service. Many of them volunteered to serve multiple tours of duty during the emergencies of 1774.

Although more proficient than the militia companies that mustered for one day every calendar quarter, the militia of the frontier counties remained part-time citizen-soldiers and not professionals. Breaches of discipline among militiamen, such as desertion on the expedition, did not result in the same severe punishment inflicted on British regulars for similar offenses. Such weakness notwithstanding, the militia establishments of the western counties had a core of men who demonstrated at least a quasi-professional level of proficiency and could be depended on in emergencies. Throughout the Revolutionary War, many veterans of Dunmore's War volunteered for service in the Continental Army, and as members of the militia defended their communities and responded to countless local alarms, and served in expeditions against British forces and their Indian allies.

To the objective observer of Dunmore's War, the righteousness of each side's cause turns on the different perceptions of the provisions of the Treaties of Hard Labor, Fort Stanwix, and Lochaber, negotiated between 1768 and 1770, as well as the Cherokee Grant of 1772. They were negotiated in good faith by representatives of the British Crown and native peoples, ratified by King George III, and of benefit to the colony, and Virginians generally accepted them as valid agreements. Although not a principal party, Virginia commissioners usually, but not always, succeeded in having the Crown's negotiators consider the colony's interests. In contrast, the Shawnees rejected the Ohio as the boundary and maintained that parties who spoke on their behalf at the treaty councils did not represent their interests. This distinction is often missing from recent studies of the conflict and its causes, which tend to focus on the Shawnee position.

Not unlike the Virginia colony's leaders, Shawnee and Mingo war chiefs took responsibility for the protection of their people and the safeguarding of their nations' territory, both homeland and hunting ground. Vacant land that Virginians may have legitimately viewed as open to settlement and improvement from their perspective and moved to occupy, Indians also rightly looked on as an invasion of an area vital to their people's economy and survival. Crossing the Ohio to raid Virginia settlements, from the Shawnee point of view, may be likened to their Big Knife opponents' conducting a defensive war with an offensive strategy and not waging one of aggression. From their respective positions, each side in Dunmore's War perceived its actions as right. The conditions that contribute to these divergent perceptions must be equally considered in order to more fully understand the conflict.

Deconstruction of the events to a struggle between the two primary combatant entities results in simplistic explanations. Dunmore's War involved more participating polities than the colony of Virginia on one side and the Shawnees, with some Mingo allies, on the other. It was much more complex, and the complexity had important effects, as has been shown.

Relations between the British Empire and its colonies on one side and Indians on the other were likewise intricate and transcend the events of 1774. For example, the sometimes-contentious relationship that existed between the various native peoples of the Ohio region and the Six Nations of Iroquois, as well as the Cherokees, are too significant to ignore. Likewise, those that existed between Great Britain and its colonies in general, as well as between the colonies of Virginia and Pennsylvania in particular, are important to the study of the causes, conduct, legacy, and memory of Dunmore's War.

The Iroquois Confederacy, or Six Nations, was an essential British ally that influenced the situation on the frontier as it pursued its national interests. Guyasuta, the confederacy's viceroy for the Ohio area, exercised direct leadership of the Six Nations' immigrant community known as the Mingoes and represented the confederacy's authority and suzerainty over other native peoples, including dependent nations such as the Delaware, and those under its dominion by right of conquest, like the Shawnees. The viceroy worked closely with the Indian Department's Alexander McKee to further the mutual interests of the Crown and the central council at Onondaga.

The Iroquois Six Nations had benefitted from its cession of Shawnee hunting ground to the British in the Treaty of Fort Stanwix. Amid growing dissatisfaction with Virginia's settlement of the ceded area, the possibility of a Shawnee-led confederation of Ohio-area Indians forming, and attempts to alienate the Mingoes from the authority of the central council at Onondaga, the Six Nations had little sympathy for the Shawnees in their dispute with Virginia. Through the efforts of Guyasuta and representative deputies the council sent to support him, the Six Nations exerted its political, diplomatic, and military power and influence to isolate the Shawnees from potential Indian allies and resolved the situation in its own favor. The Iroquois ordered member and dependent nations not to join the fight against the Virginians. The Mingo faction that followed Logan to war arguably might have refrained from its alliance and remained neutral if not motivated to avenge the Yellow Creek massacre.

The Six Nations domination of the native peoples of the region meant that the Shawnees essentially fought without allies. Various bands of Delaware warriors not only declined to join with the Shawnees but were ready to follow Chief White Eyes when he offered Dunmore their services as scouts and auxiliaries on the expedition. The Iroquois' action guaranteed the Shawnee defeat, kept Dunmore's War limited, and prevented a wider conflict from erupting between their British allies and a potential pan-Indian confederacy.

As the Six Nations of Iroquois had assumed the mantle of the most powerful Indian polity in the north, the Cherokees represented its counterpart in the south. Like the Iroquois, Cherokee leaders had also acted in their nation's interest when they ceded land the Shawnees considered their hunting ground to Virginia. Notwithstanding any resentment the transaction caused, the Shawnees also sought Cherokee assistance for their fight against the Virginians. When some vocal leaders urged military action in reprisal for the murder of a tribal member by an unapologetic settler, the Shawnees stood to benefit by having numbers of Cherokee warriors joining them in the fight against the Virginians; whether as allies or cobelligerents made little difference.

Under the leadership of Oconostota and Colonel William Preston, respectively, Cherokee and Virginia representatives engaged in meaningful long-distance diplomacy that averted war. Assisted by Indian Department deputy superintendents and facilitated by well-intentioned traders acting as intermediaries, the two sides resolved their differences without armed force. By refraining from the fight against the Virginians, the Cherokees further isolated the Shawnees and protected their own interests. Like that of the Six Nations, although more benign, Cherokee involvement had a significant influence on the outcome of Dunmore's War. An important aspect of this conclusion is that other Indian polities—namely, the Six Nations and the Cherokees—played a significant role in the Virginia victory, although not as combatants.

Lord Dunmore had assumed the royal governorship of Virginia in 1771, not long after repeal of the Townshend Acts, the second of what many colonists viewed as unconstitutional taxation laws imposed on them. The period that followed repeal began what historians describe as the "quiet time" before the Revolutionary War. Governor Dunmore took advantage of the political climate and pursued policies that at times conflicted with those of his superiors in the British government. He proposed policies and signed legislative acts that many Virginians viewed as beneficial to the colony. Although he also acted in his own self-interest, Dunmore lived in an era when using one's public office for personal gain did not necessarily constitute corruption or wrongdoing. Like many of his prominent Virginia contemporaries, he sought the acquisition of land for his own and his family's benefit. Accusing Dunmore of extending Virginia's boundaries solely for personal gain is not only inaccurate but judges his actions by the standards other than that of the time in which he lived. Virginians in general perceived many of Dunmore's policies, especially those that promoted settlement of western territories within the boundaries defined by Virginia's royal charter and valid treaties, as in the best interest of the colony entrusted to his administration.

The boundary dispute between Virginia and Pennsylvania is often explored only with regard to the Indian conflict of 1774 as an example of Dunmore's aggression. Both colonies claimed the strategic Forks of the Ohio and surrounding area in the period preceding and during the Revolutionary War. Although Pennsylvania had moved more quickly to develop the area as part of its Westmoreland County, Dunmore led a belated but effective effort to add it to Virginia's Augusta County. The area not only had tracts of land for speculation and development but was an important location for control of the lucrative trade with the Indians of the Ohio Country. The Grand Ohio Company's plan to establish the inland province of Vandalia as the fourteenth English colony further complicated the competing claims of the two older colonies. Much of the land the proposed new colony encompassed fell within the area granted by Virginia's royal charter. If any aspect of Dunmore's War may be characterized as a land grab it is the establishment of Vandalia by the Grand Ohio Company for the benefit of its London and Philadelphia investors, not Lord Dunmore. The governor countered by establishing county court and militia apparatus in the area. The competing interests and biases of each colony's partisans are reflected in the primary source documents written by these participants.

Dunmore's War was more than an armed conflict between the colony of Virginia and the Shawnee nation of Indians. Virginia viewed the conflict as a defensive war to protect its people and borders, including legally acquired land, against foreign invaders. The colony achieved victory with a limited offensive operation conducted to achieve limited objectives. The Six Nations of Iroquois, the Cherokees, and the colony of Pennsylvania had all acted in their own respective interests, and each made significant contributions to the causes, course, and outcome of Dunmore's War. The last conflict of the colonial era may have been limited, but it was nonetheless a complex and significant prelude that helped shape the events that followed.

Appendix A

Wakatomika Expedition, July 26–August 2, 1774
Order of Battle
Expeditionary Battalion (approximately 400 soldiers)
Major Angus McDonald

Companies/ Commanders:
1. Captain George Rogers Clark
2. Captain Michael Cresap
3. Captain Henry Hoagland
4. Captain Hancock Lee
5. Captain William Lynn (Linn)
6. Captain Daniel Morgan
7. Captain James Wood
8. Captain John Stephenson

Forces of the Shawnee-Led Confederation of Indians
Estimated between 30 and 50 warriors, mostly Shawnees and their
Mingo allies, plus some sympathetic individual Delawares.

Appendix B

Battle of Point Pleasant, October 10, 1774
Order of Battle
Dunmore's Virginia Expeditionary Army
Southern Division/Left Wing
Augusta, Botetourt, Fincastle Counties, plus volunteer companies from Bedford, Culpeper, and Dunmore Counties (approximately 1,100 soldiers, total)
Division Commander: Colonel Andrew Lewis (Botetourt County)

1. Augusta County Line, Detached Battalion (13 companies)
   Colonel Charles Lewis
   a. Captain John Dickinson
   b. Captain James Gilmore
   c. Captain Benjamin Harrison
   d. Captain Joseph Haynes
   e. Captain John Lewis
   f. Captain Andrew Lockridge
   g. Captain George Mathews
   h. Captain Alexander McClanahan
   i. Captain Samuel McDowell
   j. Captain George Moffat
   k. Captain William Nalle
   l. Captain John Skidmore
   m. Captain Samuel Wilson

2. Botetourt County Line, Detached Battalion (7 companies)
   Colonel William Fleming
   a. Captain Matthew Arbuckle
   b. Captain John Lewis
   c. Captain Philip Love
   d. Captain Robert McClanahan
   e. Captain John Murray
   f. Captain Henry Pauling

g. Captain John Stuart

3. Fincastle County Line, Detached Battalion (8 companies)
   Colonel William Christian
   a. Captain William Campbell
   b. Captain Walter Crockett
   c. Captain John Floyd
   d. Captain James Harrod
   e. Captain William Herbert
   f. Captain William Robertson
   g. Captain William Russell (attached to Botetourt Line)
   h. Captain Evan Shelby (attached to Botetourt Line)

4. Culpeper County Corps of Volunteers (3 companies)
   Colonel (Major/Captain) John Field
   a. Captain William Chapman
   b. Captain James Kirtley
   c. Captain George Slaughter

When accounts were settled after the war, Field received the pay of a colonel.

5. Bedford County Independent Company of Volunteers
   Captain Thomas Buford (attached to Botetourt Line)

6. Dunmore County Independent Company of Volunteers
   Captain John Tipton
   Colonel (Captain) Francis Slaughter

Forces of the Shawnee-Led Confederation of Indians
Estimated 800 warriors, mostly Shawnees with their Mingo allies, plus bands of Ottawa, Miami, Wyandot, and some volunteers from the Delaware, Cherokee, and others nations.

Notes

CHAPTER 1: OUR CUSTOMS DIFFERING FROM YOURS

1. The Virginia Colony had two competing newspapers in 1773, both named the *Virginia Gazette* and published in Williamsburg: one by the printing house of Alexander Purdie and John Dixon, the other by William Rind, and later his widow, Clementina. Hereafter, to distinguish between them, the older Purdie and Dixon newspaper will be cited as *Virginia Gazette* #1 (Purdie and Dixon), and Rind's as *Virginia Gazette* #2 (Rind). Unless otherwise specified, all are located in Special Collections, John D. Rockefeller Jr. Library, Colonial Williamsburg Foundation, Williamsburg, Virginia.

2. *Virginia Gazette* #2 (Rind), December 23, 1773; Alexander Scott Withers, *Chronicles of Border Warfare, or, A History of the Settlement by the Whites of North-Western Virginia: and of the Indian Wars and Massacres in That Section of the State, with Reflections, Anecdotes, &c.* (Clarksburg, VA: Joseph Israel, 1831; repr., ed. and annot. Reuben Gold Thwaites, Cincinnati: Stewart and Kidd, 1895), 144-146.

3. William Ogilvy to Maj. Gen. Frederick Haldimand, letter dated Charlestowne, June 8, 1774, Enclosure: Isaac Thomas deposition dated Fincastle, February 12, 1774, Thomas Gage Papers, Series 2: American Series, Subseries 1: Correspondence and Enclosures: Vol. 119, William L. Clements Library, University of Michigan (hereafter cited as Gage Papers).

4. *Virginia Gazette* #2 (Rind), December 23, 1773; Withers, *Chronicles of Border Warfare*, 144; Robert Morgan, *Boone: A Biography* (Chapel Hill, NC: Algonquin Books, 2008), 136-137. Some sources alternate spelling between "Mendenhall" and "Mendinall."

5. Withers, *Chronicles of Border Warfare*, 144-146; John Mack Faragher, *Daniel Boone: The Life and Legend of an American Pioneer* (New York: Henry Holt, 1992), 93; Morgan, *Boone*, 136-137.

6. *Virginia Gazette* #2, December 23, 1773; Withers, *Chronicles of Border Warfare*, 144; Morgan, *Boone*, 136-137. Vandalia, the proposed fourteenth colony, would have encompassed much of present-day West Virginia and Kentucky.

7. John Gass to Lyman Draper, letter dated November 6, 1847, Daniel Boone Papers, 24C79, Lyman C. Draper Collection of Manuscripts, Wisconsin Historical Society, Madison, Wisconsin (hereafter cited as Draper Manuscripts); Withers, *Chronicles of Border Warfare*, 144-146; Faragher, *Daniel Boone*, 90.

8. *Virginia Gazette* #2 (Rind), December 23, 1773; Withers, *Chronicles of Border Warfare*, 145n.

9. Daniel Boone, "The Adventures of Colonel Daniel Boone," in Samuel Metcalf, ed., *A Collection of the Most Interesting Narratives of Indian Warfare in the West Containing an Account of the Adventures of Daniel Boone* (Lexington: William G. Hunt Printers, 1821), 13; William Ogilvy to Maj. Gen. Frederick Haldimand, letter dated Charlestowne, June 8, 1774, Enclosure: Thomas Sharp deposition dated Fincastle, February 20, 1774, Gage Papers; Withers, *Chronicles of Border Warfare*, 144-145, 145n; Faragher, *Daniel Boone*, 91-92; Morgan, *Boone*, 136-137.

10. *Virginia Gazette* #2 (Rind), December 23, 1773; John Gass to Lyman Draper, later dated November 6, 1847, Daniel Boone Papers, 24C79, Draper Manuscripts.

11. Boone, "Adventures," 13; Faragher, *Daniel Boone*, 95; Morgan, *Boone*, 137-138.

12. Faragher, *Daniel Boone*, 95; Morgan, *Boone*, 137-138.

13. Withers, *Chronicles of Border Warfare*, 145n; Faragher, *Daniel Boone*, 94-95; Morgan, *Boone*, 137-138. What were believed to be Drake's remains were found two decades later about one eighth of a mile from the massacre site.

14. *Virginia Gazette* #2 (Rind), December 23, 1773.

15. *Pennsylvania Chronicle and Universal Advertiser*, December 6, 1773.

16. Dr. Hugh Mercer to Col. William Preston, letter dated Fredericksburg, January 8, 1774, William Preston Papers, Draper Manuscripts, 3QQ15; Reuben Gold Thwaites and Louise Phelps Kellogg, eds., *Documentary History of Dunmore's War 1774* (Madison: Wisconsin Historical Society, 1905), 1-2. Hereafter, if a transcript of the original document also appears in *Documentary History*, the page numbers will appear in parentheses after the manuscript citation.

17. Maj. Gen. Frederick Haldimand to Sir William Johnson, letter dated New York, March 18, 1774, in Alexander C. Flick, ed., *The Papers of Sir William Johnson* (Albany: University of the State of New York, 1933), 8:1083-1084 (hereafter cited as *Johnson Papers*).

18. Alexander McKee, journal entry dated February 27, 1774, in Milton W. Hamilton, ed., *Johnson Papers* (Albany: University of the State of New York, 1957), 12:1080; Earl of Dunmore to Earl of Dartmouth, letter dated Williamsburg, December 24, 1774, in K. G. Davies, ed., *Documents of the American Revolution 1770-1783*, vol. 8, transcripts 1774 (Shannon: Irish University Press, 1975), 258.

19. Earl of Dunmore to John Stuart, letter dated Williamsburg, December 20, 1773, and Daniel Boone Papers, 6C16, Draper Manuscripts.

20. John Stuart to Maj. Gen. Frederick Haldimand, letter dated Charles Town, February 3, 1774, Davies, *Documents*, 8:34-37.

21. Alexander Cameron to John Stuart, letter dated Keowee, March 1, 1774, Davies, *Documents*, 8:56-58. The Great Warrior was one of the names by which English settlers knew the Cherokee chief Oconostota. Variations of his name include Aganstata, Oconastota and Cunne Shote. Besides Great Warrior, he was also called First Warrior and the Warrior of Chota. At this time, he ranked second only to the First Beloved Man, or principal chief, his cousin Attakullakulla.

22. William Ogilvy to Maj. Gen. Frederick Haldimand, letter dated Charlestowne, June 8, 1774, Gage Papers.

23. Earl of Dunmore to Earl of Dartmouth, letter dated Williamsburg, December 24, 1774, Davies, *Documents*, 8:257; John Richard Alden, *John Stuart and the Southern Colonial Frontier: A Study of Indian Relations, War, Trade, and Land Problems in the Southern*

Wilderness, 1754–1775 (Ann Arbor: University of Michigan Press, 1944; repr. New York: Gordian Press, 1966), 263-24.

24. *Virginia Gazette* #1 (Purdie and Dixon), supplement, December 23, 1773; *Virginia Gazette* #2 (Rind).

25. Sir William Johnson to Earl of Dartmouth, letter dated Johnson Hall, September 22, 1773, *Johnson Papers*, 8:890.

26. Donald B. Ricky, *Indians of Maryland: Past and Present* (St. Clair Shores, MI: Somerset Publishers, 1999), 50-51. Evidence suggests the presence of a small Shawnee community in the Ohio valley sometime prior to the Beaver Wars. If so, its inhabitants would have been among those dispersed.

27. Sir William Johnson to Lt. Gen. Thomas Gage, letter dated Johnson Hall, November 18, 1772, *Johnson Papers*, 8: 640; Ricky, *Indians of Maryland*, 51-53.

28. Sir William Johnson to Lt. Gov. Richard Penn, letter dated Johnson Hall, January 29, 1772, *Johnson Papers*, 8: 938.

29. Samuel Johnson, *A Dictionary of the English Language . . .* , 5th ed., vol. 1 (London: Printed for W. Strahan, et al., 1773), DEP-DEP, TRI-TRI.

30. Lt. Gen. Thomas Gage to Sir William Johnson, letter dated New York, October 7, 1772, *Johnson Papers*, 12: 994-995.

31. Sir George Thomas, ed., *The Treaty Held with the Indians of the Six Nations at Philadelphia, in July 1742, To which is Prefix'd an Account of the first Confederacy of the Six Nations, their present Tributaries, Dependents, and Allies* (Philadelphia: B. Franklin, 1743; repr., London: T. Sowle Raylton and Luke Hinde, 1744), vi, Ratified Indian Treaties 1722-1800, Record Group 75, Microfilm Publication, M668, Roll 2, National Archives and Records Administration (hereafter cited as NARA), Washington, DC.

32. Thomas, *Treaty Held with the Indians*, vii, Ratified Indian Treaties 1722-1800, NARA.

33. Sir William Johnson to Lt. Gen. Thomas Gage, letter dated Johnson Hall, February 15, 1772, *Johnson Papers*, 8: 406.

34. *Treaty Held with the Indians of the Six Nations in the Court-House in the Town of Lancaster, on Friday the Twenty Second of June, 1744* (Philadelphia: B. Franklin, 1744), 16, Ratified Indian Treaties 1722-1800, NARA.

35. *Extracts from the Treaty with the Indians at Loggstown in the Year 1752*, 18, Ratified Indian Treaties 1722-1800, NARA.

36. Col. Guy Johnson to Lt. Gen. Thomas Gage, letter dated Johnson Hall, January 1, 1773, and Sir William Johnson to Maj. Gen. Frederick Haldimand, letter dated Johnson Hall, June 30, 1773, *Johnson Papers*, 8:688 and 837; Arthur Parker, *The Constitution of the Five Nations* (Albany: University of the State of New York, 1916).

37. Sir William Johnson to Earl of Dartmouth, letter dated Johnson Hall, December 26, 1772, Davies, *Documents*, 5:247-29.

38. Thomas Wildcat Alford, *Civilization: As Told to Florence Drake* (Norman: University of Oklahoma Press, 1936), 44; James H. Howard, *Shawnee! The Ceremonialism of a Native American Tribe and Its Cultural Background* (Athens: Ohio University Press, 1981), 107-108; Jerry E. Clark, *The Shawnee* (Lexington: University Press of Kentucky, 1977), 33. Among other variations, the Chilabcahtha are also identified as Chilicothe, Calaka, Chalaakaatha, and Chalahgawtha; the Assiwikale as Oawikila, Hathawaekela, Thawekila, Thaawikila, and Thawegila; the Spitotha as Mekoches, Mequachake, Maykujay, Mekoce,

and Mekoche; the Bicowetha as Piqua, Pekowis, and Pekowi; and the Kispokotha as Kispokos, Kiscopocoke, Kispokotha, and Spitotha.

39. Ricky, *Indians of Maryland*, 254.

40. Colonial Records of Pennsylvania, *Minutes of the Provincial Council of Pennsylvania, from the Organization to the Termination of the Proprietary Government*, vol. 8, *Containing the Proceedings of Council from January 18th, 1757, to 4th of October, 1762, Both Dates Included*, ed. Samuel Hazard (Harrisburg: Theodore Fenn, 1852), 187-88, 204.

41. Edmund Burke, ed., *Annual Register*, vol. 6 (1763), sec. 1 (London: Robert Dodsley, 1763), 208-213.

42. Robert J. Miller, *Native America, Discovered and Conquered: Thomas Jefferson, Lewis and Clark, and Manifest Destiny* (Lincoln: University of Nebraska Press, 2008), 1-5, as well as conversations and e-mail correspondence with the author.

43. John Locke, *Two Treatises of Government* (London: Black Swan in Pater Noster Row, 1698; repr., edited with an introduction and notes by Peter Laslett, Cambridge: Cambridge University Press, 2009), 2:32.

44. Johnson, *Dictionary*, DES-DES, IMP-IN.

45. John Locke, "The Second Treatise of Government: An Essay Concerning the True and Original, Extent, and End of Government," Peter Laslett, ed. (Cambridge: Cambridge University Press, 1960, repr. 2009), §42:18-20 (297).

46. Benjamin Franklin, "Observation Concerning the Increase of Mankind, Peopling of Countries, &c.," in Leonard W. Larabee, W. B. Wilcox, Claude Lopez, and Barbara B. Oberg, eds., *The Papers of Benjamin Franklin* (New Haven, CT: Yale University Press, 1959-1998), 4:229, 231.

47. Locke, *Two Treatises*, 2:32.

48. *Treaty Held with the Indians of the Six Nations in the Court-House in the Town of Lancaster, on Friday the Twenty Second of June, 1744* (Philadelphia: B. Franklin, 1744), 36, Ratified Indian Treaties 1722-1800, NARA.

49. Ibid.

50. *Minutes of a Treaty Held at Easton, in Pennsylvania, in October, 1758* (Woodbridge, NJ: James Parker, 1758; repr., edited with an introduction and notes by Peter Laslett, Cambridge: Cambridge University Press, 2009), 19. The Minisinks, also called the Munsees, were a division of the Delawares sometimes called the Wolf Clan.

51. Ibid., 19-20.

52. George Washington to Earl of Dunmore, letter dated Williamsburg, November 2, 1773, in W. W. Abbot and Dorothy Twohig, eds., *The Papers of George Washington*, Colonial Series, vol. 9, January 1772–March 1774 (Charlottesville: University Press of Virginia, 1994), 357 (hereafter cited as *Washington Papers*).

53. Burke, *Annual Register*, 208-213.

54. Earl of Shelburne to Sir William Johnson, letter dated Whitehall, January 5, 1768, in Edmund Baily O'Callahan, ed., *Documents Related to the Colonial History of New York* (Albany: Weed, Parsons, 1857), 8:3 (hereafter cited as *New York Colonial Documents*).

55. Sir William Johnson to Earl of Shelburne, letter dated Johnson Hall, March 14, 1768, in ibid., 8:36-38.

56. Executive Journals of the Council of Virginia, dated December 16, 1768, in Benjamin J. Hillman, ed., *Executive Journals of the Council of Colonial Virginia, 1754-1775*, vol. 6

(Richmond: Virginia State Library, 1966), 308-309 (hereafter cited as *Council Executive Journals*).

57. *The 1768 Fort Stanwix Boundary Line Treaty*, Ratified Indian Treaties 1722-1800, NARA; Sir William Johnson to Earl of Hillsborough, letter dated Fort Stanwix, October 21, 1768, *Johnson Papers* 16, 2007; Proceedings of Sir William Johnson with the Indians at Fort Stanwix to Settle a Boundary Line, in O'Callahan, *New York Colonial Documents*, 8:38-50.

58. *The 1768 Fort Stanwix Boundary Line Treaty*, Ratified Indian Treaties 1722-1800, NARA.

59. Council dated December 16, 1768, *Council Executive Journals*, 6:309.

60. Ibid.

61. *The 1768 Fort Stanwix Boundary Line Treaty*, Ratified Indian Treaties 1722-1800, NARA; Sir William Johnson to Lt. Gen. Thomas Gage, letter dated Johnson Hall, November 13, 1768, with deed enclosed, *Johnson Papers*, 16: 210.

62. Joseph Cabell Jr., et al., to Baron de Botetourt, petition dated December (?), 1769, in James Rood Robertson, ed., *Petitions of the Early Habitants of Kentucky to the General Assembly of Virginia,1769-1792* (Louisville: Filson Club Publication, 1914; repr., Baltimore: Genealogical Publishing, 1998), 35n.

63. John Stuart to Baron de Botetourt, letter dated Lochaber, October 18, 1770, with copy of the Cherokee deed enclosed, in John Pendleton Kennedy, ed., *Journals of the House of Burgesses for Virginia, 1770-1772* (Richmond: Library of Virginia, 1906), xv-xvii (hereafter cited as *JHB*). The Long Island of the Holston River is the site of present-day Kingsport, Tennessee.

64. Journal entry from the House of Burgesses for Friday, June 15, 1770, session, and Baron de Botetourt to John Stuart, letter dated Williamsburg, June 21, 1770, in Kennedy, *JHB, 1770-1772*, 74 and xiii.

65. John Stuart to Alexander Cochrane, letter dated Charles Town, February 23, 1771, Davies, *Documents*, 3, Transcripts 1771 (Shannon: Irish University Press, 1973), 42-43.

66. Sir William Johnson to Earl of Dartmouth, letter dated Johnson Hall, April 22, 1773, Davies, *Documents*, vol. 6, Transcripts 1773 (Shannon: Irish University Press, 1974), 129-130.

67. George II to William, third earl of Dunmore, Royal Pardon and License to Reside at Beverley in Yorkshire, dated January 21, 1748, Handwritten MSS, Dunmore Family Papers 1, 65 D92, Box III, Folder I, Special Collections, Earl Greg Swem Library, College of William and Mary.

68. Ibid.; John E. Selby, *Dunmore* (Williamsburg: Virginia Independence Bicentennial Commission, 1977), 5-6.

69. John Newcastle, writing for King George II, to John Murray, Commission as Ensign in the Foot Guards, dated Kensington, May 30, 1749, Handwritten MSS, Dunmore Family Papers; Selby, *Dunmore*, 6. Dunmore's uncle and namesake, John, second earl, had been colonel of the regiment for nearly four decades. During this period, the Crown privileged officers in the Guards Regiments with dual-rank commissions. This enabled them to hold one rank in the guards and a higher rank in the army structure. Commissions in the guards were more valuable and therefore cost more than those of the same rank in nonguards units. For example, a captaincy in the guards included a lieutenant colonelcy in the army. Subalterns (i.e., ensigns and lieutenants) like Dunmore, in the

guards, were also captains in the army. When assigned or serving outside of their regiments, guards officers functioned as, and were treated and addressed by, the higher army rank. The British army abolished the practice after the Crimean War in the 1850s.
70. John Debrett, *Debrett's Correct Peerage of England, Scotland and Ireland, with the Extinct and Forfeited Peerages of the Three Kingdoms,* vol. 2, *Scotland* (London: F. and C. Rivington, 1805), 771. In some documents, Dunmore's other titles are written as Moulin, and Tillemott, Tillemot, Tilleymount, and Taymount.
71. James Corbett David, "Dunmore's New World: Political Culture in the British Empire, 1745–1796," unpublished manuscript, PhD diss., College of William and Mary, Williamsburg, VA, 2010, 33-35.
72. Lord Shelburne to Lord Dunmore, letter dated September 23, 1762, Handwritten MSS, Dunmore Family Papers 1, 65 D92, Box 3, Folder 22; Selby, *Dunmore,* 4, 7-8. Shelburne became first lord, or president, of the Lords of the Board of Trade in 1763.
73. Earl of Dunmore to Earl of Hillsborough, letter dated Williamsburg, March (?), 1772, Davies, *Documents,* vol. 5, transcripts 1772 (Shannon: Irish University Press, 1974), 51-53; Kennedy, *JHB, 1770-1772,* xxvi. Attakullakulla is a variation of Adagal'kala.
74. William Waller Hening, ed., *Statutes at Large: Being a Collection of All the Laws of Virginia, from the First Session of the Legislature in the Year 1619* (Richmond, VA: J. and C. Cochran, 1821), 8:600.
75. Council dated October 10, 1772, *Council Executive Journals,* 6:504-506.
76. John Stuart to Earl of Hillsborough, letter dated Charles Town, April 27, 1771, Davies, *Documents,* 3:85-86.
77. Lt. Gen. Thomas Gage to Earl of Hillsborough, letter dated New York, December 4, 1771, Davies, *Documents,* 3:25-26.
78. Lt. Gen. Thomas Gage to Viscount Barrington, letter dated New York, March 4, 1772, in Clarence Edwin Carter, ed., *The Correspondence of General Thomas Gage with the Secretaries of State and with the War Office and the Treasury, 1763-1775* (Hamden, CT: Archon Books, 1969), 2:600-601 (hereafter cited as *Gage Correspondence*).
79. Lt. Gen. Thomas Gage to Earl of Dartmouth, letter dated New York, December 2, 1772, Carter, *Gage Correspondence,* 1:340-341.
80. Percy B. Caley, "Lord Dunmore and the Pennsylvania-Virginia Boundary Dispute," *Western Pennsylvania Historical Magazine* 22 (June 1939): 87.
81. Commissioners of Trade and Plantations to the King, letter dated Whitehall, May 6, 1773, Davies, *Documents,* 6:134-142; Edward Montagu to the Virginia House of Burgesses Committee of Correspondence, letter dated London, January 18, 1770, *JHB, 1770-1772,* xvi-xvii.
82. Earl of Dunmore to Earl of Hillsborough, letter dated Williamsburg, March (?), 1771, Davies, *Documents,* 5:53-54.
83. Earl of Dunmore to the Surveyor of Fincastle County [William Preston], Certificate of Military Land Claim for Alexander Waugh, dated Williamsburg, December 17, 1773, Handwritten MSS, Catalog no. 1969.51.019, Collection, History Museum of Western Virginia, Roanoke, Virginia.
84. Ibid.; and George Rogers Clark to Jonathan Clark, letter dated Grave Creek Township, January 9, 1773, in James Alton James, ed., *George Rogers Clark Papers, 1771-1781* (Springfield: Illinois State Historical Library, 1912), 32 (hereafter cited as *Clark Papers*).

85. Shawnee Deputies to *Guyasuta* and Alexander McKee, speech dated Pittsburgh, June 28, 1773, Davies, *Documents*, 6:166-167. Variations of spelling Cornstalk's Indian name include Hokolesqua and Wynepuechsika. Variations of Guyasuta's name include Keyashuta, Kayasota, Kayashuta, Gaiachuton, Geyesutha, Koyashota, and Ca-ya-sho-ta.
86. Earl of Dunmore to Earl of Dartmouth, letter dated Williamsburg, March 18, 1774, Davies, *Documents*, 8, transcripts 1774 (Shannon: Irish University Press, 1974), 65-67.
87. George Washington to Earl of Dunmore, letter dated Mount Vernon, April 13, 1773, *Washington Papers*, 9:217-218.
88. Earl of Dunmore to George Washington, letter dated Williamsburg, July 3, 1773, *Washington Papers*, 9:258-259.
89. Earl of Dunmore to Earl of Dartmouth, letter dated Williamsburg, March 18, 1774, Davies, *Documents*, 8:65-67.
90. John Connolly, "A Narrative of the Transactions, Imprisonment, and Sufferings of John Connolly, an American Loyalist and Lieutenant-Colonel in His Majesty's Service," *Pennsylvania Magazine of History and Biography* 12, no. 3.
91. John Connolly to George Washington, letter dated Pittsburgh, August 29, 1773, and George Washington to Earl of Dunmore, letter dated Mount Vernon, September 12, 1773, *Washington Papers*, 9:314-315 and 322-324.
92. Sir William Johnson to Earl of Dartmouth, letter dated Johnson Hall, September 22, 1773, Davies, *Documents*, 6:224-225.
93. Council dated October 11, 1773, *Council Executive Journals*, 6:541-543.

CHAPTER 2: EXTRAORDINARY OCCURRENCES

1. King George III to Lord Dunmore, Royal Commission and Instructions as Governor of Virginia, dated Court of St. James, February 7, 1771 (hereafter Dunmore's Commission), Aspinwall Papers, Massachusetts Historical Collection, 4th ser., vol. 10 (Boston: Massachusetts Historical Society, 1871), 659-660; George Webb, *The office and authority of a justice of peace. . . .* (Williamsburg, VA: William Parks, 1736), 18, Special Collections, John D. Rockefeller Jr. Library, Colonial Williamsburg Foundation, Williamsburg, VA); H. R. (Henry Read) McIlwaine, *JHB*, 1727-1734 (Richmond: Virginia State Library, 1910), 241; Council dated October 11, 1773, *Council Executive Journals*, 541-543; McIlwaine, 243-244 (Williamsburg, VA: Printed by William Parks, 1736), 222-223, *JHB 1727-1734* (Richmond: Virginia State Library, 1910), 241.
2. Council dated October 11, 1773, *Council Executive Journals*, 6:541-543.
3. Ibid.
4. Council dated October 11, 1773, *Council Executive Journals*, 6:541-543.
5. Smyth, J. F. D., *A Tour in the United States of America . . .*, vol. 1 (Dublin: G. Perrin, 1784), 13.
6. Capt. Augustine Prevost, diary entry dated Williamsburg, July 2, 1774, in Nicholas B. Wainwright, ed., "Turmoil at Pittsburgh: Diary of Augustine Prevost, 1774," *Pennsylvania Magazine of History and Biography* 85, no. 2 (April 1961): 123.
7.William Crawford to George Washington, letter dated Spring Garden, December 29, 1773, in Abbot and Twohig, *Washington Papers*, 9:444-445, 445n.
8. John Connolly to George Washington, letter dated Westmoreland Gaol, Pennsylvania, February 1, 1774, in ibid., 464-466. Redstone is present-day Brownsville, Pennsylvania.

9. John Connolly to George Washington, letter dated Fredericksburg, December 23, 1773, in ibid., 414.

10. Webb, *office and authority of a justice of peace*, 203.

11. Arthur St. Clair to Gov. John Penn, letter dated Ligonier, February 2, 1774, in Samuel Hazard, ed., *Pennsylvania Archives*, ser. 1, vol. 4 (Philadelphia: Joseph Severns, 1853), 476-478.

12. William Crawford to George Washington, letter dated Spring Garden, January 10, 1774, in Abbot and Twohig, *Washington Papers*, 9:418-420.

13. William Crawford to George Washington, letter dated Spring Garden, January 10, 1774, C.W. Butterfield, ed., *The Washington-Crawford Letters, Being the Correspondence between George Washington and William Crawford, from 1767 to 1781, Concerning Western Lands* (Cincinnati: Robert Clarke, 1877), 40-41.

14. John J. Jacob, *A Biographical Sketch of the Life of the Late Captain Michael Cresap* (Cumberland, MD: J. M. Buchanan, 1826), 57.

15. Arthur St. Clair to Joseph Shippen, letter dated Ligonier, January 15, 1774, in Hazard, *Pennsylvania Archives* 1, 4:471-472.

16. Aeneas Mackay to Gov. John Penn, letter dated Pittsburgh, April 4, 1774, in Peter Force, ed., *American Archives: Consisting of a Collection of Authentic Records, . . .*, vol. 1 (Washington, DC: M. St. Clair Clarke and Peter Force, 1837-1853), 269-270.

17. Aeneas Mackay to Gov. John Penn, letter dated Pittsburgh, April 4, 1774, in Force, *American Archives*, 1:269-270; Abbot and Twohig, *Washington Papers*, 9:466n.

18. Arthur St. Clair to Gov. John Penn, letter dated Ligonier, February 2, 1774, in Hazard, *Pennsylvania Archives* 1, 4:476-478.

19. Ibid.

20. Arthur St. Clair to Gov. John Penn, letter dated Ligonier, February 9, 1774, and Aeneas Mackay to Gov. John Penn, letter dated Pittsburgh, April 4, 1774, in Force, *American Archives*, 1:266-267 and 269-271; Council dated February 28, 1774, *Council Executive Journals*, 6:554-555.

21. Enclosure to St. Clair's letter to Gov. Penn, February 2, 1774, in Force, *American Archives* 1:267-268.

22. Arthur St. Clair to Gov. John Penn, letter dated Ligonier, February 9, 1774, in Force, *American Archives*, 1:266-267.

23. Paper referred to in St. Clair's letter to Penn, dated Ligonier, February 2, 1774, in Hazard, *Pennsylvania Archives* 1, 4:478-480.

24. Ibid., 478-480.

25. Arthur St. Clair to Gov. John Penn, letter dated Ligonier, February 2, 1774, in Hazard, *Pennsylvania Archives* 1, 4:476-478.

26. Gov. John Penn to Earl of Dunmore, letter dated Philadelphia, January 31, 1774, as mentioned in Dunmore's March 3 reply, in Force, *American Archives*, 1:252-255.

27. John Connolly to George Washington, letter dated Westmoreland Gaol, February 1, 1774, in Abbot and Twohig, *Washington Papers*, 9:554-556.

28. Council dated February 28, 1774, *Council Executive Journals*, 6:554-555.

29. Earl of Dunmore to Gov. John Penn, letter dated Williamsburg, March 3, 1774, in Force, *American Archives*, 1:252-255.

30. Gov. John Penn to Earl of Dunmore, letter dated Philadelphia, March 31, 1774, in Force, *American Archives*, 1:255-260, and Council dated April 20, 1774, *Council Executive Journals*, 6:556-557.

31. Earl of Dunmore to Earl of Dartmouth (extract), letter dated Williamsburg, April 2, 1774, in Hazard, *Pennsylvania Archives* 1, 4:423-424 (emphasis from text); Petition of Inhabitants of Augusta, Botetourt, and Fincastle Counties in Virginia to Earl of Dunmore, Davies, K. G., ed., *Documents of the American Revolution 1770—1783*, Davies, *Documents*, 8:85-86.

32. Joseph Spear to Arthur St. Clair, letter dated Pittsburgh, February 23, 1774, in Hazard, *Pennsylvania Archives* 1, 4:481.

33. Arthur St. Clair to Joseph Shippen, letter dated Ligonier, February 25, 1774, in Force, *American Archives*, 1:269.

34. George Croghan to David Sample, letter dated Pittsburgh, April 4, 1774, in Hazard, *Pennsylvania Archives* 1, 4:483.

35. George Croghan to the Earl of Dunmore, letter dated Fort Pitt, April 9, 1774, in Augustine Prevost, "Turmoil at Pittsburgh: Diary of Augustine Prevost, 1774," ed. Nicholas B. Wainwright, *Pennsylvania Magazine of History and Biography* 85, no. 2 (April 1961): 144-146.

36. Arthur St. Clair to Gov. John Penn, letter dated Ligonier, February 2, 1774, in Hazard, *Pennsylvania Archives* 1, 4:476-478. Redstone is now called Brownsville, in Fayette County, Pennsylvania.

37. Arthur St. Clair to Gov. John Penn, letter dated Ligonier, February 2, 1774, and Joseph Spear to Arthur St. Clair, letter dated Pittsburgh, February 23, 1774, in Hazard, *Pennsylvania Archives* 1, 4:476-478 and 481.

38. Joseph Spear to Arthur St. Clair, letter dated Pittsburgh, February 23, 1774, in Hazard, *Pennsylvania Archives* 1, 4:481.

39. Aeneas Mackay to Gov. John Penn, letter dated Pittsburgh, April 4, 1774, in Hazard, *Pennsylvania Archives* 1, 4:484-486.

40. Ibid.; William Crawford to Gov. John Penn, letter dated Westmoreland County, April 8, 1774, in Force, *American Archives*, 1:262-263; Council dated April 20, 1774, *Council Executive Journals*, 6:554-555.

41. Aeneas Mackay to Gov. Penn, letter dated Pittsburgh, April 4, 1774, in Hazard, *Pennsylvania Archives* 1, 4:484-486.

42. Ibid.

43. William Crawford to Gov. John Penn, letter dated Westmoreland County, April 8, 1774, with Enclosure 1: John Connolly to Magistrates of Westmoreland County, in Force, *American Archives*, 1:262-263.

44. Ibid.; Thomas Smith to Joseph Shippen, letter dated Westmoreland, April 7, 1774, in Force, *American Archives*, 1:262-263 and 271-273; George Wilson to William Fisher, deposition dated Philadelphia, April 25, 1774, in Hazard, *Pennsylvania Archives* 1, 4:491-492.

45. William Crawford to Gov. John Penn, letter dated Westmoreland County, April 8, 1774, in Force, *American Archives*, 1:262-263.

46. Ibid., with Enclosure 2: Magistrates of Westmoreland County to John Connolly's Address.

47. Andrew McFarlane to Gov. John Penn, letter dated Pittsburgh, April 9, 1774, in Hazard, *Pennsylvania Archives* 1, 4:487-488; Aeneas Mackay to Gov. John Penn, letter dated Pittsburgh, April 9, 1774, and Devereux Smith to Gov. John Penn, letter dated Pittsburgh, April 9, 1774, in Force, *American Archives*, 1:264-265. The text version reads "Minsworn Constable" but is corrected here to read "Missworn Constable."

48. Thomas Smith to Joseph Shippen, letter dated Bedford, April 13, 1774, in Hazard, *Pennsylvania Archives* 1, 4:488-489; Gov. John Penn to William Crawford, Esq., and Associates of Westmoreland County, letter dated Philadelphia, April 22, 1774, and Gov. John Penn to Aeneas Mackay, Devereux Smith, and Andrew McFarlane, letter dated Philadelphia, April 22, 1774, and, Gov. John Penn to James Tilghman and Andrew Allen, Instructions as Commissioners Appointed to Treat with the Governor of Virginia, dated Philadelphia, May 7, 1774, in Force, *American Archives*, 1:265-266 and 279-280.

49. Thomas Smith to Joseph Shippen, letter dated Westmoreland County, April 7, 1774, and Aeneas Mackay to Gov. John Penn, letter dated Staunton, May 5, 1774, in Force, *American Archives*, 1:271-273 and 282-283.

50. Council dated April 25, 1774, *Council Executive Journals*, 6:558.

51. Aeneas Mackay to Gov. John Penn, letter dated Staunton, May 5, 1774, and Earl of Dunmore to Daniel Smith, letter dated Williamsburg, April 26, 1774, in Force, *American Archives*, 1:282-283.

52. John Murray, Earl of Dunmore, Governor of (Colony) Virginia 1771-1775, Proclamation dated Williamsburg, April 25, 1774, in *An American Time Capsule: Three Centuries of Broadsides and Other Printed Ephemera*, portfolio 178, folder 12c, US Library of Congress, Washington, DC; and Extract of a Journal of the United Brethren's Mission on Muskingum from February 21 to 20 May 20, 1774, in Force, *American Archives*, 1:288-289. The Muskingum is a tributary of the Ohio that flows through the east-central area of present-day Ohio.

53. Alexander McKee to Sir William Johnson, letter dated Pittsburgh, March 3, 1774, *Johnson Papers*, 8:1057-1058; Earl of Dunmore to Earl of Dartmouth, letter dated Williamsburg, December 24, 1774, in Davies, *Documents*, 8:257.

54. Alexander McKee to Sir William Johnson, letter dated Pittsburgh, March 3, 1774, in Hamilton, *Johnson Papers*, 12:1082.

55. Davies, *Documents*, 53.

56. Council dated July 17, 1771, *Council Executive Journals*, 6:428.

57. Withers, *Chronicles of Border Warfare*, 136–137; Earl of Dunmore to Earl of Dartmouth, letter dated Williamsburg, December 24, 1774, in Davies, *Documents*, 8:257.

58. Withers, *Chronicles of Border Warfare*, 137–138. One of the five, John Cutright, revealed the truth in a deathbed confession in 1852, per 137n.

59. Jacob, *Biographical Sketch*, 53, and Samuel Kercheval, *A History of the Valley of Virginia* (1909; repr., Baltimore: Genealogical Publishing, 2002), 109.

60. Council dated October 14, 1773, *Council Executive Journals*, 6:544. Although the incident happened in South Carolina, Virginia officials took measures to apprehend Collins if the fugitive traveled to the colony.

61. Jacob, *Biographical Sketch*, 53.

62. John Stuart to Maj. Gen. Frederick Haldimand, letter dated Charles Town, February 3, 1774, in Davies, *Documents*, 8:34-37.

63. Andrew Lewis to George Washington, letter dated Richfield, March 9, 1774, in Abbot and Twohig, *Washington Papers*, 9:512-515; and *Virginia Gazette* #2 (Rind), March 17, 1774.

64. John Patton Pension Application R8012, dated February 11, 1835, Record Group 15, Revolutionary War Pension Applications, M805, Roll 1889, NARA.

65. Joseph Doddridge, *Notes on the Settlement and Indian Wars of the Western Parts of Virginia and Pennsylvania from 1763 to 1783, Inclusive* (Wellsburgh, VA: Office of the Gazette, 1824; repr., Pittsburgh: John S. Ritenour and William T. Lindsey, 1912), 94.

66. Andrew Lewis to George Washington, letter dated Richfield, March 9, 1774, in Abbot and Twohig, *Washington Papers*, 9:512-515.

67. Ibid.; and William Preston to Samuel McDowell, letter dated Fincastle, May 27, 1774, in Preston Papers, 3QQ27. Lewis's Richfield was on the Roanoke River in present-day Salem, Virginia. Preston's Smithfield Plantation is near present-day Blacksburg, Virginia.

68. Andrew Lewis to George Washington, letter dated Richfield Botetourt County, March 9, 1774, in Abbot and Twohig, *Washington Papers*, 9:512-515.

69. Capt. Daniel Smith to Col. William Preston, letter dated Castle's Wood, March 22, 1774, in Preston Papers, 3QQ15.

70. *Virginia Gazette* #2 (Rind), March 24, 1774.

71. *Virginia Gazette* #1 (Purdie and Dixon), March 24, 1774.

72. Capt. William Russell to Col. William Preston, letter dated Castle's Woods, May 7, 1774, and Capt. William Russell to Scouts, instructions, n.d., Preston Papers, 3QQ23 and 3QQ18.

73. Capt. William Russell to Col. William Preston, letter dated Castle's Woods, May 7, 1774, and Col. William Preston to Capt. Samuel McDowell, letter dated Richfield, May 27, 1774, Preston Papers, 3QQ23 and 3QQ27.

74. Capt. William Russell to Scouts, instructions, n.d., Preston Papers, 3QQ18.

CHAPTER 3: A WAR IS EVERY MOMENT EXPECTED

1. Thomas Hanson's Journal, extract, April 7–August 9, 1774, *George Rogers Clark Papers*, Draper Manuscripts, 14J58-84 (114-115), and Aeneas Mackay to Gov. John Penn, letter dated Pittsburgh, April 4, 1774, in Force, *American Archives*, 1:269-271.

2. Alexander McKee, journal entry dated March 8, 1774, *Johnson Papers*, 12:1083-1086.

3. Deveraux Smith to Dr. William Smith, letter dated Pittsburgh, June 10, 1774, *Pennsylvania Archives*, 1, 4:511-513; Rev. David Zeisberger letter [extract] dated Schönbrunn, May 27, 1774, in Force, *American Archives*, 1:285-286; Jacob, *Biographical Sketch*, 56, 134; John Floyd to Col. William Preston, letter dated Little Giandot, April 26, 1774, Preston Papers, Draper Manuscripts, 3QQ19 (7-9).

4. John Connolly, "Journal of My Proceedings & etc., Commencing from the late Disturbances with the Cherokees upon the Ohio," 1, handwritten manuscript, George Chalmers Papers Relating to Indian Affairs, 1750-1775, New York Public Library.

5. McKee, journal entry dated Pittsburgh, April 27, 1774, *Johnson Papers*, 12:1090-1091. Mingo Town was the location of present-day Steubenville, Ohio.

6. Deveraux Smith to Dr. William Smith, letter dated Pittsburgh, June 10, 1774, in Hazard, *Pennsylvania Archives*, 1, 4:511-513; Rev. David Zeisberger [extract] letter dated Schönbrunn, May 27, 1774, in Force, *American Archives*, 1:285-286; Jacob, *Biographical Sketch*, 56, 134; John Floyd to Col. William Preston, letter dated Little Giandot, April 26, 1774, Preston Papers, Draper Manuscripts, 3QQ19 (7-9).

7. McKee, journal entries dated Pittsburgh, April 17-25 and 27, 1774, *Johnson Papers*, 12:1090-1091, 1095.

8. Connolly, "Journal," April 20, 1774, 2.

9. McKee, journal entry dated Pittsburgh, April 27, 1774, *Johnson Papers*, 12:1095.

10. Arthur St. Clair to Gov. John Penn, letter dated May 29, 1774, in Hazard, *Pennsylvania Archives*, 1, 4:502.

11. John Floyd to Col. William Preston, letter dated Little Giandot, April 26, 1774, Preston Papers, Draper Manuscripts, 3QQ19, 7-9, and Hanson's Journal, extract, April 7–9, August 9, 1774, *Clark Papers*, Draper Manuscripts, 14J58-84 (114-115).

12. Rev. David Zeisberger letter (extract) dated Schönbrunn, May 27, 1774, in Force, *American Archives*, 1:285-286.

13. Deveraux Smith to Dr. William Smith, letter dated Pittsburgh, June 10, 1774, in Hazard, *Pennsylvania Archives*, 1, 4:511-513.

14. McKee, journal entry dated Pittsburgh, April 25, 1774, *Johnson Papers*, 12:1094-1095.

15. John Murray, Earl of Dunmore, Proclamation dated Williamsburg, April 25, 1774, portfolio 178, folder 12c, Library of Congress, Washington, DC, also at *An American Time Capsule: Three Centuries of Broadsides and Other Printed Ephemera*, http://memory.loc.gov/ammem/rbpehtml/pehome.html; Council dated April 25, 1774, *Council Executive Journals*, 6:558.

16. John Floyd to William Preston, letter dated Little Giandot, April 26, 1774, Preston Papers, Draper Manuscripts, 3QQ19.

17. John Floyd to William Preston, letter dated Little Giandot, April 26, 1774, Preston Papers, Draper Manuscripts, 3QQ19 (7-9).

18. Alexander Spottswood Dandridge to Col. William Preston, letter dated May 15, 1774, Preston Papers, Draper Manuscripts, 3QQ26 (22).

19. George Rogers Clark to Samuel Brown, Esq., letter dated June 17, 1798, *Clark Papers*, 3-9; also published in Jacob, *Biographical Sketch*, 154. Although Ebenezer Zane first settled there in 1769, Virginia did not incorporate Wheeling until 1787.

20. George Rogers Clark to Samuel Brown, Esq., letter dated June 17, 1798, *Clark Papers*, 3-9.

21. Jacob, *Biographical Sketch*, 47-50, 140; Thwaites and Kellogg, *Documentary History*, 12n; Kercheval, *History of the Valley*, 125; Withers, *Chronicles of Border Warfare*, 134n. Oldtown is near present-day Cumberland, now within Allegany County, Maryland.

22. George Rogers Clark to Samuel Brown, Esq., letter dated June 17, 1798, *Clark Papers*, 3-9.

23. Dunmore Proclamation dated Williamsburg, April 25, 1774; Council dated April 25, 1774, *Council Executive Journals*, 6:558; George Rogers Clark to Samuel Brown, Esq., letter dated June 17, 1798, *Clark Papers*, 3-9, and Alexander McKee, journal entry dated Pittsburgh, April 27, 1774, *Johnson Papers*, 12:1095-1096.

24. George Rogers Clark to Samuel Brown, Esq., letter dated June 17, 1798, *Clark Papers*, 3-9.

25. Ibid., and McKee, journal entry dated Pittsburgh, April 27, 1774, *Johnson Papers*, 12:1095-1096.

26. George Rogers Clark to Samuel Brown, Esq., letter dated June 17, 1798, *Clark Papers*, 3-9, and McKee, journal entry dated Pittsburgh, April 27, 1774, *Johnson Papers*, 12:1095-1096.

27. Ebenezer Zane to Hon. John Brown, letter dated Wheeling, February 4, 1800, and John Anderson, certificate dated Fredericksburg, June 30, 1798, in Thomas Jefferson,

Notes on the State of Virginia, ed. Frank Shuffelton (New York: Penguin Books, 1999), 242-243 and 248-249, respectively; Kercheval, *History of the Valley*, 125.

28. George Rogers Clark to Samuel Brown, Esq., letter dated June 17, 1798, *Clark Papers*, 3-9; McKee, journal entry dated Pittsburgh, April 27, 1774, *Johnson Papers*, 12:1095-1096.

29. George Rogers Clark to Samuel Brown, Esq., letter dated June 17, 1798, *Clark Papers*, 3-9; McKee, journal entry dated Pittsburgh, April 27, 1774, *Johnson Papers*, 12:1095-1096, and William Crawford to George Washington, letter dated May 8, 1774, in Butterfield, *Washington-Crawford Letters*, 46-50.

30. McKee, journal entry dated Pittsburgh, April 27, 1774, *Johnson Papers*, 12:1096.

31. George Rogers Clark to Samuel Brown, Esq., letter dated June 17, 1798, *Clark Papers*, 3-9; McKee, journal entry dated Pittsburgh, April 27, 1774, *Johnson Papers*, 12:1095-1096, and Henry Jolly, Reminiscence, Draper Manuscripts, 6NN-24 (9-13, 11n-12n).

32. John Gibson to Judge Jeremiah Baker, deposition dated Pittsburgh, April 4, 1800, in Jefferson, *Notes on the State of Virginia*, ed. Shuffelton, 239-241.

33. Shamokin was near present-day Sunbury, Pennsylvania. Variations of Shikellamy include Shikellemus and Swatana.

34. Variations of Logan's Indian name include Talgayeeta, Tah-gah-jute, Tachnechdorus, Tachnedorus, Tacaniodoragon, and Soyechtowa. Although some histories identify him as Seneca, he was born of an Oneida father and Cayuga mother, and therefore was a member of the latter in the matrilineal Iroquoian society.

35. John Sappington to Samuel McKee Jr., declaration dated Madison County, February 13, 1800, and James Chambers to Samuel Shannon, deposition dated Washington County, Pennsylvania, April 20, 1798, in Jefferson, *Notes on the State of Virginia*, ed. Shuffelton, 261-263 and 245-247, respectively; Michael Cresap Jr. to Lyman C. Draper, 1845, Draper Manuscripts, 2SS, book 5, 33-35, as noted in Thwaites and Kellogg, *Documentary History*, 15. Baker's Bottom was near present-day Newell, West Virginia. Catfish Camp is present-day Washington, Pennsylvania.

36. John Sappington to Samuel McKee Jr., declaration dated Madison County, February 13, 1800, in Jefferson, *Notes on the State of Virginia*, ed. Shuffelton, 261-263.

37. John Sappington to Samuel McKee Jr., declaration dated Madison County, February 13, 1800, William Robinson, declaration dated Philadelphia, February 28, 1800, and James Chambers to Samuel Shannon, deposition dated Washington County, Pennsylvania, April 20, 1798, in Jefferson, *Notes on the State of Virginia*, ed. Shuffelton, 261-263, 249-251, and 245-247, respectively, and Michael Cresap Jr. and Bazaleel Wells to Lyman C. Draper, 1845, *Documentary History*, 15 and 16, respectively.

38. James Chambers to Samuel Shannon, deposition dated Washington County, Pennsylvania, April 20, 1798, in Jefferson, *Notes on the State of Virginia*, ed. Shuffelton, 245-247.

39. McKee, journal entry dated May 3, 1774, *Johnson Papers*, 12:1097-1098; George Edgington to Lyman C. Draper, 1845, Draper Manuscripts, 2S book 3, 341, Thwaites and Kellogg, *Documentary History*, 16-17; James Chambers to Samuel Shannon, deposition dated Washington County, Pennsylvania, April 20, 1798, in Jefferson, *Notes on the State of Virginia*, ed. Shuffelton, 245-247; Earl of Dunmore to Earl of Dartmouth, letter dated Williamsburg, December 24, 1774, Davies, *Documents*, 8:259.

40. McKee, journal entry dated May 3, 1774, *Johnson Papers*, 12:1097-1098; John Sappington to Samuel McKee Jr., declaration dated Madison County, February 13, 1800, William Robinson, declaration dated Philadelphia, February 28, 1800, James Chambers to Samuel Shannon, deposition dated Washington County, Pennsylvania, April 20, 1798, and Harry Innes to Thomas Jefferson, declaration dated Kentucky near Frankfort, November 14, 1799, all in Jefferson, *Notes on the State of Virginia*, ed. Shuffelton, 261-263, 249-251, 245-247, and 248-249, respectively; Rev. David Zeisberger letter [extract] dated Schönbrunn, May 27, 1774, in Force, *American Archives*, 1:285-286.

41. James Chambers to Samuel Shannon, deposition dated Washington County, Pennsylvania, April 20, 1798, in Jefferson, *Notes on the State of Virginia*, ed. Shuffelton, 245-247.

42. Jolly, Reminiscences, Pittsburgh and Northwest Virginia Papers 6NN-24, Draper Manuscripts, and Thwaites and Kellogg, *Documentary History*, 9-13, 11n-12n.

43. McKee, journal entry dated May 3, 1774, *Johnson Papers*, 12:1097-1098; James Chambers to Samuel Shannon, deposition dated Washington County, Pennsylvania, April 20, 1798, and William Robinson, declaration dated Philadelphia, February 28, 1800, in Jefferson, *Notes on the State of Virginia*, ed. Shuffelton, 249-251 and 245-247, respectively; Jolly, Reminiscences, Pittsburgh and Northwest Virginia Papers 6NN-24 (9-13, 11n-12n), and Jefferson, *Notes on the State of Virginia*, ed. Shuffelton, 67.

44. James Chambers to Samuel Shannon, deposition dated Washington County, Pennsylvania, April 20, 1798, in Jefferson, *Notes on the State of Virginia*, ed. Shuffelton, 245-247.

45. Rev. David Zeisberger Journal [extract] of the United Brethren Mission on Muskingum dated Schönbrunn, May 24, 1774, in Force, *American Archives*, 1:285-286.

46. Jolly, Reminiscences, Pittsburgh and Northwest Virginia Papers 6NN-24 (9-13, 11n-12n); William Huston to David Riddick, certificate dated Washington County, Pennsylvania, April 18, 1798, and James Chambers to Samuel Shannon, deposition dated Washington County, Pennsylvania, April 20, 1798, in Jefferson, *Notes on the State of Virginia*, ed. Shuffelton, 243-244 and 245-257, respectively.

47. William Huston to David Riddick, certificate dated Washington County, Pennsylvania, April 18, 1798, in Jefferson, *Notes on the State of Virginia*, ed. Shuffelton, 243-244; Jolly, Reminiscences, Pittsburgh and Northwest Virginia Papers 6NN-24 (9-13, 11n-12n); William Crawford to George Washington, letter dated May 8, 1774, in Butterfield, *Washington-Crawford Letters*, 46-50; McKee, journal entry dated May 3, 1774, *Johnson Papers*, 12:1097-1098.

48. William Crawford to George Washington, letter dated Spring Garden, May 8, 1774, and Valentine Crawford to George Washington, letter dated Jacob's Creek, April 27, 1774, Butterfield, *Washington-Crawford Letters*, 46-50 and 84-85, respectively, and 84n.

49. Connolly, "Journal," May 1, 1774, and Hening, *Statutes*, 7:93-94, 106-107, and 110-111.

50. Connolly, "Journal," May 3, 1774.

51. Ibid., May 1, 3, and 6, 1774, and McKee, journal entry, May 2, 1774, *Johnson Papers*, 12:1096.

52. John G. E. Heckewelder, *History, Manners and Customs of the Indian Nations Who Once Inhabited Pennsylvania and the Neighboring States* (Philadelphia: Abraham Small, 1819; repr., Philadelphia: Historical Society of Pennsylvania, 1876; repr., Westminster, MD: Heritage Books, 2007), 176.

53. Connolly, "Journal," May 6, 1774, and McKee, journal entry dated May 5, 1774.

54. George Croghan to Capt. John Connolly and Alexander McKee, letter dated Pittsburgh, May 4, 1774, *Johnson Papers*, 12:1099.

55. Ibid.

56. The following discussion of the council between colonial officials and representatives of Indian nations held at Pittsburgh is based on Connolly, "Journal," May 2-7, 1774.

57. Rev. David Zeisberger Journal [extract] of the United Brethren Mission on Muskingum, dated Schönbrunn, April 30, 1774, in Force, *American Archives*, 1:283.

58. Rev. David Zeisberger, letter [extract] dated Schönbrunn, May 24, 1774, in Force, *American Archives*, 1:284-285, and Thwaites and Kellogg, *Documentary History*, 36n.

59. Netawatwes was called Newcomer by the English, and variations of his name, meaning "skilled adviser," include Netahutquemaled, Netodwehement, and Netautwhalemund.

60. Rev. John Heckewelder, declaration, in Jefferson, *Notes on the State of Virginia*, ed. Shuffelton, 253; Rev. David Zeisberger, letter dated Schönbrunn, May 27, 1774, in Force, *American Archives*, 1:285-286.

61. Sir William Johnson to Earl of Dartmouth, letter dated Johnson Hall, June 20, 1774, Davies, *Documents*, 8:133-134.

62. Rev. John Heckewelder, declaration, in Jefferson, *Notes on the State of Virginia*, ed. Shuffelton, 253; Rev. David Zeisberger, letter dated Schönbrunn, May 27, 1774, in Force, *American Archives*, 1:285-286; Arthur St. Clair to Gov. Penn, letter dated Ligonier, May 29, 1774, in Hazard, *Pennsylvania Archives*, 1, 4:502.

63. Rev. David Zeisberger Journal [extract] of the United Brethren Mission on Muskingum, dated Schönbrunn, April 30–May 20, 1774, in Force, *American Archives*, 1:285-286. Wakatomica, a Shawnee town of four villages on the Muskingum River, stood near present-day Dresden, Ohio: Wapatomica, Waketomika, Woakatameka, and Waketameki are variations of the name.

64. Ibid.

65. Rev. John Heckewelder, declaration, in Jefferson, *Notes on the State of Virginia*, ed. Shuffelton, 253.

66. Rev. David Zeisberger, letter dated Schönbrunn, May 24, 1774, in Force, *American Archives*, 1:285-286.

67. Rev. David Zeisberger Journal [extract] of the United Brethren Mission on Muskingum, dated Schönbrunn, April 30–May 20, 1774, in Force, *American Archives*, 1:283-284.

68. Connolly, "Journal," entry for May 26, 1774.

69. Capt. William Russell to Col. William Preston, letter dated Castle's Woods, May 7, 1774, Preston Papers, Draper Manuscripts, 3QQ23 (19-23).

70. William Crawford to George Washington, letter dated Spring Garden, May 8, 1774, and Valentine Crawford to George Washington, letter dated Jacob's Creek, April 27, 1774, in Butterfield, *Washington-Crawford Letters*, 46-50 and 84-85, respectively, and 84n.

CHAPTER 4: TRAINED IN MARTIAL EXERCISE

1. Connolly, "Journal," May 8-11, 1774.

2. William Crawford to George Washington, letter dated Spring Garden, May 8, 1774, in Butterfield, *Washington-Crawford Letters*, 46-50; Connolly, "Journal," May 8-11, 1774.

3. Connolly, "Journal," May 8-11, 1774.

4. Ibid., May 10-12, 1774.

5. Ibid., May 16, 1774.

6. Ibid., May 19, 1774.

7. Capt. John Connolly to Commanders of Companies, circular letter dated Fort Pitt, May 19, 1774, Connolly, "Journal," May 19, 1774.

8. Connolly, "Journal," May 20-23, 1774.

9. Rev. David Zeisberger Journal (extract) of the United Brethren Mission on Muskingum, dated Schönbrunn, April 30–May 20, 1774, in Force, *American Archives*, 1:284; Letter (extract) dated Bedford, May 30, 1774, *Virginia Gazette* #1 (Purdie and Dixon), June 23, 1774. Some sources render John Anderson's surname as "Saunderson."

10. Arthur St. Clair to Gov. John Penn, letter dated May 29, 1774, and Rev. David Zeisberger, Journal (extract) of the United Brethren Mission on Muskingum, dated Schönbrunn, February 21–May 20, 1774, in Hazard, *Pennsylvania Archives*, 1, 4:502 and 495-497, respectively; Connolly, "Journal," May 24, 1774.

11. Cornstalk to Alexander McKee, letter (speech) dated May 20, 1774, in Hazard, *Pennsylvania Archives*, 1, 4:497-498. Variations of Cornstalk's name include Hokoleskwa, Colesqua, Keightugh-qua, and Wynepuechsika.

12. Ibid.

13. Rev. David Zeisberger Journal (extract) of the United Brethren Mission on Muskingum, dated Schönbrunn, February 21–May 20, 1774, in Hazard, *Pennsylvania Archives*, 1, 4:495-497.

14. Ibid.

15. James Smith, *An Account of the Remarkable Occurrences in the Life of Col. James Smith, During His Captivity with the Indians, in the Years 1755, '56, '57, '58, & '59, Written by Himself* (Lexington, KY: John Bradford, 1799, repr., Columbus, OH: Ohio Historical Society, 1996), 33.

16. Rev. David Zeisberger Journal (extract) of the United Brethren Mission on Muskingum, dated Schönbrunn, February 21–May 20, 1774, in Hazard, *Pennsylvania Archives*, 1, 4:495-497.

17. Rev. David Zeisberger Journal (extract) of the United Brethren Mission on Muskingum, dated Schönbrunn, February 21-May 20, and May 28, 1774, and Deveraux Smith to Dr. Smith, letter dated Pittsburgh, June 10, 1774, in Hazard, *Pennsylvania Archives*, 1, 4:495-497, 498-500, and 511-513, respectively; John Campbell to L. Andrew Levy, letter dated Pittsburgh, May 30, 1774, William Vincent Byars, ed., *B. and M. Gratz, Merchants in Philadelphia, 1754-1798: Papers of Interest to Their Posterity and the Posterity of Their Associates* (Jefferson City, MO: Hugh Stephens Printing, 1916), 142-143 (hereafter cited as *Gratz Papers*).

18. Rev. David Zeisberger Journal (extract) of the United Brethren Mission on Muskingum dated Schönbrunn, May 24, 1774, in Force, *American Archives*, 1:285-286. Variations of Newcomer's Indian name are Netawatwees and Netawatenees.

19. Connolly, "Journal," May 24, 1774, 16-17; Arthur St. Clair to Gov. John Penn, letter dated Pittsburgh, May 29, 1774, in Hazard, *Pennsylvania Archives*, 1, 4:501-502.

20. Jacob, *Biographical Sketch*, 68.

21. Connolly, "Journal," May 24, 1774.

22. Connolly, "Journal," May 25, 1774, 17; McKee, "Journal," May 1, 1774; Arthur St. Clair to Gov. John Penn, letter dated May 29, 1774, in Hazard, *Pennsylvania Archives*, 1, 4:501-502; Sir William Johnson to Lt. Gen. Thomas Gage, letter dated Johnson Hall, July 4, 1774, *Johnson Papers*, 12:1114-1116.

23. Arthur St. Clair to the Six Nations and Delawares, letter (speech) dated May 25, 1774, in Hazard, *Pennsylvania Archives*, 1, 4:500.

24. William Wilson to Benjamin and Michael Gratz, letter dated Pittsburgh, May 31, 1774, *Gratz Papers*, 144; Capt. Dorsey Pentecost—for Capt. John Connolly—to Capt. Joel Reece, letter dated Pittsburgh, May 27, 1774, in Kercheval, *History of the Valley*, 131; Letter (extract), dated Pittsburgh, May 30, *Virginia Gazette #2* (Rind), June 23, 1774, and Letter (extract) dated Bedford, May 30, 1774, *Virginia Gazette #1* (Purdie and Dixon), June 23, 1774.

25. Unknown addressees, letter dated June 5, 1774, in Hazard, *Pennsylvania Archives*, 1, 4:508-509.

26. Connolly, "Journal," May 27, 1774.

27. Ibid., May 26, 1774, 17.

28. Arthur St. Clair to Gov. John Penn, letter dated Ligonier, June 12, 1774, in Hazard, *Pennsylvania Archives*, 1, 4:514-515; Connolly, "Journal," May 26, 1774, 17; Capt. Dorsey Pentecost—for Capt. John Connolly—to Capt. Joel Reece, letter dated Pittsburgh, May 27, 1774, in Kercheval, *History of the Valley*, 131.

29. Letter (extract) dated Bedford, May 30, 1774, *Virginia Gazette #1* (Purdie and Dixon), June 23, 1774.

30. Ibid.; Valentine Crawford to George Washington, letter dated Jacob's Creek, June 8, 1774, in Butterfield, *Washington-Crawford Letters*, 90-91.

31. Arthur Trader pension application S30169, December 5, 1833, Record Group 15, Revolutionary War Pension Applications, M804, Roll 2408, NARA, and Warren Skidmore and Donna Kaminsky, eds., *Lord Dunmore's Little War of 1774: His Captains and Their Men Who Opened Up Kentucky & the West to American Settlement* (Bowie, MD: Heritage Books, 2002), 34-35.

32. Letter (extract) dated Bedford, May 30, 1774, *Virginia Gazette #1* (Purdie and Dixon), June 23, 1774.

33. Arthur St. Clair to Gov. John Penn, letter dated Pittsburgh, May 29, 1774, in Hazard, *Pennsylvania Archives*, 1, 4:501-502.

34. Connolly's Journal, May 26, 1774, 17; Arthur St. Clair to Gov. John Penn, letter dated Pittsburgh, May 29, 1774, in Hazard, *Pennsylvania Archives*, 1, 4:503-504.

35. Alexander McKee to Sir William Johnson, letter [extract] dated Fort Pitt, June 10, 1774, in Force, *American Archives*, 1:466.

36. As the dates and many details found in newspaper articles and other sources agree, despite the different spellings of the surname, William Spicer and Spier (as well as Benjamin Spear in Valentine Crawford's June 8, 1774, letter to Washington) appear to be the same individual. Sources differ on whether the Spicers had five or seven children.

37. Rev. David Jones, *A Journal of Two Visits Made to Some Nations of Indians on the West Side of the River Ohio, in the Years 1772 and 1773* (Burlington, VT: Isaac Collins printer, 1774), 767; Smith, *Account*, 22-23, 29-31; Mary Jemison, *A Narrative of the Life of Mrs. Mary Jemison*, ed. James E. Seaver, Canandaigua, NY: J. D. Bemis, 1824; repr., ed. June Namias, Norman: University of Oklahoma Press, 1992), 67-71, 75-78.

38. Letters (extract) dated Fort Pitt, June 7, June 16, and 23, 1774, *Virginia Gazette* #1 (Purdie and Dixon), and *Pennsylvania Gazette*, June 12, 1774, Eighteenth Century American Newspapers, vol. 1294, Library of Congress, Washington, DC; William Crawford to George Washington, letter dated Spring Garden, June 8, 1774, and Augustine Crawford to George Washington, two letters dated Jacob's Creek, June 8, 1774, in Butterfield, *Washington-Crawford Letters*, 50-52, and 90-94, respectively; Devereux Smith to Dr. Smith, letter dated Pittsburgh, June 1774, and Aeneas Mackay to Gov. John Penn, letter dated Pittsburgh, June 14, 1774, in Hazard, *Pennsylvania Archives*, 1, 4:511-513 and 517, respectively; Jacob, *Biographical Sketch*, 27; Samuel Bates, *History of Greene County, Pennsylvania* (Chicago: Nelson Rishforth, 1888), 511-513; L. K. Evans, *Pioneer History of Greene County, Pennsylvania* (Waynesburg, PA: Waynesburg Republican, 1941; repr. Greene County Historical Society, 1969), 29-31; C. Hale Sipe, *The Indian Wars of Pennsylvania* (Butler, PA: 1931; repr., Lewisburg, PA: Wennawoods, 1999), 495.
39. Bates, *History of Greene County*, 511-513; Evans, *Pioneer History*, 29-31; Eleanor Musick, *A History of Bobtown* (Carmichaels, PA: Flemmiken Memorial Library, 1998).
40. Bates, *History of Greene County*, 239; Musick, *History of Bobtown*; James Axtell and William C. Sturtevant, "The Unkindest Cut, or Who Invented Scalping," *William and Mary Quarterly*, ser. 3, vol. 37, no. 3 (July 1980): 456, 458, 461.
41. Capt. William Crawford to George Washington, letter dated Spring Garden, June 8, 1774, and Augustine Crawford to George Washington, letter dated Jacob's Creek, June 8, 1774, in Butterfield, *Washington-Crawford Letters*, 50-52 and 92-94, respectively; Letters (extracts) dated Fort Pitt, June 16 and 23, 1774, *Virginia Gazette* #1 (Purdie and Dixon), June 9 and 16, and July 20, 1774, *Virginia Gazette* #2 (Rind), and *Pennsylvania Gazette*, June 12, 1774; Evans, *Pioneer History*, 29-31; Sipe, *Indian Wars of Pennsylvania*, 495.
42. Letters (extracts) dated Fort Pitt, June 16 and 23, 1774, *Virginia Gazette* #1 (Purdie and Dixon), June 9 and 16, and July 20, 1774, *Virginia Gazette* #2 (Rind), and *Pennsylvania Gazette*, June 12, 1774.
43. Capt. William Crawford to George Washington, letter dated Spring Garden, June 8, 1774, and Augustine Crawford to George Washington, letter dated Jacob's Creek, June 8, 1774, in Butterfield, *Washington-Crawford Letters*, 50-52 and 92-94.
44. *Virginia Gazette* #1 (Purdie and Dixon), June 27, 1774; Capt. William Crawford to George Washington, letter dated Spring Garden, June 8, 1774, and Augustine Crawford to George Washington, letter dated Jacob's Creek, June 8, 1774, in Butterfield, *Washington-Crawford Letters*, 50-52 and 92-94.
45. Aeneas Mackay to Gov. John Penn, letter dated Pittsburgh, June 14, 1774, in Hazard, *Pennsylvania Archives*, 1, 4:517; Boyd Crumrine, Franklin Ellis, and Austin N. Hungerford, *History of Washington County, Pennsylvania: With Biographical Sketches of Many of Its Pioneers and Prominent Men* (Philadelphia: L. H. Everts, 1882), 70-71.
46. Aeneas Mackay to Gov. John Penn, letter dated Pittsburgh, June 14, 1774, in Hazard, *Pennsylvania Archives*, 1, 4:517; Crumrine et al., *History of Washington County*, 70-71. The engagement took place near present-day Waynesburg, Pennsylvania. While some sources have recorded the lieutenant's name as Kinkaid, it is recorded as Kinkade in the militia muster rolls.
47. *Virginia Gazette* #1 (Purdie and Dixon), June 16, 1774; Arthur St. Clair to Gov. John Penn, letter dated Ligonier, June 8, 1774, in Hazard, *Pennsylvania Archives*, 1, 4:510.

48. *Virginia Gazette* #1 (Purdie and Dixon), June 2, 1774.

49. Rev. John Brown to Col. William Preston, letter dated Mr. Howard's, May 28, 1774, Preston Papers, Draper Manuscripts, 3QQ29 (26-27).

50. Capt. Daniel Smith to Col. William Preston, letter dated Indian Creek, May 30, 1774, Preston Papers, Draper Manuscripts, 3QQ149 (30-31); An Act for Reducing the Several Acts of Assembly, for Making Provision against Invasions and Insurrections, into One Act, Hening, *Statutes*, 7:106-107.

51. Capt. Daniel Smith to Col. William Preston, letter dated Indian Creek, May 30, 1774, Preston Papers, Draper Manuscripts, 3QQ149 (30-31); Act for the Better Regulating and Disciplining of the Militia, Hening, *Statutes*, 7:94.

52. Johnson, *Dictionary of the English Language,* 2:412.

53. Ibid., 2:465, 749.

54. Lord Edward Hyde Clarendon, first earl, *The History of the Rebellion and Civil Wars in England,* 2 vols. (London: 1696; repr., Oxford: University Press, 1843), 1:132.

55. Dunmore's Commission, 659-60; Evarts Boutell Greene, *The Provincial Governor in the English Colonies of North America* (Cambridge, MA: Harvard University Press, 1898), 99.

56. Dunmore's Commission; Greene, *Provincial Governor*, 99.

57. Hening, *Statutes*, 5:16-24, 6:530-564, 7:93-106, and 8:241-245, 503.

58. Ibid., 5:99-100; 6:112-118, 350; 7:106-116, 536-537; 8:9-12.

59. *The Militia-Man: Containing Necessary Rules for Both Officer and Soldier, with an Explanation of the Manual Exercise of the Foot* (London: circa 1740; facsimile repr., Schenectady, NY: US Historical Research Service, 1995), 4.

60. McIlwaine, *JHB*, 1752-1755 and 1756-1758, xv, 99-100.

61. Hening, *Statutes*, 7:93; 8:241, 503; McIlwaine, *JHB*, 1752-1755 and 1756-1758, xv, 99-100.

62. Hening, *Statutes*, 8:503.

63. Kennedy, *JHB*, 1773-1776, ix, xi, xiv, and xv.

64. Hening, *Statutes*, 7:93-94; Col. William Preston (extract) letter dated Fincastle, September 28, 1774, *Virginia Gazette* #1 (Purdie and Dixon), October 13, 1774, and Smyth, *Tour in the United States*, 2:115.

65. Hening, *Statutes*, 7:93-94.

66. Ibid., 4:55-56.

67. Hening, *Statutes*, 6:118.

68. Ibid., 7:95, 5:81-82, and 8:244.

69. Webb, *office and authority of a justice of peace*, 222-223, and Henning, *Statutes*, 8:243-244.

70. Hening, *Statutes*, 8:244.

71. Ibid., 7:102.

72. Ibid., 7:112.

73. Ibid., 6:530; 7:100.

74. Joseph Tennant, quoted in Peter Haught Pension Application S6981, dated August 7, 1832, Record Group 15, Revolutionary War Pension Applications, M804, Roll 1224, NARA.

75. Dunmore's Commission; Greene, *Provincial Governor*, 99.

76. Lord Norborne Berkeley Botetourt to Thomas Jefferson, Certificate of Commission, dated Williamsburg, June 10, 1770, as Commander of the Albemarle County, Virginia, Militia, Thomas Jefferson Papers, Series 1, General Correspondence, 1751-1827, Library of Congress, Washington, DC (hereafter cited as Jefferson's Commission); John Earl of Dunmore to George Rogers Clark, Certificate of Commission, dated Williamsburg, May 2, 1774, as Captain in the Augusta County, Virginia, Militia, Draper Manuscripts (microfilm edition), Historical Society of Wisconsin, 48J1 (hereafter cited as Clark's Commission), and Hening, *Statutes,* 7:106-107.

77. Jefferson's Commission; Clark's Commission; Hening, *Statutes,* 7:106-107.

78. Hening, *Statutes,* 6:541; 7:93-94.

79. Jefferson's Commission; Webb, *office and authority,* 221.

80. Hening, Statutes, 6:540; 7:102-103.

81. Ibid., 6:536.

82. McIlwaine, *JHB,* 1752-1755 and 1756-1758, xxiii-xxiv; 297-298, 321; Hening, *Statutes,* 6:527, 529-541, 530, 544-545, 559-565; 7:106-107.

83. Clark's Commission, and Hening, *Statutes,* 6:113-114; 7:95-96, 106-107; 8:244, 514; 9:23-24. Reference to the 1764 manual is found in a resolution of the March 1775 extralegal Virginia Convention that called for raising volunteer independent companies as agreed to in the Continental Association. One can safely assume the 1764 manual was most familiar to and used by the colonial militia following the French and Indian War.

84. Hening, *Statutes,* 6:113-114; 7:95-96; 8:244, 514; 9:23-24; Matthew Spring, *With Zeal and with Bayonets Only: The British Army on Campaign in North America, 1775-1783* (Norman: University of Oklahoma Press, 2008), 118; *The Manual Exercise as Ordered by His Majesty in One thousand seven-hundred sixty-four, Together with Plans and Explanations of the Method Generally Practiced at Reviews and Field Days, &c.* (Newburyport: E. Lunt and H. W. Tinges, 1774), Special Collections, the Society of the Cincinnati Library, Washington, DC, 19-21 (hereafter cited as *Manual Exercise* of 1764B).

85. J. A. Houlding, *Fit for Service: Training in the British Army, 1715-1795* (Oxford: Oxford University Press, 1981), 55-56.

86. Hening, *Statutes,* 6:113-114; 7:95-96; 8:244, 514; 9:23-24; Spring, *Zeal and Bayonetts,* 118; *Manual Exercise* of 1764B, 19-21.

87. McIlwaine, *JHB,* 1727-1734 and 1736-1740, xxxi-xxxiii, 437; Hening, *Statutes,* 5:23, 121-123.

88. McIlwaine, *JHB,* 1752-1755 and 1756-1758, xv, 99-100, 104-105; *Council Executive Journals,* 6:316, 317.

89. McIlwaine, *JHB,* 1752-1755 and 1756-1758, xv, 99-100, 104-105.

90. Ibid., xv, 99-100, 104-105.

91. James Wolfe, *General Wolfe's Instructions to Young Officers,* 2nd ed. (London: J. Millan, 1780; facsimile repr., Cranbury, NJ: Scholar's Bookshelf, 2005), v.

92. Journal of May 10, 1769, *Council Executive Journals,* 6:316; *Virginia Gazette #2* (Rind), supplement, March 22, 1770. The supplement was an extra edition of that day's paper.

93. *Virginia Gazette #2* (Rind), supp., March 22, 1770; *Virginia Gazette #1* (Purdie & Dixon), February 21, 1771.

94. Council and House of Burgesses to Governor Dunmore, broadside dated Williamsburg, May 5, 1774, Printed Ephemera Collection, portfolio 178, folders 12a and 12e, respectively, Broadsides, Leaflets, and Pamphlets from America and Europe, US Library of Congress; May 6, 1774, entry, Kennedy, *JHB*, 1773-1776, 73-74.

CHAPTER 5: THE PRESENT EXIGENCE

1. May 11 and 12, 1774, entries, *JHB* 1773-1774, 90-91, 92.
2. May 9-11, 1774, entries, *JHB* 1773-1774, 93, 97, 99-100.
3. *Virginia Gazette* #2 (Rind), May 26, 1774.
4. Ibid.
5. Hening, *Statutes*, 8: 9; Greene, *Provincial Governor*, 101; Lucille Griffith, *The Virginia House of Burgesses 1750-1774* (Tuscaloosa: University of Alabama Press, 1968), 6.
6. May 10-14, 1774, *JHB* 1773-1774, 93, 97, 99-100.
7. Ibid.
8. May 19 and 24, 1774, entries, *JHB* 1773-1774 (1905), 110 and 124.
9. May 24, 1774, entry, *JHB* 1773-1774, 124.
10. *Virginia Gazette* #1 (Purdie and Dixon), and *Virginia Gazette* #2 (Rind), May 26, 1774.
11. The Report of James Tilghman and Andrew Allen, Commissioners Appointed by the Hon. John Penn, Governor of Pennsylvania, to Treat with the Right Honourable the Earl of Dunmore, Governor of Virginia, to the Council held at Philadelphia, June 27, 1774, in Force, *American Archives*, 1:454, 462.
12. Ibid.
13. May 28, 1774, entry, *Council Executive Journals*, 6:563.
14. May 31, 1774, entry, *JHB* 1773-1774, 132.
15. *Virginia Gazette* #1 (Purdie and Dixon), and *Virginia Gazette* #2 (Rind), May 26, 1774.
16. Earl of Dunmore to Lt. Gen. Thomas Gage, letter dated Williamsburg, June 11, 1774, Gage Papers.
17. *Virginia Gazette* #1 (Purdie and Dixon), and *Virginia Gazette* #2 (Rind), May 26, 1774. Emphasis in the original.
18. John Campbell to Andrew Levy, and forwarded to Michael Gratz, letter dated Pittsburgh, May 30, 1774, Gratz Papers, 142-143. In Britain and colonial America, one hundredweight equaled 112 pounds.
19. Arthur St. Clair to Gov. John Penn, letter dated May 29, 1774, in Hazard, *Pennsylvania Archives* 1, 4:501-503; Hening, *Statutes*, 7:108, 111-112.
20. Capt. William Crawford to George Washington, letter dated Spring Garden, May 8, 1774, in Butterfield, *Washington-Crawford Letters*, 48.
21. Arthur St. Clair to Gov. John Penn, letter dated May 29, 1774, in Hazard, *Pennsylvania Archives* 1, 4:501-503.
22. Maj. Gen. Frederick Haldimand to Earl of Dartmouth, letter dated New York, June 1, 1774, Davies, *Documents*, 8:124-125.
23. Sir William Johnson to Earl of Dartmouth, letter dated Johnson Hall, June 20, 1774, Davies, *Documents*, 8:133-136.
24. Sir William Johnson to Maj. Gen. Frederick Haldimand, letter dated Johnson Hall, June 9, 1774, *Johnson Papers*, 8:1164.

25. Arthur St. Clair to Gov. John Penn, letters dated Ligonier, May 29, 1774, in Hazard, *Pennsylvania Archives* 1, 4:501-503 and 504-505.

26. John Montgomery to Gov. John Penn, letters dated Carlisle, June 3, 1774, in Hazard, *Pennsylvania Archives* 1, 4:505-506 and 506-507.

27. George Croghan to Arthur St. Clair, letter dated June 4, 1774, in Hazard, *Pennsylvania Archives* 1, 4:507-508.

28. Arthur St. Clair to Gov. John Penn, letter dated Laurel Hill, June 7, 1774, in Hazard, *Pennsylvania Archives* 1, 4:509-510.

29. Connolly, "Journal," May 26, 1774, 17.

30. Letter (extract) dated Fort Pitt, June 12, 1774, *Pennsylvania Gazette*, June 22, 1774, Eighteenth Century American Newspapers, vol. 1294, Library of Congress, Washington, DC; John Montgomery to Gov. John Penn, letter dated Carlisle, June 3, 1774, in Hazard, *Pennsylvania Archives* 1, 4:506-507.

31. Rev. John Heckewelder, declaration, printed in appendix, Jefferson, *Notes on the State of Virginia*, ed. Shuffelton, 254.

32. Ibid.

33. John Leith, *A Short Biography of John Leith: With a Brief Account of His Life among the Indians; A Reprint with Illustrative Notes*, ed. Consul W. Butterfield (Cincinnati: Robert Clarke, 1883), repr. from Ewel Jeffries, *A Short Biography of John Leeth, Giving a Brief Account of His Travels and Sufferings among the Indians for Eighteen Years, from His Own Relation* (Lancaster, OH: Gazette, 1831), Special Collections, Society of the Cincinnati Library, Washington, DC, 10-13. Some sources record John Leith's surname as "Leeth." The Indian town at Standing Stone, also called Free Stone on some period maps, was near present-day Lancaster, Ohio.

34. Ibid., 13-14.

35. Earl of Dunmore to County Lieutenants, circular letter dated Williamsburg, June 10, 1774, William Preston Papers, Draper Manuscripts, 3QQ39 (33-35).

36. Earl of Dunmore to Lt. Gen. Thomas Gage, letter dated Williamsburg, June 11, 1774, Thomas Gage Papers.

37. Dunmore's Commission, 630; Earl of Dunmore to the County Lieutenants, circular letter dated Williamsburg, June 10, 1774, William Preston Papers, Draper Manuscripts, 3QQ39 (33-35); Greene, *Provincial Governor*, 99.

38. Earl of Dunmore to the County Lieutenants, circular letter dated Williamsburg, June 10, 1774, Preston Papers, Draper Manuscripts, 3QQ39 (33-35); Earl of Dunmore to George Rogers Clark, Certificate of Commission as Captain in the Augusta County, Virginia, Militia, dated Williamsburg, 2 May 1774, Clark Papers, Draper Manuscripts, 48J1; Hening, *Statutes*, 9:23-24. The Ordinance for Raising and Embodying a Sufficient Force for the Defense and Protection of the Colony, passed by the Virginia Convention in July 1775, mandated the use of the manual, indicating a continuation of that already in use by the Virginia colonial militia before the Revolutionary War.

39. Ibid.

40. Earl of Dunmore to Lt. Gen. Thomas Gage, letter dated Williamsburg, June 11, 1774, Thomas Gage Papers.

41. Hening, *Statutes*, 7:31.

42. Ibid., 7:20.

43. Ibid., 7:31.

44. Ibid., 7:14.

45. Ibid., 7:14-16.

46. Ibid., 7:17.

47. Ibid., 7:114 and 3:17.

48. Lt. Gov. Robert Dinwiddie to Col. George Washington, letter dated Williamsburg, December 14, 1755, in R. A. Brock, ed., *The Official Records of Robert Dinwiddie, Lieutenant Governor of the Colony of Virginia, 1751-1758* (Richmond: Virginia Historical Society, 1884), 291; Col. George Washington to Capt. Andrew Lewis, letter dated Winchester, September 6, 1755, in Abbot and Twohig, *Washington Papers*, vol. 2, August 1755–April 1756 (Charlottesville: University Press of Virginia, 1983), 23-24.

49. Col. George Washington to the Officers of the Virginia Regiment, Orders dated Winchester, January 8, 1756, in Abbot and Twohig, *Washington Papers*, 2:257; Appleton P. C. Griffin, comp., *A Catalogue of the Washington Collection in the Boston Athenaeum* (Boston: Boston Athenaeum, 1997), 537.

50. Humphrey Bland, *A Treatise of Military Discipline, in which is laid down and explained the duty of the officer and soldier*, 9th ed. (London, 1762), contents, 6, 8, 143.

51. Stephen Brumwell, *Redcoats: The British Soldier and War in the Americas, 1755-1763* (New York: Cambridge University Press, 2002), 193, 217.

52. Guy Chet, *Conquering the American Wilderness: The Triumph of European Warfare in the Colonial Northeast* (Boston: University of Massachusetts Press, 2003), 144.

53. Thomas Barton, "Journal of an Expedition to the Ohio, commanded by His Excellency Brigadier General Forbes; in the Year of our Lord 1758," in William A. Hunter, ed., "Thomas Barton and the Forbes Expedition," *Pennsylvania Magazine of History and Biography* 95, no. 4 (October 1971): 449-450.

54. Hening, *Statutes*, 4:9-10, McIlwaine, *Council Executive Journals*, 3:1558-1559.

55. Hening, *Statutes*, 4:9-10.

56. Elias Hughes offered this explanation of the spy service, as quoted in an appendix based on an 1835 report by the War Department on alleged fraudulent pension awards and attached to the David W. Sleeth pension application S6111, August 7, 1832, Record Group 15, Revolutionary War Pension Applications, M804, Roll 2199, NARA.

57. Hening, *Statutes*, 4:11, 6:465.

58. Ibid., 6: 465-466.

59. Ibid., 6: 465-466; *JHB* 1752-1755 and 1756-1758, xxii, 292-294.

60. Hening, *Statutes*, 7:76, 173.

61. Ibid., 7:76, 173.

62. Withers, *Chronicles of Border Warfare*, 102.

63. Johnson, *Dictionary* (1773), 2:321.

64. William Smith pension application W6094, December 17, 1832, Record Group 15, Revolutionary War Pension Applications, M804, Roll 2237, NARA.

CHAPTER 6: THE WARLIKE NATION OF THE CHEROKEE

1. Heckewelder, *History, Manners*, 217.

2. Jemison, *Narrative*, 75.

3. Ibid.

4. Heckewelder, *History, Manners*, 192, 217.

5. Jemison, *Narrative*, 9.

6. Ibid., 63, 67. The Jemison farm was located near present-day Cashtown, near Gettysburg, in Adams County, Pennsylvania.

7. Ibid., 66-69.

8. Bates, *History of Greene County*, 239.

9. Jemison, *Narrative*, 68; Axtell and Sturtevant, "Unkindest Cut," 456, 458, 461. Mary Jemison's two older brothers escaped and avoided being captured with the rest of the family. The warrior who killed William Spicer Sr. lost the scalp before he could dress it.

10. Jemison, *Narrative*, 78.

11. Ibid.; Bates, *History of Greene County*, 239.

12. Heckewelder, *History, Manners*, 218.

13. Smith, *Account*, 22-24.

14. Heckewelder, *History, Manners*, 217-218.

15. Jemison, *Narrative*, 78.

16. Reverend David Jones, *A Journal of Two Visits Made to Some Nations of Indians on the West Side of the Ohio River, in the Years 1772 and 1773* (Burlington, VT: Isaac Collins printer, 1774; repr., New York: Arno Press, 1971), 76-77.

17. Smith, *Account*, 26.

18. Jemison, *Narrative*, 75.

19. Earl of Dunmore to Capt. John Connolly, letter dated Williamsburg, June 20, 1774, in Force, *American Archives*, 1:473; Earl of Dunmore to Col. William Preston, letter dated Williamsburg, July 3, 1774, 3QQ53, Preston Papers, Draper Manuscripts (61-63).

20. Arthur St. Clair to Gov. John Penn, letter dated Ligonier, June 16, 1774, in Hazard, *Pennsylvania Archives* 1, 4:519-520.

21. Aeneas Mackay to Gov. John Penn, letter dated Pittsburgh, June 14, 1774, and Arthur St. Clair to Gov. John Penn, letter dated Ligonier, June 16, 1774, in Hazard, *Pennsylvania Archives* 1, 4:517, 519-520; *Virginia Gazette #1* (Purdie and Dixon), June 27, 1774; Crumrine et al., *History of Washington County*, 70-71.

22. Earl of Dunmore to Capt. John Connolly, letter dated Williamsburg, June 20, 1774, in Force, *American Archives*, 1:473; Arthur St. Clair to Gov. John Penn, letter dated Ligonier, June 16, 1774, in Hazard, *Pennsylvania Archives* 1, 4:519-520.

23. Maj. Angus McDonald to Capt. Daniel Morgan, letter dated June 11, 1774. Theodorus Bailey Myers collection, Manuscripts and Archives Division, New York Public Library.

24. Earl of Dunmore to Capt. John Connolly, letter dated Williamsburg, June 20, 1774, in Force, *American Archives*, 1:473.

25. Capt. William Russell to Col. William Preston, letter dated Clinch, June 26, 1774, Preston Papers, Draper Manuscripts, 3QQ46 (49-51).

26. Alden, *John Stewart*, 263-265, 290-291. Sycamore Shoals is near present-day Elizabethton, Tennessee.

27. Maj. Arthur Campbell to Col. William Preston, letter undated Royal Oak (estimated June 20, 1774) and June 22, 1774, Preston Papers, Draper Manuscripts, 3QQ40 (38-39) and 3QQ41 (40-42). The Watauga and Nolichucky valleys now encompass present-day Washington and Carter Counties, Tennessee, with the murder believed committed near present-day Jonesborough.

28. Maj. Arthur Campbell to Col. William Preston, letter dated Royal Oak, June 22, 1774, Preston Papers, Draper Manuscripts, 3QQ41 (40-42).

29. Ibid.; Col. William Christian to Col. William Preston, letter dated Dunkard Bottom, (Morning) June 22, and Capt. William Russell to Col. William Preston, letter dated Clinch, June 26, 1774, Preston Papers, Draper Manuscripts, 3QQ41 (40-42), 3QQ42 (42-43), and 3QQ46 (49-51).

30. Maj. Arthur Campbell, letter dated Royal Oak, June 22, 1774, Preston Papers, Draper Manuscripts, 3QQ41 (40-42).

31. Maj. Arthur Campbell, letter dated Royal Oak, June 23, 1774; Maj. Arthur Campbell to Col. William Preston, letter, undated Royal Oak (estimated June 20, 1774), Preston Papers, Draper Manuscripts, 3QQ44 (47-49) and 3QQ40 (38-39); Johnson, *Dictionary*, 2:321.

32. Maj. Arthur Campbell to Col. William Preston, letters dated Royal Oak, June 23 and undated (estimated June 20, 1774), Preston Papers, Draper Manuscripts 3QQ44 (47-49) and 3QQ40 (38-39).

33. Col. William Christian to Col. William Preston, letter dated Dunkard Bottom, (Morning) June 22, 1774, Preston Papers, Draper Manuscripts, 3QQ42 (42-46).

34. Capt. William Russell to Col. William Preston, letter dated Clinch, June 26, 1774, Preston Papers, Draper Manuscripts, 3QQ46 (49-51).

35. Ibid.

36. Ibid. Mansco's Lick is in present-day Davidson County, Tennessee. The "falls" is at present-day Louisville.

37. Col. William Preston to Col. William Christian, letter dated Dunkard Bottom (Morning), June 22, 1774, Preston Papers, Draper Manuscripts, 3QQ42 (42-46).

38. Col. William Preston to Col. William Christian, Fort Chiswell, June 27, 1774, Preston Papers, Draper Manuscripts, 3QQ47 (52-56).

39. Ibid.

40. Ibid. The Middle Fork on Holston is near the present-day Smyth-Wythe County line in southwest Virginia. The Town House on the Holston site is near present-day Chilhowie, Smyth County, Virginia.

41. Ibid.

42. Bland, *Treatise*, 132.

43. Col. William Preston to Col. William Christian, letter dated Fort Chiswell, June 27, 1774, Preston Papers, Draper Manuscripts, 3QQ47 (52-55).

44. Ibid.

45. Col. William Christian to Col. William Preston, letter dated Sawyers, June 27 (evening), 1774, Preston Papers, Draper Manuscripts, 3QQ48 (55-56).

46. HeckeweLder, *History, Manners*, 89-90.

47. Ibid., 177-78.

48. Jones, *Journal of Two Visits*, 72.

49. HeckeweLder, *History, Manners*, 177.

50. Jones, *Journal of Two Visits*, 76-77; Smith, *Account*, 34.

51. HeckeweLder, *History, Manners*, 177-78.

52. Ibid.

53. Jemison, *Narrative*, 70-1.

54. HeckeweLder, *History, Manners*, 177.

55. Col. William Christian to Capt. Joseph Cloyd, letter dated Sawyers, June 29, 1774, and Col. Charles Lewis to Col. William Preston, letter dated July 9, 1774, Preston Papers,

Draper Manuscripts, 3QQ49 (56-57) and 3QQ59 (73-74); *Virginia Gazette* #1 (Purdie and Dixon), July 14, 1774. The location is in present-day Greenbrier County, West Virginia.

56. Col. William Christian to Col. William Preston, letter dated Andrew Colvill's, July 9, 1774, Preston Papers, Draper Manuscripts, 3QQ60 (75-78). In some sources, William Faulin appears as William Falling or Fallen.

57. Maj. Arthur Campbell to Col. William Preston, letter dated Holston, July 9, 1774, Preston Papers, Draper Manuscripts, 3QQ58 (72-73). The site of Chota is in present-day Monroe County, Tennessee.

58. Col. William Christian to Capt. Joseph Cloyd, letter dated Sawyers, June 29, 1774, Preston Papers, Draper Manuscripts, 3QQ49 (56-57); *Virginia Gazette* #1 (Purdie and Dixon), July 14, 1774. Walker's Creek and Blue Stone are located in present-day Giles County, Virginia, and Mercer County, West Virginia, respectively.

59. Col. William Christian to Capt. Joseph Cloyd, letter dated Sawyers, June 29, 1774, Preston Papers, Draper Manuscripts, 3QQ49 (56-57).

60. Maj. Arthur Campbell to Col. William Preston, letter dated July 1, 1774, Preston Papers, Draper Manuscripts, 3QQ50 (57-58).

61. Col. William Preston to Col. William Christian, letter (estimated) July 3, 1774, Preston Papers, Draper Manuscripts, 3QQ51 (59-61).

62. Col. William Christian to Col. William Preston, letter dated New Dublin, July 4 (Thursday), 1774, Preston Papers, Draper Manuscripts, 3QQ54 (63-66).

63. Capt. Daniel Smith to Col. William Preston, letter dated Indian Creek, July 8, 1774, Preston Papers, Draper Manuscripts, 3QQ57 (69-71).

64. Earl of Dunmore to Col. William Preston, letter dated Williamsburg, July 3, 1774, Preston Papers, Draper Manuscripts, 3QQ53 (61-63).

65. Maj. Arthur Campbell to Col. William Preston, letter dated Holston, July 9, 1774, Preston Papers, Draper Manuscripts, 3QQ58 (72-73).

66. Ibid.; Col. William Christian to Col. William Preston, letter dated Andrew Colvill's, July 9, 1774, Preston Papers, Draper Manuscripts, 3QQ58 (72-73) and 3QQ60 (75-78).

67. Oconastota to Col. Andrew Lewis and Col. William Preston, letter dated Town House in Chota, July 16, 1774, Preston Papers, Draper Manuscripts, 3QQ142.

68. Col. William Preston to Oconastota, letter (estimated July 19, 1774), and Maj. Arthur Campbell to Col. William Preston, letter dated Holston, July 9, 1774, Preston Papers, Draper Manuscripts, 3QQ142 and 3QQ58 (72-73).

CHAPTER 7: THE DRUMS BEAT UP AGAIN

1. *Virginia Gazette* #1 (Purdie and Dixon), July 14, 1774.

2. Capt. John Connolly to Arthur St. Clair, letter dated Fort Dunmore, July 19, 1774, in Hazard, *Pennsylvania Archives*, 1, 6:548.

3. Benjamin Cleaver pension application R2039, dated September 24, 1831, Record Group 15, Revolutionary War Pension Applications, M804, Roll 575, NARA.

4. Col. Charles Lewis to Col. William Preston, letter dated July 9, 1774, Preston Papers, Draper Manuscripts, 3QQ59 (73-74); *Virginia Gazette* #1 (Purdie and Dixon), July 14, 1774. Warm Springs is in present-day Bath County, Virginia.

5. Col. William Preston, letter dated Fincastle, August 13, 1774, in Force, *American Archives*, 1:707-708; John Stuart, "Narrative by Captain John Stuart of Andrew Lewis'

Expedition Against the Indians in the year 1774, and of the Battle of Pleasant Point Virginia," ed. John Austen Stevens, *Magazine of American History* 1, no. 1 (November–December 1877): 674-675; J. H. Newton, G. G. Nichols, and A. G. Sprankle, eds., *History of the Pan-Handle; Being Historical Collections of Ohio, Brooke, Marshall, and Hancock Counties, West Virginia* (Wheeling, WV: J. A. Q. Caldwell, 1889), 80.

6. Stuart, "Narrative," 674-675; John Jones pension application W7920, dated January 15, 1833, Roll 1441; Thwaites and Kellogg, *Documentary History*, 112n.

7. Col. William Preston, letter dated Fincastle, August 13, 1774, in Force, *American Archives*, 1:707-708; Stuart, "Narrative," 674-675; Thwaites and Kellogg, *Documentary History*, 112n.

8. Col. William Preston, letter dated Fincastle, August 13, 1774, in Force, *American Archives*, 1:707-708; Stuart, "Narrative," 674-675.

9. Ibid.

10. Col. Charles Lewis to Col. William Preston, letter dated July 9, 1774, Preston Papers, Draper Manuscripts, 3QQ59 (73-74); *Virginia Gazette* #1 (Purdie and Dixon), July 14, 1774; *Virginia Gazette* #2 (Rind), July 14, 1774.

11. Arthur St. Clair to Gov. John Penn, letter dated Ligonier, June 22, 1774, and Aeneas Mackay, Joseph Spear, and Deveraux Smith to Gov. John Penn, letter dated Pittsburgh, July 8, 1774, in Hazard, *Pennsylvania Archives*, 1, 6:523-525 and 540-542.

12. Arthur St. Clair to Gov. John Penn, letter dated Ligonier, June 22, 1774, and Aeneas Mackay, Joseph Spear, and Deveraux Smith to Gov. John Penn, letter dated Pittsburgh, July 8, 1774, in Hazard, *Pennsylvania Archives*, 1, 6:523-525 and 540-542.

13. Arthur St. Clair to Gov. John Penn, letter dated Ligonier, June 22, 1774, in Hazard, *Pennsylvania Archives*, 1, 6:523-525.

14. Subscribers to Gov. John Penn, Memorial dated Pittsburgh, June 25, 1774, in Hazard, *Pennsylvania Archives*, 1, 6:526-527.

15. Remarks on the Proceedings of Doctor Connolly, dated Pittsburgh, June 25, 1774, in Hazard, *Pennsylvania Archives*, 1, 6:528-529.

16. Arthur St. Clair to Gov. John Penn, letters dated Ligonier, July 4, 17, and 22, 1774, and Aeneas Mackay, Joseph Spear, and Devereux Smith to Gov. John Penn, letter dated Pittsburgh, July 8, 1774, in Hazard, *Pennsylvania Archives*, 1, 6:539, 545, 550-551, and 540-542.

17. Aeneas Mackay, Joseph Spear, and Devereux Smith to Gov. John Penn, letter dated Pittsburgh, July 8, 1774, William Wilson to Arthur St. Clair, deposition dated Pittsburgh, July 1, 1774, and Arthur St. Clair to Gov. John Penn, letter dated Ligonier, July 22, 1774, in Hazard, *Pennsylvania Archives*, 1, 6:540-542, 543-544, and 550-551.

18. Arthur St. Clair to Gov. John Penn, letter dared Ligonier, July 22, 1774, in Hazard, *Pennsylvania Archives*, 1, 6:550-551.

19. Arthur St. Clair to Gov. John Penn, letter dated Ligonier, July 4, 1774, in Hazard, *Pennsylvania Archives*, 1, 6:539.

20. Alexander McKee to Sir William Johnson, Report dated Pittsburgh, June 29, 1774, and Aeneas Mackay to Joseph Shippen, letter dated Pittsburgh, July 8, 1774, in Hazard, *Pennsylvania Archives*, 1, 6:531-533 and 540-542.

21. Arthur St. Clair to Gov. John Penn, letters dated Ligonier, July 4 and 22, 1774, and Arthur St. Clair to Gov. John Penn, letter dated Ligonier, July 22, 1774, in Hazard, *Pennsylvania Archives*, 1, 6:539 and 550-551.

22. Evan Morgan pension application S11098, dated March 7, 1833, Roll 1784; David Gamble pension application S32264, dated September 10, 1833, Roll 1044.

23. Arthur St. Clair to Gov. John Penn, letter dated Ligonier, June 26, 1774, in Hazard, *Pennsylvania Archives*, 1, 6:530.

24. Capt. William Harrod to Abraham Van Meter, receipt dated July 4, 1774, Capt. John Connolly to Capt. William Harrod, letter dated Fort Dunmore, July 16, 1774, Capt. Dorsey Pentecost to Capt. William Harrod, letter dated July 20, 1774, and Capt. William Harrod, receipt dated Fort Fincastle, August 2, 1774, Draper Manuscripts, Pittsburgh and Northwest Virginia Papers, 4NN7 (68), 4NN8, (101-102), 4NN9 (102), and 4NN9 (103).

25. Capt. William Harrod to Abraham Van Meter, receipt dated July 4, 1774, Capt. John Connolly to Capt. William Harrod, letter dated Fort Dunmore, July 16, 1774, Capt. Dorsey Pentecost to Capt. William Harrod, letter dated July 20, 1774, and Capt. William Harrod, receipt dated Fort Fincastle, August 2, 1774, Draper Manuscripts, Pittsburgh and Northwest Virginia Papers, 4NN7 (68), 4NN8, (101-102), 4NN9 (102), and 4NN9 (103).

26. John Montgomery to Gov. John Penn, letter dated Carlisle, June 30, 1774, in Hazard, *Pennsylvania Archives*, 1, 6:533-534.

27. William Robinson, declaration dated Philadelphia, February 28, 1800, printed in appendix, Jefferson, *Notes on the State of Virginia*, ed. Shuffelton, 249-251; Henry Haymond, *History of Harrison County, West Virginia* (Parsons, WV: McClain Printing, 1910; repr. Morgantown, WV: Acme Printing, 1973), 58. Prickett's fort was located near present-day Fairmont, West Virginia. The West Fork of the Monongahela is now called the West Fork River.

28. William Robinson, declaration dated Philadelphia, February 28, 1800, printed in appendix, Jefferson, *Notes on the State of Virginia*, ed. Shuffelton, 249-251; Haymond, *History of Harrison County*, 58; Skidmore and Kaminsky, *Lord Dunmore's Little War*, 34-35.

29. John Pollock, David Shelvey, and George Shervor to George Wilson, deposition dated July 15, 1774, and Capt. John Connolly to Arthur St. Clair, letter dated Fort Dunmore, July 19, 1774, in Hazard, *Pennsylvania Archives*, 1, 6:544-545 and 548.

30. Valentine Crawford to George Washington, letter dated Jacob's Creek, July 27, 1774, in Butterfield, *Washington-Crawford Letters*, 94-97, 96n; Earl of Dunmore to Col. Andrew Lewis, letter dated Rosegill, July 12, 1774, George Rogers Clark Papers, Draper Manuscripts 46J7 (8687).

31. Aeneas Mackay, Joseph Spear, and Devereaux Smith to Gov. John Penn, letter dated Pittsburgh, July 8, 1774, and Arthur St. Clair to Gov. John Penn, letter dated Ligonier, July 4, 1774, in Hazard, *Pennsylvania Archives*, 1, 6:540-542 and 539.

32. Capt. John Connolly to Arthur St. Clair, letter dated Fort Dunmore, July 19, 1774, in Hazard, *Pennsylvania Archives*, 1, 6:548.

33. Arthur St. Clair to Capt. John Connolly, letter dated Ligonier, July 22, 1774, in Hazard, *Pennsylvania Archives*, 1, 6:549-550.

34. David Griffey to Andrew McFarlane, Examination dated Hanna's Town, July 24, 1774, in Hazard, *Pennsylvania Archives*, 1, 6:555-556.

35. Arthur St. Clair to Gov. John Penn, letter dated Ligonier, July 26, 1774, in Hazard, *Pennsylvania Archives*, 1, 6:557-558.

36. Resolution of Assembly, July 20, 1774, in Hazard, *Pennsylvania Archives*, 1, 6:518-519.

37. Valentine Crawford to George Washington, letter dated Jacob's Creek, July 27, 1774, in Butterfield, *Washington-Crawford Letters*, 1877, 94-97.

38. Indian Speeches, dated Pittsburgh, July 23, 1774, in Hazard, *Pennsylvania Archives*, 1, 6:553.

39. William Robinson, declaration dated Philadelphia, February 28, 1800, printed in appendix, Jefferson, *Notes on the State of Virginia*, ed. Shuffelton, 249-251; Haymond, *History of Harrison County*, 58.

40. William Robinson, declaration dated Philadelphia, February 28, 1800, printed in appendix, Jefferson, *Notes on the State of Virginia*, ed. Shuffelton, 249-251; Maj. Arthur Campbell to Col. William Christian, enclosure to letter dated Royal Oak, October 12, 1774, Preston Papers, Draper Manuscripts, 3QQ118 (246-247).

41. Heckewelder, *History, Manners*, 176.

42. Sir William Johnson to Lt. Gen. Thomas Gage, letter dated Johnson Hall, July 4, 1774, and Col. Guy Johnson to Lt. Gen. Thomas Gage, letter dated Johnson Hall, July 12, 1774, *Johnson Papers*, 12:1113-1116 and 1121-1124.

43. Sir William Johnson to Lt. Gen. Thomas Gage, letter dated Johnson Hall, July 4, 1774, *Johnson Papers*, 12:1113-1116.

44. Col. Guy Johnson to Lt. Gen. Thomas Gage, letter dated Johnson Hall, July 12, 1774, *Johnson Papers*, 12:1121-1124; Lt. Gen. Thomas Gage to Guy Johnson, letter dated Boston, July 17, 1774, and Col. Guy Johnson to Lt. Gen. Thomas Gage, letter dated Johnson Hall, July 26, 1774, *Johnson Papers*, 13:637 and 640-643.

45. Col. Guy Johnson to Lt. Gen. Thomas Gage, letter dated Johnson Hall, July 26, 1774, *Johnson Papers*, 13:640-643.

46. Ibid.

47. Journal for July 14 and 15, Proceedings of a Congress with All the Chiefs and Warriors of the Six Nations at Johnson Hall in June and July 1774, in O'Callahan, *New York Colonial Documents*, 8:480-483.

48. Capt. William Russell to Col. William Preston, letter dated Fort Preston, July 13, 1774, and Col. William Christian to Col. William Preston, letter dated Andrew Colvill's, July 9, 1774, Preston Papers, Draper Manuscripts, 3QQ64 (88-91) and 3QQ60 (75-78).

49. Col. William Christian to Col. William Preston, letter dated Andrew Colvill's, July 9, 1774, Preston Papers, Draper Manuscripts, 3QQ60 (75-78).

50. Col. William Christian to Col. William Preston, letter dated Andrew Colvill's, July 9, 1774, and Capt. Robert Doack to Col. William Preston, letter dated July 12, 1774, Preston Papers, Draper Manuscripts, 3QQ60 (75-78) and 3QQ61 (78-80).

51. Capt. Robert Doack to Col. William Preston, letter dated July 12, 1774, Preston Papers, Draper Manuscripts, 3QQ61 (78-80); Hening, *Statutes*, 7: 114 and 3: 17. Rich Valley lies between Walker's Mountain and the North Fork of the Holston River in present-day Washington County, Virginia.

52. Capt. Robert Doack to Col. William Preston, letter dated July 12, 1774, Preston Papers, Draper Manuscripts, 3QQ61 (78-80).

53. Col. William Christian to Col. William Preston, letter dated Russell's Fort, July 12, 1774, and Capt. William Russell to Col. William Preston, letter dated Fort Preston, July 13, 1774, Preston Papers, Draper Manuscripts, 3QQ63 (80-85), and 3QQ64 (88-91).

54. Ibid.; Thwaites and Kellogg, *Documentary History,* 85n. Fort Blackmore is in present-day Scott County, Virginia.

55. Capt. William Russell to Col. William Preston, letter dated Fort Preston, July 13, 1774, Preston Papers, Draper Manuscripts, 3QQ64 (88-91).

56. Capt. William Russell to Col. William Preston, letter dated Fort Preston, July 13, 1774, Preston Papers, Draper Manuscripts, 3QQ64 (88-91).

57. Col. William Christian to Col. William Preston, letter dated Russell's Fort, July 12, 1774, Preston Papers, Draper Manuscripts, 3QQ63 (80-85).

58. Ibid.

59. Ibid.; Thwaites and Kellogg, *Documentary History*, 85n.

60. Earl of Dunmore to Col. Andrew Lewis, letter dated Rosegill, July 12, 1774, George Rogers Clark Papers, Draper Manuscripts 46J7 (86-87).

61. Col. Andrew Lewis to Col. William Preston, letter [fragment, presumably] dated Richfield, July 12, 1774, Preston Papers, Draper Manuscripts, 3QQ62 (87-88).

62. Col. William Preston circular letter dated Smithfield, July 20, 1774, Preston Papers, Draper Manuscripts, 3QQ139 (91-93).

63. George Farquhar, *The Recruiting Officer*, ed. S. Trussler (London: 1706; repr., London: Nick Hern Books, 1997); *Virginia Gazette* (published by William Parks), September 10, 1736; Arthur Hornblow, *A History of the Theater in America from Its Beginnings to the Present Time*, vol. 1 (Philadelphia: J. B. Lippincott, 1919), 42.

64. Thomas D'Urfey, *Wit and Mirth, or Pills to Purge the Melancholy*, vol. 5 (London: J. Tonson, 1719-1720), 319-321.

65. Indian Speeches, dated Pittsburgh, July 23, 1774, in Hazard, *Pennsylvania Archives*, 1, 4:552-554.

66. Aeneas Mackay to Arthur St. Clair, letter dated Pittsburgh, July 25, 1774, in Hazard, *Pennsylvania Archives*, 1, 4:556.

67. Arthur St. Clair to Gov. John Penn, letter dated Ligonier, July 26, 1774, in Hazard, *Pennsylvania Archives*, 1, 4:557-558.

68. *Virginia Gazette* #2 (Rind), August 4, 1774; McIlwaine, *JHB*, 6:223-224.

CHAPTER 8: ON HIS MAJESTY'S SERVICE

1. *Virginia Gazette* #1 (Purdie and Dixon), October 13, 1774. The author's inclusion of John Stephenson is based on an educated guess in the absence of specific documentary evidence.

2. Ibid., in Butterfield, *Washington-Crawford Letters*, 96n; Withers, *Chronicles of Border Warfare*, 153-155; Thwaites and Kellogg, *Documentary History*, 156n. The mouth of Fish Creek is in present-day Marshall County, West Virginia. Captina Creek enters the Ohio in present-day Belmont County, Ohio, approximately 120 miles downstream from Pittsburgh.

3. Bland, *Treatise*, 136-137.

4. Lyman Draper, McDonald's Expedition, handwritten Mss., Border Forays 2D5-11, Draper Manuscripts Collection, Wisconsin Historical Society; June 14, 1775 entry, *JHB*, 1773-1774, xx, 218, 225, 249, 265, and 274.

5. *Virginia Gazette* #1 (Purdie and Dixon), October 13, 1774.

6. Draper, McDonald's Expedition; June 14, 1775 entry, *JHB*, 1773-1774, xx, 218, 225, 249, 265, and 274.

7. Bland, *Treatise*, 137.

8. Draper, McDonald's Expedition.

9. Bland, *Treatise*, 144-45; *Virginia Gazette* #1 (Purdie and Dixon), October 13, 1774.

10. Col. William Christian to Col. William Preston, letter dated Camp Union at Great Levels, September 7, 1774, Preston Papers, Draper Manuscripts, 3QQ92 (185-188); Draper, McDonald's Expedition.

11. Evan Morgan pension application S11098, March 7, 1833, Roll 1784; *Virginia Gazette* #1 (Purdie and Dixon), October 13, 1774; Col. William Christian to Col. William Preston, letter dated Camp Union at Great Levels, September 7, 1774, Preston Papers, Draper Manuscripts, 3QQ92 (185-188).

12. Draper, McDonald's Expedition.

13. Bland, *Treatise*, 159.

14. *Virginia Gazette* #1 (Purdie and Dixon), October 13, 1774.

15. Maj. Angus McDonald to Maj. John Connolly [extract] letter dated Fort Fincastle, August 9, 1774, enclosed with Thomas Walpole to Earl of Dartmouth, letter dated Lincoln's Inn Field, October 27, 1774, in W. O. Hewlett, ed., *Manuscripts of the Earl of Dartmouth*, vol. 2 (London: Her Majesty's Stationary Office, 1887), 359 (151-153) (hereafter cited as *Dartmouth Manuscripts*).

16. *Virginia Gazette* #1 (Purdie and Dixon), October 13, 1774.

17. Maj. Angus McDonald to Maj. John Connolly [extract] letter dated Fort Fincastle, August 9, 1774, in Hewlett, *Dartmouth Manuscripts*, 359 (151-153); Draper, McDonald's Expedition.

18. *Virginia Gazette* #1 (Purdie and Dixon), October 13, 1774.

19. Ibid.

20. Draper, McDonald's Expedition; Jacob, *Biographical Sketch*, 70.

21. *Virginia Gazette* #1 (Purdie and Dixon), October 13, 1774.

22. Maj. Angus McDonald to Maj. John Connolly [extract] letter dated Fort Fincastle, August 9, 1774, in Hewlett, *Dartmouth Manuscripts*, 359 (151-153); *Virginia Gazette* #1 (Purdie and Dixon), October 13, 1774; Draper, McDonald's Expedition.

23. *Virginia Gazette* #1 (Purdie and Dixon), October 13, 1774.

24. Ibid.; Draper, McDonald's Expedition.

25. *Virginia Gazette* #1 (Purdie and Dixon), October 13, 1774; Draper, McDonald's Expedition.

26. Maj. Angus McDonald to Maj. John Connolly [extract] letter dated Fort Fincastle, August 9, 1774, in Hewlett, *Dartmouth Manuscripts*, 359 (151-153); Draper, McDonald's Expedition.

27. *Virginia Gazette* #1 (Purdie and Dixon), October 13, 1774; Draper, McDonald's Expedition.

28. Col. William Christian to Col. William Preston, letter dated Camp Union at Great Levels, September 7, 1774, Preston Papers, Draper Manuscripts, 3QQ92 (185-188); Maj. Angus McDonald to Maj. John Connolly [extract] letter dated Fort Fincastle, August 9, 1774, in Hewlett, *Dartmouth Manuscripts*, 359 (151-153).

29. Maj. Angus McDonald to Maj. John Connolly [extract] letter dated Fort Fincastle, August 9, 1774, in Hewlett, *Dartmouth Manuscripts*, 359 (151-153); Draper, McDonald's Expedition; Thwaites and Kellogg, *Documentary History*, 156n.

30. Draper, McDonald's Expedition; William Greenway pension application S1907, September 12, 1832, Roll 1784; Evan Morgan pension application S11098, March 7, 1833, Roll 1784; Brantz Mayer, *Tay-gah-jute or Logan and Captain Michael Cresap* (Baltimore: Maryland Historical Society, 1851), 58.

31. *Virginia Gazette* #1 (Purdie and Dixon), August 18, 1774; *Journal of the House of Delegates of the Commonwealth of Virginia* (Richmond: Samuel Shepherd, 1828), 22 (Dec. 9, 1776).

32. Maj. James Robertson to Col. William Preston, letter dated Culbertson's Bottom, August 1, 1774, Preston Papers, Draper Manuscripts, 3QQ69 (103-106); Stuart, "Narrative," 674-675.

33. Maj. James Robertson to Col. William Preston, letter dated Culbertson's Bottom, August 1, 1774, Preston Papers, Draper Manuscripts, 3QQ69 (103-106); Col. William Preston, letter dated Fincastle, August 13, 1774, in Force, *American Archives*, 1:707-708; Stuart, "Narrative," 674-675; Newton et al., *History of the Pan-Handle*, 80.

34. Col. William Preston to Capt. Evan Shelby, letter dated August 2, 1774, Tennessee Papers, Draper Manuscripts 5XX4 (106-108).

35. Ibid.

36. Thomas Hanson Journal entries dated August 6–9, 1774, George Rogers Clark Papers, Draper Manuscripts 14J58-84, in Thwaites and Kellogg, *Documentary History*, 133; Col. William Preston to George Washington, letter dated Smithfield, August 15, 1774, in Abbot and Twohig, *Washington Papers*, 10:151-152.

37. Maj. Arthur Campbell to Col. William Preston, letter dated McCauls, August 3, 1774, Preston Papers, Draper Manuscripts, 3QQ70 (108-109); Thwaites and Kellogg, *Documentary History*, 108n.

38. Maj. Arthur Campbell to Col. William Preston, letter dated McCauls, August 3, 1774, Preston Papers, Draper Manuscripts, 3QQ70 (108-109).

39. Maj. Arthur Campbell to Col. William Preston, letter dated August 9, 1774, Preston Papers, Draper Manuscripts, 3QQ79 (135-136).

40. Col. William Preston to Maj. James Robertson, letter [undated], Preston Papers, Draper Manuscripts, 3QQ138 (95-97).

41. Ibid.

42. Maj. James Robertson to Col. William Preston, letters dated July 19 and 20, 1774, Preston Papers, Draper Manuscripts, 3QQ66 (94-95).

43. Maj. James Robertson to Col. William Preston, letter dated Fort Dunmore (Fincastle County), July 26, 1774, Preston Papers, Draper Manuscripts, 3QQ67-68 (99-100).

44. Maj. James Robertson to Col. William Preston, letter dated Fort Byrd (Culbertson's), July 28, 1774, Preston Papers, Draper Manuscripts, 3QQ67-68 (100-101).

45. Col. William Preston to Maj. Arthur Campbell, letter dated August 25, 1774, Preston Papers, Draper Manuscripts, 3QQ82 (161-162).

46. Maj. James Robertson to Col. William Preston, letter dated Fort Byrd (Culbertson's), July 28, 1774, Preston Papers, Draper Manuscripts, 3QQ67-68 (100-101).

47. Maj. James Robertson to Col. William Preston, letters dated Fort Byrd and Culbertson's Bottom, July 28, August 1, and August 12, 1774, Preston Papers, Draper Manuscripts 3QQ67-69, 74 (100-101, 103-106, 140-142).

48. Maj. James Robertson to Col. William Preston, letter dated Culbertson's Bottom, August 6, 1774, Preston Papers, Draper Manuscripts, 3QQ71 (109-110).

49. Maj. James Robertson to Col. William Preston, letter dated Culbertson's Bottom, August 1, 1774, Preston Papers, Draper Manuscripts, 3QQ69 (103-106).

50. Maj. James Robertson to Col. William Preston, letter dated Culbertson's Bottom, August 11, 1774, Preston Papers, Draper Manuscripts, 3QQ73 (138-140).

51. Maj. James Robertson to Col. William Preston, letter dated Culbertson's Bottom, August 6, 1774, Preston Papers, Draper Manuscripts, 3QQ71 (109-110).

52. Maj. James Robertson to Col. William Preston, letter dated Culberston's Bottom, August 11, 1774, Preston Papers, Draper Manuscripts, 3QQ73 (138-140).

53. Maj. Arthur Campbell to Capt. Daniel Smith, letter dated Royal Oak, August 9, 1774, William Henry Harrison Papers, Draper Manuscripts, 4X43 (134); Maj. James Robertson to Col. William Preston, letter dated Culbertson's Bottom, August 12, 1774, Preston Papers, Draper Manuscripts, 3QQ74 (140-142); Col. William Preston to George Washington, letter dated Smithfield, August 15, 1774, in Abbot and Twohig, *Washington Papers*, 10:151-152; John Lybrook to Draper, Lyman Draper Notebook, 31S433; Jacob Sidnow pension application R9903 Roll 2241; Thwaites and Kellogg, *Documentary History*, 134n. Sinking Creek is in present-day Giles County, West Virginia.

54. Maj. Arthur Campbell to Capt. Daniel Smith, letter dated Royal Oak, August 9, 1774, William Henry Harrison Papers, Draper Manuscripts, 4X43 (134); Maj. James Robertson to Col. William Preston, letter dated Culbertson's Bottom, August 12, 1774, Preston Papers, Draper Manuscripts, 3QQ74 (140-142); John Lybrook to Draper, Lyman Draper Notebook, 31S433.

55. Maj. Arthur Campbell to Capt. Daniel Smith, letter dated Royal Oak, August 9, 1774, William Henry Harrison Papers, Draper Manuscripts, 4X43 (134); Maj. James Robertson to Col. William Preston, letter dated Culbertson's Bottom, August 12, 1774, Preston Papers, Draper Manuscripts, 3QQ74 (140-142); John Lybrook to Draper, Lyman Draper Notebook, 31S433; David E. Johnson, *A History of the Middle New River Settlements and Contiguous Territory* (Huntington, WV: Standard Printing & Publishing, 1906), 42-44.

56. Maj. Arthur Campbell to Capt. Daniel Smith, letter dated Royal Oak, August 9, 1774, William Henry Harrison Papers, Draper Manuscripts, 4X43 (134); Maj. James Robertson to Col. William Preston, letter dated Culbertson's Bottom, August 12, 1774, Preston Papers, Draper Manuscripts, 3QQ74 (140-142); Col. William Preston to George Washington, letter dated Smithfield, August 15, 1774, in Abbot and Twohig, *Washington Papers*, 10:151-152; John Lybrook to Draper, Lyman Draper Notebook, 31S433; Johnson, *History of the Middle New River Settlements*, 42-44.

57. Maj. Arthur Campbell to Capt. Daniel Smith, letter dated Royal Oak, August 9, 1774, William Henry Harrison Papers, Draper Manuscripts, 4X43 (134); Maj. James Robertson to Col. William Preston, letter dated Culbertson's Bottom, August 12, 1774, Preston Papers, Draper Manuscripts, 3QQ74 (140-142); Col. William Preston to George Washington, letter dated Smithfield, August 15, 1774, *Papers of George Washington*, Colonial Series 10: 151-152; John Lybrook to Draper, Lyman Draper Notebook, 31S433; and Thwaites and Kellogg, *Documentary History*, 134n; Johnson, *History of the Middle New River Settlements*, 42-44. Tradition holds that remains found nearby years later confirmed that McGriff's shot mortally wounded the warrior.

58. Maj. James Robertson to Col. William Preston, letter dated Culbertson's Bottom, August 12, 1774, Preston Papers, Draper Manuscripts, 3QQ74 (140-142).

59. Maj. James Robertson to Col. William Preston, letter dated Culbertson's Bottom, August 11, 1774, Preston Papers, Draper Manuscripts, 3QQ73 (138-140).

60. Maj. James Robertson to Col. William Preston, letter dated Culbertson's Bottom, August 12, 1774, Preston Papers, Draper Manuscripts, 3QQ74 (140-142); Draper's Notes, Draper Manuscripts Collection, Wisconsin Historical Society, 31S433,; Johnson, *History of the Middle New River Settlements*, 42-44.

61. Maj. James Robertson to Col. William Preston, letter dated Culbertson's Bottom, August 12, 1774, Preston Papers, Draper Manuscripts, 3QQ74 (140-142); Draper's Notes, Draper Manuscripts, 31S433; Johnson, *History of the Middle New River Settlements*, 45-46. The location is believed to be the vicinity of Pipestem Knob in present-day Summers County, West Virginia. Theophilus Snidow was eventually adopted by and lived with the Indians for fourteen years following his capture.

62. Maj. James Robertson to Col. William Preston, letter dated Culberston's Bottom, August 11, 1774, Preston Papers, Draper Manuscripts, 3QQ73 (138-140).

63. Ibid.

64. Maj. James Robertson to Col. William Preston, letter dated Culbertson's Bottom, August 12, 1774, Preston Papers, Draper Manuscripts, 3QQ74 (140-142); Draper's Notes, Draper Manuscripts, 31S433; Johnson, *History of the Middle New River Settlements*, 45-46.

65. Maj. James Robertson to Col. William Preston, letter dated Culbertson's Bottom, August 12, 1774, Preston Papers, Draper Manuscripts, 3QQ74 (140-142).

66. The following discussion of the council of war is based on Council of War, report dated Richfield, Botetourt, August 12, 1774, Bullitt Family Papers, Oxmoor Collection, Filson Historical Society, Louisville; and Col. Preston to Maj. Arthur Campbell, letter dated Smithfield, August 13, 1774, Preston Papers, Draper Manuscripts, 3QQ76 (145-146).

67. Jacob Gillespie pension application S3398, dated October 4, 1832, and Samuel Gwinn pension application S17992, dated March 12, 1834, Roll 1149. Clover Lick is in present-day Pocahontas County, West Virginia.

68. Maj. James Robertson to Col. William Preston, letter dated Culbertson's Bottom, August 12, 1774, Preston Papers, Draper Manuscripts, 3QQ74 (140-142); Johnson, *Dictionary* (1773), vol. 2, ROU-RUB. Johnson defined "rub up" as "to excite; to awaken."

69. Maj. James Robertson to Col. William Preston, letter dated Culbertson's Bottom, August 12, 1774, Preston Papers, Draper Manuscripts, 3QQ74 (140-142).

70. Col. William Preston to Capt. John L. Joanes, letter dated Smithfield, August 13, 1773, Preston Papers, Draper Manuscripts, 3QQ147 (146-147).

71. Col. William Preston to Capt. David Long, letter dated Smithfield, August 13, 1774, Preston Papers, Draper Manuscripts, 3QQ140 (147-148).

72. Maj. Arthur Campbell to Capt. Daniel Smith, letter dated Royal Oak, August 9, 1774, William Henry Harrison Papers, Draper Manuscripts, 4X43 (134).

73. Ibid.

74. Maj. Arthur Campbell to Capt. Daniel Smith and Col. William Preston, letters dated Royal Oak, August 9, 1774, William Henry Harrison Papers 4X43 (134) and Preston Papers, Draper Manuscripts, 3QQ79 (135-136).

75. Maj. Arthur Campbell to Col. William Preston, letter dated Royal Oak, August 12, 1774, Preston Papers, Draper Manuscripts, 3QQ75 (142-144).

76. Ibid.

77. Col. William Preston to Maj. Arthur Campbell, letter dated Smithfield, August 13, 1774, Preston Papers, Draper Manuscripts, 3QQ76 (145-146).

78. Maj. Arthur Campbell to Col. William Preston, letter dated Royal Oak, August 12, 1774, Preston Papers, Draper Manuscripts, 3QQ75 (142-144).

79. Col. William Preston to Maj. Arthur Campbell, letter dated Smithfield, August 13, 1774, Preston Papers, Draper Manuscripts, 3QQ76 (145-146).

80. Col. William Preston, letter dated Fincastle, August 13, 1774, in Force, *American Archives*, 1:707-708.

81. Col. William Preston to George Washington, letter dated Smithfield, August 15, 1774, in Abbot and Twohig, *Washington Papers*, 10:151-152.

82. Earl of Dunmore to Earl of Dartmouth, letter dated Frederick County August 14, 1774, Davies, *Documents*, 8:160.

83. Earl of Dunmore to Col. Andrew Lewis, letter dated Winchester, July 24, 1774, Preston Papers, Draper Manuscripts, 3QQ141 (97-98).

84. *Virginia Gazette* #1 (Purdie and Dixon), August 4 and 11, 1774, and *Virginia Gazette* #2 (Rind), August 11, 1774. Among the earliest examples of officers adding "On His Majesty's Service" to the addresses in their correspondence is Maj. Arthur Campbell to Capt. Daniel Smith, letter dated August 9, 1774, Preston Papers, Draper Manuscripts, 4X43 (134).

CHAPTER 9: EQUAL TO ANY TROOPS

1. Provincial Council at Philadelphia, Minutes dated August 4, 1774, and Gov. John Penn to Capt. Arthur St. Clair, letter dated Philadelphia, August 6, 1774, Colonial Records of Pennsylvania, *Minutes of the Provincial Council of Pennsylvania, from the Organization to the Termination of the Proprietary Government*, vol. 10, *Containing the Proceedings of Council from October 18th 1771, to 27th of September, 1775, Both Dates Included: Together with Minutes of the Council of Safety from June 30th, 1775 to November 12th, 1776, Both Dates Included*, ed. Samuel Hazard (Harrisburg: Theodore Fenn, 1852), 201 and 202-203.

2. Ibid., August 4, 1774, 201.

3. Gov. John Penn to Capt. Arthur St. Clair, letter dated Philadelphia, August 6, 1774, ibid., 202-203.

4. Ibid.; Capt. Arthur St. Clair to Gov. John Penn, letter dated Ligonier, August 25, 1774, in Hazard, *Pennsylvania Archives*, 1, 4:573-576.

5. Arthur St. Clair to Gov. John Penn, letter dated Ligonier, August 25, 1774, *Pennsylvania Archives*, 1, 4:573-576.

6. Gov. John Penn to the Chiefs and Warriors of the Delaware Indians, message dated Philadelphia, August 6, 1774, *Pennsylvania Archives*, 1, 4:204-205.

7. Arthur St. Clair to Gov. John Penn, letter dated Ligonier, August 25, 1774, *Pennsylvania Archives*, 1, 4: 573-576.

8. Gov. John Penn to the Chiefs and Warriors of the Shawanese Indians, message dated Philadelphia, August 6, 1774, *Pennsylvania Archives*, 1, 4:203-204.

9. Col. Andrew Lewis to Col. William Preston, letter dated Richfield, August 14, 1774, Preston Papers, Draper Manuscripts, 3QQ77 (149).

10. Capt. William Russell to Col. William Preston, letter dated August 16, 1774, Preston Papers, Draper Manuscripts, 3QQ78 (156-158).

11. Capt. William Russell to Col. William Preston, letter dated August 28, 1774, Preston Papers, Draper Manuscripts, 3QQ84 (172-173).

12. Col. William Preston to Maj. Arthur Campbell, letter dated August 25, 1774, Preston Papers, Draper Manuscripts, 3QQ82 (161-162).

13. Maj. Arthur Campbell to Col. William Preston, letter dated Royal Oak, August 26, 1774, Preston Papers, Draper Manuscripts, 3QQ83 (162-163).

14. Capt. William Russell to Colonel William Preston, letters dated Town House, August 28, 1774, and Fort Preston, August 16, 1774, Preston Papers, Draper Manuscripts, 3QQ84 (172-174) and 3QQ78 (157).

15. Capt. William Russell to Col. William Preston, letter dated August 16, 1774, Preston Papers, Draper Manuscripts, 3QQ78 (156-158).

16. Capt. John Floyd to Col. William Preston, letters dated or estimated Royal Oak and Town House, August 26–28, 1774, Draper's Notes, Draper Manuscripts, 33S35-49 (163-168); Maj. Arthur Campbell to Col. William Preston, letter dated Town House, August 28, 1774, Preston Papers, Draper Manuscripts, 3QQ85 (170-172).

17. Ibid.

18. Maj. Arthur Campbell to Col. William Preston, letter dated Town House, August 28, 1774, Preston Papers, Draper Manuscripts, 3QQ85 (170-172).

19. Capt. John Floyd to Col. William Preston, letters dated or estimated Royal Oak and Town House, August 26–28, 1774, Draper's Notes, Draper Manuscripts, 33S35-49 (163-168); Maj. Arthur Campbell to Col. William Preston, letter dated Town House, August 28, 1774, Preston Papers, Draper Manuscripts, 3QQ85 (170-172).

20. Capt. John Floyd to Col. William Preston, letters dated or estimated Royal Oak and Town House, August 26–28, 1774, Draper's Notes, Draper Manuscripts, 33S35-49 (163-168).

21. Col. William Christian to Col. William Preston, letter dated Head of Rich Creek, September 3, 1774, Preston Papers, Draper Manuscripts, 3QQ89 (176-179); (enclosure) Return of Militia from Fincastle County, dated Camp Union, September 7, 1774, Preston Papers, Draper Manuscripts, 3QQ92 (189); John Canterbury pension application R1667, dated February 3, 1834, Roll 465.

22. Col. William Christian to Col. William Preston, letter dated Head of Rich Creek, September 3, 1774, Preston Papers, Draper Manuscripts, 3QQ89 (176-179).

23. Maj. James Robertson to Col. William Preston, letter dated September 1, 1774, Preston Papers, Draper Manuscripts, 3QQ88 (174-175).

24. D'Urfey, *Wit and Mirth*, 5:319-321.

25. Maj. James Robertson to Col. William Preston, letters dated September 1 and 4, 1774, Preston Papers, Draper Manuscripts, 3QQ88 (174-175) and 3QQ91 (179-180).

26. Maj. James Robertson to Colonel William Preston, letter dated September 4, 1774, Preston Papers, Draper Manuscripts, 3QQ91 (179-180).

27. Capt. Michael Woods to Col. William Preston, letter dated September 3, 1774, Preston Papers, Draper Manuscripts, 3QQ88 (175-176).

28. Col. William Christian to Col. William Preston, letter dated Head of Rich Creek, September 3, 1774, Preston Papers, Draper Manuscripts, 3QQ89 (176-179).

29. Rev. John Brown to Col. William Preston, letter dated August 22, 1774, Preston Papers, Draper Manuscripts, 3QQ81 (159-161).

30. Benjamin Cleaver pension application R2039, dated September 24, 1831, Roll 575; John Cox pension application R2404, dated October 16, 1834, Roll 671.

31. Rev. John Brown to Col. William Preston, letter dated August 22, 1774, Preston Papers, Draper Manuscripts, 3QQ81 (159-161).

32. Col. William Christian to Col. William Preston, letter dated Head of Rich Creek, September 3, 1774, Preston Papers, Draper Manuscripts, 3QQ89 (176-179); Thwaites and Kellogg, *Documentary History,* 223n.

33. Hening, *Statutes,* 6:268-70; Nicholas Cresswell, *The Journal of Nicholas Cresswell, 1774–1777* (London: Jonathan Cape, 1925), 49.

34. Col. Adam Stephen to Richard Henry Lee, letter dated Berkeley Courthouse, August 27, 1774, Richard H. Lee, *Memoir of the Life of Richard Henry Lee, and His Correspondence,* ed. Richard H. Lee, vol. 1 (Philadelphia: M. C. Carey and I. Lea, 1825), 207.

35. Augustine Prevost, diary entry dated Pittsburgh, September 12, 1774, in Prevost, "Turmoil at Pittsburgh," 133.

36. Gov. Dunmore to Maj. Horatio Gates, Commission dated Williamsburg, 6 April 1773, Horatio Gates Papers, 1760-1804, Microfilm Publication, Manuscripts and Archives Division, Special Collections, New York Public Library, New York, Microfilm Collection M2135, reel 2, 1769–1776 (NYHS viHi 1719), 0458-60, copy in the John D. Rockefeller Jr. Library, Colonial Williamsburg Foundation, Williamsburg, Virginia.

37. Col. Adam Stephen to Lt. Col. Horatio Gates, letter dated Winchester, 24 August 1774, Gates Papers.

38. Lt. Col. Horatio Gates to Col. Adam Stephen, letter dated Traveler's Rest, 26 August 1774, Gates Papers.

39. Col. William Fleming to Mrs. Nancy Fleming, letter dated Union Camp on the Levels of Green Brier, September 7, 1774, Virginia Papers, Draper Manuscripts, 2ZZ2 (183-184); Col. William Christian to Col. William Preston, letter dated Camp Union at the Great Levels, September 7, 1774, Preston Papers, Draper Manuscripts, 3QQ92 (185-189); Capt. Dorsey Pentecost to Capt. William Harrod, letter dated September 16, 1774, Pittsburgh and Northwest Virginia Papers, Draper Manuscripts, 4NN12 (201-202).

40. Col. William Fleming to Mrs. Nancy Fleming, letter dated Union Camp on the Levels of Green Brier, September 7, 1774, Virginia Papers, Draper Manuscripts, 2ZZ2 (183-184); Col. William Christian to Col. William Preston, letter dated Camp Union at the Great Levels, September 7, 1774, and Col. Andrew Lewis to Col. William Preston, letter dated Camp Union on the Great Levels, September 8, 1774, Preston Papers, Draper Manuscripts, 3QQ92 (185-189) and 3QQ93 (190-192); Valentine Crawford to George Washington, letter dated Fort Fincastle, October 1, 1774, in Butterfield, *Washington-Crawford Letters,* 97-100; Capt. Augustine Prevost, diary entry dated Pittsburgh, September 6, 1774, 128, and Capt. Dorsey Pentecost to Capt. William Harrod, letter dated September 16, 1774, Pittsburgh and Northwest Virginia Papers, Draper Manuscripts, 4NN12 (201-202).

41. Col. William Fleming to Mrs. Nancy Fleming, letter dated Union Camp on the Levels of Green Brier, September 7, 1774, Virginia Papers, Draper Manuscripts, 2ZZ2 (183-184); Col. William Christian to Col. William Preston, letter dated Camp Union at the Great Levels, September 7, 1774, and Col. Andrew Lewis to Col. William Preston, letter

dated Camp Union on the Great Levels, September 8, 1774, Preston Papers, Draper Manuscripts, 3QQ92 (185-189) and 3QQ93 (190-192); Valentine Crawford to George Washington, letter dated Fort Fincastle, October 1, 1774, in Butterfield, *Washington-Crawford Letters*, 97-100; Capt. Augustine Prevost, diary entry dated Pittsburgh, September 6, 1774, 128, and Capt. Dorsey Pentecost to Capt. William Harrod, letter dated September 16, 1774, Pittsburgh and Northwest Virginia Papers, Draper Manuscripts, 4NN12 (201-202).

42. Col. William Fleming to Mrs. Nancy Fleming, letter dated Union Camp on the Levels of Green Brier, September 4, 1774, and Col. William Fleming Journal, Virginia Papers, Draper Manuscripts, 2ZZ1 (181-182) and 2ZZ71 (231); Bland, *Treatise*, 296; Captain George Smith, *An Universal Military Dictionary: A Copious Explanation of the Technical Terms &c., Used in the Equipment, Machinery, Movements, and Military Operations of an Army* (London: J. Milan, 1779; facsimile repr., Ottawa, ON: Museum Restoration Services, 1969), DRU-DUT.

43. Col. William Fleming to Mrs. Nancy Fleming, letter dated Union Camp on the Levels of Green Brier, September 4, 1774, Virginia Papers, Draper Manuscripts, 2ZZ1 (181-182).

44. William Kennerly pension application S8781, dated July 22, 1833, Roll 1473. Warwick's Fort was near what is present-day Huttonsville, West Virginia.

45. Col. William Fleming to Mrs. Nancy Fleming, letter dated Union Camp on the Levels of Green Brier, September 4, 1774, to William Bowyer, undated Point Pleasant, and Journal, Virginia Papers, Draper Manuscripts, 2ZZ1 (181-182), 2ZZ7 (254-257), and 2ZZ71 (232).

46. Col. William Fleming, Orderly Book dated Camp Union, September 4, 1774, Virginia Papers, Draper Manuscripts, 2ZZ71 (313); Bland, *Treatise*, 245, 254.

47. Col. William Fleming, Orderly Book dated Camp Union, September 4, 1774, Virginia Papers, Draper Manuscripts, 2ZZ71 (313); Bland, *Treatise*, 254, 256-258, 260.

48. Col. William Fleming, Journal and Orderly Book dated Camp Union, September 4, 1774, Virginia Papers, Draper Manuscripts, 2ZZ71 (232) and 2ZZ72 (313).

49. Ibid.; Col. William Christian to Col. William Preston, letter dated Camp Union at the Great Levels, September 7, 1774, Preston Papers, Draper Manuscripts, 3QQ92 (185-189).

50. Col. William Fleming, Journal and Orderly Book dated Camp Union, September 5, 1774, Virginia Papers, Draper Manuscripts, 2ZZ71 (232) and 2ZZ72 (314).

51. Col. William Fleming, Orderly Book dated Camp Union, September 4, 1774, Virginia Papers 2ZZ72 (313).

52. Col. William Fleming, Orderly Book dated Camp Union, September 7, 1774, Virginia Papers 2ZZ72 (315-316).

53. Col. William Christian to Col. William Preston, letter dated Camp Union at the Great Levels, September 7, 1774, Preston Papers, Draper Manuscripts, 3QQ92 (185-189).

54. Samuel Lightfoot to Joseph Wright, John Mickle Jr., James Hammond, Patrick Quinn, and Christian Miller, Agreement dated York, March 1, 1759, in Samuel Parrish, ed., *Several Chapters in the History of the Friendly Association for Regaining and Preserving the Peace with the Indians by Pacific Measures* (Philadelphia: Friends Historical Association, 1877), 109; Erna Risch, *Supplying Washington's Army* (Washington, DC: US Army Center of Military History, 1981), 66-71, 75.

55. Col. Andrew Lewis to Col. William Preston, letter dated Richfield, August 14, 1774, Preston Papers, Draper Manuscripts, 3QQ77 (149).

56. Col. William Fleming, Orderly Book dated Camp Union, September 6, 1774, Virginia Papers, Draper Manuscripts, 2ZZ72 (314).

57. Col. William Christian to Col. William Preston, letter dated Head of Rich Creek, September 3, 1774, Preston Papers, Draper Manuscripts, 3QQ89 (176-179).

58. Smyth, *Tour in the United States*, 2:115-116.

59. Col. Andrew Lewis to Col. William Preston, letter dated Camp Union on the Great Levels, September 8, 1774, and Col. William Christian to Col. William Preston, letter dated Camp Union at the Great Levels, September 7, 1774, Preston Papers, Draper Manuscripts, 3QQ93 (190-192) and 3QQ92 (185-189).

60. Col. Andrew Lewis to Col. William Preston, letter dated Camp Union on the Great Levels, September 8, 1774, Preston Papers, Draper Manuscripts, 3QQ93 (190-192).

61. Col. William Christian to Col. William Preston, letter dated Camp Union, September 12, 1774, Preston Papers, Draper Manuscripts, 3QQ146 (196-199); Col. William Fleming, Journal and Orderly Book entries dated Camp Union, September 6, 1774, Virginia Papers, Draper Manuscripts, 2ZZ71 (282) and 2ZZ72 (314).

62. Col. William Fleming, Journal and Orderly Book dated September 6, and to Mrs. Nancy Fleming, letter dated Camp Union, September 7, 1774, Virginia Papers, Draper Manuscripts, 2ZZ71 (283-284), 2ZZ72 (313), and 2ZZ2 (183-184).

63. Col. Andrew Lewis to Col. William Preston, letter dated Camp Union on the Great Levels, September 8, 1774, Preston Papers, Draper Manuscripts, 3QQ93 (190-192).

64. Ibid.; Col. William Fleming Journal and Orderly Book entries dated Camp Union, September 6, 1774, Virginia Papers, Draper Manuscripts, 2ZZ71 (282) and 02ZZ72 (314-315).

65. Col. William Fleming, Journal and Orderly Book dated Camp Union, September 6, 1774, Virginia Papers 2ZZ71 (283-284) and 2ZZ72 (315-316); Col. William Christian to Col. William Preston, letter dated Camp Union at the Great Levels, September 7, 1774, Preston Papers, Draper Manuscripts, 3QQ92 (185-189); Bland, *Treatise*, 296; Smith, *Universal Military Dictionary*, DRU-DUT.

66. Col. William Fleming to Mrs. Nancy Fleming, letter dated Union Camp, September 7, 1774, Virginia Papers, Draper Manuscripts, 2ZZ2 (183-184).

67. Col. William Christian to Col. William Preston, and Col. Andrew Lewis to Col. William Preston, letters dated Camp Union on the Great Levels, September 7 and 8, 1774, Preston Papers, Draper Manuscripts, 3QQ92 (185-189) and 3QQ93 (190-192).

68. Col. William Christian to Col. William Preston, letter dated Camp Union at the Great Levels, September 7, and Col. Andrew Lewis to Col. William Preston, letter dated Camp Union on the Great Levels, September 8, 1774, Preston Papers, Draper Manuscripts, 3QQ92 (185-189) and 3QQ93 (190-192); Hening, *Statutes*, 7:114 and 3:17 (1823).

69. Col. William Preston [extract] letter dated Fincastle, September 28, 1774, *Virginia Gazette* #1 (Purdie and Dixon) October 13, 1774, also in Force, *American Archives*, 1:808.

CHAPTER 10: TO HOLD THEMSELVES IN READINESS

1. The following section about events that transpired in and around Pittsburgh in early September 1774 is based on Prevost, "Turmoil at Pittsburgh," 123-132.

2. Earl of Dunmore to Earl of Hillsborough, letter dated New York, December 6, 1770, in O'Callahan, *New York Colonial Documents*, 8:259.

3. Prevost, "Turmoil at Pittsburgh," 132-133, 137.

4. *Virginia Gazette* #2 (Pinkney), supplement, October 13, 1774. Also in Force, *American Archives*, 1:871-878, and Prevost, "Turmoil at Pittsburgh," 135.

5. Prevost, "Turmoil at Pittsburgh," 138.

6. Ibid., 135, 136, 138, 139.

7. *Virginia Gazette* #2 (Pinkney), supplement, October 13, 1774. Also in Force, *American Archives*, 1:871-878; and Prevost, "Turmoil at Pittsburgh," 138-139.

8. *Virginia Gazette* #2 (Pinkney), supplement, October 13, 1774. Also in Force, *American Archives*, 1:871-878.

9. Prevost, "Turmoil at Pittsburgh," 140, *Virginia Gazette* #2 (Pinkney), supplement, October 13, 1774, and Force, *American Archives*, 1:871-878. Another variation of Pluggy's Mohawk name was Tecanyaterighto.

10. Ibid. Prevost, "Turmoil at Pittsburgh," 140, *Virginia Gazette* #2 (Pinkney), supplement, October 13, 1774, and Force, *American Archives*, 1:871-878.

11. Prevost, "Turmoil at Pittsburgh," 142, and Valentine Crawford to George Washington, letter dated Fort Fincastle, October 1, 1774, in Butterfield, *Washington-Crawford Letters*, 97-99.

12. Col. William Fleming, Orderly Book September 13, 1774, Virginia Papers, Draper Manuscripts, 2ZZ72 (320).

13. Col. William Fleming, Orderly Book September 12, 1774, Virginia Papers, Draper Manuscripts, 2ZZ72 (319), Col. William Fleming Journal, September 12, 1774, Virginia Papers, Draper Manuscripts, 2ZZ71 (284); Col. William Christian to Mrs. Nancy Fleming, letter dated Camp Union, September 18, 1774, Virginia Papers, Draper Manuscripts, 2ZZ10 (205); Withers, *Chronicles of Border Warfare*, 166.

14. Letter (extract) from an (unnamed) Officer Late Under the Command of Lord Dunmore Against the Indians, dated Fort Augusta, November 21, 1774, *American Archives*, 1:1017-1018. Elk River Camp was located near present-day Charleston, West Virginia.

15. Col. William Fleming Journal, September 6, 1774, Virginia Papers 2ZZ71 (283-284), and Col. William Christian to Col. William Preston, letter dated Camp Union, September 12, 1774, Preston Papers, Draper Manuscripts, 3QQ146 (196-199).

16. Maj. Arthur Campbell to Col. William Preston, letter dated Royal Oak, September 29, 1774, Preston Papers, Draper Manuscripts, 3QQ106 (216-2192).

17. Maj. Arthur Campbell to Col. William Preston, letter dated Royal Oak, September 17, 1774, Preston Papers, Draper Manuscripts, 3QQ98 (202-205).

18. Maj. Arthur Campbell to Col. William Preston, letter dated Royal Oak, September 9, 1774, and Maj. Arthur Campbell to Col. William Preston, letter dated Royal Oak, September 17, 1774, Preston Papers, Draper Manuscripts, 3QQ94 (192-195) and 3QQ98 (202-205).

19. Maj. Arthur Campbell to Col. William Preston, letter dated Royal Oak, October 1, 1774, Preston Papers, Draper Manuscripts, 3QQ109 (219-222).

20. Maj. Arthur Campbell to Col. William Preston, letter dated Royal Oak, September 9, 1774, and Maj. Arthur Campbell to Col. William Preston, letter dated Royal Oak, September 17, 1774, Preston Papers, Draper Manuscripts, 3QQ94 (192-195) and 3QQ98 (202-205). List of Men in Captain Daniel Smith's Company, muster rolls dated

August 13 and 29, 1774, Tennessee Papers 5XX2, 5XX3, and 6XX16; also in Lloyd De-Witt Bockstruck, *Virginia's Colonial Soldiers* (Baltimore: Genealogical Publishing, 1988), 154-155.
21. Maj. Arthur Campbell to Col. William Preston, letter dated Royal Oak, September 17, 1774, Preston Papers, Draper Manuscripts, 3QQ98 (202-205).
22. Ibid.; Col. William Preston [extract] letter dated Fincastle, September 28, 1774, in Force, *American Archives*, 1:808.
23. Maj. Arthur Campbell to Col. William Preston, letter dated Royal Oak, September 17, 1774, Preston Papers, Draper Manuscripts, 3QQ98 (202-205).
24. Ibid.
25. Maj. Arthur Campbell to Col. William Preston, letter dated Royal Oak, October 1, 1774, Preston Papers, Draper Manuscripts, 3QQ109 (219-222).
26. Maj. Arthur Campbell to Col. William Preston, letter dated Royal Oak, September 9, 1774, and Maj. Arthur Campbell to Col. William Preston, letter dated Royal Oak, September 17, 1774, Preston Papers, Draper Manuscripts, 3QQ94 (192-195) and 3QQ98 (202-205).
27. Maj. Arthur Campbell to Col. William Preston, letter dated Royal Oak, September 9, 1774, and Maj. Arthur Campbell to Col. William Preston, letter dated Royal Oak, September 17, 1774, Preston Papers, Draper Manuscripts, 3QQ94 (192-195) and 3QQ98 (202-205).
28. Maj. Arthur Campbell to Col. William Preston, letter dated Royal Oak, September 9, 1774; Maj. Arthur Campbell to Col. William Preston, letter dated Royal Oak, September 17, 1774, Preston Papers, Draper Manuscripts, 3QQ94 (192-195) and 3QQ98 (202-205); Thwaites and Kellogg, *Documentary History,* 194n. The locations are in present-day Russell County, most in the vicinity of Castlewood, or in the case of Elk Garden, near Lebanon, Virginia.
29. Maj. Arthur Campbell to William Preston, letters dated September 26, 1774, Preston Papers, Draper Manuscripts, 3QQ104 and 3QQ105 (209-211); Thwaites and Kellogg, *Documentary History*, 85n, 209n.
30. Captain William Cocke to Inhabitants on the Frontier of Holston, circular letter dated September 25, 1774; Maj. Arthur Campbell to Col. William Preston, letters dated Royal Oak, September 26 and October 3, 1774, Preston Papers, Draper Manuscripts, 3QQ103 (208-209), 3QQ104 (209-211), and 3QQ111; Col. William Preston [extract] letter dated Fincastle, September 28, 1774, in Force, *American Archives*, 1:808; Thwaites and Kellogg, *Documentary History*, 208n, 218n-219n.
31. Maj. Arthur Campbell to Col. William Preston, letter dated Royal Oak, October 12, 1774, Preston Papers, Draper Manuscripts, 3QQ118 (244-245); John Montgomery to Gov. John Penn, letter dated Carlisle, June 30, 1774, *Pennsylvania Archives,* 1, 4:533-534.
32. Maj. Arthur Campbell to Col. William Preston, letters dated Royal Oak, October 3 and 6, 1774, Preston Papers, Draper Manuscripts, 3QQ111 and 3QQ116 (233); Thwaites and Kellogg, *Documentary History*, 218n-219n.
33. Captain William Cocke to Inhabitants on the Frontier of Holston, circular letter dated September 25, 1774, and Maj. Arthur Campbell to William Preston, letter dated September 26, 1774, Preston Papers, Draper Manuscripts, 3QQ103 (208-209) and 3QQ104 (209-211); Thwaites and Kellogg, *Documentary History*, 208n.

34. Maj. Arthur Campbell to William Preston, letter dated September 26, 1774, Preston Papers, Draper Manuscripts, 3QQ104 (209-211).

35. Ibid.; Col. William Preston [extract] letter dated Fincastle, September 28, 1774, in Force, *American Archives*, 1:808.

36. Maj. Arthur Campbell to William Preston, letter (addendum) dated September 26, 1774, Preston Papers, Draper Manuscripts, 3QQ104 (211-212); Thwaites and Kellogg, *Documentary History*, 210n.

37. Maj. Arthur Campbell to Col. William Preston, letter dated Royal Oak, September 29, 1774, Preston Papers, Draper Manuscripts, 3QQ106-107 (216-219).

38. Maj. Arthur Campbell to Col. William Preston, letters dated Royal Oak, September 29 and October 1, 1774, Preston Papers, Draper Manuscripts, 3QQ106-107 (216-219) and 3QQ109 (219-222).

39. Maj. Arthur Campbell to Col. William Preston, letter dated Royal Oak, September 29, 1774, Preston Papers, Draper Manuscripts, 3QQ106-107 (216-219).

40. Ibid.

41. Maj. Arthur Campbell to Col. William Preston, letter dated Royal Oak, October 1, 1774, Preston Papers, Draper Manuscripts, 3QQ109 (219-222).

42. Withers, *Chronicles of Border Warfare*, 161.

43. Maj. William Crawford to George Washington, letter dated Stewart's Crossing, September 20, 1774, and Valentine Crawford to George Washington, letter dated Fort Fincastle, October 1, 1774, in Butterfield, *Washington-Crawford Letters*, 52-53 and 97-99.

44. Valentine Crawford to George Washington, letter dated Fort Fincastle, October 1, 1774, in Butterfield, *Washington-Crawford Letters*, 97-99.

45. Maj. William Crawford to George Washington, letter dated Stewart's Crossing, September 20, 1774, and Valentine Crawford to George Washington, letter dated Fort Fincastle, October 1, 1774, in Butterfield, *Washington-Crawford Letters*, 52-53 and 97-99; Withers, *Chronicles of Border Warfare*, 179n. Present-day Parkersburg, West Virginia, is at the mouth of the Little Kanawha River. Present-day Hockingport, Ohio, is at the mouth of the Hocking River.

46. Maj. William Crawford to George Washington, letter dated Stewart's Crossing, September 20, 1774, and Valentine Crawford to George Washington, letter dated Fort Fincastle, October 1, 1774, in Butterfield, *Washington-Crawford Letters*, 52-53 and 97-99; Withers, *Chronicles of Border Warfare*, 179n.

47. Valentine Crawford to George Washington, letter dated Fort Fincastle, October 1, 1774, in Butterfield, *Washington-Crawford Letters*, 97-99; Jacob, *Biographical Sketch*, 72; Governor Earl of Dunmore to Earl of Dartmouth, Official Report dated Williamsburg, December 24, 1774, Davies, *Documents*, 8:261; Thwaites and Kellogg, *Documentary History*, 285n.

48. Col. Andrew Lewis to Col. William Preston, letter dated Camp Union on the Great Levels, September 8, 1774, and Col. William Christian to Col. William Preston, letter dated Camp Union, September 12, 1774, Preston Papers, Draper Manuscripts, 3QQ93 and 3QQ146 (196-199 and 190-192); Joseph Duncan pension application S1809, dated September 14, 1832, Roll 864.

49. Col. William Christian to Col. William Preston, letter dated Camp Union at the Great Levels, September 7, 1774, Preston Papers, Draper Manuscripts, 3QQ92 (185-189).

50. Col. William Fleming, Orderly Book/journal entry September 9, 1774, Virginia Pa-

pers, 2ZZ72 (317-318); Col. Andrew Lewis to Col. William Preston, letter dated Camp Union on the Great Levels, September 8, 1774, Preston Papers, Draper Manuscripts, 3QQ93 (190-192).

51. Col. William Christian to Col. William Preston, letter dated Camp Union, September 12, 1774, Preston Papers, Draper Manuscripts, 3QQ146 (196-199); Col. William Fleming, Journal, September 6, 1774, Virginia Papers, Draper Manuscripts, 2ZZ71 (283-284).

52. Col. William Fleming, Orderly Book, September 9-11, 1774, Virginia Papers, Draper Manuscripts, 2ZZ72 (317-319).

53. Col. William Christian to Col. William Preston, letter dated Camp Union, September 12, 1774, Preston Papers, Draper Manuscripts, 3QQ146 (196-199); Col. William Fleming, Journal, September 6, 1774, Virginia Papers, Draper Manuscripts, 2ZZ71 (283-4).

54. Col. William Fleming, Orderly Book September 15, 1774, Virginia Papers, Draper Manuscripts, 2ZZ72 (321).

55. Col. William Christian to Col. William Preston, letter dated Camp Union, September 12, 1774, Preston Papers, Draper Manuscripts, 3QQ146 (196-199).

56. Col. William Christian to Col. William Preston, letter dated Camp Union, September 12, 1774, Preston Papers, Draper Manuscripts, 3QQ146 (196-199); Capt. John Floyd to Col. William Preston, letter (fragments) dated September 18, 1774, Draper's Notes, 33S42, 43 (206-208).

57. Maj. James Robertson, Captain Michael Woods, and Maj. James Robertson to Col. William Preston, letters dated Rich Creek, September 15 and 16, 1774, Preston Papers, Draper Manuscripts, 3QQ96 and 3QQ97 (199-201).

58. Col. William Christian to Mrs. Nancy Fleming, letter dated Camp Union, September 18, 1774, Virginia Papers, Draper Manuscripts, 2ZZ10 (205); Sergeant James Newell, Journal, September 23, 1774; Thwaites and Kellogg, *Documentary History*, 327n.

59. Capt. John Floyd to Col. William Preston, letter dated September 28, 1774, Draper's Notes, 33S43, 44 (214-215).

60. Capt. Anthony Bledsoe to Col. William Preston, letter dated Camp Union, October 1, 1774, Preston Papers, Draper Manuscripts, 3QQ108 (222-224).

61. Col. William Christian to Col. William Preston, letter dated Camp Union at the Great Levels, September 7, 1774, Preston Papers, Draper Manuscripts, 3QQ92 (185-189); Col. William Fleming, Journal and Orderly Book, September 23, 1774, Virginia Papers, Draper Manuscripts, 2ZZ71 and 2ZZ72 (284, 327). The site of the camp at Elk River is near present-day Charleston, West Virginia.

62. Col. William Fleming, Journal, September 24-30, 1774; and Col. William Fleming, Orderly Book, September 23-30, 1774, Virginia Papers, Draper Manuscripts, 2ZZ71 (284-285) and 2ZZ72 (327-333). The mouth of the Coal River is near present-day St. Albans, West Virginia.

63. Col. William Fleming to Mrs. Nancy Fleming, letter dated Mouth of Elk River, September 27, 1774, Col. William Fleming, Journal, September 24-30, 1774, and Col. William Fleming, Orderly Book, September 23-30, 1774, Virginia Papers, Draper Manuscripts, 2ZZ5 (212-214), 2ZZ71 (284-285), and 2ZZ72 (327-333).

64. Col. William Fleming, Journal, September 24-30, 1774, and Col. William Fleming, Orderly Book September 23-30, 1774, Virginia Papers, Draper Manuscripts, 2ZZ71 (284-285) and 2ZZ72 (327-333).

65. Col. William Fleming, Journal, September 24-30, 1774, and Col. William Fleming, Orderly Book, September 23-30, 1774, Virginia Papers, Draper Manuscripts, 2ZZ71 (284-285) and 2ZZ72 (327-333); Col. William Fleming to Mrs. Nancy Fleming, letter dated Mouth of Elk River, September 27, 1774, Virginia Papers, Draper Manuscripts, 2ZZ5 (212-214).

CHAPTER 11: A HARD FOUGHT BATTLE

1. Guy Chet, *Conquering the American Wilderness* (Boston: University of Massachusetts Press, 2003), 139.
2. Smith, *Account*, 22, 34.
3. Thomas Hutchins, "A List of Different Nations and Tribes of Indians in the Northern District of North America, with the Number of their Fighting Men &c., In the Year 1778," in *A Topographical Description of Virginia, Pennsylvania, Maryland, and North Carolina; reprinted from the original ed. of 1778*, ed. Frederick Charles Hicks (Cleveland: Burrows Brothers, 1875), 135-137; Thomas Hutchins, "A List of the Number of Fighting Men of the Different Indian Nations," enclosure, Col. George Croghan to Gen. Jeffrey Amherst and Sir William Johnson, letters dated Fort Pitt, October 5, 1762, *Johnson Papers*, 10: 543-546; George Croghan Journal, September 26, 1765, Reuben Gold Thwaites, ed., *Early Western Journals, 1748-1765* (Cleveland: Arthur Clark, 1904), 167-169, and Sir William Johnson, "Enumeration of Indians Within the Northern Department, November 18, 1763," in *Documents Relative to the Colonial History of New York*, ed. Edmund B. O'Callaghan, vol. 7 (Albany: Weed, Parsons, 1856), 135-137; Smyth, *Tour in the United States*, 1:229; Col. William Fleming to Mrs. Nancy Fleming, letter dated Point Pleasant, October 13, 1774, Virginia Papers, Draper Manuscripts, 2ZZ6 (253254).
4. Governor Earl of Dunmore to Earl of Dartmouth, Official Report dated Williamsburg, December 24, 1774, Davies, *Documents*, 8:261; Colonel William Fleming to William Bowyer, undated letter, Virginia Papers, Draper Manuscripts, 2ZZ7 (254-257); Thwaites and Kellogg, *Documentary History*, 256n, 302n; Kevin P. Kelly, "John Montour: The Life of a Cultural Go-Between," *Colonial Williamsburg Interpreter* (Winter 2000/2001): 1-4.
5. Governor Earl of Dunmore to Earl of Dartmouth, Official Report dated Williamsburg, December 24, 1774, Davies, *Documents*, 8:261; Colonel William Fleming to William Bowyer, undated letter, Virginia Papers, Draper Manuscripts, 2ZZ7 (254-257); Thwaites and Kellogg, *Documentary History*, 256n, 302n; Kevin P. Kelly, "John Montour: The Life of a Cultural Go-Between," *Colonial Williamsburg Interpreter* (Winter 2000/2001), 1-4.
6. Valentine Crawford to George Washington, letter dated Fort Fincastle, October 1, 1774, in Butterfield, *Washington-Crawford Letters*, 97-99; Governor Earl of Dunmore to Earl of Dartmouth, Official Report dated Williamsburg, December 24, 1774, Davies, *Documents*, 8:261; Col. William Christian to Col. William Preston, letter dated Camp on Point Pleasant, October 15, 1774, Bullitt Family Papers, Filson Historical Society (260-263); Jacob, *Biographical Sketch*, 72; Thwaites and Kellogg, *Documentary History*, 285n.
7. Governor Earl of Dunmore to Earl of Dartmouth, Official Report dated Williamsburg, December 24, 1774, Davies, *Documents*, 8:261.
8. Col. William Fleming, Journal, and Orderly Book, October 1, 1774, Virginia Papers, Draper Manuscripts, 2ZZ71 and 2ZZ72 (283, 285, 334); Bland, *Treatise*, 143-144; Thomas Hutchins, alias A Lover of His Country, *An Historical Account of the Expedition*

Against the Ohio Indians, in the Year 1764 (Philadelphia: William Bradford, 1765; facsimile repr., Hinesville, GA: Nova Anglia, 2005), 8-9.

9. Col. William Fleming, Orderly Book, October 2, 1774, Virginia Papers, Draper Manuscripts, 2ZZ72 (334-337).

10. Col. William Fleming, Journal, and Orderly Book, October 6, 1774, Virginia Papers, 2ZZ71 and 2ZZ72 (285-286, 339); William Sharp pension application R9429, dated September 4, 1832, Roll 2158; Thwaites and Kellogg, *Documentary History*, 285n.

11. Capt. John Floyd to Col. William Preston, letter dated Mouth of the Great Kanawha (Point Pleasant), October 16, 1774, Draper's Notes, Draper Manuscripts, 33S44-49 (266-269).

12. Capt. Anthony Bledsoe to Colonel William Preston, letter dated October 15, 1774, Preston Papers, Draper Manuscripts, 3QQ122 (260-261).

13. Col. William Fleming, Journal, October 10, 1774, and Orderly Book, October 7, 1774, Virginia Papers, Draper Manuscripts, 2ZZ71 (288) and 2ZZ72 (339-340).

14. Col. William Fleming, Orderly Book, October 8, 1774, Virginia Papers, Draper Manuscripts, 2ZZ72 (340).

15. Col. William Fleming, Orderly Book, October 7, 1774, Virginia Papers, 2ZZ72 (339-340); Thwaites and Kellogg, *Documentary History*, 340n.

16. Col. William Fleming to Col. Adam Stephen, letter dated Point Pleasant, October 8, 1774, Virginia Papers, 2ZZ71 (236-238).

17. Col. William Fleming to Col. Adam Stephen, letter dated Point Pleasant, October 8, 1774, Col. William Fleming, Journal, and Orderly Book, October 6, 1774, Virginia Papers, 2ZZ71 (236-238, 285-286) and 2ZZ72 (339).

18. Col. William Fleming, Journal, and Orderly Book, October 8, 1774, Virginia Papers, Draper Manuscripts, 2ZZ71 and 2ZZ72 (285-286, 340); Stuart, "Narrative," 675; William Sharp pension application R9429, dated September 4, 1832, Roll 2158; Governor Earl of Dunmore to Earl of Dartmouth, Official Report dated Williamsburg, December 24, 1774, Davies, *Documents*, 8:261.

19. Capt. William Ingles to Col. William Preston, letter dated Point Pleasant, October 14, 1774, Preston Papers, Draper Manuscripts, 3QQ121 (257-259); Col. William Fleming, Orderly Book, October 8 and 9, 1774, Virginia Papers 2ZZ72 (340-341).

20. Stuart, "Narrative," 675-676.

21. Capt. William Ingles to Col. William Preston, letter dated Point Pleasant, October 14, 1774, Preston Papers, Draper Manuscripts, 3QQ121 (257-259).

22. Ibid.

23. Ibid.; Col. William Christian to Col. William Preston, letter dated Camp at Point Pleasant, October 15, 1774, Bullitt Family Papers, Filson Historical Society (265); Col. William Preston to Patrick Henry, letter dated Springfield, October 31, 1774, Preston Papers, Draper Manuscripts, 3QQ128 (292).

24. Smith, *Account*, 161-162, 169-170.

25. Capt. William Ingles to Col. William Preston, letter dated Point Pleasant, October 14, 1774, Preston Papers, Draper Manuscripts, 3QQ121 (257-259); Col. William Fleming to William Bowyer, undated letter, Virginia Papers, Draper Manuscripts, 2ZZ7 (254-257); Col. William Christian to Col. William Preston, letter dated Camp at Point Pleasant, October 15, 1774, Bullitt Family Papers, Filson Historical Society (264).

26. Smith, *Account*, 161-164, 169-170.

27. Capt. William Ingles to Col. William Preston, letter dated Point Pleasant, October 14, 1774, Preston Papers, Draper Manuscripts, 3QQ121 (257-259); Col. William Fleming, Journal, October 10, 1774, Virginia Papers, Draper Manuscripts, 2ZZ71 (286-287),

28. Thwaites and Kellogg, *Documentary History*, 271-272n; Withers, *Chronicles of Border Warfare*, 168n.

29. Smith, *Account*, 161-162.

30. Lieut. Isaac Shelby to John Shelby, letter dated Camp Opposite the Great Kanawha (Point Pleasant), October 16, 1774, Virginia Papers, Draper Manuscripts, 7ZZ2 (269-277); Col. William Fleming, Orderly Book, October 10, 1774, Virginia Papers, Draper Manuscripts, 2ZZ72 (341); Stuart, "Narrative," 676; Smith, *Universal Military Dictionary*, DRU-DUT (79).

31. Bland, *Treatise*, 146.

32. Lieut. Isaac Shelby to John Shelby, letter dated Camp Opposite the Great Kanawha (Point Pleasant), October 16, 1774, Virginia Papers, Draper Manuscripts, 7ZZ2 (269-277); Col. William Fleming, Journal, and Orderly Book, October 10, 1774, Virginia Papers, Draper Manuscripts, 2ZZ71 (286-287) and 2ZZ72 (341).

33. Lieut. Isaac Shelby to John Shelby, letter dated Camp Opposite the Great Kanawha (Point Pleasant), October 16, 1774, Virginia Papers, Draper Manuscripts, 7ZZ2 (269-277); Col. William Fleming, Journal, and Orderly Book, October 10, 1774, Virginia Papers, Draper Manuscripts, 2ZZ71 (286-288) and 2ZZ72 (341-344).

34. Stuart, "Narrative," 676.

35. Col. William Fleming, Journal, and Orderly Book, October 10, 1774, Virginia Papers, Draper Manuscripts, 2ZZ71 (286-289) and 2ZZ72 (341-344).

36. Col. William Fleming, Journal, October 10, 1774, Virginia Papers, Draper Manuscripts, 2ZZ71 (286-287).

37. Lieut. Isaac Shelby to John Shelby, letter dated Camp Opposite the Great Kanawha (Point Pleasant), October 16, 1774, Virginia Papers 7ZZ2 (269-277); Col. William Fleming, Orderly Book, October 10, 1774, Virginia Papers, Draper Manuscripts, 2ZZ72 (341-344).

38. Capt. William Ingles to Col. William Preston, letter dated Point Pleasant, October 14, 1774, Preston Papers, 3QQ121 (257-259); Lieut. Isaac Shelby to John Shelby, letter dated Camp Opposite the Great Kanawha (Point Pleasant), October 16, 1774, Virginia Papers, Draper Manuscripts, 7ZZ2 (269-277).

39. Capt. William Ingles to Col. William Preston, letter dated Point Pleasant, October 14, 1774, Preston Papers, Draper Manuscripts, 3QQ121 (257-259); Col. William Fleming, Orderly Book, October 10, 1774, Virginia Papers, Draper Manuscripts, 2ZZ72 (341-344).

40. Lieut. Isaac Shelby to John Shelby, letter dated Camp Opposite the Great Kanawha (Point Pleasant), October 16, 1774, Virginia Papers, Draper Manuscripts, 7ZZ2 (269-277); Col. William Fleming, Orderly Book, October 10, 1774, Virginia Papers, Draper Manuscripts, 2ZZ72 (341-344).

41. Col. William Fleming, Orderly Book, October 10, 1774, Virginia Papers, Draper Manuscripts, 2ZZ72 (341-343).

42. Lieut. Isaac Shelby to John Shelby, letter dated Camp Opposite the Great Kanawha (Point Pleasant), October 16, 1774, Virginia Papers, Draper Manuscripts, 7ZZ2 (269-277); Col. William Fleming, Orderly Book, October 10, 1774, Virginia Papers, Draper Manuscripts, 2ZZ72 (341-343).

43. Lieut. Isaac Shelby to John Shelby, letter dated Camp Opposite the Great Kanawha (Point Pleasant), October 16, 1774, Virginia Papers, Draper Manuscripts, 7ZZ2 (269-277); Col. William Christian to Col. William Preston, letter dated Camp at Point Pleasant, October 15, 1774, Bullitt Family Papers, Filson Historical Society (265); *Pennsylvania Gazette*, November 16, 1774, 18th Century American Newspapers, V1294, Library of Congress.

44. Lieut. Isaac Shelby to John Shelby, letter dated Camp Opposite the Great Kanawha (Point Pleasant), October 16, 1774, Virginia Papers, Draper Manuscripts, 7ZZ2 (269-277); Col. William Fleming, Orderly Book, October 10, 1774, Virginia Papers, Draper Manuscripts, 2ZZ72 (341-343).

45. Col. William Fleming, Orderly Book, October 10, 1774, Virginia Papers, Draper Manuscripts, 2ZZ72 (341-343); Bland, *Treatise*, 158-159.

46. Col. William Fleming, Orderly Book, October 10, 1774, and Lieut. Isaac Shelby to John Shelby, letter dated Camp Opposite the Great Kanawha (Point Pleasant), October 16, 1774, Virginia Papers, Draper Manuscripts, 2ZZ72 (341-344) and 7ZZ2 (269-277).

47. Capt. William Ingles to Col. William Preston, letter dated Point Pleasant, October 14, 1774, Preston Papers, Draper Manuscripts, 3QQ121 (257-259).

48. Col. William Fleming, Journal, and Orderly Book, October 10, 1774, Virginia Papers, Draper Manuscripts, and 2ZZ71 (286-287, 341-343).

49. Lieut. Isaac Shelby to John Shelby, letter dated Camp Opposite the Great Kanawha (Point Pleasant), October 16, 1774, Virginia Papers, Draper Manuscripts, 7ZZ2 (269-277); Col. William Fleming, Orderly Book, October 10, 1774, Virginia Papers, Draper Manuscripts, 2ZZ72 (341-343).

50. Col. William Fleming, Journal, and Orderly Book, October 10, 1774, and Col. William Fleming to Mrs. Nancy Fleming, letter dated Point Pleasant, October 13, 1774, Virginia Papers, Draper Manuscripts, 2ZZ71, 2ZZ72 (286-287, 341-343), 2ZZ72, and 2ZZ6 (253-254).

51. Col. William Christian to Col. William Preston, letter dated October 15, 1774, Handwritten MSS, Bullitt Family Papers, Filson Historical Society (261-266); John W. Howe pension application W8938, dated June 3, 1833, Roll 1345; James Brown pension application S15347 dated March 25, 1834, Roll 367; Capt. John Floyd to Col. William Preston, letter dated Mouth of the Great Kanawha (Point Pleasant), October 16, 1774, Draper's Notes, Draper Manuscripts, 33S44-49 (266-269); Col. William Fleming, Journal, October 10, 1774, Virginia Papers, Draper Manuscripts, 2ZZ71 (288); Joseph Duncan pension application S1809, dated September 14, 1832, Roll 864.

52. Col. William Christian to Col. William Preston, letter dated October 15, 1774, Bullitt Family Papers, Filson Historical Society (262).

53. Col. William Fleming, Journal, and Orderly Book, October 10, 1774, and Col. William Fleming to Mrs. Nancy Fleming, letter dated Point Pleasant, October 13, 1774, Virginia Papers, Draper Manuscripts, 2ZZ71, 2ZZ72 (286-287, 341-343), 2ZZ72, and 2ZZ6 (253-254).

54. Capt. William Ingles to Col. William Preston, letter dated Point Pleasant, October 14, 1774, Preston Papers, Draper Manuscripts, 3QQ121 (257-259).

55. Col. William Fleming, Journal, October, and Orderly Book, October 11-12, 1774, Virginia Papers, Draper Manuscripts, 2ZZ71 and 2ZZ72 (288, 292, 347).

56. Col. William Fleming, Journal, and Orderly Book, October 11, 1774, Virginia Papers, Draper Manuscripts, 2ZZ71 and 2ZZ72 (288, 345-346).

57. Ibid.

58. Col. William Fleming, Journal, October, and Orderly Book, October 11-12, 1774, Virginia Papers, Draper Manuscripts, 2ZZ71 and 2ZZ72 (288, 292, 347).

CHAPTER 12: THE TREATY OF CAMP CHARLOTTE AND BEYOND

1. Governor Earl of Dunmore to Earl of Dartmouth, Official Report dated Williamsburg, December 24, 1774, Davies, *Documents*, 8:261; Col. William Fleming, Journal, and Orderly Book, October 13, 1774, Virginia Papers, Draper Manuscripts 2ZZ71, 2ZZ72 (288, 348). Thwaites and Kellogg, *Documentary History*, 307n.

2. Thwaites and Kellogg, *Documentary History*, 302n.

3. Col. William Preston to Patrick Henry, letter dated October 31, 1774, Preston Papers, Draper Manuscripts, 3QQ128 (292); Thwaites and Kellogg, *Documentary History*, 302n. The site of this Chillicothe is near present-day Circleville, Ohio.

4. Governor Earl of Dunmore to Earl of Dartmouth, Official Report dated Williamsburg, December 24, 1774, Davies, *Documents*, 8:262; Draper's Notes, Draper Manuscripts, 3S517 (302n); Thwaites and Kellogg, *Documentary History*, 301n.

5. Governor Earl of Dunmore to Earl of Dartmouth, Official Report dated Williamsburg, December 24, 1774, Davies, *Documents*, 8:261; Col. William Fleming, Journal, and Orderly Book, October 13, 1774, Virginia Papers, Draper Manuscripts, 2ZZ71 and 2ZZ72 (288, 348).

6. John Gibson, deposition sworn to Judge Jeremiah Baker, April 4, 1800, at Pittsburgh, in Thomas Jefferson, *Notes on the State of Virginia*, ed. William Peden (Chapel Hill: University of North Carolina Press, 1982), 234; Col. William Christian to Col. William Preston, letter dated Smithfield, November 8, 1774, Preston Papers, Draper Manuscripts, 3QQ130 (301-307).

7. Jefferson, *Notes on the State of Virginia*, ed. Peden, 63.

8. Col. William Christian to Col. William Preston, letter dated Smithfield, November 8, 1774, Preston Papers, Draper Manuscripts, 3QQ130 (301-307); Earl of Dunmore to Shawnee Nation of Indians, message, undated, Camp Charlotte, Chalmers Collection, Mss 507, catalog number b11822957, i.d. 2098264.

9. Col. William Fleming, Journal, and Orderly Book, October 12-14, 1774, Virginia Papers, Draper Manuscripts, 2ZZ71, 2ZZ72 (288-289, 347-349).

10. Col. William Fleming, Journal, and Orderly Book, October 13, 1774, Virginia Papers, Draper Manuscripts, 2ZZ71 and 2ZZ72 (288, 348).

11. Ibid.

12. Col. William Fleming, Journal, October 13-16, 1774, Virginia Papers, Draper Manuscripts, 2ZZ71 (288).

13. Col. William Fleming, Orderly Book, October 15-18, 1774, Virginia Papers, Draper Manuscripts, 2ZZ72 (349-350).

14. Col. William Fleming, Orderly Book, October 17-18, 1774, Virginia Papers, Draper Manuscripts, 2ZZ72 (352-353); Ens. James Newell, Orderly Book, October 27, 1774, Virginia Papers, Draper Manuscripts, ZZ1-12 (367); Joseph Handly pension application S5581, dated September 4, 1832, Roll 1368.

15. Lt. James Newell, Orderly Book, and Journal, dated Camp on Point Pleasant, October 17, 1774, Virginia Papers, Draper Manuscripts, 11ZZ1 (361-362).

16. Governor Earl of Dunmore to Earl of Dartmouth, Official Report dated Williamsburg, December 24, 1774, Davies, *Documents*, 8:261; Earl of Dunmore to Shawnees and Mingo Indians, speech, undated, Camp Charlotte, Chalmers Collection, Mss 50, catalog i.d. b11822957, i.d. 2098263.

17. Ibid.

18. Cornstalk to Big Knife, speech, undated, Camp Charlotte, Chalmers Collection, Mss 507, catalog b11822957, i.d. 2098268, NYPL.

19. Col. William Fleming, Journal, and Orderly Book, October 28-29, 1774, Virginia Papers, Draper Manuscripts, 2ZZ71 and 2ZZ72 (289-291, 355-356); Col. William Christian to Col. William Preston, letter dated Smithfield, November 8, 1774, Preston Papers, Draper Manuscripts, 3QQ130 (301-307).

20. Maj. William Crawford to George Washington, letter dated Stewart's Crossing, November 14, 1774, in Butterfield, *Washington-Crawford Letters*, 54-57.

21. John W. Howe pension application W8938, dated June 3, 1833, Roll 1345.

22. Maj. William Crawford to George Washington, letter dated Stewart's Crossing, November 14, 1774, in Butterfield, *Washington-Crawford Letters*, 54-57.

23. Leith, *Short Biography*, 17-18, 19. A "match-coat" was basically a wool blanket with decorative gold trim to give it a distinguished appearance.

24. Force, *American Archives*, 1:962-963.

25. Nicholas Cresswell, *The Journal of Nicholas Cresswell, 1774-1777*, ed. Lincoln MacVeagh (New York: Dial Press, 1924), 49.

26. Force, *American Archives*, 1:1019, 1020.

27. Thomas Cresap to Earl of Dunmore, letter not dated, Chalmers Collection, NYPL.

28. Henning, *Statutes*, 9:61-65.

29. Virgil A. Lewis, *History of the Battle of Point Pleasant* (Charleston: West Virginia Department of Archives and History, 1909; repr. Westminster, MD: Willow Bend Books, 1999), 74, 128.

30. Henning, *Statutes*, 9:61-65.

31. Ibid., 9:63-64.

Bibliography

Primary Sources

GOVERNMENTAL ARCHIVES, STATE PAPERS, AND PUBLISHED DOCUMENTARY SOURCES

GREAT BRITAIN

Burke, Edmund, ed. *Annual Register*, vol. 6 (1763), sec. 1. London: Robert Dodsley, 1763.

Davies, K. G. ed. *Documents of the American Revolution 1770-1783 (Colonial Office Series)*. 21 vols. Shannon: Irish University Press, 1972-1981.

UNITED STATES

Force, Peter, ed. *American Archives: Consisting of a Collection of Authentic Records, State Papers, Debates, and Letters and Other Notices of Publick Affairs, the Whole Forming a Documentary History of the Origin and Progress of the North American Colonies*. 9 vols. Washington, DC: M. St. Clair Clarke and Peter Force, 1837-1853.

Ratified Indian Treaties 1722-1800. Record Group 75, Microfilm Publication, M668, Roll 2. National Archives and Records Administration, Washington, DC.

Records of the Department of Veterans Affairs, Record Group 15, Revolutionary War Pension and Bounty-Land Warrant Application Files, Microfilm Publication M805, National Archives and Records Administration, Washington, DC.

NEW YORK

O'Callaghan, Edmund B., ed. *Documents Relative to the Colonial History of New York.* Vol. 8. Albany: Weed, Parsons, 1857.

PENNSYLVANIA

Colonial Records of Pennsylvania. *Minutes of the Provincial Council of Pennsylvania, from the Organization to the Termination of the Proprietary Government,* vol. 8, *Containing the Proceedings of Council from January 18th, 1757, to 4th of October, 1762, Both Dates Included.* Edited by Samuel Hazard. Harrisburg: Theodore Fenn, 1852.

————. *Minutes of the Provincial Council of Pennsylvania, from the Organization to the Termination of the Proprietary Government,* vol. 10, *Containing the Proceedings of Council from October 18th, 1771, to 27th of September, 1775, Both Dates Included: Together with Minutes of the Council of Safety from June 30th, 1775 to November 12th, 1776, Both Dates Included.* Edited by Samuel Hazard. Harrisburg: Theodore Fenn, 1852. Pennsylvania Archives. Ser. 1, vol. 4, Commencing 1760 (to 1775). Edited by Samuel Hazard. Philadelphia: Joseph Severns, 1853.

————. Ser. 4, vol. 3, Papers of the Governors, 1759-1785. Edited by George Edward Reed. Harrisburg: J. Severns, 1900.

VIRGINIA

Hall, Wilmer L. ed., *Executive Journals of the Council of Colonial Virginia.* Vol. 5 (1739-1754). Richmond: Virginia State Library, 1945.

Hillman, Benjamin J., ed., *Executive Journals of the Council of Colonial Virginia,* Vol. 6 (June 20, 1754-May 3, 1775). Richmond: Virginia State Library, 1966.

Hening, William Waller, ed. *Statutes at Large: Being a Collection of All the Laws of Virginia, from the First Session of the Legislature in the Year 1619.* 13 vols. Richmond, VA: J. and C. Cochran, 1819-1823. Facsimile reprint on CD-ROM. Westminster, MD: Heritage Books, 2003.

McIlwaine, Henry Reed, ed. *Journals of the Council of the State of Virginia.* Vol. 1, July 12, 1776-October 2, 1777. Richmond: Virginia State Library, 1931.

————. *Legislative Journals of the Council of Colonial Virginia.* Vol. 3, 1754-1775. Richmond: Colonial Press, 1919.

McIlwaine, Henry Reed, and John Pendleton Kennedy, eds. *Journals of the House of Burgesses of Virginia, 1619-1776.* 13 vols. Richmond: State of Virginia, 1905-15. Facsimile reprint on CD-ROM. Westminster, MD: Heritage Books, 2003.

McIlwaine, Henry Reed, and Wilmer L. Hall, eds. *Executive Journals of the Council of Colonial Virginia*. 6 vols. Richmond: State of Virginia, 1930-1966.

Proceedings of the Convention of the Delegates in the Colony of Virginia, Held at Richmond. Williamsburg, VA: Alexander Purdie, 1776. Reprint, Richmond: Ritchie, Trueheart and Du-Val Printers, 1816.

Virginia (Colony). *Colonial Papers*, 1630-1778. Accession 36138. Microfilm Publication Rolls 609-612. State Records Collection, Library of Virginia.

DOCUMENT COLLECTIONS, PERSONAL PAPERS, AND CORRESPONDENCE

UNPUBLISHED PAPERS AND MANUSCRIPT COLLECTIONS

Bullitt Family Papers. Oxmoor Collection. Filson Historical Society, Louisville, KY.

Connolly, John. "Journal of My Proceedings & etc., Commencing from the late Disturbances with the Cherokees upon the Ohio." Handwritten manuscript. George Chalmers Papers Relating to Indian Affairs, 1750-1775. Special Collections, Mss. Film. 637. New York Public Library, New York.

Croghan, George. Papers, 1744-1826. Cadwalader Collection. Ser. 4, box 5. Historical Society of Pennsylvania, Philadelphia.

Draper, Lyman C. Draper Collection of Manuscripts. Wisconsin Historical Society, Madison. Microfilm collection copies at David Library of the American Revolution, Washington Crossing, PA, and John. D. Rockefeller Jr. Library, Colonial Williamsburg Foundation, Williamsburg, VA.

Dunmore Family Papers 1 (1650-1899) and 2 (1768-1804), relating to John Murray, 4th Earl of Dunmore, last royal governor of Virginia, MSS, 65 D92 and 74s D92, respectively. Early American Historical Research Center, Earl Gregg Swem Library. College of William and Mary, Williamsburg, VA.

Earl of Dunmore to the Surveyor of Fincastle County [William Preston], Certificate of Military Land Claim for Alexander Waugh, dated Williamsburg, December 17, 1773. Handwritten MSS. Catalog no. 1969.51.019. Collection, History Museum of Western Virginia, Roanoke, Virginia.

Gage, Thomas. Papers, 1754-1783. William Clements Library, University of Michigan, Ann Arbor.

Gates, Horatio. Papers, 1760-1804. Microfilm. Manuscripts and Archives Division, Special Collections, New York Public Library, New York. Microfilm Collection M2135, reel 2, 1769-1776, copy in John D. Rockefeller Jr. Library, Colonial Williamsburg Foundation, Williamsburg, VA.

Jefferson, Thomas. Papers, Ser. 1, General Correspondence, 1751-1827. US Library of Congress, Washington, DC.

McKee, Alexander. "Extract from My Journal from the 1st May 1774 containing Indian Transactions &ca." Handwritten MS. George Chalmers Papers Relating to Indian Affairs, 1750-1775. Special Collections, MSS Film 637. New York Public Library. New York.

PUBLISHED PERSONAL PAPERS, MEMOIRS, AND DOCUMENT COLLECTIONS

Abbot, W. W., ed. *The Papers of George Washington, Colonial Series.* 10 vols. Charlottesville: University Press of Virginia, 1983-1995.

Barton, Thomas. "Journal of an Expedition to the Ohio, commanded by His Excellency Brigadier General Forbes; in the Year of our Lord 1758." In William A. Hunter, ed., "Thomas Barton and the Forbes Expedition." *Pennsylvania Magazine of History and Biography* 95, no. 4 (October 1971): 431-483.

Brock, R. A., ed. *The Official Records of Robert Dinwiddie, Lieutenant-Governor of the Colony of Virginia, 1751-1758.* 2 vols. Richmond: Virginia Historical Society, 1884.

Butterfield, Consul W., ed. *The Washington-Crawford Letters, Being the Correspondence between George Washington and William Crawford, from 1767 to 1781, Concerning Western Lands.* Cincinnati: Robert Clarke, 1877. Rare book collection, David Library of the American Revolution, Washington Crossing, PA.

Byars, William Vincent, ed. *B. and M. Gratz, Merchants in Philadelphia, 1754-1798: Papers of Interest to Their Posterity and the Posterity of Their Associates.* Jefferson City, MO: Hugh Stephens Printing, 1916.

Clark, George Rogers. *George Rogers Clark Papers, 1771-81.* Edited by James Alton James. Springfield: Illinois State Historical Library, 1912.

Connolly, John. "A Narrative of the Transactions, Imprisonment, and Sufferings of John Connolly, an American Loyalist and Lieutenant Colonel in His Majesty's Service." *Pennsylvania Magazine of History and Biography* 12, no. 2 (1888): 310-324; no. 4 (1888): 407-420; and vol. 13, no. 1 (1889): 61-70; no. 2 (1889): 153-167; no. 3 (1889): 281-291.

Cresswell, Nicholas. *The Journal of Nicholas Cresswell, 1774-1777.* Edited by Lincoln MacVeagh. New York: Dial Press, 1924.

Doddridge, Joseph. *Notes on the Settlement and Indian Wars of the Western Parts of Virginia and Pennsylvania from 1763 to 1783, Inclusive.* Wellsburgh, VA: Office of the Gazette, 1824. Reprint, Pittsburgh: J. S. Ritenour and W. T. Lindsey, 1912.

Franklin, Benjamin. *The Papers of Benjamin Franklin.* 34 vols. Edited by Leonard W. Larabee, W. B. Wilcox, Claude Lopez, and Barbara B. Oberg. New Haven, CT: Yale University Press, 1959-1998.

Gage, Thomas. *The Correspondence of General Thomas Gage with the Secretaries of State and with the War Office and the Treasury, 1763-1775.* 2 vols. Edited by Clarence Edwin Carter. New Haven, CT: Yale University Press, 1931-33. Reprint, Hamden, CT: Archon Books, 1969.

Hewlett, W. O., ed. *Manuscripts of the Earl of Dartmouth.* Vol. 2, London: Her Majesty's Stationary Office, 1887.

Hutchins, Thomas. *A Topographical Description of Virginia, Pennsylvania, Maryland, and North Carolina; reprinted from the original ed. of 1778.* Edited by Frederick Charles Hicks. Cleveland: Burrows Brothers, 1875.

Jefferson, Thomas. *The Papers of Thomas Jefferson.* 21 vols. Edited by Julian P. Boyd and L. H. Butterfield. Princeton, NJ: Princeton Press, 1950-1951.

Jemison, Mary. *A Narrative of the Life of Mrs. Mary Jemison.* Edited by James E. Seaver. Canandaigua, NY: J. D. Bemis, 1824. Reprint edited by June Namias. Norman: University of Oklahoma Press, 1992.

Johnson, William. *The Papers of Sir William Johnson.* 8 vols. Edited by Milton W. Hamilton. Albany: University of the State of New York, 1962, and the Division of Archives and History, 1921-1933.

Jones, Reverend David. *A Journal of Two Visits Made to Some Nations of Indians on the West Side of the Ohio River, in the Years 1772 and 1773.* Burlington, VT: Isaac Collins printer, 1774. Reprint, New York: Arno Press, 1971.

Lee, Richard Henry. *Memoir of the Life of Richard Henry Lee, and His Correspondence.* 2 vols. Edited by Richard H. Lee. Philadelphia: M. C. Carey and I. Lea, 1825.

Nelson, William. *The Correspondence of William Nelson as Acting Governor of Virginia, 1770-1771.* Edited by John C. Van Horne. Charlottesville: University Press of Virginia, 1975.

Newell, James. "Journal and Orderly Book of Ensign James Newell." *Virginia Magazine of History and Biography* 11 (1904): 242-253.

Preston, William. *The Preston and Virginia Papers of the Draper Collection of Manuscripts.* Edited by Lyman Draper. Madison: State Historical Society of Wisconsin, 1915.

Prevost, Augustine. "Turmoil at Pittsburgh: Diary of Augustine Prevost, 1774." Edited by Nicholas B. Wainwright. *Pennsylvania Magazine of History and Biography* 85, no. 2 (April 1961): 111-162.

Robertson, James Rood, ed. *Petitions of the Early Inhabitants of Kentucky to the General Assembly of Virginia, 1769-1792.* Louisville: Filson Club Publication no. 27, 1914. Reprint, Baltimore: Genealogical Publishing, 1998.

Smith, James. *An Account of the Remarkable Occurrences in the Life of Col. James Smith, During His Captivity with the Indians, in the Years 1755, '56, '57, '58, & '59, Written by Himself.* Lexington, KY: John Bradford, 1799. Reprinted as *Scoouwa: James Smith's Indian Captivity Narrative.* Edited by William M. Darlington and John J. Barsotti. Columbus: Ohio Historical Society, 1996.

Smyth, John Ferdinand Dalziel. *A Tour in the United States of America; containing an account of the present situation of that country; the population, agriculture, commerce, customs, and manners of the inhabitants . . . With a description of the Indian nations, the general face of the country, mountains, forests, rivers, and the most beautiful grand, and picturesque views throughout that vast continent. Likewise improvements in husbandry that may be adopted with great advantage in Europe.* 2 vols. Dublin: G. Perrin, 1784. Special Collections, John D. Rockefeller Jr. Library, Colonial Williamsburg Foundation, Williamsburg, VA.

Stuart, John. "Narrative by Captain John Stuart of General Andrew Lewis' Expedition against the Indians in the year 1774, and of the Battle of Pleasant Point, Virginia." *Magazine of American History* 1, no. 1 (November–December 1877): 668-679, 740-750.

Wolfe, James. *General Wolfe's Instructions to Young Officers.* 2nd ed. London: J. Millan, 1780. Facsimile reprint, Cranbury, NJ: Scholar's Bookshelf, 2005.

PUBLISHED MISCELLANEOUS DOCUMENT COLLECTIONS

Bockstruck, Lloyd DeWitt. *Virginia's Colonial Soldiers.* Baltimore: Genealogical Publishing, 1988.

Crozier, William Armstrong, ed. *Virginia Colonial Militia, 1651-1776.* New York: Genealogical Association, 1905. Reprint, Baltimore: Southern Book Co., 1954. Reprint, Baltimore: Genealogical Publishing, 1965.

Eckenrode, Hamilton J. *List of the Colonial Soldiers of Virginia: Special Report of the Department of Archives and History for 1913.* Richmond: Virginia State Library, 1917. Reprints, Baltimore: Genealogical Publishing, 1961 and 1980.

King George III Instructions to John Murray, Earl of Dunmore, commission as governor of Virginia, dated the Court of St. James, February 7, 1771, 630-666, and King George III Orders and Instructions to John Murray, Earl of Dunmore, governor of Virginia, dated Court of St.

James, February 7, 1771, 667-691. Aspinwall Papers. *Massachusetts Historical Collection.* 4th ser., vol. 10. Boston: Massachusetts Historical Society, 1871.

Leith, John. *A Short Biography of John Leith: With a Brief Account of His Life among the Indians; A Reprint with Illustrative Notes.* Edited by W. Consul Butterfield, Cincinnati: Robert Clarke, 1883. Reprinted from Ewel Jeffries. *A Short Biography of John Leeth, Giving a Brief Account of His Travels and Sufferings among the Indians for Eighteen Years, from His Own Relation.* Lancaster, OH: Gazette, 1831. Special Collections, Society of the Cincinnati Library, Washington, DC.

Metcalf, Samuel, ed. *A Collection of the Most Interesting Narratives of Indian Warfare in the West Containing an Account of the Adventures of Daniel Boone.* Lexington, KY: William G. Hunt Printers, 1821. Special Collections, Society of the Cincinnati Library, Washington, DC.

Skidmore, Warren, and Donna Kaminsky, eds. *Lord Dunmore's Little War of 1774: His Captains and Their Men Who Opened Up Kentucky & the West to American Settlement.* Bowie, MD: Heritage Books, 2002.

Thwaites, Reuben Gold, ed. *Early Western Journals, 1748-1765.* Cleveland: Arthur Clark, 1904.

Thwaites, Reuben G., and Louise P. Kellogg, eds. *Documentary History of Dunmore's War 1774.* Madison: Wisconsin Historical Society, 1905. Reprint, Bowie, MD: Heritage Books, 1989.

CONTEMPORARY PUBLICATIONS AND BROADSIDES
(ORIGINAL AND REPRINTED)

NEWSPAPERS, BROADSIDES, AND OTHER PUBLIC DOCUMENT COLLECTIONS

American Weekly Mercury (Philadelphia), August 19-26, 1736. Newspapers and Circulating Periodicals Collection, Eighteenth Century American Newspapers, vol. 1073, box 24, fol. 2. US Library of Congress, Washington, DC.

Early American Imprints. 1st ser., 1639-1800. Also available on electronic database through Readex. http://infoweb.newsbank.com.

New York Weekly Journal, January 17, 1743. Newspapers and Circulating Periodicals Collection, Eighteenth Century American Newspapers, no. 458, box 23, fol. 4, v-940 and Microfilm Roll 2904. US Library of Congress, Washington, DC.

Pennsylvania Gazette. Special Collections, Library Company of Philadelphia, Philadelphia, Pennsylvania.

Printed Ephemera Collection, portfolio 178, folder 12c. Library of Congress. Also at *An American Time Capsule: Three Centuries of Broadsides and Other Printed Ephemera.* http://memory.loc.gov/ammem/rbpehtml/pe-home.html.

Virginia Gazette. Special Collections, John D. Rockefeller Jr. Library, Colonial Williamsburg Foundation, Williamsburg, VA.

Virginia Gazette #1. Printed in Williamsburg by Alexander Purdie and John Dixon from 1766 to 1775, and John Dixon and William Hunter from 1775 to 1778.

Virginia Gazette #2. Printed in Williamsburg by William Rind from 1766 to 1773, Clementina Rind from 1773 to1774, and John Pinckney from 1774 to 1776.

Virginia Gazette #3. Printed in Williamsburg by Alexander Purdie from 1775 to 1779.

CONTEMPORARY PUBLICATIONS

D'Urfey, Thomas. *Wit and Mirth, or Pills to Purge the Melancholy.* Vol. 5. London: J. Tonson, 1719-20. Facsimile reprint, New York: Folklore Library Publishers, 1876. Reprint, New York: Noble Offset Printers, 1959.

Farquhar, George. *The Recruiting Officer.* London: 1706. Reprint, S. Trussler, ed. London: Nick Hern Books, 1997.

Heckewelder, John G. E. *History, Manners and Customs of the Indian Nations Who Once Inhabited Pennsylvania and the Neighboring States.* Philadelphia: Abraham Small, 1819. Reprint, Philadelphia: Historical Society of Pennsylvania, 1876. Reprint, Westminster, MD: Heritage Books, 2007.

Hutchins, Thomas, alias A Lover of His Country. *An Historical Account of the Expedition Against the Ohio Indians, in the Year 1764.* Philadelphia: William Bradford, 1765. Facsimile reprint, Hinesville, GA: Nova Anglia, 2005.

Hyde, Lord Edward, first Earl of Clarendon. *The History of the Rebellion and Civil Wars in England.* 2 vols. London: 1696. Reprint, Oxford: University Press, 1843.

Jefferson, Thomas. *Notes on the State of Virginia.* France: 1785. Revised 1800. Edited with an introduction and notes by William Peden. Chapel Hill: University of North Carolina Press, 1954. Reprint, Chapel Hill: University of North Carolina Press, 1982.

———. *Notes on the State of Virginia.* France: 1785. Revised 1800. Edited with an introduction and notes by Frank Shuffelton. New York: Penguin Books, 1999.

Johnson, Samuel. *A Dictionary of the English Language, in which the Words are deduced from their Originals; Explained in their Different Meanings and Authorized by the Names of the Writers in whose Works they are found.* 2 vols. London: 1766. Special Collections, Harvard University Library, Cambridge, MA.
————. *A Dictionary of the English Language . . . .* 5th ed. London: Printed for W. Strahan, et al., 1773. Society of the Cincinnati Library, Washington, DC.
Locke, John. *Two Treatises of Government.* London: Black Swan in Pater Noster Row, 1698. Reprint, edited with an introduction and notes by Peter Laslett. Cambridge: Cambridge University Press, 2009.
Smith, George. *An Universal Military Dictionary: A Copious Explanation of the Technical Terms &c. Used in the Equipment, Machinery, Movements and Military Operations of an Army,* London: J. Millan, 1779. Facsimile reprints, Ottawa, ON: Museum Restoration Services, 1969, and London: Gale Cenage Learning—Eighteenth Century Collectibles Online, 2010.
Thomas, Sir George, ed. *The Treaty Held with the Indians of the Six Nations at Philadelphia, in July 1742, To which is Prefix'd an Account of the first Confederacy of the Six Nations, their present Tributaries, Dependents, and Allies.* Philadelphia: B. Franklin, 1743. Reprint, London: T. Sowle Rayton and Luke Hinde, 1743. Special Collections, Pennsylvania Archives.
Webb, George. *The office and authority of a justice of peace. And also the duty of sheriffs, coroners, church-wardens, surveiors of highways, constables, and officers of militia. Together with precedents of warrants, judgments, executions, and other legal process, issuable by magistrates within their respective jurisdictions, in cases civil or criminal. And the method of judicial proceedings, before justices of peace, in matters within their cognisance out of sessions. Collected from the common and statute laws of England, and acts of Assembly, now in force; and adapted to the constitution and practice of Virginia.* Williamsburg, VA: William Parks, 1736. Special Collections, John D. Rockefeller Jr. Library, Colonial Williamsburg Foundation, Williamsburg, VA.

CONTEMPORARY MILITARY MANUALS AND TREATISES

Bland, Humphrey. *A Treatise of Military Discipline, in which is laid down and Explained the Duty of the Officer and Soldier, Thro' the Several Branches of the Service.* London: S. Buckley, 1727. 6th ed., 1759. 9th ed., *Corrected and Altered to the Present Practice of the Army,* 1762. Special Collections, Society of the Cincinnati Library, Washington, DC.

———. *A Treatise of Military Discipline. . . .* 9th ed. London: W. Johnson, B. Law, and T. Caslon, 1762. Reprint, London: Military and Naval Press, 2010.

The Manual Exercise as Ordered by His Majesty in 1764 Including the Fundamentals of Marching and Maneuvering. London: J. Millan, 1770. Special Collections, Society of the Cincinnati Library, Washington, DC.

The Manual Exercise as Ordered by His Majesty in One thousand seven-hundred sixty-four, Together with Plans and Explanations of the Method Generally Practiced at Reviews and Field Days, &c. Newburyport: E. Lunt and H. W. Tinges, 1774. Special Collections, Society of the Cincinnati Library, Washington, DC.

The Militia-Man: Containing Necessary Rules for Both Officer and Soldier, with an Explanation of the Manual Exercise of the Foot. London, circa 1740. Facsimile reprint, Schenectady, NY: US Historical Research Service, 1995.

A Plan of Discipline of the Militia of the County of Norfolk, for 1759. London: J. Millan, 1768. Facsimile reprint, Ottawa: Museum Restoration Services, 2004.

Secondary Sources

Alden, John Richard. *John Stuart and the Southern Colonial Frontier: A Study of Indian Relations, War, Trade, and Land Problems in the Southern Wilderness, 1754-1775.* Ann Arbor: University of Michigan Press, 1944. Republished, New York: Gordian Press, 1966.

Alford, Thomas Wildcat. *Civilization: As Told to Florence Drake.* Norman: University of Oklahoma Press, 1936. Reprinted as *Civilization and the Story of the Absentee Shawnee,* Norman: University of Oklahoma Press, 1980.

Axtell, James, and William C. Sturtevant. "The Unkindest Cut, or Who Invented Scalping." *William and Mary Quarterly,* ser. 3, vol. 37, no. 3 (July 1980): 451-472.

Bates, Samuel P. *History of Greene County, Pennsylvania.* Chicago: Nelson Rishforth, 1888.

Caley, Percy B. "The Life Adventures of Lieutenant Colonel John Connolly: The Story of a Tory." *Western Pennsylvania History* 11, no. 1 (January 1928): 10-49; no. 2 (April 1928): 76-111; no. 3 (July 1928): 144-156; and no. 4 (October 1928): 225-259. Special Collections, Society of the Cincinnati Library, Washington, DC.

———. "Lord Dunmore and the Pennsylvania–Virginia Boundary Dispute." *Western Pennsylvania Historical Magazine* 22 (June 1939): 573-586.

Chet, Guy. *Conquering the American Wilderness*. Boston: University of Massachusetts Press, 2003.

Clark, Jerry E. *The Shawnee*. Lexington: University Press of Kentucky, 1977.

Crumrine, Boyd, Franklin Ellis, and Austin N. Hungerford. *History of Washington County, Pennsylvania: With Biographical Sketches of Many of Its Pioneers and Prominent Men*. Philadelphia: L. H. Everts, 1882.

David, James Corbett. *Dunmore's New World: The Extraordinary Life of a Royal Governor in Revolutionary America—with Jacobites, Counterfeiters, Land Schemes, Shipwrecks, Scalping, Indian Politics, Runaway Slaves, and Two Illegal Royal Weddings*. Charlottesville: University Press of Virginia, 2013.

———. "Dunmore's New World: Political Culture in the British Empire, 1745-1796." PhD diss., College of William and Mary, Williamsburg, VA, 2010.

Debrett, John. *Debrett's Correct Peerage of England, Scotland and Ireland, with the Extinct and Forfeited Peerages of the Three Kingdoms*. 2 vols. London: F. and C. Rivington, 1805.

Evans, L. K. *Pioneer History of Greene County, Pennsylvania*. Waynesburg, PA: Waynesburg Republican, 1941.

Faragher, John Mack. *Daniel Boone: The Life and Legend of an American Pioneer*. New York: Holt, 1992.

Greene, Evarts Boutell. *The Provincial Governor in the English Colonies of North America*. Cambridge, MA: Harvard University Press, 1898.

Greene, E. B., and V. D. Harrington. *American Population before the Federal Census of 1790*. New York: Columbia University Press, 1932.

Griffith, Lucille. *The Virginia House of Burgesses 1750-1774*. Tuscaloosa: University of Alabama Press, 1968.

Hamilton, Emory L. "Frontier Forts of Southwest Virginia." *Historical Sketches of Southwest Virginia*, no. 4 (1968): 1-26.

Haymond, Henry. *Historical Reference to Prickets' Fort and Its Defenders, with Incidents of Border Warfare in the Monongahela Valley, and Ceremonies at Unveiling of Monument Marking Site of Pricketts' Fort, Erected in 1774*. Clarksburg, WV: printed by author, [1914?].

———. *History of Harrison County, West Virginia*. Parsons, WV: McClain Printing, 1910. Reprint, Morgantown, WV: Acme Printing, 1973.

Hornblow, Arthur. *A History of the Theater in America from Its Beginnings to the Present Time*. 2 vols. Philadelphia: J. B. Lippincott, 1919.

Houlding, J. A. *Fit for Service: Training in the British Army, 1715-1795.* Oxford: Oxford University Press, 1981.

Howard, James H. *Shawnee!: The Ceremonialism of a Native American Tribe and Its Cultural Background.* Athens: Ohio University Press, 1981.

Jacob, John J. *A Biographical Sketch of the Life of the Late Captain Michael Cresap.* Cumberland, MD: J. M. Buchanan, 1826. Rare book collection, New York Historical Society Library. Reprint, Cincinnati: John. F. Uhlhorn, 1866. Reprint, New York: Arno Press, 1971.

Kelly, Kevin P. "John Montour: The Life of a Cultural Go-Between," *Colonial Williamsburg Interpreter* (Winter 2000/2001): 1-4.

Kercheval, Samuel. *A History of the Valley of Virginia.* Winchester, VA: Samuel H. Davis, 1833. Reprint, Woodstock, VA: John Gatewood, printer, 1850. Reprint, Woodstock, VA: W. N. Grabill, 1909. Facsimile reprint, Baltimore: Genealogical Publishing, 2002.

Lewis, Virgil A. *History of the Battle of Point Pleasant.* Charleston: West Virginia Department of Archives and History, 1909. Reprint, Westminster, MD: Willow Bend Books, 1999.

Miller, Robert J. *Native America, Discovered and Conquered: Thomas Jefferson, Lewis and Clark, and Manifest Destiny.* Lincoln: University of Nebraska Press, 2008.

Morgan, Robert. *Boone: A Biography.* Chapel Hill, NC: Algonquin Books, 2008.

Newton, J. H., G. G. Nichols, and A. G. Sprankle, eds. *History of the Pan-Handle; Being Historical Collections of Ohio, Brooke, Marshall, and Hancock Counties, West Virginia* (Wheeling, WV: J. A. Q. Caldwell, 1889), 80.

Parker, Arthur. *The Constitution of the Five Nations.* Albany: University of the State of New York, 1916.

Parrish, Samuel, ed. *Several Chapters in the History of the Friendly Association for Regaining and Preserving the Peace with the Indians by Pacific Measures.* Philadelphia: Friends Historical Association, 1877.

Ricky, Donald B., ed. *Indians of Maryland: Past and Present.* St. Clair Shores, MI: Somerset, 1999.

Risch, Erna. *Supplying Washington's Army.* Washington, DC: US Army Center of Military History, 1981.

Sanchez-Saavedra, E. M. *A Guide to Virginia Military Organizations in the American Revolution, 1774-1787.* Richmond: Virginia State Library, 1978.

Selby, John E. *Dunmore.* Williamsburg: Virginia Independence Bicentennial Commission, 1977.

Spring, Matthew H. *With Zeal and With Bayonets Only: The British Army on Campaign in North America, 1775-1783.* Norman: University of Oklahoma Press, 2008.

White, Claire. *William Fleming, Patriot.* Baltimore: Gateway Press, 2001.

Withers, Alexander Scott. *Chronicles of Border Warfare: or, A History of the Settlement by the Whites, of North-Western Virginia, and of the Indian Wars and Massacres in that Section of the State, with Reflections, Anecdotes, &c.* Clarksburg, VA: Joseph Israel, 1831. Reprint edited and annotated by Reuben Gold Thwaites, Cincinnati: Stewart and Kidd, 1895. Reprint, Whitefish, MT: Kessinger, 2010.

Acknowledgments

W HILE IT is a standard practice to name one's spouse at the end, my loving wife, Patricia "Trish" Williams, she has allowed me to let this project dictate how we spent much of our "leisure time" for way too long. I think it is therefore appropriate to express my sincere thanks to her first, for her total support and understanding, not to mention the sacrifice she endured. I love you and thank you from the bottom of my heart.

I am grateful to the many individuals and institutions that have assisted in this project. Among the first is the library at the National Headquarters of the Society of the Cincinnati in Washington, DC. Not only did the society honor me with its Tyree-Lamb Fellowship, but the library's collection on eighteenth-century military manuals and treatises make this resource one of the go-to places for researching military history of the period. The library's Directoress (yes, that's how it reads on her door), Ellen McMasters Clark, and her staff are not only helpful but intuitive in locating research documents that ultimately prove helpful, many times, before you even ask.

Similarly, the David Library of the American Revolution in Washington Crossing, Pennsylvania, is an excellent place to research and write in a contemplative and relaxing setting. The library kindly awarded me a residency, and frequent trips to do research there always proved fruitful. Executive Director Meg McSweeney, librarian Kathy Ludwig, and Administrative Officer Brian Graziano always went out of their way to assist me.

I am indebted to the Colonial Williamsburg Foundation for its invaluable assistance. I spent many hours in its John D. Rockefeller Jr. Research Library, which houses many pertinent and useful primary and secondary sources, and I wish to acknowledge Del Moore, George Yetter, Marianne Martin, and Doug Mayo for their help. The staffs of the Museums of Colonial

Williamsburg were also most helpful, and I thank Mary Cottrill, Carl Louns-
bury, and Ed Chappell in particular. I am especially appreciative of two museum professionals on the foundation's curatorial staff. James Mullins,
exhibit graphics artist at the DeWitt Wallace Museum, gave me his personal
tour of the eighteenth-century military objects on display. I would particularly like to thank Erik Goldstein, curator of the mechanical and numis-
matic objects collection, for his behind-the-scenes tour of Dunmore-related
objects in the storage facility not normally on exhibit, and for allowing me
to not only see but touch and hold objects such as Lord Dunmore's brace
of pistols and the fusé he carried on the Indian campaign. It was a special
treat for me to connect with his lordship through this material culture.
Other members of the Colonial Williamsburg Foundation staff; Peter Wrike,
the foundation's Dunmore scholar; Phil Shultz, Dunmore interpreter; Lance
Pedigo, head of the military field musick program; Scott Krogh, interpreter
at the Governor's Palace; Robert Hill, the now-retired manager of CWF
Booksellers; and others too numerous to mention shared their knowledge
of 1774 Virginia. And, quite frankly, as a historian who specializes in the
eighteenth century, I just like being in Colonial Williamsburg and took advantage of every opportunity to visit for research, as well as attend inform-
ative and entertaining programs.

In addition to the Dunmore sources at the Rockefeller Library, the Earl
Gregg Swem Library at the nearby College of William and Mary also had
collections of the Dunmore family papers. I would like to thank Susan A.
Riggs of the manuscripts and rare books collection and Bea Hardy for their
assistance.

I cannot fail to mention the staff at the Fort Pitt Museum—or Fort Dunmore, as it was known in 1774. I am particularly grateful to Director Alan
Gutchess and especially my former shipmate from the USS *Constellation*,
Education Manager Kathleen McLean, for their assistance and hospitality
during my visit and participation in a program on Dunmore's War.

A number of other institutions and their staffs also proved most helpful.
In no particular order, these include Laura Ruttum and Megan O'Shea,
Manuscripts and Archives Division, New York Public Library; Heather
Stone and Scott Scarboro of the Filson Historical Society, Louisville, Ken-
tucky; Joan Stahl, librarian, George Washington's Mount Vernon Estate and
Gardens; Brian Leigh Dunnigan and Janet Bloom of the William L.
Clements Library at the University of Michigan; Samantha Winn, librarian
at Virginia Polytechnic Institute; and Jessica Miller of the Flenniken Public
Library in Carmichaels, Pennsylvania. I would like to express my thanks to
the Society of Colonial Wars in the State of New York for its extraordinary

and far-sighted endorsement of this then unfinished work with the honor of its annual book award in 2013. I also wish to additionally thank the Society of Colonial Wars in the both the States of New York and New Jersey for their generous support of this project.

My good friends and colleagues, as well as my favorite musicologist and period music interpreters, David and Ginger Hildebrand of the Colonial Music Institute, gave excellent advice on incorporating information about performing arts in 1774 Virginia.

Numerous friends and colleagues have supported this endeavor, and I want to thank Robert Selig, John Maass, Joseph Seymour, James Kelly, Stan Berry, Kenneth Smith-Christmas, Grant "Scotty" Knight, William Welsch, Bruce Venter, Edward Lengel, James Kirby Martin, Daniel Tortora, David Preston, Mark Lender, Andrew O'Shaughnessy, Patrick O'Donnell, James Corbett David, Robert J. Miller, Todd Braisted, Don Hagist, Todd Post, Holly Mayer, Kim Burdick, William Fowler, Scott Stephenson, and my cousin Dr. Vera Ellen Kaminski-Saxton, as well as my friend, fellow historian, coffee brewer, and wardrobe critic, Gina DiNicolo.

I wish to thank the staffs and volunteers at numerous historic sites and museums not already mentioned who also assisted in this endeavor or help to preserve the cultural resources and artifacts associated with this period of history. At the risk of leaving any out—and I probably will unintentionally—these include, but are not limited to, the sites of Camp Union, Point Pleasant, Fort Fincastle/Henry, Fort Gower, Prickett's Fort, the Frontier Culture Museum, Hanna's Town, Logan Elm Park, and Camp Charlotte, and a special mention to Jilla Smith of the Irvin Allen/Michael Cresap House Museum in Oldtown, Maryland.

As I worked on this manuscript concurrent with my doctoral dissertation, I would like to express my gratitude to my adviser, professor Jon T. Sumida, and the other members of my committee, professors Richard Bell, Colleen Woods, and Mary Corbin Sies of the University of Maryland, College Park, and Dr. Dennis Conrad of the US Navy History and Heritage Command. Their exacting standards and helpful comments on the dissertation version not only enabled me to earn my doctorate but made this book a better narrative.

Finally, I wish to thank Bruce H. Franklin and Westholme Publishing for giving me the opportunity to write about Dunmore's War and being extremely patient with my work schedule, Ron Silverman for his copyediting support, Trudi Gershenov for the cover design, and Pamela Patrick White of White Historic Art for permission to use her painting.

Index